Diversity and Integration in Private International Law

Edited by Verónica Ruiz Abou-Nigm
and María Blanca Noodt Taquela

EDINBURGH
University Press

Edinburgh University Press is one of the leading university presses in the UK. We publish academic books and journals in our selected subject areas across the humanities and social sciences, combining cutting-edge scholarship with high editorial and production values to produce academic works of lasting importance. For more information visit our website: edinburghuniversitypress.com

Edinburgh University Press Ltd
The Tun – Holyrood Road
12(2f) Jackson's Entry
Edinburgh EH8 8PJ

Typeset in 11/13pt Times New Roman by
Servis Filmsetting Ltd, Stockport, Cheshire
and printed and bound by CPI Group (UK) Ltd, Croydon, CR0 4YY

A CIP record for this book is available from the British Library

ISBN 978 1 4744 4785 0 (hardback)
ISBN 978 1 4744 4787 4 (webready PDF)
ISBN 978 1 4744 4788 1 (epub)

Contents

Foreword

This edited collection is one of the outputs of the Private International Law and Integrated Markets (PILIM) project. This project (2014–17) has been a very successful platform for cross-regional collaboration, facilitating interaction between private international law scholars in Europe and South America. Led by Verónica Ruiz Abou-Nigm (University of Edinburgh) and María Blanca Noodt Taquela (University of Buenos Aires), and funded by the British Academy, it was also made possible by the invaluable support of the American Association of Private International Law (ASADIP) and the Hague Conference (HCCH) Regional Office in Buenos Aires.

The project explored the conceptual and methodological discourse of private international law and its impact on the European Union and the Mercosur zone. It aimed to contribute to improving the understanding of private international law as a discipline, advocating for a more inclusive discourse that in turn would be more conducive to committing to the reality of regional integration. A study of this kind should also shed light on how to rethink the great question of the relations between the different legal orders at stake, a subject that is examined with great attention by a rich and very recent European doctrine, including many of the contributions in this book. This is particularly useful in present times, within Europe as a whole and especially with regard to Brexit, and may lead to an eventual future programme of research and further normative developments in the field. Although the PILIM project was launched at a time when the UK exit from the EU was not yet on the horizon, it became necessary during the later stages of the project to consider the possible scenarios of legal cooperation between the UK and continental Europe in the event where the rules of private international law that are currently in force in the EU no longer exist.

I was invited to participate in the event at which the project was launched – a scoping workshop in Buenos Aires. There, the bases and objectives of the project were identified. The central theme of the scoping workshop was the methodological difficulties of private international law discourse: how to overcome them and make the discourse more accessible. This event took due note of what happens in reality in terms of the study and understanding of our discipline, and its interpretation and application by judges and arbitrators. Several issues were examined, including arbitration, family law matters and international jurisdictional cooperation, the latter in light of the operational difficulties it presents when it involves the UK on the one hand, and Argentina, Uruguay and other South American countries on the other. To these difficulties one may add that private international law is often perceived as not sufficiently grounded in reality – perhaps because of exacerbated 'theoreticism'; a certain absence of input from the 'judicial family' itself, all of which increases the difficulties of grasping its contribution in practice. 'Theoreticism', I add, connatural to a branch of law that opens, in one way or another, the borders of the state to the foreign state in the matter of private relations, without diminishing state sovereignty.

To a certain extent, PILIM went down a route already explored in the past for the purposes of private international law codification in the Americas. The Inter-American Specialized Conference of Private International Law (CIDIP) is the greatest development of multilateral regional codification fulfilled by the OAS (Organization of American States), which from 1975 has generated seven conferences and more than twenty international conventions in force among many countries of the Americas, although this codification is yet to be fully recognised in Europe.

A second workshop, focused on some of the key themes identified in this first stage of the project, took place in Porto Alegre in October 2014 as a side event to the annual congress of the American Association of Private International Law (ASADIP). The PILIM project may be perceived as complementary to the agenda of ASADIP, the scope and institutional format of each, as well as their autonomy, all remaining unaffected by the existence of the other. I fully support these practices of 'multilateral' knowledge exchange, as they provide many real opportunities for specialists from our region to participate in fruitful dialogue with colleagues from other countries.

The third major international event of the project took place in Edinburgh in February 2015. It focused on international arbitration as one of the spheres where private international law could do more and could do better. International commercial arbitration plays a key role in the interface between ideas of conflict of laws and jurisdictions, applicable law, self-regulation and public policy; all of these themes are key components of private international law's contemporary discourse, as examined in the excellent contribution of Cordero-Moss and Fernández Arroyo in this collection.

Throughout the three years of this project several other collaborative workshops took place. These events offered an extremely valuable opportunity to gather information from practice on the ground and to steer the project towards more impactful outcomes. One of the most important outcomes of these workshops was the idea generated in the Buenos Aires workshop to join efforts with the pivotal and pioneer international organisation in the field, the Hague Conference (HCCH). Born of that idea was the very successful event that took place at the University of Buenos Aires on 9 November 2016, in which I participated, that brought together more than ninety participants, including judges from across Argentina, Peru, Paraguay, Brazil and Uruguay, together with world-renowned academics, legal practitioners and government officials, to exchange experiences on the role of the judiciary in private international law cases. The importance of the role of the judiciary cannot be overestimated and the joint contribution by Ignacio Goicoechea and Hans van Loon in this collection pays due tribute to that.

The final conference of the project took place in Edinburgh in February 2017. Entitled 'Private International Law: Embracing Diversity', it saw the participation of established experts and new voices from the UK, Europe and the Americas.

My vision of PILIM is that of a bridge between systems of private international law; perhaps its greatest specific contribution is that one of the project leaders is based in Scotland – from a Brexit perspective, a national space where the popular vote supported the link with continental Europe from the valuable perspective of belonging. In this sense PILIM fills a space of knowledge that demands greater dissemination each day, not only as a result of the demands of globalisation, but also because of the need to consolidate and deepen cooperation pathways.

At this point – at the end of the three-year project – an examination of PILIM and its outcomes demands certain general reflections including some suggestions for future research, in tune with the progressive development of private international law.

Considering the central role of the judge, it is possible to argue that a teleological interpretation and application of the rules of private international law in the resolution of cases makes equity characteristic of the judicial office, deriving from it an approximation of the juridical families of common law and Roman-Germanic law, imposed by the nature of the legal situation rather than by any prescriptive normative position embodied in positive law. Likewise, the judge in private international law scenarios must adjudicate cross-border cases without ignoring that his or her decision may affect various legal orders. In several instances, the judge could become a 'legislator' in a specific case; this is a hypersensitive point that could not be left out of the debate. It goes beyond the purpose of this foreword to dwell on my resistance to accept a transfer to the arbitrator of faculties similar to those of the judge, at least in what refers to the alleged capacity to create a sort of *lex arbitralis*, with my greatest intellectual respect towards those who postulate it, although I disagree with the radicalism with which this is done at times. I cannot hide that the 'finality' of the solution (an expression of tragic historical evocation) contains risks that are not easily conjugated. Another issue worthy of debate is the so-called best interest of the child, as the guiding and true heart of internal and international jurisprudence in matters of family relations. Such primacy is not exempt, in my opinion, from certain procedures that, in the absence of a binding definition, allow it to be viewed as an objective or even qualify as a totally autonomous category and still as a new connection that would work in the system of conflict of laws.

The determination of certain guiding criteria – here the usefulness of soft law might be emphasised – is an issue that would require a multidisciplinary consideration in which private international law techniques and methodologies could not be absent, and, of course – if I dare suggest it – PILIM itself has been a promoter of such a multidisciplinary approach.

Similarly, procedural law solutions play a central role in inter-system cooperation and constitute an irreplaceable contribution to the operation of private international law, especially when the objective is to facilitate access to justice and promote the recognition and enforcement of foreign judgments.

In this sense the knowledge and application of foreign law with the so-called controls of conventionality and constitutionality takes the judge to a role as inescapable as responsible, as well recognised by positive law and contemporary doctrine.

All in all, PILIM has clearly and accurately demonstrated the role that it plays in the progressive development of private international law by serving as a 'bridge' between legal families whose main difference lies, *inter alia*, in the role of the judges and their sources. The project is remarkable and the inclusiveness of approach, as shown in the call for participants, is commendable.

I am sure that projects such as PILIM are, in these times of turbulence, one of the greatest contributions we can build from our modest redoubt in favour of a better coexistence between countries and people.

Prof. Dr Didier Opertti Badán
Montevideo, 15 August 2018

Contributors

María Mercedes Albornoz, Professor of Private International Law, Centro de Investigación y Docencia Económicas (CIDE) (Mexico)

Beatriz Añoveros Terradas, Associate Professor of Private International Law, ESADE Law School Universitat Ramon Llull, Barcelona (Spain)

Nadia de Araujo, Professor of Private International Law, Pontificia Universidade Católica de Rio de Janeiro (Brazil)

Guillermo Argerich, Professor of Private International Law, University of Buenos Aires (Argentina)

María Laura Capalbo, Associate Professor of Private International Law, Universidad de la República (Uruguay)

Laura Carballo Piñeiro, Professor, Nippon Foundation Chair, World Maritime University, Malmö (Sweden)

Janeen M. Carruthers, Professor of Private Law, University of Glasgow (Scotland)

Giuditta Cordero-Moss, Professor of Private International Law, University of Oslo (Norway)

Rosario Espinosa Calabuig, Professor of Private International Law, Universitat de Valencia (Spain)

Diego P. Fernández Arroyo, Professor of Law, SciencesPo, Paris (France)

Cecilia Fresnedo de Aguirre, Professor of Private International Law, Universidad de la República (Uruguay)

Ignacio Goicoechea, Representative for Latin America and the Caribbean of the Hague Conference on Private International Law (Argentina)

Kasey McCall-Smith, Lecturer in Public International Law, University of Edinburgh (Scotland)

David McClean, Emeritus Professor of Private International Law, University of Sheffield (England)

Ralf Michaels, Arthur Larson Professor of Law, Duke University (United States)

María Blanca Noodt Taquela, Professor of Private International Law, Universidad de Buenos Aires (Argentina)

Didier Opertti Badán, Emeritus Professor of Private International Law, Universidad de la República (Uruguay)

Sebastián Paredes, Assistant Professor of Private International Law, Universidad de Buenos Aires (Argentina)

Fabricio B. Pasquot Polido, Associate Professor of Private International Law, Universidade Federal de Minas Gerais (Brazil)

Marta Requejo Isidro, Senior Research Fellow, Max Planck Institute (Luxembourg)

Nieve Rubaja, Assistant Professor of Private International Law, University of Buenos Aires (Argentina)

Verónica Ruiz Abou-Nigm, Senior Lecturer in International Private Law, University of Edinburgh (Scotland)

Katarina Trimmings, Senior Lecturer, University of Aberdeen (Scotland)

Hans van Loon, independent consultant, former Secretary-General of the Hague Conference on Private International Law (1996–2013) (Netherlands)

Nicola Wisdahl, Legal Officer, Scottish Government Office in Brussels (Scotland)

Burcu Yüksel, Lecturer in Law, University of Aberdeen (Scotland)

Introduction: Private International Law and Cosmopolitan Integration

Verónica Ruiz Abou-Nigm

Opening Remarks

Private international law embraces legal diversity and pluralism. Different legal traditions continue to meet, interact and integrate in different forms of integration, at the national, regional and international levels. Different systems of substantive law couple with divergent systems of private international law (designed to accommodate the former in cross-border situations). This complex legal landscape impacts individuals and families in cross-border scenarios and international commerce broadly conceived. Private international law methodologies and techniques offer means for the coordination of this constellation of legal orders and value systems in cross-border situations. This is essential in integration processes as it is for furthering 'global' interconnectivity.

This edited collection is one of the outputs of the PILIM[1] project (2014–17) led by the editors. PILIM has been a very successful platform for collaboration, facilitating the interaction between private international law scholars in Europe and in South America. As a cross-regional research project, it aimed to reflect on the role and contribution of private international law in regional integration. The project explored a variety of themes. This edited collection focuses on the connective capabilities of private international law in bridging and balancing legal diversity as a corollary for the development of integration. Resulting from research conducted mainly in Europe and in South America, regions where private international law has a long-standing tradition, the book explores how private international law's connective capacity could be enhanced by more inclusive methodologies and techniques that might better respond to the reality of the integration that it is there to promote.

[1] Private International Law and Integrated Markets: A Cross-Regional Collaboration (PILIM). http://www.pilim.law.ed.ac.uk, British Academy funded project 2014–17. The editors of this book would like to thank the British Academy for its financial support of this project.

The diversity of the contributions, bringing together a wide range of expertise, including the work of world-leading scholars alongside new voices, coming from very different backgrounds and traditions, speaking different languages, thinking about private international law and integration in different ways, and engaging with various private international law topics and perspectives, taken as a whole, portrays precisely the sort of 'pluralistic thinking'[2] and open dialogue this book advances: this volume aims to serve as a conduit for delivering cross-regional dialogue on private international law in this era of interdependence and interconnectivity.

Diversity in this collection refers mainly to legal diversity, as a manifestation of cultural diversity. Yet, diversity is also manifest in the different contributions themselves: the diverse range of approaches mentioned above reflect disciplinary diversity, that is, differences in underlying disciplinary paradigms. In turn, integration is understood in its broadest sense – not limited to economic nor to regional integration. Yet, many contributions focus on regional integration in the European Union and in the Mercosur zone.

To explain the vision that infuses this volume I borrow two concepts from other social sciences: (1) pluralistic thinking as coined in social psychology, and (2) cosmopolitan integration as described in social theory – the latter with caveats. Pluralistic thinking is a deep form of open-mindedness, involving the recognition and endorsement of multiplicity and complexity in the world. Pluralism has been broadly described as positively valuing multiplicity and I explore that concept in connection with private international law thinking in the final chapter of this volume. In turn, cosmopolitan integration is based on a paradigm shift whose principle is that diversity is not the problem but the solution.[3] And this volume as a whole contributes to developing the claim that this paradigm can extend to legal diversity in integration precisely via the connective capacity of private international law methodologies and techniques.

Contributions explore inter-related dimensions: private international law as a field of knowledge, private international law normativity, and legal practice, including the practice of international commercial arbitration. Central to the connective capacity of private international law is international judicial cooperation, hence an entire part of the book is dedicated to examining cooperation practices through an eminently practical lens.

Private international law and its connective capabilities, in the words of Hans van Loon, 'play a vital role in the global legal architecture needed to support our emerging multicultural world society'.[4] In particular, the development of private international law in some South American countries has been distinctive due to its openness to the rest of the world. Private international law techniques, methods and solutions developed in South America have been informed by a cosmopolitan vision

[2] See the final chapter by Ruiz Abou-Nigm in this volume.
[3] Beck, U. and C. Cronin (2014) *Cosmopolitan Vision*, Polity Press.
[4] See the chapter by van Loon in this volume.

of private international law. In turn, the Europeanisation of private international law has often been perceived as more concerned with the development of the internal European market rather than the connective capacity of private international law beyond Europe. Notwithstanding the foregoing, both these approaches have generated a non-inclusive discourse. This may be changing as the views shared in the contributions to this volume show.

On these lines, this volume celebrates private international law for engaging with the Other, embracing diversity and pluralism.

To set us off on this journey, in the first chapter, Ralf Michaels invites us to think about private international law as an ethic of a particular kind, an ethic of responsivity, that operates as such through its technique.[5] As Michaels explains, 'Private international law provides us with a technique of ethics, a technique that helps us conceptualise and address some of the most pressing issues of our time. It is not only ethically relevant, it is itself an ethic.'[6]

Part I – Legal Diversity and Integration

In our deeply pluralistic world legal diversity is a valuable asset. However, in certain legal fields harmonisation has been pursued at regional and global levels to facilitate commerce and to minimise the hurdles of accommodating diversity in cross-border cases. Though the contributions to this first part of the book cover a wide range of topics, the thread which links them is the ability of private international law methodologies and techniques to accommodate legal diversity, their pitfalls, tensions and challenges. Diversity and pluralism bring richness but also complexity to international legal relations between private parties. The selection of chapters within Part I show how private international law is able to maximise the opportunities to capture that richness while aiming to facilitate connectivity (that is, aiming to ease the hurdles posed to parties by the differences in the laws of different countries). Traditionally private international law has done this using a plurality of methodologies, including harmonisation via multilateral treaties, soft law instruments and, in the European Union, the Europeanisation of the rules of private international law, mostly in the form of European regulations. This part brings to the fore the inclusiveness needed for any of these normative processes aimed at tackling legal diversity to succeed.

The leading international forum for private international harmonisation is the Hague Conference (HCCH). In the first chapter of Part I, Hans van Loon, former Secretary-General of the HCCH (1996–2013), analyses the wide range of techniques developed by the HCCH to accommodate the multiple and very different facets of legal diversity. Efforts to harmonise the rules of private international law started in the late nineteenth century, first in Latin America, then among a select group of continental European civil law states. Tobias Asser, founder of the Hague Conference,

[5] See the chapter by Michaels in this volume.

[6] Ibid.

deliberately chose the method of unification not of substantive law, but of private international law. This was only realistic, he felt, in a world characterised by legal diversity. From bridging the divide between civil (continental) law and common law systems – although in some areas the divergent approaches between the United States and other common law countries may be no less challenging – to reconciling the realities of federal and quasi-federal systems with those of unitary systems, this chapter discusses the evolving role of the Hague Conference. An important contemporary aspect of legal diversity in the HCCH relates to cross-border issues involving legal systems based on religious, in particular Jewish and Sharia, law, and secular legal systems. After analysing these different facets of legal diversity and the efforts of the HCCH to accommodate them, this contribution concludes by highlighting the role of inclusiveness in this process and the unifying force of global and regional human rights instruments.

A different strategy to manage diversity is that used by the private international law rules in the United Kingdom's legal systems in the context of the law of succession. Instead of opting to be part of the EU's harmonised rules of private international law in this sphere, the UK has instead adopted the scission principle and its supporting connecting factors of *lex situs* and *lex ultimi domicilii.* Janeen Carruthers examines this strategy of managing legal diversity giving consideration to the initiatives of the HCCH, and of the EU in the field of succession, remarking that, from a UK perspective, neither initiative has proved to be successful. From the European perspective, diversity among Member States has been tackled through the Succession Regulation, which provides harmonised rules of jurisdiction, applicable law, and recognition and enforcement of decisions. The visible increase in the availability of party autonomy in the Regulation, although policed, is evidence of a new (to UK eyes) technique in this sphere by which parties may seek to manage diversity in succession. Appreciating that it is the function of private international law (Carruthers refers to international private law, as the discipline is also known in Scots law) to recognise legal diversity, to anticipate conflict and thereby to manage the substantive outcome, in ways that may differ according to whether a legal system adopts jurisdiction-selection or rule-selection methodology. The chapter demonstrates that when it comes to private international law, harmonisation in the EU has been partial and yet the prospects of not being part of the ongoing harmonisation process in the EU after Brexit poses many questions. Continuing with this inchoate and fragmented feature of EU private international law, in the next chapter in Part I Rosario Espinosa Calabuig analyses challenges in the family law sphere, examining EU case law to assess the success of EU private international law regulations in the fields of divorce, matrimonial property, maintenance obligations and cross-border rights of access to children. This chapter points to the difficulties facing judges, national courts and legal professionals in the application of EU regulations in this sphere. These challenges are not exclusively derived from normative complexity but may lie elsewhere. This is explained in Chapter 4 by Katarina Trimmings and Burcu Yüksel. Distilling insights from their empirical research conducted in the context of the EUPILLAR project they show that the uniform rules of EU private international law are not always interpreted and applied uniformly in all EU Member States. They argue that one of the main reasons for this divergence is the different legal thinking across EU Member States, each state having its own legal traditions and heritages. Legal actors are naturally and subconsciously inclined to follow a particular way of legal thinking connected to the legal system that has shaped their legal matrix, which evidence shows may be particularly problematic in this context when using characterisation as a private international law technique. This jeopardises the functioning of the harmonised rules of private international law in the EU regime governing private relationships with a transnational element and cross-border dispute litigation. Despite these hurdles, there is a key value embedded in the EU regime: legal certainty, as explained by Marta Requejo Isidro in the final chapter of Part I. Requejo Isidro examines the impoverishment that Brexit would represent in the specific context of private international law and transnational litigation, in both commercial and family law, as this exit would mean a significant loss in terms of legal certainty for all parties involved. Admittedly, the hurdles of uncertainty regarding jurisdiction, or the disadvantages of losing a swift system for passporting UK judgments into Europe will not affect all stakeholders equally: some groups of the population, such as consumers, employees, small businesses, children or maintenance creditors, are likely to endure worse experiences than major litigants in complex corporate litigation. This chapter analyses the complexities of Brexit in this field as well as the contributions of English and Scottish legal systems to the development of EU private international law from a continental European perspective. It concludes that Brexit means overall impoverishment. EU law is as it is – not civil law, not common law, not even mixed, but European – thanks to many influences, including the very important British common law perspective.

Part II – Cooperation, the Architecture of Engagement

International cooperation nowadays appears to be one of the cornerstones of the necessary engagement between states in this sphere. It encompasses the practical mechanisms operationalising the methodologies and techniques of private international law in relation to the issues of jurisdiction, applicable law, and recognition and enforcement of foreign judgments in the day-to-day lives of people and courts. How do judges communicate in cases of international child abduction? What is the role of Central Authorities in locating the child? How does the court find out the content of foreign law? How is it possible to effectuate service of process in a foreign country? What sort of formalisms do legal documents issued in foreign countries need to be effective outside their country of origin? What are the effects of foreign judgments? These and many other practical questions are addressed in international judicial cooperation frameworks. These kinds of provision appear in different levels of normativity in place in the multilateral, regional, bilateral, supranational and internal (national) spheres.

This second part of the book shows, in turn, the importance of these different frameworks and the interplay between them, and reflects on the robust architecture of international judicial cooperation and its pivotal role for the development of private international law. The contributions in this part are eminently practical, focusing on the Hague Conference Conventions, the Inter-American Conventions and the instruments on international judicial cooperation adopted in Mercosur and the EU; the differences in approach in the common law tradition as compared to civilian systems; and the current situation of international judicial cooperation in Scotland.

In the first chapter of Part II María Blanca Noodt Taquela examines the key role of international judicial cooperation in modern society and introduces suggestions to further this 'architecture of engagement' following models from the neighbouring field of international commercial arbitration and to enhance the role of administrative cooperation. Following on from this, David McClean in Chapter 8 focuses on the differing approaches to judicial cooperation between the civil law and common law traditions. These differences are explored together with the efforts made, especially by the HCCH and the EU, to find procedures acceptable to both traditions. This has been especially successful in the case of the service of process, while in other processes, such as the taking of evidence, it has been less so.

International judicial cooperation has its different shades not only between the civil and common law traditions but also between different regions of the world. Nadia de Araujo's Chapter 9 examines international judicial cooperation instruments in force in Latin America. It sheds light on how international treaties have influenced the rules on enforcement and recognition of foreign decisions in the regional instruments adopted within Mercosur, particularly the Las Leñas Protocol. Moving afterwards to national perspectives, Chapter 10, by Nicola Wisdahl, focuses on Scotland as a legal jurisdiction within a multi-jurisdictional state, which itself is experiencing a period of constitutional upheaval. Given the current Brexit scenario, future political and constitutional developments may present a challenge to maintaining pre-existing methods of cooperation available through the European legal infrastructure. Finally, after tackling the regional and national dimensions, the final chapter of Part II looks at the international scenario. Fabrício B. Pasquot Polido critically reviews some of the foundational concepts and inspirational ideas underlying the current negotiations for a convention on recognition and enforcement of foreign judgments at the HCCH. Much has been written about the draft text of the convention prepared by the Hague Special Commission (its Final Draft of May 2018), particularly in terms of doctrinal analysis focused on the technicalities and legal aspects of the Draft's main provisions, such as its general bases for recognition, exclusive bases for recognition, jurisdictional filters and even its compatibility with domestic laws and regional European instruments, such as the Brussels I *bis* Regulation. Pasquot Polido takes a different angle. He argues that beyond the project's desired result, that is, a multilateral treaty establishing uniform rules for recognition and enforcement of judgments in civil and commercial matters (the ultimate stage of international judicial cooperation), the negotiation process appears to meet some old expectations of convergence between the theoretical enterprises of private international law both in strengthening 'recognition' as one of its main paradigms and in highlighting the increasing relevance of coordination of judicial dispute resolution systems with respect to transnational civil and commercial litigation.

Part III – The Evolving Focus on the Individual

The third part of the book presents a wide spectrum of parties affected by private international law issues, far beyond the more obvious cases of parties engaged in international commercial transactions and parties pertaining to a cross-border family, to showcase the role of private international law in the construction of a more equal multicultural society. The narrative thread of this third part of the book is the evolving focus of private international law normativity and practice on the needs of individuals and, therefore, the need for successful coordination frameworks. The themes in this section reveal the expansive potential of private international law in its tackling of issues and problems that perhaps would not traditionally have been considered to be within the remit of the discipline from a more orthodox (and possibly outdated) perspective. Some of these themes are also perceived to benefit from interdisciplinary approaches, so 'coordination' in this section relates not only to the necessary coordination between states, but also to the coordination in terms of normative accommodation between different related layers of legality, and even more so (and arguably much more ambitiously) the coordination between diverse policies and interests at play. In the first chapter in Part III, Kasey McCall-Smith, a scholar of public international law, uses the global migration phenomenon to explore how private and public international law can integrate in order to facilitate the contributions of migrants to cultural, social and financial change in this age of global interconnectivity and interdependence. There is a general understanding that the economic, social and private dimensions of migration need to be addressed holistically. Adopting a boundary-spanning approach, this chapter examines the 2018 UN Global Compact for Safe, Orderly and Regular Migration and considers how private international law could facilitate many of the aims of the Compact, which was adopted in the week that this volume went to press. Engaging further with the increasingly important phenomenon of migration, the next chapter explores more specifically the challenges of labour migration for private international law. In our increasingly globalised world, businesses relocate workers to low-wage countries, moving them across borders. Laura Carbalho Piñeiro challenges the suitability of the classical submission of individual employment relationships to the law of the habitual place of work. Her chapter examines whether or not the principle of worker protection has been domestically and internationally jeopardised in favour of furthering economic integration. In doing so, the chapter sheds light on the policy coordination needed to make the normative accommodation efficient.

Continuing with the narrative thread of this third part of the book and focusing on the protection of weaker parties, Beatriz Añoveros provides an in-depth examination of cross-border consumer protection in e-commerce in the EU private international law regime. This chapter shows that although the European regime offers the same level of protection for European consumers entering into transactions with suppliers domiciled outside the EU and those who benefit from the internal market, equal treatment is not yet achievable due to the differing aims of *ad intra* and *ad extra* consumer protection. Changing regions, Part III then moves onto the evolving focus on the individual in the new private international law codifications in Latin American countries. Sebastián Paredes' Chapter 15 examines normative and jurisprudential developments of private international law in Argentina, Uruguay, Brazil, Panama, Dominican Republic and Paraguay, among many others that have amended their civil codes or drafted private international law acts after years of passivity. This chapter examines the extent to which these developments have captured and maintained the traditional cosmopolitan vision of Latin American countries in cross-border solutions. As a final contribution in this part, Nieve Rubaja and Mercedes Albornoz address the variations in the conception of families that have taken place in substantive private law in many countries and reveal the recognition challenges in the Latin American context. The authors show how IT and biomedical advances have influenced and favoured international legal cooperation, facilitated parent-child contact in cross-border situations and helped intending parents to procreate. However, the need for further coordination remains blatant to effectively support individuals in these circumstances. The contribution analyses the most relevant multilateral legal instruments currently in force in Latin American countries aiming to provide solutions to day-to-day private international law problems in this constantly evolving regional reality. By bringing to the fore the importance of the role of judges, Central Authorities and judicial networks in this field, this chapter provides a valuable segue to the final part of this volume.

Part IV – Private International Law in Practice

The themes of this final part are purposely diverse, as the common thread is engagement with the Other, understood as the fibre across the breadth and depth of private international law thinking. In the day-to-day practice of cross-border civil and commercial cases judges and courts play a central role in that engagement. Ignacio Goicoechea and Hans van Loon open this final part with their analysis of the key role of judges in the development of the discipline, focusing on the enormous contribution of the HCCH to the development of judicial networks and databases, such as that on the case law of the Hague Child Abduction Convention. Another scenario where theory meets practice is that of international commercial arbitration. Giuditta Cordero-Moss and Diego P. Fernández Arroyo in Chapter 18 debate the relevance of private international law for the practice of international commercial arbitration. The contribution follows a keynote delivered by the authors in one of the PILIM project's international events in Edinburgh, devoted to examining private international law in arbitration practice. Their debate highlights the relevance of private international law thinking for the practice of international commercial arbitration and discusses the advantages and disadvantages of conflict rules in arbitration proceedings where the parties have made a choice of law, pointing to the limitations of choice of law clauses in commercial contracts. The reference to the latter provides a link to the next chapter, which looks specifically at commercial contracts. Premised on the motivation of demystifying the difficulty that understanding private international law frameworks presents to legal practitioners who are not specialised in private international law, the contribution by Guillermo Argerich and Laura Capalbo provides a simplified picture of the current legal landscape relevant to international commercial contracts in Argentina and Uruguay. The contribution is based on the assumption that the relentless process of globalisation requires private international law methodologies to be understood by all legal operators, particularly practitioners in charge of drafting international commercial contracts. Argerich and Capalbo emphasise the simplicity of their description by doing what they believe is necessary for further engagement of practitioners with private international law, that is, explaining in a simplified fashion what the implications of private international law issues – such as the ascertainment of the applicable law and the identification of the competent courts, or the choice of arbitration as an alternative dispute resolution mechanism in the eventuality of a dispute – are for the governance of international commercial contracts.

Still focusing on the need for meaningful engagement with the Other, and based also on a perspective from Uruguay and Mercosur countries, the next chapter moves onto an examination of a quintessential technique of private international law practice: the public policy exception. Cecilia Fresnedo de Aguirre analyses the public policy exception as a technique to deal with diversity and pluralism. The public policy exception is in fact a barrier to the application of foreign law and to the recognition or enforcement of a foreign judgment when doing so contravenes a fundamental principle on which the court's state bases its legal individuality. Yet, it can also be said that the public policy exception is each state's guardian that protects its legal coherence within its frontiers as preventing the application of a foreign law or the recognition of a foreign judgment may endanger the set of fundamental principles that constitute the international public policy of the concerned state. This chapter examines this essential concept from a South American perspective, highlighting the role that Uruguay has had in promoting a restrictive (and therefore more open) approach to the scope of the public policy exception.

To conclude, in the final chapter of this book I offer my own contribution and insights, and an overall reflection on the insights derived from this volume as a whole. When we started thinking about the PILIM project several years ago, our concern was that there was something in the narrative and discourse of private international law that was preventing greater engagement of the discipline with the integration processes, both in Europe and in the Mercosur countries. At that time the waves of isolationism threatening integration processes regionally were not at the forefront. Throughout the life of the project it became clear that part of the problem surrounding private international law's outreach was the lack of awareness of the potential that its methodologies and techniques have in contributing to the necessary accommodation of different legal cultures, and therefore for the difficult task of bridging, *inter alia*, traditions; parties' and states' interests; capitalist pressures; social and ethnographic cultural differences; and the provincial, national, regional, international and transnational normative spaces. Balancing these tensions between competing rationalities is a crucial ingredient for the success of inclusive integration processes. Bridging legal diversity is more often than not a complex task. Private international law thinking, however, is developed to do just that. The challenge is how to tailor the streaming of private international law thinking in a manner that becomes relevant to the day-to-day life of lawyers and ordinary people. The question is how to do so openly and effectively. To that purpose, I introduce the concept of 'pluralistic thinking' as developed in social psychology, with the aim of grasping where the cognitive barriers come from and of generating ideas in relation to the building blocks for further embracement of diversity. This final chapter engages with culturalist approaches to provide insights that could prove enlightening to private international law practice, particularly in the context of regional integration. Bringing together several threads in this book, this final chapter portrays private international law as a methodology that embraces multiplicity and pluralism in the accommodation of legal diversity.

Opening Inclusive Dialogue

This book opens a cross-regional dialogue and shifts the Eurocentric discussion on diversity and integration to a more inclusive engagement with South America in private international law issues. It promotes a contemporary cosmopolitan vision of private international law as a discipline enabling legal interconnectivity, with the potential to transcend its disciplinary boundaries to further promote the reality of cross-border integration, and with its focus on the ever-increasing cross-border mobility of individuals. At the beginning of the project leading to this publication, the waves of isolationism presenting further challenges for the world today were not so blatant. This reality calls for rethinking cosmopolitan integration and in turn promoting the role of private international law in this context and, more broadly, in our increasingly multicultural globalised society.

1

Private International Law as an Ethic of Responsivity

Ralf Michaels

Introduction

The world is a mess. Populism, xenophobia and Islamophobia; misogyny and racism; the closing of borders against the neediest – the existential crisis of modernity calls for a firm response from ethics. Why, instead of engaging with these problems through traditional ethics, worry about private international law, that most technical of technical fields of law? My claim in this chapter: not despite, but because of its technical character. Private international law provides such an ethic, an ethic of responsivity. It provides us with a technique of ethics, a technique that helps us conceptualise and address some of the most pressing issues of our time. It is not only ethically relevant, it is itself an ethic. Let me explain.[1]

Private International Law and Ethics

Whether private international law has an ethical dimension is a question that has long been discussed.[2] On one level, the relevance should be obvious. First, private international law decisions often have to grapple with the ethical challenges listed above; indeed, it is often in private international law cases that these issues come up concretely. Xenophobia and populism regularly occur as refusals to apply foreign

[1] This is the expanded written version of my keynote address at the Edinburgh Conference entitled, 'Private International Law: Embracing Diversity'. I thank Verónica Ruiz Abou-Nigm and María Blanca Noodt Taquela for the invitation and the participants for a lively and very helpful discussion.

[2] The most comprehensive such project, one that has influenced the argument in this chapter, is Muir Watt, H. (2017) 'Hospitality, Tolerance, and Exclusion in Legal Form: Private International Law and the Politics of Difference', *Current Legal Problems*, vol. 70, no. 1, 111–47; Muir Watt, H. (2018) 'Discours sur les méthodes du droit international privé (des formes juridiques de l'inter-altérité)', *Recueil des cours*, vol. 389. See also, for example, some of the contributions in Childress, D. E. III (ed.) (2012) *The Role of Ethics in International Law*, Cambridge University Press.

law (even though the reverse is not true: such refusals are not necessarily evidence of xenophobia).[3] Islamophobia in particular frequently appears as 'Shariaphobia', fear of Islamic law, and thus in the context of private international law. The backlash against the Archbishop of Canterbury's proposal to give Islamic law a place in Britain is one example; another is the foreign law amendments and laws in the United States, which ostentatiously ban courts from applying any foreign law but are really mostly directed against the application of Islamic law.[4] Misogyny and racism are both issues for private international law, especially where feminism and multiculturalism come to a clash in view of a foreign law that discriminates against women.[5]

Second, even where such ethical challenges are discussed without reference to private international law, private international law often remains relevant. Take, as an important example, the current refugee crisis. Numerous questions related to it – whether a refugee's child marriage should be recognised, what the refugee's domicile is and so forth – concern, at heart, issues of private international law. Moreover, even the refugee's status itself is, to a considerable extent, a question of private international law, in accordance with what Karen Knop has called private citizenship.[6] It goes largely unrecognised (though it ought not to) that Hannah Arendt, when she discusses the famous 'right to have rights' as a defence of refugee rights, uses a private international law example to make her point: 'a German citizen under the Nazi regime might not be able to enter a mixed marriage abroad because of the Nuremberg laws'.[7] Private international law is present even where it is not recognised.

Three Positions against Ethics

If, therefore, private international law is somehow related to questions of ethics, a direct importance is nonetheless often denied. Three positions can be separated, each related to one term in the discipline's name: private, international, law. Because it is *international*, it is considered *incapable* of dealing with ethical questions. Because

3 See also Clermont, K. M. and T. Eisenberg (2007) 'Xenophilia or Xenophobia in American Courts? Before and After 9/11', 4 *Journal of Empirical Legal Studies*, 441–64.

4 On the former, see Griffith-Jones, R. (ed.) (2013) *Islam and English Law*, Cambridge University Press. On the latter, see Fellmeth, A. (2012) 'U.S. State Legislation to Limit Use of International and Foreign Law', 106 *Am. J. Int'l L.* 107; Volokh, E. (2014) 'Religious Laws (Especially Islamic Law) in American Courts', 66 *Okla. L. Rev.*; and, for a broader reading of foreign law bans as directed not just against Islamic law but against foreign law in general, Rahdert, M. C. (2016) 'Exceptionalism Unbound: Appraising American Resistance to Foreign Law', 65 *Cath. U. L. Rev.* 537.

5 See Knop, K., R. Michaels and A. Riles (2012) 'From Multiculturalism to Technique: Feminism, Multiculturalism, and the Conflict of Laws Style', 64 *Stan. L. Rev.* 589; for a feminist approach, see also Banu, R. (2017) 'A Relational Feminist Approach to Conflict of Laws', 24 *Michigan Journal of Gender and Law* 1.

6 Knop, K. (2008) 'Citizenship, Public and Private', 71 *L. & Contemp. Probs.* 309. In French law, the law of aliens is part of private international law.

7 Arendt, H. (1994) *The Origins of Totalitarianism*, Schocken Books, 294. For the historical background, see, for example, Caestecker, F. and D. Fraser (2008) 'The Extraterritorial Application of the Nuremberg Laws. Rassenschande and Mixed Marriages in European Liberal Democracies', 10 *J. Hist. Int'l L.* 35.

it is *private*, it is considered *irrelevant* to questions of ethics. And because it is *law*, more precisely technical law, it is considered *inadequate*. Each of these critiques shall be briefly discussed in turn.

The first position is that private international law, as an international technical discipline, is incapable of dealing with matters of private international law. Understood as a discipline that merely allocates substantive and ethical decisions to the proper sovereign – whether based on comity, the seat of a legal relation, or the closest connection – private international law wears a 'blindfold' with regard to the ethical content of these laws themselves. Private international law, in this sense, is ethically 'neutral'.

Among those who hold this view, differences exist as to what a proper response would be. While some support such neutrality, others believe that ethical concerns must be taken seriously within private international law. A narrower response is to use the public policy exception as an 'ethical moment',[8] the application of substantive and ethical ideas to avoid application of a law that had been designated as applicable before, without consideration to its substance. A broader response is to replace the technical conflict of laws altogether with a method that focuses on the 'real conflicts,' which are, in principle, substantive conflicts.[9]

A second position is that private international law is irrelevant because it deals with small questions without ethical relevance. For this perspective, ethical questions are, by contrast, big questions and are, as such, the business of public, not private, international law. Robert Wai could be understood to hold such a view when he says that

> [w]ar and depression, the twin nightmares of public international lawyers and international trade lawyers . . . are not the overriding concerns of private international law. Private law conflicts are instead disputes among private parties about a defective product, an accident, or a violated contract. Focusing away from the extremes of international anarchy permits a calmer view of the role of contestation and dissensus.[10]

Even granting that war and depression are the more important ethical issues, private international law is related to these issues as well: it has long (though intermittently) been discussed as a response to the enmity that spurs war,[11] and it

[8] Knop et al. (2012), above fn. 5, at 640–2.

[9] Singer, J. W. (1989) 'Real Conflicts', 69 *B.U. L. Rev.* 1, 74ff.

[10] Wai, R. (2005) 'Transnational Private Law and Private Ordering in a Contested Global Society', 46 *Harv. Int'l L.J.* 471, 472–3.

[11] Schulze, G. (2016) 'Die Überwindung von Feindschaft durch Kollisionsrecht – Ein Grundgedanke des Internationalen Privatrechts von der Antike bis zu seiner Vergemeinschaftung', in Strangas et al. (eds), *Kollision, Feindschaft und Recht*, Nomos, 1097–128; see also Spain, A. (2013) 'International Dispute Resolution in an Era of Globalization', in Byrnes, A., M. Hayashi and C. Michaelsen (eds), *International Law in the New Age of Globalization*, Martinus Nijhoff, 41, 68–9. The Hague Academy of International Law was explicitly set up as an instrument for the promotion of peace through law;

deals with those trade relations that make up the financial markets and thus can contribute to depression.[12] But it seems questionable already whether the core issues of private international law are really less relevant from an ethical perspective, merely because they (often) deal with fewer individuals. Ethics is relevant in the particular, the concrete.

A third position is that private international law, at least in its traditional form, is inadequate to deal with questions of private international law because it is technical. In this realm, Joel Paul deplores the isolation of private international law from public international law (and therefore from politics),[13] and Horatia Muir Watt criticises private international law for its 'epistemological tunnel-vision, actively providing immunity and impunity to abusers of private sovereignty'.[14] These authors, and like-minded others, do not think of private international law as intrinsically incapable of dealing with ethical questions, but they do think that it is incapable in its current form. They ask us, in other ways, to rethink private international law fundamentally, in order to move it from a technical to a political understanding.

The Other in Private International Law

Against all these critiques, how do we get at the ethical dimension of private international law? Think of what ethics is about at its core: it is about our relation to the Other.[15] Ethics may be, abstractly, the discipline of right and wrong, but most of that is focused on how we should 'do unto others', on our relation with an Other. This Other is a fascinating concept. 'Je est un autre,' says Rimbaud famously – 'I is an Other' – and though here the focus is more on the I than on the Other, the quote expresses very well the complex dual nature of the Other in relation to the self. The Other is like me in that she is another sentient being. And the Other is unlike me because she is different, an Other. She is both, me and not me. My relation to the Other involves me as an actor, but it also involves me in the Other: how I relate to the Other says something about me, it says something about how I relate to me.

This should suggest how private international law is related to ethics. Let us leave aside, for a moment, both its specific doctrines and tools – its technical character and its ultimate goals – its results that are usually discussed when questions of ethics and

it fulfils this in part through courses in both public and private international law. Nonetheless, public international lawyers tend to ignore the role of private international law; for example, it is absent from Bailliet, C. M. and K. Mujezinovic Larsen (eds) (2015) *Promoting Peace Through International Law*, Oxford University Press.

12 See Riles, A. (2014) 'Managing Regulatory Arbitrage: A Conflict of Laws Approach', 47 *Cornell Int'l L.J.* 63.

13 Paul, J. R. (1988) 'The Isolation of Private International Law', 7 *Wis. J. Int'l L.* 149, 164ff; see also Paul, J. R. (2008) 'The Transformation of International Comity', 71 *L. & Contemp. Probs.* 19.

14 Muir Watt, H. (2011) 'Private International Law Beyond the Schism' 2 *Transnational Legal Theory* 347, 374.

15 On this theme, see, for example, Waldenfels, B. (2007) *The Question of the Other*, State University of New York Press.

politics are at stake. Let us instead focus on the core situation that private international law addresses. In private international law, we deal with something foreign: a foreign party, a foreign contact, a foreign law. We do not face the 'normal' case in which law, parties, facts all belong to the same order; we have to relate our normative order to this foreign element. We deal, then, with an Other.[16] That Other can be a foreign law, it can be a foreign party, or it can be another foreign element. But insofar as a foreign element is necessary to trigger a meaningful conflict of laws analysis, the foreign, the Other, is a constant of private international law regardless of what else one thinks the discipline is about.

Is, however, the foreign element that triggers a conflict of laws analysis an Other in the sense of ethics? Conflict of laws deals with foreign laws; ethics deals with persons. Are those the same thing? It is not necessary to think we have ethical obligations towards foreign law, as Pierre Legrand has frequently argued:[17] our ethical obligations are towards people, not laws. But laws matter only insofar as they apply to people, and people in return come with laws. This means that treating people and treating laws are interrelated: our treatment of foreign law is our treatment of people. The Afghani couple who come to our court carry with them the laws under which they got married. A refusal to apply that law (or recognise their marriage under that law) concerns not only, not even primarily, the law, but instead the persons who rely on it. Our attitude towards the law under which a contract was formed is closely related to the contract itself, and thereby to the persons who entered into that contract and who constituted their interrelation, and thus their identity, through it.

Three Attitudes

Foreign law is, then, like the Other: similar and different at the same time. Foreign law is similar because it is law, just like the law of the forum is law. Foreign law is different because it is foreign law, not the law of the forum. If this is correct, then one minimum ethical demand within private international law is to acknowledge this situation of the Other as both different and similar to us. Such acknowledgment is denied both where difference is denied and where similarity is denied.

Denial of difference is the easier variant. It occurs where the law of the forum is applied as a matter of course (*lex fori* approach), regardless of the foreign element involved in a fact pattern, because it is assumed that the foreign element is in all relevant regards similar to the local elements that domestic law has in mind. In this case, the law ignores that the claimant before the court is a foreigner; it ignores that the tort before the court occurred elsewhere; it ignores that the intentions of the parties to the contract were built against background expectations different from those existing in the forum's state. If there were no private international law, then difference would

16 Berman, P. S. (2010) 'Conflict of Laws and the Negotiation of Difference', in Sarat, A. D., M. Umphrey and L. Douglas (eds), *Law and the Stranger*, Stanford University Press, 141, 143ff.

17 For example, Legrand, P. (2012) 'Foreign Law in the Third Space', *juridikum* 32.

always be denied, and that would be unethical. It is through private international law that it is acknowledged.

Similarity, by contrast, is denied where foreign law is rejected *tout court*, without specific consideration of how it plays out in the concrete context. The foreign law amendments in the US and the English aversion to Islamic law, mentioned before, are two examples of such fundamental rejection. They are based on the idea of fundamental otherness. We find this idea of fundamental otherness especially vis-à-vis religious laws.[18] But the idea goes beyond this where American exceptionalism is invoked to justify a fundamental otherness of any foreign law as a reason for its irrelevance. That would be unethical in its refusal to acknowledge similarity.

Both the denial of difference and the denial of similarity thus lead to the same result: application of forum law, rejection of foreign law. In part, they rest on a similar attitude, namely a facile unwillingness to understand the Other, to deal with it. That unwillingness plays out in different methods, however: the *lex fori* approach occurs without consideration of otherness, the principled rejection of foreign law follows from an exaggeration of otherness. And although they reach the same result in the area of choice of law (because in each case forum law applies), they play out differently for the recognition of foreign judgments. Where difference is denied, foreign judgments will be recognised without any limits; where similarity is denied, foreign judgments will never be recognised.

It is necessary, therefore, to accept the Other as Other in private international law, and that means as similar and different alike. This creates a first, and important, ethical position. Paul Schiff Berman has helped explain this position, which he calls cosmopolitan,[19] although it is arguably not new, but actually intrinsic to private international law itself. Such a position creates the discipline's proper attitude, which is one in which the possibility of deference to foreign law should be considered. But the attitude itself does not tell us when and how such deference should take place. Something more must be involved. What should it be?

Three Ethics of Private International Law[20]

An Ethic of Tolerance?

A first ethic in private international law would be an ethic of tolerance. Tolerance certainly would offer a huge improvement over the 'zero tolerance' approach the US

[18] Michaels, R. (2016) 'Religiöse Rechte und postsäkulare Rechtsvergleichung', in Zimmermann, R. (ed.), *Zukunftsfragen der Rechtsvergleichung*, Mohr Siebeck, 40, 53ff.

[19] Berman, P. S. (2005) 'Towards a Cosmopolitan Vision of Conflict of Laws: Redefining Governmental Interests in a Global Era', 153 *U. Pa. L. Rev.* 1819.

[20] H. Muir Watt has, in two recent publications (above fn. 2), helpfully linked certain ethical positions to certain private international law doctrines. My typology is inspired by hers, although there are differences in the types I distinguish and the implications I draw for the relation between private international law and ethics.

administration has taken on its border towards refugees,[21] the archetypical Others to whom ethical conduct is owed. In sharp contrast, private international law can be understood as the discipline that encapsulates toleration of the Other. Werner Goldschmidt based his whole private international law on the idea of tolerance;[22] other authors express similar ideas.[23] Benjamin Cardozo, writing for the New York Court of Appeals in 1918, expressed the attitude in a way that has become widely cited: 'We are not so provincial as to say that every solution of a problem is wrong because we deal with it otherwise at home.'[24]

Tolerance is, at first, only an attitude, but it appears also in form of a doctrine. That doctrine is comity, which the US Supreme Court once defined, tellingly, as follows:

> 'Comity,' in the legal sense, is neither a matter of absolute obligation, on the one hand, nor of mere courtesy and good will, upon the other. But it is the recognition which one nation allows within its territory to the legislative, executive or judicial acts of another nation, having due regard both to international duty and convenience, and to the rights of its own citizens, or of other persons who are under the protection of its laws.[25]

Foreign law, thus, is tolerated, though not as a matter of legal obligation but instead as a matter of 'international duty and convenience'. As a consequence, the extent of this tolerance is unclear. And unclear also are the precise limits on this tolerance, which are expressed through the public policy (or *ordre public*) exception, which serves as a 'limit of tolerance'.[26]

The vagueness of both doctrines, comity and public policy, is not an accident; it is a sign of a deeper problem with understanding private international law as

[21] Office of the Attorney General, Memorandum for Federal Prosecutors Along the Southwest Border—Zero-Tolerance for Offenses Under 8 U.S.C. § 1325(a), https://www.justice.gov/opa/press-release/file/1049751

[22] Goldschmidt, W. (1977) *Derecho Internacional Privado. Derecho de la Tolerancia*, 3rd edn, Depalma, Prologue; see Oyarzábal, M. J. A. (2017) 'Goldschmidt, Werner', in *Elgar Encyclopedia of Private International Law*, Elgar, vol. 1, 852, 857–8.

[23] See, for example, Katzenbach, N. de B. (1956) 'Conflicts on an Unruly Horse: Reciprocal Claims and Tolerances in Interstate and International Law', 65 *Yale L.J.* 1087.

[24] *Loucks* v. *Standard Oil Co. of New York*, 224 N.Y. 99, 111.

[25] *Hilton* v. *Guyot*, 159 U.S. 113, 143 (1895). For the history of comity in US conflict of laws, see, most comprehensively, Dodge, W. S. (2015) 'International Comity in American Law', 115 *Colum. L. Rev.* 2071. For a plea to re-establish the private international law underpinnings of comity, see Childress III, D. E. (2010) 'Comity as Conflict: Resituating International Comity as Conflict of Laws', 44 *U.C. Davis L. Rev.* 11.

[26] Struycken, A. V. M. (2004) 'Co-ordination and Co-operation in Respectful Disagreement', *Recueil des cours*, vol. 311, 9, 395. For a central role of the public policy doctrine, see also Boden, D. (2005) 'Le pluralisme juridique en droit international privé', 49 *Arch. phil. droit* 275–316.

tolerance. Tolerance, although discussed already in antiquity, is an achievement of the Enlightenment. When Locke, Bayle and Voltaire, among others, write about it, what they have in mind is the treatment of religious difference.[27] It thus correlates, historically, with competing truth claims. Toleration is a way to live with the Other while being able to maintain the idea that the Other is wrong. It is in this sense that tolerance is another word for indifference, as Somerset Maugham allegedly said.[28] Indifference, in turn, is described by Karl Jaspers as 'the mildest form of intolerance: secret contempt – let others believe what they like, it doesn't concern me'.[29]

This idea of toleration as secret disdain can be found in private international law understood as comity and public policy: foreign law is applied not because of, but in spite of, its own value, through the forum's enlightened tolerance for what it, in principle, disagrees with. Such tolerance is therefore limited when that disagreement becomes too great. True understanding of the Other is not required and often does not take place. Where a US Court dismisses antitrust claims from Ecuadorian victims of a global cartel and defers to the regulatory interests of the Ecuadorian government, such application of comity smacks of Jasper's kind of secret disdain if the court never truly assesses what those regulatory interests are.[30] And, indeed, as critics of comity have often pointed out: if the foreign law is considered wrong, how can its application ever be justified? It can only be tolerated as long as it is harmless, and like the refugees at the US–Mexican border, that tolerance is withdrawn once the Other is viewed as dangerous.[31]

[27] See, generally, Forst, R. (2017) 'Toleration', *The Stanford Encyclopedia of Philosophy*, available at: https://plato.stanford.edu/entries/toleration

[28] The quote seems apocryphal. It does appear, however, in the Monthly Summary of the Religious Press, *The Japan Weekly Mail*, 14 Jan 1905, 44, at 45, where it is attributed to an article by a writer calling himself Entei in the publication Koye (Roman Catholic).

[29] Jaspers, K. [1953] (2014) *Origin and Goal of History* (transl. M. Bullock), Routledge, 221. Jaspers himself distinguishes indifference from tolerance, which he defines as 'open-minded: it knows its own limitations and seeks to integrate them humanly into diversity, without reducing the notions and ideas of faith to a common denominator'. Ibid., 221.

[30] *F. Hoffman-La Roche Ltd* v. *Empagran S.A.*, 542 U.S. 155, 165 (2004). For my critique of the Court, see Michaels, R. (2011) 'Empagran's Empire: International Law and Statutory Interpretation in the U.S. Supreme Court of the Twenty-First Century', in Sloss, D. L. et al. (eds), *International Law in the U.S. Supreme Court: Continuity and Change*, Cambridge University Press, 533. For discussion of developing nations' interests and how to accommodate them, see Michaels, R. (2016) 'Supplanting Foreign Antitrust', 79 *L. & Contemp. Probs*. 223.

[31] Cf. Treitschke, H. von (1916) *Politics* (transl. B. Dugdale and T. de Bille), Macmillan, vol. II, 605: 'Let us make as many treaties as we like about international civil law [German original: Internationales Privatrecht, private international law], but they must all presuppose that the alien is not troublesome to ourselves. Should he become so, the State must have power to expel him without giving reasons, even if it has signed a treaty which, as a rule, ensures security of residence to the subjects of another Government.'

An Ethic of Recognition?

Goethe thought so, too: 'Tolerance should really be only a temporary attitude; it must lead to recognition. To tolerate means to offend.'[32] Is recognition therefore a better approach for private international law? Recognition of the Other looks, at first, like a unidirectional relation between a recognising subject and a recognised object. However, since Hegel, recognition is often viewed as a mutual, reciprocal process: it is through recognition of the Other as an intentional person that we manage to recognise ourselves. If tolerance was the ethical position of the eighteenth century, recognition was the position of the nineteenth century: now, minorities – religious or otherwise – demanded more than mere toleration; they demanded to be recognised in their identity. But recognition has also become a core concern in the late twentieth century, encouraged especially through the neo-Hegelian theories of, respectively, Charles Taylor and Axel Honneth.[33] Charles Taylor argues that the need for recognition is universal; the risk of its absence arises with modernity. Recognition accounts for the fact, described earlier, that the Other is both similar and different: recognition accounts equal dignity to the Other, but it also enables a politics of difference, in which the unique identity of the Other is recognised. Axel Honneth expands such ideas to focus more on the specific relations between the self and the Other and distinguishes three: love (for self-confidence), rights (for self-respect) and solidarity (for self-esteem).

Clearly, such ideas find responses in the law. Private international law in particular is amenable to ideas of recognition, given the central role that recognition plays for the discipline. Foreign judgments are recognised, as were, for a long time, so-called 'vested rights'[34] established under foreign law. Within the European Union, there is even discussion of resting an entire system of private international law on ideas of mutual recognition.[35] And indeed, as in ethics, so in private international law the idea of recognition has gained much support.[36]

And yet, recognition is insufficient as well, both in ethics and in private international law. Nancy Fraser voices an important concern that is mirrored in private international law: the focus on recognition is insufficient for justice unless it is

[32] 'Toleranz sollte eigentlich nur eine vorübergehende Gesinnung sein; sie muss zur Anerkennung führen. Dulden heißt Beleidigen.' Goethe, J. W., 'Maximen und Reflexionen', *Werke* XII, Beck (1981), 385, no. 151.

[33] Taylor, C. (1992) 'The Politics of Recognition', in Taylor, C., *Multiculturalism and the Politics of Recognition*, Princeton University Press, 23–73; Honneth, A. (1992) *The Struggle for Recognition: The Moral Grammar of Social Conflicts*, Polity Press.

[34] Dicey, A. V. (1896) *A Digest of the Law of England with Reference to the Conflict of Laws*. Stevens and Sons Limited, 24–25, and 28 et seq.

[35] Lagarde, P. (ed.) (2013) *La reconnaissance des situations en droit international privé*, A. Pedone.

[36] Isailovic, I. (2016) 'La reconnaissance politique en droit transnational: Les identités, les marginalisations et le droit international privé', in Tourmé Jouannet, E., H. Muir Watt, O. Frouville and J. Matringe (eds), *Droit international et reconnaissance*, A. Pedone, 301.

coupled with a focus on issues of distribution.[37] We find a similar concern in private international law, in particular in the debate over the application of foreign law: how can we reconcile the recognition and applicability of an unjust law with our commitment to substantive justice? Jacques Rancière goes further in his critique when he questions what it is that is being recognised: the identity of the Other, he suggests, does not predate the act of recognition.[38] And, indeed, foreign legal systems do not fully exist prior to their recognition,[39] and foreign law is always applied in a way different from how it exists in the foreign system.[40]

Two examples demonstrate these shortcomings. When the Court of Justice of the European Union, in its Grunkin Paul decision, required German authorities to recognise a newborn's name under Danish law, it did so on the basis of a duty to recognise the child's status.[41] The child is thus recognised, essentially, as having a Danish identity, as demonstrated in his or her name. This may be a defensible result. But does such recognition not ignore the multifaceted identity of the individual who is, as is always the case in private international law, caught between different orders? Rather than recognising a pre-existing identity, it is the decision itself that constructs this identity. A second example arises from the French refusal to recognise unilateral divorces under Moroccan law as violating a woman's equal rights.[42] The woman is here recognised as equal to the man, but in refusing to recognise her divorce, courts recreate her as a split personality: considered divorced in her country of origin (and in her faith community) yet considered married in the court's country.

Indeed, one problem of recognition can be that it goes too far: by creating identities, recognition cuts through the fluidity of the private international law individual who exists between legal systems. As a consequence, and perhaps perversely, recognition can enhance separation and thereby lead to discrimination. Elizabeth Povinelli describes such a process in the context of the recognition of aborigines in Australia: although ostensibly a benevolent act, the recognition actually hardens the distance between aborigines and the Australian state and confines them within their identity.[43]

[37] Fraser, N. (2001) 'Recognition without Ethics?', 18 *Theory, Culture & Society* 21–42; for the discussion with Honneth, see Fraser, N. and A. Honneth (2003) *Redistribution or Recognition: A Political-Philosophical Exchange*, Verso.

[38] See Deranty, J. P. (2003) 'Jacques Rancière's contribution to the ethics of recognition', 31 *Political Theory* 136; Honneth, A. and J. Rancière (2016), *Recognition or Disagreement*, Columbia University Press.

[39] Michaels, R. (2017) 'Law and Recognition – Towards a Relational Concept of Law', in Roughan, N. and A. Halpin (eds), *In Pursuit of Pluralist Jurisprudence*, Cambridge University Press, 90–115.

[40] See Jansen, N. and R. Michaels (2003) 'Die Auslegung iund Fortbildung ausländischen Rechts', 116 *Zeitschrift für Zivilprozess*, 3–56.

[41] CJEU, 14 October 2008, C-353-06, Grunkin and Paul.

[42] Fournier, P. (2016) *Muslim Marriage in Western Courts: Lost in Transplantation*, Routledge, 54–5 with references.

[43] Povinelli, E. A. (2002) *The Cunning of Recognition: Indigenous Alterities and the Making of Australian Multiculturalism*, Duke University Press.

An Ethic of Hospitality?

If tolerance is insufficient, and recognition is intrusive, the solution may lie in an ethic of hospitality. This ethic can be grounded in Martin Buber's philosophy, as developed further by Emmanuel Levinas and Jacques Derrida. Buber suggests that the world always exists in relation to the self, but it does so in two very different relations that he calls I-It and I-Thou.[44] Simplified, I-It relations treat the other as an object, whereas I-Thou relations treat the other as a subject, as an Other. This is related to the Kantian idea of treating others as ends in themselves. But it goes beyond that because Buber's focus is less on the Other and more on the relation itself. The Other is simultaneously recognised as an Other and intrinsically put in relation to the self.

This is the thought that Levinas develops further and turns into a meta-ethical position that transcends the is/ought separation: the relation itself creates a normative claim on the self.[45] For Levinas, insofar like Buber, the Other is always already in a relation to me (I-Thou). But the relation is not formal and abstract: the Other comes as a concrete person with specifics (a 'face') and with concrete needs: the Other is poor, or dirty, or sick, or helpless. This Other therefore commands me through his very existence and his very needs; he demands from me: let me live. That ethical demand has priority over the ontology of the Other, meaning the Other comes to me already in an ethical relation, with a command. And I can respond to this command by following it, or not, but I cannot ignore the command.

This has surprising parallels with private international law. The foreign law already stands in a relation with the forum's law; it is never 'merely there'.[46] That law is specific – it is not 'foreign law' in the abstract, or the law of a fictitious entity like Ruritania. It has needs: it has no force in our courts, without the help of the judge who is willing to enforce it. Its command to the forum is: help me in this. Do not kill me. Do not be jurispathic, to use Robert Cover's term.[47] And so the forum can yield to this command or not, but it cannot escape it.

Take, for example, partners in a same-sex marriage celebrated elsewhere, asking for recognition of their marriage. The marriage under foreign law is part of their identity, the plea for recognition is clear (and, where the status of being married can prevent deportation, it is literally a plea to save their lives).[48] Now the court cannot

[44] Buber, M. (1970) *I and Thou*, T. & T. Clark.

[45] Levinas' position is developed at several places, especially in his Levinas, E. (1961) *Totality and Infinity*, Kluwer. For helpful introductions, see Levinas, E. (1995) *Ethics and Infinity—Conversations with Philippe Nemo*, Duquesne University Press; Morgan, M. L. (2011) *The Cambridge Introduction to Emmanuel Levinas*, Cambridge University Press, Ch. 3, 59ff.

[46] Michaels, 'Law and Recognition', above fn. 39.

[47] Cover, R. M. (1983) 'The Supreme Court, 1982 Term' Foreword: Nomos and Narrative, 97 *Harv. L. Rev.* 4, 40ff.

[48] Jessurun d'Oliveira, H. U. (1999) 'The Artifact of "Sham Marriages"', *Yearbook of Private International Law*, vol. 1, 49–83.

escape the demand: even if it denies the claim for recognition, it cannot thereby avoid the relation.[49]

Horatia Muir Watt, drawing on Derrida (who was in this respect influenced by Levinas) has demonstrated how such thoughts can inform an understanding of private international law.[50] Traditional private international law, she suggests, recognises foreign law merely under certain conditions, namely a certain level of similarity; it is based only on ideas of tolerance. Hospitality as unconditional acceptance, by contrast, can be found in unilateral approaches to private international law. Here, the foreign law necessarily appears in its concrete specificity and gets applied because it wants (needs) to be applied according to the doctrine of unilateralism. Unilateralism is often rejected in private international law as an is/ought crossover: the fact that the foreign law wants to be applied (a fact) has no normative implication that the forum should apply it.[51] A response can invoke Levinas: the mere fact that the foreign law appears related to us, in its specificity and with its needs (in this case: to be applied), creates an ethical plea for such application, but not yet more. The is/ought crossover is not the only criticism of unilateralism, however. The bigger problem is, arguably, that unilateralism is too powerful: by ceding to the other entirely, we give foreign law more force than domestic law. The US Supreme Court once discussed this possibility as absurd:

> A rigid and literal enforcement of the full faith and credit clause, without regard to the statute of the forum, would lead to the absurd result that, wherever the conflict arises, the statute of each state must be enforced in the courts of the other, but cannot be in its own.[52]

Muir Watt suggests that this is not an insoluble problem: applicability of foreign law is not unlimited, but instead remains under control of the public policy exception.[53] But this seems incompatible with the idea she draws on. Derrida in particular suggests that hospitality is not only unconditional, but also unlimited; it requires to receive the stranger not just without any conditions (of similarity, even of giving her name), but also without any limitations: the host is required to offer literally everything: his house, his wealth, his family. Such absolute hospitality is an impossibility, while

[49] See Cossman, B. (2008) 'Betwixt and Between Recognition: Migrating Same-Sex Marriages and the Turn Toward the Private', 71 *L. & Contemp. Probs.* 153–68.

[50] Muir Watt (2017), above fn. 2, draws on Derrida, J. (2000) *Of Hospitality—Anne Dufourmantelle Invites Jacques Derrida to Respond*, Stanford University Press; see also Derrida, J. (2001) *Cosmopolitanism and Forgiveness*, Routledge. Levinas' influence on Derrida's concept of hospitality, palpable throughout both texts, becomes even clearer in Derrida, J. (1999) *Adieu to Emmanuel Levinas*, Stanford University Press.

[51] Schurig, K. (1986) 'Lois d'application immédiate und Sonderanknüpfungzwingenden Rechts: Erkenntnisfortschritt oder Mystifikation?', in Holl, W. and U. Klinge (eds), *Internationales Privatrecht—Internationales Wirtschaftsrecht* 55.

[52] *Alaska Packers Ass'n* v. *Industrial Accident Commission of California*, 294 U.S. 532, 547 (1935).

[53] Muir Watt (2017) 'Politics of Difference', above fn. 2, at 138.

Muir Watt's restriction is possible. At the same time, hospitality limited by a public policy exception is no longer hospitality in the sense of Derrida; at its core it is again merely limited deference.

An Ethic of Responsivity

What, then, should an ethical approach to private international law look like? Some progress has been made. In the first section of this chapter, I demonstrated that the ethical relevance of private international law lies in its focus on the Other, and that it must recognise the Other as both similar and different, as both independent and related. That created an attitude of a principled willingness to defer to foreign law, but not more. In the second section, I discussed different ethical positions towards the Other – tolerance, recognition, hospitality – and related these to different approaches to private international law. These positions describe different degrees of willingness to defer to foreign law, as Muir Watt describes in her somewhat parallel project: apply foreign law never, sometimes, always.[54] Different ethical positions do not, however, only differ in the degree of deference to the foreign. They also differ in the kind of relation they construct. Tolerance creates a relation of wilful ignorance; recognition creates a relation of hierarchy; hospitality rests on a relationship of need.

And the positions differ in the degree to which they view the Other as independent from that relation. Tolerance assumes the other to be independent, though it may require the Other to become more similar in order to justify being tolerated. Comity can be remarkably blind for the actual content of the foreign law. Recognition is more ambivalent: insofar as it is the act of recognition that constructs the Other, recognition becomes a violent act, one that defines the Other. Povinelli's example, discussed before, comes to mind. Hospitality, finally, is the ethical position that positions the relation as irreducibly linked to the Other: the Other appears only in relation (Buber), and that relation is ethical before it is ontological (Levinas).

This suggests that it is worthwhile to shift the gaze from the Other to the relation in which the self stands to the Other, from the foreign law as such to the relation in which that foreign law stands to the forum. What is lacking here is a finer analysis of what exactly that relation entails. Both a plea for survival (Levinas) and unlimited hospitality (Derrida) are in themselves insufficient: mere survival is too minimal, unlimited hospitality is too maximal. Both can generate discussions about concrete ethical problems, but they do not entail them through logical deduction. Once we focus on the relation, we no longer ask what is owed to the foreign law; instead, we ask what the relation entails.

[54] Ibid., at 115, 126.

The Relevance of Technique

This is where technique becomes relevant. After all, in private international law we do not confine ourselves to a two-step analysis, in which we first define a deferential relation to the Other and then limit it through the public policy exception. Instead, the relation to the Other is established through a number of devices that are used in the analysis of private international law: characterisation, *renvoi*, adaptation, substitution, public policy and so on. These devices, which are 'merely technical', are often thought of as anathema to questions of ethics. At best, they are insufficient devices to avoid outcomes that are normatively undesirable – the US debate speaks in this context of 'escape devices'.[55] At worst, they are devices that blind the analyst for the actual ethical relevance in the case – this is what the European reception of the US conflicts revolution emphasised, and what new critical approaches to private international law re-establish.[56]

Technique is often thought to be merely that: opposed to theory and opposed to ethics. Muir Watt suggests, apodictically: 'Often described as "theoretical", these aspects of private international law are essentially technical and have little relationship with the great questions of legal theory.'[57] This may be true for the practical application of private international law, but it seems untrue for the field in general. Justice Frankfurter referred to Joseph Beale's conflict of laws course as a course in jurisprudence, and Beale was arguably the most technical of conflicts scholars in the US.[58] It is not only the case that private international law provides fruitful inspirations for legal theory;[59] it is also the case that private international law can itself be viewed as a legal theory, and that its technical devices do not avoid difficult questions of politics and ethics, but instead serve to formulate them in a way that is more prone to allowing responses.[60]

The theoretical and ethical content of the techniques of private international law cannot here be demonstrated with sufficient specificity. Two examples must suffice.

[55] Currie, B. (1959) 'Notes on Methods and Objectives in the Conflict of Laws', *Duke L.J.* 171, 175.

[56] Muir Watt (2011), 'Private International Law Beyond the Schism', above fn. 14.

[57] Ibid., at 380, fn. 163.

[58] Frankfurter, F. (1943) 'Henry Joseph Beale', 56 *Harv. L. Rev.* 701, 703. Beale is almost universally rejected today; see only Symeonides, S. (2007) 'The First Conflicts Restatement through the Eyes of Old: As Bad as its Reputation?', 32 *Southern Ill. L.R.* 39. See also Freund, P. A. (1946) 'Chief Justice Stone and the Conflict of Laws', 59 *Harv. L. Rev.* 1210: 'Chief Justice Stone . . . would regard Conflict of Laws as a study serving in place of a course in Jurisprudence', with citation to the passage by Frankfurter.

[59] Maurer, A. and M. Renner (2010) 'Kollisionsrechtliches Denken in der Rechtstheorie', in Schramm, E. et al., *Konflikte im Recht –Recht der Konflikte* 125 *Archiv für Rechts- und Sozialphilosophie* 207–24.

[60] Or so I have argued: Michaels, R. (2014) 'Post-Critical Private International Law: From Politics to Technique', in Fernández Arroyo, D. P. and H. Muir Watt (eds), *Private International Law and Global Governance*, Oxford University Press, 54–67.

The first concerns the application of foreign law itself.[61] True deference to foreign law puts the judge before an ethical dilemma: respect for the foreign law requires the judge, on the one hand, to get foreign law right and, on the other hand, to realise that he or she is not a part of the foreign law and can therefore not make authoritative claims to its meaning. The discipline of anthropology has, for the parallel problem that truly 'going native' is impossible, developed the device of 'lateral thinking': thinking through the Other, thinking 'as if' one were part of the Other.[62] In private international law, the 'foreign court theory', according to which a judge is supposed to apply foreign law 'as if' he or she were sitting in the foreign court, takes a similar move. The foreign court theory must then be seen, not as an impossibility, but instead as a sophisticated and attractive ethical move.

Or take the aforementioned public policy exception. It is the response to another ethical dilemma: the conflict between the duty of deferring to foreign law and the duty to avoid the application of a law that is incompatible with fundamental values. The public policy exception actually responds in a very subtle way to minimise the conflict. First, it is directed not against the foreign law itself, but only against the result of its application in the forum state. Second, the standard of review is not some supposed universal set of values, but instead the values of the forum state. Third, the public policy exception only sets in when there are sufficient connections to the forum state. All of this is like saying to the Other: I respect you, I do not question your identity and I do not suggest that my values are better than yours merely because they are mine. I merely minimise the impact of your identity insofar as it fundamentally upsets my home. And I do so because, in this concrete case, my home is so directly affected, because of the strong relationship between the conduct and my home. Seen like this, the public policy exception is not merely the ethical stop gap against the mechanical application of foreign law; it is itself a deeply ethical device.

Note what role ethics plays here. Ethics does not come before the devices of private international law, as a normative foundation to inform them. Nor does ethics come after them, as an *ex post* tool to evaluate their quality. Instead, ethics is within these devices themselves. These technical devices are themselves ethical constructions: it is through private international law itself that an ethical position is formulated and at the same time put into practice. This is what it means to understand private international law as an ethic, not merely as grounded in one.

An Ethic of Responsivity

Finally, what kind of an ethic is it? The technique of private international law is not merely a device of fine-tuning comity to determine the exact border between deference and its limits. Instead, the technique of private international law is an ethic of a particular nature: it is, to borrow a concept from Bernhard Waldenfels, an ethic

[61] For the following, see Riles, A. (2008) 'Cultural Conflicts', 71 *L. & Contemp. Probs.* 273, 296ff.

[62] For a summary, see Gad, C. and C. B. Jensen (2016) 'Lateral Concepts', 2 *Engaging Science, Technology, and Society* 3–12.

of responsivity.[63] Responsivity is different from both intentionality and regularity: 'that with which I respond owes its meaning to the challenge to which it responds'.[64] Through the application of complicated technique vis-à-vis the foreign law, private international law takes the Other more seriously than mere deference would. The application of private international law rules is never purely mechanical; it always operates in response to the concrete Other law, and therefore private international law is always necessarily open.[65] Thereby, private international law engages the Other. It takes the Other's plea more seriously than mere deference would. It grapples with the Other. It puts the positions taken by the Other in perspective and in context. It creates a hypothetical dialogue with the Other – hypothetical because the dialogue takes place within private international law's own position,[66] but therefore no less real. The response can lead to a result that a conflict remains, just as in conflicts among individuals the ethically required result is sometimes that the conflict remains. Responsivity does not merely equate deference. But responsivity makes rejection justifiable.

Private international law can act as an ethic of responsivity because it is not a merely theoretical position. It shares that emphasis on practice with existing positions in the discipline of ethics. It is, then, a practical ethic, but one of a specific kind because its practice consists of legal doctrine, in a particular kind of technical argument. Where the Other is a legal order, legal doctrine becomes the practice to which private international law responds: the Other is law, the relation to it is law and the ethic that emerges from that is law, too.

Conclusion

I have argued that private international law not only has ethical relevance, but that it is itself an ethic, namely an ethic of responsivity. That ethic relies on three foundational building blocks, discussed in three sections: the Other, the relation to the Other and the technique of responsivity. The two first blocks exist in ethics more generally. The third is specific to private international law, simply because the technique of private international law is specific to private international law. The first two blocks do not need private international law. The third one is private international law's own contribution to ethics.

63 See Waldenfels, B. (2003) 'From Intentionality to Responsivity', in Bernet, R. and D. J. Martino (eds), *Phenomenology Today: The Schuwer Spep Lectures, 1998–2002*, Simon Silverman Phenomenology Center, Duquesne University, 23–35; Waldenfels, *The Question of the Other*, above fn. 15, at 21ff.; Leistle, B. (2016) 'Responsivity and (Some) Other Approaches to Alterity', *Anthropological Theory* vol. 16, no. 1, 48–74. Waldenfels distinguishes responsivity as a creative process from technical responses as results from a programme: Waldenfels, B. (2015) *Sozialität und AlteritätModi sozialer Erfahrung*, Suhrkamp, 18–19. My use of technique encompasses the creativity, which is arguably always present in the process of private international law.

64 Waldenfels, 'From Intentionality to Responsivity', above fn. 63, at 24.

65 Schurig, K. (1981) *Kollisionsnorm und Sachrecht. Zu Struktur, Standort und Methode des internationalen Privatrechts*, Duncker and Humblot, 170–6.

66 See Knop et al. 'From Multiculturalism to Technique', above fn. 5, at 648–9.

What follows for the way in which we engage in private international law? If we feel that private international law is of ethical importance – and how could we not? – then the findings here should be reason for hope. The hope is that the relation to the Other, that hugely important ethical issue of our times, can find an adequate ethical response, although in an unexpected place. Private international law, understood as an ethic, is not a mere technical device that leads to arbitrary responses. Nor is it a field that needs to be completely reinvented in order to be ethically relevant. What is necessary is to understand that, and how, private international law itself operates as an ethic, and that it does so through its technique.

That in itself is not a small step. It does not require a radical reinvention of the field, but it requires a fairly radical reorientation of our thinking of the field. To know that we are, when we apply doctrines of private international law, operating in ethical theory and practice, is empowering, but it also creates a great responsibility. Private international law, far from being at the margin of the big issues of our world, stands in its centre. The biggest ethical issues of our world require us to define our relation to the Other. Let us see how private international law as an ethic of responsivity can do this.

PART I

LEGAL DIVERSITY AND INTEGRATION

2

Embracing Diversity – The Role of the Hague Conference in the Creation of Universal Instruments

Hans van Loon

Legal Diversity in the Hague Conference

The Hague Conference on Private International Law is naturally predicated on legal diversity: without the large variety of approaches, systems, rules and practices of civil and commercial law and civil procedure in our world, there would be no Hague Conference.[1]

Tobias Asser, the founder of the Conference,[2] was driven by his frustration as a practising lawyer in Amsterdam that a judgment, properly obtained from a court in one country, could be a worthless piece of paper in another. Or that a contract, a will, a marriage or a divorce valid in one country could be considered invalid in another: very concrete day-to-day problems resulting from legal diversity faced by people in their relationships and activities, private and commercial, across borders. It was the practical need to overcome such problems that inspired Asser to look for solutions.

His efforts took shape in the late nineteenth century, within a small community of continental European civil law states.[3] Even so, Asser deliberately chose the route of unification not of substantive law, but of private international law. This was only realistic, he felt, in a world where a large part of civil law, and in particular of family law, stood under the influence of '*coutumes locales, des originalités de la race, des*

[1] This chapter draws, in part, on work first published as 'Legal Diversity in a Flat, Crowded World: The Role of the Hague Conference', in *Revue hellénique de droit international*, vol. 62, no. 2 (2009), 494–509; as well as in the *International Journal of Legal Information*, vol. 39, no. 2 (Summer 2011), 172–85.

[2] See Eyffinger, A. (2011) *Dreaming the Ideal, Living the Attainable T.M.C. Asser [1838-1913] Founder of the Hague Tradition*, T. M. C. Asser Press. Van Loon, H. (2012) 'The Hague Conference on Private International Law: Asser's Vision and an Evolving Mission', *Hague Yearbook of International Law/Annuaire de La Haye de droit international*, vol. 24, 3–10.

[3] A stimulus for these efforts also came from the successful Latin American work on the unification of private international law, in particular the 1889 *Montevideo Treaties on Private International Law*.

mœurs, du climat etc.', other parts of civil law were related to political institutions and still others bore the imprint of convictions held by the country's jurists[4] – or, in modern terms, in a world characterised by (legal) diversity.

It was Mancini's cosmopolitan nationality concept that provided the cornerstone for an ambitious programme for the unification of private international law. Nationality, as the principal connecting factor to identify the applicable law in cases involving a foreign element, left maximum scope for diversity at the level of substantive law. Moreover, the assumption was that the various legal systems represented in The Hague were essentially equivalent: Italian authorities would, as a firm rule, apply French law to the marriage of a French couple and French courts would apply Italian law to an Italian couple. The early Hague Conventions did not even contain the safety valve of the public policy exception.[5]

But during the run-up to the First World War it already appeared that this approach was far too naive. Then, in the interbellum period, some dreadful court decisions were rendered, which applied German law, including the Nuremberg laws steeped in anti-Semitism, with the argument that the 1902 Hague Marriage Convention did not allow a refusal to apply foreign law. In retrospect such decisions clearly violated human rights.[6]

The Hague Conventions negotiated after the Second World War introduced the criterion of habitual residence as a primary connecting factor, as well as the possibility for the courts not to give effect to the foreign law or judgment simply '*pour un motif d'ordre public*'. But this unrestricted public policy clause moved the pendulum too far to the other side, because if any public policy consideration is sufficient to set aside the foreign law or foreign decision, then respect for diversity is at risk.

Therefore, the early Hague Conventions on child support, the 1956 Convention on the Law Applicable to Maintenance Obligations towards Children[7] and the 1958 Convention Concerning the Recognition and Enforcement of Decisions relating to Maintenance Obligations towards Children,[8] introduced the now common and famous

[4] Asser, T. M. C. (1880) 'Droit international privé et droit uniforme', *Revue de droit international et de législation comparée*, vol. 12, 5–22, at 12–13.

[5] On the public policy exception see further the chapter by Fresnedo in this volume.

[6] For example, Art. 12 of the European Convention on Human Rights read in conjunction with its Art. 14. The Convention for the Protection of Human Rights and Fundamental Freedoms was concluded in Rome on 4 November 1950 and entered into force on 3 September 1953. Its status is available at: www.coe.int/en/web/conventions/full-list

[7] The Hague Convention on the Law Applicable to Maintenance Obligations towards Children was concluded on 24 October 1956 and entered into force on 1 January 1962; 14 States Parties, status as at 15 October 2018; Art. 4.

[8] The Hague Convention Concerning the Recognition and Enforcement of Decisions relating to Maintenance Obligations towards Children was signed on 15 April 1958 and entered into force on 1 January 1962; 20 States Parties, status as at 15 October 2018; Art. 2 (5): Decisions must be recognised and enforced if '*la décision n'est pas manifestement incompatible avec l'ordre public de l'Etat où elle est invoquée*'.

formula according to which the application of a foreign law, or the recognition of a foreign judgment, may be refused only if this is manifestly incompatible with the public policy of the forum.[9] The formula has done wonders in practice: it has helped to keep the refusal to apply foreign laws or to recognise foreign decisions to a bare minimum. Its effect is enhanced by the fact that the post-war choice of law (or applicable law) Conventions[10] apply universally, that is, whether or not the law designated by the Convention is that of a State Party to the treaty.[11] The formula stands out as a marker of respect for legal diversity and the universal equivalence, in principle, of legal systems, while reserving the application of fundamental values (increasingly including regionally and globally shared values)[12] embraced by the forum.[13]

The states that in the 1950s gave the Hague Conference its permanent status were, as in the early period, largely continental European civil law countries, plus Japan and the United Kingdom. As in the case of the European Union, the basis for the unification efforts was therefore laid predominantly by civil law systems.

In the EU context of work on private international law, civil law continues to dominate, sometimes, especially in the Court of Justice's case law, excessively.[14] And the common law influence is likely to further diminish if Brexit becomes a reality.[15]

The Hague Conference, on the other hand, has gradually included an ever-widening circle of legal systems.[16] In the 1960s, the United States, Canada and other common law countries joined. A development began which still continues today, aimed at bridging not only civil law and common law systems, which now hold each other pretty much in balance within the Conference, but also the varieties *within* each of these two families, and unitary and federal systems, which in some cases include both civil and common law (such as Quebec within the Canadian federal system). Later, the Conference included China, other Asian countries and a large number of Latin American states. Furthermore, in this century dialogue with the Islamic systems has become a focal point.

9 For the origins and justification of this formula, see de Winter, L. I. (1957) 'Rapport de la Commission Spéciale', *Documents relatifs à la Huitième Session de la Conférence de La Haye*, 3–14 October 1956, 124–33, at 131–2.

10 An exception, however, may be found in the 1956 Hague Convention on the Law Applicable to Maintenance Obligations towards Children (Art. 6: '*La Convention ne s'applique qu'aux cas où la loi désignée par l'article premier, est celle d'un des Etats contractants*').

11 In this context 'universal' means relating to 'abandonment of reciprocity with regards to choice of law'; in the words of Basedow, 'the modern conventions are *lois uniformes* that apply regardless of whether the designated law is the law of a Contracting State'; see Basedow, J. (2018) 'The Hague Conference and the Future of Private International Law – A Jubilee Speech' *RabelsZ* vol. 82, no. 4, 922–43.

12 Cf. 'The Unifying Force of Global Human Rights', below.

13 Cf. van Loon (2015) 'The Global Horizon of Private International Law', *Recueil des cours*, vol. 380, 9–108 (para. 15; 55–6, 59).

14 See also Hartley, T. (2005) 'The European Union and the Systematic Dismantling of the Common Law of Conflict of Laws', *ICLQ*, vol. 54, 813–28.

15 On private international law and Brexit see the chapter by Requejo Isidro in this volume.

16 See overview at HCCH Members' tab, available at: www.hcch.net/en/states/hcch-members

In relation to each new issue in the Hague Conference agenda, Members of the Conference are invited to deepen a common international perspective on how to handle legal diversity and to work together on instruments to permit coordination of legal systems, and increasingly also to facilitate direct cross-border communication and cooperation among national administrative authorities and courts.

Of the many aspects of legal diversity that present a challenge to the Conference, this chapter will concentrate briefly on three: we will discuss, first, how the Conference has dealt with federal, quasi-federal and unitary legal systems; second, how it has attempted to bridge the divide between common law and civil law systems; and, third, how it has dealt with legal systems based on, or influenced by, religion or faith. This will be followed by some concluding remarks on the importance of inclusiveness as a working method of the Conference, and also on the relevance of the global human rights framework.

Federal, Quasi-federal and Unitary Jurisdictions

When the US first attended a Session of the Hague Conference in 1956, as an invited observer, Kurt Nadelmann argued on behalf of the American delegation that, given the prerogatives of the states within the federal system, it would be very difficult for the US to bind itself to international treaties on private international law. He proposed to broaden the working methods of the Conference, and to move towards the adoption of non-binding model laws, the uniform law method widely used within the US. Although this proposal was not rejected, the Conference has during the past sixty years quietly continued to work on binding multilateral treaties. And, thanks to the efforts of the State Department and countless groups and individuals, the US is now a Party to seven Hague Conventions: the 1961 Convention Abolishing the Requirement of Legalisation (Apostille Convention);[17] the 1965 Convention on the Service Abroad of Judicial and Extrajudicial Documents in Civil and Commercial Matters;[18] the 1970 Hague Convention on the Taking of Evidence Abroad in Civil and Commercial Matters;[19] the 1980 Hague Convention on the Civil Aspects of International Child Abduction;[20] the 1993 Convention on Protection of Children and

[17] The Convention Abolishing the Requirement of Legalisation for Foreign Public Documents was concluded in The Hague on 5 October 1961 and entered into force on 24 January 1965; 117 States Parties, status as at 15 October 2018.

[18] The Hague Convention on the Service Abroad of Judicial and Extrajudicial Documents in Civil or Commercial Matters was concluded on 15 November 1965 and entered into force on 10 February 1969; 73 States Parties, status as at 15 October 2018.

[19] The Hague Convention on the Taking of Evidence Abroad in Civil or Commercial Matters was concluded on 18 March 1970 and entered into force on 7 October 1972; 61 States Parties, status as at 15 October 2018.

[20] The Convention on the Civil Aspects of International Child Abduction was concluded in The Hague on 25 October 1980 and entered into force on 1 December 1983; 99 States Parties, status as at 15 October 2018.

Co-operation in Respect of Intercountry Adoption;[21] the 2007 Convention on the International Recovery of Child Support and Other Forms of Family Maintenance;[22] and the 2006 Convention on the Law Applicable to Certain Rights in Respect of Securities Held with an Intermediary.[23] Moreover, the US has signed, but not yet ratified, the 1985 Convention on the Law Applicable to Trusts and on their Recognition;[24] the 1996 Convention on Jurisdiction, Applicable Law, Recognition, Enforcement and Co-operation in Respect of Parental Responsibility and Measures for the Protection of Children;[25] and the 2005 Convention on Choice of Court Agreements.[26]

This has been made possible by a major process within the US of rethinking the relationship between federal and state law in the field of 'civil procedure, family law, estate law and the law applicable to international business transactions . . . areas of the law left, for the most part, to the states . . .'[27] Ways have been found to combine the uniform law technique with the treaty engagements. With 'conditional spending', the federal government uses its purse to encourage a state legislature to act; if it does not, the state will lose federal subsidies. This has worked as an effective means to ensure the implementation of the 2007 Child Support Convention. Another technique, which has been considered in connection with the efforts towards ratification of the 2005 Choice of Court Convention, is that of 'cooperative federalism'.[28]

In addition to the US, the number of federal systems or quasi-federal systems within the Conference has steadily grown. It has developed techniques to allow ratification of Conventions regarding only one or more sub-units, thus respecting federal diversity. This has been important to Canada but has also been used by

[21] The Hague Convention on Protection of Children and Co-operation in Respect of Intercountry Adoption was adopted on 29 May 1993 and entered into force on 1 May 1995; 99 States Parties, status as at 15 October 2018.

[22] The Hague Convention on the International Recovery of Child Support and Other Forms of Family Maintenance was concluded on 23 November 2007 and entered into force on 1 January 2013; 39 States Parties, status as at 15 October 2018.

[23] The Convention on the Law Applicable to Certain Rights in Respect of Securities held with an Intermediary was adopted in The Hague on 5 July 2006 and entered into force on 1 April 2017; 3 States Parties, status as at 15 October 2018.

[24] The Hague Convention on the Law Applicable to Trusts and on their Recognition was concluded on 1 July 1985 and entered into force on 1 January 1992; 14 States Parties, status as at 15 October 2018.

[25] The Convention on Jurisdiction, Applicable Law, Recognition, Enforcement and Co-operation in Respect of Parental Responsibility and Measures for the Protection of Children was concluded in The Hague on 19 October 1996 and entered into force on 1 January 2002; 49 States Parties, status as at 15 October 2018.

[26] The Hague Convention on Choice of Court Agreements was adopted on 30 June 2005 and entered into force on 1 October 2015; 32 States Parties, status as at 15 October 2018.

[27] Pfund, P. (1994) 'Contributing to Progressive Development of Private International Law: the International Process and the United States Approach', *Recueil des cours*, vol. 249, 11–144, at 51.

[28] In the case of the Choice of Court Convention, this would lead to a combination of legislative action at the federal level and election of a uniform state law at the state level, so that states, while maintaining state law, would make sure to follow the Convention.

the UK in respect of Scotland regarding the 2000 Convention on the International Protection of Adults. Moreover, the Hague Conference has developed rules to allocate the competence of courts, and to determine the applicable law, within a federal system.[29]

The EU is not a federation, of course. Yet, since the entry into force of the Amsterdam Treaty in 1999, the EU is leading the negotiations for its Member States in the Conference. Legal diversity within the EU is channelled, so to speak, through EU consultations, and expressed by one voice. Recent Conventions have opened up the possibility for the EU, in matters within its competence, to become itself a Party to the Convention. The EU has taken advantage of this opportunity in the case of three Hague Conventions: the 2005 Choice of Court Convention, the 2007 Child Support Convention and the 2007 Protocol on the Law Applicable to Maintenance Obligations.[30]

The transfer of legislative powers from Member States to the EU in the field of private international law made possible by the Amsterdam Treaty[31] has made the EU more receptive to certain ideas developed within federal systems. An example is the mechanism of transfer of adjudicatory jurisdiction across (state or provincial) borders, known in the US and Canada, which found its place in the 1996 Protection of Children Convention[32] and 2000 Convention on the Protection of Adults,[33] and, via these international treaties, in Regulation 2201/2003 (EC) Concerning Jurisdiction and the Recognition and Enforcement of Judgments in Matrimonial Matters and the Matters of Parental Responsibility (Brussels IIa).[34]

As the Supreme Court of Canada pointed out in *Hunt* v. *T&N plc*,[35] federal sys-

[29] See, for example, Art. 47 of the 1996 Protection of Children Convention, and Art. 45 of the Convention on the International Protection of Adults which was adopted in The Hague on 13 January 2000 and entered into force on 1 January 2009; 12 States Parties, status as at 15 October 2018.

[30] The Protocol on the Law Applicable to Maintenance Obligations was adopted in The Hague on 23 November 2007 and entered into force on 1 August 2013; 30 States Parties, status as at 15 October 2018.

[31] See van Loon, H. and A. Schulz (2008) 'The European Community and the Hague Conference on Private International Law', in Martenczuk, B. and S. van Thiel (eds), *Justice, Liberty, Security*, VUB Press, 257–99.

[32] Arts 8 and 9.

[33] Art. 8.

[34] Art. 15. Cf. also Regulation 650/2012 on jurisdiction, applicable law, recognition and enforcement of decisions, and acceptance and enforcement of authentic instruments in matters of succession and on the creation of a European Certificate of Succession, Art. 6(a) (Possibility of declining jurisdiction, at the request of one of the parties, in favour of the courts of the EU Member State whose law has been chosen by the deceased).

[35] [1993] 4 *S.C.R.* 289 (Judgment of the Court delivered by La Forest J.): 'Legal systems and rules are a reflection and expression of the fundamental values of a society, so to respect diversity of societies it is important to respect differences in legal systems . . . Developing such coordination in the face of diversity is a common function of both public and private international law. It is also one of the major objectives of the division of powers among federal and provincial governments in a federation. This

tems face a double challenge for the coordination of diversity. On the one hand, the challenge for a federation is to ensure the coordination of the values and norms of its own society with that of foreign legal systems. On the other hand, it needs to ensure the coordination of the diversity of its federal system and its sub-units (in Canada, the provinces). This second task may be at least as demanding as the first, and there is therefore a risk that federal systems will develop an inward-looking attitude, focusing only on the federal diversity balance and losing sight of the need for transnational balancing.

The complex EU system is not immune to this inward-looking trend. This is why it is so important that the EU has itself become a Member of the Conference alongside the individual country Members, and that both the EU and its Member States work with a wide range of other Members of the Conference towards global solutions for global issues. It is a fact that several EU members have strong cultural links with third countries, and a balance must be found between reinforcing community integration and respecting such links extending beyond the EU.

One of the effects of increased regional activity on private international law within the Conference has been that, sixty years after the US plea for non-binding instruments, the Conference in 2015 adopted the Principles on Choice of Law in International Commercial Contracts.[36] That the Principles are non-binding – soft law – has much to do with the fact that the 2008 Rome I Regulation on the Law Applicable to Contractual Obligations[37] is a binding text, and, moreover, has a universal scope of application, as has the 1994 Inter-American Convention on the Law Applicable to International Contracts.[38]

The Hague Principles do not seek to replace or duplicate Rome I or the Mexico Convention, but instead to provide states that are not yet familiar with party autonomy with guiding principles on the possibility of choosing the law applicable to international dealings. In a globalising world economy, this is also in the interest of businesses in legal systems that have long known the concept, with a view to their dealings with companies in third countries who are not familiar with party

appeal raises issues that lie at the confluence of private international law and constitutional law. In seeking to find a workable balance between diversity and uniformity, one must be aware of the similarities but also the differences that exist in the balances represented in the rules in these two areas of law . . .'

36 The Hague Principles on Choice of Law in International Commercial Contracts were approved on 19 March 2015; the full text is available at: www.hcch.net/en/instruments/conventions/full-text/?cid=135

37 Regulation (EC) No. 593/2008 of the European Parliament and of the Council on the Law Applicable to Contractual Obligations was concluded at Strasbourg on 17 June 2008 (Rome I) and entered into force on 24 July 2008; application from 17 December 2009; the Regulation replaced the 1980 Rome Convention in the EU Member States.

38 The Inter-American Convention on the Law Applicable to International Contracts was signed in Mexico City, Mexico, on 17 March 1994 and entered into force on 15 December 1996 between Mexico and Venezuela, the only two States Parties, status as at 15 October 2018.

autonomy – after all these transactions may lead to litigation in these third countries. Moreover, the Principles provide guidance in the context of international arbitration.[39]

Common Law and Civil Law

As noted previously, from the 1960s onwards bridging the divide between the civil (continental) law and the common law systems grew into a central concern for the Conference. Accommodating their diverse approaches in family law, contracts, torts, property law and succession, and civil procedure became an ongoing challenge, with the 1985 Trusts Convention perhaps the icon of bridge-building between the two systems. And this remains a challenge, although in some areas the divide between the approaches of the US and of other, including common law, systems may be no less challenging than that between civil and common law.

The 1970 Hague Convention on the Taking of Evidence offers an illustration of both types of differences. This treaty not only accommodates differences between civil and common law methods of the taking of evidence in general, but it also permits a reservation specifically regarding 'fishing expeditions' through pre-trial discovery of documents, as practised in the US.

Accommodating Civil and Common Law

In civil proceedings in common law, generally speaking the parties lead and the judge acts more like a neutral arbiter, deferring to procedural party autonomy. In contrast, in the civil or continental law tradition, the judge is more active and the judicial process more structured, more controlled by the courts. So, regarding the taking of evidence in common law systems, the witness's statement will be recorded in full, read to the witness and then signed by him or her. In civil law systems, on the other hand, the judge will question the witness and dictate a summary of the questions and answers to a court officer. Likewise, in common law cross-examination of witnesses is possible but this is not generally the case in civil law systems. To bridge these differences, Article 9 of the 1985 Hague Convention on the Taking of Evidence begins by stating: 'The judicial authority which executes a Letter of Request shall apply its own law as to the methods and procedures to be followed'. But it continues:

> However, it will follow a request of the requesting authority that a special method or procedure be followed, unless this is incompatible with the internal law of the State of execution or is impossible of performance by reason of its internal practice and procedure or by reason of practical difficulties.

'Incompatible' and 'impossible of performance' are strong terms: clearly this rule is encouragement to accede to a request to apply a foreign method of obtaining evidence. And it has worked: in Germany and France the common law methods of

[39] Van Loon, 'The Global Horizon', above fn. 13, paras 48–59.

full recording of witness statements and cross-examination have been applied at the request of common law courts, and France has even amended its legislation to make this possible. Conversely, French and German judges have appeared in New York courtrooms and have interrogated witnesses according to their own system.[40]

UK versus US: Article 23 (Reservations) in the 1985 Evidence Convention

According to Article 23: 'A Contracting State may reserve the right not to execute a request for legal assistance for the purpose of obtaining pre-trial discovery of documents as known in Common Law countries'. One might think that this rule was prompted by civil law countries. It is, however, actually the result of a UK proposal. The UK realised, at a late stage in the negotiations, that its own method of pre-trial discovery of documents was much more limited and specific than the American method, and proposed this reservation in order to be able to refuse execution of 'fishing expeditions', and therefore insisted on the inclusion of this provision.[41] This also illustrates how, despite a common source and a common name, an institution may develop in divergent ways, so much so that some of its manifestations are no longer acceptable to another system of the same origin.

Challenges for the Ongoing Negotiations on a Hague Judgments Convention

The current preliminary draft for a global Hague Convention on the Recognition and Enforcement of Judgments also illustrates both differences.[42] The draft, like the Brussels I Regulation,[43] has a specific provision dealing with the basis for recognition of a judgment concerning trusts, unknown in most civil law countries (Article 5(1)(k)). It also has a provision on the recognition of judgments awarding punitive or exemplary damages (Article 10). Punitive or exemplary damages are most widely used in the context of proceedings in the US.

Yet the most fundamental issue is the difference in approach between the US on the one hand and practically all the other systems on the other regarding jurisdiction of the courts. In the US, jurisdiction is a constitutional matter – in that respect

[40] Report on the work of the Special Commission of May 1985 on the operation of the Hague Evidence Convention, 24 *I.L.M.*, 1668.

[41] See McClean, J. D. (2012) *International Co-operation in Civil and Criminal Matters*, 3rd edn, Oxford University Press, Ch. 3, I.

[42] The Draft Convention on the Recognition and Enforcement of Foreign Judgments was adopted by the Special Commission that met in The Hague on 24–9 May 2018. On this Draft Convention see the chapter by Pasquot Polido in this volume.

[43] The Council Regulation (EC) No. 44/2001 on jurisdiction and the recognition and enforcement of judgments in civil and commercial matters was adopted at Brussels on 22 December 2000 and entered into force on 1 March 2002; OJ L 12, 16.1.2001. The Regulation replaced the 1968 Brussels Convention in the Member States. No longer in force, it was repealed by Regulation (EU) No. 1215/2012 of the European Parliament and of the Council on jurisdiction and the recognition and enforcement of judgments in civil and commercial matters, adopted at Strasbourg on 12 December 2012; application from 10 January 2015; OJ L 351, 20.12.2012.

it is rather unique. In a long series of judgments, starting with *Pennoyer* v. *Neff* (1877),[44] the US Supreme Court has developed a doctrine on adjudicatory jurisdiction that protects the defendant based on the due process clauses of the 5th and 14th Amendments of the US Constitution. Hence, while the European approach, including that of the UK, focuses on the relationship between the dispute and the forum, the US approach focuses on the defendant and the forum. That eliminates, for example, the possibility that a provision for *forum actoris* in consumer and employment disputes would be considered desirable. At the same time, in the US the defendant is located for jurisdictional purposes not only where he or she (or it, in the case of legal persons) is domiciled – as in the Brussels-Lugano system[45] – but also where that defendant is (economically) active in a jurisdiction or directs activity into a jurisdiction.[46]

The result is that from a US perspective the European approach to jurisdiction is sometimes too broad and sometimes too narrow. Take the court-dispute connection based on the place of performance of the contract found in Article 7(1) of the Brussels I *bis* Regulation and Article 5(1)(a) of the Lugano Convention. In the US view, this base is on the one hand too narrow, because it does not provide for jurisdiction for acts of the defendant outside the state of the court causing effects within the state, in other words, when the defendant 'purposefully' directs its activity into that state. On the other hand, it is too broad, because it may lead to jurisdiction in a state in which the defendant has no activities and into which the defendant has not directed any activities.

The preliminary draft for a global Hague Convention on the Recognition and Enforcement of Judgments deals with the second aspect. Article 5(1)(g),[47] on contracts, with its place of performance criterion is based on the court-dispute connection, but takes into account the court-defendant idea by excluding cases where the 'defendant's activities in relation to the transaction clearly did not

[44] 95 US 714 (1878).

[45] The Convention on Jurisdiction and the Recognition and Enforcement of Judgments in Civil and Commercial Matters was adopted at Lugano on 30 October 2007, OJ L 339, 21.12.2007, date of effect 1 January 2010; the 2007 Convention repealed the Lugano Convention of 16 September 1988 on jurisdiction and the enforcement of judgments in civil and commercial matters, OJ L 319, 25.11.1988, which extended the application of the rules of the 1968 Brussels Convention to certain Member States of the European Free Trade Association.

[46] In its decisions *Goodyear Dunlop Operations S.S.* v. *Brown*, 131 S. Cr. 2846 (2011) and *Daimler AG* v. *Bauman et al.* 134, S. Ct 746 (2014), the US Supreme Court has reduced the exposure of foreign corporate defendants to the assertion of such general jurisdiction on the basis of 'doing business'.

[47] Article 5: 'A judgment is eligible for recognition and enforcement if one of the following requirements is met – g) the judgment ruled on a contractual obligation and it was given in the State in which performance of that obligation took place, or should have taken place, in accordance with
(i) the parties' agreement, or
(ii) the law applicable to the contract, in the absence of an agreed place of performance,
unless the defendant's activities in relation to the transaction clearly did not constitute a purposeful and substantial connection to that State'.

constitute a purposeful and substantial connection' to the forum. In practice, this exclusion will probably not severely limit the indirect base of jurisdiction in contractual cases.[48]

By contrast, Article 5(1)(j),[49] on torts 'arising from death, physical injury, damage to or loss of tangible property', which requires that 'the act or omission directly causing the harm occurred in the State of origin, irrespective of where that harm occurred', excludes judgments rendered by a court of the state where the injury arose if that is a state different from that where the act or omission took place. However, contrary to Article 5(1)(g) for contracts, Article 5(1)(j) does not make any exception for an act intentionally or foreseeably causing damage in the state where the harm occurred.[50] Conversely, the (direct) base of jurisdiction for torts in the Brussels/Lugano regime has been considered to include both the location of the act causing the harm and the location where the harm materialised.[51] The exclusion of this dual formula in the preliminary draft reduces its usefulness, in particular in cross-border environmental cases.[52]

[48] But it could lead to uncertainty: Bonomi, A. (2016) 'Courage or Caution? A Critical Overview of the Hague Preliminary Draft on Judgments', *Yearbook of Private International Law*, vol. 17, 1–31, at 22–3.

[49] Art. 5: 'A judgment is eligible for recognition and enforcement if one of the following requirements is met – j) the judgment ruled on a non-contractual obligation arising from death, physical injury, damage to or loss of tangible property, and the act or omission directly causing such harm occurred in the State of origin, irrespective of where that harm occurred'.

[50] And may thus go beyond what is required under the case law of the US Supreme Court in, for example, *Asahi Metal Industry Co.* v. *Superior Court*, 480 US 102 (1987), *J. McIntyre Machinery* v. *Nicastro*, 564 US 873 (2011); but see also *Walden* v. *Fiore et al.*, 25, 134 S Ct. 1115 (2014).

[51] Following the world-renowned interpretation of the Court of Justice of the European Union (CJEU) in case 21/76 [1976] ECLI:EU:C:1976:166 (*Handelskwekerij Bier* v. *Mines de Potasse*).

[52] Even if the judgment results in local damages only (EUCJ C-68/93), ECLI: EU:C:1995:61 (Shevill). This is unfortunate, in particular given the urgent need for at least basic 'rules of the game' for civil tort litigation across borders in environmental matters. Cf. van Loon, 'The Global Horizon', above fn. 13, Ch. III B, at 105–6. See also Bonomi, 'Courage or Caution', above fn. 48, 25–6. In previous texts, in the context of the original attempt to draw up a 'double convention', the base for jurisdiction in tort matters was broader, while reconciling the court-defendant and the court-dispute approach, thus paralleling Art. 5 (g) of the May 2018 draft on contractual obligations. Cf. Art. 10 of the 2001 Interim text:
'1. A plaintiff may bring an action in tort [or delict] in the courts of the State –
a) in which the act or omission that caused injury occurred, or
b) in which the injury arose, unless the defendant establishes that the person claimed to be responsible could not reasonably foresee that the act or omission could result in an injury of the same nature in that State'.

Secular and Religious Legal Systems

Hague Conventions and Religious Law: Personal Laws, Repudiation, Kafala, Islamic Securities

An important contemporary aspect of legal diversity that the Hague Conference is facing relates to cross-border issues involving countries whose legal systems are based on religion, in particular Jewish and Sharia law. In the 1960s, when Egypt and Israel joined the organisation, the Conference started to make provision in the Conventions for the fact that these countries have a legal system based upon personal laws, so that different laws apply to Muslims, Jews and Christians, for example. The 1970 Hague Convention on the Recognition of Divorces and Legal Separations[53] provides a framework for accommodating religious divorces, in particular repudiations. Provided they are subject to a procedure before or in the presence of an authority and prescribed or permitted by the law of the state where they are made, these acts are to be recognised under the Convention. The Convention links Egypt with nineteen Western states. Another example is the 1996 Child Protection Convention[54] that expressly provides for cross-border *kafala* arrangements, a form of foster care that is structurally different from adoption – and that is why it is not included in the 1993 Intercountry Adoption Convention – but that may offer a functional substitute.[55] On similar considerations, 'Islamic securities' were taken into account in the negotiations of the 2006 Securities Convention.

Cross-cultural Dialogue: The Malta Process

The aftermath of 9/11 greatly increased the role of the religious factor in international relations, and complicated respect for diversity by the international community. The recent refugee crises have not made things any easier. Yet, family contacts and relationships across the Mediterranean and beyond continue to increase (such as in the Gulf States, Pakistan, India, Malaysia and Indonesia, for example). The human pain involved in the separations and divorces of mixed couples is considerable, and children may suffer as a result of their wrongful removal and the loss of contact with one of their parents.

There are bilateral arrangements dealing with trans-frontier family relations between some Western countries and Egypt, Tunisia, Algeria, Morocco and Lebanon. However, their success has been very limited. Why? Because they seek to achieve

[53] The Hague Convention on the Recognition of Divorces and Legal Separations was adopted on 1 June 1970 and entered into force on 24 August 1975; 20 States Parties, status as at 15 October 2018. It was the first Hague Convention to make provision for legal systems applying different laws to different categories of persons. See Arts 15 and 16, and the Explanatory Report by Bellet, P. and B. Goldman (1970) *Actes et Documents de la Onzième Session, 7–26 octobre 1968*, vol. II, 210–23, at 222.

[54] Above fn. 25.

[55] See Duncan, W. (1998) 'Children's Rights, Cultural Diversity and Private International Law', in Douglas, G. and L. Sebba (eds), *Children's Rights and Traditional Values*, Ashgate, 31–46.

a solution through voluntary settlements but they lack clear rules on jurisdiction, recognition and enforcement of decisions, as well as on cooperation, which the 1980 Hague Child Abduction Convention and the 1996 Hague Child Protection Convention do provide. The post 9/11 political climate has not made it any easier to persuade countries whose laws are based on Sharia to join these Conventions.

Faced with this dilemma, and building on the goodwill and enthusiasm of affected states, the Hague Conference has chosen a novel approach. A series of conferences including judges and high-level administrative representatives has been organised in Malta to discuss how to secure better protection for cross-border rights of contact between parents and their children and solutions to the problems posed, in particular, by the wrongful removal of children across borders. Judges from some thirty countries, many of which are neither a Party to the Hague Conventions nor a Member of the Conference, have taken part in these judicial conferences. Starting from the United Nations Convention on the Rights of the Child[56] as a general normative framework, these meetings have enabled the participating judges to better understand each other's systems. They have agreed that common rules are needed to specify which country's courts are competent to make decisions concerning custody and contact, and that such decisions made by a competent court in one country should be respected in other countries.

This initiative, known as the Malta process,[57] has led to an increasing interest among the participants, in the course of the four conferences, in the solutions of the 1996 Child Protection Convention, the 1980 Child Abduction Convention and, at the fourth conference (2014), the 2007 Child Support Convention.[58] The collective ratification by the EU Member States of the 1996 Convention and side conferences has given a further impetus to this growing interest. The recent accessions by Pakistan[59] and Tunisia[60] to the 1980 Child Abduction Convention may also be seen as a fruit of the Malta process.

Meeting the Challenge of Diversity

As these examples show, in the face of growing diversity within the Conference a variety of approaches and techniques are needed, not so much to substitute the traditional Convention negotiation method, but to support and adapt the Convention's implementation and operation to new environments. Overall inclusiveness is critical

[56] The Convention on the Rights of the Child was concluded in New York on 20 November 1989 and entered into force on 2 September 1990; 196 States Parties, status as at 15 October 2018.

[57] Duncan, W. (2013) 'Reflections on the Malta Process', in Permanent Bureau of the Hague Conference on Private International Law (eds), *Essays in Honour of Hans van Loon: A Commitment to Private International Law*, Intersentia,135–42.

[58] Above fn. 22.

[59] Pakistan acceded to the 1980 Child Abduction Convention on 22 December 2016; entry into force 1 March 2017.

[60] Tunisia acceded to the 1980 Child Abduction Convention on 10 July 2017; entry into force 1 October 2017.

to this. At the same time, there are unifying forces, in particular the steadily increasing global human rights framework.

Inclusiveness

Regarding inclusiveness, the emergence of the EU in the Conference has given an impetus to a switch from the traditional voting procedure to the consensus principle, which is now also enshrined in the HCCH Statute.[61] Consensus has its price in terms of negotiation time, but recent experience tends to show its benefits with regard to greater inclusiveness. The negotiations on the 2007 Child Support Convention offer an example. Western countries wanted a high level of legal assistance in matters of cross-border child and family support, and minimal checks regarding the recognition and enforcement of foreign decisions. China and other countries felt that they were unable to meet the Western standards. Applying the voting system would not have brought relief, because it would have favoured one solution, leaving the losing side at most with the option of a reservation. However, consensus has made it possible to achieve a system with two variants for both legal assistance (Articles 15 and 16) and enforcement of decisions (Articles 23 and 24), acceptable to all.

The Unifying Force of Global Human Rights

The 2007 Child Support Convention not only coordinates and provides channels for communication and cooperation between legal systems, it also implements a human rights imperative. The Convention is a response to the call made by the United Nations Convention of 20 November 1989 on the Rights of the Child (CRC)[62] to its States Parties to secure the international recovery of child support. The CRC does not deal directly with the private international law aspects of

[61] Traditionally, negotiations at the Hague Conference took place through voting, although there was always an understanding that in certain cases a vote could be reconsidered, and wise Chairs always took consensus-building as their prime objective. Increasing coordination among EU Member States of their positions and narrow majorities during the negotiations on the Hague Judgments Convention in the late 1990s stimulated the formal switch from voting to consensus, now enshrined in Art. 8 (2) of the HCCH Statute. Art. 8 of the Statute of the Hague Conference on Private International Law: [. . .] (2) 'The Sessions, Council and Special Commissions shall, to the furthest extent possible, operate on the basis of consensus'. The Statute was adopted during the Seventh Session of the Hague Conference on Private International Law on 31 October 1951 and entered into force on 15 July 1955. Amendments were adopted during the Twentieth Session on 30 June 2005 (Final Act, C), approved by Members on 30 September 2006, and entered into force on 1 January 2007. See also van Loon and Schulz, 'The European Community and the Hague Conference on Private International Law', above fn. 31, 263–4, 293.

[62] Above fn. 56. Art. 27 [. . .] '4. States Parties shall take all appropriate measures to secure the recovery of maintenance or the child from the parents or other persons having financial responsibility for the child, both within the State Party and from abroad, in particular, where the person having financial responsibility for the child lives in a State different from that of the child, States Parties shall promote the accession to international agreements or the conclusion of such agreements, as well as the making of other appropriate arrangements'.

child support cases; that would be beyond its reach. Instead, it sets the principle and urges states to promote the accession to, or conclusion of, international agreements. The 2007 Child Support Convention implements this human rights imperative 'vertically', at the same time ensuring the respect and coordination of the differences between legal systems 'horizontally'. In varying degrees the 1980 Child Abduction Convention, the 1996 Child Protection Convention and the 1993 Intercountry Adoption Convention perform a similar function towards the CRC. The CRC provides the general framework; the Hague Conventions implement the framework's human rights principles and coordinate the diverse legal systems. As a result, the need to use the public policy exception to safeguard fundamental values of the forum is heavily reduced.[63]

In a similar way, the 2000 Convention on the International Protection of Adults[64] may complement the recent United Nations Convention of 13 December 2006 on the Rights of Persons with Disabilities,[65] in particular its provisions on equal recognition before the law[66] and on international cooperation.[67]

There is potential for more complementarity, for example between the 1966 United Nations Covenant on Civil and Political Rights[68] and various Hague Conventions, including the Conventions on Marriage, Divorce, the four modern Children's Conventions (Abduction, Child Protection, Adoption and Child Support) and the Conventions on legal cooperation (1965 Service of Documents, 1970 Taking of Evidence, 1980 Access to Justice).[69] As the European Court of Human Rights has interpreted various provisions of the European Convention on Human Rights (in particular, Articles 6, 8 and 14)[70] in the light of Hague Conventions (in particular the 1980 Child Abduction Convention), so the UN Human Rights Committee might likewise interpret the UN Covenant, under the (first) Optional Protocol to the Covenant, in the light of relevant Hague Conventions.

In this way the 'vertical' human rights dimension and the 'horizontal' private international law dimensions of coordination, communication and cooperation

63 Cf. van Loon, H. (2017) 'Protecting Children Across Borders: The Interaction between the CRC and the Hague Children's Conventions', in Liefaard, T. and J. Sloth-Nielsen (eds), *The United Nations Convention on the Rights of the Child – Taking Stock after 25 Years and Looking Ahead*, Brill Nijhoff, 31–46.

64 Above fn. 29.

65 The Convention on the Rights of Persons with Disabilities was adopted in New York on 13 December 2006 and entered into force on 3 May 2008; 177 States Parties, status as at 15 October 2018.

66 Art. 12 of the 2006 Convention on the Rights of Persons with Disabilities.

67 Art. 32 of the 2006 Convention on the Rights of Persons with Disabilities.

68 The International Covenant on Civil and Political Rights was concluded in New York on 16 December 1966 and entered into force on 23 March 1976; 172 States Parties, status as at 15 October 2018.

69 The Convention on International Access to Justice was concluded in the Hague on 25 October 1980 and entered into force on 1 May 1988; 28 States Parties, status as at 15 October 2018.

70 Cf. Marchadier, F. (2007) 'La contribution de la Cour européenne des droits de l'homme à l'efficacité des conventions de La Haye de coopération judiciaire et administrative', 4. *Rev. crit. DIP* 677–715.

reinforce each other. Private international law, informed by globally established fundamental rights, is instrumental in ensuring respect for legal diversity in our world, and the unification of private international law plays a vital role in the creation of the global legal architecture needed for our emerging multicultural world society.

3

Managing Diversity in Cross-border Succession Problems: A British Perspective

*Janeen M. Carruthers**

Introduction

In considering the management of diversity in the area of the law of succession, two obvious diversities may be noted, namely, the diversity of substantive rules of succession among the legal systems of the European Union and beyond,[1] and, separately, the diversity of approach among legal systems to the resolution of conflict of laws problems arising in relation to wills and succession.[2]

The United Kingdom provides an excellent example of neighbouring independent legal systems, as between which the substantive rules of succession differ in some aspects of primary importance (for example, family rights of succession in intestate estates),[3] and some of interesting, but secondary note (for instance, the formal validity of wills),[4] as a result of their distinct histories and legal development, but which, by contrast, have demonstrated for at least two centuries and still,

* The author wishes to record her thanks to Professor Elizabeth B. Crawford, School of Law, University of Glasgow, for her very helpful comments and suggestions.

1 For detail regarding different civilian and common law heritage, see Zimmermann, R., M. J. de Waal and K. G. C. Reid (2011) , vol. 1: *Testamentary Formalities*, Oxford University Press; and Zimmermann, R., M. J. de Waal and K. G. C. Reid (2015) *Comparative Succession Law*, vol. II: *Intestate Succession*, Oxford University Press.

2 For background, see, for example, Hague Conference on Private International Law, Proceedings of the Sixteenth Session (1990) vol. II, 19 (Droz, G. A. L. 'Questionnaire and Commentary on Succession in PIL').

3 See, for example, Zimmermann et al., *Comparative Succession Law*, vol. II, above fn. 1, Ch. 14, 'Intestate Succession in England and Wales' (Kerridge, R.) and Ch.16, 'Intestate Succession in Scotland' (Reid, K. G. C.).

4 See Zimmermann et al., *Comparative Succession Law*, vol. 1, above fn. 1, Ch. 13, 'Testamentary Formalities in England and Wales' (Kerridge, R.) and Ch. 17, 'Testamentary Formalities in Scotland' (Reid, K. G. C.).

congruence of approach to the formulation and application of choice of law rules in succession.[5]

In Scotland and England, respectively, the twentieth-century legal practitioner would have encountered conflict of laws problems principally in the context of the winding-up of an estate in which the deceased (who, let it be assumed, had personal connections with both Scotland and England, rendering his domicile at death potentially contentious) had left immoveable and/or moveable estate in different parts of the UK. The existence of adjoining countries having different legal systems with distinct rules of succession (the application of which could affect putative beneficiaries markedly, sometimes favourably, sometimes adversely) fostered the development of conflict of laws expertise in this field of private law. There are very few areas of difference in the choice of law rules in wills and succession applied, respectively, by Scots and English courts.

Looking outwards from the UK, however, the diversity of approach is well known between the 'British' method of resolution of cross-border succession problems and the civilian approach, represented now by Rome IV (see below).[6]

The Function of International Private Law

It is the function of international private law to recognise legal diversity,[7] to anticipate conflict and thereby to manage the substantive outcome in ways that may differ according to whether a legal system adopts jurisdiction-selection or rule-selection methodology. This chapter will not rehearse the various arguments in favour of and against jurisdiction-selection and rule-selection,[8] and merely notes that the two conflict of laws methodologies differently manage the fact of legal diversity.

Diversity among legal systems' substantive rules is managed by the provision of

[5] See, for choice of law rules operative in Scotland, Crawford, E. B. and J. M. Carruthers (2015) *International Private Law: A Scots Perspective*, 4th edn, W. Green, Ch. 18 and, for equivalent rules in England and Wales, Collins, L. et al. (eds) (2012) *Dicey, Morris & Collins, The Conflict of Laws*, 15th edn, Sweet & Maxwell, para. 27R-010 et seq.

[6] Crawford and Carruthers, *International Private Law* above fn. 5, para 18–40 et seq.

[7] See, for detailed treatment, van Loon, J. H. A. (2015) 'The Global Horizon of Private International Law', *Receuil des cours*, vol. 380; and Morris, P. S. (2016) 'The Modern Transplantation of Continental Law in England: How English Private International Law Embraces Europeanisation, 1972–2014', *Journal of Private International Law*, vol. 12, no. 3, 587–607.

[8] For detail on choice of law methodology, see Cavers, D. F. (1933) 'A Critique of the Choice-of-Law Process' 47 *Harv. L. Rev.* 173; Kegel, G. (1961) 'The Crisis of Conflict of Laws' *Recueil des cours*, vol. 112, 95; Hancock, M. (1961) 'Three Approaches to the Choice-of-Law Problem: the Classificatory, the Functional and the Result-Selective', in Nadelmann, K. H. (ed.), *XXth Century Comparative and Conflicts Law; Legal Essays in Honor of Hessel E. Yntema*, Sijthoff, 367; Rosenberg, M. (1981) 'The Comeback of Choice-of-Law Rules', 81 *Colum. L. Rev.* 946; Sauveplanne, J. G. (1982) 'New Trends in the Doctrine of Private International Law and their Impact on Court Practice', *Recueil des cours*, vol. 175, 13; Juenger, F. K. (1982) 'American and European Conflicts Law' 30 *American Journal of Comparative Law* 117; and Trautman, D. T. (1986) 'The Revolution in Choice of Law: Another Insight' 99 *Harv. L. Rev.* 1101.

conflict of laws rules of jurisdiction and choice of law, increasingly on a harmonised or assimilated regional or international basis. The first part of this chapter will examine the management of diversity in the law of succession through international agreement, and the second part will consider such management by means of 'national' private international law rules in the UK.

Managing Diversity through International Agreement

Major international efforts to manage diversity in the private international law of succession were made over decades by the Hague Conference on Private International Law,[9] ending in the 1989 Convention on the Law Applicable to Succession to the Estates of Deceased Persons (an instrument which, however, failed),[10] and, subsequently, by the EU institutions and Member States, culminating on 4 July 2012 in the finalisation of the Regulation (EU) No. 650/2012 (hereinafter 'Rome IV').[11] From a UK perspective, neither initiative proved to be attractive.

Examining the subject of cross-border succession from a European perspective, it is self-evident that legal diversity has been minimised by the assimilation of the private international law rules of twenty-five out of twenty-eight European Member States. Rome IV closely follows the modern pattern of European regulations: the instrument is quadruple in nature, laying down harmonised rules of jurisdiction (Chapter II), applicable law (Chapter III), recognition, enforceability and enforcement of decisions (Chapter IV), and introducing the European Certificate of Succession (Chapter VI). The essence and purpose of the instrument are encapsulated in Recital (37), to the effect, first, that harmonised conflict of laws rules should enable 'citizens' to know in advance which law will apply to their succession; second, that the succession to a qualifying person's estate should be governed by a predictable law of close connection; and, finally, that those harmonised rules should operate to avoid contradictory results.

Most notably in relation to choice of law, the Regulation introduces a unitary rule,[12] in terms of which the law applicable to the succession to the estate as a whole of a deceased person shall be the law of the state in which the deceased had his or her habitual residence at the time of death, unless, by way of exception,[13] it is clear from all the circumstances of the case that, at the time of death, the deceased was manifestly more closely connected with another state, in which case the law of that state shall apply.

[9] For the work of the Hague Conference more generally see van Loon's chapter in this volume.

[10] The Convention attracted only four signatures and, ultimately (following the Netherlands' denouncement of the Convention in 2014), three.

[11] Regulation (EU) No. 650/2012 of the European Parliament and of the Council on jurisdiction, applicable law, recognition and enforcement of decisions and acceptance and enforcement of authentic instruments in matters of succession and on the creation of a European Certificate of Succession, applicable to the succession of persons who died on or after 17 August 2015.

[12] Art. 21: Applicable law: 'General rule'.

[13] Art. 21.2.

Further, by Article 22.1 ('Choice of law'), 'a person' may choose[14] as the law to govern his succession as a whole the law of the state whose nationality he possesses at the time of making the choice or at the time of death.[15] Party autonomy features in this limited, controlled way as a tool in the hands of an individual testator to manage legal diversity. Party autonomy in relation to choice of law is a means of optimising legal diversity, to positive effect as far as the (informed)[16] testator is concerned regarding the matter of succession to his or her estate, but to potential negative effect as far as concerns some potential beneficiaries.

It is not the purpose of this chapter to critique the express provisions of Rome IV.[17] Rather, it is the intention to ponder the consequences, so far as concerns the management of legal diversity, of failure to secure participation in the European harmonisation exercise by all EU Member States.

Managing Diversity in Hybridity

The problem of 'hybridity', a term coined in the private international law context to describe the interface between a European regulatory regime and the world beyond that regime, manifests in various guises,[18] and is well known. Problems of geographical hybridity exist when it is necessary to determine the physical extent of application, if any, of a European regulation's rules in circumstances where there are factual and/or legal connections with an EU Member State (or non-compliant Member State; see below) and a Third State.[19] Such problems have been the impetus for recourse

[14] Recitals (38), (39) and (41).

[15] Where a person possesses multiple nationalities, he may choose the law of any of the states whose nationalities he possesses at the time of choice or death. Art. 22.4 makes clear that a change of mind as to applicable law is permitted, by way of modification or revocation of the choice of law. Where a choice of law has been made, and the choice is that of a (compliant) Member State law, the 'parties concerned' [undefined] may agree that the courts of that Member State are to have exclusive jurisdiction to rule on any succession matter (Art. 5).

[16] Contrast, a few years in advance of Rome IV, the difficulties encountered by the testator in *Scarfe* v. *Matthews* [2012] EWHC 3071 (Ch).

[17] For full commentary on Rome IV, see Calvo Caravaca, A-L., A. Davì and H.-P. Mansel (eds) (2016) *The EU Succession Regulation: A Commentary*, Cambridge University Press; Bergquist, U., D. Damascelli, R. Frimston, P. Lagarde, F. Odersky and B. Reinhartz (2015) *EU Regulation on Succession and Wills: Commentary*, Sellier European Law Publishers; Pfeiffer, M. (2016) 'Legal Certainty and Predictability in International Succession Law' *Journal of Private International Law*, vol. 12, no. 3, 566–86, and Marongiu Buonaiuti, F. (2016) 'The EU Succession Regulation and Third Country Courts' *Journal of Private International Law* vol. 12, no. 3, 545–65.

[18] See, regarding difficulties in delimiting the European legal sphere, Crawford and Carruthers, *International Private Law*, above fn. 5, para. 7-62.

[19] See, for example, in the context of the Brussels I Regulation, problems concerning delineation of the geographical ambit of operation of the rules, e.g. *Owusu* v. *Jackson (t/a Villa Holidays Bal-Inn Villas)* C-281/02 [2005] QB 801; and *Orams* v. *Apostolides* [2007] 1 WLR 241. Cf. regarding conflicting jurisdiction in the family law sphere, difficulties of demarcation between the scheme set out in Domicile and Matrimonial Proceedings Act 1973, Sch.3.9, and that in Brussels II *bis*, Art. 19: *JKN*

to reflexive reasoning,[20] according to which a UK court seised on a ground of jurisdiction contained, say, in the Brussels I Regulation cedes jurisdiction to the court of a Third State on the rationale of applying the spirit of, or reflecting 'outwards', the Brussels regime.[21] The hybridity problem which presents in the context of Rome IV, however, is of a different type and level of complexity, concerning delineation of the extent of operation of that instrument within the EU vis-à-vis those EU Member States which, *ex facie*, are not bound by the Regulation.

Enhanced Cooperation Procedure

Recognition and management of legal diversity among the Member States of the EU is explicit in the 'enhanced cooperation procedure'.[22] According to Article 328(1) of the Treaty on the Functioning of the European Union, when enhanced cooperation is being established, participation shall be open to all Member States (subject to compliance with conditions of participation laid down by the authorising decision). Any resulting regulation, however, shall be binding and directly applicable only in those Member States which choose to participate.

This was the procedure by which the instrument known as Rome III (Council Regulation (EU) No. 1259/201 of 20 December 2010 implementing enhanced cooperation in the area of the law applicable to divorce and legal separation)[23] came into effect on 21 June 2012. In order to delimit clearly the geographical or territorial scope of Rome III, Member States which elected to participate in that cooperative scheme – of which the UK is not one[24] – are specified in the Regulation.[25] The enhanced cooperation procedure, in admitting parallel schemes to operate within the one supranational

v. *JCN*. [2010] EWHC 843 (Fam), and *AB* v. *CB (Divorce and Maintenance: Discretion to Stay)* (also known as *Mittal* v. *Mittal*) [2014] Fam 102.

[20] Crawford and Carruthers, *International Private Law*, above fn. 5, para. 7-63.

[21] For example, *Ferrexpo AG* v. *Gilson Investments Limited and ors* [2012] EWHC 721 (Comm); *Konkola Copper Mines Plc* v. *Coromin Ltd* [2006] EWHC 1093; *Goshawk Dedicated Ltd* v. *Life Receivables Ireland Ltd* [2009] I.E.S.C. 7. See also *Samengo-Turner* v. *J & H Marsh & McLennan (Services) Ltd* [2007] EWCA Civ. 723.

[22] See further, on the enhanced cooperation procedure in relation to other private international family law matters, Espinosa Calabuig's chapter in this volume.

[23] OJ L 343, 29.12.10, 10–16. See, for detail, Fiorini, A. (2008) 'Rome III – Choice of Law in Divorce: Is the Europeanization of Family Law Going Too Far?' *International Journal of Law, Policy and the Family* 178; and Fiorini, A. (2010) 'Harmonizing the Law Applicable to Divorce and Legal Separation – Enhanced Co-operation as the Way Forward?' 59 *International and Comparative Law Quarterly*, 1143.

[24] The UK exercised its right not to opt into the proposed measure: Hansard 18 Apr 2007: Col WS7. For background, see House of Lords EU Committee (2005–6) 'Rome III – Choice of Law in Divorce, Report with Evidence' (2006).

[25] Austria, Bulgaria, France, Spain, Italy, Luxembourg, Hungary, Romania, Slovenia, Germany, Belgium, Latvia, Malta and Portugal (Rome III, Recitals (6) and (11)). Greece, which had been one of the petitioners, withdrew its request to participate in the instrument. Lithuania subsequently adopted the measure (European Commission Press Release, Brussels, 7 June 2012 (IP/12/590)).

group of legal systems, plainly accepts legal diversity within the regional block. Rome III, which is commendable for its explicit recognition of the non-uniform status of European Member States, is an exemplar of the accommodation of legal diversity within a choice of law instrument.

Rome IV – the Consequences of Exercise of the 'Opt-out'

Recital (82) of the Rome IV Regulation states that, in accordance with Articles 1 and 2 of Protocol No. 21 on the position of the UK and Ireland in respect of the area of freedom, security and justice, annexed to the Treaty on European Union and to the Treaty on the Functioning of the European Union,[26] those Member States are not taking part in the adoption of Rome IV and are not bound by it or subject to its application. Despite early intimation of non-participation by the UK in this harmonisation initiative, the final version of Rome IV, though stating starkly the 'opt-out' in Recital (82), seems wilfully blind to the end position that not all EU Member States adopted the Regulation, and to the repercussions of such an outcome.

A defect by way of omission in the drafting of Rome IV is the absence of any acknowledgment that, as a result of the decision by the UK and Ireland not to opt in, there exist three categories of state for the purpose of dealing with cross-border successions in an EU context. Rome IV can be criticised for failure to differentiate in its substantive provision between Member States which are bound by the Regulation and in which it is directly applicable, and those three Member States which are not bound by it. Comprehensive drafting of the Regulation should have identified distinct categories, namely: (1) Member States which are bound by the Regulation or subject to its application; (2) Member States which are not bound by the Regulation or subject to its application (that is, the United Kingdom, Ireland and Denmark); and (3) Third States (sovereign states which are not EU Member States). This manifestation of diversity, the challenge of diversity within the EU, is a modern phenomenon.

Paradoxically, although the UK did not take part in the adoption of Rome IV, the facts of life and death are such that the estates of British nationals and/or assets situated in the UK may be affected, in certain circumstances, by the European Regulation. It is not merely 'bound' or compliant Member States which may be affected by Rome IV, or parties who are habitually resident or domiciled therein or nationals thereof. Rather, where the estate of a deceased person, habitually resident in a compliant Member State, includes immoveable property situated in a non-compliant Member State, or in a Third State, his or her assets there situated are liable to be affected by operation of the Regulation. Equally, a party who is, say, a domiciliary or national of a non-compliant Member State such as the UK, but who is habitually resident in a compliant Member State, is likely to be subject to the provisions of the Regulation.[27]

[26] [2008] OJ C115/295.

[27] For conjecture on different sets of circumstances, see Crawford, E. B. and J. M. Carruthers (2014) 'Speculation on the Operation of Succession Regulation 650/2012: Tales of the Unexpected' 22 *European Review of Private Law* 6, 847–78, where the questions 'which persons are affected by

A result which has surprised commentators is that the option to choose the applicable law, provided by Article 22, is not restricted to the nationals of compliant Member States. The 'constituency of electors'[28] extends to nationals of non-compliant Member States and Third States. Accordingly, 'British people', whether at a date when the UK is a non-compliant Member State or after it becomes a Third State,[29] have the benefit of the use of the party autonomy tool provided by a European regulation which the UK did not adopt.

The operation of the Regulation by compliant Member States is likely to be made more complicated, and in certain cases compromised, by the refusal by the UK and Ireland to opt in. Recital (37) of Rome IV contains an arrogant boast, namely that

> [f]or reasons of legal certainty and in order to avoid the fragmentation of the succession, [the *lex successionis*] should govern the succession as a whole, that is to say, all of the property forming part of the estate, irrespective of the nature of the assets and regardless of whether the assets are located in another Member State or in a third State.

This claim must be subject in relevant cases to the acquiescence of a non-compliant Member State or of a Third State, with which the deceased had a personal law connection or in which he or she held assets.

As to the outcome in any given case, much will depend upon the identity of forum, that is, the court which is most likely on the facts to take jurisdiction, being that which has the preponderant interest in the subject of the proceedings, normally, in this context, the court in the state where the bulk of the deceased's estate is situated and/or where the deceased was last habitually resident[30] and upon the operation of the enforcement rules contained in Chapter IV of the Regulation, which, as far as non-compliant Member States are concerned, are nothing more than aspirational.

In assessing the implications of Rome IV for non-compliant Member States, it is necessary always to interpret the phrase 'Member State' wherever it appears in the Regulation. On the assumption that the UK cannot be considered a 'Member State', at least for the purposes of Chapter II (Jurisdiction), it should be regarded as a *faux* Third State upon which no jurisdiction can be conferred by the rules in Chapter II, even by submission of parties per Article 9. Since Chapter III (Applicable law) opens by enunciating the principle of universality, it is apparent that the Regulation broadens its intended ambit in relation to choice of law, and the terminology changes

Rome IV, and to what extent?' are posed. The article examines those provisions of Rome IV which are capable of affecting succession to the estates of persons having a personal law connection with non-compliant Member States, and/or succession to estates containing property situated in such states, and seeks to show that it would be naive to assume that UK courts and UK citizens and residents are insulated from the effects of the operation of Rome IV.

[28] Crawford and Carruthers, ibid., 867.

[29] On Brexit and private international law, see Requejo Isidro's chapter in this volume.

[30] For compliant Member States, see detailed rules of jurisdiction contained in Rome IV, Chapter II.

accordingly from to 'Member State' to 'State'. Article 20, in securing application of the principle of universality, is an important nod to the accommodation of legal diversity, providing that any law specified by the Regulation shall be applied, whether or not it is the law of a Member State. With regard to Chapter IV (Recognition, Enforceability and Enforcement of Decisions), legislative *vires* would suggest that, as with Chapter II, the rules are intended to apply only within the net of compliant Member States.

As far as the UK is concerned, any objection concerning ambiguity of terminology will be superseded as and when the proposed exit from the EU by the UK comes to pass,[31] at which stage the status of the UK as a Third State will be irrefutable. Potential problems of interpretation, however, will persist in relation to the status of Ireland and Denmark in the operation of Rome IV.

Despite the advent of a harmonisation instrument to regulate cross-border succession problems, it will not always be straightforward to determine when the harmonised private international law rules in Rome IV will apply and when national rules of private international law of non-compliant Member States or of Third States should govern. In relevant cases, in order to function effectively as a harmonisation instrument, Rome IV will require cooperation between compliant and non-compliant Member States 'to fend off the chaos which otherwise will be likely to occur at the boundary between the harmonised system and residual national systems'.[32]

Managing Diversity through 'National' Private International Law

In the private international law of the legal systems of the UK, legal diversity in succession, in a private international law sense, is managed by operation of several devices. The primary technique has long been, and continues to be, the scission principle, with its supporting connecting factors of *lex situs* and ultimate domicile of the deceased. Other choice of law devices act as secondary techniques for the management of diversity, namely alternative reference choice of law rules, such as that contained in the Wills Act 1963, the process of characterisation, and *renvoi* reasoning. This section will consider each of these techniques in turn.

The Primary Technique: The Scission Principle

Adherence to the scission principle, which insists upon the application of a different choice of law rule according to the nature, as moveable or immoveable, of the property in question, immediately puts the legal systems of the UK into a situation of

[31] On 23 June 2016, the UK voted to leave the EU. In principle, the process of exiting the EU, after the invocation of Article 50 of the Treaty on European Union, ought to be accomplished within two years (that period elapses on 29 March 2019). Difficult problems of a transitional nature may be expected to emerge.

[32] Crawford and Carruthers, 'Speculation on the Operation of Succession Regulation 650/2012', above fn. 27, 847, at 852–3. On international cooperation, see further Part II of this volume.

divergence from many other legal systems, not least most other Member States of the EU which, *en bloc*, by virtue of Rome IV, apply a unitary choice of law rule.[33]

The characterisation of property

For as long as the scission rule continues to operate in the legal systems of the UK, it is essential for any British forum to determine whether property is to be treated as immoveable or moveable. Scots and English courts rely upon a decision of 1932, *Macdonald* v. *Macdonald's Executrix*,[34] in which the House of Lords ceded to the Canadian provincial *lex situs* the power to classify the deceased's various property interests situated in Canada. Lord Tomlin articulated the principle that

> [English law and Scots law, respectively . . .] when brought into contact with a foreign system, does, in accordance with the principles of what is called private international law, recognise the antithesis *for the purpose of applying the rule of comity* that, in matters of succession, moveables devolve according to the law of the domicile of the deceased and immoveables devolve according to the *lex rei sitae*.[35]

It is noteworthy that the scission rule was conceived as an enlightened, outward-looking technique, a rule based in, or even fostering, comity.

Though characterisation normally is the function of the forum, the exception concerning the characterisation of property as a private international law technique (generally, and not only for the purposes of the law of succession) is well established.[36] The rule has been long held that 'It is the law of the country where the subject is situated that must regulate the character of the subject as heritable or moveable.'[37]

In contrast, as regards operation of the other half of the scission principle, British courts have never deviated from their insistence that it is the forum's task to identify the domicile of the *propositus*, whether it be the last domicile for succession purposes or domicile at any other point in his or her life. This is demonstrated by *Re Annesley*,[38] in which Russell J insisted that Mrs Annesley, of English domicile of origin, died domiciled in France, having lived there for fifty-six years. A French court would not

33 Rome IV, Arts 21.1, 22.1 and 23.1.

34 1932 S.C. (HL) 79. See also *Robinson* v. *Robinson's Trustees* 1930 S.C. (H.L.) 20; *Re Berchtold* [1923] 1 Ch. 192; *Re Hoyles (No.1)* [1911] 1 Ch. 179; *Duncan* v. *Lawson* (1889) L.R. 41 Ch. D. 394; *Freke* v. *Lord Carbery* (1873) L.R. 16 Eq. 461; and *Jerningham* v. *Herbert* 38 E.R. 851; (1828) 4 Russ. 388.

35 1932 S.C. (HL) 79, at 84 (emphasis added).

36 Carruthers, J. M. (2005) *The Transfer of Property in the Conflict of Laws*, Oxford University Press, paras 1.01–1.19.

37 *Newlands* v. *Chalmers' Trustees* (1832) 11 S 65, per Lord Glenlee at 65. See also *Downie* v. *Downie's Trustees* (1866) 4 M 1067; *Monteith* v. *Monteith* (1882) 19 ScLR 740; *Moss' Trustees* v. *Moss* (1916) 2 SLT 31, per Lord Hunter at 34; *Re Berchtold, Berchtold* v. *Capron* [1923] 1 Ch. 193, per Russell J at 199; and *Re Cutliffe's Will Trusts, Brewer* v. *Cutliffe* [1940] 1 Ch. 565, per Morton J at 571.

38 [1926] Ch. 692.

have reached this conclusion on domicile,[39] for Mrs Annesley had not completed documentation indicating her intention to become a French domiciliary.[40] Despite demonstrating divergence of opinion in relation to the deceased's domicile, the case evinces a strenuous desire on the part of the English judge to achieve consensus between English law and French law through the operation of *renvoi* reasoning, and to that extent *Annesley* is an object lesson in managing diversity in succession.[41]

The *situs* principle

At the heart of the scission principle is the recognition that immoveable property is a special type of property and that, ultimately, for title to pass from the deceased, the *lex situs* must be satisfied, and the heir identified according to that law.[42] For centuries, even where the deceased's personal law has applied as the choice of law rule governing the devolution of his or her moveable property, whether in the event of death or bankruptcy,[43] the law of the *situs* at the date of death has governed succession to immoveable property.[44]

For over three decades, however, British conflict lawyers have questioned the need for this bifurcated approach, against a backdrop of many, if not most, other legal systems now having adopted a single choice of law rule for all types of property.[45]

[39] Ibid., per Russell J at 706: 'I hold that the question whether Mrs. Annesley died domiciled in France must be answered by ascertaining whether she had abandoned her English domicil and had acquired a French domicil of choice *in accordance with the requirements of English law* – namely, by the *factum* of residence coupled with the *animus manendi*, and that regardless of the question whether she had or had not complied with the formalities required by French law to be carried out by her before she could rank in its eyes as a domiciled Frenchwoman'.

[40] Ibid., at 693–4. Mrs Annesley never took the steps prescribed by Article 13 of the French Civil Code with a view to obtaining a formal French domicile according to French law (though an unsigned, printed form of application for this purpose was found among her personal papers).

[41] Cf. *Haji-Ioannou* v. *Frangos* [2009] EWHC 2310 (QB).

[42] In relation to the 'land taboo' (a phrase coined in 1938 by the undisclosed author of 'Choice of Law for Land Transactions' (1938) 28 *Colum. L. Rev.* 1939, at 1051, and associated with Moffat Hancock, who described the term as referring to the rule whereby 'every conceivable question affecting the transfer of title to land must invariably be determined by the domestic law of the *situs*' (Hancock, M. (1967) 'Conceptual Devices for Avoiding the Land Taboo in Conflict of Laws: The Disadvantages of Disingenuousness' 20 *Stanford Law Review* 1), see Carruthers, *The Transfer of Property*, above fn. 36, Ch. 2, and para. 2.06 in particular.

[43] *Sill* v. *Worswick* (1791) 1 HB 1 665; *Bell* v. *Kennedy* (1868) 6 M. (H.L.) 69; *Train* v. *Train's Executor* (1899) 2 F. 146; *Provincial Treasurer for Alberta* v. *Kerr* [1933] AC 701, 721; and *Bank voor Handel en Scheepvaart NV* v. *Slatford* [1953] 1 QB 248, per Devlin J at 257.

[44] *Fenton* v. *Livingstone* (1859) 21D (HL) 10; *Downie* v. *Downie's Trustees* (1866) 4 M 1067; and *Train* v. *Train's Executrix* (1899) 2F 146. See Crawford and Carruthers, *International Private Law* above fn. 5, para. 18-05.

[45] In a commentary on a succession questionnaire completed by the various Contracting States to the Hague Conference on Private International Law, Droz concluded that a rule of unity of inheritance (in terms of which succession to the entire estate of a deceased person would be governed by a single legal system, regardless of where the assets are situated) generally was provided for,

Notably a central feature of the 1989 Hague Convention on the Law Applicable to Succession to the Estates of Deceased Persons was the adoption of a unity principle, whereby a single law governed the succession to both moveable and immoveable property in the deceased's estate.[46] Subject to party choice of governing law (Article 5), the Convention favours (Article 3) application of the law of the state in which the deceased was habitually resident at the time of his or her death, and the law of his or her nationality, subject to application of the law of the state with which the deceased was manifestly more closely connected.[47]

A unitary choice of law rule is a feature also of Rome IV.[48] Although loss of the scission principle was not the UK's major concern with that instrument, it was one of the features of the proposal which gave some British lawyers pause for thought.[49] However, with regard to the Government's decision to opt in, or not, to the European Commission proposal for a regulation on wills and succession, the House of Lords European Union Committee found itself in agreement with the proposed change to a unitary choice of law rule to apply to the whole of the estate of a deceased.[50] Even in domestic law in the UK special rules governing the devolution of heritage/realty have died, or are dying, out[51] (so to speak), and support in the UK for the now idiosyncratic scissionist rule has weakened significantly.[52]

even if the connecting factor utilised by states was not the same in all cases: Hague Conference on Private International Law, Proceedings of the Sixteenth Session, vol. II (1990), 19 (Droz, G. A. L., *Questionnaire and Commentary on Succession in PIL*).

46 Arts 3–7. See Hague Conference on Private International Law, Proceedings of the Sixteenth Session, vol. II (1990), Waters, D. W. M., 'Report of the Special Commission', 241–3.

47 Art. 3(1) and (2).

48 Arts 21.1, 22.1 and 23.1. See above fn. 11.

49 Crawford and Carruthers, *International Private Law*, above fn. 5, para. 18-41.

50 *House of Lords European Union Committee, 6th Report of Session 2009–10, The EU's Regulation on Succession: Report with Evidence* (The Stationery Office, 2010), HL Paper No. 75 (Session 2009/10), para. 58.

51 The Succession (Scotland) Act 1964 removed many differences that previously had existed in domestic Scots law between succession to heritage and succession to moveables, albeit remnants of the distinction remain in domestic law. In England and Wales, see Collins et al., *Dicey, Morris & Collins*, above fn. 5, para. 27-018; and the Administration of Estates Act 1925.

52 See Carruthers, *The Transfer of Property*, above fn. 36, para. 2.76 et seq; and Crawford and Carruthers, *International Private Law*, above fn. 5, para. 18-05. In England, see Collins et al., *Dicey, Morris & Collins*, above fn. 5, para. 27-018. By the end of the 1980s, the Scottish Law Commission had come to the view that the last domicile of the deceased should regulate the devolution of the whole (intestate) estate: Scottish Law Commission, *Some Miscellaneous Topics in the Law of Succession*, 1986, *Scot. Law Com.* Memo. No. 71, para. 6.4; Scottish Law Commission, *Report on Succession*, 1990, *Scot. Law Com.* No. 124, para. 10.5; Scottish Law Commission, *Discussion Paper on Succession*, 2007, DP No. 136, para. 4.77 and *Report on Succession*, 2009, *Scot. Law Com.* No. 215), para. 5.3. Most recently, see Scottish Government Consultation on Technical Issues Relating to the Law of Succession (August 2014), followed by the passing of the Succession (Scotland) Act 2016 (which, however, did not address the private international law point). For responses to the Scottish Government's June 2015 Consultation on the Law of Succession, wherein the Government

Ultimate domicile

Turning to the other limb of the scission rule, the application to the devolution of a deceased person's moveable property of the law of his or her ultimate domicile, a rule long favoured by Scots[53] and English choice of law rules,[54] is not uncontroversial, but remains extant. In the UK, the evolution of domicile as a connecting factor has been one of common law development, interspersed with occasional statutory changes, some of great moment (for example, removal of the unity of domicile rule by the Domicile and Matrimonial Proceedings Act 1973;[55] and, in Scots law, by virtue of Section 22 of the Family Law (Scotland) Act 2006, ascription of domicile to persons aged under 16); and other, less far-reaching changes (for example, of dependent domicile of children in English law).[56] Domicile has withstood many attempts at wholesale reform and the general belief that reform was abandoned because the ambit of its operation was forecast to suffer attrition has proved to be correct.[57] Yet, domicile prevails in the UK in the area of choice of law rules concerning succession to moveable property, and the rule determines such matters as the rights of children in testate and intestate succession;[58] the essential validity of wills;[59] priority of deaths in a common calamity;[60] and collation *inter liberos*. When English domestic law limited freedom of testation by means of the Inheritance (Family Provision & Dependents) Act 1975, so as to allow a discontented family member to claim a discretionary award out of the deceased's estate, the gateway through which the claimant is required to pass before seeking a discretionary award from the court is to persuade the court that the deceased died domiciled in England and Wales.[61]

asked consultees if rights in intestacy should be 'property-specific' (p. 18), see www.gov.scot/Publications/2015/07/6682/0. The Consultation did not address the issue of retention, or not, of the scission principle, except in relation to the matter of capacity to make or revoke a will (para. 5.1) (re. recommendation 45, namely: 'Capacity to make or revoke a will should, in the case of a will or revocation executed after commencement, be determined (whether the will disposes of moveables or immoveables) by the law of the testator's domicile at the time of making or revoking the will.').

53 *Bell* v. *Kennedy* (1868) 6 M. (H.L.) 69; and *Train* v. *Train's Executor* (1899) 2 F. 146.

54 *Sill* v. *Worswick* (1791) 1 HB 1 665; *Provincial Treasurer for Alberta* v. *Kerr* [1933] AC 701, 721; and *Bank voor Handel en Scheepvaart NV* v. *Slatford* [1953] 1 QB 248, per Devlin J at 257.

55 Section 1.

56 Domicile and Matrimonial Proceedings Act 1973, Section 4.

57 Crawford and Carruthers, *International Private Law*, above fn. 5, paras 6-37 and 6-47.

58 *Bell* v. *Kennedy* (1868) 6 M. (H.L.) 69; *Train* v. *Train's Executor* (1899) 2 F. 146; *Re Groos* [1915] 1 Ch. 572; and *Reddington* v. *Riach's Executor* 2002 S.L.T. 537.

59 *Fuld (No.3)* [1968] P. 675.

60 *Re Cohn* [1945] Ch. 5.

61 See Crawford, E. B. and J. M. Carruthers (2014) 'The Law of Unintended Consequences: The Inheritance and Trustees' Powers Bill' 18(1) *Edin.L.R.* 133 for discussion of proposals at the Bill stage to 'widen the gateway'. In the face of opposition, the Inheritance and Trustees' Powers Act 2014 rightly did not create any additional jurisdictional criterion on which to make a family provision claim.

Towards a unitary choice of law rule?

Criticism of the scission principle in Scots and English choice of law rules has tended to relate to the *situs* limb, not the personal law limb. However, even allowing that domicile as a choice of law rule has its critics, the UK Government was not prepared to accept an undefined 'habitual residence of the deceased' as the connecting factor to govern all essential matters of succession per Rome IV.[62]

There is value in reflecting on Lord Tomlin's statement in 1932 in *Macdonald* v. *Macdonald's Executrix*,[63] that Scots and English law '*recognise the antithesis for the purpose of applying the rule of comity* that, in matters of succession, moveables devolve according to the law of the domicile of the deceased and immoveables devolve according to the *lex rei sitae*'.[64] The scission principle may be said to accommodate diversity by recognising and evaluating the different interests of different legal systems in the distribution of the component parts of an individual's estate. It manages diversity by prioritising legal systems' interests (or perceived interests) according to the nature of property. The problem, however, is that, while the *situs* rule developed at a time when wealth was equivalent to land ownership, which, in turn, was to be equated with rights of suffrage,[65] as the economy and domestic private law have evolved, the *situs* principle in UK choice of law rules of succession has remained static.[66] The rule now appears anachronistic:[67] although succession problems increasingly have become internationalised, 'stemming from an increasingly peripatetic society',[68] this is to be contrasted in UK choice of law rules with the 'tradition-bound character of the law of inheritance'.[69]

Given that the distinction between succession to immoveables and succession to moveables has been rendered less significant both in Scots domestic law[70] and in English domestic law,[71] the rationale of the scission principle is less convincing, and the rule is a stumbling block to achieving harmony in the handling of cross-border successions and a barrier to the smooth operation, in some cases at least, of the EU

62 Arts 21–3 and Recital (25). See also Hansard, HL vol. 502, part no. 17, col. 141 (16 December 2009).

63 1932 S.C. (HL) 79.

64 1932 S.C. (HL) 79, at 84 (emphasis added).

65 Weintraub, R. J. (1966) 'An Inquiry into the Utility of "Situs" as a Concept in Conflicts Analysis' 52 *Cornell Law Quarterly* 1, at 19.

66 Carruthers, *The Transfer of Property*, above fn. 36, para. 2.81; and Scoles, E. F. (1988) 'Choice of Law in Family Property Transactions' *Recueil des cours*, vol. 13, at 63.

67 Professor Anton observed in 1967 that '[t]he rule that succession to immoveables is governed by the *lex situs* was one of the first rules of private international law to be clearly enunciated in Scotland'. Anton, A. E. (1967) *Private International Law*, W. Green, 512, n. 52, citing Craig, *Jus Feudale*, 3.7.4, Lord Clyde's Translation, vol. II, 1058.

68 Carruthers, *The Transfer of Property*, above fn. 36, para. 2.81.

69 Hague Conference on Private International Law, Proceedings of the Sixteenth Session, vol. II (1990), van Loon, H., 'Update on the Commentary', 107, at 155.

70 Crawford and Carruthers, *International Private Law*, above fn. 5, para. 18-05.

71 Collins et al., *Dicey, Morris & Collins*, above fn. 5, para. 27-018.

Succession Regulation. Conceived as a measure to safeguard the different interests of different legal systems, the scission principle is more likely now to foster conflict rather than comity.

If Scots and English law were to abandon the scission principle, this would go a long way to reducing diversity of choice of law rules, minimising complexity and rendering easier coexistence among legal systems – particularly with those European legal systems most proximate to the UK – as regards succession to the estates of an increasingly mobile population. But there is a question, given the UK's hesitation with regard to harmonisation efforts in the law of succession, of whether or not the UK is ready to embrace a common approach to the private international law of succession.

Secondary Techniques for the Management of Diversity

Alternative reference choice of law rules

The scission rule comprises, in effect, two discrete choice of law rules, whereas the choice of law rule provided for the UK by the Wills Act 1963, regarding the formal validity of wills, is one of alternative (multi-)reference. The 1963 Act, which derives from deliberations at the Hague Conference on Private International Law,[72] is a triumph of harmonisation. The legislation manages diversity by placing on a par more than seven laws, each of which can be said to have an interest in determining the formal validity of a will. In Scots and English private international law, a will is to be regarded as validly executed in form if it complies with any of the following laws:[73] the law of the place of execution;[74] the law of the testator's domicile at the date of execution or at his or her death; the law of the testator's habitual residence at the date of execution or at his or her death; the law of the testator's nationality at the date of execution or at his or her death;[75] the law of the territory with which a vessel or aircraft is most closely connected in the case of a will executed on board a vessel or aircraft; or the law of the territory in which property is situated in the case of a will purporting to dispose of immoveable property.[76] This statutory rule, which is notably and patently easier to satisfy than a rule of cumulative reference[77] (whereby more than one *lex causae* requires to be satisfied), is liable to have a positive, *in favorem*

[72] The 1961 Hague Convention on the Conflict of Laws relating to the Form of Testamentary Dispositions entered into force on 5 January 1964. There are 44 States Parties as at 15 October 2018.

[73] In each case the law in question is the internal law of the country: Section 6(1).

[74] Even if the testator was on a temporary visit there: *Re Wynn (Deceased)* [1983] 3 All E.R. 310.

[75] Or, in the case of dual nationals, the law of either nationality: Mann, F. A. (1986) 'The Formal Validity of Wills in Case of Dual Nationality' 35 *International and Comparative Law Quarterly* 423.

[76] Section 1 (general rule as to formal validity); and Section 2 (additional rules).

[77] Such as is found, for example, in Section 38(2) of the Family Law (Scotland) Act 2006 concerning capacity and consent to marry. A rule so formulated acts as a brake upon, or barrier to, validity.

result in terms of upholding the formal validity of a will, and in that respect is a useful choice of law device for managing diversity, to positive benefit.

The characterisation process

An essential technique used in the operation of choice of law rules is the power of the forum to characterise the legal issue arising in any given dispute. Characterisation is central to orthodox jurisdiction-selection methodology.[78] Arguably that most important distinction, between that which is substantive and that which is procedural, is at the root of many, if not all, cross-border succession cases. In the same way that the scission principle may be said to manage diversity by recognising and evaluating the different interests of different legal systems in the distribution of the component parts of an individual's estate, so too the forum's characterisation of an issue as pertaining to form or substance constitutes an exercise in prioritisation of different legal systems' interests. Choice of law rules in succession constitute an *a priori* identification of the legal system which is deemed to be most appropriate to determine, or which is most interested in the resolution of, the issue in question.

The characterisation process makes one pause to consider if the legal issue in question might legitimately (in the view of the forum) be diverted to some other legal system having an interest, or greater interest, in the outcome. This is apparent in the distinction between the formal and the essential validity of a will, as, for example, in the characterisation of a rule that prohibits the witnessing of a will by the spouse of a beneficiary.[79] Similarly, a Scottish or English forum, having characterised an issue as pertaining to the interpretation of a will (what do the provisions of a will mean?) rather than to its essential validity (to what extent are the provisions of a will valid and enforceable?), will refer it to the law governing interpretation, which may differ from the *lex successionis*,[80] since in this instance only will 'UK' choice of law rules determine the applicable law by ascertaining the law which the testator intended, or may be said to have intended, should govern the will's interpretation[81] – a very restrained nod to party autonomy as a choice of law rule.

An unusual case where the forum ceded to the *lex causae* the power to characterise is *In re Maldonado*,[82] in which the English Court of Appeal yielded to the Spanish law characterisation of the Spanish state's entitlement to a deceased's intestate estate, in circumstances where the deceased, who had no heirs, left moveable property in England. The question was whether the Spanish government, by Spanish law, was properly to be regarded as the ultimate heir in succession or as the recipient of *bona*

[78] See, in detail, Robertson, A. H. (1940), *Characterization in the Conflict of Laws*, Harvard University Press.

[79] *Re Priest (Deceased)* [1944] Ch. 58.

[80] *Mitchell & Baxter* v. *Davies* (1875) 3 R. 208.

[81] *Philipson-Stow* v. *Inland Revenue Commissioners* [1961] A.C. 727, per Lord Denning at 760–1. See also *Re Levick's Will Trusts* [1963] 1 W.L.R. 311.

[82] [1954] P. 223.

vacantia. The Court of Appeal held that Spanish law was the *lex causae qua lex successionis*: the state of Spain, in the view of Spanish law, was the true heir, not merely the fiscal recipient of ownerless property.

In cases such as those concerning *bona vacantia*,[83] and other well-known characterisation exercises such as those between the law of succession and that of matrimonial property or contract,[84] or between the law of marriage and the law of succession,[85] or between succession and donation,[86] the forum, in following its preferred characterisation, is not so much managing diversity by prioritising the different interests of different legal systems, as making a choice which, to the cynic, is tantamount to result-selection.

A more impartial example of diversity management is provided by *Re Cohn*,[87] in which Uthwatt J strove to characterise the nature of the presumption regarding *commorientes* found, respectively, in the English law of the forum and in the German law of the deceased persons' ultimate domicile. Both legal systems' rules being held to be substantive in character, the judge considered himself bound to apply the rule of the German *lex successionis*, the parties having died domiciled in Germany. Though both the German rule and its English equivalent were classified as substantive, the content of the respective rules was diametrically opposed.

Renvoi

Historically, *renvoi* as a technique has played a very significant part, at least in English choice of law rules, in the recognition and management of diversity in international private law, and could fairly be described as the pinnacle of any legal system's endeavours to accommodate legal diversity. The law of succession is the natural home of this methodological device, the classic *renvoi* problem presenting in a case of succession to the moveable estate in England (or Scotland) of a British subject who died intestate, and domiciled abroad, in a country the law of which refers questions of succession to the law of the deceased's nationality.

As with the Wills Act 1963, an *in favorem* impetus lies behind the genesis of *renvoi* thinking in England. In *Collier* v. *Rivaz*[88] the diversity of connecting factor opened up by the *renvoi* reasoning which was inherent in the choice of law rule was embraced as a positive attribute. *Renvoi* reasoning was invoked to alleviate the strictness of the then English rule,[89] by providing additional (domestic) laws against which to test the formal validity of a testamentary instrument. By acknowledging that

[83] *Re Barnett* [1902] 1 Ch. 867; *Re Musurus* [1936] 2 All E.R. 1666; *Goold Stuart's Trustees* v. *McPhail* 1947 S.L.T. 221; and *In re Maldonado* [1954] P. 223.

[84] *De Nicols* v. *Curlier (No 1)* [1900] A.C. 1.

[85] *In re Martin* [1900] P. 211; and *Westerman* v. *Schwab* (1905) 8 F. 132.

[86] *Re Korvine's Trust* [1921] 1 Ch. 343.

[87] *Re Cohn* [1945] Ch. 5.

[88] *Collier* v. *Rivaz* (1841) 2 Curt. 855.

[89] Cf., in tort, *Neilson* v. *Overseas Projects Corp of Victoria Ltd* [2005] HCA 54.

the choice of law rule of the *lex causae* identified by the forum may favour for the distribution of the estate the internal law of the forum, or the law of a Third State, the forum, in effect, concedes that another legal system has a greater interest in the determination of the issue, or at least that the other legal system has a justifiable claim to be applied, in the hope of producing a positive result (for some).[90]

An English court is free to deploy *renvoi* as a technique in succession matters, except in relation to formal validity, where the Wills Act 1963 (generous already in its choice of law provision) refers to the internal law in force in the territories listed.[91]

European Member State courts operating Rome IV are required to follow the complex *renvoi* provision contained in Article 34 of that instrument. Article 34 authorises the operation of *renvoi* outwards, that is, where a (compliant) Member State court has identified as the applicable law under the Regulation the law of a Third State. There would be no point in admitting the *renvoi* process within the net of compliant Member States, for that would generate never-ending circularity.[92] Where a Third State law 'in the round' makes a remission to the law of a (compliant) Member State, the *renvoi* process is permitted, and Recital (57) encourages the compliant Member State to accept the reference back. Clearly it is beyond the power of the Regulation to dictate the approach which a Third State court should take to the *renvoi* process in a cross-border succession litigation.

If an English court were to engage in *renvoi* reasoning in a case where, in its view, the *lex causae* is that of a compliant Member State, that English court would be required, at second remove, to apply Article 34, being part of the private international law of the compliant Member State.

Conclusion

This chapter started by noting two obvious diversities: the diversity of substantive rules of succession among the legal systems of the EU and beyond, and, separately, the diversity of approach among legal systems to the resolution of conflict of laws problems. Diversity among legal systems' substantive rules is managed by means of private international law rules (and the techniques embedded therein), those rules operating sometimes on an international basis and sometimes, as in the case of the UK, on a national basis.

All European Member States, except Denmark and Ireland, now operate a harmonised approach to conflict of laws rules in matters of succession, embracing a unitary approach. The UK's refusal to embrace Rome IV is likely to undermine the instrument's operation elsewhere in Europe, unless, for the sake of practicality, convenience and comity, Scots and English courts are prepared to acquiesce in the operation of its rules. Had the UK opted into Rome IV, would this have evidenced an embracing of diversity through the subordination of our native, scissionist rule to

[90] *In the Estate of Fuld (Deceased) (No 3)* [1968] P. 675.

[91] Section 1.

[92] Crawford and Carruthers (2015), above fn. 5, para. 18-49. See also Recital (57).

the approach agreed among the continental majority? As it is, the UK has preferred to adhere to its insular approach, by retaining, for the time being, a bifurcated rule, which, though conceived as fostering comity, now is capable of fomenting conflict. To this important extent, diversity remains in the private international law of succession.

4

Cross-border Family Issues in the EU: Multiplicity of Instruments, Inconsistencies and Problems of Coordination

Rosario Espinosa Calabuig

Introduction

According to the European Commission there are currently around 16 million international couples in the European Union. Cross-border family issues are therefore likely to occur frequently. When a couple breaks up, family members including children often end up living in different countries and their legal disputes become more complex. The statistics show that the number of international divorces and separations has increased in the EU in recent years.[1] At the same time, legal alternatives to marriage, like registered partnerships, have become more widespread and national legislations have conferred rights on unmarried and same-sex couples.[2] In 2019, the legal systems of fifteen of the total Member States of the EU provide for same-sex marriage.[3] This generates a potential increase in the number of legal separations and divorces in these states.

The constant and increasing flow of citizens from one state to another, with the consequent Europeanisation and internationalisation of family relations, has given rise for some time to a growing increase in cross-border family conflicts. Challenges are many and concern categories such as divorce, matrimonial property, cross-border maintenance obligations and cross-border rights of access to children, *inter alia*. To

[1] Denmark, Latvia, Lithuania and Portugal are the countries with the most divorces per year in the EU. See http://ec.europa.eu/eurostat/statistics-explained/index.php/Marriage_and_divorce_statistics

[2] See Dethloff, N. (2011) 'New Models of Partnership: The Financial Consequences of Separation', 12 *Journal of the Academy of European Law*, 89–102.

[3] In particular Austria (2019), Malta (2017), Finland (2017), Germany (2017), Slovenia (2015), Luxembourg (2015), Ireland (2015), United Kingdom (2014, with the exception of Northern Ireland), France (2013), Denmark (2012), Portugal (2010), Sweden (2009), Spain (2005), Belgium (2003), Netherlands (2001). Outside the EU, countries such as Canada, South Africa, Norway, Argentina, Brazil, Uruguay, New Zealand and some states of the USA and Mexico also recognise same-sex marriages.

face these challenges and in trying to offer EU citizens legal certainty several instruments have been adopted in the EU with the objective of creating a uniform regime of jurisdiction and conflict of laws rules.[4] To maximise the efficiency of these instruments all EU countries should agree to them unanimously. Unfortunately, however, this is not the case. Only the Brussels IIa Regulation[5] and the Maintenance Regulation[6] are applicable in all Member States. The Succession Regulation ('Rome IV')[7] was adopted in all Member States except the United Kingdom, Ireland and Denmark. The other three Regulations approved in this field have needed the route of enhanced cooperation foreseen by Article 20 of the European Union treaty and Articles 326–34 of the Treaty on the Functioning of the European Union.[8] This has been the only

[4] For the advantages and disadvantages of the process of unification in the EU see, among others, Jäntera Jareborg, M. (2003) 'Unification of International Family Law in Europe – A Critical Perspective', in Boele-Woelki, K., *Perspectives for the Unification and Harmonisation of Family Law in Europe*, Intersentia, 194–216; Martiny, D. (2002) 'The Harmonisation of Family Law in the European Community. Pro and Contra', in Faure, M., *Towards a European Ius Commune in Legal Education and Research. Proceedings of the Conference Held on the Occasion of the 20th Anniversary of the Maastricht Faculty of Law*, Intersentia, 191–201; Campuzano Díaz, B. (2011) 'The Coordination of the EU Regulations on Divorce and Legal Separation with the Proposal on Matrimonial Property Regimes', *Yearbook of Private International Law*, vol. 13, 233–53; Dethloff, N. (2003) 'Arguments for the Unification and Harmonization of Family in Europe', in Boele-Woelki, K., *Perspectives for the Unification and Harmonisation of Family Law in Europe*, Intersentia, 54–64; Harding, M. (2011) 'The Harmonization of Private International Law in Europe: Taking the Character out of Family Law', *Journal of Private International Law*, 203–29.

[5] Council Regulation (EC) No. 2201/2003 of 27 November 2003 concerning jurisdiction and the recognition and enforcement of judgments in matrimonial matters and parental responsibility (which repeals Regulation (EC) No. 1347/2000) OJ L 338, 23.12.2003. See proposals for reform COM (2016) 411 final, Brussels 30.6.2016, as well as the Opinion of the European Economic and Social Committee on the Proposal for a Council Regulation on the competence, recognition and enforcement of decisions on matrimonial matters and parental responsibility, published on 26 February 2017 (COM(2016) 411 final –2016/0190 (CNS)).

[6] Council Regulation (EU) No. 4/2009 of 18 December 2008 on jurisdiction, applicable law, recognition and enforcement of decisions and cooperation in matters relating to maintenance obligations OJ L 7, 10.01.2009.

[7] Council Regulation (EU) No. 605/2012 of 4 July 2012 on jurisdiction, applicable law, recognition and enforcement of decisions and acceptance and enforcement of authentic instruments in matters of succession and on the creation of a European Certificate of Succession OJ L 201, 27.07.2012, applicable to the succession of persons who died on or after 17 August 2015.

[8] See, in general, Boele-Woelki, K. (2010) 'For Better or for Worse: the Europeanisation of International Divorce Law', *Yearbook of Private International Law*, vol. 12, 21–5; Cannone, A. (2005) *Le cooperazione rafforzate. Contributo allo studio dell'integrazione differenziata*, Cacucci, 10; Pocar, F. (2011) 'Brevi note sulle cooperazione rafforzate e il diritto internazionale privato', *Rivista di Diritto Internazionale privato e processuale*, 297–306; Franzina, P. (2011) 'Una "cooperazione rafforzata" fra l'Italia e altri tredici stati membri dell'Unione Europea per determinare la legge applicabile alla separazione e al divorzio', *Int'l Lis*, 7–11; Fiorini, A. (2013) 'Bruxelles sans Rome: La réticence du Royaume-Uni face à l'harmonisation du droit européen du divorce', in Corneloup, S. (ed.), *Droit européen du divorce*, LexisNexis, 701; Fiorini, A. (2010) 'Harmonizing the Law Applicable to Divorce and Legal Separation – Enhanced Co-operation as the Way Forward?' 59 *International and*

possible way to adopt Regulations in matters such as divorce and legal separation ('Rome III'),[9] matrimonial property regimes[10] and property-related consequences of registered partnerships.[11] Due to this European mechanism of enhanced cooperation, the latter group of Regulations are only applied in some of the twenty-eight Member States, referred to as 'participating Member States'[12] or 'compliant Member States'.[13] Therefore, the objective of the legal unification in cross-border family issues has been frustrated and the 'two-speed Europe' seems to be a fact. The limitations in their geographical and substantial scope of application can motivate the heavily criticised 'race to the courts' depending on the interests and expectations of the parties and as a result of the divergences existing in the substantive laws of the Member States in matters such as same-sex marriage.

The number of proceedings pending in more than one country has multiplied in recent years,[14] as have cases in which the recognition of a divorce in a certain country constrained the possibility of celebrating a new marriage or even the legitimate nature of filiation in another state. The so-called limping marriages, those dissolved in one country but considered valid in another, have also increased as have cases of international child abduction.[15] It has therefore become urgent to provide a unified response at a European level through a coordinated and effective system of rules on jurisdiction and the recognition and enforcement of judgments. Such a system would replace the current one in the European states, based – for the most part – in a plurality of alternative fora, which has often caused a high number of conflicts of jurisdiction. However, the result of the multiplicity of new instruments (the aforementioned

Comparative Law Quarterly 1143; Baruffi, M. C. (2011) 'Il regolamento sulla legge applicabile ai "divorzi europei"' 4 *Diritto dell'Unione europea* 841–5; Ottaviano, I. (2011) 'La prima cooperazione rafforzata dell'Unione europea: una disciplina comune in materia d legge applicabile a separazione e divorzi trasnazionali', *Diritto dell'unione europea*, 113–44.

9 Council Regulation (EU) No. 1259/2010 of 20 December 2010 implementing enhanced cooperation in the area of the law applicable to divorce and legal separation OJ L 343, 29.12.2010, came into effect on 21 June 2012.

10 Council Regulation (EU) 2016/1103 of 24 June 2016 implementing enhanced cooperation in the area of jurisdiction, applicable law and the recognition and enforcement of decisions in matters of OJ L 183, 8.7.2016. It applies from 29 January 2019, except for Arts 63 and 64 which apply from 29 April 2018, and Arts 65, 66 and 67, which apply from 29 July 2016.

11 Council Regulation (EU) 2016/1104 of 24 June 2016 implementing enhanced cooperation in the area of jurisdiction, applicable law and recognition and enforcement of decisions in matters of OJ L 183, 8.7.2016. It applies from 29 January 2019, except for Arts 63 and 64 which apply from 29 April 2018, and Arts 65, 66 and 67, which apply from 29 July 2016.

12 In the case of the Rome III Regulation there are so far seventeen participating Member States (Austria, Belgium, Bulgaria, Estonia, France, Germany, Greece, Hungary, Italy, Latvia, Lithuania, Luxembourg, Malta, Portugal, Romania, Slovenia and Spain).

13 This is the expression used by Carruthers in her chapter in this volume.

14 See www.eufams.unimi.it

15 For details, see Espinosa Calabuig, R. (2007) *Custodia y visita de menores en el Espacio judicial europeo*, Marcial Pons, 38–78.

Regulations) have rendered the solution of a cross-border family dispute very complicated and are likely to continue to obstruct the work of any legal professional dealing with international family litigation. The coexistence of all these instruments forces national legal practitioners to ascertain the appropriate coordination, not only among the EU Regulations, but also with the international Conventions which might be applied, such as the 1996 Hague Convention on Jurisdiction, Applicable Law, Recognition, Enforcement and Co-operation concerning Parental Responsibility and Measures for the Protection of Children,[16] the 2007 Hague Convention on the International Recovery of Child Support and Other Forms of Family Maintenance[17] or the 2007 Hague Protocol on the Law Applicable to Maintenance Obligations.[18] This coordination is indeed complex, due to the difficulties stemming from the multiplicity of instruments and their limitations, deficiencies and interpretative problems. Besides, the fragmentation of the legal framework contrasts with the practice of family law, where causes of action such as marriage, divorce, maintenance and parental responsibility tend to be intertwined in a single case scenario. In particular, in order to deal with international family litigation, several issues should be ascertained: (1) the legal framework (European, international or national); (2) the status of the states involved (Member State, participating Member State, Member State bound or not by the 2007 Hague Protocol, or a Third State); (3) the legal categories involved in the dispute (divorce, separation, annulment, maintenance, which usually requires the private international law technique of characterisation to be used to determine them); and (4) scope of application of the relevant instruments of the legal framework to identify the issues not covered or excluded from the EU Regulations which in turn make necessary the application of the forum's national rules of private international law. Therefore, it is not surprising how fearful legal practitioners are of facing the complexity and intricacy of this kind of case and dealing with it with expertise and professionalism.

This chapter focuses only on some of the problems and difficulties arising from the aforementioned multiplicity and complexity, and aims particularly to illustrate some of the more striking inconsistencies and conflicting aspects that their application can generate in practice.

[16] The Convention on Jurisdiction, Applicable Law, Recognition, Enforcement and Co-operation in Respect of Parental Responsibility and Measures for the Protection of Children was concluded in The Hague on 19 October 1996 and entered into force on 1 January 2002; 49 States Parties, status as at 15 October 2018.

[17] The Hague Convention on the International Recovery of Child Support and Other Forms of Family Maintenance was concluded on 23 November 2007 and entered into force on 1 January 2013; 39 States Parties, status as at 15 October 2018.

[18] The Protocol on the Law Applicable to Maintenance Obligations was adopted in The Hague on 23 November 2007 and entered into force on 1 August 2013; 30 States Parties, status as at 15 October 2018.

Matrimonial Crisis: Inconsistencies between the Brussels IIa Regulation and the Rome III Regulation

The drafting of the Rome III Regulation has seen its original objective of creating uniform conflict of law rules consistent with the rules of jurisdiction of the Brussels IIa Regulation frustrated.[19] The attainment of this objective would have made possible the long-awaited alignment *forum-ius* that is so advisable in family matters where substantive and procedural rules work closely together.[20] However, its limited scope of application – with remarkable omissions like marriage annulment – can motivate the mentioned race to the courts, for example, in cases of same-sex couples who want to divorce.

Jurisdiction: Regulation (EC) No. 2201/2003 and the Proposal to Recast the Regulation

The rules on jurisdiction of the courts of the European Member States in cases of divorce, legal separation or marriage annulment are provided for in the Brussels IIa Regulation. This Regulation is undoubtedly 'the cornerstone of judicial cooperation in family matters in the Union',[21] and in turn 'judicial cooperation between the Member States of the Union must gradually improve and adapt to the reality of an increasing number of citizens throughout the Union who move, get married and have children'.[22] The Regulation has a limited scope of application, since it 'should apply only to the dissolution of matrimonial ties and should not deal with issues such as the grounds for divorce, property consequences of the marriage or any other ancillary measures' (Recital (8)). This can raise problems in countries where the judge is competent to dissolve the marriage and also to rule on the liquidation of the matrimonial property regimes and to fix the subsequent framework of parent-child relationships.[23]

[19] See Loquin, E. 'La création d'un marché européen du divorce', in Corneloup, *Droit européen du divorce* above fn. 8, 741–51; Kruger, T. and L. Samyn (2016) 'Brussels IIa: Successes and Suggested Improvements' 12 *Journal of Private International Law*, 132–68.

[20] They are like two sides of the same coin; see Franzina, 'Una "cooperazione rafforzata"', above fn. 8, 95–6.

[21] Opinion of the European Economic and Social Committee on the Proposal for a Council Regulation on the competence, recognition and enforcement of decisions on matrimonial matters and parental responsibility, 26 February 2017 (C. Bäumler).

[22] (COM (2016) 411 final – 2016/0190 (CNS)). See Kruger and Samyn, 'Brussels IIa: Successes and Suggested Improvements', above fn. 19, 132–68; de Boer, Th. M. (2015) 'What We Should Not Expect From a Recast of the Brussels II bis Regulation', *Nederlands Internationaal Privaatrecht* (*NIPR*), Afl.1, 10–19. See also Campuzano Díaz, B. (2017) 'La Propuesta de reforma del Reglamento 2201/2003: ¿Se introducen mejoras en la regulación de la competencia judicial internacional', in Guzmán Zapatero, M. and C. Esplugues Mota, *Persona y familia en el nuevo modelo español de Derecho internacional privado*, Tirant lo Blanch, 91–102.

[23] This is the case, for example, in Spain. See Iglesias Buhigues, J. L., C. Esplugues Mota and G. Palao Moreno (2017), *Derecho internacional privado*, 11th edn, Tirant lo Blanch, 460; Añoveros Terradas, B. (2007) 'The Impact and Application of the Brussels II bis Regulation in Spain', in Boele-Woelki,

Article 3 of the Regulation provides for seven grounds of concurrent jurisdiction, six territorial ones (habitual residence of one or both spouses) and one more based on the common nationality of the parties (in the case of the UK and Ireland, the common 'domicile'). There is no hierarchy established between these alternative competent fora according to *Hadady*.[24] This multiplicity of competent fora in matrimonial matters is likely to increase the cases of *lis pendens*, as well as – and in particular – the phenomenon of 'forum shopping'.[25] For the Court of Justice of the European Union (CJEU) the fora of Article 3 must be interpreted autonomously, without regard to the law of the various Member States. In this framework it is perfectly possible to have two different courts competent to hear the case (concurrent jurisdiction), since Article 3.1(b) refers generically to the common nationality of the spouses, without qualifying this in any way. The risk of parallel proceedings before various courts is tackled by Article 19 of the Regulation (*lis pendens* and dependent actions).[26] The risks evidenced in *Hadady* explain some of the criticisms that have been levelled at the multiplicity of fora of Article 3 of the Regulation. The aforementioned risk of forum shopping may be increased as well as the possibility of 'manipulation' that could result from the voluntary use by the spouses of any of the grounds of jurisdiction. They could, by mutual agreement or not, change their nationality or even more easily their habitual residence and thus exert an influence on the facts and, ultimately, on the jurisdiction of one or other of the courts.[27] These risks are exacerbated, as explained below, by the limited scope of application of the Rome III Regulation.

The criteria of jurisdiction foreseen in Article 3 are, moreover, accompanied by a set of rules that specify the operation of these criteria. On one hand, Article 4 states that the court before which there are proceedings for marriage annulment, legal separation or divorce, as provided for Article 3 of the Regulation, should also be competent to examine the counterclaim, provided that it comes within the scope of the Regulation. On the other hand, Article 5 considers that, without prejudice to Article 3, the court that has given a judgment on legal separation shall also have jurisdiction for converting that judgment into a divorce, if the law of that Member State so provides. These grounds of jurisdiction are considered to be the only available ones within the scope of application of the Regulation, as it is clear from Article 6 to the effect that a spouse who has his or her habitual residence in the territory of a Member

K. and C. González Beilfuss (eds) (2007), *Brussels II bis: Its Impact and Application in the Member States*, Intersentia, Commission on European Family Law, 279–95.

24 *Laszlo Hadadi (Hadady)* v. *Csilla Marta Mesko, wife of Hadadi (Hadady)* (Case C-168/08) (2009) ECR I-6871.

25 See de Vareilles-Sommières, P. (1999) 'La libre circulation des jugements rendus en matière matrimoniale en Europe. Convention de Bruxelles II du 28 mai 1998 et proposition de règlement (C.E.) du Conseil' *Gazette du Palais*, 17–18 December, 22–3; Ricci, C. (2017) 'Jurisdiction in matrimonial matters', in Honorati, C. (ed.), *Jurisdiction in Matrimonial Matters, Parental Responsibility and International Abduction*, Giappichelli, 37–59.

26 Following *Hadady* (paras 43 and 56).

27 See de Vareilles-Sommières, 'La libre circulation des jugements', above fn. 25, 22–3.

State, or is a national of a Member State, or in the case of the UK and Ireland has his or her 'domicile' in the territory of one of the latter Member States, may be sued in another Member State only in accordance with Articles 3, 4 and 5. As stated by the CJEU in *Sundelind López*,[28] Article 6 would allow a defendant who does not fit within the requirements of that provision and who therefore has no habitual residence in a Member State (and who does not have the nationality of or is not domiciled in a Member State) to be brought before the courts of a Member State in accordance with the rules of jurisdiction provided in the domestic law of that state, pursuant to the provisions of Article 7 of the Regulation. However, this will only be possible provided that for such a case there is no competent court according to Articles 3, 4 and 5 of the Regulation. On the other hand, by way of 'residual jurisdiction' (Article 7) it is possible in the latter cases to take recourse to the otherwise applicable jurisdiction rules of the forum.[29] Doubts raised in the application of Articles 6 and 7 explain the elimination of the first and the reformulation of the second in the Proposal to recast the Brussels IIa Regulation launched in June 2016.[30] The removal of Article 6 can be seen as a success as it is only considered to be a source of confusion in its current terms. The Proposal combines both Articles in a single provision entitled 'residual jurisdiction', which refers to domestic rules on jurisdiction when it is not possible to establish in accordance with Articles 3, 4 and 5 the jurisdiction of any Member State authority. However, there is again one limitation, that is, domestic rules on jurisdiction shall not apply when the defendant has his or her habitual residence in a Member State or is a national/domicilee of a Member State. In this sense the Proposal could have avoided a reference to the domestic legislation; instead it could have provided for *forum necessitatis*.[31]

Applicable Law: Rome III

The main purpose of the Rome III Regulation was to avoid the risk of forum shopping and the consequent race to the courts to obtain a judicial response more in line with

[28] *Kerstin Sundelin López* v. *Miguel Enrique López Lozazo* (Case C-68/07) (2007), ECR-I-10403. See also Requejo Isidro, M. (2008) 'Regulation (EC) 2201/03 and its Personal Scope' *Yearbook of Private International Law*, 579–91.

[29] Art. 7 of the Regulation has also been interpreted by the CJEU in *Sundelind López*. It raised a question concerning the divorce of a Swedish national residing in France, whose husband, a Cuban national, was in Cuba at the time of the application to the Swedish courts. They declared themselves incompetent, deciding that the French courts were the only ones competent under Art. 3 of the Regulation. This interpretation was supported by the CJEU which considered that, according to Art. 7, the Swedish courts had to declare their lack of competence *ex officio* in the event that the French courts or any other court of a Member State were competent under Art. 3 of the Regulation.

[30] Proposal COM (2016) 411 final, 2016/0190 (CNS), above fn. 22.

[31] In the case of Spain this rule could avoid the reference to the national provisions, that is, *Ley Orgánica del Poder Judicial* (*LOPJ*). After its reform by Act 7/2015 of 7 July 2015, the special forum on matrimonial matters, Art. 22 (c) of *LOPJ*, is a copy of the Regulation, thus litigants in Spain can only use the criteria established by the Brussels IIa Regulation.

the interests of one party or the other. Flexibility, predictability and legal certainty were thus sought.[32] To this end, a series of subsidiary connecting factors (Article 8) were introduced to ascertain the applicable law, which apply in the absence of choice of law by the parties (Article 5), such as: (1) the habitual residence of the spouses at the time the court is seized; or failing that (2) where they were last habitually resident, provided that the period of residence did not end more than one year before the court was seized, in so far as one of the spouses still resides in that state at the time the court is seized; or, failing that (3) the country of common nationality of the spouses at the time the court is seized; or, failing that (4) where the court is seized. Lastly, Article 10 provides for the *lex fori* as a last recourse.

The Regulation proclaims freedom of choice that allows the parties to select a law from the exhaustive list provided by the Regulation. For the first time the autonomy of the parties has become the bastion of private international law regulation of family law in the EU, in particular, divorce and judicial separation. And it has raised many 'sensitivities' based on the social, cultural and legal diversity in the European Member States in this field, which have made it impossible to achieve unanimity in the approval of this and other instruments regarding cross-border family issues.[33]

Another feature of Rome III is that, although it is concerned with regulating divorce (apart from separation) in the EU, it does not promote *favor divortii* at all costs, although certain provisions do. In particular, if the applicable law were to run counter to divorce, it would not apply because it would be understood that public policy would be violated. Thus, according to Article 12, 'application of a provision of the law designated by virtue of this Regulation may be refused only if such application is manifestly incompatible with the public policy of the forum'. Other provisions of the Regulation would also facilitate *favor divortii* as is the case of Article 9.2, which regulates the conversion of judicial separation into divorce. In this case, 'if the law applied to the legal separation does not provide for the conversion of legal separation into divorce, Article 8 shall apply, unless the parties have agreed otherwise in accordance with Article 5'. Besides, Article 10 provides that

32 See Espinosa Calabuig, R. 'Elección de una ley por las partes al divorcio y separación judicial: la solución limitada del Reglamento Roma III', in Queirolo, I., A. M. Benedetti and L. Carpaneto (2014) *Le nuove famiglie tra globalizzazione e identità statuali. Scritti di diritto privato europeo ed internazionale*, Aracne, 211–37.

33 On the assessment of party autonomy in family disputes in the UK see Carruthers, J. (2012) 'Party Autonomy in the Legal Regulation of Adult Relationships: What Place for Party Choice in Private International Law?', *International and Comparative Law Quarterly*, vol. 61, no. 4, 881. Regarding countries such as Italy, Germany, Belgium or the Netherlands, see Viarengo, I. (2010) 'Il regolamento UE sulla legge applicabile alla separazione e al divorzio e il criterio della volontà delle parti', *Rivista di diritto internazionale privato e processuale*, 611. See, in general, Añoveros Terrades, B. (2013) 'La Autonomía de la voluntad como principio rector de las normas de derecho internacional privado comunitario de familia', in Forner Delaygua, J., C. González Beilfuss and E. Viñas Ferrer, *Entre Bruselas y La Haya. Estudios sobre la unificación internacional y regional del Derecho internacional privado. Liber Amicorum Alegría Borras*, Marcial Pons, 119–33.

> where the law applicable pursuant to Articles 5 or Article 8 makes no provision for divorce or does not grant one of the spouses equal access to divorce or legal separation on grounds of their sex, the law of the *forum* shall apply.

On the contrary, other provisions contained in the Regulation would prevent or at least restrict the *favor divortii*. This would be the case of Article 13 concerning 'Differences in National Law'.[34] On the one hand, the rule seems consistent with the current EU process which is still very much dependent on the idiosyncrasies of the EU Member States taken individually. It seems, therefore, to be a justifiable compromise in favour of legal diversity on a key legal instrument.[35] But, on the other hand, it is also an objectionable rule from several points of view, as explained below.

Objectionable limitations in the scope of application of Rome III

The Regulation only deals with the dissolution or loosening of marriage ties[36] without contemplating other issues that in some EU Member States are resolved concurrently in the same proceedings. The applicable law to these other issues must be ascertained following a different conflict of laws rule. This kind of fragmentation related to issues of characterisation also occurs within the scope of Brussels IIa which, likewise, leaves outside its scope of application aspects such as the causes of divorce, the property consequences of marriage or other ancillary measures.

Apart from the above shortcoming, Article 1.2 of Rome III excludes a number of private situations, 'even if they arise merely as a preliminary question within the context of divorce or legal separation proceedings', such as (1) the legal capacity of natural persons; (2) the existence, validity or recognition of a marriage; (3) the annulment of a marriage; (4) the name of the spouses; (5) the property consequences of the marriage; (6) parental responsibility; (7) maintenance obligations; (8) trusts or successions. Once again, the legal practitioner is forced to make considerable efforts to ascertain the applicable law to these other related issues to complete an applicable law mosaic enabling them to deal with a divorce case as a whole, including issues such as parental responsibility or child maintenance, as well as other ancillary issues. The fragmentation in the regulation of these matters is clearly contrary to the objective of creating uniform standards in the EU.[37]

Among all the exclusions made by Rome III the most strikingly unjustified,

[34] For the *favor divortii* in the Regulation see Carrascosa González, J. (2012) 'The Law Applicable to Judicial Separation and Divorce in Default of Choice of Law by the Spouses. Analysis of Article 8 of Regulation 1259/2010 of December 20, 2010', 4 *Cuadernos de Derecho Transnacional*, 58–60.

[35] Following Guzmán Zapater, M. (2012) 'Divorcio, matrimonio y ciertas diferencias nacionales: a propósito de su tratamiento en el art. 13 del Reglamento Roma III', in Esplugues Mota, C. and P. Palao Moreno (eds), *Nuevas fronteras del Derecho de la Unión europea. Liberamicorum José Luis Iglesias Buhigues*, Tirant lo Blanch, 52.

[36] Recital 10, Rome III Regulation.

[37] See Nascimbene, B. (2012) 'Le norme di conflitto in tema di separazione e divorzio nel regolamento 1259/2010' *Diritto del commercio internazionale*, 349.

since it is within the scope of Brussels IIa, is that relating to marriage annulment. Attention is drawn to the explanation given in Recital (10) of the Regulation: 'The scope and purpose of this Regulation should be consistent with those of Regulation (EC) No. 2201/2003. However, this Regulation should not apply to the annulment of the marriage'. So what is the justification for the exclusion of the latter?[38] On the one hand, it does not make sense in relation to the key objective of the Regulation: to avoid the race to the courts and favour legal certainty; these are objectives that would impact separation and divorce and marriage annulment to the same extent. On the other hand, it cannot be argued that the autonomy of the parties is not appropriate to regulate matrimonial annulment, since it would have been sufficient to introduce a different rule to exclude party autonomy in the annulment context. Likewise, it is also meaningless to argue that there are countries where marriage annulment is not recognised – as is clear from the preparatory work of the Regulation – since there are others (such as Germany, Greece and Finland) that do not recognise separation.[39]

Another issue that is excluded from the scope of application, and equally objectionable, is the 'existence, validity or recognition of a marriage' (Article 1.2). Different situations are left unresolved, for example, those in which a divorce is sought in relation to a marriage that was potentially null and void or non-existent under the *lex fori*, such as marriage between minors or the marriage of the second wife of a polygamous couple or resulting from a fixed marriage.[40] This exclusion can also lead to the aforementioned race to the courts for the dissolution of a same-sex marriage; it is an exclusion, above all, linked to Article 13, which seems to be aimed at appeasing the sensitivities of some states in which same-sex marriage is not recognised. In this sense Article 13 would prevent any interpretive risk in favour of a possible recognition of marriages which, although valid in certain Member States, are not in many others.[41] It is suggested that in this context a provision for *forum necessitatis* would have been preferable as recognised by the Council of the EU in its Declaration requesting that the Brussels IIa Regulation be reformed to include *forum*

[38] According to the preparatory works of the Regulation and following the criticisms of Orejudo Prieto de los Mozos, P. (2012) 'La nueva regulación de la ley aplicable a la separación judicial y al divorcio: aplicación del reglamento Roma III en España' *Diario La Ley*, no. 7913, 5–6. See also Herranz Ballesteros, M. (2012) 'Régimen jurídico de las crisis matrimoniales internacionales y derecho aplicable: el reglamento (UE) nº 1259/2010, del Consejo, de 20 de diciembre de 2010, por el que se establece una cooperación reforzada en el ámbito de la ley aplicable al divorcio y a la separación judicial' 22 *Revista de Derecho de la Unión Europea* 46–7; Campuzano Díaz, B. (2011) 'El reglamento (UE) 1259/2010, del Consejo, de 20 de diciembre de 2010, por el que se establece una cooperación reforzada en el ámbito de la ley aplicable al divorcio y a la separación judicial', *Revista de derecho comunitario europeo*, 565.

[39] See Magnus, U. and P. Mankowski (2012) *Brussels IIbis Regulation*, Sellier, 69. In particular, legal separation is not known in the legal systems of Austria, the Czech Republic, Cyprus, Estonia, Finland, Germany, Greece, Hungary, Latvia, the Netherlands, Slovakia, Slovenia and Sweden.

[40] See Guzmán Zapater, 'Divorcio, matrimonio y ciertas diferencias nacionales', above fn. 35, 528.

[41] This explains the 'reassuring tone' of Recital 26.2 of the Regulation.

necessitatis for cases in which the competent courts were in countries that do not recognise same-sex marriages.[42] Furthermore, practice demonstrates that the courts of some Member States in which same-sex marriage is not recognised, as in the case of Italy, are recognising the registration of such marriages that have been celebrated in a state where they are recognised,[43] by virtue of the respect for the *status familiae* and Article 12 of the European Convention on Human Rights (ECHR).[44] Moreover, in *Orlandi and Others* v. *Italy*[45] the European Court of Human Rights (ECtHR) held that the lack of legal recognition of same-sex unions in Italy violated the rights of six couples who married abroad. In particular, it was considered a violation of Article 8 (right to respect for private and family life) of the ECHR.[46] Lastly, regarding the future of the Regulation it has been suggested that the use of gender-neutral and inclusive terminology in it ('spouse' instead of 'husband or wife') will eventually facilitate coverage of same-sex marriages.[47]

Objectionable limitations to freedom of choice in Rome III

The statement of freedom of choice as the main connecting factor in Article 5 collides with the private international law rules in some EU Member States where this principle has traditionally been rejected in family law, and instead they have preferred the other classical criteria in this field, mainly the application of the *lex fori*.[48] However,

[42] Council Document of 26 November 2010, 17046/10, JUSTCIV 214, JAI 100. In this vein see also the European Parliament Resolution of 15 November 2010.

[43] For details, see Marinai, S. (2016) 'Recognition in Italy of Same-Sex Marriages Celebrated Abroad: The Importance of a Bottom-up Approach' 9 *European Journal of Legal Studies*, 10.

[44] The judgment of the Italian Supreme Court of 31 January 2017 recently confirmed the decision of the Court of Appeal of Naples that had ordered the registration of a French marriage between two women. On the other hand, the Italian Government introduced the Private International Law Act of 31 May 1995, n. 218, Art. 32 bis (and thanks to a legislative decree of action of the Italian Same-Sex Civil Partnership Act of 20 May 2016, n. 76), according to which 'the civil union or other similar institution, constituted abroad between Italian citizens of the same sex habitually resident in Italy produces the effects of civil unions regulated by Italian law'.

[45] Judgment of the ECHR of 14 December 2017, Application no. 26431/12; 26742/12; 44057/12 and 60088/12.

[46] The case concerned a complaint by six same-sex couples that they had been unable to have their marriages, which they had contracted abroad, registered or recognised in any form as a union in Italy. They alleged, among other things, discrimination on the grounds of their sexuality. The Court noted that states had wide discretion on the question of whether or not to allow or register same-sex marriages. However, it found that there had been a violation of the couples' rights after they had married abroad because Italian law had not provided any legal protection or recognition for them before 2016 when legislation on same-sex civil unions had come into force.

[47] See Swennen, F. (2007) 'Atypical Families in EU (Private International) Family Law', in Meeusen, J., G. Straetmans, M. Pertegas and F. Swennen (eds), *International Family Law for the European Union*, Intersentia, 396.

[48] Regarding the development of the choice of law in the EU and the use of the *lex fori* in some states, such as the UK, see Boele-Woelki, 'For Better or for Worse', above fn. 8, 26–7; Carruthers, 'Party Autonomy in the Legal Regulation of Adult Relationships', above fn. 33, 888–92; Queirolo, I. and

the freedom of choice in this type of litigation presents undoubted advantages, in particular in cases of divorces by mutual consent, encouraging amicable divorces that are crucial for couples with children.[49] It should also help third-country nationals to integrate by affording them the opportunity to substitute the law of their new residence for their national law. Article 5 limits the parties' choice to some specific connecting factors such as: (1) the law of the state where the spouses are habitually resident at the time the agreement is concluded; (2) the law of the state where the spouses were last habitually resident, in so far as one of them still resides there at the moment the agreement is concluded; (3) the law of the state of nationality of either spouse at the time the agreement is concluded; or (4) the law of the forum. In practice, such advantages and objectives may be frustrated by this exhaustive list of possibilities; by all the other limitations of the Regulation and its shortcomings examined in this chapter.[50] Notwithstanding these limitations, freedom of choice can offer the parties great opportunities to regulate their divorce or separation following standards that may be more or less restrictive depending on the substantive law that they choose.

In the case of same-sex couples who marry in a state in which their marriage is recognised as valid, both in one of the participants' Member States (for example, Belgium, France or Spain) and in the other Member States (for example, Denmark, Portugal, Sweden and the Netherlands) or in a Third State in which it is permitted (for example, Argentina, Uruguay, Canada or Brazil), they may choose the law of any of those countries, provided that it coincides with the country indicated by any of the criteria of Article 5 of the Rome III Regulation and the dispute is settled according to Brussels IIa. Protecting legal diversity in relation to the validity of same-sex marriages may therefore lead to the undesirable result of the race to the court already mentioned.

Another risk derived from the freedom of choice regulated in Article 5 relates to the criterion of habitual residence in which this provision is supported (paragraphs a and b, but also paragraph d based on *lex fori* that will tend to coincide with the residence of one or both spouses). The concept of habitual residence should be qualified autonomously in accordance with the CJEU case law which favours a factual interpretation.[51] Yet, the determination of the common habitual residence of the parties

L. Carpaneto (2012) 'Considerazioni critiche sull'estensione dell'autonomia privata a separazione e divorzio nel regolamento "Roma III"', *Rivista di diritto internazionale privato e processuale*, 59–62; Franzina, 'Una cooperazione rafforzata', above fn. 8, 94–6; Viarengo, 'Il regolamento UE', above fn. 33, 611.

49 See Regulation proposal. COM (2010) 105 final.

50 For the limitations and shortcomings of rules regulating the party autonomy in Rome III, including the regulation on the choice of law agreement, see Queirolo and Carpaneto, above fn. 48, 59–62; Espinosa Calabuig, 'Elección de una ley', above fn. 32, 230–6.

51 For instance, the judgment of the CJEU 02.04.2009, case C-523/07, in relation to the habitual residence of the child in Regulation 2201/2003. See Viarengo, 'Il regolamento UE', above fn. 33, 611. See also Silberman, L. (2008) 'Rethinking Rules of Conflict of Laws in Marriage and Divorce in the United States: What Can We Learn from Europe?' *Tulane Law Review*, 2011.

may give rise to practical difficulties, because of its mutable nature, which prevents the establishment of such a place when the spouses of a different nationality have never lived in the same state or lived together in more than one state, or one of them after a period of residence in common moves to live in another state. Therefore, a broader and more flexible range of connections could have been included. The option for the common habitual residence of the parties is not very useful, since in addition to the above, it coincides with the criteria established to determine the applicable law in the absence of agreement between the parties in Article 8. Greater flexibility in the connecting factors would have favoured coordination between the conflict of law rules regarding divorce and other instruments which also allow the choice of the parties in favour of one of the spouses' residence.[52]

Child Protection: Inconsistencies between Regulation (EC) No. 2201/2003 and Regulation (EC) No. 4/2009

The EU private international law framework for custody and access rights of children as well as maintenance obligations give rise to very similar conflicts. These issues are governed by different instruments at the international and European levels. The patrimonial nature of child maintenance obligations and the breadth of their concept, as well as the notion of debtors and creditors, seem to have justified, at EU level, their provision in the already mentioned Regulation (EC) No. 4/2009[53] and their exclusion from Brussels IIa. The plurality of instruments not only contributes to increasing the confusion, even the perplexity, of practitioners, but is at odds with the usual practice in relation to this kind of dispute, whereas these issues, though separable legal categories for the purposes of characterising private international law, are usually dealt with jointly in the same proceedings. Furthermore, the analysis of both Regulations as examined in the following section shows certain inconsistencies which are to the detriment of child protection.

Rules on Parental Responsibility and Maintenance Obligations

Despite the breath of the concept of parental responsibility contained in Brussels IIa, maintenance obligations have been excluded from this concept; the latter is regulated by the Maintenance Regulation, which, however, does not define the concept.[54] The possibility of reaching agreements between the parties on maintenance obligations has generally been regulated as a means of increasing legal certainty, predictability

[52] As explained by Viarengo, 'Il regolamento UE', above fn. 33, 612–14, in relation to the maintenance obligations regulated by Art. 8 of the 2007 Hague Protocol or the matrimonial economic regime in the proposed Regulation in Art. 16 (now Art. 22 of Regulation (EU) No. 2016/1103).

[53] OJ L 7, 10.01.2009.

[54] More broadly, see Espinosa Calabuig, R. (2009) 'Maintenance Obligations Towards the Child and Their Relation to Parental Responsibility: The Regulations 4/2009 and 2201/2003', in Baruffi, M. C. and R. Caffari-Panico, *Le nuove competenze comunitarie. Obbligazioni alimentari e le sucessioni*, Cedam, 51–61.

and autonomy of the parties, as explained in the Preamble of the Regulation. Yet, it has been excluded with respect to children under the age of 18 'to protect the weaker party'.[55] It is not clear, however, whether freedom of choice may jeopardise the protection of the child and, in particular, the payment of maintenance by the debtor, contrasting with the objectives of the Brussels IIa Regulation with regard to disputes relating to parental responsibility, both when they are linked to a matrimonial dispute and when they are independent of them (according to the conditions established in Article 12). Furthermore, since the Maintenance Regulation has established a forum on child maintenance in cases related to parental responsibility litigation, it indirectly considers freedom of choice. This would happen when the judge who decides the custody rights and access of a child according to the *porrogatio fori* (Article 12) also resolves the child maintenance dispute, in accordance with Article 3 (d).

Rules on International Child Abduction

Among the rules in Brussels IIa, the child abduction provisions, that is, those provisions on the return of the child wrongfully removed or retained, stand out. A brief visit to the INCADAT[56] database is enough to show that this phenomenon, far from diminishing, continues to increase worldwide. This, coupled with the new case law generated in recent times,[57] the length of the proceeding, especially in the courts of some Member States, and the outdated legal framework in some countries justifies the interest of the EU in further reforming in this context. This explains why the proposal for a Brussels IIa Regulation recast adds new provisions on child abduction,[58] proposing rules that would promote better mechanisms for protecting the best interests of the children.[59] The proposals include suggestions for realigning the Regulation with the

[55] Recital 19 of Regulation (EC) No. 4.

[56] International Child Abduction Database, available at: www.incadat.com

[57] In particular, there has been an increase in the cases of wrongful removal of the child carried out by the holder of the custody rights, as well as for reasons of gender-based violence by the abused parent in order to distance the child from the abuser. See Kaye, M. (1999) 'The Hague Convention and the Flight from Domestic Violence: How Women and Children are Being Returned by Coach and Four' 13 *International Journal Law Policy Family*, 191.

[58] See further van Loon's chapter in this volume.

[59] See van Loon, H. (2015), 'The Brussels IIa Regulation: Towards a Review?', in *Cross-border Activities in the EU – Making Life Easier for Citizens*, available at: www.europarl.europa.eu/RegData/etudes/STUD/2015/510003/IPOL_STU(2015)510003_EN.pdf. See also the interesting proposals of Beaumont, P., L. Walker and J. Holliday (2016), 'Parental Responsibility and International Child Abduction in the Proposed Recast of Brussels IIa Regulation and the Effect of Brexit on Future Child Abduction Proceedings', *Journal of Private International Law*, 211–60. Some of these proposals and keys of the future regulation focus on: (1) Concentration of jurisdiction for child abduction cases; (2) Limiting appeals and making the whole process timely; (3) Reversal of *Povse*; (4) Hearing the child; (5) Protective measures and links to the 1996 Convention; (6) Central Authorities. Very interesting also are the reflections made by Rodriguez Pineau, E. (2017) 'Regulation Brussels II bis Recast: Reflections on the Role of European Private International Law', *Revista Española de Derecho Internacional*, vol. 69, 1, 139–66.

1996 Hague Convention[60] and harmonising the protection of children within the EU and in relation with third States Parties to the 1996 Convention; adding provisions to speed up return proceedings, including agreed solutions through mediation and promoting judicial and administrative cooperation.[61]

It should be recalled that the main objective of the 1980 Hague Convention[62] was to ensure the immediate return of the child after a wrongful removal or retention committed by one of the 'holders of parental responsibility'.[63] It was this objective that justified the introduction of rules in relation to child abduction[64] (controversial indeed) in the Brussels IIa Regulation.[65] It is no longer the judge of the state to where the child has been removed who controls the enforcement of the return decision, but the judge of the habitual (original) residence of the child by issuing a certificate which must satisfy specific conditions.[66] Despite the difficulties caused by these rules (because they may put in conflict the views of two different courts),[67] the

[60] The Convention on Jurisdiction, Applicable Law, Recognition, Enforcement and Co-operation in Respect of Parental Responsibility and Measures for the Protection of Children was concluded in The Hague on 19 October 1996 and entered into force on 1 January 2002; 49 States Parties, status as at 15 October 2018.

[61] More broadly see Baruffi, M. C. (2017) 'Uno spazio di libertà, sicurezza e gisutizia a misura di minori: la sfida (in)compiuta dell'Unione europea nei casi di sottrazione internazionale', *Freedom, Security & Justice: European Legal Studies*, 2–25; Honorati, C. (2017) 'La proposta di revisione del regolamento Bruxels II-bis: più tutela per I minori e più efficacia nell'esecuzione delle decisioni', *Rivista di diritto internazionale private e processuale*, 247–82; Beaumont et al. 'Parental Responsibility and International Child Abduction', above fn. 59 211–60; Rodriguez Pineau, 'Regulation Brussels II bis Recast', above fn. 59, 139–66.

[62] The Convention on the Civil Aspects of International Child Abduction was concluded in The Hague on 25 October 1980 and entered into force on 1 December 1983; 99 States Parties, status as at 15 October 2018.

[63] Using the terminology of Regulation 2201/2003, up until now the Hague Convention has focused on cases of wrongful removal by the holder of the access rights.

[64] (EC) No. 2201/2003, Art. 11.8 (and Art. 42 to which reference is made).

[65] The case law of the CJEU on Regulation 2201/2003, including Art. 11.8, is already abundant. For example, judgments such as those of Case C-195/08 PPU, 11 July 2008; Case C-168/08, 16 July 2009; Case C-403/09, 23 December 2009; Case C-211/10 PPU, 1 July 2010; Case C-256/09, 15 July 2010; C-400/10 PPU, 5 October 2010; Case C-296/10 PPU, 9 November 2010; Case C-491/10, 22 December 2010; C-497/10 PPU, 22 December 2010; Case C-498/14, 9 January 2015; and Case C-455/15, 10 November 2015.

[66] For a critical analysis of Art. 11.8 of the Regulation see Espinosa Calabuig, R. 'La sottrazione di minori nell'Unione Europea: tra Regolamento n. 2201/2003 e Convenzione dell'Aja del 1980', in Carbone, S. M. and I. Queirolo (2008) *Diritto di familia e Unione Europea*, Chiappichelli, 283; Espinosa Calabuig, R. (2016) 'Traslado o retención ilícitos de menores tras la reforma de 2015: rapidez, especialización y . . . algunas ausencias', 68 *Revista española de derecho internacional* 347. See also Beaumont, P., L. Walker and J. Holliday (2016) 'Conflicts of EU Courts on Child Abduction: The Reality of Article 11 (6)–(8) Brussels IIa proceedings across the EU' *Journal of Private International Law*, vol. 12, no. 2, 211–60.

[67] To the extent that, once the certificate has been issued, it is no longer possible to oppose the recognition in the requested state of the decision to return the child, nor to appeal the issuing of the certificate,

prioritisation of the judgment of the state of the habitual resident of the child prior to his or her wrongful removal or retention has received the support of the CJEU without any room for exceptions. This has led to a clear interpretive conflict regarding the protection of fundamental rights and the concept of the child's best interest in these cases, as was shown by the ECtHR in *Sofia Povse*[68] and by the CJEU in *Aguirre Zárraga.*[69] The insistence on defending the application of Article 11.8 does not seem to be consistent with the defence of what may constitute the best interests of the child in each particular case, even if an act has been committed which, in principle, can be classified as wrongful under the terms of the rules intended to protect the child from being abducted in both instruments. The reform of Article 11.8 of the Regulation must consider the difficult balance between the assessment of the child's best interests in each case and the risk of manipulations such as those that have until now been carried out within the scope of the 1980 Hague Convention. The proposal for reform includes new time limits for the return proceedings established by the 1980 Hague Convention. The departing of the proposal from the maximum six-week period mentioned in the Convention should be revised to the extent that, although not realistic, in practice this period puts pressure on courts to satisfy the return proceeding as soon as possible; the new time limits risk putting an end to that pressure.[70]

In any case the accomplishment of a short deadline for the return of the child will only be possible with an inter-state cooperation framework. This will require direct communication, without intermediaries, among authorities and courts of different countries.[71] In particular, it will require the assistance of the Central Authorities involved, the existing networks of judicial cooperation, the members of the International Hague Network of Judges and the liaison judges. This could

and the law of the state of origin will regulate any possible rectification (Art. 43, 1 and 2, in relation to Arts 41.1 and 42.1).

68 Case C-211/10 PPU *Povse* v. *Alpago* (2010) ECR I-00673 (*Povse*). For detail see Lazic, V. (2015) 'Family Private International Law Issues Before the European Court of Human Rights: Lessons to be Learned from Povse v. Austria in Revising the Brussels IIa Regulation', in Paulussen, C., T. Takacs, V. Lazić and B. Van Rompuy (eds), *Fundamental Rights in International and European Law*, Springer, 161–83. Previously the Court of Justice of the European Union (CJEU) had ruled in accordance with the judgment of 1 July 2010, in C-211/10 PPU.

69 Case C-491/10 PPU (Indent 75), 22 December 2010. In the opinion of the CJEU, 'the Court with jurisdiction in the Member State of enforcement cannot oppose the enforcement of a certified judgment ordering the return of a child who has been wrongfully removed on the ground that the Court of the Member State of origin which handed down that judgment may have infringed art. 42 of the Regulation, interpreted in accordance to art. 24 of the Charter of fundamental Rights of the EU, since the assessment of whether there is such an infringement falls exclusively within the jurisdiction of the courts of the Member State of origin'.

70 See Espinosa Calabuig, R. and L. Carballo Piñeiro, 'Report on the Spanish Good Practices', *Planning the Future of Cross-border Families: A Path Through Coordination 'EUFam's'*, Spanish Exchange Seminar, 24 October 2016, available at: www.eufams.unimi.it, 13.

71 On the importance of direct communications and the role of judges see Goicoechea and van Loon's chapter in this volume.

be enhanced, presumably, by the concentration and specialisation of jurisdiction as provided for in the proposal for reform. This cooperation is the only way to reduce the risk of manipulation in time limits in cases where, for example, a removal that began as lawful has become wrongful, so that when the request for the return of the child is received the child is already settled in his or her new environment (in line with Article 12 of the 1980 Hague Convention). However, the requirement for speedy proceedings will continue to present difficulties in important matters such as, for example, the hearing of the child. This is due in part to the legal diversity inherent in Europe (for example, in certain countries, such as Germany, it is regarded as a principle of constitutional rank, and in others it has been practically non-existent for years).[72] *Aguirre Zárraga* is a good example of this conflict, as well as the ECtHR's response in *Sofia Povse.*[73]

Final Remarks

The multiplicity of instruments adopted in the EU to regulate cross-border family issues and the difficulties of achieving unanimity in their approval show that, for the time being, the objective of unification in this field has been frustrated and that 'two-speed Europe' is a reality.

The limitations in the geographical and substantial scope of application of many of the instruments regarding family law can motivate the heavily criticised 'race to courts'. This depends on the interests and expectations of the parties and it is a result of the legal diversity inherent to Europe. Even though throughout this volume there is recognition of the importance of private international law methodologies and techniques to embrace legal diversity, this chapter has shown some of the problems associated with its management, illustrated particularly through the EU private international law provisions on divorce and the diversity in relation to substantive laws of the Member States in matters such as same-sex marriage.

Furthermore, the chapter has shown the difficulties posed by the multiplicity of sources – a perennial struggle in private international law governance. It has shown, for instance, in relation to the Rome III Regulation, how its provisions have frustrated its original objectives of creating uniform conflict of law rules in consistency with the rules of jurisdiction of the Brussels IIa Regulation. Attainment of this prime objective would have rendered possible the long-awaited alignment of *forum-ius* that is so advisable in family matters where substantives and procedural rules work closely together.

The coexistence of all these instruments exacerbates the complexity of the legal

[72] See Völker, M. (2005) 'Le règlement "Bruxelles II bis" du point de vue d'un juge aux affaires familiales allemand', in Fulchiron, H. and C. Nourissat, *Le nouveau droit communitaire du divorce et de la responsabilité parentale*, Dalloz, 293–302.

[73] See Kinsch, P. (2014) 'Harroudj v. France: Indications from the European Court of Human Rights on the Nature of Choice of Law Rules and on their Potentially Discriminatory Effect', *Journal of Private International Law*, 39–44.

framework, and this fragmentation contrasts with the practice of family law, where all these causes of action and private international law categories tend to come together and become intertwined in the same proceedings.

In addition, there are rules which are unknown to the legal tradition of many Member States. For instance, the concept of parental responsibility, the criteria of *forum non conveniens* or the role of the freedom of choice in family matters. This explains the slow learning process in some states in the understanding and application of these instruments and the great number of decisions of the Court of Justice of the European Union in these fields. An analysis of the case law in the Member States[74] reveals the progressive implementation, with uneven success, of EU Regulations by national judges.

Bearing in mind the proposal to recast the Brussels IIa Regulation launched in June 2016, it would be essential for the best operation of all these instruments to include rules of coordination between private international law rules on matrimonial and parental responsibility issues as well as other family matters regulated by other instruments. The 'dialogue of the sources',[75] an expression coined by Erik Jayme, becomes as useful as ever in this context.

The silence of the proposal with regard to some important points (such as a rule comparable to Article 13 of the Rome III Regulation or Article 9 of the Regulation on matrimonial property regimes and a *forum necessitatis* provision for cases in which the competent authorities are in countries that do not admit same-sex marriages) should be reconsidered in the interests of consistency between all the European and international instruments.

Finally, the principle of mutual recognition and the objective of constructing the European Judicial Area also raise doubts in relation to issues such as same-sex marriages and the respect of the *status familiae*, and child abduction and the 'best interest' of the child. Judicial cooperation has to be significantly improved in the European area of justice as key to a successful and consistent application of these Regulations, in particular when it comes to their provisions on jurisdiction. The role of the European Judicial Network, as well as the continuing training of legal practitioners, needs to be reinforced to face all these challenges that derive from the richness of legal diversity in Europe.

[74] See EU Fam's project, available at: www.eufams.unimi.it

[75] For the relationship between instruments in the context of the HCCH Judgments Project see Noodt Taquela, M. B. and V. Ruiz Abou-Nigm (2018) 'The Draft Judgments Convention and its Relationship with Other International Instruments', *Yearbook of Private International Law*, vol. 19, 449–74.

5

Non-uniform Application of European Union Private International Law

Katarina Trimmings and Burcu Yüksel

Introduction

Private international law has been largely harmonised in a wide range of areas in the European Union in order to increase legal certainty and predictability in cross-border legal situations. Since 2002, the private international law framework in the EU has been deliberately built through a number of European regulations which, in principle, are binding on and directly applicable in all Member States under Article 288 of the Treaty on the Functioning of the EU.[1] One of the objectives behind this is to ensure that the same rules are applied in the same manner in all twenty-eight Member States. However, a recent comparative empirical study conducted by the Centre for Private International Law at the University of Aberdeen under an EU-funded project entitled 'Cross-Border Litigation in Europe: Private International Law Legislative Framework, National Courts and the Court of Justice of the European Union' (EUPILLAR – EU PIL: Legal Application in Reality)[2] on the Brussels I,[3] Brussels

[1] [2012] OJ C 326/47.

[2] JUST/2013/JCIV/AG/4635. The EUPILLAR Project, which was coordinated by Professor Paul Beaumont from the University of Aberdeen, involved Dr Katarina Trimmings and Dr Burcu Yüksel from the University of Aberdeen, Dr Mihail Danov from the University of Leeds (UK), Professor Stefania Bariatti from the University of Milan (Italy), Professor Jan von Hein from the University of Freiburg (Germany), Professor Carmen García-Castrillón Otero from Complutense University of Madrid (Spain), Professor Thalia Kruger from the University of Antwerp (Belgium) and Dr Agnieszka Frąckowiak-Adamska from the University of Wroclaw (Poland). Further information about the EUPILLAR Project is available at: www.abdn.ac.uk/law/research/eupillar.php

[3] Council Regulation (EC) No. 44/2001 of 22 December 2000 on jurisdiction and the recognition and enforcement of judgments in civil and commercial matters, [2001] OJ L 12/1. The Brussels Ia Regulation (Regulation (EU) No. 1215/2012 of the European Parliament and of the Council of 12 December 2012 on jurisdiction and the recognition and enforcement of judgments in civil and

IIa,[4] Rome I,[5] Rome II[6] and the Maintenance Regulations,[7] indicates that in reality these uniform private international law rules are not always interpreted and applied uniformly in all EU Member States.[8]

The purpose of this chapter is to provide a range of illustrations of these different interpretations and applications of the same EU private international law rules in the EU through examples from various EU Member States; to analyse the reasons why the interpretation and application of the same rules are sometimes divergent in the EU; and to suggest specific ways to improve the degree of uniformity in application. Where necessary, this analysis is supported by the EUPILLAR Project data gathered from over 2,300 judgments,[9] qualitative interviews involving 181 participants[10] and national reports from twenty-six EU Member States[11] on the application of the Brussels I, Brussels IIa, Rome I, Rome II and Maintenance Regulations.

Divergent Application of the EU Private International Law Rules: Selected Examples

The evidence indicates that the EU private international law rules are not always interpreted and applied uniformly throughout the EU.

In relation to jurisdiction and the recognition and enforcement of judgments in civil and commercial matters, there are divergent practices on the application of the special jurisdiction rules under Article 5 of Brussels I, which corresponds to Article 7 of the Brussels I *bis* Regulation. These rules provide, *inter alia*, that a person domiciled in a Member State may be sued in another Member State in

commercial matters (recast)) replaced Brussels I which, however, continues to apply to proceedings instituted before Brussels Ia came into application on 10 January 2015.

4 Council Regulation (EC) No. 2201/2003 of 27 November 2003 concerning jurisdiction and the recognition and enforcement of judgments in matrimonial matters and the matters of parental responsibility, repealing regulation (EC) No. 1347/2000, [2003] OJ L 338/1.

5 Regulation (EC) No. 593/2008 of the European Parliament and of the Council of 17 June 2008 on the Law Applicable to Contractual Obligations (Rome I), [2008] OJ L 177/6.

6 Regulation (EC) No. 864/2007 of the European Parliament and of the Council of 11 July 2007 on the Law Applicable to Non-contractual Obligations (Rome II), [2007] OJ L 199/40.

7 Council Regulation (EC) No. 4/2009 of 18 December 2008 on jurisdiction, applicable law, recognition and enforcement of decisions and cooperation in matters relating to maintenance obligations, [2009] OJ L 7/1.

8 For the research findings of the EUPILLAR Project, see Beaumont, P., M. Danov, K. Trimmings and B. Yüksel (eds) (2017) *Cross-Border Litigation in Europe*, Hart Publishing.

9 These judgments were rendered between 1 March 2002 and 31 December 2015 concerning the Brussels I, Rome I, Rome II, Brussels IIa and Maintenance Regulations in the Court of Justice of the European Union (CJEU) and in Germany, Belgium, Poland, the UK, Italy and Spain. English summaries of all judgments are available on the EUPILLAR Database at: www.w3.abdn.ac.uk/clsm/eupillar/#/home

10 The interviews were conducted with legal practitioners, judges and representatives of the EU institutions across Europe.

11 The national reports were provided from all EU Member States except Denmark and Estonia.

(1) matters relating to a contract, in the courts for the place of performance of the obligation in question; and (2) in matters relating to tort, delict or quasi-delict, in the courts for the place where the harmful event occurred or may occur. The concepts of 'matters relating to contract' or 'matters related to tort' within the meaning of Article 5 of the Brussels I Regulation are sometimes interpreted differently in different Member States. Belgium is one example where the courts often rely on national law in interpreting these terms, which results in either the non-application of the provisions of the Regulation or the incorrect application of the provisions.[12] In Luxembourg, the courts have had difficulties in applying Article 5 of the Brussels I Regulation and a tendency is noted for the first instance courts to apply Article 5(1)(a) providing for the courts of the place of performance of the obligation in question instead of Article 5(1)(b) that specifies the previous rule in relation to contracts for the sale of goods and contracts for the provision of services, respectively, at the place in a Member State where, under the contract, the goods were delivered or should have been delivered, and at the place in a Member State where, under the contract, the services were provided or should have been provided. This results in wrongfully declining jurisdiction particularly in the case of the contract for the provision of services.[13] The Court of Justice of the European Union (CJEU) has dealt with a number of preliminary ruling requests concerning Article 5 of Brussels I which also demonstrates the difficulties that national courts have experienced in this respect.[14]

In relation to the law applicable to contractual obligations, although only a limited number of reported cases are available on the Rome I Regulation, there are notable divergent practices among different Member States, particularly on the scope of application of the Regulation. For instance, in Greece, the courts in a limited number of cases applied the provisions of Rome I to non-contractual obligations or to contractual obligations involving no international element.[15] There are also cases where the Greek courts applied Rome I to contracts concluded before 17 December 2009 and where they applied the Rome Convention[16] and the Rome I Regulation together.[17] In Bulgaria, in some cases, the applicable law was not analysed under Rome I at all which resulted in the application of Bulgarian substantive law.[18] In the Czech

[12] See Kruger, T. and E. Ulrix (2017) 'National Report: Belgium', in Beaumont et al., *Cross-Border Litigation*, above fn. 8.

[13] See Camara, C. (2017) 'National Report: Luxembourg', in Beaumont et al., *Cross-Border Litigation*, above fn. 8.

[14] See Beaumont, P. and B. Yüksel (2017) 'Cross-Border Civil and Commercial Disputes Before the Court of Justice of the European Union', in Beaumont et al., *Cross-Border Litigation*, above fn. 8.

[15] See Archontaki, A. and P. Simsive (2017) 'National Report: Greece', in Beaumont et al., *Cross-Border Litigation*, above fn. 8.

[16] 1980 Rome Convention on the Law Applicable to Contractual Obligations, [1980] OJ L 266/1.

[17] See Archontaki and Simsive, 'National Report: Greece', above fn. 15.

[18] See Tsenova, T. and A. Petrov (2017) 'National Report: Bulgaria', in Beaumont et al., *Cross-Border Litigation*, above fn. 8.

Republic, there are cases where the courts applied the Czech Private International Law Act although they should have applied Rome I.[19]

In relation to the law applicable to non-contractual obligations, although there is only a limited number of reported cases available on the Rome II Regulation, divergent practices on the Regulation among different Member States are apparent. For instance, in Greece, in a number of cases the courts applied the Regulation to events that had occurred before its date of application.[20] Similar examples are found also in Italian case law.[21] In Italy, the material scope of application also raises issues, particularly as regards the matters which are treated as non-contractual under the Regulation but not under Italian law.[22] The national courts seem to struggle with deciding on the delimitation between Rome I and Rome II also in Spain,[23] Lithuania[24] and the Netherlands,[25] which inherits the risk of divergent application of the Regulations. In Bulgaria, the main problem in the context of Rome II is considered to be the misunderstanding of the distinction between direct and indirect damages by the Bulgarian judges, which has led to the application of the incorrect law to some cases.[26] In Portugal, the interpretation of the concept of direct damage by the courts in some cases is also considered to be problematic.[27]

In relation to jurisdiction and the recognition and enforcement of judgments in matrimonial matters and matters of parental responsibility, divergent practices are seen in relation to the scope of application of the Brussels IIa Regulation. For instance, in Belgium, the courts do not always apply Brussels IIa and there are cases where they revert immediately to the Belgian Code on Private International Law.[28] Similar examples are found also in the Croatian case law where the courts have invoked the Croatian Private International Law Act, instead of applying Brussels IIa.[29] In Italy, despite the fact that the Brussels IIa Regulation should apply only to the dissolution of matrimonial ties and it should not deal with issues such as the grounds

[19] See Pauknerová, M., M. Zavadilová and J. Grygar (2017) 'National Report: the Czech Republic', in Beaumont et al., *Cross-Border Litigation*, above fn. 8.

[20] Archontaki and Simsive, 'National Report: Greece', above fn. 15.

[21] See Bariatti, S., I. Viarengo, F. C. Villata, S. Bernasconi and F. Marchetti (2017) 'National Report: Italy', in Beaumont et al., *Cross-Border Litigation*, above fn. 8.

[22] Ibid.

[23] See García-Castrillón Otero, C. (2017) 'National Report: Spain', in Beaumont et al., *Cross-Border Litigation*, above fn. 8.

[24] See Praneviciene, K. (2017) 'National Report: Lithuania', in Beaumont et al., *Cross-Border Litigation*, above fn. 8.

[25] See van Hoek, A., I. Curry-Sumner and C. van der Plas (2017) 'National Report: the Netherlands', in Beaumont et al., *Cross-Border Litigation*, above fn. 8.

[26] See Tsenova and Petrov, 'National Report: Bulgaria', above fn. 18.

[27] See Dias Oliveira, E., J. Almeida, S. Maltez and R. Correia, 'National Report: Portugal', in Beaumont et al., *Cross-Border Litigation*, above fn. 8.

[28] See Kruger and Ulrix, 'National Report: Belgium', above fn. 12.

[29] See Kunda, I., 'National Report: Croatia', in Beaumont et al., *Cross-Border Litigation*, above fn. 8.

for divorce, property consequences of the marriage or any other ancillary measures,[30] there are cases where the courts applied the Regulation also when required to adjudicate on a legal separation on fault grounds.[31] In Luxembourg, due to following an approach which is not in line with the CJEU's interpretation, there are cases where the courts misapplied the residual grounds of jurisdiction under Article 7 where the defendant is neither an EU national nor resident in the EU.[32]

In relation to jurisdiction, applicable law, recognition and enforcement of decisions and cooperation in matters relating to maintenance obligations, divergent practices are seen in the scope of application of the Maintenance Regulation. In Greece, the incorrect application or non-application of the Regulation is apparent particularly in determining the law applicable to maintenance obligations.[33] In Italy, it is indicated that the courts experience some difficulties with interpreting and applying the Regulation, since the concept of a maintenance obligation is narrower under Italian substantive law compared to the autonomous notion used in the Regulation.[34]

Reasons for the Non-uniform Interpretation and Application of EU Private International Law Rules

It might be thought at first glance that the divergent interpretation and application of the EU private international law rules might result from simply favouring one's own jurisdiction to hear and decide the case, and one's own law to be applied to the case. To a certain extent, there is evidence which affirms this for some jurisdictions in the EU. For instance, in Greece the courts generally interpret the Regulations in a way which allows them to establish jurisdiction and apply Greek law.[35] The homeward trend is also visible in Belgium with respect to both jurisdiction and applicable law.[36] However, favouring one's own jurisdiction and law is not the only reason for the divergent interpretation and application of the EU private international law rules. Empirical evidence indicates that there are indeed several other reasons why the same private international law rules are not always interpreted and applied in the same manner in all EU Member States. In the following paragraphs the authors analyse some of these reasons to bring to the fore the roots of these divergences.

Legal Thinking

One of the main reasons for the divergent interpretation and application of the EU private international law rules in the EU is the existence of different legal thinking in different EU Member States. There are twenty-eight Member States in the EU,

30 See Recital 7 to the Brussels IIa Regulation.
31 See Bariatti et al., 'National Report: Italy', above fn. 21.
32 See Camara, 'National Report: Luxembourg', above fn. 13.
33 See Archontaki and Simsive, 'National Report: Greece', above fn. 15.
34 See Bariatti et al., 'National Report: Italy', above fn. 21.
35 See Archontaki and Simsive, 'National Report: Greece', above fn. 15.
36 See Kruger and Ulrix, 'National Report: Belgium', above fn. 12.

each with its own legal tradition and heritage. Civil law, common law and mixed legal systems come together under this union. The civil law tradition is rooted in Roman law and developed in continental Europe during the Middle Ages. One of the distinctive characteristics of all systems based on the civil law tradition is that they are codified – that is, they have comprehensive, continuously updated legal codes and supplementary legislation, which together represent the key source of law within the given jurisdiction. In a civil law system, the judge's role is to establish the facts of the case and to apply the relevant legislative provisions.[37] The common law tradition developed in England during the Middle Ages and was later distributed throughout the British Empire. Common law systems are characterised by the lack of codification, meaning that there is no comprehensive compilation of legal rules and statutes. While common law does rely on some scattered legislative statutes, it is largely based on precedent, that is, a legal rule established through a judicial decision in a previous case involving similar issues or facts. Of the current twenty-eight EU Member States, only the legal systems of England and Ireland are regarded as pure common law systems.[38] The fact that most of the EU Member States have a civil law tradition, however, does not guarantee uniformity in legal thinking. This is because the civil law tradition itself is not a homogeneous group of legal systems, as a number of 'sub-groups' can be identified within this legal tradition.[39] Accordingly, legal systems based on the civil law tradition often show different characteristics as they may be originally based on the French model or the German model.[40] There are also Scandinavian Member States which have a civil law tradition but, compared to German and French laws, often have a more practical and pragmatically orientated and less conceptualistic approach.[41] In addition, there are the Member States historically coming from a socialist legal culture.[42] In this diversity, legal actors are natu-

[37] For a comprehensive overview of the civil law tradition see Glendon, M. A., P. Carozza and C. Picker (2016) *Comparative Legal Traditions in a Nutshell*, West Academic Publishing, 19–174; and Glenn, H. P. (2014) *Legal Traditions of the World*, Oxford University Press, 132–79.

[38] The legal systems of Scotland, Cyprus and Malta contain elements of both civil and common law, and are therefore regarded as 'mixed legal systems'.

[39] See, for example, Zweigert, K. and H. Kötz (1998) *Introduction to Comparative Law*, Oxford University Press. The authors identify and treat as separate legal families the 'Romanistic legal family' (74–132), the 'Germanic legal family' (132–80) and the 'Nordic legal family' (276–86).

[40] Zweigert and Kötz term these two models as the 'Romanistic legal family' and the 'Germanic legal family' respectively. See above fn. 39.

[41] Bogdan, M. and U. Maunsbach, 'National Report: Sweden', in Beaumont et al., *Cross-Border Litigation*, above fn. 8. See also above fn. 39, where it is explained that Zweigert and Kötz have termed this sub-group of the civil law tradition the 'Nordic legal family'.

[42] For the analysis that identifies four groups of private law regimes within the EU (that is, common law countries, traditional civil law countries, Scandinavian Member States and countries that entered the EU in 2004) and that notes the existence of considerable differences in substance within these groups, see Smits, J. M. (2007) 'Convergence of Private Law in Europe: Towards a New Ius Commune?', in Örücü, E. and D. Nelken (eds), *Comparative Law: A Handbook*, Hart Publishing, 219–40. See also Siems, M. (2014) *Comparative Law*, Cambridge University Press, 74–80.

rally and subconsciously inclined to follow a particular way of legal thinking within their own legal system. This is particularly apparent in relation to characterisation. Characterisation is defined as 'the allocation of the question raised by the factual situation before the court to its correct legal category'.[43] The interpretation of legal concepts may, however, differ from one jurisdiction to another in the EU, based on their national meanings and understandings in each jurisdiction. In Belgium, characterisation is considered to be a challenge and, as indicated by evidence, the courts too often rely on national legal categories rather than the autonomous concepts.[44] In Italy, there are cases where difficulties appeared in the process of abandoning domestic legal categories in favour of autonomous EU concepts.[45] In Poland, a tendency is noted as regards both parties' representatives and the lower courts interpreting the EU private international law regulations from the perspective of national law, a deficit that is normally corrected at the higher courts stage.[46] In the Czech Republic, it is assessed that the courts can sometimes project their specific perception into the interpretation of uniform EU private international law rules.[47] Even in jurisdictions where the courts have a good knowledge of EU private international law Regulations, such as Scotland, the judges and practitioners seem to struggle with interpreting the legal concepts autonomously, free from the national meanings and understanding in their jurisdiction.[48] An analysis of the CJEU case law also demonstrates that characterisation, particularly in civil and commercial law matters, is a significant issue on which the national courts need guidance.[49]

Insufficient Knowledge of and Training in EU Private International Law on the Part of Judges and Practitioners

Another reason for the non-uniform application of European private international law is insufficient knowledge of and training in the specific EU private international law instruments on the part of the relevant actors, in particular judges and legal practitioners. In practical terms, the lack of expertise is demonstrated in the erroneous application of the Regulations, combined with the lack of familiarity on the part of the judges with the relevant case law of the CJEU. For example, in both Latvia and Greece, the application of the Maintenance Regulation in particular is poor, the

[43] Torremans, P., U. Grušić, C. Heinze, L. Merrett, A. Mills, C. O. García-Castrillón, Z. S. Tang, K. Trimmings and L. Walker (eds) (2017) *Cheshire, North & Fawcett: Private International Law*, Oxford University Press, 42.

[44] See Kruger and Ulrix, 'National Report: Belgium', above fn. 12.

[45] See Bariatti et al., 'National Report: Italy', above fn. 21.

[46] Frąckowiak-Adamska, A., A. Guzewicz and Ł. Petelski, 'National Report: Poland', in Beaumont et al., *Cross-Border Litigation*, above fn. 8.

[47] See Pauknerová et al., 'National Report: the Czech Republic', in Beaumont et al., *Cross-Border Litigation*, above fn. 8.

[48] See Beaumont, P., M. Danov, K. Trimmings and B. Yüksel, 'National Report: Great Britain', in Beaumont et al., *Cross-Border Litigation*, above fn. 8.

[49] See Beaumont and Yüksel, 'Cross-Border Civil and Commercial Disputes', above fn. 14.

judgments lack analysis and reasoning and the Regulation tends to be misapplied.[50] In Ireland, the interaction between return proceedings in child abduction cases, substantive custody proceedings and enforcement of existing custody orders is not 'well understood', which leads to 'multiplication of legal proceedings and delays for the parents involved'.[51] Even more alarmingly, in Greece, in some child abduction cases courts have ignored the fact that return proceedings are not substantive proceedings[52] and have decided in such proceedings on the rights of custody and access too.[53] In extreme cases, the Regulations are not applied at all as no examination of jurisdiction and/or applicable law is carried out by the judge even if the facts of the case indicate the presence of an international element.[54] In some child abduction cases, judges have erroneously relied solely on the 1980 Hague Abduction Convention, without making any reference to Brussels IIa.[55] The national reports prepared as a part of the EUPILLAR project have revealed that the problem of the lack of knowledge is exacerbated by two factors in particular, as detailed in the sections below.

No concentration of jurisdiction for cross-border cases

First, generally, there is no or only limited concentration of jurisdiction for cross-border cases across EU Member States. Consequently, judges lack the opportunity to develop the required expertise in applying European private international law. This appears to be an issue especially in relation to first instance judges[56] and the problem is even more obvious in smaller jurisdictions where judges encounter cross-border cases only infrequently.[57]

Complexity of the legal framework

Second, in family law specifically, the problem is exacerbated by the complexity of the instruments and the fact that their application has to be 'fitted around' various domestic rules.[58] For example, under Czech law, parental responsibility and divorce cannot be combined in one action as parental responsibility (and maintenance) must

50 See Kucina, I., 'National Report: Latvia', in Beaumont et al., *Cross-Border Litigation*, above fn. 8, and Archontaki and Simsive, 'National Report: Greece', above fn. 15.

51 See Harding, M., 'National Report: Ireland', in Beaumont et al., *Cross-Border Litigation*, above fn. 8.

52 See Hague Convention of 25 October 1980 on the Civil Aspects of International Child Abduction, Article 16. See also Pérez-Vera, E., *Explanatory Report*, para. 121, available at https://assets.hcch.net/upload/expl28.pdf

53 See Archontaki and Simsive, 'National Report: Greece', above fn. 15.

54 See Tsenova and Petrov, 'National Report: Bulgaria', above fn. 18.

55 See Archontaki and Simsive, 'National Report: Greece', above fn. 15, and Beaumont et al., 'National Report: Great Britain', above fn. 48. The most worrying effect of such practice is that the child's right to be heard guaranteed by Article 11(2) of Brussels IIa is ignored.

56 See Frąckowiak-Adamska et al., 'National Report: Poland', above fn. 46.

57 See Kraljić, S. 'National Report: Slovenia', in Beaumont et al., *Cross-Border Litigation*, above fn. 8.

58 See Trimmings, K. 'Matrimonial Matters under the Brussels IIa Regulation', in Beaumont et al., *Cross-Border Litigation*, above fn. 8. See further the chapter by Espinosa Calabuig in this volume.

be judicially resolved before a divorce can be granted.[59] In contrast, domestic law in other EU jurisdictions requires that divorce, parental responsibility and maintenance proceedings (or a combination of any two of these) are joined in one action. For instance, in Lithuania and Poland, divorce cannot be resolved separately from parental responsibility and maintenance.[60] These issues have to be joined in one action, although they are covered by different sets of jurisdictional rules contained in Brussels IIa for divorce and parental responsibility and the Maintenance Regulation for maintenance. A negative effect of this fragmentation of jurisdiction is that, often due to a lack of expertise, judges in some Member States tend to misapply the jurisdictional rules, for example by incorrectly extending the material scope of Brussels IIa to maintenance obligations and automatically applying the Brussels IIa regime of jurisdiction for parental responsibility to the issue of maintenance also.[61] Alternatively, where all three causes are joined in one action, judges may correctly base the jurisdiction in divorce on the Brussels IIa Regulation, but automatically linking this issue with parental responsibility and maintenance, without examining whether they can indeed establish jurisdiction in these matters in accordance with Article 12(1) of the Brussels IIa Regulation[62] and the Maintenance Regulation.[63] Problems may also arise in situations where under domestic law divorce and parental responsibility proceedings have to be conducted jointly. This leads to spouses with common nationality being prevented from obtaining divorce in their 'home' jurisdiction where Article 8 Brussels IIa points to a different forum for parental responsibility proceedings, and prorogation under Article 12(1) of Brussels IIa is not forthcoming.[64]

[59] See Pauknerová et al., 'National Report: the Czech Republic', above fn. 19.

[60] See Praneviciene, 'National Report: Lithuania', above fn. 24, and Frąckowiak-Adamska et al., 'National Report: Poland', above fn. 46.

[61] See Archontaki and Simsive, 'National Report: Greece', above fn. 15. In this context, see the CJEU decision in Case C-184/14 *A* v. *B*, EU:C:2015:479, which dealt with the interpretation of Art. 3(c) and (d) of the Maintenance Regulation. For a detailed critical analysis of this judgment see Beaumont, P. and K. Trimmings, 'Court of Justice of the European Union's Case Law on Family Law Matters under Brussels IIa and Maintenance', in Beaumont et al., *Cross-Border Litigation*, above fn. 8.

[62] See Vozáryová, M. and K. Burdová, 'National Report: Slovakia', in Beaumont et al., *Cross-Border Litigation*, above fn. 8., and Frąckowiak-Adamska et al., 'National Report: Poland', above fn. 46. In Luxembourg, 'the litigants tend to rely on Article 12 while not fulfilling the strict conditions therein, especially the condition of an express agreement between the parties'. See Camara, 'National Report: Luxembourg', above fn. 13. In Lithuania, the courts 'do not appreciate the prorogation option in Article 12 and they do not take advantage of it'. See Praneviciene, 'National Report: Lithuania', above fn. 24. In contrast, Bulgarian courts 'often rely on Art. 12'. See Tsenova and Petrov, 'National Report: Bulgaria', above fn. 18.

[63] See Vozáryová and K Burdová, 'National Report: Slovakia', above fn. 62.

[64] See Frąckowiak-Adamska et al., 'National Report: Poland', above fn. 46, and Praneviciene, 'National Report: Lithuania', above fn. 24. Cf. Ní ShúilleabFháin, M. (2010) *Cross-Border Divorce Law*, Oxford University Press, 166, suggesting that 'Brussels II bis achieves a reasonable level of harmony between parental responsibility and divorce jurisdiction'.

Lack of Networking and Communication among Judiciary within the EU

Another problem that leads to the non-uniform application of the European private international law framework is an insufficient level of interaction among the EU judiciary, either in the form of networking activities that would facilitate exchange of experience and best practices in the application of private international law instruments, or in the form of direct contact between judges in relation to specific cases.[65] Direct judicial communication may be advantageous in particular in certain family law cases, for example in child abduction cases when assessing the availability of protective measures in the requesting state pursuant to Article 11(4) of Brussels IIa.

Yet another possible, although still infrequent, form of engagement by national judges with the work of their counterparts in other EU Member States is through accessing and studying case law from other EU jurisdictions. The lack of comparative law analysis in this sense is partly due to the lack of public availability of case law in most civil law jurisdictions and partly due to limited linguistic skills on the part of the judges. The problem of inaccessibility of case law was highlighted in a number of the national reports. For example, in Romania, some court decisions are freely available online; however, the majority of relevant jurisprudence 'escapes public knowledge' either because the courts do not make judgments publicly available or because access is 'restricted by paid subscription'.[66] In Sweden, first instance decisions remain 'generally unpublished and unknown' and only a small fraction of the courts of appeal judgments are published.[67] In Luxembourg, there is 'neither a systematic publication of decisions nor a publicly accessible repository of case law'.[68] Similarly, in Poland, 'there is no common framework for case-law repositories', and the decision as to whether a particular judgment will be made publicly available rests with the president of the given court.[69]

Suggestions and Concluding Remarks

A number of ways can be suggested to facilitate the uniform application of the EU private international law rules moving forward.

[65] On the work of the Hague Conference on this issue in relation to the HCCH instruments see the chapter by Goicoechea and van Loon in this volume.

[66] Smeureanu, I. M., L. Ilie and A. E. Dobre, 'National Report: Romania', in Beaumont et al., *Cross-Border Litigation*, above fn. 8.

[67] See Bogdan and Maunsbach, 'National Report: Sweden', above fn. 41. These judgments are published in annual volumes of *Rättsfall från hovrätterna* (RH). Decisions of the Swedish Supreme Court are published in annual volumes of *Nytt Juridiskt Arkiv* (NJA). Ibid.

[68] See Camara, 'National Report: Luxembourg', above fn. 13.

[69] See Frąckowiak-Adamska et al., 'National Report: Poland', above fn. 46.

Role of the CJEU

The CJEU, as part of its mission, gives preliminary rulings, at the request of courts or tribunals of the Member States, on the interpretation of EU law.[70] The issue of preliminary rulings by the CJEU is one of the available tools to reduce divergences and to facilitate the uniform application of the EU private international law rules, as they bind not only the referring national court in deciding the dispute before it but also other national courts before which the same problem is raised. A careful case law analysis indicates that although there are some controversial interpretations of the CJEU, overall the role of the CJEU in relation to its preliminary rulings is helpful.[71] Indeed, the uniformity in the interpretation and application of EU private international law that has been achieved through the preliminary rulings procedure has led to an increased level of legal certainty and predictability of thc outcome of litigation, whilst furthering the aim of the protection of the parties' legitimate expectations.[72] By way of example, the interpretation of the concept of habitual residence of a child in cross-border parental responsibility proceedings by the CJEU for the purposes of the Brussels IIa Regulation has given an autonomous meaning to a factual concept which had naturally been prone to divergent interpretations under domestic laws of the EU Member States.[73]

It goes without saying that in order to enhance the uniformity in applying EU private international law, judges dealing with cross-border cases have to be familiar with the jurisprudence of the CJEU.[74] In addition, they should use the preliminary ruling mechanism appropriately.[75]

Case Law Databases

Another tool to reduce the divergences in the application of EU private international law would be further access to case law databases facilitating access to cases decided

[70] For an empirical analysis on the effectiveness of the CJEU in interpreting EU private international law regulations, see Yüksel, B. 'An Analysis of the Effectiveness of the EU Institutions in Making and Interpreting EU Private International Law Regulations', in Beaumont et al., *Cross-Border Litigation*, above fn. 8.

[71] See Beaumont, P. and B. Yüksel, 'Cross-Border Civil and Commercial Disputes before the Court of Justice of the European Union', in Beaumont et al., *Cross-Border Litigation*, above fn. 8; Beaumont and Trimmings, 'Court of Justice of the European Union's Case Law', above fn. 61.

[72] See García-Castrillón Otero, C., 'Legal Certainty and Predictability in the EUPILLAR Project's Regulations An Assessment', in Beaumont et al., *Cross-Border Litigation*, above fn. 8.

[73] See Kruger, T., 'Habitual Residence: The Factors that Courts Consider', in Beaumont et al., *Cross-Border Litigation*, above fn. 8.

[74] This links with the need for better education of judges, which is addressed below.

[75] For example, resorting to a request for a preliminary ruling only in genuine circumstances where there is no prior CJEU ruling on the question referred; or, on the other hand, not shying away from seeking a preliminary ruling from the CJEU where the case before the judge requires it. More generally, see Yüksel, B., 'An Analysis of the Effectiveness of the EU Institutions in Making and Interpreting EU Private International Law Regulations', in Beaumont et al., *Cross-Border Litigation*, above fn. 8.

in the courts of the EU Member States. Indeed, in order to enhance the uniformity in the application of EU private international law, a systematic publication of case law of domestic courts on the EU private international law Regulations is necessary. This will allow judges to see how the Regulations are applied by their colleagues in other EU jurisdictions, and thus facilitate a level of uniformity. Therefore, a systematic electronic publication of case law, preferably with at least summaries in English, as the language that is most frequently spoken as a common language throughout the EU, such as the EUPILLAR Database,[76] is very much needed.

Education to Facilitate Dialogue

Last but not least, the availability of further continuing education for judges in the form of workshops and training sessions is essential to enhance the uniform application of EU private international law. Ideally, this should be preceded by concentration of jurisdiction for cross-border cases, at least in family law,[77] to ensure that the training sessions are directed at the relevant group of judges who in turn have the opportunity to develop the required level of expertise in handling cross-border cases. It has also been suggested that practical guides to the application of the Regulations should be made available in local languages.[78]

At the same time, enhancing the linguistic skills of the judges dealing with cross-border cases is necessary. A working knowledge of English,[79] as the language that is most frequently used as the language of understanding between the different languages of the EU Member States, will enable further networking, facilitate direct judicial communication and enable judges to make the most of case law databases from other EU Member States. The networking activities should build on the existing European Judicial Network (EJN) in civil and commercial matters,[80] which was created in 2002 and seeks to bring together judicial authorities from all EU Member States in order to streamline and support judicial cooperation between Member States.[81]

[76] See above fn. 9.

[77] This has been acknowledged by the European Commission in the Proposal for the Recast of the Brussels IIa Regulation. See European Commission, 'Proposal for a Council Regulation on Jurisdiction, the Recognition and Enforcement of Decisions in Matrimonial Matters and the Matters of Parental Responsibility, and on International Child Abduction (recast)' COM(2016) 411 final, in particular Recital 26 and Art. 22.

[78] See Frąckowiak-Adamska et al., 'National Report: Poland', above fn. 46.

[79] Despite the promotion of linguistic diversity and multilingualism in Europe, it is a matter of fact that English has over the past couple of decades become the de facto lingua franca within the EU. See, for example, Cogoa, A. and J. Jenkins (2010) 'English as a Lingua Franca in Europe: A Mismatch between Policy and Practice', *European Journal of Language Policy*, October, 271–94.

[80] See further on the EJN the chapters by van Loon and Wisdahl, respectively, in this volume.

[81] See European E-Justice Portal, 'EJN in Civil and Commercial Matters', available at: https://e-justice.europa.eu/content_ejn_in_civil_and_commercial_matters-21-en.do. See, for example, European Commission (2015) *Judicial Cooperation in Civil Matters in the European Union: a Guide for Legal Practitioners*, Publications Office of the European Commission.

6

On Private International Law, the EU and Brexit

*Marta Requejo Isidro**

Introduction

On 23 June 2016 a referendum was held in the United Kingdom to decide whether the country should leave or remain in the European Union. Leave won by 52 per cent to 48 per cent. On 29 March 2017, Sir Tim Barrow, as British ambassador to the EU, delivered the official Article 50 notice to the European Council President, Donald Tusk. The exit of the UK raises many doubts as to the legal regime of cross-border private relationships, both ongoing and to be entered into in the future. The landscape gets gradually clearer as the expectations and objectives of both parties come to light and the negotiations that started in June 2017 progress. On the side of the EU the Commission acts as the negotiator on instructions (directives) given by the Council for a two-phased process: the first phase intends to provide clarity and legal certainty regarding the separation of the UK from the EU; the second-stage negotiations aim at reaching an agreement on a future relationship.

On November 2018, on the verge of running out of time, a Draft Withdrawal Agreement (DWA) was agreed, approved by the UK Prime Minister's Cabinet and endorsed by all the leaders of the EU27 nations.[1] The Agreement addresses the UK's withdrawal from the EU on 29 March 2019 and a transition period until the end of 2020, with one possible extension. At the time of writing the agreement is awaiting ratification from the UK Parliament, as well as consent from the EU Parliament. Regarding the future relationship, a Political Declaration[2] was published to accompany the DWA, setting out the principles for the future partnership. No

* The last version of this text was finished on 26 November 2018.

[1] Available at: www.consilium.europa.eu/media/37095/draft_withdrawal_agreement_incl_art132.pdf

[2] Available at: https://assets.publishing.service.gov.uk/government/uploads/system/uploads/attachment_data/file/756378/14_November_Outline_Political_Declaration_on_the_Future_Relationship.pdf

single reference is made therein to judicial cooperation in civil and commercial matters. In what follows we will briefly address the DWA before moving on to comment on the future and the likeliness of a bespoke agreement between the EU and the UK in the field of judicial cooperation in civil and commercial matters.

Transition Period: State of Play

A Brief Insight into the Negotiations

The negotiations for an orderly withdrawal of the UK from the EU started in June 2017. Following the Council Directives for the negotiation of an agreement with the United Kingdom of Great Britain and Northern Ireland setting out the arrangements for its withdrawal from the European Union, approved on 22 May 2017, the Commission's Position paper of 29 June 2017 transmitted to EU27 on Judicial Co-operation in Civil and Commercial Matters set out the main principles to be applied on the withdrawal date to the winding down of the existing relationship between the EU and the UK. In response to this document the UK Government published on 22 August 2017 a paper entitled *Providing a cross-border civil judicial cooperation framework: a future partnership paper*[3] that stressed the need to agree on a new civil judicial cooperation framework for future cases mirrored on existing provisions. Judicial cooperation in civil and commercial matters in the context of separation was addressed only in an Annexe. The documents prove the EU and the UK shared the same view as to the material scope of any withdrawal agreement vis-à-vis the instruments to be considered in the field of cross-border judicial cooperation in civil and commercial matters. On the contrary, the EU Position paper and the response of the UK Government in the abovementioned Annexe showed differences about the specific solutions, particularly in relation to the time limit determining which judgments benefit from the EU instruments on recognition and enforcement: according to the EU, the provisions on recognition and enforcement 'should continue to govern all judicial decisions given *before the withdrawal date*' (italics added), whereas in the UK's view, the existing EU rules on recognition and enforcement should also apply to judgments given *after the withdrawal date in proceedings which were instituted before it*.

A Joint Report from the negotiators of the EU and the UK Government regarding Phase 1 of the talks under Article 50 TEU was adopted on 8 December 2017, where cooperation in civil and commercial matters for the UK's orderly withdrawal from the EU was addressed at paragraph 91.[4] Subsequently, a first DWA by the European Commission was transmitted to EU27 on 28 February 2018, and to the UK on 13 March. On 19 March 2018, a colour text was published reflecting the progress made in the EU/UK negotiation round between 16 and 19 March:[5] the text in green had been

[3] Available at: www.gov.uk/government/publications/providing-a-cross-border-civil-judicial-cooperation-framework-a-future-partnership-paper

[4] Available at: https://ec.europa.eu/commission/sites/beta-political/files/joint_report.pdf

[5] Draft Agreement on the Withdrawal of the United Kingdom of Great Britain and Northern Ireland

agreed at the negotiators' level and was only subject to technical legal revisions at a later stage. Yellow meant the text had been agreed with regard to the policy objective but drafting changes or clarifications were still required. The text in white corresponded to proposals by the EU on which discussions were pending, that is, no agreement had yet been reached. Title VI of Part Three, 'Ongoing judicial cooperation in civil and commercial matters', covering Articles 62 to 65, was coloured green except for Article 63 – jurisdiction, recognition and enforcement of judicial decisions, and related cooperation between Central Authorities – which remained white. Some months later, on 19 June 2018, a Joint Statement from the negotiators of the EU and the UK Government on the progress of negotiations under Article 50 TEU on the United Kingdom's orderly withdrawal from the European Union (incorporating a DWA), announced further progress;[6] a new Article 63 was enclosed, coloured in green. Articles 62 to 65 of the DWA of March 2018 have been copied almost to the letter in the document of November 2018 with a different numbering – Articles 66 to 69.

The current DWA distinguishes two relevant periods after Brexit, which occurs on 29 March 2019: first (Article 126), a transition period from 30 March 2019 until 31 December 2020, where following Article 127 EU law shall be applicable to and in the UK unless otherwise provided in the Agreement, and any reference to Member States in the Union law applicable pursuant to paragraph 1, including as implemented and applied by Member States, shall be understood as including the United Kingdom.[7] Second, after 31 December 2020, where according to Article 185 specific provisions of the Agreement shall apply, including those on ongoing judicial cooperation in civil matters.

Ongoing Civil Judicial Cooperation: Open Questions

Articles 66 to 69 of the current DWA address four areas of private international law – applicable law, jurisdiction, recognition and enforcement, and cooperation in the broad sense – including all the EU instruments, be they regulations, directives or decisions, binding upon the UK.[8] With the exception of Article 66 on the Rome I and Rome II Regulations, which for obvious reasons is only directed at the UK,[9] the

from the European Union and the European Atomic Energy Community highlighting the progress made (coloured version) in the negotiation round with the UK of 16–19 March 2018. Available at: https://ec.europa.eu/commission/sites/beta-political/files/draft_agreement_coloured.pdf

6 Available at: https://ec.europa.eu/commission/publications/joint-statement-negotiators-european-union-and-united-kingdom-government-progress-negotiations-under-article-50-teu-united-kingdoms-orderly-withdrawal-european-union_en

7 According to Art. 132.1, notwithstanding Art. 126, before 1 July 2020 the competent body may adopt a single decision extending the transition period for up to one or two years.

8 The UK has a right to decide on a case-by-case basis whether or not to opt in to proposals relating to the areas of freedom, security and justice: Protocol No. 4 to the Amsterdam Treaty in 1997, confirmed by the Treaty of Lisbon in 2009.

9 The Regulations being of universal application there is no need to remind the Member States about their compulsory applicability in all situations falling under their material and temporal scope.

provisions set obligations for the UK and for the Member States; no qualification is required for the former, whereas for the Member States the situation at stake needs to be one 'involving the UK'. The – quite unfortunate – expression is surely meant to embrace in one term all the circumstances required for each of the EU Regulations to apply: for instance, the domicile of the defendant in a Member State (or the UK) for the Brussels I *bis* Regulation; the habitual residence of a child in an action on parental responsibility in a Member State (or the UK) under the Brussels II *bis* Regulation; or the habitual residence of the creditor, or of the debtor, in a Member State (or the UK) under the Maintenance Regulation.[10]

In our mind, there is no doubt that EU/UK agreement upon a text must be welcome: at this stage we cannot yet count on it. However, the current document gives rise to uncertainties which may ruin its main purpose – a swift, orderly exit of the UK from the EU, for the benefit of all stakeholders. Article 67 provides some juicy examples:[11] to start with, reference is made under paragraphs (1) and (2) to 'legal proceedings instituted before the end of the transition period', and to 'requests and applications received by the Central Authority of the requested state before the end of the transition period', under Article 67(3), but no indication is provided as to how to determine when legal proceedings have been instituted (or when a request is deemed to have been received). The provisions of the in-force procedural EU Regulations on pending cases relate primarily to *lis pendens* and related actions and use a different terminology (see for instance Article 16, Regulation Brussels II *bis*, Article 9 Maintenance Regulation); the possibility of extending the criteria to Article 67 is at the very least disputable.

A second example is provided by the expression 'provisions regarding jurisdiction'. Under Article 67 it comprises indisputably the grounds for jurisdiction established in each EU Regulation. However, doubts may arise about choice of court clauses. Under Article 63 DWA of March 2018, Article 25 Regulation (EU) No. 1215/2012 and Article 4 Maintenance Regulation would have applied for the purposes of assessing the legal force of agreements on jurisdiction or choice of court agreements concluded before the end of the transition period; however, the rule has disappeared in the November 2018 version of the DWA.

[10] Regulation (EU) No. 1215/2012 of the European Parliament and of the Council of 12 December 2012 on jurisdiction and the recognition and enforcement of judgments in civil and commercial matters, [2012] OJ L 351/1; Council Regulation (EC) No. 2201/2003, of 27 November 2003, concerning jurisdiction and the recognition and enforcement of judgments in matrimonial matters and the matters of parental responsibility, repealing Regulation (EC) No. 1347/2000, [2003] OJ L 338/1; Council Regulation (EC) No. 4/2009 of 18 December 2008 on jurisdiction, applicable law, recognition and enforcement of decisions and cooperation in matters relating to maintenance obligations, [2009] OJ L 7/1.

[11] We take up here our study (together with T. Amos, P. de Miguel, A. Dutta and M. Harper) *The Future Relationship between the UK and the EU following the UK's Withdrawal from the EU in the Field of Family Law*, commissioned by the European Parliament's Policy Department for Citizens' Rights and Constitutional Affairs at the request of the Committee on Legal Affairs, October 2018.

Doubts may also be expressed regarding rules which are not aimed directly at distributing jurisdiction among the Member States, but rather at indicating how to exercise it under specific circumstances. Significant examples are Articles 27 and 28 Brussels I *bis* Regulation, Article 11 Brussels II *bis*, Articles 17 and 18 of the same Regulation, and Articles 10 and 11 Maintenance Regulation. Before June 2018, the rules on *lis pendens* and related actions in the Regulations raised similar doubts. In this respect the text of Article 63 DWA June 2018, Article 67 DWA November 2018, entails a significant development in comparison with the wording which was used in March 2018: it clarifies that Articles 19 to 31 Brussels I *bis*, 19 Brussels II *bis* and Articles 12 and 13 Maintenance Regulation will apply in respect of proceedings or actions related to legal proceedings instituted before the end of the transition period. This explanation is particularly important since the coexistence of several courts having jurisdiction is expressly provided for in those Regulations, and legal certainty in the treatment of parallel actions is of the essence. The question remains open, however, as to the remaining provisions such as those mentioned above.

The Future Partnership: Judicial Cooperation on Civil and Commercial Matters

The Baseline

The UK's wish for a bespoke agreement mirroring existing law

In response to the European Commission Position Paper on Judicial Cooperation in Civil and Commercial Matters, on 22 August 2017 the UK published *Providing a cross-border civil judicial cooperation framework: a future partnership paper.*[12] The document reveals the UK's ambitions for a deep and special future partnership in the area, so as to provide a clear legal basis to support cross-border activities after the UK's withdrawal: the solutions therein would mirror closely the current EU system; however, direct jurisdiction of the Court of Justice of the European Union (CJEU) would no longer exist.[13] The UK Government's White Paper of July 2018 on the future relationship between the UK and the EU points in the same direction:

> The UK is therefore keen to explore a new bilateral agreement with the EU, which would cover a coherent package of rules on jurisdiction, choice of jurisdiction, applicable law, and recognition and enforcement of judgments in civil, commercial, insolvency and family matters. This would seek to build on the principles established in the Lugano Convention and subsequent developments at EU level in civil judicial cooperation between the UK and MS. This would also reflect the

[12] Above fn. 3.

[13] Paras 17–20. It is unclear what 'direct' means. For the purposes of this paper we assume it is equivalent to the taking due account or giving due regard to the case law of the Court.

> long history of cooperation in this field based on mutual trust in each other's legal systems . . .[14]

Why this interest in continuity after leaving the EU? There is one keyword to describe the EU legal regime governing private relationships with a transnational element and cross-border dispute litigation, and that is 'certainty'. Scholars, professionals and politicians in the UK are all well aware of it. Even before the Brexit referendum, uncertainty was singled out by UK academics and lawyers as the fear par excellence.[15] In the specific context of private international law and transnational litigation, both in commercial and in family law, it was immediately understood that moving outside the EU will entail a significant loss in terms of legal certainty. Several aspects appear particularly sensitive: the validity of English jurisdiction agreements in the area of commercial litigation, and the protection against child abduction in the field of family law. In the domain of recognition and enforcement of judgments, uncertainty will be the outcome of the withdrawal from a single, simple and streamlined recognition/enforcement regime. Evidence Sessions held from December 2016 to January 2017 at the House of Lords before the Select Committee on the EU Justice Sub-committee[16] gathered expert witnesses to explain the significance for everyday life of EU procedural Regulations in the field of judicial cooperation – Brussels I *bis*, Brussels II *bis*, the Maintenance Regulation. A large majority of the evidence conveyed the wish to keep the current EU-law-based regime, and, failing this, a regime replicating it, for the post-Brexit situation.[17] At the end of January 2017, the Minister of State for Courts and Justice gave the Committee details as to the hope on the side of the UK regarding the post-Brexit best-case scenario, which in a nutshell would rely on two main pillars: a set of common rules in the form of new agreements with the EU taking

[14] HM Government, 'The Future Relationship between the United Kingdom and the European Union', Cm. 9593, July 2018.

[15] A joint MPI/BIICL seminar was held in London in May 2016 under the title 'Post Brexit: The Fate of Commercial Dispute Resolution in London and on the Continent', at which English and continental scholars and lawyers expressed their views.

[16] Hereinafter 'Evidence Sessions'. The Committee looked at a certain number of issues in order to assist the Government, alerting it to areas where the law might be impacted upon due to the withdrawal from the EU so that they can be part of any negotiation. The transcriptions of the oral evidence are downloadable in pdf format at: www.parliament.uk/business/committees/committees-a-z/lords-select/eu-justice-subcommittee/inquiries/parliament-2015/brexit-civil-justice-cooperation. See also House of Lords European Union Committee, *Brexit: Justice for Families,Iindividuals and Businesses?*, 17th Report of Session 2016–17, published 20 March 2017, available at: https://publications.parliament.uk/pa/ld201617/ldselect/ldeucom/134/134.pdf; House of Lords, Select Committee on the European Union, Justice Sub-Committee, oral evidence, *Civil Justice Co-operation Post Brexit – Follow-up Inquiry*, published 22 May 2018, at: http://data.parliament.uk/writtenevidence/committeeevidence.svc/evidencedocument/eu-justice-subcommittee/civil-justice-cooperation-post-brexit-followup/oral/84128.pdf

[17] To some extent a different view is represented by Richard Fentimann, Evidence Session No. 1, answer to Q1 where the author recalls the virtues of the common law rules and suggests they could be a short-term solution to fill any temporary gap.

up the contents of the European rules, to ensure mutuality and reciprocity; and the absence of any post-Brexit role for the Court of Justice.[18] As already seen, the same idea prevails in the UK Government's plans for the post-transition relationship with the EU27, disclosed in July 2018.

EU law as a melting pot: relevance of the UK's input

In 2014, the former President of the CJEU, Vassilios Skouris, 'observed that the relationship between the common law tradition, the civil law tradition and European Union law is a circular one. Relying on the words of Lord Neuberger,[19] he considered this relationship to be one of cross-fertilisation, and advised to look at European law as a synthesis of several legal traditions'.[20]

The influence of the UK's legal systems in shaping the rules in the European Regulations is well recognised at both a scholarly and a political level: 'What has become very clear is the extent to which British lawyers have been actively involved and [have been] major contributors to [EU] law'.[21] The UK has fully participated in the negotiations of EU instruments, sometimes even after announcing in the initial stages its intention to not opt in: this was the case with the Rome I Regulation, where there was, in the end, a decision to opt in, and also with the European Account Preservation Order, with the opposite result.[22]

The impact of the common law tradition can certainly be traced in the EU conflict of law rules in contractual matters, first in the Rome Convention of 1980 and later in the Rome I Regulation. A prominent example would be the first connection to determine the law applicable to a contract, which is the one chosen by the parties: there are English decisions on this point dating back to the end of the eighteenth century. Further rules inspired by the common law culture are the following: the law applicable to a contract can only be that of a state; the scope of the law applicable to the contract, so that in relation to the manner of performance and the steps to be taken in the event of defective performance regard shall be had to the law of the country in which performance takes place.

In the field of procedural law it is habitual to point to Article 15 Brussels II *bis* Regulation as a rule the adoption of which was encouraged by existing common law

[18] Available at: www.parliament.uk/business/committees/committees-a-z/lords-select/eu-justice-sub committee/news-parliament-2015/brexit-cjc-justice-minister

[19] Who at the time was the President of the Supreme Court of the UK.

[20] See www.kcl.ac.uk/law/newsevents/newsrecords/2014-15/cel-president-skouris-lecture.aspx

[21] Baroness Kennedy of The Shaws, Chairman of the Justice Subcommittee, Evidence Session No. 1, Q2; reproduced with similar words in the following sessions.

[22] Regulation (EC) No. 593/2008 of the European Parliament and of the Council of 17 June 2008 on the Law Applicable to Contractual Obligations (Rome I) [2008] OJ L 177/6; Regulation (EU) No. 655/2014 of the European Parliament and of the Council of 15 May 2014 establishing a European Account Preservation Order procedure to facilitate cross-border debt recovery in civil and commercial matters, [2014] OJ L 189/59.

solutions,[23] even if in its final shape the solution does not fully match the Anglo-Saxon figure: under Article 15 some degree of interaction between the courts involved is needed which is not required within the unilateral *forum non conveniens* doctrine.

An English flavour is also discernible in the *lis pendens* rule of Article 33 of the Brussels I *bis* Regulation, where 'the proper administration of justice' is a key element in the decision of the seized court to stay the proceedings in favour of a Third State court. According to some scholars 'the proper administration of justice' is a sort of *forum non conveniens* rule: 'the *lis pendens* rule for actions pending in third States introduces some of the elements of the *forum non conveniens* doctrine . . . into the Brussels I *bis* Regulation, albeit not the entire doctrine itself'.[24] Other views which at first glance would disagree also end up accepting that the proper administration of justice 'can be interpreted as referring to the ends of justice in the individual case, thereby allowing discretionary considerations such as the availability of proof and witnesses'.[25]

Articles 41 onwards of the latest EU Insolvency Regulation,[26] on cooperation, communication and coordination between the courts, provide for a further example of the UK's influence on EU law. The previous Regulation[27] required the liquidators of the main and secondary proceedings of the insolvency to communicate; they were literally duty bound to do so by Article 31. In contrast, the question of whether the judges seized respectively of the main and secondary proceedings were under a similar obligation was controversial. In this framework there had already been some indications from the UK pointing to an affirmative answer. A well-known example comes from the High Court of Justice in Birmingham on 11 May 2005 in the case of *MG Rover*. The Court opened a main proceeding against the Rover group comprising the subsidiaries in Germany, France, Holland, Belgium, Luxembourg, Spain, Ireland,

[23] González Beilfuss, C. (2012) '*Forum non conveniens* a la europea: el mecanismo de transmisión del asunto al juez mejor situado', in Borras, A. and G. Garriga (eds), *Adaptación de la legislación interna a la normativa de la Unión Europea en materia de cooperación civil. Homenaje al Prof. Dr. Ramón Viñas Farré*, Marcial Pons, 125.

[24] Heinze, C. and B. Steinrötter (2017) 'The Revised *lis pendens* Rules in the Brussels Ibis Regulation', in Laczic, V. and S. Stuij (eds), *Brussels Ibis Regulation. Changes and Challenges of the Renewed Procedural Scheme*, Springer, 12. This is a view shared by British scholars: Roggerson, P. (2014) 'Arts. 32–34', in Dickinson, A. *The Brussels I Regulation Recast*, Oxford University Press, para. 11.78.

[25] Weber, J. (2011) 'Universal Jurisdiction and Third States in the Reform of the Brussels I Regulation', 75 *RabelsZ* 634, 637. The author starts by stating that the concept of 'proper administration of justice' should be construed with the help of principles that mirror preferences of the regulation itself: the *prior in tempore* principle, and the requirement that the jurisdiction of the Third State is based on criteria similar to those in the regulation. This understanding would allow for a standardised method in assessing the appropriateness of Third State proceedings.

[26] Regulation (EU) 2015/848 of the European Parliament and of the Council of 20 May 2015 on insolvency proceedings, [2015] OJ L 141/19.

[27] Council Regulation (EC) No. 1346/2000 of 29 May 2000 on insolvency proceedings, [2000] OJ L160/1.

Italy and Portugal. In this context, with the aim of limiting the likelihood of the opening of secondary proceedings, the English court adopted orders addressed to the courts of other Member States describing the purpose of the main proceedings in England and the powers and responsibilities of the administrators, with particular reference to the power to make payments to workers of the European subsidiaries, so that they received the same amount as they would have received through a secondary procedure.[28]

It goes without saying that the inclusion of this element – or of any other of the elements referred to above – in the EU Regulations is not solely the outcome of the UK's influence: the background to EU law background is certainly broader than that. However, the source of inspiration is easily identifiable and, what is more, important: in the future, for the application of the texts, the English experience would be very valuable. In this regard, the general attitude of the English courts towards EU law, characterised by goodwill and good work, is worth mentioning. Recalling the UK's reluctance to become a Party to the Rome Convention, it was said that the agreement was not well regarded 'within a legal system that was pleased with the virtues of its private international law system', but that 'as is generally the case, the British system takes writing law quite seriously, and once it opts for or incorporates European law, it offers guarantees of a compromised application'.[29] In the practical application of the Regulations English judges have also proven their high technical quality.[30] The same can be said as regards their relation with the CJEU.

Interplay with the CJEU: was it so excruciating?

There is one point of the future negotiations where the UK seems to be adamant: there is no direct post-Brexit role for the CJEU.

Nevertheless, the dialogue between the British courts and the CJEU through the preliminary ruling system has, as a matter of fact, been a fruitful one. Between 1973 and 2016 the UK had referred some 700 preliminary questions to the CJEU. It is not one of the most active Member States (this position is occupied by Italy and Germany), but it is clearly not a passive country either. In addition, scholars highlight an evolution in this sense:

> English courts have traditionally been selective in the use of the preliminary reference procedure. The data suggest that there are fewer references by UK courts in

[28] High Court of Justice Chancery Division Birmingham, 18 April 2005, [2005] EWHC 874.

[29] Sánchez Lorenzo, S. (2013) *El Derecho inglés y los contratos internacionales*, Tirant lo Blanch, 136.

[30] See also below, text to fn. 43. On the Rome II Regulation, *Winrow* v. *Hemphill*, [2014] EWHC 3164, on the analysis of Art. 4 (3) Rome II and the escape clause in detail, see the positive assessment by van Calster, G. (2016) *European Private International Law* 2nd edn, Hart Publishing, 256: 'the judgment is to my knowledge one of few discussing Article 4 (3)'s escape clause in such detail. A judgment which does justice to both the exceptional nature of the provision, and the need to consider all relevant factors'. Another example of correct application of EU as interpreted by the CJEU is provided by the same author, at 300–1, regarding insolvency law: *Northsea Base Investments et al.*, [2015] EWHC 121.

> comparison to courts of other Member States of equivalent or even smaller population, although in recent years references from UK courts have grown.[31]

The reluctance of English courts to make references is explained as the consequence of a number of factors, including cultural ones: 'in a culture where the judge makes the law, passing the resolution of the dispute to another authority may be viewed as indecisiveness'.[32] Judging from the words of Hon Sir Oliver Heald QC MP, Minister of State for Courts and Justice, 'We have taken back the power to make our own laws and to have our judges decide what those laws mean',[33] it is legitimate to conclude that the idea still features strongly in the British mind.

And yet, the UK courts have referred questions to the CJEU. In the above-mentioned speech given in 2014, Vassilios Skouris explained how the common law tradition has contributed to the development of EU law as a result of three important elements, one of which is precisely the preliminary rulings sent by the common law courts, the excellence of which was highly praised by the speaker.[34] There can be no doubt that the choice of the questions, as well as the way they are drafted, are distinctive features of the UK's preliminary references. In the field of private international law two further characteristics are worth recalling: first, some of the requests were (from the perspective of the common law and in view of the clear civil law penchant of the Court) risky questions; and indeed the common law was scorched by the answers, as shown by the Court's rulings regarding secular institutions like the *forum non conveniens* and the antisuit injunctions. Academics reflected this with papers bearing particularly poignant titles, such as T. Hartley's 'The EU and the Systematic Dismantling of the Common Law of Conflict' in 2005, or H. Seriki's 'Anti-Suit Injunctions and Arbitration: A Final Nail in the Coffin'.[35]

Private international law preliminary references by English courts have proved to be seminal and in the general interest of all Member States: this would be the second relevant feature. Until 2016 twenty-two requests had been referred to the Court, only three relating to family law and one to the temporal scope of the Rome II Regulation. The rest concerned the Brussels system (Brussels Convention, Brussels I Regulation). For those familiar with European procedural law there is no need to insist on the relevance of cases such as the following: case C-185/07, *Allianz*, on the jurisdiction of a court of a Member State to issue an order restraining a party from commencing or continuing proceedings before a court of another Member State on the ground that those proceedings would be contrary to an arbitration agreement;[36] case C-281/02,

[31] Tridimas, T. (2003) 'Knocking on Heaven's Door: Fragmentation, Efficiency and Defiance in the Preliminary Reference Procedure', 40 *Common Market L.Rev*. 9, 38.

[32] Ibid.

[33] Evidence Session No. 6, Q46.

[34] Above fn. 20.

[35] (2005) 45 *ICLQ* 813, for the first, and (2006) 23 *J. Int'l Arb*. 25, for the latter.

[36] ECLI:EU:C:2009:69.

Owusu, on the compatibility of the *forum non conveniens* doctrine within the EU;[37] case C-159/02, *Turner*, on antisuit injunctions, allowing for pivotal considerations on mutual trust;[38] case C-163/95, *von Horn*, on the transitional application of the *lis pendens* rules, and the systematic interpretation of the different parts of the Brussels Convention;[39] case C-68/93, *Shevill*, on the mosaic principle to establish jurisdiction over plurilocalised tort claims;[40] case C-406/92, *the Tatry*, on the relation with other conventions;[41] case C-351/89, *Overseas Union Insurance Ltd*, on the applicability of the *lis pendens* rule independently of the defendant's domicile;[42] case C-190/89, *Marc Rich*, on the material scope of the Brussels Convention and arbitration.[43]

The dialogue between UK courts and the CJEU continues in other ways: for instance, as citations to the latter's case law far beyond the mere formal reference to the ECLI number. By way of example, *Canyon Offshore Limited* v. *GDF Suez EP Netherland BV* has been referred to in academic writings as a case of perfect application of the current Article 7.1 Brussels I *bis* Regulation (at the time Article 5.1)

> starting with the very discussion of whether there has been a contract between the parties . . . into the discussion of 'goods' v. 'services'; back to the at first sight very, very puzzling fall back provision of the third indent of the Article ('(c) if subparagraph (b) does not apply then subparagraph (a) applies'); finally, to the determination of the place of performance of the obligation in question . . . Mackie J did an absolute perfect job of taking the case through Article 7's cascade, with impeccable reference to relevant CJEU case law.[44]

In a similar vein, in the field of family law it has not been unusual that a solution developed in the context of a European instrument becomes generalised and is applied to other settings.[45] A striking example is the abandon of the ascertainment of the habitual residence of the child through an adult-focused approach, to be substituted by a child-centred approach. It is now settled law that the same definition of habitual residence applies in all children cases and mirrors that adopted by the CJEU.[46] The Court of Appeal has also endorsed the suggestion that the requirement under Brussels

[37] ECLI:EU:C:2005:120.

[38] ECLI:EU:C:2004:228.

[39] ECLI:EU:C:1997:472.

[40] ECLI:EU:C:1995:61.

[41] ECLI:EU:C:1994:400.

[42] ECLI:EU:C:1991:279.

[43] ECLI:EU:C:1991:319.

[44] Van Calster, *European Private International Law*, above fn. 30, 144.

[45] The pervasiveness of EU law and case law is much easier to observe in family law than in commercial law, where English courts are less willing to extend the EU solutions beyond what is strictly necessary. An example is that the exercise of discretion and considerations of *forum conveniens* are maintained in non-EU cases; see *Pike and Doyle* v. *The Indian Hotels Company Ltd*, [2013] EWHC 4096 (QB).

[46] See *In the matter of B (A child)*, [2016] UKSC 4, at 31.

II *bis* to ascertain the views of children of sufficient age of maturity is not restricted to intra-European Community cases of child abduction, but is a principle of universal application.[47]

The (Un)likeliness of an EU/UK Agreement on Civil Judicial Cooperation

Third-state UK: what is so special?

It is indeed sensible to have solutions on cross-border jurisdiction and recognition and enforcement of decisions which enhance certainty for the continental citizens with interests in Third States; this is a general truth. With the UK having been a Member State for more than forty years, British negotiators would not need to prove what is so particular about the UK that an EU/UK convention is of the essence for the post-Brexit period. On the other hand, they will have to convince the EU that the solutions to be agreed are precisely those currently contained in the European regulations; and, in addition, about the CJEU not being part of the agreement. For the endeavour to succeed fundamental obstacles relating to the systemic nature of the EU and of EU law must be overcome: the following elaborates on this.

EU law is purpose-oriented

The unlikelihood of an uprooted EU-like bilateral convention. As a matter of principle, an EU-like agreement with a state willing to abandon the EU project is a puzzling idea. It suffices to recall the basis for the private international law legislation in the EU: Article 65 of the Treaty of Amsterdam, Article 81 TFEU. These provisions represent the evolution from the isolated, imprecise hint in Article 220 in the Treaty of Rome to the Member States prompting them to conclude international conventions, to a standard competence of the EU subject to flexible limits (proportionality, subsidiarity). They mirror the political, economic and social development of the European project itself: a project of integration. An essential part of this integration venture is a 'genuine European area of justice', intended to prevent individuals and businesspeople from feeling discouraged from exercising their rights.[48] Accordingly, Article 67.4 of the TFEU states today that 'The Union shall facilitate access to justice, in particular through the principle of mutual recognition of judicial and extrajudicial decisions in civil matters'. But this intention is not meant as a holistic one: it is European-focused. Needless to say, this is also the case of the Charter of Fundamental Rights of the EU, Article 47. There is no interest in easing access to justice *per se*; it is associated with the EU project.

Inadequacy of the technical solutions. Certain mechanisms and technical solutions of the EU procedural law instruments, such as the abolition of *exequatur*, have been endorsed only for integration – a multi-factor, dynamic process which

[47] *Re M. (A Child) (Abduction: Child's Objections to Return)*, [2007] EWCA Civ 260, [2007] 2 FLR 72.
[48] Tampere Summit of the EU Council, 15 and 16 October 1999.

surpasses mutual respect for the legal system of other States to entail assimilation and inclusiveness. Throughout the Evidence Sessions before the House of Lords in 2016–17, allusions were made to reciprocity and mutuality as overarching principles of the (yet to come) EU-UK agreement. Indeed, reciprocity as such is not indicative of any legal regime; it does not guarantee the suppression of barriers to enforcement. In fact, it only ensures the equality of treatment in two normative spaces; *a priori* any technical solution may be agreed upon to be reciprocally applied. However, it is doubtful whether the far-reaching solutions – in terms of removal of obstacles to the circulation of judgments – of the current EU procedural regulations are exportable to a context not led by the philosophy of integration. Within the EU, the sacrifices imposed by mutual trust to the individual right to due process are endurable in the name of integration as a greater, common good; the reality remains that the procedural laws of Member States differ, and that they do not always meet the same standards of respect of the fundamental rights. In the absence of any integration goal there is no apparent reason for an all-embracing blind reciprocal trust.

EU priorities are set according to predominant purpose. Integration is the overarching inspiring strategy of the EU rules on cross-border judicial cooperation, but it is not the only strategy. The EU private international law and procedural law regulations also respond to other policies, such as the protection of the child, the protection of the maintenance creditor, and so on. Nonetheless, in case of a conflict between them and the integration policy the tendency is that the latter prevails.[49] Will the UK be willing to accept this for an EU-UK agreement? We will come back to this later in this chapter.

Keeping pace? Integration is an organic process: it evolves. The likely-to-be future development of private international law and EU procedural law has been addressed in the *EU Justice Agenda for 2020 – Strengthening Trust, Mobility and Growth within the Union*: codification, consolidation and complementing the acquis are the keywords. Along the same lines, the Commission has started to think about reviewing the current instruments of EU procedural law in light of specific EU needs relating to the free circulation of judgments. The proposed actions range from no intervention at all to a full-scale harmonisation of procedural law. Further developments are expected for single regulations currently in force: see, for instance, Article 79 Brussels I *bis* Regulation, hinting at the further extension of the rules on jurisdiction to defendants not domiciled in Member States and the abolition of residual fora. It is unlikely that any bilateral conventional agreement will be reviewed to align with the EU rules each time these are amended. In any event, the UK will have no say in these developments, and once it is no longer a Member State there will be no need for the EU to show deference to its legal system or traditions.[50]

[49] As demonstrated by case C-491/10, *Aguirre Zarraga*, ECLI:EU:C:2010:828.

[50] According to Art. 67.1 *in fine* of the TFEU: 'The Union shall constitute an area of freedom, security and justice with respect for fundamental rights and the different legal systems and traditions of the Member States'.

EU law (and case law) is a system

The *acquis communautaire* is built as a system. This results in several consequences affecting the UK proposal, though admittedly they differ in how serious they are.

Inextricably intertwined components. The EU legal instruments complement and reinforce one another: any proposal to reproduce single, isolated elements of the system in a bilateral convention ignores this fact. In fact, the Evidence before the House of Lords suggests the contrary: 'We should not take Brussels as a simple picture . . . we should be looking at the complexity that lies behind Brussels – the Regulations and the other Directives that are relevant to it'.[51] There is indeed much more to cross-border judicial cooperation than meets the eye. The EU system does not start, nor does it end, with the three regulations examined at the Evidence Sessions. Many private international law and procedural rules for cross-border cases are set in EU acts with a broader content and purpose. Let us consider one of the most recent, the EU General Data Protection Regulation, which entered into force in May 2016 and has applied since May 2018.[52] Article 82 accords all persons who have suffered damage as a result of an infringement of this Regulation the right to receive compensation from the controller or processor for the damage suffered. In addition, the regulation, Article 79.2, provides for specific fora for proceedings against a controller or a processor in cross-border settings: claims shall be lodged with the courts of the Member State where the controller or processor has an establishment; alternatively, proceedings may be brought before the courts of the Member State where the data subject has his or her habitual residence. A special regime is thus set up: how it relates to the Brussels I *bis* Regulation (whether it completely replaces it or whether new fora are added to the old ones) remains to be decided. What does the UK suggest in this regard in the post-Brexit scenario?

Ties and links among the components of legal systems may be stronger or looser. When confronted with a proposal such as the UK's, one of the unavoidable questions to be answered is to what extent the EU instruments can have a separate, independent life from each other. Formal cross-references within a regulation to other regulations will of course make it difficult (and there are many of these); one may wonder whether the bridges created between regulations by the CJEU work to the same effect.[53] But in the event EU rules do not include formal *renvois*, the question remains whether they make sense when removed from their natural environment. One cannot help regarding them as a single package; at any rate, it is in the context of the package that they work well.

[51] Greene, D., Evidence Session No. 4, answer to Q22.

[52] Regulation (EU) 2016/679 of the European Parliament and of the Council of 27 April 2016 on the protection of natural persons with regard to the processing of personal data and on the free movement of such data, and repealing Directive 95/46/EC, [2016] OJ L 119/1.

[53] For instance, when interpreting the Brussels Regulations and the Insolvency Regulations in case C- 157/13, *Nickel & Goeldner Spedition GmbH*, ECLI:EU:C:2014:2145, para. 21.

Member States, actors under constraints. Member States are actors in the system; they must remain loyal to it and they cannot escape from it. When applying their laws and when legislating, even as sovereign powers beyond the sphere of direct influence/competence of the EU,[54] they are subject to the overarching obligation of doing so in a way that preserves the *effet utile* of the EU rules; see, for instance, case C-533/08, *TNT Express Nederland BV*.[55] In a similar vein, principles such as those of equivalence and effectiveness condition and shape their freedom as to the content and the application of their own laws.

Controls of inadequate legal measures of Member States are foreseen at the institutional level: first and foremost by the CJEU, whose preliminary ruling may trigger severe consequences such as changes in the Member States' law in domains not directly covered by EU law.[56] The Commission is also entrusted with monitoring powers to ensure the correct application of EU law.[57] The examination may be carried out on its own initiative or in response to a request from the European Parliament (EP) or to complaints received from citizens, businesses, NGOs and other interested parties which reveal possible violations of EU law.[58]

Of course, there is no question of the UK accepting any of the above described

[54] As opposed to 'delegated powers', to be used to implement or complement EU law.

[55] ECLI:EU:C:2010:243, para. 49, on the application of specialised conventions signed by the Member States: 'the fact remains that their application cannot compromise the principles which underlie judicial cooperation in civil and commercial matters in the European Union, such as the principles . . . of free movement of judgments in civil and commercial matters, predictability as to the courts having jurisdiction and therefore legal certainty for litigants, sound administration of justice, minimization of the risk of concurrent proceedings, and mutual trust in the administration of justice in the European Union'. See also paras 50 and 56.

[56] See case C-618/10, *Banco Español de Crédito*, ECLI:EU:C:2012:349, on the *ex officio* assessment of the fairness of contractual terms, triggering the amendment of the Spanish *Ley de Enjuiciamiento Civil* (Art. 815) by the *Ley 42/2015, de 5 de octubre, de reforma de la Ley 1/2000, de 7 de enero, de Enjuiciamiento Civil*.

[57] The Commission's control over the activities of the Member States concentrates typically on the full and correct transposition of the directives and the correct application of the EU acquis. There are nonetheless examples of further areas of control: for instance, proceedings against Member States for failing to adopt measures to enable the application of Regulations within a certain time limit, even where such time limit was not fixed in the Regulation itself (see case 30/72, *Commission* v. *Italia*, ECLI:EU:C:1973:16; case C-403/98, *Azienda Agricole Monte Arcosu*, ECLI:EU:C:2001:6).

[58] In the framework of the *Šneersone and Kampanella* litigation the Republic of Latvia denounced Italy to the Commission in October 2008 under Art. 227 TCE (now Art. 259 TFEU); see ECtHR, 12 July 2011, *Sneersone y Kampanella* c. *Italia*, application no. 14737/09, para. 39ff. The Commission has expressed its views on national procedural rules in the context of the individual right of petition lodged with the Parliament: see European Parliament (Committee on Petitions) document on the meeting of 4 and 5 May 2015, PETI_PV(2015)242_1. The annual reports on the monitoring of the application of EU law, published by the Commission, show further research initiated by the Commission at the request of the European Parliament. See Report No. 31, Com (2014) 612 final, which refers to the follow-up of an infringement procedure against Belgium for the incorrect application of the Regulation on the European Enforcement Order.

mechanisms as necessary companions to any agreement with the EU; they are meant to fulfil a nomofilactic function of surveillance of the integrity and consistency of the EU system that ultimately benefits the EU citizen – an issue that will no longer concern the UK. However, the EU Member States will still be bound by them. This creates a structural imbalance among the Contracting States to any international agreement: should tensions arise regarding its interpretation and application, the Member States enjoy very little, if any, leeway to deviate from the constraint of remaining EU-consistent. Indeed, a similar situation might arise in connection to any other agreement, but it is likely to be more problematic in the case of conventions which replicate the content of regulations but not their (EU) purposes.

'Getting out in order to be free of the CJEU'[59]

Symbolic role and practical unavoidable function (for the EU) of the Court. The UK's intention to dispense with the CJEU may prove difficult. Beyond the political, symbolic dimension of the institution, there is the functional one: from a practical point of view the CJEU is not easily expendable.[60] The Court gives cohesion to the EU system and ensures the uniformity and coexistence of the EU legal instruments, delimiting them and interpreting them to preserve the internal consistency of the whole. Preliminary references submitted to the CJEU focus most of the time on single EU rules; however, the Court does not usually elaborate on them as isolated instruments, but rather with the system in mind.[61]

Moreover, the CJEU is a meeting point for disparate national approaches to legal problems; the preliminary reference is a vehicle for cultural legal exchange.

It is established that international agreements concluded by the EU (as opposed to those signed by the Member States) form an integral part of its legal order and can therefore be the subject of a request for a preliminary ruling by the Member State;[62] and there is no doubt that an international convention on jurisdiction and enforcement in civil and commercial matters, such as the one the UK has in mind, falls within the scope of the exclusive external competences of the EU.[63] The interpretation of agreements containing provisions on the jurisdiction of courts or on the recognition

[59] Quotation from Evidence Session No. 3, 13 December 2016, Baroness Ludford.

[60] Even according to some evidence before the House of Lords: a negotiation to keep the EU procedural instruments without any role for the Court is out of the question, Williams, D., Evidence Session No. 2, answer to Q12; Harris, J., Evidence Session No. 3, answer to Q18.

[61] See, for instance, case C-92/12, *Health Service Executive*, ECLI:EU:C:2012:255, para. 142, recalling principles elaborated under the Brussels I Regulation to apply them to the interpretation of the Brussels II *bis* Regulation.

[62] See para. 60 of case C- 533/08, *TNT Express Nederland BV*, ECLI:EU:C:2010:243.

[63] Opinion 1/03, on the Competence of the Community to Conclude the New Lugano Convention on the jurisdiction and the recognition and enforcement of judgments in civil and commercial matters. See also Opinion 1/13, regarding the Union's competence as to the acceptance of the accession of Third States to the Hague Convention of 1980 on international child abduction. It is also the view of the witnesses before the House of Lords: Harris, J., Evidence Session No. 3, answer to Q14.

and enforcement of judgments is capable of affecting EU rules; the possibility to refer requests to the CJEU must remain open in order to guarantee compatibility with the EU rules. Besides, as things stand today, the instrument to be agreed would replicate the content of the EU regulations. A uniform application in the Member States is required for the sake of certainty and manageability. In other words, fragmentation of interpretation must be avoided.

How will consistency be ensured? Replication of the case law of the Court. De iure, once the UK is no longer an EU Member State the CJEU findings will not be binding on it.[64] The fact remains that diverging interpretations – one for the Member States and another for the UK – of the same bilateral instrument will jeopardise its very purpose. As a workable compromise, it has been posited that the CJEU could retain a role similar to the one it has under the Lugano Convention: the jurisdiction of the CJEU applies to the Member States and Norway, Iceland and Switzerland are not directly subject to it, although their courts are nevertheless bound to 'have regard' to CJEU case law. A second possibility would be the obligation on the side of the UK courts to take 'due account' of the case law of the Court. Let's assume we accept one of these offers: will the UK retain an EU-like interpretation? Several questions arise: first, is it technically possible to reproduce – or to anticipate, as the case may be – the jurisprudence of the CJEU? When confronted with doubts on the interpretation of an agreement between the UK and the EU, would a court of the UK be able to reason in the same way as the CJEU? An affirmative answer should not be excluded from the outset. Indeed, the interpretation of EU law is not a task of the CJEU alone; national courts are main actors and only selected cases get as far as the CJEU.[65] Besides, the UK courts' attitude in relation to the preliminary reference seems to be one of restriction; they have not been particularly CJEU-dependent, but rather confident in their skills to properly understand EU law without the help of the CJEU. However, it must be clear that the 'accurate understanding of EU law' also entails, beyond the need to reach EU-oriented interpretations, a Europe-specific approach, coupled with particular syntax, grammar, language, categories and ideological assumptions. Examples of the difficulty of the task may be put forward. Let us compare the presentation by the House of Lords and the UK Government in case C-159/02, *Turner*, and the arguments of the CJEU in the same case.[66] The former revolved around the idea of 'parties' and 'good or bad faith', with the aim of protecting the legitimate interest of the applicant

[64] Although the possibility exists, in the light of Opinions 1/91, 1/92 and 1/00, for an extension by an international agreement concluded with Third States of the powers of the EU Courts to give binding preliminary rulings on the interpretation of such an agreement, and of the rules established pursuant to it, on questions submitted by courts of the Third States concerned. See Rosas, A. (2012) 'The National Judge as EU Judge: Opinion 1/9', in Cardonnel, P., A. Rosas and N. Wahl (eds), *Constitutionalising the EU Judicial System. Essays in Honour of Pernilla Lindh*, Hart Publishing, 105, 112–17.

[65] For a long time only courts of last instance could send preliminary references to the CJEU. Only a very small number of cross-border litigation cases make it to the Court.

[66] ECLI:EU:C:2004:228.

in the English proceedings; very little attention was paid to the jurisdiction of the foreign court. The CJEU narrative starts and ends with mutual trust:

> the Convention is necessarily based on the trust which the Contracting States accord to one another's legal systems and judicial institutions. It is that mutual trust which has enabled a compulsory system of jurisdiction to be established . . . and as a corollary, the waiver by those States of the right to apply their internal rules on recognition and enforcement of foreign judgments . . .[67]

The language, the syntax, the assumptions are all different.

Second, will the UK be willing to make an EU-like interpretation? It is uncertain what the compromise solution of 'having regard' or the – in all evidence fairly flexible – 'taking due account' solution actually implies. At any rate, the impact of the CJEU case law will not *per se* be accorded more than a persuasive value, as opposed to a binding one.[68] How persuasive it may be, once there is no possibility for UK representatives to intervene in any way, neither to influence the court nor simply to try to explain the national legal culture, remains to be seen. Moreover, the CJEU will not be the only court to be looked at; regard to other courts will be permitted as well.

There are examples of UK legal concepts being challenged and finally rejected within the EU domain, entailing the need to adjust or to abandon domestic doctrines: very well-known examples in the field of civil and commercial matters are the antisuit injunctions and the *forum non conveniens* doctrines. In insolvency matters it is worth recalling *In re Collins*[69] where groups of companies were treated as a single unit for the purposes of the centre of main interest (COMI); it was overruled by case C-341/04, *Eurofood.*[70] Regarding choice of court clauses, the non-formalistic approach adopted in *BNP Parisbas* v. *Anchorage Capital Europe et al.*[71] runs counter to case C-352/13 of the CJEU, *CDC*,[72] thus laying the foundations for further clashes. Potential confrontation has been avoided by not submitting preliminary references to the CJEU, in spite of the timeliness of the occasion: an example would be *Ferrexpo AG* v. *Gilson Investment Ltd and Other*, on the reflexive effect of (today's) Article 24 Brussels I *bis* when the defendant is domiciled in a Third State.[73]

In the light of the foregoing, it is legitimate to doubt the willingness of a British court, once the UK is no longer a Member State, to renounce legal concepts or institutions on its own motion, putting at risk the internal consistency and integrity of its

[67] Para. 24.

[68] Among others, Fentiman, R., Evidence Session No. 1, answer to Q1. Renton, J., Evidence Session No. 2, answer to Q11, refers to the model applied to ECtHR decisions.

[69] [2005] EWHC 1754 (Ch).

[70] ECLI:EU:C:2006:281.

[71] [2013] EWHC 3073.

[72] ECLI:EU:C:2015:335.

[73] [2012] EWHC 721.

own domestic system, giving up elements considered as benchmarks and competitive advantages of the system, and all for the sake of an alien project – EU integration.

DWA November 2018 and accompanying political declaration

At the time of writing it is indeed too early for any statement on the content of a future EU/UK partnership agreement. Indeed, according to the DWA November 2018, Article 184

> [t]he Union and the United Kingdom shall use their best endeavours, in good faith and in full respect of their respective legal orders, to take the necessary steps to negotiate expeditiously the agreements governing their future relationship referred to in the political declaration of [DD/MM/2018] and to conduct the relevant procedures for the ratification or conclusion of those agreements, with a view to ensuring that those agreements apply, to the extent possible, as from the end of the transition period.

However, regarding in particular judicial cooperation in civil and commercial matters the EU Council Guidelines of 23 March 2018 show a very cautious approach to judicial cooperation in civil matters: first, no reference is made to 'civil and commercial matters', but only to 'matrimonial, parental responsibility and other related matters'; second, the guideline proposes to explore 'options' for judicial cooperation 'taking into account that the UK will be a third country outside Schengen and that such cooperation would require strong safeguards to ensure full respect of fundamental rights'.[74] And even more telling, the *Outline of the Political Declaration Setting out the Framework for the Future Relationship between the European Union and the United Kingdom*, published on 14 November 2018 and accompanying the DWA, includes no mention at all of judicial cooperation in civil and commercial matters.

Conclusions

Brexit means impoverishment. EU law is as it is – not civil law, not common law, not even mixed law, but *European* law – thanks to many influences. The UK's influence is a unique one. The distinctive features of UK law, together with the country's loyalty and willingness to comply with EU law, have allowed the consolidation of relevant features of today's European private international law and procedural law. It will always be possible for Europe to look at the UK, its legal doctrines and practices and learn from them, but the channels allowing for direct communication and exchange may not remain open.

A transition time is of the essence for both the UK and the EU to prepare for the future. As of November 2018, substantial progress has been made as to the organisation of the transition period. The ratification of the DWA is still pending, however.

[74] Guideline 10. Interestingly, the draft document of 7 March 2018 contained no single reference to civil judicial cooperation.

Should the text of the current DWA become law, interpretative doubts will arise. In this regard it is worth noting that according to the current DWA the UK is no longer entitled to submit preliminary references to the CJEU on the interpretation of Part III of the withdrawal agreement.[75]

While it can be reasonably assumed that the interest in common rules for UK/continental private relations will diminish once the UK is no longer a partner in the EU project, the fact remains that cross-border commerce, trade and family relationships will continue. The UK's prospect of replicating in a bilateral instrument the content of the EU regulations presumes that their rules can be exported and applied in a non EU-principled setting. This assumption may prove to be a fundamental misrepresentation. On the one hand, European private international law rules are – both content-wise and technically – deeply rooted in the EU project; they do not make sense or work properly out of that context and in isolation. On the other hand, the attempt to give the conventionally agreed new rules an EU-independent meaning is doomed to fail, on the European side, each time it clashes with European objectives. At the end of the day this means that EU views must prevail, for no agreement should be given a different (and in the worst-case scenario, irreconcilable) interpretation by each of the parties thereto.

The UK's will to break free from the CJEU may be feasible on paper. However, the Court will remain competent to interpret whatever international agreement is concluded by the EU and the UK, since such agreement will be an integral part of the EU legal order. This entails that compatibility with EU law and with the EU project of integration will be the primary driver of the interpretation. Member States will be bound by the CJEU case law. To prevent jeopardising the very purpose of the planned agreement, the UK is well-advised to follow the Court too.

The burden of proof regarding the benefits of an EU-like partnership proposal lies largely with the UK. In this context it is worth recalling the remark made by former MEP Diana Wallis in May 2016: 'Don't expect this to be easy; we have exhausted everybody's patience'.[76]

[75] See Title I of Part VI of the DWA.

[76] At the BIICL, May 2016, see above fn. 15.

PART II

COOPERATION, THE ARCHITECTURE OF ENGAGEMENT

7

International Judicial Cooperation as the Architecture of Engagement

María Blanca Noodt Taquela

Introduction

The exponential expansion of cross-border movement of persons and goods and the economic integration of regional markets in recent decades have encouraged individuals and corporations to engage in cross-border legal relationships more frequently than ever before. This increase of private international law cases has in turn generated a notorious increase in the need for international judicial cooperation between states. Ascertaining the international jurisdiction and determining the applicable law are clearly not enough to provide an effective solution to private international law cases. In other words, effective practical solutions to cross-border cases require international cooperation between courts and other authorities of different countries.

This chapter explores the idea that international judicial cooperation shows the level of engagement of one state with others and with people all over the world: the breadth of international judicial cooperation of a country shows its commitment to other countries in terms of private international law. As explained in the introduction of this book, private international law reflects how a legal system understands the world around it, either individually or as a network of smaller legal systems, in the shape of a regional integration project, or as States Parties to an international treaty, or as state members of a federal system or a multi-national state. By a similar measure, to what extent a country is keen to facilitate international judicial cooperation and cooperation in administrative matters in the sphere of cross-border private relations reflects a particular vision of the world. The concept of international cooperation is therefore central not only to a private international law normative framework generally, but also to the specific operationalisation of private international law in integrated regions. Different theoretical underpinnings have been thought to sustain different frameworks of international judicial cooperation, from the open-ended concept of comity to the more robust construction of mutual trust in the European Union, to the 'sheer practical necessity' demanded by the peripatetic lives we live as citizens of the world in this day and age.

The chapter is developed using the 'architectural' conceptualisation, as follows: first, the place of international judicial cooperation in private international law is discussed; second, the use of the arbitration framework as a model to enhance international cooperation is explored; third, the importance and role of administrative cooperation is highlighted and finally the rise of networks and the possible role of non-governmental organisations (NGOs) and other private actors to facilitate international cooperation is suggested.

The Place of International Judicial Cooperation in Present Times

It is submitted that the increasing importance of international judicial cooperation places these issues at the core of the discipline in such a way that the traditional pillars of private international law as understood more broadly, that is, jurisdiction, applicable law, and recognition and enforcement of foreign judgments, could be rethought to recognise how foundational international cooperation is to the operationalisation of private international law's disciplinary goals nowadays. Instead of mentioning the recognition and enforcement of foreign judgments, it is submitted that the third issue should be widened to include international judicial cooperation considered more broadly, including recognition and enforcement of foreign judgments. Thus, this chapter is premised on the understanding that the three issues that private international law addresses are international jurisdiction, applicable law and international judicial cooperation.[1]

Recognition of foreign judgments has traditionally been understood as the third pillar of private international law, and certainly it is extremely important for the efficiency of the solutions delivered. Nevertheless it is not enough to fulfil the goals and objectives of the discipline. Private international law cases also need an effective and quick service of process and taking of evidence abroad, access to foreign law, recognition of foreign documents and particularly the enforcement of provisional measures abroad.

Provisional measures are essential for international judicial cooperation and for the efficient solving of cross-border cases. Recognition of foreign judgments becomes an almost too-late stage of cooperation if enforcement of provisional measures abroad is not allowed by international treaties or domestic rules, and more importantly admitted by case law and practice of the relevant courts. Certainly, provisional measures play a very important role in any proceeding, but when the defendant's assets are located out of the jurisdiction and the claimant must seek enforcement abroad, the existence of mechanisms that facilitate the enforcement of provisional measures abroad becomes of crucial importance.

[1] Noodt Taquela, M. B. (2016) 'Applying the Most Favourable Treaty or Domestic Rules to Facilitate Private International Law Co-operation', *Recueil des cours*, vol. 377, 121–318, at 168.

The Hague Conference on Private International Law has not yet adopted international instruments on provisional measures, but in the American hemisphere, the Inter-American Convention on Execution of Preventive Measures, signed in Montevideo on 8 May 1979, is in force in seven Latin American states.[2] There is also a regional instrument to that effect, the Protocol on Provisional Measures adopted in Ouro Preto, on 16 December 1994, that is in force in Argentina, Brazil, Paraguay and Uruguay.

International Arbitration as a Model

The New York Convention: The Framework of International Commercial Arbitration

International arbitration may be a model to follow for some issues in international judicial cooperation. I shall explain this idea in more detail: states decided to support arbitration as a private way to solve international disputes more than sixty years ago. The Convention on the Recognition and Enforcement of Foreign Arbitral Awards, concluded in New York on 10 June 1958,[3] is the architecture that allows the system of international commercial arbitration to work efficiently worldwide; the Convention is a kind of network for international arbitration, as suggested by Guillermo Argerich elsewhere.[4]

For the most part it may be argued that the application and interpretation of the Convention contributes to the main aim of private international law, that is, to provide an appropriate solution to cross-border cases, with an outcome that may be enforced almost worldwide.

The system adopted by the New York Convention has proved to be very efficient: it is based on a limited number of grounds of denial of recognition or enforcement of foreign arbitral awards. The paradigm of international arbitration since the adoption of the New York Convention is that a foreign arbitral award must be recognised and enforced in other countries and the limited grounds for refusal are the exception; the principle is that an arbitral award may circulate almost around the world.

In addition, chambers of commerce worldwide have been facilitating arbitration proceedings for decades. The International Chamber of Commerce, the organisation that brings together chambers of commerce all over the world, supports

[2] The Inter-American Convention on Execution of Preventive Measures was concluded in Montevideo on 8 May 1979 and entered into force on 14 June 1980; 7 States Parties: Argentina, Colombia, Ecuador, Guatemala, Paraguay, Peru and Uruguay, status as at 30 November 2018. Available at: http://www.oas.org

[3] The Convention on the Recognition and Enforcement of Foreign Arbitral Awards was concluded in New York on 10 June 1958 and entered into force on 7 June 1959; 159 States Parties, status as at 30 November 2018.

[4] Argerich, G. (2018) 'La Convención sobre reconocimiento y ejecución de sentencias arbitrales extranjeras. Una red de cooperación jurídica internacional', *Revista La Ley*, 30 November 2018, 1–3.

operationalising the practice of international commercial arbitration. This network may be developed further to support arbitration practice not only when the parties have chosen the rules of the International Chamber of Commerce, but also in arbitration proceedings more broadly.

Recognition and Enforcement of Foreign Judgments

This is not the case with the recognition and enforcement of foreign judgments: the party requesting the recognition must produce evidence and fulfil certain procedural requirements in order to obtain recognition; in most of the treaties and domestic rules that deal with this subject there are a number of conditions or requirements that must be satisfied by the claimant in order to obtain recognition.

Moreover, in some countries, recognition of foreign judgments depends on the existence of a bilateral or multilateral treaty on the matter, as in China, for example. As Qisheng He explained

> although the requirement of reciprocity has been an individual ground for recognizing and enforcing foreign judgments, before 2016, in judicial practice, without a bilateral treaty with China, it was hard for a foreign judgment to be recognized and enforced in the Chinese courts.[5]

Other countries require reciprocity to recognise a foreign judgment, a condition that jeopardises access to justice and thus the trend is to eliminate this requirement. Latin American countries, and Mercosur[6] countries in particular, have never required reciprocity as a condition to recognise foreign judgments.

The situation of recognition and enforcement of foreign judgments in the EU is completely different: the mutual trust principle between Member States is the basis for recognition, presently under Regulation (EU) No. 1215/2012 of the European Parliament and of the Council on Jurisdiction and the Recognition and Enforcement of Judgments in Civil and Commercial Matters, adopted at Strasbourg on 12 December 2012;[7] the Regulation replaced the Council Regulation (EC) No. 44/2001 on Jurisdiction and the Recognition and Enforcement of Judgments in Civil and Commercial Matters, adopted at Brussels on 22 December 2000.[8]

[5] He, Q. (2017), 'Dilemma and Its Way out in Judgments Reciprocity: From Sino-Japan Model to Sino-Singapore Model', in *Global Forum on Private International Law. Cooperation for Common Progress: Evolving Role of Private International Law,* 22–23 September 2017, Wuhan, China, 314–43, at 316.

[6] Mercosur is the acronym in Spanish for the South Common Market. The original Member States are Argentina, Brazil, Paraguay and Uruguay; in 2006 the Bolivarian Republic of Venezuela was incorporated but was later suspended in all the rights and obligations inherent to its status as a State Party of Mercosur; since 2015 the Plurinational State of Bolivia has been in the process of accession.

[7] Application from 10 January 2015; OJ L 351, 20.12.2012.

[8] Regulation 44/2001 entered into force on 1 March 2002; OJ L 12, 16.1.2001 and replaced the 1968 Brussels Convention between the Member States.

The Hague Conference's Approach to the Arbitration Model

The 'arbitration model' was followed by the Hague Conference (HCCH) with the adoption of the Convention on Choice of Court Agreements, signed on 30 June 2005;[9] the Explanatory Report explained that the Member States of the Working Group 'viewed the proposed Convention as achieving for such agreements and the resulting judgments what the 1958 New York Convention on the Recognition and Enforcement of Foreign Arbitral Awards accomplishes for agreements to arbitrate and the resulting awards'.[10]

The idea of the Judgments Project[11] was also to follow the 'New York Convention arbitration model' (Article 7); nevertheless the jurisdictional criteria of the Draft Judgments Convention (Article 5) put the proposed instrument quite far from this model.

The increasing presence of international judicial cooperation in private international situations, the need to provide effective judicial protection, the change of paradigm of comity and reciprocity in international judicial cooperation that upgraded to the obligation to cooperate with other states are all circumstances that make clear that recognition and enforcement of foreign judgments must be facilitated by all means.

Following this idea that foreign judgments must be recognised unless there is a ground for refusal, denial of recognition should only be permitted when the judgment is manifestly incompatible with the public policy of the requested state, or when there has been a fundamental breach of due process. According to this understanding, the jurisdictional requirements should be set aside and may not be a ground for refusal.

Uniform Interpretation and Application

The interpretation and application of the New York Convention by national courts has been decisive to the effective success of the international instrument, so any efforts made to disseminate how courts in different jurisdictions interpret and apply the New York Convention provisions is welcomed. The creation and management of databases on this Convention is the best way to generate knowledge and understanding and also to raise awareness of the many pitfalls that judges and courts face daily on the interpretation of the provisions of this Convention; thus, the work done by UNCITRAL in this sphere is of enormous importance.[12]

9 The Hague Convention on Choice of Court Agreements was adopted on 30 June 2005 and entered into force on 1 October 2015; 32 Contracting Parties, status as at 30 November 2018.

10 Hartley, T. and M. Dogauchi (2013) 'Explanatory Report on the 2005 Hague Choice of Court Agreements' 787, [27].

11 On the Judgments Project see the chapters by Polido and by Araujo in this volume.

12 Bermann, G. A. (2017) *Recognition and Enforcement of Foreign Arbitral Awards: the Interpretation and Application of the New York Convention by National Courts*, Springer; UNCITRAL (2014) *Guide on the Convention on the Recognition and Enforcement of Foreign Arbitral Awards (New York, 1958)*, available at: www.newyorkconvention1958.org. See also UNCITRAL (2012) *Digest of Case Law on the Model Law on International Commercial Arbitration*, United Nations, available at: www.uncitral.org/uncitral/en/case_law/digests/mal2012.html

The experience of facilitating access to databases is also something that can be taken from the arbitration model: international organisations may create and administer single databases on international judicial cooperation as a whole or separate bases for recognition of foreign judgments, service of process abroad, taking of evidence abroad and so on. The Organization of American States (OAS) as depositary of the Inter-American Conventions adopted in the CIDIPs – nine of which deal with international judicial cooperation – may provide access to case law on the application of the cooperation conventions.[13]

A different possibility would be for a private association – such as the American Association of Private International Law (ASADIP)[14] – to undertake the task of the management of these databases: experts from different countries in the American hemisphere could generate a repository of case law and best practices on international judicial cooperation and contribute to the databases. Some case law, in fact, has already been uploaded to the ASADIP website, but it is only from some countries and it is not completely up to date;[15] it is quite an undertaking to gather this empirical information in particular in relation to international judicial cooperation, because when petitions of recognition of foreign judgments, provisional measures or assistance are granted, usually the relevant judicial order does not get publicity. At a global level the collection and streaming of empirical data could be undertaken by the HCCH; its experience in the administration of other databases such as INCADAT could be very useful for the proper management of these databases.[16]

Increasing Role of Administrative Cooperation

A great number of cross-border conflicts are solved by administrative cooperation, more quickly and in a more satisfactory way than through judicial adjudication. The New York Convention on the Recovery Abroad of Maintenance adopted in 20 June 1956[17] is perhaps one of the oldest instruments focused on administrative cooperation. The Convention does not deal with international jurisdiction and has only one rule on applicable law (Article 6.3);[18] nevertheless, for six decades the 1956 New York Convention has played an important role in international cooperation.

The Hague Convention on Maintenance adopted in 2007[19] is another example of

[13] Available at: www.oas.org/en/sla/dil/treaties_agreements.asp

[14] ASADIP drew up the *ASADIP Principles on Transnational Access to Justice (TRANSJUS)* and has taken part as observer in the Special Commissions on the Judgments Project at the HCCH.

[15] See www.asadip.org/v2

[16] See www.incadat.com

[17] The Convention on the Recovery Abroad of Maintenance was adopted in New York on 20 June 1956 and entered into force on 25 May 1957; 64 States Parties, status as 30 November 2018.

[18] Art. 6.3 of the Convention on the Recovery Abroad of Maintenance, adopted in New York in 1956, is not very frequently applied, due to the existence of other instruments that deal with applicable law to maintenance obligations, in particular the Hague Conventions of 1956 and 1973.

[19] The Hague Convention on the International Recovery of Child Support and Other Forms of Family

the increasing importance of administrative cooperation. The Convention is focused on administrative cooperation, while the issue of applicable law is only ruled in the Protocol[20] adopted jointly with the Convention.

Central Authorities play an important role and are main players in international cooperation, because they constitute specialised bodies, in many cases including staff who are fluent in several languages; they may work in a more informal way than courts, they establish direct communication with the Central Authorities of other countries and they are empowered to facilitate mediation and conciliation agreements between the parties. All this work constitutes administrative cooperation carried out to facilitate international cooperation.

In addition to the administrative cooperation that Central Authorities and other bodies already participate in, other administrative authorities recognise judgments and documents that do not require to be enforced; that is the case of divorce, filiation, adoption, surrogacy and other judgments and documents related to the civil status of individuals.

Other situations may be facilitated through administrative cooperation, for example when an individual must show evidence of his or her civil status in order to be granted a state pension or other social security benefits.

We must also bear in mind the importance of administrative recognition of foreign documents in relation to migrants. The enormous problems that migrants face may be partially alleviated through expeditious recognition of their documents, and consequently their civil status. In this sphere the important work developed by the International Commission on Civil Status – best known by its French name, Commission Internationale de l'État Civil (CIEC) – should be noted. This is an international intergovernmental organisation, founded in 1948, whose aim is 'to facilitate international cooperation in civil-status matters and to further the exchange of information between civil registrars'. To this end, the Commission has drawn up thirty-four Conventions, twenty-eight of which are currently in force, and eleven Recommendations; unfortunately only European countries are party to these Conventions which might be very useful worldwide.[21]

Rise of Networks and Possible Role for NGOs and Other Private Actors to Facilitate International Cooperation

Rise of Networks and the Existing Instruments of International Cooperation

The rise of networks in the late decades of the twentieth century is evident; the internet may be the most famous of them but it is, of course, not the only one. The

Maintenance was concluded on 23 November 2007 and entered into force on 1 January 2013; 39 States Parties, status as at 15 October 2018.

[20] The Protocol on the Law Applicable to Maintenance Obligations was adopted in The Hague on 23 November 2007 and entered into force on 1 August 2013; 30 States Parties, status as at 15 October 2018.

[21] The Conventions and their respective statuses are available at: http://www.ciec1.org

opportunities it provides to enhance communication all over the world in real time is remarkable; law in general, and private international law in particular, should do all they can to derive the greatest benefits from these technological resources. In the day-to-day practice of courts, it may in some countries (including European ones) take several months – sometimes even more than a year – to fulfil the transmission of judicial documents for service of process.[22] It is difficult to justify why some countries continue to ask for the issue of a letter rogatory for service or taking of evidence abroad. This requirement is sometimes established by domestic rules,[23] and in other cases by reservations made to international treaties on this matter.

For example, the Hague Convention on the Service Abroad of Judicial and Extrajudicial Documents in Civil or Commercial Matters, concluded on 15 November 1965,[24] allows transmission of judicial or extrajudicial documents for service abroad through Central Authorities, and by other means of transmission, provided that the state of destination does not object to them. Thus, Article 10, paragraph (a) of the 1965 Hague Convention permits the sending of judicial documents by post directly to the relevant person(s) abroad. Taking into account that the Service Convention was adopted more than five decades ago, we understand that a considerable number of countries, in fact almost half of the Contracting States, have declared their opposition to the transmission by postal channels according to Article 10, paragraph (a) and Article 21, second paragraph, (a); several countries are also opposed to service done through diplomatic or consular agents, according to Article 8. Yet nowadays, in our view, these reservations jeopardise international cooperation; they go against the underlying rationale of international cooperation in the age of interconnectivity. It would take as little as withdrawing these reservations that were made in a context very different from today's reality. In this sense, it is interesting to follow the 'post-ratification' work of the Hague Conference through its Special Commissions on the practical operation of the different Conventions; for example, Switzerland answered the questionnaire of July 2008 relating to the 1965 Hague Convention considering that it was a criminal offence to execute acts in Swiss territory without the authorisation of Swiss authorities.[25] Conversely, the Special Commissions of the Hague Conference understand that requests for service transmitted under the main channel of transmission (the Central Authority) may be executed by electronic means under Article 5. In addition, the Special Commissions

[22] According to the Hague Conference on Private International Law, 'statistical data shows that 66% of requests are executed within 2 months', *Outline of the Convention.* Available at: www.hcch.net

[23] This is the case with Argentina under Article 2612 of the Civil and Commercial Code enacted in 2014, among other countries.

[24] The Hague Convention on the Service Abroad of Judicial and Extrajudicial Documents in Civil or Commercial Matters was concluded on 15 November 1965 and entered into force on 10 February 1969; 74 States Parties, status as at 30 November 2018.

[25] Hague Conference on Private International Law, *Answers to the Questionnaire of July 2008 Relating to the Hague Convention of 15 November 1965 on the Service Abroad of Judicial and Extrajudicial Documents in Civil or Commercial Matters*: Response 41 of Switzerland.

also encourage the use of information technology under the alternative channels of Article 10.[26]

Role of Non-governmental Organisations and Other Private Actors

Why do we not take advantage of public and private networks to make international cooperation easier and quicker? Several networks come to mind – although they are not necessarily recognised as facilitating international judicial cooperation – such as the International Bar Association and the International Union of Notaries, both of which have an excellent network of lawyers or notaries public through national associations. The International Bar Association, established in 1947, is an international organisation of legal practitioners, bar associations and law societies that has more than 190 members spanning over 170 countries.[27] Another NGO is the International Union of Notaries; established in 1948 it includes eighty-eight countries and is based in Rome. It has close links with the Permanent Notarial Office of International Exchange (ONPI), based in Buenos Aires, whose fundamental mission is to provide information to notaries and other persons working for or with the International Union of Notaries.[28]

Private actors may be very helpful in facilitating international judicial cooperation, and their participation in this sphere, as in many others, does not threaten national sovereignty. Lawyers may collaborate further in the operationalisation of international judicial cooperation, and civil law countries may consider following some common law practices in relation to the responsibilities that lawyers undertake. Notaries public may also play an important role in international judicial cooperation; they may participate in the service of process, the taking of evidence and other forms of international judicial cooperation.

Service of process by private means may be transmitted through bar associations very quickly. Even if service of process must be done by a letter rogatory, if courts issue a digital letter rogatory it could be transmitted either by Central Authorities or by bar associations, and transmission from one country to another should not take more than a day or two. Even more expeditious may be other encrypted means available through the internet. There are concerns regarding issues of confidentiality and legal certainty that it may not be so straightforward to provide for, but technological advances have made it possible to work much more expeditiously than is currently possible in a great number of legal systems.

We suggest that the International Bar Association, the International Union of Notaries and similar associations operate as private networks that not only contribute to facilitating international judicial cooperation, but also continue to lobby to get

[26] Hague Conference on Private International Law, *Conclusions and Recommendations of the Special Commission on the Practical Operation of the Hague Service, Evidence and Access to Justice Conventions, 20–3 May 2014*, para. 37.

[27] See www.ibanet.org/barassociations/bar_associations_home.aspx

[28] See www.uinl.org/onpi

the necessary financial support to the judiciary with a view to making the most of developments in IT in this context. These associations have strong control over their members' activities, which may be a safeguard for good practice for the professionals involved in the transmission.

IberRed and other Regional Networks

The establishment of regional networks based on common heritage and common cultural roots is a possible way of encouraging direct communication not only between judges but also between administrative authorities. Such is the case with IberRed, created by the Member States of the Ibero-American Community of Nations.[29]

This network operates in the two mother tongues of its member states – Spanish and Portuguese – for judicial cooperation in civil and criminal matters. The IberRed network will be used, among other things, to resolve difficulties in processing letters rogatory, the request of information, documentation and formalities, and the coordination of special procedures or proceedings in advance, allowing the use of available technological means and facilitation for ongoing international investigations and coordination of joint actions.[30]

Conclusions

For more than a century international judicial cooperation has appeared as the architecture of the engagement between states in relation to tackling solutions for the management of private cross-border relations. The role of international judicial cooperation is ever increasing but what may make this architecture more robust in present times is the further inclusion of administrative organisations and private individuals, including NGOs in the operationalisation of international cooperation.

While states adopt international treaties and domestic laws on international judicial cooperation that provide the legal framework of the subject, administrative entities, NGOs and other private actors may facilitate international cooperation, in a similar way as chambers of commerce do in relation to international commercial arbitration.

Service of process, for example, may be completed quickly if the mechanism is provided for private organisations to contribute to the task; the linkages between the

[29] The Ministries of Justice, representatives of the Public Prosecutor's Offices or State Prosecuting Offices and the Courts of the Member Countries of the Ibero-American Community of Nations created IberRed: the Ibero-American Network for Judicial Co-operation in Civil and Criminal Matters for the twenty-two Member States of the Ibero-American Community of Nations: Andorra, Argentina, Bolivia, Brazil, Chile, Colombia, Costa Rica, Cuba, Dominican Republic, Ecuador, El Salvador, Guatemala, Honduras, Mexico, Nicaragua, Panama, Paraguay, Peru, Portugal, Spain, Uruguay and Venezuela and Puerto Rico as an organised and unincorporated territory of the USA. The website is available at: www.iberred.org

[30] See Pérez Manrique, R. (2009) 'The Hague Network and IberRed in Latin America', in *The Judges' Newsletter on International Child Protection*, vol. XV Special Focus, Theme 2; available at: www.hcch.net/upload/newsletter/JN15_Perez_Manrique.pdf

NGOs of one country and another may be immediate if technological means are used. The taking of evidence may be facilitated and made less onerous for the parties if private actors help to gather information and other pieces of evidence. Lawyers must present evidence, in particular documents and information, directly to the arbitral tribunal; it is not necessary that the arbitral tribunal issues a procedural order to allow parties to take evidence. This model that applies in international arbitration may be also useful in international litigation.

All in all, as discussed further in the next chapter, by David McClean, the move is towards informality, and bearing in mind that the focus should be on the individuals and their needs in cross-border cases, no efforts should be spared to make the most of ICT developments and other technological advances to enhance international cooperation in this sphere.

8

Judicial Cooperation: Resolving the Differing Approaches

David McClean

Introduction

A subtitle for this chapter might well be 'From formality to informality'. It is concerned with the way in which judicial cooperation, notably in the fields of service of documents and the taking of evidence abroad, has developed over the last century, with a discernible movement from a formal approach to one that allows much more rapid processing of matters. There are several different strands in this development. Some are not at all legal in origin but reflect scientific and social changes. The civil procedure conventions agreed at the end of the nineteenth and the beginning of the twentieth century, for example those negotiated at the Hague Conference (HCCH) in 1896 and 1905, antedate not only the telephone as an easy method of international communication but also such developments as fax and email. Video conferencing may come to have a major effect on the taking of evidence abroad.[1] Social exchanges have become progressively less formal and this has come to influence even such conservative bodies as the courts. In England, for example, robes and wigs (once essential features of the higher courts) are increasingly dispensed with, and legal terms derived from Latin or Norman French are being expelled from the legal lexicon. But it would have been inconceivable to the authors of the 1896 Hague Convention that technological progress and a greatly relaxed approach to protocol

[1] A Special Commission of Hague Conference in 2009 made a series of recommendations showing how video technology could assist the working of the Convention: Conclusions and Recommendations, paras 55–7. Cf. Davies, M. (2007) 'By-Passing the Hague Evidence Convention' 55 *Am. J. Comp. L.* 205. See *Asic* v. *Rich* [2004] NSWSC 467, with a full review of (mainly Australian) case law noting some practical issues including the difficulty created by differences in time zones, the assessment of credit where evidence is given by audiovisual link and difficulties raised by the use of documents for cross-examination in audiovisual evidence; and *Nichia Corporation* v. *Arrow Electronics Australia Pty Ltd (No 3)* [2016] FCA 466.

would allow the relevant officials in different states actually to speak directly one to the other.

A relatively early example is the movement away from modes of communication between states such as the diplomatic channel, a notoriously slow process but one of what was seen as of appropriate formality and dignity. That was the preferred channel in the Hague Convention of 1896, but it was replaced in that of 1905 by the 'indirect consular channel', communication between a consul of the state of origin and an authority designated for the purpose by the state of destination. In the most recent international instruments, whether they be Hague Conventions or European Union Regulations, the involvement of foreign ministries is largely no more, and simpler and more direct means of communication are preferred.

Accompanying that development has been the adoption of procedures that are operated by specialist personnel for whom cross-border litigation becomes a principal concern, so that they acquire expertise in the workings of the relevant international instruments.

Differing Legal Approaches: Service

Part of the story, however, concerns the different approaches of the common law and civil law traditions. Just over a century ago, in 1918, the United Kingdom Government established a Committee on British and Foreign Legal Procedure. It examined the then state of international arrangements for judicial cooperation in the service of process and the taking of evidence, especially the Civil Procedure Convention agreed at the HCCH in 1905.[2] The Convention did not find favour: its service provisions were too much concerned with the use of official channels; less formal methods were seen as much more desirable, and it was recommended that the UK should work to promote that informality, initially through bilateral negotiations.[3]

In microcosm, that reveals a fundamental difference of approach as between the common law tradition and that found in mainland Europe and South America. Reducing the discussion to two broad traditions may be justified as a necessary convenience, but it does of course obscure many local variations. Ironically, the common law tradition, first developed in the courts of England, has given way in the matters to be examined in this chapter to EU Regulations. To that extent the common law no longer prevails in England or in Cyprus, Ireland and Malta; but it remains the basis of the legal systems of most Commonwealth countries. The roots of United States practice lie in common law soil, but the resulting plant has developed in ways very different from those found elsewhere.

There would be universal agreement that the administration of justice is an

[2] Convention on Civil Procedure, concluded in The Hague on 17 July 1905; 22 States Parties. It was replaced by the Convention of 1 March 1954 on Civil Procedure, available at: www.hcch.net/en/instruments/the-old-conventions

[3] Report, Cmd 251, paras 43–4.

important function of the state. If one looks behind that agreement, differences soon emerge. In the common law tradition, the conduct of litigation is essentially a matter for the parties; a common lawyer would find that a statement of the obvious, hardly worth saying. Its implications do, however, need to be noted. In common law jurisdictions, the responsibility for the service of process, the documents initiating legal proceedings,[4] rests with the claimant[5] or the agents (solicitors, process-servers) acting for the claimant. Service is a quite informal affair: under the English Civil Procedure Rules, for example, 'a document is served personally on (a) an individual by leaving it with that individual; (b) a company or other corporation by leaving it with a person holding a senior position within the company or corporation'.[6] The document will usually have been issued by a court office, but that does not entail any active involvement; service is not in any sense a judicial function.

In modern English practice, personal service has been largely supplanted by the use of the post or electronic means of communication, and service of English claim forms within England is now usually effected by the court office. The traditional approach is reflected in the rule that the claimant can always insist on serving the document rather than having the court office act.[7] It continues to be the case that there is nothing in a common law jurisdiction that reflects the distinctions drawn in many civil law systems between 'formal' and 'informal' service, or between service 'accepted voluntarily' and 'enforced' service.

In many civil law systems, on the other hand, service is regarded as a formal, official act, closely regulated by legislation. There may be less formal methods but they are used principally in the case of documents originating from abroad.[8] It will be appreciated that when the 1918 report in Britain called for 'informal' methods of service, it was using 'informal' to mean the direct action by the parties or their agent, as opposed to the use of official channels of any sort.

This common law approach is all the more surprising to those from other legal traditions when the significance of service in the common law is appreciated. It may seem to undermine the statement that service is not a judicial function. In the common law tradition, service of process has two purposes: it notifies the defendant of the claim and it also – and this is the bewildering bit – gives the court jurisdiction. The court has jurisdiction if, and only if, the defendant is served with process whether that be within the country in which the court sits or outside it.[9] In some cases, the leave

[4] Usually 'the writ', though now in England this is 'the claim form'.

[5] Or plaintiff, petitioner, etc.

[6] CPR, r 6.5(3)(a)(b).

[7] CPR, r 6.4(1)(b).

[8] The Hague Convention on the Service Abroad of Judicial and Extrajudicial Documents in Civil or Commercial Matters was concluded on 15 November 1965 and entered into force 10 February 1969; 74 States Parties, status as at 30 November 2018: see Art. 5, referring to this informal method as 'delivery to an addressee who accepts it voluntarily'.

[9] See Lord Collins of Mapesbury and J. Harris (eds) (2012) *Dicey, Morris & Collins on the Conflict of Laws*, 15th edn, Sweet and Maxwell, Rule 29, 371. See *Abela* v. *Baadarani* [2013] UKSC 44;

of the court is required before there can be service in another country: the court will exercise a discretion, aware that it may be trespassing on the jurisdiction of a foreign court.[10] This is decision about jurisdiction, and the common law rules as to jurisdiction have an element of discretion alien to civil law practice. If the court grants leave, and in the many cases in which leave is not required, the relevant document is served and the practical steps are matters for the claimant.

Differing Legal Approaches: Evidence

The differences between the common law and civil law traditions are sharper in the context of evidence. Gathering evidence is seen by those in the civil law tradition as essentially a judicial function. A civilian may be surprised to read this authoritative statement of the common law approach:

> Under the civil procedure of the [English] High Court the court does not, in general, exercise any control over the manner in which a party obtains the evidence which he needs to support his case. The court may give him help, certainly; for instance by discovery of documents *inter partes* . . .; by allowing evidence to be obtained or presented at the trial in various ways . . .; and by the issue of subpoenas . . . Subject, however, to the help of the court in these various ways, the basic principle underlying the preparation and presentation of a party's case in the High Court in England is that it is for that party to obtain and present the evidence which he needs by his own means, provided always that such means are lawful in the country in which they are used.[11]

As between states in the civil law tradition, the taking of evidence abroad traditionally required the prior permission of the authorities of the state in which action was to be taken. This involved a formal request, initiated by a court or some related official, formerly transmitted via the diplomatic channel, and ultimately considered by a court or other authority in the state of destination. The document which set out what was required was referred to as a 'letter (or letters) of request' or 'letter rogatory'.[12] As in common law states the service of process and the gathering of evidence was essentially for the parties, this procedure was relatively little known in such states.

Reasons for Late Resolution of these Differences

Given that international trade has existed for many centuries, one may wonder why these examples of legal diversity, this contrast between common law and civil law

[2013] 1 WLR 2043 and the critical note by Dickinson, A. (2014) 'Service Abroad – An Inconvenient Obstacle?' 130 *LQR* 197.

10 Ibid., Rule 34, 428ff. The defendant, once served, may apply for a stay of proceedings under the doctrine of *forum non conveniens*, in effect requiring the court to exercise its discretion afresh: see ibid., Rule 38, 533ff.

11 *South Carolina Insurance Co* v. *Assurantie Maatschappij 'De Zeven Provincien' NV* [1987] AC 24 (HL), 41–2.

12 The latter term is prevalent in United States usage.

approaches, was not resolved long ago. The answer may lie in political geography. When the English courts began to have dealings with their counterparts in other countries, the other country was often one in the common law tradition, indeed often a British possession, so exposure to different practices was limited. The same could be said of countries in mainland Europe with their colonial empires and with trading links with neighbouring states, all in the civil law tradition. There was a lasting blindness to legal diversity, and assumption (still, it has to be said, evident in some courts in the United States) that other countries did, and certainly should, follow the familiar practices known to the judge.

The very term 'judicial cooperation' identifies the judge as a key player.[13] That may obscure the fact that the role of the judge is itself seen in different ways, reflecting the manner in which judges are appointed. In England, a judge will almost always be appointed after many years of work as a barrister (or occasionally as a solicitor or legal academic); judges are treated with great respect and decisions are seldom appealed. In some other states work as a judge may be one part of a legal career begun at a young age; in some jurisdictions, cases are very commonly taken to a second instance. The common law tradition is more inclined to recognise the role of the judge in developing the law; in many contexts, he or she is allowed a broad discretion. The civil law experience favours detailed regulation, and so more formal procedures.

More generally, it is certainly the case that many matters which in the UK would seem best dealt with by 'soft law', by guidance, circulars or notices issued by the appropriate Government department or agency, would in mainland Europe (and in the EU) be spelt out in detailed legislation.

Service: Party-based Approaches in the Hague Conventions

An important issue is the extent to which the informal, party-based approach of the common law has a place in international agreements.

Even the earlier Hague Conventions dealing with the service of documents, conventions in the negotiation of which common law countries played no part, mentioned service by post. The 1896 Convention allowed service by post, but only so far as the laws of the concerned states or conventions entered into between them allowed.[14] In the 1905 text, service by post was mentioned, but it could only be used where it was permitted under a bilateral convention, or, in the absence of a convention, if the state of destination did not object.[15]

It has already been mentioned that the view in the UK was that the 1905 Convention was unsatisfactory. The UK was anxious to ensure that its informal approach to service was accepted in civil law countries, even where the foreign

[13] In relation to the role of judges in international judicial cooperation see in particular the chapter by Goicoechea and van Loon in this volume.

[14] Convention on Civil Procedure signed in The Hague on 14 November 1896, Art. 6. It was replaced by the Convention on Civil Procedure of 1905.

[15] Convention on Civil Procedure of 1905, Art. 6, status fn. 2.

state did not use informal methods in its own practice. It took this policy forward by negotiating twenty-two bilateral conventions in the years from 1928 to 1936. In nineteen of these conventions, service by post was allowed; in sixteen service by an agent appointed by the claimant (though in some cases with restrictions, for example only on nationals of the state of origin).[16]

The most recent Hague Convention is that of 15 November 1965 on the Service Abroad of Judicial and Extrajudicial Documents in Civil or Commercial Matters.[17] The Convention is a detailed one, with prescribed forms, and quite elaborate rules as to translations. It introduced a new and tailor-made system for communication from the state of origin to the state of service, using designated Central Authorities, typically located in the Ministry of Justice.[18]

The success of the Convention is due in large part to the Central Authorities system. Those Authorities acquire expertise, becoming aware of common mistakes made in the Convention process, so that they (or at least some of them) will respond to a defective request not by rejecting it but by using informal means of communication to have the mistake corrected. Many States Parties use their Central Authority to transmit documents as well as to fulfil the Convention obligation to receive them and arrange for their service.[19] The use of a Central Authority as a transmitting agency does add a degree of complication, but this is outweighed by the likelihood that the Authority will complete the request accurately, and by the ability of pairs of Authorities dealing with a particular case to speak to, or email, one another to resolve any problems. The regular Special Commissions of the Hague Conference to review the workings of this, and the Evidence, Convention serve not only to promote the Convention and encourage other states to accede, but provide a valuable meeting point for the officials who operate the various Central Authorities.

Someone else, however, has to initiate the request in the state of origin, and here the differing approaches remain relevant. Many countries in the civil law tradition insist that an outgoing request must emanate directly from a court (and tend to resist the use of the Central Authority as a transmitting agency, for this would be to use an administrative agency to oversee a judicial function). The Convention provides that the request is initiated by an 'authority or judicial officer competent under the law of the state in which the documents originate'.[20] In some countries, including Ireland and Canada, and in some US states, lawyers acting for the claimant are within this category.

The Convention allows the use of the post, speaking of 'the freedom to send judicial documents, by postal channels, directly to persons abroad',[21] but makes

[16] For a full list see McClean, D. (2012) *International Co-operation in Civil and Commercial Matters*, 3rd edn, Oxford University Press, 16.

[17] The Convention has 74 States Parties, status as at 30 November 2018.

[18] Convention, Arts 8 and 9.

[19] Convention, Arts 2–6.

[20] Convention, Art. 3(1).

[21] Convention, Art. 10(a).

it clear that this is subject to any objection by the state of destination.[22] Some Contracting States have indicated their objection, including, disappointingly, some (Belgium, Germany, Greece, Hungary and Poland) that had agreed to permit the use of the post in their bilateral conventions with the UK. Some US courts have reached the extraordinary decision that the Convention does not in fact allow service via the postal channel, as Article 10(a) uses the word 'send' rather than 'serve'.[23]

Subject to any objection by the state of destination, 'any person interested in a judicial proceeding' may effect service directly through the judicial officers, officials or other competent persons of the state of destination.[24] In the UK, this is limited to a direct approach to the Central Authority; but that does not preclude any person in another Contracting State who is interested in a judicial proceeding (including that person's lawyer) from effecting service in the UK 'directly' through a competent person other than a judicial officer or official, for example a solicitor.[25]

Mention has already been made of the tendency of some jurisdictions to cling to their own practices and to minimise the effect of international conventions. Although in the context of service US practice is seen as a prime example,[26] the broader issue can arise in many jurisdictions whenever the defendant is a corporation or some other form of association. In many countries, service can be effected on a foreign corporation or business association at its place of business or registered address;[27] if there is no 'occasion to transmit a . . . document for service abroad', then the Convention does not apply.

The matter has been repeatedly discussed at Special Commissions of the Hague Conference held to review the operation of the Convention, and the meetings in 2003 and 2009 both accepted that the Convention had 'a non-mandatory but exclusive character'. More fully,

> [t]he language [of Art. 1] 'where there is occasion to transmit' is understood as meaning that the Service Convention is non-mandatory in the sense that it is a matter for the *lex fori* to determine whether a document must be transmitted for service abroad. The use of the word 'shall' is understood as meaning that the Service Convention is exclusive, in the sense that once the law of the forum has determined that a document must be transmitted abroad for service, the channels of transmission

22 Convention, Arts 10 and 21(2)(a).

23 For example *Bankston* v. *Toyota Motor Corpn* 889 F 2d. 172 (8th Cir, 1989); but see to the contrary *Ackermann* v. *Levine* 788 F 2d 830 (2nd Cir, 1986); *Nuovo Pignone* v. *Storman Asia M/V* 310 F 3d 374 (5th Cir, 2002); *Brockmeyer* v. *May* 383 F 3d 798 (9th Cir, 2004).

24 Convention, Arts 10(c), 21(2)(a).

25 The Irish declaration objecting to the mode of service under Art. 10(c) expressly saves service via a solicitor in Ireland.

26 See *Volksvagenwerk AG* v. *Schlunk* 486 US 694 (1988) (subsidiary company agent by operation of law of a foreign parent company).

27 In England rules to this effect are to be found both in the Civil Procedure Rules and the Companies Act 2006.

expressly available or otherwise permitted under the Hague Service Convention are the *only* channels that may be used.[28]

Service: Party-based Approaches in the EU Instruments

Within the EU, the service in the Member States of judicial and extrajudicial documents in civil or commercial matters is governed by Regulation 1393/2007[29] which came into force on 13 November 2008. The Regulation builds on the experience gained in the operation of the Hague Service Convention, but whereas the Hague text enshrines a preference for communication between Central Authorities, the policy of the Regulation is that 'efficiency and speed in judicial procedures in civil matters means that the transmission of judicial and extrajudicial documents is to be made direct and by rapid means between local bodies designated by the Member States'.[30]

Although the Regulation provides for the appointment of a 'central body' in each Member State, this will only exceptionally be involved in the actual processes of service. The operational agencies are the transmitting and receiving agencies designated under the Regulation. They are specified 'public officers, authorities or other persons' competent either to transmit or receive documents, or to carry out both functions.[31] In most Member States, the transmitting and receiving agencies are the local courts. For example, in Italy well over 100 local *tribunali* or *corti d'appello* are designated as transmitting agencies but only an office in the Rome Court of Appeal as a receiving agency. *Huissiers de justice* or the equivalent act in Belgium, France, Luxembourg and the Netherlands.

Although the possibility under the Regulation of direct transmission from local court to local court may seem the ultimate decentralisation, there is a price to be paid. Individual local courts, perhaps with limited numbers of cross-border cases, may lack the expertise that the Hague Central Authorities have built up; and may be reluctant to use informal methods of communication to resolve the difficulties that inevitably occur from time to time.

Although transmission via the transmitting and receiving agencies is the preferred method, the Regulation also allows use of the post. A Member State may not refuse to allow the use of the postal channel but may specify 'the conditions under which' it will accept service of judicial documents by post by registered letter with acknowledgment of receipt or equivalent.[32] In language following that of the Hague Convention, the Regulation also preserves the freedom of any person interested in

28 Preliminary Document 10 for the Special Commission of 2009, para. 6.

29 European Parliament and Council Regulation (EC) No. 1393/2007 of 13 November 2007 on the service in the Member States of judicial and extrajudicial documents in civil and commercial matters (service of documents) and repealing Council Regulation (EC) 1348/2000, [2007] OJ L324/79. This replaced the earlier Regulation 1348/2000, [2000] OJ L160/37.

30 Regulation 1393/2007, Recital (6).

31 Regulation 1393/2007, Art. 2(1)(2)(3).

32 Regulation 1393/2007, Art. 14.

a judicial proceeding to effect service of judicial documents directly through the judicial officers, officials or other competent persons of the Member State addressed, where such direct service is permitted under the law of that Member State.[33]

It will be seen from this brief account of the Hague Convention and the EU Regulation that the use of informal methods of service has a place in both texts. Service by post is guaranteed a place under the EU Regulation, subject to prescribed conditions; both texts allow for 'direct service'.

Evidence: Work at The Hague Conference

Work under the auspices of the Hague Conference on the taking of evidence abroad followed a similar course to that in the context of service of documents. Provisions as to the taking of evidence abroad were included in the Civil Procedure Conventions of 1896, 1905 and 1954; they were all primarily concerned with the use of letters rogatory. The 1896 Convention specified the use of the diplomatic channel as the primary route; in the 1905 text, the primary or preferred mode of transmission was the indirect consular channel, from the consul of the requesting state to an authority designated for the purpose by the state addressed.

The Hague Convention on the Taking of Evidence Abroad in Civil or Commercial Matters was signed on 18 March 1970.[34] It contains a detailed code on the use of Letters of Request and other means of securing evidence.

As in the Service Convention, each Contracting State must establish a Central Authority to receive Letters of Request,[35] and there is freedom to designate additional 'other authorities' or, in the case of federal states, more than one Central Authority. It is customary for the same body to be designated as the Central Authority for other Hague Conventions dealing with civil procedure, notably that on service. To ensure the simplicity of the system, it is expressly provided in Article 2 that no intervening agency in the requested state is to deal with the Letter of Request on its way to the Central Authority.

The Convention prescribes in detail the contents of Letters of Request,[36] the language to be used,[37] defines the narrow circumstances in which execution may be refused[38] and contains provisions under which a Contracting State may declare that 'judicial personnel of the requesting authority' are allowed to be present at the execution of the letter.[39]

[33] Regulation 1393/2007, Art. 14.

[34] The Hague Convention on the Taking of Evidence Abroad in Civil or Commercial Matters was concluded on 18 March 1970 and entered into force on 7 October 1972; 61 States Parties, status as at 30 November 2018.

[35] Convention, Art. 2.

[36] Convention, Art. 3.

[37] Convention, Art. 4.

[38] Convention, Art. 12.

[39] Convention, Art. 8.

The judicial authority executing the request applies its own laws and procedures, save where a request is made to follow a special method or procedure, which is not incompatible with the law of the state of execution or impossible of performance by reason of its internal practice and procedure or by reason of other practical difficulties.[40] Some requesting states may only accept evidence taken in a particular way and the Convention tries to ensure that a request for a special procedure (for example, for verbatim transcripts or, on the other hand, for a summary of the evidence in deposition form; or for videotaped evidence) will not be refused merely because it is inconvenient to the requested state. 'Incompatible with' internal law does not mean simply 'different from' such law, but that there must be some constitutional or statutory prohibition. It is, of course, for the requested state to determine whether the special method is impractical or impossible of performance.

It is for the court in which the legal proceedings are taking place to decide whether evidence is to be taken abroad. From the common law perspective, evidence before a commissioner from the requesting state can be very convenient. The Commissioner can carry out the special method or procedure requested, for example to overcome the difficulty which a civil law state may have in satisfying a request from a common law state to take evidence under cross-examination, because no judge or local lawyer in the requested state had any experience in that field.

The drafting of the Convention brought out interesting differences between the common law and civil law countries as to the degree of acceptability of consuls and commissioners. In a common law country, the preparation of a case for trial is the private responsibility of the parties, and so the taking of evidence, without compulsion, by a consul or a commissioner does not necessarily offend such a country's concept of judicial sovereignty. So, to cite a summary prepared as part of the preliminary work leading up to the Convention:

> There is no legal objection to the taking of evidence in England for use outside the jurisdiction without the intervention of the English court. Evidence can be freely taken by agents acting on behalf of foreign litigants; but no compulsory processes may be used, nor may the evidence be taken on oath. A foreign court is at liberty to appoint a consul in England of its own country, or any other person it desires as an examiner to take evidence. So long as the witnesses are willing to attend to give evidence the examination may be completed and the result returned to the foreign court without the intervention of the court in England. The administration of an oath in England without lawful authority is an offence, but a person appointed by order of a foreign court or other judicial authority has the necessary authority by virtue of section 1 of the Oaths and Evidence (Overseas Authorities and Countries) Act 1963, for use in civil proceedings carried on under the law of that country, and a consul may administer an oath under certain other statutory provisions.

[40] Convention, Art. 9.

The position may be very different where, as in many civil law countries, the obtaining of evidence is part of the judicial function, and official permission is required before the evidence can be taken privately. The Convention, partly drawing on UK bilateral conventions, sought to harmonise these different concepts by providing a procedural device acceptable to all systems. In so doing, it achieved a successful bridge between the two systems.

Civil law countries take a much stricter line on the permissibility of such actions in their jurisdiction by the agents of foreign courts. For this reason the whole of Chapter II of the Convention, while providing much fuller and clearer guidance than the earlier 1954 text, is subject to optional clauses and rights of reservation. Indeed the whole Chapter may be excluded by a reservation under Article 33 and several countries have taken this course.

The Convention provides first that a diplomatic officer and consular agent may take evidence without compulsion in civil or commercial matters from nationals of the accrediting state in aid of proceedings commenced in the courts of the state represented.[41] However, even the exercise of this right may, by the declaration of the Contacting State in which the evidence is to be taken, be made subject to the permission of the appropriate authority designated by that state.[42] In contrast, Article 16 provides that a diplomatic officer or consular agent may only take evidence, without compulsion, of nationals of the state in which he or she exercises his or her functions, or of third states, if a competent authority in the requested state has given its permission, either generally or in the particular case, and subject to any conditions imposed. A state may, however, by declaration dispense with the need for such permission.[43] Many states have made such declarations, albeit subject to a variety of conditions, mainly requiring the requested state to be informed about, or to be present at, the taking of the evidence.

A state may declare that a diplomatic officer, consular agent or commissioner may apply to the designated competent authority for 'appropriate' assistance to obtain evidence by compulsion.[44] The declaration may impose conditions. The measures of compulsion will be those prescribed by law for use in internal proceedings.[45]

As has already been noted, the development of the common law in the US has not followed that found in England and more generally in the Commonwealth. The very extensive pre-trial discovery practices in the US have led to complex litigation within that country, focusing on the mandatory or optional character of the Convention[46]

[41] Convention, Art. 15(1).
[42] Convention, Art. 15(2).
[43] Convention, Art. 16(2).
[44] Convention, Art. 18.
[45] Convention, Art. 18(2).
[46] See *Société Nationale Industrielle Aérospatiale* v. *US District Court for the Southern District of Iowa* 482 US 522 (1987). See, generally, Black, S. F. (1991) 'United States Transnational Discovery: The Rise and Fall of the Hague Evidence Convention' 40 *ICLQ* 901.

and to opposition from other states to the use of the extensive powers asserted by US courts in cross-border cases.

Evidence: The EU Regulation

In 2001, the EU adopted a Council Regulation on cooperation between the courts of the Member States in the taking of evidence in civil or commercial matters.[47] The Regulation builds on the Hague Convention of 1970, a major difference being that the Regulation provides for the direct transmission of requests from court to court, dispensing with the Central Authorities which are such an important feature of the Hague Convention, though preserving a limited role for what are termed 'central bodies', responsible for (1) supplying information to the courts; (2) seeking solutions to any difficulties which may arise in respect of a request; and (3) forwarding, 'in exceptional cases', at the request of a requesting court, a request to the competent court.[48] One type of request may be routed through a central body: this is a request for the direct taking of evidence by the requesting court under Article 17, considered further below.

Requests are to be transmitted by the court before which the proceedings are commenced or contemplated, 'the requesting court', directly to the competent court of another Member State, 'the requested court', for the performance of the taking of evidence.[49] For this procedure to be effective, information must be available as to the competent courts in each Member State: which court, for example, has jurisdiction in respect of commercial matters in, say, Barcelona? To make this possible, each Member State must draw up a list of the courts competent for the performance of taking of evidence under the Regulation, indicating the territorial and, where appropriate, the special jurisdiction of those courts.[50]

Requests are not normally routed via any central agency in the requested state, but are to be transmitted by the swiftest possible means which the requested state has indicated it can accept: in many cases this will include electronic means. The only essential is that the document received accurately reflects the content of the document forwarded and that all information in it is legible.[51]

The Regulation makes an advance on the Hague text by including developed provisions as to the taking by the requesting court of evidence on the territory of another Member State.[52] In this type of case, the request is submitted to the designated central body of the requested state. The direct taking of evidence may only take place if it can

[47] Council Regulation (EC) No. 1206/2001 of 28 May 2001, [2001] OJ L174/1. Available at: https://publications.europa.eu

[48] Regulation, Art. 3(1).

[49] Regulation, Art. 2(1).

[50] Regulation, Art. 2(2). The information is available on the website of the European Judicial Network: http://eurojust.europa.eu; see Arts 19, 22.

[51] Regulation, Art. 6.

[52] Little used in practice: see the Commission's 2007 report, para. 2.7.

be performed on a voluntary basis without the need for coercive measures.[53] Where the direct taking of evidence means that a witness is required to testify, the requesting court must inform the person concerned that this can only be on a voluntary basis. The evidence is taken by a member of the judicial personnel of the requesting court or by any other person such as an expert, designated in accordance with the law of requesting state.

Judicial Networks and Similar Arrangements

Experience has demonstrated the great value of direct communication between the different officials working on the processes involved in cross-border cases. In the context of the Hague Conventions dealing with child abduction and the protection of children, a Hague Network of Judges was established in 1999. By 2015, it had 101 judges in membership, from seventy-five different states. The Hague Conference supports the Network by publishing regular bulletins and has also prepared the Hague General Principles for Judicial Communications, first issued in 2013.[54]

In England, Lord Justice Thorpe, during his service as Head of International Family Justice, was a strong advocate of the value of judicial networks in family cases; indeed it was he who suggested the establishment of the Hague Network. For example, In *Re H (a child)*,[55] a complicated child abduction case, he said

> It would appear that those proceedings will be here in London and the primary responsibility will be on a judge of the Family Division. But nothing that is decided in London is likely to be wide enough in extent for this child, whose heritage and future lie between two different jurisdictions, two different continents, and two different cultures.
>
> Thus, it is essential that there should be close judicial collaboration, to ensure that her future is not abused by any unilateral wrongful action that either parent might be tempted to take. Fortunately, Mexico has appointed a judge to the Hague International Judicial Network. It has been my experience and the experience of my office that we have always received the most generous and swift assistance from the Mexican Network Judge whenever we have asked for it, so I have no doubt at all that, insofar as judicial collaboration can be needed, it is assured.

However in *Re B (A Child) (Care Proceedings: Jurisdiction)*,[56] the English Court of Appeal emphasised that the role of the Judicial Network was not to provide a mechanism for obtaining binding rulings from the requested Network Judge. The emphasis was upon the practical aspects of resolving international cases, including the provision of 'information as to the law', rather than upon obtaining concluded free-standing determinations on matters of jurisdiction or status. In the context of

[53] Regulation, Art. 17(2).
[54] Cf. Diamond, R. M. 'Canadian Network of Contact Judges' [2012] *IFL* 84.
[55] [2013] EWCA Civ 148 [29] and [30].
[56] [2013] EWCA Civ 1434, [2014] Fam 139 [59]ff.

liaison between judges in Europe, each will be governed by the fair trial requirements of Article 6 of the European Convention on Human Rights. As McFarlane LJ put it

> One only has to contemplate a requested judge issuing a determination in circumstances where they have not heard any of the parties or their advocates, they probably have not been exposed to all, or to any, of the key documentation in the case and almost certainly, where there are no extant court proceedings, they do not have any jurisdiction to make a binding determination under their domestic law.

Also in the 1990s a number of countries appointed 'liaison magistrates', sometimes based in their home country and sometimes in a foreign centre with whose courts and authorities there was a great deal of 'trade'. In 1996 the EU provided a formalised framework for the exchange of liaison magistrates in a Joint Action.[57] This provided guidelines for the posting or the exchange of magistrates (in the civil law sense, which includes judges) or officials with special expertise in judicial cooperation procedures as between Member States, on the basis of bilateral or multilateral arrangements.

The main aim of creating a framework for the exchange of liaison magistrates was declared to be to increase the speed and effectiveness of judicial cooperation and to promote the pooling of information on the legal and judicial systems of the Member States and to improve their operation.[58] The Joint Action defined the functions of liaison magistrates as normally including any activity designed to encourage and accelerate all forms of judicial cooperation, in particular by establishing direct links with the competent departments and judicial authorities of the host state. If the two states so agreed, liaison magistrates could also undertake any activity connected with handling the exchange of information and statistics designed to promote mutual understanding of the legal systems and legal databases of the states concerned and to further relations between the legal professions of each of those states.[59]

In 2001, on the model of an earlier network concerned only with criminal cases, the EU created the European Judicial Network in civil and commercial matters.[60] The Network as originally established was composed of (1) a contact point designated by each Member State, or when local circumstances so require a 'limited number' of contact points;[61] (2) central bodies and Central Authorities provided for

[57] Joint Action of 22 April 1996 adopted by the Council on the basis of Art. K.3 of the Treaty on European Union, concerning a framework for the exchange of liaison magistrates to improve judicial cooperation between the Member States of the European Union, [1996] OJ L105/1.

[58] Joint Action, Art. 1.

[59] Joint Action, Art. 2.

[60] Council Decision 2001/470/EC of 28 May 2001 establishing a European Judicial Network in civil and commercial matters. See the Report from the Commission to the Council, the European Parliament and the European Economic and Social Committee on the application of Council Decision 2001/470/EC establishing a European Judicial Network in civil and commercial matters, COM(2006) 203 final, 16.5.2006. A second report is overdue.

[61] See Council Decision, Art. 2(2). Detailed provisions as to the duties of contact points and their relationship to other relevant authorities are in Arts 5 to 8.

in Community instruments, instruments of international law to which the Member States are parties or rules of domestic law in the area of judicial cooperation in civil and commercial matters; (3) the liaison magistrates to whom the Joint Action of 22 April 1996 applies, where they have responsibilities in cooperation in civil and commercial matters; and (4) any other appropriate judicial or administrative authority with responsibilities for judicial cooperation in civil and commercial matters whose membership of the Network is considered to be useful by the Member State to which it belongs. Meetings of the contact points are to be held at least once each half-year.[62] There are over 400 members of the Network, with some eighty contact points.

A principal function of the Network is to seek to ensure the smooth operation of the effective and practical application of EU instruments or conventions in force between two or more Member States and more generally of procedures having a cross-border impact and the facilitation of requests for judicial cooperation between the Member States, in particular where no Community or international instrument is applicable.[63]

An amending decision in 2009[64] added a new category of members of the Network, 'professional associations representing, at national level in the Member States, legal practitioners directly involved in the application of Community and international instruments concerning judicial cooperation in civil and commercial matters'.[65] It also provided for closer links with national judiciaries: if the designated contact point is not a judge, the Member State concerned must provide for effective liaison with the national judiciary and may designate a judge to support this function, that judge being a member of the Network.

The Network is increasingly being mentioned in the English courts: recent examples show it referred to as providing on its website translations of foreign codes;[66] and as containing in the European Judicial Atlas (a website maintained by the Network) information as to the practice followed in the service of documents.[67]

Conclusion

Progress has been made in accommodating within international instruments the differing approaches of the common law and civil law traditions to judicial cooperation.

[62] Council Decision, Art. 9(1).

[63] Council Decision, Art. 3, which was amended in detail by Decision No. 568/2009.

[64] Decision No. 568/2009/EC of the European Parliament and of the Council of 18 June 2009 amending Council Decision 2001/470/EC establishing a European Judicial Network in civil and commercial matters, [2009] OJ L168/35.

[65] Council Decision, Art. 2(1)(e) and 2(4A) both as inserted by Decision 568/2009. The scope of this provision is described in Recital (12) to the latter Decision, referring to 'lawyers, solicitors, barristers, notaries and bailiffs directly involved in the application of Community and international instruments concerning civil justice'.

[66] *Puceviciene* v. *Prosecutor General's Office of the Republic of Lithuania* [2016] EWHC 1862 (Admin).

[67] *Asefa Yesuf Import and Export* v. *A.P. Møller – Mærsk A/S trading as Mærsk Line* [2016] EWHC 1437 (Admlty).

Those differences will remain, for they grow out of the nature of legal systems and the role of the judiciary within them. In practical terms, the existing international legal instruments meet most needs, especially if they are operated with flexibility and an understanding of the needs of different states. The development of judicial networks and the holding of regular meetings of those charged with operating the instruments are very positive developments.

It remains to be seen if further changes in international practice and the growing use of electronic means of communication including videoconferencing will make the current conventions and arrangements seem as dated as the very first Hague Conventions.

9

Judicial Cooperation in South America: A Regional Perspective

Nadia de Araujo

Introduction

The key to efficient international commerce lies in the element of trust: trust between the parties that decide to invest in international business relations, and trust between the legal systems that may need to deal with disputes arising from a contract gone sour. In addition to disputes of a commercial nature, courts often handle cross-border tort cases, the solution of which becomes problematic if evidence needs to be collected and damages assessed in another jurisdiction. The fact that the state that issues the judgment may not be the same one that enforces it adds another layer of difficulty to the fulfilment of the outcomes of the proceedings.

When a party turns to the judiciary in order to solve a domestic case, the question of which judge within the forum will adjudicate the case poses no dilemma. The local rules of civil procedure easily provide an answer to that, as well as to all questions pertaining to the specificities of the proceedings. However, when a case is connected to more than one state, 'complexity' is the word that comes to mind, beginning with the very ascertainment of the court where the prospective claimant may bring his or her suit. If not provided for in a choice of court agreement, one needs to tread carefully when selecting a forum. Many a forum may be internationally competent to adjudicate the case, but determining which one is the best equipped to do so requires an in-depth assessment, one that parties are not always prepared – time and budget-wise – to conduct. As is common in cross-border cases, the court that adjudicates the case may not be able to enforce its own judgment because the defendant's assets may be located in another jurisdiction and, if so, the claimant's success will only be secure if the forum where enforcement is sought is receptive of (or responsive to)[1] foreign judgments. What is more, during the course of the proceedings, the adjudicating

[1] See the chapter by Michaels in this volume.

judge may find him- or herself in need of evidence that may only be collected abroad. The outcome of the proceedings will then depend on active cooperation between authorities from different countries.

Claimants, defendants and courts worldwide continuously struggle with the complexities of international civil and commercial litigation, and Latin America is no exception. For that very reason, the movement towards the development of international agreements for bilateral, regional or multilateral international judicial cooperation (IJC), which started in the late nineteenth century, shows no signs of abating. IJC embraces two very different stages of cooperation. The first involves inter-state assistance during the course of proceedings for carrying out certain judicial acts, such as service of process and taking evidence. The second stage, known as post-trial assistance, addresses the recognition and enforcement of foreign judgments. This chapter focuses on the latter.[2]

Enforcing a judgment abroad may prove to be too onerous a task, the costs of which may exceed the very indemnification amount that the claimant is seeking to recover in the first place. In addition, the shortcomings of cross-border enforcement are detrimental to the development of international commerce itself, as many business players perceive an international business relation – relying as they do on its lack of legal certainty – as a way of evading the fulfilment of their obligations. Adopting further international IJC rules for the recognition and enforcement of foreign judgments may put us all on the right track towards access to justice and cost-efficient and risk-free (at least from a legal perspective) transnational relations.

This chapter will first map out Latin America's many initiatives for the harmonisation of private international law rules in the field of IJC promoted by the Organization of American States (OAS) and Mercosur. It will then examine briefly the Judgments Project of the Hague Conference on Private International Law (HCCH) and its eventual impact for Latin America.[3] The chapter draws a parallel between these two approaches and examines how they may highlight avenues for mutual enhancement. The assumption here is that the conventions currently in force in Latin America and the HCCH's Judgments Project provide common ground for IJC. Latin American countries in general, and the Mercosur Member States in particular, would benefit greatly from the adoption of a global convention on the recognition and enforcement of foreign judgments, as it would promote stronger ties for IJC both within and beyond Latin America.

[2] For a comprehensive analysis of international cooperation see McClean, D. (2012) *International Co-operation in Civil and Criminal Matters*, 3rd edn, Oxford University Press. See also the chapter by McClean in this volume.

[3] See also Noodt Taquela, M. B. and V. Ruiz Abou-Nigm (2018) 'The Draft Judgments Convention and its Relationship with other International Instruments', *Yearbook of Private International Law*, vol. 19, 449–74. The Judgments Project in general is the sole object of study of the chapter by Pasquot Polido in this volume.

The Latin American Approach to International Judicial Cooperation

In the context of the Americas, the harmonisation and codification of private international law rules providing for the cross-border circulation of individuals and businesses has been ongoing since the closing decades of the 1800s.[4] The Lima Treaty of 1878, though ratified by a few countries, set the stage for substantive developments in this field in the subsequent decades. The Montevideo Treaties of 1888–9 saw the uniformisation of private international law rules gaining momentum, with the adoption of no fewer than eight treaties. In 1928, the Havana Conference saw the legendary Bustamante Code come to life. These international treaties constitute landmarks in the establishment of the legal framework for private international law rules in Latin America and are exemplars to the world.

In 1975, the OAS restarted the process of regional codification of private international law, embarking on a journey inspired by the specialised conventions of the HCCH. In a series of Specialized Conferences on Private International Law, known by the Spanish acronym CIDIP,[5] the OAS promoted the elaboration of more than twenty inter-American conventions on private international law.[6]

[4] The first codification of private international law occurred in Latin America in 1878, while the first European initiative at the HCCH was not until 1893.

[5] Art. 122 of the Charter of the OAS describes Specialized Conferences as 'intergovernmental meetings to deal with special technical matters or to develop specific aspects of inter-American cooperation'. To this date, seven CIDIPs have been held and twenty-six instruments have been adopted on various matters.

[6] In 1975, at CIDIP-I, OAS Member States adopted six conventions covering international trade and procedural law. These are the Inter-American Conventions on Conflict of Laws concerning Bills of Exchange, Promissory Notes and Invoices; Conflict of Laws concerning Checks; International Commercial Arbitration; Letters Rogatory; Taking of Evidence Abroad; and the Legal Regime of Powers of Attorney to be used Abroad. In 1979, at CIDIP-II, OAS Member States adopted eight international instruments concerning aspects of international trade law and international procedural law, as well as conventions on legal institutions relating to the general aspects of this branch of the law. The conventions on international trade law include the Inter-American Conventions on Conflicts of Laws Concerning Checks and Conflicts of Laws Concerning Commercial Companies. The conventions regarding procedural law include the Inter-American Conventions on Extraterritorial Validity of Foreign Judgments and Arbitral Awards; Execution of Preventive Measures; Proof and Information on Foreign Law; and the Additional Protocol to the Inter-American Convention on Letters Rogatory. General aspects of private international law were addressed in the Inter-American Conventions on the Domicile of Natural Persons in Private International Law and on General Rules of Private International Law. In 1984, at CIDIP-III, OAS Member States adopted international instruments on international civil law and international procedural law. The first group includes the Inter-American Conventions on Conflict of Laws Concerning the Adoption of Minors and on Personality and Capacity of Juridical Persons in Private International Law. The second group includes the Inter-American Convention on Jurisdiction in the International Sphere for the Extraterritorial Validity of Foreign Judgments and the Additional Protocol to the Inter-American Convention on the Taking of Evidence Abroad. In 1989, at CIDIP-IV, OAS Member States approved the Inter-American Conventions on International Return of Children; Support Obligations; and Contracts for the International Carriage of Goods by Road. In 1994, at CIDIP-V, OAS Member States approved the Inter-American Convention on Law Applicable

In the 1990s, Mercosur, the South American economic and political bloc established in 1991 by the Treaty of Asunción, comprising Argentina, Brazil, Paraguay and Uruguay, took on the task of harmonising the existing private international law rules within its Member States. Mercosur's treaties on private international law were well received and have since been governing IJC between the Member States, superseding the OAS's treaties within the bloc.[7]

The Montevideo Treaties

Argentina, Paraguay and Uruguay were the first countries in Latin America to embark on a multilateral initiative for the harmonisation of private international law rules and the improvement of IJC. Their initiative is embodied in a collection of eight multilateral agreements adopted between 1888 and 1889 and known as the Montevideo Treaties. The Montevideo Treaties were amended in 1939–40 and are currently still in force.

The rules on jurisdiction are to be found in the Montevideo Treaty on International Civil Law, in Articles 56 to 67.[8] The treaty adopts an interesting direct approach towards the harmonisation of private international law rules, by commanding States Parties to follow the rules on applicable law as connecting factors to also ascertain jurisdiction. The concept is that the country whose law applies to a certain case will also be the one to exercise jurisdiction over it. This is known as the parallelism criterion: that is, the two-way system provided for by Article 56 of the 1889 Montevideo Treaty creates an interesting parallel between applicable law and jurisdiction.[9] In 1939–40, the Montevideo Treaty was reformed. The amended Article 56, in addition to the parallelism criterion, allows for the choice of forum

to International Contracts and the Inter-American Convention on International Traffic in Minors. In 2002, at CIDIP-VI, OAS Member States adopted the Model Inter-American Law on Secured Transactions and the Inter-American Uniform Through Bill of Lading for the International Carriage of Goods by Road. In 2009, at CIDP-VI, the Model Registry Regulations under the Model Law was adopted. OAS, Department of International Law, available at: www.oas.org/en/sla/dil/private_international_law_history_cidip_process.asp

7 See Protocol for Cooperation and Jurisdictional Assistance in Civil, Commercial, Labor and Administrative Matters, known as the Protocol of Las Leñas, which was adopted in Las Leñas, Argentina, on 27 June 1992, and entered into force on 2 August 1996; 4 States Parties, status as at 15 November 2018, as well as the Protocol on International Jurisdiction in Disputes Relating to Contracts, adopted in Buenos Aires, 5 August 1994; 4 States Parties, status as at 15 November 2018.

8 Arts 56 and 67 are particularly important, as they state the following: Art. 56: '*Las acciones personales deben entablarse antes los Jueces del lugar de cuya ley está sujeto el acto jurídico materia del juicio*'. Art. 67: '*Las acciones reales y las denominadas mixtas, deben ser deducidas ante los jueces del lugar en el cuial exista la cosa sobre que la acción recaiga. Si comprendieren cosas situadas en distintos lugares, el juicio debe ser promovido ante los Jueces del lugar de cada una de ellas*'.

9 See Fernández Arroyo, D. (ed.) (2003), *Derecho Internacional Privado de los Estados del Mercosur*, Zavalia, 169. See Art. 56: '*las acciones personales deben entablarse ante los Jueces del lugar a cuya ley está sujeto el acto jurídico materia del juicio. Podrán entablarse igualmente ante los Jueces del domicilio del demandado*'.

after the lawsuit has started, if the defendant voluntarily allows it, and only for patrimonial matters.

The rules for recognition and enforcement of foreign judgments are found in the Montevideo Treaty on International Civil Procedure Law.[10] The treaty starts with a general rule determining that the procedural law of the place of the act always determines the communication of all acts.

Articles 5 to Article 8 set out the rules for recognition of foreign judgments. According to the treaty, a judgment in civil or commercial matters issued in a Member State is due recognition in the territory of other Member States if rendered by a competent tribunal in the international sphere.[11] Nonetheless, there is nothing in the treaty suggesting which criteria should be used to determine if the jurisdiction of the foreign judge was correctly ascertained, that is, there are no provisions on 'indirect jurisdiction'.

The requirements for recognition and enforcement are: (1) the decision must be final; (2) service of the defendant must have been done according to the principles of due process; and (3) the judgment is not against the public policy of the recognition and enforcement state. Furthermore, Article 6 states the necessary formalities: an integral copy of the decision as well as other relevant information, such as the proof of service, and a declaration that the decision is *res judicata*. Nonetheless, the enforcement of the decision will follow the procedural rules of the country of enforcement. Although still in force, the use of the Montevideo Treaties is rare nowadays because the members are parties to the Inter-American Convention on Recognition of Decisions of 1979, analysed later in the chapter.

The Bustamante Code

The Montevideo Treaties were only ratified by Argentina, Paraguay and Uruguay. Thus, the majority of Latin American countries lacked common private international law rules. Efforts in the direction of further unification were made at the Second Pan-American Conference, held in Rio de Janeiro in 1901. In 1906, a commission of jurists was appointed to draw up codes on public and private international law; the commission began its activity in Rio de Janeiro in 1912.[12] At the time, Lafayette Rodrigues Pereira completed a new project, later abandoned, for a code of private international law. The First World War stalled codification in the Americas and the work resumed only in 1924. This time, Antonio S. Bustamante was appointed with

[10] Adopted on 19 March 1940, at Montevideo, Uruguay, at the Second South American Congress on Private International Law.

[11] Art. 5: 'Judgments and arbitral awards rendered in civil and commercial matters in one of the signatory States shall have in the territory of the other signatories the same force as in the country where they were pronounced provided that they comply with the following requirements: (a) They must have been rendered by a tribunal competent in the international sphere . . .'

[12] See Lorenzen, E. G. (1930) 'Pan-American Code of Private International Law', *Yale Faculty Scholarship Series*, Paper 4578.

other jurists to draw up a code of private international law. The draft prepared by Bustamante was discussed and approved by the American Law Institute in 1925 and by the Commission of Jurists in Rio de Janeiro in 1927. It was finally approved at the Sixth Pan-American Conference, held in Havana in 1928. It is still in force today in eighteen countries.[13]

The Bustamante Code sets forth general conditions for Member States to exercise their jurisdiction over civil and commercial matters. This treaty leaves each Member State the task of providing for the international jurisdiction of its own courts as well as for the conditions for the recognition and enforcement of a foreign judgment in its territory. It sets forth in Article 317 that States may not establish jurisdiction in *ratione materiae* and *ratione personae* matters solely based on the nationality criteria, if the application of such criteria is prejudicial to the parties. Contrary to the Montevideo Treaties, the Bustamante Code fully embraces party autonomy. In the absence of choice, however, the Bustamante Code sets the following rules on direct jurisdiction: (1) States Parties may adjudicate cases when at least one of the parties is a national of that state and (2) States Parties must not hold ad hoc tribunals.[14] Despite being a cutting-edge legislation for its time in the field of IJC, it remains unclear whether States Parties actually applied the rules on general jurisdiction provided for by the Bustamante Code.

In addition, the Bustamante Code provides a list of objective requirements for judgments to freely circulate among its States Parties. They are the following: (1) the court of origin must have abided by the rules of jurisdiction in place therein;[15] (2) the judgment must not be subject to appeal; (3) the defendant must have been duly notified thereof. In addition to these requirements – which can be said to pertain to the forum where the decision was held – the Bustamante Code sets forth two requirements, one of a formal nature and the other of a substantive nature. These requirements must be fulfilled in the forum where recognition is sought: (4) the judgment must be legalised and translated and (5) the judgment must not contravene the public policy of the receiving forum.[16] To this day, the Bustamante Code remains influential even beyond its States Parties.[17]

The Inter-American Convention on Extraterritorial Validity of Foreign Judgments and Arbitral Awards – CIDIP II

Although the Bustamante Code and the Montevideo Treaties remain in force to this day, the Inter-American Convention on Extraterritorial Validity of Foreign Judgments

[13] The countries that ratified the Bustamante Code are Bahamas, Bolivia, Brazil, Chile, Colombia, Costa Rica, Cuba, Dominican Republic, Ecuador, El Salvador, Guatemala, Haiti, Honduras, Nicaragua, Panama, Peru, and Venezuela.

[14] Arts 318 and 321 of the Bustamante Code.

[15] Art. 423 of the Bustamante Code.

[16] The research conducted has not detected case law related to this matter and the Bustamante Code.

[17] See Michaels, R. (2017) 'Recognition and Enforcement of Foreign Judgments', in Basedow, J. et al., *Encyclopaedia of Private International Law*, Elgar.

and Arbitral Awards, adopted in 1979 (CIDIP II Convention) superseded them on the matter of recognition and enforcement of foreign judgments. Its scope is similar to the convention under negotiation in the HCCH's Judgments Project, as it covers foreign judgments held on civil and commercial matters. However, the scope of the CIDIP II Convention is wider than the HCCH's current project as it also applies to labour matters, although states may make a reservation on this point and exclude such an application.

The requirements set forth in the CIDIP II Convention for the recognition and enforcement of foreign judgments do not deviate from those established in the previous international multilateral agreements adopted in Latin America (that is, the Montevideo Treaties and the Bustamante Code).[18] However, the CIDIP II Convention brought an interesting change when it came to jurisdiction, stating the following:

> d. The judge or tribunal rendering the judgment is competent in the international sphere to try the matter and to pass judgment on it in accordance with the law of the State in which the judgment, award or decision is to take effect . . .[19]

This provision marks a shift from the Bustamante Code and even from the fluid rule of the Montevideo Treaty, which entrusted the court of origin with the task of controlling the exercise of its own jurisdiction. In the eyes of the CIDIP II Convention, it is up to the receiving state to assess whether the court of origin had grounds to adjudicate the case.[20] This provision opened the door to the use of indirect bases of jurisdiction, which appeared five years later in the CIDIP III Convention. It is fair to say that OAS had in mind the use of both conventions in a complementary manner. This, however, did not occur, as the CIDIP III Convention was not well received among Member States of the OAS.[21]

The Inter-American Convention on Jurisdiction in the International Sphere for the Extraterritorial Validity of Foreign Judgments – CIDIP III

Following the approval in 1979 of the Inter-American Convention on Extraterritorial Validity of Foreign Judgments and Arbitral Awards, a meeting of experts convened

[18] See Arts 2 and 3 of the CIDIP II Convention, available at: www.oas.org/juridico/english/treaties/b-41.html

[19] Art. 2 of the CIDIP II Convention.

[20] Tellechea Bergman, E. (2016) 'La jurisdicción internacional como requisito para el reconocimiento del fallo extranjero. Necessidad de una nueva regulación en el ámbito interamericano', RSTRP, n. 7, 24. The author criticises the use of *lex fori* to determine the jurisdiction of the court of origin in the receiving state. He contends that this rule is not adequate to facilitate the circulation of foreign judgments and that it adds to the insecurity in the field.

[21] The Inter-American Convention on Extraterritorial Validity of Foreign Judgments and Arbitral Awards, adopted in 1979 (CIDIP II), was ratified by Argentina, Bolivia, Brazil, Colombia, Ecuador, Mexico, Paraguay, Peru, Uruguay and Venezuela. Conversely, the Inter-American Convention on Jurisdiction in the International Sphere for the Extraterritorial Validity of Foreign Judgments, adopted in 1984 (CIDIP III), was ratified only by Mexico and Uruguay.

in Washington in 1980 to discuss the remaining issue of the establishment of common rules on jurisdiction of the rendering court of a judgment that would later circulate to another state, a need felt by OAS Member States to guarantee the applicability of the above convention. The Inter-American Convention on Jurisdiction in the International Sphere for the Extraterritorial Validity of Foreign Judgments (the CIDIP III Convention) was adopted in 1984. Although the Convention entered into force in the international sphere, only Mexico and Uruguay have in fact ratified it, considerably undermining the significance of its provisions for the harmonisation of private international law rules in Latin America. The CIDIP III Convention's main concern is with the establishment of common rules of indirect jurisdiction, the compliance with which is mandatory for a judgment to be recognised and enforced in a country other than its country of origin. These rules, however, do not apply if said judgment does not leave its court of origin – in this case, Member States are free to set their own rules on jurisdiction and need not amend their domestic laws in this respect. This is precisely why the Convention set up a system of indirect basis of jurisdiction, albeit in a simpler manner than the model under discussion at the HCCH. Its aim is to unify the criteria to control the requirement of 'jurisdiction in the international sphere' for the purposes of the extraterritorial validity of foreign judgments as established in the 1979 Convention, examined above.[22] The idea underpinning this treaty is to ensure recognition and enforcement of judgments within the territory of States Parties by agreeing first on the grounds on which their courts may adjudicate cases,[23] without imposing a change in their domestic jurisdictional rules. The treaty also establishes common bases of exclusive jurisdiction, which serve as grounds for refusing recognition and enforcement of judgments held against their terms.[24] It is quite remarkable that OAS Member States managed to make progress in the negotiations and actually adopt a convention that so deeply touches on the sensitive issue of a state's sovereign power to exercise jurisdiction, albeit in an indirect manner. Still, it is no wonder why only two states saw their motivation through and actually ratified the CIDIP III Convention.

The Las Leñas Protocol

The Las Leñas Protocol is a multilateral treaty adopted by Mercosur's Member States in 1992. It addresses several matters in the field of IJC, with a view to improving mutual juridical assistance within the bloc. The recognition and enforcement of foreign judgments is provided for in Articles 18 to 24. The requirements set forth in Article 20 are similar to those of the CIDIP II Convention. The Las Leñas Protocol incidentally touches on the issue of jurisdictional control,[25] providing that foreign

[22] See Fresnedo de Aguirre, C. (2017), 'Cidip', in Basedow et al., *Encyclopedia of Private International Law*, above fn. 17.

[23] Art. 1.

[24] Art. 5 of the CIDIP III Convention.

[25] Art. 20 (c).

judgments are recognisable and enforceable within the territory of Member States if the law of the state where recognition is sought determines that the court of origin had valid grounds for adjudicating the case.[26]

The Buenos Aires Protocol

The Buenos Aires Protocol, adopted by Mercosur's Member States in 1994, is the most recent initiative affecting IJC in the region. The treaty establishes common rules of jurisdiction for cases arising out of civil and commercial contracts entered into between individuals or legal persons. It is, in this sense, far less comprehensive than the CIDIP III Convention.

The Protocol fully embraces party autonomy.[27] In the absence of choice, it sets forth direct bases of jurisdiction, deeming the Member State internationally competent to adjudicate a case if (1) it is the place of performance of a contract; (2) the place where the defendant is domiciled; or (3) the place where the claimant has his or her domicile or place of business, if the claimant has fulfilled its obligation. Furthermore, Article 14 supersedes the Las Leñas Protocol provisions on indirect jurisdiction. Before the Buenos Aires Protocol was enacted, the indirect rules on jurisdiction of each State Party to the Las Leñas Protocol were valid. Once the Buenos Aires Protocol came into force, however, its rules on direct jurisdiction became mandatory for the purposes of the Las Leñas Protocol also, given that the recognition and enforcement of a foreign judgment became subject to compliance with the rules on jurisdiction of the Buenos Aires Protocol. In that sense, it is fair to say that the Buenos Aires Protocol not only harmonised private international law rules on direct jurisdiction, but also subjected the very application of the Las Leñas Protocol for the recognition and enforcement of a foreign judgment to its terms.

The HCCH's Judgments Project

In Europe, the HCCH first began its work in 1893, focusing on the uniformisation of private international law rules through the adoption of multilateral treaties addressing specific issues of civil and family law.[28] After becoming an international organisation

[26] The Las Leñas Protocol is widely used in Brazil and there is case law in the Superior Court of Justice, in matters of recognition and enforcement of foreign decisions coming from Mercosur countries. See, for example, SEC 6855, foreign decision, judgment issued 16 August 2017; and SEC 14077, judgment issued 15 March 2017, where legalisation was deemed unnecessary because of the Las Leñas Protocol; CR 398 (letter rogatory). judgment issued 29 June 2010, where a foreign decision granting a divorce in Argentina was transmitted by a letter rogatory and duly recognised in Brazil, according to the Las Leñas Protocol, Arts 19 and 20. CR 10.750 (letter rogatory), a decision on an adoption of a minor, was validated and registered after being recognised through the Las Leñas Protocol. CR 10.300 (letter rogatory), also concerning a divorce in Chile, was recognised after transmission through the Las Leñas Protocol.

[27] Art. 4.

[28] For a brief history of the HCCH, see van Loon, H. (2015) 'The Global Horizon of Private International Law', *Recueil des cours*, vol. 380, 9–108. Between 1893 and 1904, four diplomatic conferences were

in the 1950s, the HCCH invested more and more in IJC. There has since been a tremendous increase in the HCCH's codification activity, influenced greatly, no doubt, by the organisation's new outreach: from a modest start with sixteen members in the 1950s, the HCCH grew to thirty-five in the 1990s, then to forty-seven in the 2000s and now boasts eighty-three members.[29] The HCCH's statutory mission is to work towards the progressive unification of private international law rules. By setting internationally agreed approaches to issues such as jurisdiction of the courts and the recognition and enforcement of foreign judgments, the HCCH aims at building strong foundations upon which individuals and companies can expand their businesses.

Of the many projects under discussion at HCCH, the Judgments Project is one of the most relevant for IJC. This project, which dates back to the end of the twentieth century, aims at minimising the existing legal barriers for the international circulation of judgments. The ultimate goal is to mitigate uncertainty in international private relations, by ensuring that judgments rendered in a given country are enforceable where claimants need them to be. The creation of a reliable legal environment will encourage parties to comply with the rules of law and act in good faith in their contractual or non-contractual relations.

To this date, the Special Commission for the Judgments Project – set up by the HCCH's Council on General Affairs and Policy – held four meetings to work on a Draft Convention providing common ground for the recognition and enforcement of foreign judgments on civil and commercial matters.[30] The Special Commission took up the work developed in the course of four years by a Working Group comprising specialists in the field. After the fourth meeting, in May 2018, the Special Commission considered that the work on the Draft Convention was complete and a Diplomatic Session was scheduled for June 2019. [31]

In order to achieve its goal of establishing a facilitated system for the circulation of foreign judgments, the Judgments Project aims at setting certain parameters to assess whether jurisdiction over a case that is theoretically linked to more than one state has been exercised in a legitimate manner for the purposes of having it recognised and

held at the Hague, at which seven multilateral treaties were concluded. These early conventions were largely based on the nationality principle, which later became its Achilles heel (ibid., 28). It was only after World War II that the world became more aware that international cooperation was essential and HCCH was established as an intergovernmental organisation. Today, the HCCH has eighty-three members, eighty-two states and one Regional Economic Integration Organization (the EU), and a more globalised outlook. With the adoption of the 1956 Hague Convention on Child Support, the HCCH has embraced the concept of habitual residence – in lieu of the nationality principle – as its main personal connecting factor.

[29] See van Loon, 'The Global Horizon of Private International Law', above fn. 28, 44.

[30] The meetings of June 2016, February 2017, November 2017 and May 2018 had more than 150 participants from fifty-three states and sixteen international organisations and NGOs, including ASADIP (American Association of Private International Law), represented by the editors of this volume.

[31] 31. For more information on the work carried out by the Working Group and on the Judgments Project in general, see www.hcch.net/en/projects/legislative-projects/judgments

enforced in another country. These parameters serve only to enable recognition and enforcement of a judgment in a jurisdiction other than its jurisdiction of origin. They do not purport to change states' domestic rules on international jurisdiction.

In many countries throughout the world, a foreign judgment may only be recognised and enforced if the court where recognition and enforcement is sought finds that the court of origin had factual ties to adjudicate the case.[32] It fell to the Special Commission to determine – if possible – which of these factual ties are generally agreed upon among HCCH Member States.

The Preliminary Draft Convention

The preliminary Draft Convention on the Recognition and Enforcement of Judgments in Civil and Commercial Matters of May 2018 was submitted to the HCCH's Council on General Affairs and Policy in 2019. The Convention takes the form of a binding document. This means that, if adopted by the Diplomatic Conference that will be convened in 2019, the Convention will then become part of the domestic legislation of each HCCH Member State that ratifies it.

The entry into force of this Convention would mean the achievement of the HCCH's long-standing mission of harmonising IJC rules in the field of post-trial assistance. Such harmonisation, however, would be limited to the criteria for recognition and enforcement of foreign judgments. The Convention will not establish direct bases of international jurisdiction. The new Convention would add to the now in force 2005 Convention on Choice of Court Agreements.[33] The HCCH intends for it to be used in coordination with the other conventions sponsored by the organisation, such as the Convention of 23 November 2007 on the International Recovery of Child Support and Other Forms of Family Maintenance, currently in force in forty countries. The HCCH is confident that this Convention will avoid unnecessary duplication

[32] For instance, see the parallel drawn by Paul Beaumont between the issue of recognition of foreign judgments and Brexit: 'The decision of a majority of the UK to vote to leave the European Union on Thursday 23 June 2016 means that in the not too distant future the UK will not be a Member State of the European Union. This is likely to have the consequence that once the UK has left the Union it will not apply the Brussels I Regulation or the Lugano Convention to provide for recognition and enforcement of judgments from courts in the EU and in the Lugano Contracting States and vice versa.18 Clearly the Brussels I Regulation will not apply to a State outside the EU – apart from transitional arrangements for cases already in the pipeline at the time of the UK exit from the EU – and the Lugano Convention is not likely to be a model acceptable to a newly liberated UK . . . It may very well be the case that the future Hague Convention on Recognition and Enforcement of Foreign Judgments in Civil or Commercial Matters, alongside the 2005 Convention, will be the best basis for ensuring appropriate recognition and enforcement of judgments from UK courts in other States in the EU and the current Lugano Contracting States and vice versa'. Beaumont, P. (2016) *Respecting Reverse Subsidiarity as an Excellent Strategy for the European Union at The Hague Conference on Private International Law – Reflections in the Context of the Judgments Project?*, CPIL Working Paper, 4.

[33] For more information and a status table of the Choice of Court Convention, see www.hcch.net/en/instruments/conventions/status-table/?cid=98

of proceedings in different states and reduce transaction and court costs. It will also promote greater predictability with regard to the circulation of judgments, assisting the parties in their commercial decisions.

Indirect Bases for Recognition and Enforcement

The establishment of generally agreed-upon bases for the indirect control of international jurisdiction[34] has been the driving force behind the Judgments Project. These bases should enable courts that are asked to recognise a foreign judgment to assess the grounds on which the courts of origin adjudicated the case, without contravening states' sovereignty. The Special Commission was only able to make progress in the negotiations concerning the indirect bases of jurisdiction by limiting such control to very precise requirements, the presence of which the majority of the states seemed to converge on.[35] These requirements all relate to there being a reasonable connection between the case and the court of origin that makes the judgment eligible for recognition and enforcement in other states. The absence of these requirements, in turn, would enable states other than the state of origin to refuse recognition.

The Draft Convention lists well-known connection points between the case and courts of origin, such as, but not limited to:[36]

(1) The court of origin should be the place where the natural person has his or her habitual residence;[37]
(2) The court of origin should be the place where the defendant maintained a branch, agency, or other establishment;[38]
(3) The court of origin should be the parties' choice of forum;[39]
(4) The court of origin should be the place where the performance of the contractual obligation on which the judgment was held took place;[40] and
(5) The court of origin should be the place where the act or omission directly causing a non-contractual obligation arising from death, physical injury, damage to or loss of tangible property took place.[41]

[34] Hartley, T. and M. Dogauchi (2013) *Convention of 30 June 2005 on Choice of Court Agreements: Explanatory Report.* Available at: www.hcch.net/en/publications-and-studies/details4/?pid=3959

[35] Ibid., 785: 'it became apparent as work proceeded that it would not be possible to draw up a satisfactory text for a "mixed" convention within a reasonable period of time. The reasons for this included the wide differences in the existing rules of jurisdiction in different States and the unforeseeable effects of technological developments, including the Internet, on the jurisdictional rules that might be laid down in the Convention'.

[36] HCCH, *2018 Preliminary Draft Convention*, available at: https://assets.hcch.net/docs/23b6dac3-7900-49f3-9a94-aa0ffbe0d0dd.pdf

[37] Art. 5.1(a) of the Draft Convention.

[38] Art. 5.1(d) of the Draft Convention.

[39] Art. 5.1(g) of the Draft Convention.

[40] Art. 5.1(j) of the Draft Convention.

[41] Art. 5.1(j) of the Draft Convention.

The provision on indirect bases of jurisdiction is the most extensive and complex article of the Draft Convention. The absence of international criteria with which to define international jurisdiction in the first place made the task of harmonising the bases for the indirect control thereof all the more difficult.

Exclusive Bases for Recognition and Enforcement and Grounds for Refusal

Article 6 of the Draft Convention provides that the recognition and enforcement of a foreign judgment may be refused in the event that there is a close connection between the dispute and the requested state. A closer reading of this provision reveals that it translates, by exclusion, a harmonisation of PIL rules on jurisdiction: states that accede to the future Convention will agree that for the matters dealt with in Article 6 the only acceptable bases for jurisdictional control are those declared there.

Article 7 of the Draft Convention provides for the grounds on which recognition and enforcement of a foreign judgment may be refused. The Draft Convention does not innovate with regard to this point: the grounds listed therein are very much common to all states, including the public policy ground.[42]

What is There to Gain from the New Convention?

Latin American countries have a long-standing tradition of cooperation. The legal framework in place for the recognition and enforcement of foreign judgments ensures a high level of receptiveness for foreign judgments.[43] However, judgments from Latin America are not met with the same level of acceptance in other parts of the world. This means that while Latin American private international law rules are a great mechanism to secure the recognition and the enforcement of foreign judgments among the Member States, they do nothing to improve the acceptance of their own judgments outside the region. As it stands, judgments from Latin American countries may not be recognised in countries that are not signatories of the CIDIP II Convention or the Las Leñas Protocol.

The rules on direct jurisdiction provided for in the Montevideo Treaties and in the Bustamante Code did not achieve broad acceptance at their time. The subsequent initiative – the CIDIP III Convention – set aside the ambition of establishing common jurisdictional rules in order to focus on the harmonisation of indirect rules of jurisdiction, the same concept embraced by the HCCH in the Judgments Project. While the CIDIP III Convention did develop sophisticated IJC rules, especially in the field of post-judgment assistance, it failed to inspire Member States to actually use them. Its applicability is limited to the countries involved that already have similar rules on direct jurisdiction.

[42] The wording of the Article employs the term 'manifestly' to lend greater qualification to the public policy exception.

[43] Especially because there are no rules in place for indirect basis of jurisdiction as the Inter-American Convention on Jurisdiction in the International Sphere for the Extraterritorial Validity of Foreign Judgments that set out these bases is not in force in Latin American countries.

Hence, the new Convention being prepared by the HCCH should hopefully allow Latin American judgments not only to find the receptivity that they now lack in a broader geographical arena, while also helping their regional rules come to light once again, as they do not deviate greatly from the HCCH model. The Draft Convention on recognition and enforcement of foreign judgments will ensure that judgments from Latin American countries face fewer barriers in other countries, especially in North America, Europe and Asia. It would also contribute to an already sympathetic scenario to foreign decisions in Latin America. As highlighted by the Chair of the Special Commission in his introductory remarks to the first meeting in 2016,[44] the Convention will serve two purposes:

> (a) enhance access to justice; and (b) facilitate cross-border trade and investment by reducing the costs and risks associated with cross-border dealings, an objective that was particularly relevant when we worked on the Choice of Court Convention, and that remains centrally relevant to what we are doing here today.

In light of his very optimistic discourse, one can say for the Member States in general and for Latin American countries in particular that the new Convention would allow parties to concentrate more on their core businesses instead of worrying whether they will be able to enforce a judgment on their behalf wherever they need to, should a dispute arise:

> a clear, certain and predictable framework for recognition and enforcement of judgments, will enable people deciding where to bring claims to make more informed choices about where to bring those initial proceedings. If you have the choice between bringing proceedings in one of two States, and a judgment in one State will circulate under a widely ratified convention, while a judgment in another will not, that is an important factor that will guide parties in making informed, sensible, efficient choices about where to litigate in the first place.[45]

[44] Record of the introductory remarks made by the Chair of the Special Commission (1–9 June 2016), available only in the secure portal of the HCCH website for the time being. Hard copy with the author.

[45] Ibid.

10

Civil Judicial Cooperation: A Scottish Experience

Nicola Wisdahl[1]

Introduction

Any contemporary look at the settled practice and experience of most disciplines is likely to amount to a simple observation of a particular time. While it may be trite that a legal system does not exist in a vacuum, economic and socio-political factors have recently tested the constitutional arrangements of the United Kingdom more than ever.[2] At the time of writing, Scotland remains part of both the UK and in turn the European Union. Within Europe over the past few decades, a gradual shift has begun to take place in the field of private international law. The increasing 'Europeanisation' of this discipline has sought to enable EU citizens to fully realise the potential of their free movement rights. Measures adopted at this level bring the discipline to life by giving it practical, real-life meaning.

European private international law has focused on active cooperation – the engagement across borders for the benefit of citizens on either side of a (legal) boundary. This emerging discipline has been described in European Commission guidance as remaining 'largely unnoticed by legal practitioners'.[3] However, as the active embodiment of private international law, judicial cooperation exemplifies the thesis that private international law is a form of engaging with the 'Other'. For measures to be effective, they must be used. However, frequency of use of EU law varies throughout the Union for a variety of social and cultural reasons. This chapter explores the Scottish position, drawing in part on the recent – and

[1] Any views expressed in this chapter are those of the writer alone.

[2] Burrows, N. and M. Fletcher (2017) 'Brexit as Constitutional "Shock" and its Threat to the Devolution Settlement: Reform or Bust', *Juridical Review* 1, 49–57.

[3] European Commission DG Justice: 'Judicial Cooperation in Civil Matters in the European Union. A Guide for Legal Practitioners', available at: https://publications.europa.eu/en/publication-detail/-/publication/a9da11b8-0a6a-491e-8ae9-a0ff9d7e8535/language-en

first – comprehensive study of the impact of EU law before the Scottish (civil) courts.[4]

In addition to considering emerging concepts and ideas inherent in this form of 'doing' private international law, this chapter presents a (or, rather, one) Scottish experience of such cooperation between and among parties. To set the context there is brief reference to the historical setting of Scotland's place within the modern British state. Some readers might be more familiar with how things came to be as they are: in that case, a starting point would be the brief background of EU private international law, taking into account the Scottish context – including how 'making' private international law is largely separated from 'doing' it. Finally, from an anthropological perspective, this chapter includes some reflections about identifying the required 'Other' for judicial cooperation, as well as commenting on the extent of Scottish participation in this nascent European judicial area. In short, the following observations are recorded as a snapshot of what seems likely, one way or another, to be the end of an era.

History

Describing Scotland's place within the UK is the work of political scientists and historians, although a brief overview will help to understand the present-day position of the Scottish legal system. Today's constitutional set-up is the result of familial relations and of geopolitics. In 1603, King James VI of Scotland, the only child of Queen Mary of Scotland, inherited the throne of Elizabeth I, Queen of England and Ireland. With two Crowns united, one monarch – James VI and I – reigned in both kingdoms for over a century of relative stability. James sought closer political union between his two realms. In the early eighteenth century, articles of union were debated. Both the Scottish and English Parliaments passed legislation in favour,[5] and the Scottish Parliament was dissolved on 28 April 1707. The English Parliament was not dissolved; its members instead became members of the Parliament of Great Britain,[6] now the UK Parliament.

Between 1707 and 1999, the UK Parliament enjoyed a domestic legislative monopoly, as well as parliamentary sovereignty. The nature and extent of the government of constituent parts of the UK diverged even after 1707, with 'broad toleration of such differences by the Imperial Government'.[7] In the second half of the twentieth

[4] Rodger, B. (2017) 'The Application of EU Law by the Scottish Courts: an Analysis of Case Law Trends over 40 Years', *Juridical Review* 2, 59–84. For its part, the Commission has produced a variety of guides for both practitioners and citizens. These sit on the 'portal' for civil justice matters; contact points on the European Judicial Network for civil and commercial matters (EJN) should make use of the guides and the portal. The e-Justice portal and the role of the EJN will also be considered in more detail.

[5] Union with England Act 1707 and Union with Scotland Act 1706.

[6] Discussion of the constitutional relations between the UK and Ireland is beyond this chapter's remit.

[7] Shiels, R. (2018) 'The Emerging Authority of Crown Office in the Imperial Age: A Discussion Paper', *Law, Crime and History* vol. 8, no. 1, 127.

century, however, European law entered the domestic sphere. After the UK's first two applications to join the (then) European Economic Community were effectively vetoed by France, the third attempt proved successful.[8] Conservative Prime Minister Edward Heath signed the Accession Treaty providing for the UK's entry to what is now the EU. The UK's accession took place on 1 January 1973, marked by events branded as a 'Fanfare for Europe'.[9] No referendum on membership was held before accession but, following a change of government, the new Labour Government held a referendum in 1975. With a 67.2 per cent vote in favour of remaining in the 'Common Market',[10] the question of the UK's membership was settled – at least for a generation or so. A few years later, a referendum was held about a possible transfer – 'devolution' – of legislative power from UK level to Scotland. While the majority vote was in favour, the minimum turnout of the total electorate was not met and so the proposal failed.[11] The issue was not put to the population again until 1997 when, in a referendum without such a minimum threshold, a 74.29 per cent vote in favour paved the way for modern devolution.

Legal Tradition

Reflecting this uniting of different kingdoms, each with its own governing regime, since inception the UK has accommodated more than one legal system. Scots law, protected by the Treaty of Union, is one such system. The others are those of England and Wales[12] on the one hand, and Northern Ireland on the other.

Such legal pluralism might not always be obvious to a casual observer, particularly as there was only one national parliament for almost 300 years. However, that single legislative body had a variable effect throughout the country. From a Scottish perspective the UK Parliament, or Westminster Parliament, passed Acts which applied either as UK law or as Scots law.

According to the 'prevalent and authoritative narrative among Scottish legal academics'[13] Scotland has a mixed legal system. This 'mix' is one of civil law on the one hand, and the common law on the other. By civil law what is usually meant is

[8] For a full description of the applications, including Westminster parliamentary involvement, see Wall, S. (2013) *The Official History of Britain and the European Economic Community, Volume II: From Rejection to Referendum, 1963–1975*, Routledge.

[9] Ibid., 453.

[10] Ibid., 588.

[11] On the third reading of the Bill paving the way for the referendum, Labour MP George Cunningham MP proposed an amendment requiring 40 per cent turnout.

[12] Although Wales has a devolved legislature and executive, it remains part of the unified legal jurisdiction of England and Wales. At least one academic commentator has recently considered whether primary legislation made for Wales by a Welsh legislature might be 'the laws of Wales', separate from English law: Gwynedd Parry, R. (2017) 'Is Breaking up Hard to Do? The Case for a Separate Welsh Jurisdiction' *Irish Jurist* 57, 61–93.

[13] Rahmatian, A. (2017) 'The Political Purpose of the "Mixed Legal System" Conception of the Law of Scotland', *Maastricht Journal of European and Comparative Law* vol. 24, no. 6, 843–86.

the continental European civil law system; common law is as found in England. As Rahmatian observes, this description refers only to 'private law and the commercial law aspects of private law only; it does not cover all areas of Scots law, namely not criminal law, and it does not refer to public law (constitutional law and administrative law)'.[14]

In any event, the separateness of the Scottish legal system predates by several centuries the existence of the present Scottish Parliament. Legal education in Scotland prepares practitioners for entry to the Scottish profession, making clear that the system is a hybrid within a multi-jurisdictional state. Solicitors qualified to practise in Scotland have no automatic rights of audience elsewhere in the UK – and vice versa. A qualified solicitor in England and Wales or Northern Ireland may requalify in Scotland via the Intra-UK transfer test; a separate regime exists for EU-qualified solicitors.

Devolution, Private International Law and International Relations

Following the second devolution referendum, the Scotland Act 1998 established a Scottish Parliament and an executive body now known as the Scottish Government. The competence of both is restricted to those spheres of power that have been 'devolved' (transferred) from London to Edinburgh. Powers are devolved unless they are specifically reserved; the Scotland Act sets out matters that have *not* been devolved: these are known as 'reserved matters' and are outside the legislative competence of the Scottish Parliament.[15] An Act of the Scottish Parliament is not law insofar as any provision is outside its legislative competence. In short, the Scottish Parliament is 'not a sovereign legislature but one for which constitutional limits have been enshrined in statute'.[16]

The aspiration of the framers of the Scottish Parliament was that it 'should distinguish itself from Westminster on the question of sovereignty'.[17] A generation of politicians, civil servants, legal practitioners and indeed individuals and non-governmental organisations is familiar with the concept of laws passed by a parliament then being reviewed by judges – or at least *reviewable*. In this way, the Scottish Parliament 'has simply joined that wider family of parliaments' – it is Westminster that is rather the exception with regard to legislative supremacy.[18]

Civil law – the 'general principles of private law', including private international law[19] – is within the legislative competence of the Scottish Parliament. However, the operation of the Scotland Act is such that although private international law is

[14] Ibid., 843.

[15] Schedule 5 to the Scotland Act 1998 and Section 29(2)(b).

[16] McCorkindale, C. and J. Hiebert (2017) 'Vetting Bills in the Scottish Parliament for Legislative Competence', 21 *Edinburgh Law Review* 3, 319–51.

[17] Ibid., 322.

[18] Ibid., 320, referring to *Whaley* v. *Watson* 2000 SC 340, 349 per Lord Rodger.

[19] Section 126(4) of the Scotland Act 1998.

devolved, private international law aspects of reserved matters are also reserved.[20] Foreign affairs are reserved, namely: 'international relations, including relations with territories outside the UK, the European Union and other international organisations . . .'[21] This reservation does not extend to 'observing and implementing international obligations, obligations under the Human Rights Convention and obligations under EU law'.[22] Within the domestic constitutional framework, EU law is therefore treated separately to international law. Indeed, Section 126(10) defines 'international obligations' as 'any international obligations of the United Kingdom other than obligations to observe and implement EU law or the Convention rights'.[23]

International (non-EU) obligations may be found both in customary international law and in provisions of international treaties or conventions. In public international law terms the UK is a 'dualist' state: an international agreement entered into by the UK Government does not alter the domestic position until incorporated into national law. International treaties have no legal effect in the UK 'unless and until . . . incorporated into national law by legislation'.[24] In Scotland it is clear that, if proved, 'a rule of customary international law is a rule of Scots law'.[25]

As conclusion of an international treaty is generally the result of foreign affairs in action, it is the UK Government that concludes treaties involving the UK as a nation state. While individual government departments may lead on negotiations, the Foreign and Commonwealth Office (FCO) has the overall interest in form and procedure, as well as considerations of international law. The FCO provides information on treaties to which the UK is a party.[26]

International Obligations and the UK's Constituent Legal Systems

While the UK Government has the authority to bind the UK to certain treaty obligations, it is not always initially responsible for performance of those obligations. The process by which the UK's international obligations become effective and enforceable in Scotland is a matter of constitutional and administrative law. In a dualist state, both treaty-making powers and treaty implementation are required for international law to bite. While the UK Government remains responsible for treaty making, the Scottish Government has responsibility for implementation of international obligations (and indeed EU law). There is an obvious political, if not legal, interest of the Scottish Government in UK Government policy-making and

[20] Ibid., Section 29(4)(b).

[21] Ibid., para. 7(1) of Schedule 5.

[22] Ibid., para. 7(2) of Schedule 5.

[23] Ibid, Section 126(10).

[24] See https://publications.parliament.uk/pa/cm201011/cmselect/cmeuleg/633/63304.htm for a description of the consequences of this dualism.

[25] *Lord Advocate's Reference (No.1 of 2000), Lord Advocate* v. *Zelter and ors.* 2001 SCCR 296 at para. 23; para. 24 continues: 'any analogy between such foreign law and customary international law is false'.

[26] Available at: www.gov.uk/guidance/uk-treaties

treaty-conclusion in subject matters falling within the Scottish Government's range of devolved functions.

While performance of the dualist function in terms of bringing international obligations into Scots law is *prima facie* devolved to the Scottish Ministers, these functions are shared between Scottish and UK Ministers.[27] Where the UK Government enters into an international agreement, committing the UK to bind itself to certain obligations, the Government must be sure that those obligations can actually be given effect to throughout the whole of its territory. Information must be provided to the devolved administrations: according to the Memorandum of Understanding in relation to treaties, either the FCO or lead UK Government department notifies the devolved administration of any new international commitment which the devolved administration requires to implement.[28]

More broadly, the 2013 Memorandum of Understanding and Supplementary Agreements (MoU) between the UK Government and devolved administrations[29] give further insight into the principles underlying these international functions. Although devolution is a relatively recent phenomenon, since 1999 at least seven versions of the MoU have been produced.[30] The MoU is a 'statement of political intent' which, according to the introductory text, 'does not create legal obligations between the parties'.[31]

The structure of the MoU reinforces the distinction between EU issues and matters of international relations, as bilateral 'concordats' between the UK Government and each devolved administration are provided for both EU and non-EU routes. For Scotland, concordat D1 (non-EU) provides that, under the devolution settlement, the UK Government is responsible for international relations: 'the Secretary of State for Foreign and Commonwealth Affairs is responsible for the foreign policy of the United Kingdom, and has overall responsibility for concluding treaties and other international agreements on behalf of the United Kingdom'. Under D1.4 'the UK Government recognises that the devolved administrations will have an interest in international policy making in relation to devolved matters and also in obligations touching on devolved matters'. While the MoU and concordats provide structure to the working relationship, in legal terms the Scotland Act provides the UK

[27] Section 57 of the Scotland Act 1998.

[28] FCO Treaty Section *Treaties and Memoranda of Understanding – Guidance on Practice and Procedures*, available at: www.gov.uk/government/uploads/system/uploads/attachment_data/file/293976/Treaties_and_MoU_Guidance.pdf

[29] Memorandum of Understanding and Supplementary Agreements between the United Kingdom Government, the Scottish Ministers, the Welsh Ministers and the Northern Ireland Executive Committee (the MoU). Available at: https://assets.publishing.service.gov.uk/government/uploads/system/uploads/attachment_data/file/316157/MoU_between_the_UK_and_the_Devolved_Administrations.pdf

[30] Scottish Parliament Information Centre briefing. Available at: www.parliament.scot/S4_ScotlandBillCommittee/General%20Documents/2015.03.24_SPICe_note_on_Memorandums_of_understanding.pdf

[31] The MoU. Available at: https://assets.publishing.service.gov.uk/government/uploads/system/uploads/attachment_data/file/316157/MoU_between_the_UK_and_the_Devolved_Administrations.pdf

Government with power to ensure that the devolved administrations give effect to the UK's international obligations and do not act incompatibly with those obligations.[32] The UK Government has the power to prevent or require action in order to maintain compatibility with international obligations.[33] The UK Government has the power to intervene in the passage of devolved legislation in order to maintain compatibility with the UK's international obligations.[34]

Finally, although the UK Government is responsible for concluding treaties in which the UK, as a Contracting State, commits itself to certain international obligations, it need not be the case that all parts of the UK commit to the same obligations. Where only part of the UK seeks to be bound by such obligations, an international agreement may be entered into in respect of only that system. Substantively, the Hague Convention on the International Protection of Adults is presently irrelevant;[35] nonetheless, it is a precedent for internationally enforceable obligations entering into force in only one UK legal system. UK ratification in 2003 was 'ratification for Scotland only'.[36] In 2003, devolution was in its infancy: at both UK and Scottish levels the Labour Party had been in power throughout. Whether this precedent holds in a different political environment remains a matter of conjecture.

These processes have emerged and evolved between 1999 and the present day, during which time the EU system has also developed and begun to influence domestic laws. The UK has been a member of the EU since 1973 – essentially a generation before the establishment of the present Scottish Parliament and the remainder of the devolution structures set within the context of EU membership. EU law produces rights and obligations which must be given effect: on this basis, the role of the Scottish legislature, executive and indeed judiciary are relevant to considering how EU policy and legislation is made reality. The first comprehensive study of the impact of EU law in Scotland recently examined the application of this body of law before the Scottish (civil) courts.[37] In an article presenting the findings of the project, Professor Barry Rodger accounts for the role that EU law has played in the Scottish legal system, while acknowledging challenges of data analysis. Professor Rodger notes a 'clear general upward trajectory in the frequency of case law in the Scottish courts involving the consideration and application of EU law'. Between the UK's accession in 1973 and the end of 2015, the final count of potential EU law cases in the various Scottish courts was 534. This tendency is increasing: 69.5 per cent of the total has been since 2004, with 42.5 per cent of the total figure since 2010 alone.[38]

32 Section 58 of the Scotland Act 1998.

33 Ibid.

34 Ibid., Section 35.

35 Though related to the one of the earliest Acts of the Scottish Parliament, the Adults with Incapacity (Scotland) Act 2000.

36 http://treaties.fco.gov.uk/treaties/treatyrecord.htm?tid=4603 and www.hcch.net

37 Rodger, 'The Application of EU Law by the Scottish Courts', above fn. 4, 7.

38 Ibid.

Case law was coded on the basis of subject matter, the third most frequent of which was private international law (fifty-eight cases).[39] Of the cases involving an indirect application of EU law within the domestic order, a slight majority involved EU private international law. This latter category is referred to as 'spillover' cases, involving domestic rules and laws modelled on EU law provisions without any EU imperative or required harmonisation. Among a fairly limited but increasing number of EU law cases, there is a slight prominence of EU private international law. What that involves – and how judicial cooperation fits into the equation – is considered in the following section. Exploring the EU's increasing role in broader international affairs is of related interest, particularly vis-à-vis the Hague Conference on Private International Law. Space does not permit this here but this would be worth further study.

EU Private International Law – Judicial Cooperation

Private international law provides a framework for dealing with the possible divergence of legal systems, particularly when people and companies cross borders. While the discipline is generally viewed as containing three key pillars (jurisdiction, choice of law, and the recognition and enforcement of foreign judgments), international judicial cooperation emerges as a fourth, supporting pillar.

Early judicial cooperation tended to involve international agreements entered into by governments on behalf of their states.[40] However, during the post-*Wende*[41] phase of European integration, a gradual shift took place: civil judicial cooperation was described as a matter of Member States' 'common interest' in helping to realise the free movement of persons.[42] With the Treaty of Amsterdam,[43] the EU institutions acquired a role. By the time that treaty came into force in 1999, a decade had passed since the curtain dividing Europe had begun to be lifted. Internal borders were disappearing and Member States agreed to give the (then) European Community legislative competence in relation to civil judicial cooperation, with the purpose of making European citizens' lives easier including 'by improving and simplifying the rules and procedures on cooperation and communication between authorities and on enforcing decisions'.[44] The goal was the creation of a 'genuine European area of justice', in which individuals are able to use another country's courts and authorities

39 Ibid., 8 and fn. 91.

40 For example, the 1968 Brussels Convention on Jurisdiction, Recognition and the Enforcement of Judgments (which came into force in 1973) and the 1980 Rome Convention on the Law Applicable to Contractual Obligations.

41 Literally, 'the turn' but relating to the period since the fall of the Berlin Wall.

42 Art. K.1 of the Treaty on the European Union (TEU), usually 'the Maastricht Treaty'.

43 Treaty of Amsterdam amending the Treaty on European Union, the Treaties Establishing the European Communities and Certain Related Acts 1997 OJ C 340-1.

44 Action Plan of the Council and the Commission on how best to implement the provisions of the Treaty of Amsterdam on an area of freedom, security and justice (1999/C 19/01).

as easily as their own[45]. In the decade that followed, a number of key regulations were adopted.

The EU underwent further changes: in 2009 two treaties were adopted, making up what is known as the Lisbon Treaty: the Treaty on European Union (TEU), which forms the basis of EU law and sets out general principles and purpose; and the Treaty of the Functioning of the European Union (TFEU), which sets out more detailed and updated provisions of EU law.

Article 67 TFEU provides that 'the Union shall constitute an area of freedom, security and justice with respect for fundamental rights and the different legal systems and traditions of the Member States'.[46] Along with other provisions relating to the 'area of freedom, security and justice', Title V of the TFEU contains the most recent provisions on civil judicial cooperation.

EU policy-making and legislation relying on Title V is particularly important for the UK because the UK has a default opt-out to measures adopted under this title.[47] The UK is not bound by Title V measures unless it chooses to opt into them. 'Title V measures' therefore attract specific procedure within the UK but from a Scottish perspective it should be noted that the opt-in decision is one for the UK Government to take, following Westminster parliamentary procedure. In practice, the opt-in is often used – the majority of Title V measures apply in the UK, particularly for civil and commercial matters.[48] However, the UK Government elected not to opt into the EU Regulation establishing the Justice (funding) programme for the period 2014–20.[49] Under that programme, funds are allocated to specific aims including to 'facilitate and support judicial cooperation in civil and criminal matters' (30 per cent of the total share). Without opting in, the UK and its constituent parts are not eligible to apply for EU funding under this programme: for example, the 2018 'Call for proposals for action grants to support transnational projects to promote judicial cooperation in civil and criminal matters'.[50]

[45] The Tampere (Council) Conclusions of a special European Council meeting in October 1999 in Tampere, Finland.

[46] Art. 67 of the Treaty on the Functioning of the European Union, signed on 13 December 2007, *Official Journal C* 326, 26.10.2012 P. 0001–0390.

[47] Protocol 21 on the position of the United Kingdom and Ireland in respect of the Area of Freedom, Security and Justice, annexed to the Treaty on the Functioning of the European Union.

[48] www.gov.uk/government/publications/jha-opt-in-and-schengen-opt-out-protocols--3

[49] Regulation (EU) 1382/2013 of the European Parliament and of the Council of 17 December 2013 establishing a Justice Programme for the period 2014 to 2020 (2013). Available at: https://eur-lex.europa.eu/legal-content/EN/TXT/?uri=CELEX%3A32013R1382. For an overview of the programme, see http://ec.europa.eu/justice/grants1/programmes-2014-2020/justice/index_en.htm

[50] JUST-AG Justice Action Grant, JUST-JCOO-AG-2018. Available at: https://ec.europa.eu/research/participants/portal/desktop/en/opportunities/just/topics/just-jcoo-ag-2018.html

Civil Judicial Cooperation in the Treaty on the Functioning of the European Union

Article 81(1) TFEU requires the Union to 'develop judicial cooperation in civil matters having cross-border implications'. Judicial cooperation 'may include measures for the approximation of the laws and regulations of the Member States'. For the purposes of developing cooperation, the European Parliament and the Council shall adopt measures, 'particularly for the functioning of the Single Market'. Those measures are aimed at ensuring

> (a) the mutual recognition and enforcement between Member States of judgments and of decisions in extrajudicial cases; (b) the cross-border service of judicial and extrajudicial documents; (c) the compatibility of the rules applicable in the Member States concerning conflict of laws and of jurisdiction; (d) cooperation in the taking of evidence; (e) effective access to justice; (f) the elimination of obstacles to the proper functioning of civil proceedings, if necessary by promoting the compatibility of the rules on civil procedure applicable in the Member States; (g) the development of alternative methods of dispute settlement; (h) support for the training of the judiciary and judicial staff.[51]

As the general principle of subsidiarity governs the exercise of the EU's competence, the requirement for harmonisation must first be established.[52] EU competence manifests itself in a number of ways but legislative acts in this field have tended to take the form of Regulations (eighteen in total). While 'transposition' of Regulations into domestic law is generally inappropriate, legislation might be required in order to amend inconsistent existing provisions. However, a Directive allows greater discretion.[53] Where, as in the case of the UK, responsibility for implementation lies with more than one authority, Directives might allow for greater variation. A valid object of future study might be whether the EU's use of Regulations has maintained an intra-UK consistency to judicial cooperation – and/or to private international law more generally. While space does not permit a full consideration of all aims of judicial cooperation as set out in Article 81, the following section provides some insights from a Scottish perspective.

Mutual Recognition and Enforcement of Judgments

With mutual recognition and enforcement of judgments, a judgment from one jurisdiction can be recognised and then enforced in another. The principal EU regulation in this area, the Brussels I *bis* Regulation,[54] effectively created a geographical area

[51] Art. 81(2) of the TFEU.

[52] Stürner, M. (2015) 'Die justizielle Zusammenarbeit im Privatrecht in der EU', *Jura: juristische Ausbildung*; vol. 37, no. 8, 813–21, at 814.

[53] Art. 288 of the TFEU.

[54] Regulation (EU) 1215/2012 of the European Parliament and of the Council of 12 December 2012 on jurisdiction and the recognition and enforcement of judgments in civil and commercial matters (recast).

in which judgments enjoy free movement, subject to certain conditions. A court in one Member State no longer requires to declare enforceable a judgment of another Member State – the administrative validation process of *exequatur* has been abolished. Newer regulations have made similar provisions – the trend is in favour of the abolition of this administrative step. In Scotland this removes the role of the Court of Session, to which a petition for registration of a judgment previously required to be made.[55]

The Cross-border Service of Judicial and Extra-judicial Documents

Judicial and extra-judicial documents (judgments and other legal documents) are generally served within the jurisdiction in which they were issued. Agreeing to allow service in one country of documents originating from another is one way in which states agree to cooperate not necessarily for their own sake as states, but rather for the benefit of their citizens. Service of documents rules within the EU require Member States to designate bodies called 'transmitting agencies' and 'receiving agencies', responsible for transmission and receipt of documents.[56] At least one central body supplies information to the transmitting agencies. Within the UK, the various legal systems make separate provisions. For Scotland both approved solicitors, and messengers-at-arms and sheriff officers, are designated as transmitting and receiving agencies.[57] The Scottish Ministers are designated as a central body; a team in the Justice Directorate of the Scottish Government carries out these functions. This team acts as the central body for Scotland for a wide range of international conventions and EU regulations. The Central Authority is the main point of contact for incoming and outgoing cases involving Scotland. Officials from other Member States, as well as practitioners and courts in Scotland, have recourse to this team for matters covered by those instruments and agreements.[58]

Effective Access to Justice

EU citizens' effective access to (cross-border) justice is a central concept, supported by the establishment of the European Judicial Network on Civil and Commercial Matters (EJN). The legal basis for the EJN is a 2001 Council decision and a 2009

[55] Chapter 62 (recognition, registration and enforcement of foreign judgments, etc.) of the Rules of the Court of Session contains relevant rules for Brussels Ibis among others: see www.scotcourts.gov.uk/docs/default-source/rules-and-practice/rules-of-court/court-of-session/chap62.pdf

[56] Regulation (EC) 1393/2007 of the European Parliament and of the Council of 13 November 2007. See further, 'Judicial Cooperation in Civil Matters in the EU: A Guide for Legal Practitioners', published by the European Commission DG Justice and Consumers and available at: https://publications.europa.eu/en/publication-detail/-/publication/a9da11b8-0a6a-491e-8ae9-a0ff9d7e8535/language-en

[57] European Communities (Service of Judicial and Extrajudicial Documents) (Scotland) Regulations 2001 (SSI 2001/172).

[58] See the Scottish Parliament Information Centre's factsheet: 'Brexit: Impact on the Justice System in Scotland', 16, available at: www.parliament.scot/ResearchBriefingsAndFactsheets/S5/SB_16-83_Brexit_Impact_on_the_Justice_System_in_Scotland.pdf

decision of the European Parliament and the Council;[59] the EJN is not a Commission proposal but rather a commitment by the Member States themselves. The existence of multiple legal systems and traditions within the EU – both in substantive and procedural terms – might create an obstacle to the use of free movement rights. The purposes of the EJN might be seen as assisting to overcome this barrier by: providing information to the public, practitioners, judges and others on the working of EU instruments on judicial cooperation in civil and commercial matters, including information about the relevant laws and legal practices of other Member States; helping judges and relevant national authorities to resolve difficulties that may arise in the interpretation or application of EU legislation; and providing a means of communication to judges in different Member States.

The EJN consists of a number of national 'contact points' – a maximum of six per Member State. The UK has one contact point for England and Wales, one for Scotland and one for Northern Ireland. Contact points attend a number of EJN meetings each year: these provide opportunities for officials in Ministries across the EU to meet, share best practice, resolve issues that have been raised with them and maintain communications with officials in the European Commission. Agendas and details of meetings are available online.[60] Some EJN meetings involve Central Authorities, whose representatives might meet bilaterally to discuss particular cases of note, interest or difficulty. The Commission facilitates this practical cooperation, with Central Authorities' representatives discussing cases in detail. Meetings might involve an element of cultural 'translation' as insight is given into the workings of a legal profession or tradition. Understanding the specifics of one case might require more knowledge of the dominant legal culture – familiar to those in the know but quite foreign in the 'unknown' sense of the word. Reflecting the separate nature of the legal systems and contact point nomination, Scotland's Central Authority may be invited or itself invite other Central Authorities to bilateral discussions.

All EU Member States except Denmark participate in the EJN, although Denmark may nonetheless attend meetings. Candidate countries Serbia and Montenegro participated for the first time as observers to the EJN at the 2017 annual meeting.[61] Third countries that are party to international agreements on civil judicial cooperation may also be invited to attend certain meetings as observers. An observer state may send a maximum of three representatives.

Another key feature of the work of the EJN is its provision of information to citizens, businesses and practitioners by the use of the e-Justice portal.[62] Member States

[59] Consolidated EJN decision available at: http://eur-lex.europa.eu/legal-content/EN/TXT/?uri=CELEX:02001D0470-20110101

[60] See https://e-justice.europa.eu/content_eventsnews-438-en.do

[61] See https://e-justice.europa.eu/content_eventsnews-438-en.do

[62] See https://e-justice.europa.eu/content_ejn_in_civil_and_commercial_matters-21-en.do and the new BETA site https://beta.e-justice.europa.eu/?action=home&plang=en

commit themselves to provide (and update) information online using this portal.[63] In 2016, the Commission presented to the European Parliament, the Council, and the European Economic and Social Committee a report on the activities of the EJN.[64] The report analyses the network's role in developing day-to-day judicial cooperation, stating that the EJN was, through both its 'purpose and design', a tool which contributes to building bridges and thereby creating mutual trust.[65] While 'mutual trust' might be EU theology – and in any event hard to measure – the report offers a recent and thorough look at a network of officials and practitioners whose role in judicial cooperation is of targeted and practical import.

As contact points get to know one another regularly and informally, the value of a network such as the EJN is how it extends beyond the legal requirements of cooperation. Regularly meeting counterparts from across the EU helps give cooperation a human face and increases awareness of practice. Knowledge of other EU languages can be put to good use but the key is to provide an effective translation of culture and practice. An equivalent network exists for criminal matters and the two networks occasionally interact.[66]

Support for the Training of the Judiciary and Judicial Staff

In practice it is often the judiciary and judicial staff whose role determines whether or not cross-border cooperation works in practice.[67] The e-Justice portal is open to practitioners, laypersons and also to members of the judiciary. Domestic judges may on occasion – and depending on the topic – accompany national contact points to EJN meetings and meet their EU judicial counterparts. Some national contact points are themselves judges, particularly from states where judges may be seconded into a Ministry for a period of time. Such a move is not typical in Scotland, nor indeed elsewhere in the UK, where judges are not 'career judges' as with most of their mainland European counterparts.

A separate network, the European Judicial Training Network (EJTN) supports

[63] The portal contains information about practitioners and agencies in a Member State: solicitors in Scotland can check for equivalents in, say, Spain, while French practitioners can use a postcode in Scotland to find a sheriff officer in a particular area. On specific pages there are flags for each country but the UK flag takes users to separate sub-pages: one each for England and Wales, Northern Ireland, Scotland and Gibraltar. The Scottish Government maintains the pages relating to Scots law and practice. Information provided in one language is (gradually) being translated into others: a Polish speaker in Scotland can look up information about the sources of Scots law in Polish, or search for the same in English in respect of Poland. In addition to being a source of information about the EJN and national systems, the portal also outlines the various EU legislative instruments in civil judicial cooperation.

[64] See http://eur-lex.europa.eu/legal-content/EN/TXT/PDF/?uri=CELEX:52016DC0129&from=EN

[65] http://eur-lex.europa.eu/legal-content/EN/TXT/?qid=1458206470776&uri=CELEX%3A52016DC0129

[66] Basic information about the EJN for criminal matters is on the e-Justice portal, while the EJN (criminal) has its own website at www.ejn-crimjust.europa.eu/ejn/EJN_Home.aspx

[67] On the role of judges see further Goicoechea and van Loon's chapter in this volume.

and promotes training for the European judiciary including on 'civil, criminal and commercial law, and linguistics and societal issues'.[68] European judicial training for justice professionals encompasses 'the practitioners involved in the justice system such as judges, prosecutors, court staff, bailiffs or enforcement officers, lawyers, notaries, mediators, legal interpreters and translators, [and] court experts'.[69] The 2011 Commission strategy on European judicial training[70] sets objectives to be reached by 2020, with a 2018 consultation[71] seeking to gather views on that strategy and proposals for 2019–25. As the UK Government did not opt into the Justice Funding Regulation for 2014–20, the UK jurisdictions are not eligible to apply for funding for training under this regulation.[72]

Civil Judicial Cooperation: Private International Law in Practice

Within this context, some observations follow on how private international law is given effect, or 'done' in practice. Many private international law texts refer both to the existence of an 'Other' and the condition that that Other be foreign. If private international law is to be celebrated as a form of engaging with the 'Other' then who or what, in a Scottish practitioner's context, is that 'Other'? Judicial cooperation overcomes the reality that one party cannot unilaterally oblige another to do something. Cooperation implies acknowledgment, acceptance and an element of reciprocity between or among parties. Who or what are those parties? Using the Westphalian construction, cooperation is a voluntary limitation of state sovereignty: a sovereign state commits itself to cooperate with another sovereign state only within 'the framework of pre-established conditions of its own acceptance'.[73]

The Scottish perspective challenges this construction: can judicial cooperation be an exercise in the voluntary limitation of state sovereignty when Scotland is not a sovereign state? If the UK as sovereign state commits its various constituent jurisdictions to cooperate with other sovereign states, what does it mean when the framework of pre-established conditions of the UK's acceptance come to bear on,

[68] http://www.ejtn.eu/About-us

[69] https://ec.europa.eu/info/consultations/training-justice-professionals-eu-law-evaluation-new-2019-2025-strategy_en

[70] Commission Communication, *Building Trust in EU-wide Justice: A New Dimension to European Judicial Training*. COM/2011/0551, available at: http://eur-lex.europa.eu/legal-content/EN/ALL/?uri=CELEX:52011DC0551

[71] https://ec.europa.eu/info/consultations/training-justice-professionals-eu-law-evaluation-new-2019-2025-strategy_en

[72] Regulation (EU) No. 1382/2013 of the European Parliament and of the Council of 17 December 2013 establishing a Justice Programme for the period 2014 to 2020 (2013), available at https://eur-lex.europa.eu/legal-content/EN/TXT/?uri=CELEX%3A32013R1382; for an overview of the programme, see http://ec.europa.eu/justice/grants1/programmes-2014-2020/justice/index_en.htm

[73] 'Upcoming Issues of EU Law', analysis of issues compiled for the JURI committee hearing on 24 September 2014, PE 509.987, available at: www.europarl.europa.eu/document/activities/cont/201409/20140924ATT89662/20140924ATT89662EN.pdf

say, the Scottish legal system? If cooperation requires two parties who or what, in the Scottish context, are those parties?

On the other hand, Ralf Michaels[74] contends that the 'Other' being engaged in private international law terms is *another law* – '[f]oreign law is similar because it is law, just like the law of the forum is law. Foreign law is different because it is foreign law, not the law of the forum.'[75] One understanding of 'foreign' can be seen in the German Act of Introduction to the civil code, which defines private international law as 'the law to be used where the facts of a case have a connection to a foreign country'.[76] International judicial cooperation presumably follows that same pattern: the website of the German Federal Office of Justice[77] states that the role of the EJN is to assist people concerned with 'cross-border legal cases' with information about the different national legal systems. In his introduction to EU private international law, Bogdan offers the following description: 'Whenever a private law relationship having connections to more than one country (and thereby to more than one legal system) gives rise to a legal controversy . . . should the court apply its own law or foreign law'.[78] Both the German law and the position reflected by Bogdan in this text about EU private international law reflect a dominant understanding that this area of law is about 'foreignness', presumed to relate to another country. If the 'Other' must be foreign then what does that mean in a UK context? Both Scotland and England are constituent parts of the UK and as such neither is 'foreign' to each other in the most common sense of being 'of, from, in or characteristic of a country or language other than one's own'.[79] However, in legal terms, the respective jurisdictions have boundaries: lawyers qualified in Scotland have no rights of audience or practice in England and vice versa. The binary can be established. Words have shades of meaning: the guidance accompanying the Adults with Incapacity Act 2000[80] describes the provisions of that Act as applying to guardians appointed 'under the law of another country, including that of England, Wales and Northern Ireland'. Indeed, the Faculty of Advocates' response to the UK Government's Balance of Competences Review highlighted that

> [w]hen considering cross-border judicial cooperation among the UK jurisdiction in criminal matters, the House of Lords, in 1999, recalled that, although Scotland and England are politically united, for jurisdiction purposes, the two legal systems are to

[74] See the first chapter of this volume.

[75] See Michaels' chapter in this volume.

[76] *Sachverhalten mit einer Verbindung zu einem ausländischen Staat*: Art. 3 of the EGBGB, the (German) Act of Introduction to the Civil Code, available online in English at: www.gesetze-im-internet.de/englisch_bgbeg/englisch_bgbeg.html#p0015

[77] See www.bundesjustizamt.de/DE/Themen/Gerichte_Behoerden/EJNZH/Start/Ueberblick_node.html

[78] Bogdan, M (2006) *Concise Introduction to European Union Private International Law*, Europa Law Publishing, 3.

[79] Definition from the *Oxford English Dictionary*.

[80] See www.gov.scot/Publications/2008/03/20114619/11

> be considered as 'independent foreign countries'. The same principle applies in civil matters.[81]

Although the legal systems may be independent, in many situations there is no such binary: there is Scots private law and there is English private law, but there is also the jurisdiction of the UK Supreme Court which applies equally to both. At around the same time as the Faculty of Advocates set out the position above, the then President of the UK Supreme Court, Lord Neuberger, gave a public lecture on 'the British and Europe' in which the risk of 'eliding or confusing the UK with England' was said to be 'inevitable because England represents over 85% of the UK's population'.[82] Lord Neuberger continued

> If I were to identify and discuss every distinction between England and other parts of the UK on the points made in this talk, it would become tedious – or perhaps I should say even more tedious. So I apologise in advance if, at times, I appear to be subsuming the other parts of the UK into England.[83]

What, if anything, does it mean for the existence of the private international law binary if the other parts of the UK are subsumed into England? Where there is more than one legal system, there is a possibility for more than one response to the same issue. Otherwise there would be no reason for certain jurisdictions to attract cross-border litigation and others not to do the same. The UK highlights that legal diversity is possible not only among nation states but within a nation state. That diversity manifests itself in legislative bodies, in government administrations, and in court structures and judicial interpretation. That diversity is the result of historical evolution, as well as modern-day political realities.

If this volume highlights the ability of private international law methodologies and techniques to manage legal diversity, the specific role of judicial cooperation within that context must surely be in its active engagement with the Other. It is first important to know your own system, before engaging with representatives of another system about the individualities of each. In explaining those idiosyncrasies, one must – for a moment – take a look back from the perspective of the Other. Acting as a cultural ambassador, or mere interpreter, it falls to one party to explain, for example, that his or her system does not presuppose the existence of state-held details of all repossessed properties in the country. Looking at the 'domestic' system and being required to justify the differences between it and the non-domestic offers an opportunity both for greater understanding of one's own position and for the chance to revisit that position and potentially – on the basis of the other party's points – even revise

[81] Faculty of Advocates response to 'Review of the Balance of Competences between the UK and the EU: Civil Judicial Cooperation', February 2014, available at: www.gov.uk/government/uploads/system/uploads/attachment_data/file/279228/civil-judicial-cooperation-report-review-of-balance-of-competences.pdf

[82] See www.supremecourt.uk/docs/speech-140212.pdf

[83] Ibid.

it. For by seeing yourself as others see you, there is chance for reflection and perhaps even change. However, for any of this to be possible, there must first be acceptance of the validity of the existence of more than one possible outcome to the same set of facts and circumstances.[84]

An important caveat to these points takes into account the UK's dualist status: obligations entered into on the international stage require to be brought into force by domestic legislation. 'Making' private international law in terms of entering into arrangements with other states for judicial cooperation is within the competence reserved to the UK institutions. But there are responsibilities (outlined above) for the devolved administrations to ensure those obligations form part of the laws for which they are responsible. From a Scottish perspective, then, the power to 'make' private international law is often disassociated from the responsibility to 'do' private international law.

On the other hand, if the substantive rules of private international law are to be changed, this would be devolved and a matter for the Scottish legislature and executive. Indeed, it is only in relation to the international aspects of private international law that the competence to make private international law is separate from the obligation to perform it. Cooperation between and among judicial actors operating within the devolved sphere of competence – whether judicial, prosecutorial or executive – would not seem to rely on the existence of those international arrangements.

Conclusion

Following devolution there was a period of relative constitutional stability until the 2014 referendum in which voters in Scotland were asked whether Scotland should be an independent country. A total of 55.3 per cent voted against the proposition. Less than two years later, voters in the UK were asked in a referendum: should the UK remain a member of the EU or leave the EU? A 1.9 per cent majority (51.9 per cent to 48.1 per cent) voted to leave the EU. In these times of manifold challenges, domestic constitutional tensions coexist with those on the EU – and, thus, soon likely to be 'international' – front. Within the EU, the 'Europeanisation' of private international law has been achieved through legislative acts, cooperation mechanisms and also through a gradual process of training and exchange. Rühl and von Hein concluded in 2015 that the time had 'not yet come' for a comprehensive code, preferring a 'creeping' codification by the gradual creation of a more coherent framework.[85] Without the UK and its special position on Title V measures, this Europeanisation process can continue – indeed, presumably, at pace. Whether judicial cooperation will broaden and perhaps deepen remains to be seen, but the latest EJN funding call

[84] On 'pluralistic thinking' as essential to 'do' private international law see Ruiz Abou-Nigm's final chapter in this volume.

[85] Von Hein, J. and G. Rühl (2015) 'Towards a European Code on Private International Law?', in the European Parliament's Legal Affairs Committee (JURI) 2015 workshop 'Cross-border Activities in the EU – Making Life Easier for Citizens'.

proposes to allocate funds to national networks as well as cross-border ones. The external dimension to the EU's competence adds another dimension.

Within the UK it seems as though the common umbrella of Europeanised private international law is to be withdrawn. Within constitutional limits, each constituent jurisdiction has choices to make about judicial cooperation with EU neighbours: will this be maintained, decline or even deepen in the near future? Rodger's study of the impact of EU law in Scotland showed a general increase in the number of EU law cases, and a gradually increasing number of requests for a preliminary reference from Scottish courts to the Court of Justice of the European Union.[86] Practitioners in Scotland appear to be making an increasing recourse to EU law arguments: perhaps this was all just a matter of time for a generation born after UK accession to the EU and who have no recollection of professional life before the establishment of the present Scottish Parliament. On the other hand, for those who only know devolution for Scotland within the context of the UK's membership of the EU, change would seem to be on the cards.

[86] Rodger, B. (2017), above fn. 4.

11

The Judgments Project of the Hague Conference on Private International Law: A Way Forward for a Long-awaited Solution

Fabrício B. Pasquot Polido

Introductory Remarks

In April 2011, the Council for General Affairs and Policy of the Hague Conference on Private International Law (HCCH) resumed activities on the 'Judgments Project', an enterprise addressing the negotiations of a multilateral convention on recognition and enforcement of foreign judgments in civil and commercial matters.[1] Unsurprisingly, the Project re-emerged as an important forum for debate and reflection about the precise scope and current functions of recognition regimes, reaching a very representative audience from the Members and from scholarly circles in the field of private international law worldwide. In spite of the expectations created in the past by the original proposal presented by the delegation of the United States in the early 1990s – with the remarkable intellectual support of Professor Arthur von Mehren – and the subsequent development of the Project, with the backlashes and controversies that led to the unsuccessful negotiations by Hague Members in 2001, the relaunch of the HCCH initiative appears to be a real opportunity to connect recognition and jurisdictional 'normative spaces' to some universal private international law goals.

[1] The Judgments Project, as the Hague Conference's project is known, constitutes the initiative arising from the successive negotiations in the organisation since the 1990s on the possible adoption of a multilateral convention on the jurisdiction and recognition and enforcement of Judgments. For a historical retrospective on the Judgments Project, see www.hcch.net/en/projects/legislative-projects/judgments. As to the date of conclusion of this chapter, the HCCH convened four meetings of the Special Commission for the Judgments Convention (respectively 1–9 June 2016; 16–23 February 2017; 12–17 November 2017; and 24–9 May 2018). Upon the end of its Fourth Meeting, in May 2018, the Special Commission considered that it had completed the mandate conferred on it by the Council for General Affairs and Policy and that the work on the Draft Convention on Recognition and Enforcement of Foreign Judgments on Civil or Commercial Matters had reached the stage where a Diplomatic Session could be convened in mid-2019. The Draft Convention of May 2018 is available at https://assets.hcch.net/docs/23b6dac3-7900-49f3-9a94-aa0ffbe0d0dd.pdf

Much has been already written about the current negotiations taking place at the HCCH in connection with the Judgments Project since the first Draft Convention was prepared by the delegates of Member States in the course of work of the Special Commission's First Meeting in June 2016.[2] A considerable part of the literature, however, provides a doctrinal analysis focused on the technicalities and legal aspects of the draft's main provisions, such as general exclusion of subject matters from its scope of application; exclusive bases for recognition, jurisdictional filters and the draft's 'compatibility' with domestic laws and European instruments (namely Brussels I recast – Regulation No. 1215/2012).[3]

The Project, however, may not simply strategically result in a draft treaty in terms of a long-awaited solution by the Hague Conference, where a multilateral convention establishing uniform rules for recognition and enforcement of judgments in civil/commercial matters is likely to be concluded. Rather, the Judgments Project appears to meet some long-held expectations and converge on the theoretical enterprises of private international law both in strengthening 'recognition' as one of its main operative pillars (as proposed generally, for instance, by Paul Lagarde as a path for the 'future of private international law').[4] Likewise, any undertaking at multilateral level by an international organisation in the domain of private international law, such as the Hague Conference, also highlights the increasing relevance of coordination of the judicial dispute resolution systems with respect to transnational civil and commercial litigation and cross-border litigation planning.

Here, recognition may be also understood in a broader context, as one of the overarching principles, like mutual trust, for the proper political and normative functioning of the international legal cooperation regimes, jurisdictional shared spaces and for the adequate protection of interests and rights of individuals, families and companies. At best, the Judgments Project is a vital facade of this wider shifting normative landscape.

I contend further that the 'way forward' for the Judgments Project, in addition

[2] The documents of the four Meetings of the Special Commission are available on the Judgments website at:: www.hcch.net/en/projects/legislative-projects/Judgments/special-commission1. For the purposes of this chapter, the Draft Judgments Convention refers to the text consolidated after the conclusion of the Fourth Meeting of the Special Commission in May 2018 (hereinafter 'Draft Judgments Convention – Version May 2018', HCCH, Working Document No. 262 Revised).

[3] See, for instance, Brand, R. (2012) 'Recognition and Enforcement of Foreign Judgments', *International Litigation Guide*, 1; Bonomi, A. (2016) 'Courage or Caution? A Critical Overview of the Hague Preliminary Draft on Judgments', *Yearbook of Private International Law*, vol. XVII, 1–36; Wagner, R. (2016) 'Ein neuer Anlauf zu einem Haager Anerkennungs- und Vollstreckungsübereinkommen' *IPRax: Praxis des Internationalen Privat und Verfahrensrecht*, vol. 36, 9; Beaumont, P. and L. Walker (2015) 'Recognition and Enforcement of Judgments in Civil and Commercial Matters in the Brussels I Recast and Some Lessons from it and the Recent Hague Conventions for the Hague Judgments Project', *Journal of Private International Law*, vol. 11, 31.

[4] Lagarde, P. (2014) 'La méthode de la reconnaissance est-elle l'avenir du droit international privé?', *Recueil des cours*, vol. 341, 7.

to the desired conclusion and adoption of a multilateral convention by the 2019 Diplomatic Conference, has been the development of some important results from the standpoint of private international law policy-making and scholarly engagement. Successful outcomes of the Project may strive for minimum standards of uniformity (with diversity being preserved at domestic normative levels) and predictability. They consolidate a balanced framework for end-users in transnational litigation in civil and commercial matters at global level. In this sense, the Judgments Project is naturally and maturely much more ambitious, tenacious and technical than the 1958 New York Convention on Recognition and Enforcement of Foreign Arbitral Awards.[5]

This chapter critically assesses some of the foundational benchmarks and inspirational ideas underlying the current negotiations for the future convention, based on the ongoing work carried out by the HCCH. In addition, it deals with some issues of importance for 'global facilitated regimes' for transnational civil and commercial litigation.

Strengthening Institutional Goals and Facilitating a 'Global Recognition Regime'

The evolving institutional framework of the HCCH in the past three decades has confirmed the organisation's mission to reorganise the existing and open regulatory clusters in the field of private international law and international litigation. While keeping a consistent normative agenda in dialogue with the UNCITRAL and UNIDROIT, the Hague Conference appears to have established a safe harbour for the promotion of private international law related harmonisation and uniformisation goals and outcomes. The adoption of instruments minimally driven by the continuous demands of states, individuals, companies and non-governmental organisations (NGOs) reveals an integrated approach of private international law rules and principles existing and operating within a highly diverse societal context at transnational level.

It is not surprising that a private international law policy agenda – though not ranked in the top priority list of states and their governmental bodies – still remains highly adaptable and sensible to the increasingly changeable reality of international family and business affairs, as well as to the current institutionalisation patterns of international procedural and administrative and judicial cooperation frameworks dealing with specific domains of the 'global movers' (for example, from persons to tangible and intangible assets, such as goods, services, technology and information).[6] All these features represent a normative space for the inexorable blend of substantive and procedural rules intertwined with the traditional three areas of private

[5] The Convention on the Recognition and Enforcement of Foreign Arbitral Awards was adopted in New York on 10 June 1958 and entered into force on 7 June 1959; 159 States Parties, status as at 15 October 2018 [hereinafter the 'New York Convention' or the '1958 New York Convention'].

[6] For instance, a variety of topics is covered by private international law interfaces, such as environmental and human rights related issues; global governance issues; the global movement towards new technologies and the internet; the relationship with international labour law and investments.

international law – governing law, jurisdiction and recognition, and enforcement of foreign judgments.

In fact, modernisation trends and a sort of 'global legal awareness'[7] emerged from the HCCH's recent initiatives, particularly with regard to the enhancement of legislative projects, the 'treaty-based institutional direct transnational co-operation model' relating to private cross-border relationships[8] and a deep commitment to maintaining an awareness of the importance of private international law objectives. In my view, such objectives still comprise legal diversity and tolerance;[9] coordination and interaction between legal systems and solutions;[10] facilitation of recognition of legal relationships; and the guarantee of access to justice at a multijurisdictional level. It is not necessary to reinvent the wheel or to introduce private international law in an unfairly aesthetic and merely technical-procedural fashion as if it were something unknown, uncanny and mysterious.

The Judgments Project, in turn, is not only about ensuring a 'pro-enforcement' approach for judicial decisions across different legal systems and their jurisdictional normative spaces. In spite of the difficulties of consensus in some areas, the Draft Convention re-emerges as a conscious commitment of the Hague Members with coordinated solutions for the proper functioning of global systems of dispute resolution. In general, this refers to the ultimate goal of uniformisation of private international law rules in their procedural variants. Although it is submitted that the main objective of the planned Hague Judgments Convention is to facilitate cross-border enforcement of foreign judgments, it also covers certain expectations of the 'global legal movement' in civil and commercial matters, in particular efficiency and legal cooperation.[11]

[7] Let us contend that 'global legal awareness' may represent a conceptual understanding committed with international legal values and education, international legal practice and international commonalities, all of them highly sensitive to diversity in legal traditions and legal cultures across the globe and requiring a critical, politically engaged and innovative enterprise in thinking around global issues. This is precisely where international legal thinking and international policies in different perspectives and regions comes into play, whereby international, transnational and global spheres are becoming narrow. See, for instance, Trubek, D. M., Y. Dezalay, R. Buchanan and J. R. Davis (1993) 'Global Restructuring and the Law: Studies of the Internationalization of Legal Fields and the Creation of Transitional Arenas', *Case Western Reserve Law Review*, vol. 44, 407.

[8] For different perspectives, see the illustrative overview provided by van Loon, J. H. A. (2015) 'The Global Horizon of Private International Law', *Recueil des cours*, vol. 380, 9–108, at 73 (containing an analysis of examples of post-convention work of the HCCH in the field of family law and international legal cooperation in civil and commercial matters).

[9] See, for instance, Yntema, H. E. (1953) 'The Historic Bases of Private International Law', *The American Journal of Comparative Law*, vol. 2, 300; Goldschmidt, W. (1990) *Derecho internacional privado: Derecho de la tolerancia*, Depalma.

[10] Picone, P. (1999) 'Les méthodes de coordination entre ordres juridiques en droit international privé', *Recueil des cours*, vol. 276, 9–296.

[11] For different views, see, for instance, Slaughter, A. M. (2005) *A New World Order*, Princeton University Press, 85 (which explores the general framework and international politics of coordination of judicial cooperation networks and transnational litigation).

In fact, these assumptions might be best grasped from two different normative perspectives: the first is related to the scope and reach of a special procedural single convention to be adopted by Hague Member States and having the precise objective of setting uniform rules, principles and standards dealing with recognition of foreign judgments at multilateral level. As to cross-border dispute settlement frameworks, for example, the future regime could be seen as complementary to and interactive with the pre-existing recognition regime of foreign arbitral awards, as established by the 1958 New York Convention and corresponding state practice in that field. Yet, the future convention has been evolving to set minimum standards or degrees of uniformity in recognition regimes, while at the same time preserving legal diversity in domestic normative spaces.[12]

In addition to an attempt to fill existing normative gaps in terms of effectiveness of dispute settlement regimes (for example, the powerful transnational arbitration regime coexisting with an incipient transnational civil/commercial litigation regime), the Draft Convention reinstates a long-awaited goal as to the channelling of civil and commercial proceedings in particular jurisdictions. In fact, with the adoption of a global instrument, as the Draft Judgments Convention is intended to be, some Member States could become exporting states of civil/commercial judgments and could also stand out as global commercial jurisdictions, with the potential of becoming 'global commercial courts'.

The literature consistently recalls that a multilateral convention on recognition and enforcement of foreign judgments would allow above all a general expectation that rulings would be recognised in all participating Member States. This reveals the crucial element of a multilateral obligation to be implemented in good faith and with binding force.[13] In addition, as Dreyfuss and Ginsburg remark, such a convention could 'reduce costs for all sides, conserve judicial resources on an international basis

[12] One could remark that the emergence of a multilateral regime for recognition and enforcement of foreign judgments, such as the one envisaged by the HCCH, allows Member States to retain their domestic rules on recognition and enforcement for those residual cases not encompassed by the Convention (for example, non-signatory parties and subject matters excluded from its scope of application). Likewise, future signatory countries may have the opportunity to review existing state practices in the field and additionally to make a decision on individual cases concerning the application of bilateral treaties involving jurisdiction and recognition and enforcement. For instance, von Mehren sustained that one of the reasons for states to refrain from (or be reluctant to) engage in multilateral negotiations on a treaty establishing uniform rules on recognition and enforcement of judgments was the preference for bilateral agreements in this field. According to him, bilateral treaties would reduce the diplomatic distances and interests among states (for instance, the recurrent idea of 'mutual mistrust' involved in a larger jurisdictional context). See von Mehren, A. T. (1994) 'Recognition and Enforcement of Foreign Judgments: A New Approach for the Hague Conference?', *Law and Contemporary Problems*, vol. 57, 277. Two decades after his seminal contributions, the development of the HCCH Project suggests that the design of facilitated recognition regimes may have the advantage of generating outputs reducing the asymmetries related to dispute resolution systems in civil and commercial litigation.

[13] See the section on Aspirational Ideas for the Judgments Project and the Future Hague Convention below.

and promote consistent outcomes',[14] fostering the institutional features of transnational civil and commercial litigation.[15]

The second normative issue relates to the main structures and governance of cross-border private litigation. The technical features of the current Draft Convention are focused on three bundles of rules. They cover rules on exclusion from scope of application (Art. 2); rules on recognition of judgments rendered by the national courts of Hague Member States (such as provisions dealing with general bases of recognition: Arts 4 and 5; and exclusive bases of recognition: Art. 6) to rules of non-recognition or refusal (namely, provisions dealing with cases where state courts can refuse recognition and enforcement of foreign judgments: Art. 7). From the standpoint of international litigation, parties and courts in Hague Member States will probably benefit from predictability, in particular with regard to the following litigation planning profiles: (1) which subject matters are expressly excluded from the scope of application of the convention and hence should not be taken to recognition; (2) how both recognition and enforcement of a decision given in a particular Member State are processed under the regime of the proposed Convention, that is to say, how it circulates within the territorial domain created by the Convention; (3) what are the potential bases for refusal of recognition (that is, cases where public policy will play a residual role, judgments obtained by fraud, or further filters ensuring the refusal of recognition of judgments resulting from proceedings incompatible with fundamental principles of procedure of the state addressed, including the right of the parties to be heard by an impartial and independent court).

The themes described above appear to be conducive to the consolidation of a balanced framework for state courts and governmental bodies acting in administrative and judicial cooperation, and the parties in dispute – the end-users in global transnational litigation in civil and commercial matters. In any event, the 'way forward' in the Judgments Project, apart from the desired adoption of a multilateral convention, will be to guide Hague Members into a complete informed decision in reaching the minimum standards or degree of uniformity for recognition rules at transnational level. The design of such rules has to take into account the needs of the final addressees: binding provisions to be consistently applicable by domestic courts and able to promote effectively the 'global facilitated recognition regime' envisaged by participating states.

[14] Dreyfuss, R. C. and J. C. Ginsburg (2001) 'Draft Convention on Jurisdiction and Recognition of Judgments in Intellectual Property Matters', *Chicago-Kent Law Review*, vol. 77, 1066.

[15] If one could go beyond the argument consistently advocated by Hartley, T. (2013) *International Commercial Litigation* 3rd edn, Cambridge University Press, 5, any desired and successful 'outcome of a case' does not depend only on jurisdiction (to the detriment of choice of law, as he contends), but rather on the certainty related to recognition of Judgments as to their effectiveness at transnational level. Thus, even if we admit that choice of law has a 'limited influence on the outcome of litigation', exercise of adjudicatory authority will also likely be subject to a degree of relativism where recognition and enforcement regimes are not properly coordinated at a global level.

Furthermore, the Judgments Convention may reconcile procedural uniformity with diversity in domestic normative spaces. It is evident that domestic legal systems may have distinct default rules in cases of recognition that does not fall within the material scope of application of a future instrument in that field. This is precisely the objective of provisions dealing with exclusion of scope (Art. 2 of the Draft Convention). They serve either to neutralise mutual or collective mistrust and irreconcilable interests among signatory parties or to avoid any policy overlaps with further existing regional and multilateral regimes on recognition. Nevertheless, there will still be a sufficient degree of predictability for the recognition and enforcement of judgments ruling on civil/commercial matters in line with the scope of application of the proposed Convention and not expressly excluded for its text. Ambiguities could be resolved at the request of the parties before the court of origin, in a consistent litigation-based strategy that may ensure that the outcome of the dispute is efficiently streamlined with the parties' interests in recognition and enforcement in the destination state of the Judgment.[16] Clearly, one of these interests also relies on the guarantee that the decision as rendered by the court of the state of origin is not subject to any kind of re-examination by the court of the state of recognition.[17]

In a nutshell, the proper functioning of a facilitated global recognition regime also depends on the institutionalisation of a balanced framework for the end-users in transnational civil litigation, with a clear guidance on what is 'in' and 'out' of the Convention and how courts are expected to treat foreign judgments under the Convention.

Fostering Global Convergence

Apart from the concern about institutional and normative frameworks for recognition regimes, the ongoing negotiations undertaken by the Hague Conference within the context of the Judgments Project reflect the power-shifting within the global trade system. Not surprisingly, they have also been connected to voices coming from Member States representing the booming Global South. The Hague Conference no longer has a Eurocentric vein. Since Japan and the US joined the organisation and the Conference's Statute was reformed, other Members had a number of incentives to engage in proactive participation in favour of a broad and flourishing agenda. Australia, China, Russia, Singapore, South Korea and Latin American countries such as Argentina, Brazil, Chile, Ecuador, Mexico and Uruguay[18] have been increasingly

[16] Dreyfuss and Ginsburg, 'Draft Convention', above fn. 14, 1140 (highlighting the potential difficulties concerning enforceability of Judgments within the subject matter of a convention in the field of recognition and enforcement).

[17] Ibid., 1140.

[18] Some of the Latin American participants at HCCH integrate the so-called GRULAC (the Latin American and Caribbean Regional Group within the United Nations). As a non-binding dialogue Regional Group, GRULAC represents 17 per cent of all UN members. It is one of five UN Regional Groups, the others being the African Group, the Asia-Pacific Group, the Eastern European Group, and the Western European and Others Group (WEOG). For further information, see www.un.org/depts/DGACM/RegionalGroups.shtml. The HCCH itself does not officially accept GRULAC as a separate or steering group of Members.

active players. Such a diplomatic involvement associated with the participation of private international law academics and experts has been guiding the Hague Conference through a gradual development of the main clusters of policy activity. They encompass 'legislative projects' (cohabitation outside marriage; family agreements involving children; the Judgments Project; parentage/surrogacy, protection orders and protection of tourists) and 'post-convention projects' (child abduction and use of video links in the taking of evidence).[19]

The initiative equally considers the relevance of the stakes that Member States that are developing countries have in the negotiations. They take into consideration the environments of emerging business and investments and new mobility trends of legal entities on a global scale (for example, small and medium-sized companies doing business overseas), particularly those based in the southern hemisphere.[20] Some regions in Asia, Africa and Latin America are increasingly becoming part of a more interconnected commercial and business community, relying on business counterparts in the South and the North. These regions are also very reactive to new trends in information and communication technologies and digital business models, as well as to innovative mass consumer trends affecting cross-border trade.

As an insightful exercise engaged with the analysis of diplomatic behaviour and trends on multilateral negotiations, the four Meetings of the Special Commission on the Judgments Project illustrated that the two major political forces – the US and the EU – are not alone at the Hague Conference. Distinct coalitions among delegates of Member States are taking place within the Judgments Project in a strategic fashion. They either converge on or divert from specific normative and conceptual issues, for example with regard to the goals of uniformisation in the field of recognition and enforcement; distinct knowledge on international litigation planning and management; autonomous interpretation of the future convention; discretionary powers for domestic legislators in the field of private international law and international civil procedural law. Other policy issues are relevant within the Judgment Project: maximalist principles in relation to state immunity; opportunities for the insertion of intellectual property and privacy matters within a global recognition regime; the operation of 'common courts' existing in regional organisations;[21] the everlasting

[19] A comprehensive description of the projects and instruments adopted by the HCCH is available at: www.hcch.net/en/instruments/conventions. See also van Loon, ''The Global Horizon of Private International Law', above fn. 8, 9–108.

[20] According to the last UNCTAD World Investment Report 2018 (Geneva, 2018), the foreign direct investment (FDI) inflows of developing economies reached a new figure of \$671 billion – still representing a drop in relation to the same figure as to 2016 (\$765 billion). Developing countries in Asia have FDI inflows surpassing half a trillion dollars, making it the largest FDI recipient region in the world. Emerging economies still comprise half of the top ten host economies for FDI inflows.

[21] See, for instance, Art. 5(5) of the 2018 Draft Convention. The provision reflects the outcome of the Working Group on Common Courts, headed by Prof. Marcelo de Nardi (from the delegation of Brazil), and points to the different scenarios of alternative proposals on this matter. There is still a lack of consensus regarding the concept of 'common courts' (as a court pertaining to two or more states

dilemma on the widening or narrowing of the scope of the public policy exception; and different approaches to jurisdictional filters and exclusive bases of recognition.

In sum, converging and diverging approaches channel the conflicts of interest and conflicts of conception vis-à-vis a facilitated and uniform recognition and enforcement regime. Based on that, one could make a rudimentary attempt to group the major voices among Member States according to their main national or regional interests, perceptions and defensive approaches: (1) United States; (2) EU, Switzerland, Norway; (3) Canada, Australia, Japan; (4) GRULAC (Argentina, Brazil, Chile, Ecuador, Mexico, Peru and Uruguay); (5) Russia, China, Israel. In some areas, Russia, Japan, China, Israel, Brazil, Argentina, Uruguay, Japan and South Korea firmly converge, in particular on issues covering national interests, state immunity and property/land law. Singapore has been also playing an important role in the negotiations, as a strategic counterpart in Asia and a very promising hub for the settlement of international commercial disputes.[22]

Since the first meeting of the Special Commission in June 2016, Member States have expressed distinct views in relation to desired uniformisation goals and the functioning of recognition and enforcement regimes. The EU advocated for a smooth transposition of some indirect jurisdictional rules and jurisdictional filters from the EU Brussels I recast[23] Regulation to the current Draft Convention. China, Russia and Israel, acting in their national interests, engaged in different narratives related to sovereignty and territoriality and how these principles could not be simply overlooked within the existing private international law negotiation arena. The US, in turn, appears to be expressing a single voice in some negotiation clusters, such as in relation to indirect jurisdictional rules,[24] rules on appearance in court,[25] fundamental procedural policy and 'lack of due process' as potential grounds both for refusal

within the framework of a regional international organisation and taken as such to be a court of origin of a decision taken for recognition in a Contracting State). China, Russia and Israel strongly oppose the adoption of such a model, based on the lack of information about the operation of such courts, as provided by the EU delegation. This conflict of conceptions is also illustrated in the first part of Art. 5(5) and the conditions established by the said provision ('For purposes of paragraph 1, a Judgment given by a court common to two or more States shall be deemed to be a Judgment given by a court of a Contracting State if the Contracting State has identified the common court in a declaration to that effect'.).

22 See, for example, Singapore International Commercial Court (SICC). Officially established in 2015, the SICC is a state-based court aimed at boosting dispute resolution service sectors in the region and expanding the scope for the 'internationalisation and export of Singapore law'. See www.sicc.gov.sg. This specialised domestic court is an example of a global commercial court as opposed to its international commercial arbitration counterpart.

23 Regulation (EU) No. 1215/2012 of the European Parliament and of the Council of 12 December 2012 on jurisdiction and the recognition and enforcement of judgments in civil and commercial matters, OJ L 351, 20.12.2012, 1–32 ('Brussels I Recast').

24 Art. 5(1) of the 2018 Draft Convention.

25 Art. 5(1)(f) of the 2018 Draft Convention.

of recognition and for a declaration mechanism.[26] In other areas, however, the US converges with the positions of other Member States, namely Australia, Brazil and Japan.[27]

Notwithstanding the risks of a generalisation from the standpoint of Members' views and policy analysis, the proposals originated by Members supporting defensive approaches turn back to national interests, national security and approaches based on state sovereignty lagging behind domestic laws governing recognition and enforcement systems. In particular, China's main initial proposals on intellectual property rights (exclusion of the subject matter from the scope of application of the Convention; non-recognition of judgments given in connection with intellectual property rights) invoked a universal maximalist approach to the principle of territoriality.[28]

GRULAC proposals are based only to a certain degree on national interest; they are generally focused on the foundational rules and principles mainly deriving from Inter-American Conventions while at the same time preserving the necessary policy issues underlying the Judgments Project.[29] Brazil, for instance, was supportive of proposals addressing the necessary fine-tuning between normative spaces for exclusive jurisdiction rules and exclusive bases of recognition (for example, in rights *in rem*, intellectual property rights granted or registered in the state of origin of the judgment), while also ensuring certain necessary filters. Such filters refer to the express consent of defendants, in the case of consumer and employees, to proceedings taking place in the court of origin of the judgment.

In addition, Argentina, Brazil and Uruguay are supportive of the importance

[26] This issue originated from a joint proposal originally made by the US and Switzerland in the Fourth Meeting of the Special Commission, held in May 2018. It attempted to provide some procedural standard rule for refusal of recognition or a declaration mechanism in the case of procedural fairness concerns related to the state of origin of the Judgment. After much discussion between the delegations, there was insufficient support for the inclusion of any of the proposed texts from the US and Switzerland on these issues in the Draft Convention. China, Brazil and Russia strongly opposed the inclusion of any provision that could potentially induce a unilateral scrutiny, by the courts of the state of recognition, of the practices and procedural standards of the state of origin's legal system.

[27] For example, during the Second Meeting of the Special Commission, held in February 2017, the US, Brazil and Japan expressed their concerns relating to the uncertainty of the timeframe necessary for the defendant to appear before the court that rendered the Judgment in the state of origin. There seems to be no consensus regarding 'express consent' or whether the defendant is required to physically appear, in the reading of Art. 5.1(e): '1. A Judgment is eligible for recognition and enforcement if one of the following requirements is met – (e) the defendant expressly consented to the jurisdiction of the court of origin in the course of the proceedings in which the Judgment was given'.

[28] It is important to highlight, however, that the involvement of a high-level group of discussants on intellectual property matters throughout the Special Commission meetings and intersessional working groups led to a gradual change in China's reluctance to treat intellectual property matters within the Judgment Project. The US, in turn, dramatically changed its initial approach in the negotiations, and moved to a more defensive approach demanding the exclusion of intellectial property matters from the scope of the Draft Convention.

[29] For an overview of the interactions of recognition regimes in the Americas and Inter-American private international law, see de Araujo's chapter in this volume.

of the optimal interaction between Hague Conventions and the future Judgments Convention, and further international instruments concluded under the auspices of Mercosur. Unlike the EU regulations in the field of private international law, Mercosur and Inter-American instruments still fail, with minor exceptions, to achieve mutual trust goals in regional legal cooperation. They reveal a weaker degree of acceptance amongst national courts, particularly because those instruments are based on the traditional legal interplay between international law and municipal law, very often dependent on the incorporation or transposition by national statutory laws, in a different vein than the European Regulations based on EU law.

The above summary of the stakes and interests at the Hague's negotiation forum may lead to key conclusions regarding the Members' stakes and converging interests. In more integrated and interconnected markets in distinct perspectives – north-north, north-south and south-south hemispheres – one should not overlook the strong legal narrative and imaginative forces of a multilateral treaty dealing with recognition of foreign judgments in commercial matters. Here, the primary goals of private international law come into play again. Even for the success of the Judgment Project and the current initiatives carried out by the Hague Conference in the field of international procedural law and transnational litigation, Members shall be encouraged to undertake a true exercise of policy-oriented engagement with private international law's foundational purposes. Such foundational purposes recall the relevance of legal and cultural diversity for the functioning of legal systems; the respect for the 'foreign element' or the 'international character' of personal status and legal relationships; protection of the parties' interests; and the continuity and stability of legal relationships across different legal systems.

Aspirational Ideas for the Judgments Project and the Future Hague Convention

A further argument in favour of an integral view of the Judgments Project is the balance between the 'one single approach' taken by the drafters for the sake of uniformity and the diversity of legal solutions. Uniform solutions are different from minimum standards. Within the context of a multilateral instrument on recognition and enforcement of judgments, uniform rules are those agreed between the Hague Member States to shape a facilitated regime of international legal cooperation and access to justice at global level. The entire system is not dependent on reciprocity – a feature already exceptional in contemporary legal cooperation regimes; rather, it entails, as explored later in this chapter, internationally binding obligations targeting Members' domestic practices and institutions in the field of recognition and enforcement of foreign judgments.[30]

[30] In my view, this echoes one of the fundamental components of the public/private international law interplay, as a natural result of the scope of application of the Draft Convention and the general provision of Art. 4(1) ('A Judgment given by a court of a Contracting State (State of origin) shall be recognised and enforced in another Contracting State (requested State) in accordance with the

Within the Project's framework, diplomatic and institutional compromises converge in order to ensure that uniform rules on recognition (such as exclusion of subject matters from scope of application; general and exclusive bases for recognition and enforcement; and grounds for refusal)[31] are counterbalanced with specific and residual escape clauses. These clauses, for instance, apply national recognition laws in those cases where the multilateral recognition and enforcement regime structured by the future Hague Convention does not operate or is modulated by the proposed grounds for refusal of recognition or enforcement.[32] Furthermore, the interplay between global and national regimes on recognition and enforcement offers the opportunity to re-engage in some fundamental questions of private international law and international civil procedure law. They comprise, for instance, the roles broadly performed by recognition and enforcement regimes in different normative and jurisdictional (regional and domestic) systems; or even whether recognition systems may be designed to ensure the stability and continuity of legal relationships and parties' interests across borders.

The authoritative literature on this topic appears to be clear enough to respond to both questions starting from distinct but complementary perspectives. The first endorses a view of the 'public side' of recognition systems as conducive to a re-characterised form of comity in current international affairs, interdependency of state and non-state actors in a globalised world,[33] strengthened economic integration[34] or a matter of openness to the 'legitimacy of foreign norms'.[35] From the perspective of the 'private side', foreign judgments can be seen as the result of a time-consuming international litigation process, or the 'end game', as contended by Ronald Brand.[36] Arguably, thanks to the predictability of a comprehensive regime for recognition and enforcement of judgments, litigants shall benefit from legal certainty in terms of how and to what extent a judgment targeting property or assets of the foreign debtor is enforceable in another country than the state of origin of said judgment. Consequently, any sound legal recognition regime would be 'important from the

provisions of this Chapter. Recognition or enforcement may be refused only on the grounds specified in this Convention'.). Theoretically speaking, that provision equally epitomises both sovereignty and common and shared jurisdictional spaces within the territorial reach of the future Convention (as adopted by the Fourth Meeting of the Special Commission).

31 See, respectively, Arts 2, 4, 5, 6 and 7 of the Revised Draft Text as of May 2018.

32 Art. 16 of the 2018 Revised Draft Text.

33 See, for instance, Nygh, P. (1997) 'Towards a Global Judgments Convention: The Proposed New Hague Convention on the Recognition and Enforcement of Judgments in Civil and Commercial Matters', *Australian International Law Journal*, 96, 111; von Mehren, 'Recognition and Enforcement of Foreign Judgments', above fn. 12, 271.

34 Brand, R. A. (2014) *Transaction Planning Using Rules on Jurisdiction and the Recognition and Enforcement of Judgments*, Brill, 115.

35 Mills, A. (2009) *The Confluence of Public and Private International Law: Justice, Pluralism and Subsidiarity in the International Constitutional Ordering of Private Law*, Cambridge University Press, 18–19.

36 Ibid., 118.

outset of cross-border litigation'.[37] A multilateral treaty dealing with recognition and enforcement of foreign judgments in civil and commercial matters is likely to shape an adequate framework for the circulation of decisions rendered by domestic courts. Hence, with regard to cross-border litigation, the future instrument would equally create a fertile terrain for globalising the results of that 'end game', as Ronald Brand explained during Special Commission discussions, and for ensuring parties' interests wherever that judgment circulates.

I believe that the previous and existing debate among private international law scholars and specialists could be further refined at a certain stage of this challenging and necessary journey toward the conclusion of a Convention by the Hague Conference. Even though the Draft Convention mainly refers to judicial decisions involving commercial/business disputes,[38] an instrument in this field is not only to be seen as targeting private actors, for instance businesspeople or economic agents, represented by an ordinary legal category of subjects, such as 'litigants'. It paves the way to strengthening domestic institutions dealing both with legal cooperation and recognition regimes. Any single request for recognition and enforcement of foreign judgments made by parties in cross-border disputes will generate ancillary benefits for the advancement of institutional capacities and roles of domestic courts and administrative bodies directly implicated in transnational civil proceedings.

The existence of a facilitated regime for recognition of foreign judgments may also lead to different reactions from the private international law community and stakeholders in terms of systemic objectives, interests of individuals and access to justice. Indeed, in a 'global regime', parties could rely on the legitimate expectation (in part similar to that in the field of international commercial arbitration deriving from the 1958 New York Convention) that a claim for recognition and enforcement of a judgment given in a foreign state constitutes a 'fundamental right', connected to a broad conception of access to justice at global level.[39]

As anticipated, the adoption of a multilateral convention dealing with recognition and enforcement of judgments may be also conducive to empowerment and deepening asymmetries between some state/domestic courts, which may soon become

[37] Ibid., 118–19.

[38] For a detailed discussion on the categories of legal transactions and related judgments in civil and commercial matters, see the background note circulated for the Special Commission: HCCH, Prel. Doc. No. 4 of December 2016 – *Note on Article 1(1) of the 2016 Preliminary Draft Convention and the Term 'Civil or Commercial Matters'*, available at: https://assets.hcch.net/docs/9be83162-a32b-457c-8232-16748c841789.pdf

[39] Soft law instruments are using this rationale, for example ASADIP Principles on Transnational Access to Justice, available at: www.asadip.org/v2/wp-content/.../TRANSJUS-texto-final.pdf. Its Art. 7(1) reads: 'The extraterritorial effect of a foreign judgment is a fundamental right, closely linked with the right of access to justice and with the fundamental rights of due process. Judges and further State authorities shall seek to promote the effectiveness of said Judgment and interpret and apply all the requirements with which they shall enforce said Judgment'.

global commercial courts, or have already done so.[40] It is not just a debate on specialisation or expertise in business environment and dispute settlement mechanisms. The Judgments Project, at best, symbolises an international cooperative commitment to facilitate judgments' mobility, while at the same time ensuring that the parties' rights and interests are protected at a global level and are likely to be recognised by any Member States of this cooperative community.

On the other hand, the precise scope of a multilateral treaty providing rules for jurisdictional filters and exclusive bases for recognition will define roles for domestic courts in countries from which judgments in certain subject matters are rendered. Such normative spaces can foster predictability in terms of which Hague Member States will serve as states of origin of the judgment whose recognition is sought and those requested to recognise and enforce a judgment circulating within the facilitated recognition regime.

In addition to normative spaces, a future convention in this field should allow the creation of jurisdictional dialogue at global level. An integrated multilateral recognition regime might pave the way for a number of situations where there is international legal cooperation. In which sense precisely? In a similar fashion to the global governance and global constitutionalist debate,[41] by which local/domestic courts are requested to take a more pervasive attitude to ensure that individuals' rights and interests – once adjudicated overseas – are also equitably treated in the forum.[42] Accordingly, both courts of the state of origin of the judgment and of the requested state under the proposed Judgments Convention engage in an exercise of improvement of protection of parties' rights, be it in pure recognition situations or in connection with international civil and commercial disputes. This sort of pervasive attitude can deal with the legitimate expectations of stakeholders of a global regime for recognition and enforcement, where at least a certain degree of uniformity is envisaged.

[40] For a similar debate, see Hartley, T. C. (2006) 'The Modern Approach to Private International Law: International Litigation and Transactions from a Common-Law Perspective', *Recueil des cours*, vol. 319, 111.

[41] See, for instance, MacDonald, E. and E. Shamir-Bohrer (2010) 'Meeting the Challenges of Global Governance', in Ruiz Fabri, H., R. Wolfrum and J. Gogolin (eds), *Select Proceedings of the European Society of International Law*, vol. 2, Bloomsbury, 228.

[42] The proposed text for Art. 14 of the 2017 Draft Judgments Convention originally dealt with the equivalent effects of foreign judgments circulating under the Judgments Convention, so as to deal precisely with the broad objective of non-discrimination of judgments ('A Judgment recognised or enforceable under this Convention shall be given the same effect it has in the State of origin. If the Judgment provides for relief that is not available under the law of the requested State, that relief shall, to the extent possible, be adapted to relief with effects equivalent to, but not going beyond, its effects under the law of the State of origin'). The 2018 Draft reflected a narrowed version of the provision in Art. 3(3) ('A Judgment shall be recognised only if it has effect in the State of origin, and shall be enforced only if it is enforceable in the State of origin').

The Quest for Effectiveness of Multilateral Obligations of Recognition and Enforcement and Private International Law General Principles

The desired success of a multilateral convention on recognition and enforcement of foreign judgments in civil and commercial matters is not immune from political scrutiny. States cannot simply serve as mere 'passive actors' within recognition and enforcement frameworks. Their domestic institutions, administrative bodies and courts involved in international legal cooperation structures will certainly be requested to engage in the formulation of uniform interpretations around the proposed future convention's obligations and the general principles guiding a global recognition and enforcement regime.[43]

What would be the main reasons for reluctant or ambivalent discourses in diplomatic meetings against the success and feasibility of the Draft Convention? Apart from the apparent lack of historical memory of some delegates in the meetings (at both the previous Experts Group/Working Group Meetings held between 2014 and 2015, and the Special Commission meetings held between June 2016 and May 2018), there are still some shades of 'mutual mistrust' among some Members. Mistrust may be reflected in the rationale underlying a particular state's decision to recognise or not recognise 'extraterritorial effects of foreign acts of sovereignty', or may refer to the potential risks to the private interests of individuals and companies involved in litigation. Indeed, those approaches tend to oscillate between concurrent factors. The first group represents both a variable 'openness' to the circulation of 'acts of sovereignty' of states expressed by judicial decisions and a fecund pro-recognition environment. Such factors resemble, in distinct perspectives, the basic components of the multilateral/regional system previously achieved by the 1968 Brussels Convention[44] (subsequently replaced by Brussels I, and currently the Brussels I *bis* Regulation in the EU).[45] The second group, in turn, is tributary to a stringent and – paradoxically – broad and maximalist approach in relation to the existing legal procedural requirements under domestic laws of the requested states and to diplomatic flags vesting national interests in this realm.

It is imperative in this regard not simply to look at the conceptual differences or conflicting approaches between EU and US models, such as those referencing the insuperable divide on general jurisdictional grounds affecting recognition of judgment at a later stage. This would reduce the potential of the Judgments Project to

[43] See, for instance, Art. 21 of the 2018 Draft Convention on uniform interpretation rule ('In the interpretation of this Convention, regard shall be had to its international character and to the need to promote uniformity in its application').

[44] Brussels Convention on jurisdiction and the enforcement of judgments in civil and commercial matters, as of 27 September 1968, OJ L 299, 31.12.1972, 32–42.

[45] The European legal domain has been characterised by a gradual strengthening of a market-driven approach and the goal of the creation of a 'common Judicial area'. See von Mehren, 'Recognition and Enforcement of Foreign Judgments, above fn. 12, 275.

apparent policy issues or the pure legal question of whether a global instrument should be guided by different criteria – habitual residence of the defendant, as favoured by the EU, or due process clause, as generally advocated by the US. As von Mehren articulated, the actual accounts for the ambitious way forward towards the success of negotiations of the embryonic version of the Judgments Convention in the mid-1990s and early 2000s, for what he called the 'merits and demerits of various approaches to jurisdiction and recognition problems'.[46] Unlike the doctrinal debate about dissenting approaches, the negotiation bottlenecks both in the past and in present times continue to delve into different paradigms of jurisdiction,[47] generating miscommunication and mutual distrust among Members.

Are these bottlenecks surmountable? It would be premature at this stage to list all the areas where there is no consensus at all. It is important to highlight, however, that any attempt to stay or block negotiations can be neutralised by the engagement of all stakeholders, such as Members, the Council for General Affairs and Policy of the Hague and with the support of academia and NGOs. Within the draft's legal structure, it appears to be intuitive that those subject matters or substantive areas implying mutual distrust (due to the clash of legal cultures and diverging perceptions and interests of Members) or areas governed by special private international law related treaties should be completely excluded from the scope of application of the Convention.[48] As Prof. von Mehren remarked, 'it is preferable the devil we know than the one we did not'.[49]

Even if mutual mistrust is a recurrent political and systemic feature of international affairs in the fields of private international law and international procedural law (for example, in relation to the functioning of judiciary systems; trends in the application of foreign law; national laws of recognition and enforcement), one can nevertheless see promising consistencies of the Judgments Project through different lenses. As previously remarked, the upcoming adoption of the proposed Convention can be linked to Members' opportunities to enjoy a higher degree of acceptability and mobility of their judgments abroad, both attributes assured by binding multilateral obligations to be undertaken by Hague Members. Here, public international law also plays an important role in the development and enhancement of an integrated

46 Ibid., 271.

47 See Michaels, R. (2006) 'Two Paradigms of Jurisdiction' 27 *Mich.Jo.Int.L.* 1003.

48 This recommendation applies to those areas that are frequently troublesome from the standpoint of both substantive and procedural harmonisation and unformisation, such as consumer law, product liability, punitive damages, insurance law, bankruptcy law, and those dealing with hybrid legal regimes. In the latter case, specifically, true policy issues may arise in the field of privacy, rights of personality v. rights of publicity. Not accidentally, these areas are all surrounded by authentic legal cultural clashes and underlying corporate interests of some Members' industry sectors. On the other hand, judgments in family law matters are extensively covered by existing UN, Hague and Inter-American Conventions in that field, comparable to arbitral awards, which are covered by the successful regime consolidated by the 1958 New York Convention.

49 Von Mehren, 'Recognition and Enforcement of Foreign Judgments', above fn. 12, 274.

framework for circulation of foreign judgments addressing private interests of individuals and companies, similar to other undertakings at regional and global levels.

In line with those arguments, Members could perform a true role as active actors (as requesting states) in the realm of cross-border civil/commercial litigation and not merely 'states of origin' of judgments. This approach could be of the utmost importance for smaller countries and regions deprived of specific domestic procedural rules (codes, statutes, regulations) or treaties dealing with the recognition and enforcement of foreign judgments. By the same token, the ongoing Judgments Project is likely to be converted into a meaningful platform to overcome any circumstantial 'mutual mistrust' in terms of the functioning of domestic legal systems. The Project paves the way for a serious discussion about the underlying reasons behind any eventual negotiation's schism or clashes, such as dissenting views on a purely pragmatic market-driven approach for enforcement of foreign judgments in commercial matters[50] or misconceptions about exclusive jurisdiction rules and scope of the territoriality principle.

The Project refreshes the normative debate about the interactions between private international law and international procedural law related conventions,[51] focused *inter alia* on the pervasive power of the 1958 New York Convention and the relationship between the proposed Judgments Convention and the 2005 Convention on Choice of Court Agreement.[52] This debate goes far beyond the mere replication of correlated treaty patterns in the draft text as it stands in the Special Commission's work. In addition, the gradual progress of negotiations, endorsed by the Hague Council for General Affairs since 2011, sets the diplomatic compromise towards the establishment of uniform rules for recognition and enforcement of foreign judgments. This is a remarkable achievement in a time where Members are aware of the disadvantages of keeping the manifest imbalance between the 1958 New York Convention binding regime on recognition and enforcement of foreign arbitral awards and a parallel regime – that currently does not exist – for recognition of foreign judgments. Without any deliberate and strategic action by the international private international law community and stakeholders, international civil/commercial litigation will remain relegated to a serious competitive disadvantage in relation to its international commercial arbitration counterpart.

There is a workable comparison between a desired global regime for recognition and enforcement of foreign judgments in civil and commercial matters and the

[50] This approach could be, in distinct variants, associated with circulation of money judgments, effectiveness of cross-border debt collection or the creation of common judicial areas anchored in market freedoms.

[51] For the Judgments Project and the relation between Conventions see Noodt Taquela, M. B. and V. Ruiz Abou-Nigm (2018) 'The Draft Judgments Convention and its Relationship with Other International Instruments', *Yearbook of Private International Law*, vol. 19, 449–74.

[52] The Hague Convention on Choice of Court Agreements was adopted on 30 June 2005 and entered into force on 1 October 2015; 32 States Parties, status as at 15 October 2018.

well-established regime constituted by the 1958 New York Convention. This comparison appears to enjoy a twofold advantage in relation to the generally adopted techniques of harmonisation and uniformisation in private international law. It allows, for instance, domestic courts to use the practice of treaty law within HCCH Members' legal systems in order to solve any conflict related to interpretation and application of general rules and multilateral obligations to enforce judgments arising under the future Judgments Convention. Perhaps for those HCCH Members which are signatories to the 1958 New York Convention, this exercise would not be difficult.

For HCCH Members that are not party to that Convention, there will be additional reasons for the Hague Conference to take a step further in the design of a platform for information exchange in a highly innovative fashion. First, this platform could have the advantage of facilitating access to the practice of treaties and conventions related to recognition and enforcement of foreign judgments in different fora (for example the EU, the OAS/CIDIPs and Mercosur) and the Judgments Convention itself. Similarly, it may be the most appropriate site for the establishment of a Guide on the Judgments Convention, in a similar vein as has been adopted by UNCITRAL with regard to the 1958 New York Convention related practice – the New York Convention Guide.[53] This aspect highlights a 'post-conventional' pillar within the global recognition and enforcement regime and profiles of international legal cooperation in civil and commercial matters. The scope of Article 4(1) of the Draft Judgments Convention expressly refers to a binding obligation of a Contracting State – the 'requested state' – to recognise and enforce a judgment given in another Contracting State, the 'state of origin', in accordance with the provisions of Chapter II and refusal of recognition based on specific grounds. It is a similar approach to what is sought by Article III of the 1958 New York Convention, according to which Contracting States shall recognise arbitral awards as binding. The Article enshrines a 'pro-enforcement' principle, to be respected by domestic courts for the sake of effectiveness of international commercial arbitration.[54]

The interplay between a facilitated global regime for recognition and enforcement of foreign judgments and the respect of multilateral obligations undertaken under the proposed HCCH Judgment Convention is also instrumental to a wider scrutiny of transnational dealings by general principles in the field of private international law. Apart from a pro-enforcement principle, further principles include: (1) application of most-favourable treaties in respect of recognition and enforcement of foreign

[53] Available at: http://newyorkconvention1958.org

[54] According to an authoritative commentary, Art. III entails a 'pro-enforcement bias', with the main obligation for Contracting States to recognise and enforce foreign arbitral awards under the rules of procedure in the country where the award is being relied on, unless one of the refusal grounds of Art. V is proven (see Börner, A. (2010) 'Article III', in Kronke, H., P. Nacimiento, D. Otto and N. C. Port (eds), *Recognition and Enforcement of Foreign Arbitral Awards: A Global Commentary on the New York Convention*, Kluwer Law International, 115.

judgments[55] (benefiting from the distinct views and practices arising from regional regimes of legal cooperation); (2) optimal circulation of foreign judgments guided by the preservation of due process and fair hearing; (3) equivalent effects between foreign and domestic judgments;[56] (4) protection of *res judicata* effects in recognition and enforcement regimes.[57]

The articulation between a multilateral regime anchored in binding obligations and general principles underlying in the operation of a future Hague Convention equally consolidates a general mutually assisted system forging prospective cooperative frameworks in the field of recognition of judgments. A convention of such nature can induce positive effects over domestic legal systems by creating new solutions or adapting national practices in terms of laws of recognition. Furthermore, as discussed in this chapter, the successful adoption of the Judgments Convention could launch the minimum basis for ensuring the protection of parties' rights and interests in a fair operation of international civil/commercial litigation at a global level.

Concluding Remarks

The adoption of a convention comprising rules on recognition and enforcement of foreign judgments is conducive to the political engagement and maturity of approach related to the ultimate goals of uniformisation and convergence in private international law. In addition to providing for specific rules at global level, the Convention may ensure an appropriate level of diversity among regional systems and national laws on recognition, particularly in view of competing constitutional and civil procedural rules involved in recognition and enforcement frameworks. At the current stage of the negotiations of the Draft Judgments Convention by the HCCH Special Commission, Members should be encouraged to find a compromise for the sake of the success and future of the desired instrument. It appears to me that the optimal functioning of the 'facilitated regime' for circulation of judgments at a global level depends on a balanced approach, linked to both the preservation of differences (without generalisations, imposition of legal transplants or hegemonic concepts) and full commitment to ensure the realisation of recognition as a pivotal principle in private international law. Recognition is not something only based on legal claims

[55] See Noodt Taquela, M. B. (2016), 'Applying the Most Favourable Treaty or Domestic Rules to Facilitate Private International Law Co-operation', *Recueil des cours*, vol. 377, 121–317.

[56] See Art. 14 of the 2017 Draft and Art. 3(3) of the 2018 Draft Judgments Convention.

[57] These pivotal principles on the functioning of dispute settlement systems, particularly in relation to adjudicatory authority and international civil/commercial litigation, are addressed by the literature in distinct approaches. See Hartley, *International Commercial Litigation*, above fn. 15, 14; Schack, H. (2014) *Internationales Zivilverfahrensrecht*, 6th edn, C. H. Beck, 13; Fernández Arroyo, D. P. (2004) 'Exorbitantant Exclusive Grounds of Jurisdiction in European Private International Law: Will They Ever Survive?', in Mansel, H. P. (ed.), *Festschrift für Erik Jayme*, Sellier, 169; Fentiman, R. (2010) *International Commercial Litigation*, Oxford University Press; Polido, F. B. P. (2013) *Direito Processual Internacional e o Contencioso Internacional Privado*. Juruá, 36; Vescovi, E. (2000) *Derecho Procesal Civil Internacional*, Idea,17.

or expectations. It comprises the realisation of private rights and legitimate interests of individuals, families, companies and organisations when engaged in international dealings. Ultimately, recognition is a part of life for citizens of the world.[58]

In view of further potential political constraints at HCCH or even the unilateral resistance of certain Members, it is important to give the Judgments Project a chance. I see it as a genuine private international law enterprise, as Arthur von Mehren and Peter Nygh once idealised. As stated above, the future instrument could be conducive to the establishment of a true global integrated network aimed at facilitating, by means of the Members' compromise, a 'generally accepted global regime' for recognition and enforcement of foreign judgments in civil and commercial matters, expressing the potential to include several other Members. A Convention of that magnitude can also promote the commitment of international civil and commercial litigation stakeholders and domestic legal systems to enhance the existing dispute resolution mechanisms focused on recognition and enforcement, all of them taken as alternatives (and not second-best options) to international commercial arbitration, particularly where certain industry sectors, amounts or complexity of the dispute are at stake.

[58] See Knop, K. (2016) 'Lorimer's Private Citizens of the World', *European Journal of International Law* vol. 27: 447–75.

PART III

THE EVOLVING FOCUS ON THE INDIVIDUAL

12

Integrating Legal Approaches to Migration

Kasey McCall-Smith

Introduction

Migration is one of the oldest phenomena in human history. The origins of diplomatic protection in the field of public international law speak to this, not only as protections for state representatives but also for the protection of common individuals crossing borders for a range of reasons: trade, entrepreneurship and, dare it be written, love. The final two of these exemplar enterprises are often facilitated by private international law. In fact, migration can be traced in the earliest annals of civilisation, with foreign travellers trekking great distances to peddle their wares or to negotiate with foreign powers. Yet recent political discourse on migration has turned the term into a 'dirty' word, leading the public across many transit or receiving states to decry all forms of migration and to suggest that all individuals from foreign lands are of some lesser value. This sour, inward turn has been enabled by the incoherence of the laws that speak to migration issues. The blurring of individuals' rights, coordinated mobility, jurisdictional competition and protectionist policies currently delivers an unintelligible melee of competing rules and norms. This chaotic legal situation facilitates a hostile environment toward migrants and the policies that facilitate their movement.

For some years now, the international community has recognised the need to recalibrate migration discourse and clarify the distinct, positive and necessary features of migration.[1] Furthermore, the recognition is underpinned by the practical reality that only a coordinated effort across states will be successful, which is logical considering that migration will always, by definition, engage at least two states and it

[1] See, for example, Crépeau, F. and I. Atak (2016) 'Global Migration Governance: Avoiding Commitments on Human Rights, yet Tracing a Course for Cooperation' 34(2) *Netherlands Quarterly of Human Rights* 113; Castles, S. and N. van Hear (2011) 'Root Causes', in Betts, A. (ed.), *Global Migration Governance*, Oxford University Press, 287.

is a primary conduit through which cosmopolitan aims might be achieved. The many rounds of discussions surrounding the development of a Global Compact for Safe, Orderly and Regular Migration (Migration Compact) have clearly revealed that the only chance at delivering a framework for enhanced cooperation is to ensure that the Compact takes a coordinated, holistic and cross-cutting approach.[2] To manage the complexities of global migration and not waste effort reinventing the wheel, it is crucial to build on existing law and policy frameworks in all efforts to address today's global frenzy over migration, particularly the 2030 Agenda for Sustainable Development and its seventeen sustainable development goals (SDGs).[3] The challenge in connecting global migration with other processes, promoting linkages and avoiding overlap, is one that must be deftly navigated. This chapter examines the proposed Migration Compact as an avenue for maximising the efficiency of current regulatory frameworks, identifying gaps, promoting synergies and utilising the connective capabilities of public and private international law to foster further integration in a highly diverse panoply of governance frameworks.

As has been examined through this volume, private international law is instrumental in developing the global legal architecture necessary to facilitate the accommodation of different legal systems and frameworks in modern society through clearly defined processes that enable and balance the cross-border application of law. This chapter explores the nexus points between public and private international law to reinforce the potential impact of the forthcoming Migration Compact and how private international law could play a crucial role in developing the architecture through which these two fields of law could realise positive migration solutions. The second section delivers a brief overview of contemporary migration highlighting the key sticking points that have driven recent political and legal debates. The third section will then introduce the predominant legal frameworks triggered by migration. The fourth will discuss how the Migration Compact seeks to maximise the coordinated capabilities of existing international law to deliver holistic responses to migration problems, both real and potential. It concludes with thoughts about the role of sustainable, humanised migration approaches in the continued evolution of contemporary global society. In the words of Cançado Trindade, 'we can contribute to enabling the humanised law of nations . . . to provide responses to the basic needs and aspirations of the international community as a whole, and, ultimately, of human

[2] United Nations Global Compact for Safe, Orderly and Regular Migration (Migration Compact), Final Draft, 11 July 2018, para. 13ss, available at: www.iom.int/global-compact-migration. The final round of negotiations and adoption of the Compact is set for 10–11 December 2018. See also UN General Assembly, Resolution 71/1. New York Declaration for Refugees and Migrants of 19 September 2016, UN Doc. A/RES/71/1 (3 October 2016) (hereinafter 'New York Declaration').

[3] United Nations General Assembly, Resolution 70/1. Transforming our world: the 2030 Agenda for Sustainable Development, UN Doc. A/RES/70/1 (21 October 2015) (hereinafter '2030 Development Agenda'), para. 59ss. sets out the sustainable development goals.

kind. This is the great task before us today.'[4] This contribution demonstrates that in aiming to harmonise and coordinate the multifarious regulatory frameworks while simultaneously adhering to global norms, the international community can not only entrench a more humanised law of nations, but can also aid in delivering a more productive and sustainable global economy and society.

On Contemporary Migration

Before examining the law relating to migration, it is useful to first contextualise the subject of migration and define its borders (to the extent to which they are identifiable). Much like Dauvergne's observation about the term globalisation, migration, too, is a label attached to any and all aspects of transboundary movement by individuals. Thus, migration, just like the term globalisation, presents 'an ironic mirroring of the phenomenon it describes, the term [sic] has grown out of control . . . it makes sense to use it with full consciousness of its fluidity'.[5] In the national context, migration and immigration are used interchangeably and their accompanying connotations are often derived from national laws focused predominantly on the task of 'othering' non-citizens of the state or defining who is, and who is not, a citizen.[6] Increasingly, the term is slanted entirely toward public international law norms, which serves to detract from the more fundamental purposes traditionally facilitated by migration. It is a term applied unapologetically and without distinction to the situations of refugees, asylum seekers, temporary labourers filling workforce gaps, highly skilled professionals recruited for specific industries and those in search of economic opportunity in a new land. For this reason and for present purposes, it is sufficient to define migration as the movement of an individual – the migrant – from one state to another state for whatever reason, be it political, economic, social or otherwise. Therefore a migrant could be a refugee, an asylum seeker, an economic migrant or anyone crossing a border with the purpose of residing in a place different from his or her country of origin without drawing distinctions, while also acknowledging that specific rules will apply to individuals qualifying as refugees or asylum seekers under international law.[7] For this reason, this chapter adopts the term 'migrant' to include all individuals

[4] Cançado Trindade, A. A. (2014) 'The Universality of International Law, its Humanist Outlook, and the Mission of the Hague Academy of International Law', 32 *Netherlands Quarterly of Human Rights* 109, 115.

[5] Dauvergne, C. (2008) *Making People Illegal: What Globalization Means for Migration and Law*, Cambridge University Press, 29.

[6] Plender, R. (2015) 'Nationality Law and Immigration Law', in Plender, R. (ed.), *Issues in International Migration Law*, Brill Nijhoff, 1.

[7] Notably, the Convention relating to the Status of Refugees, 28 July 1951, 189 U.N.T.S. 150, as amended by the Protocol relating to the Status of Refugees, 31 January 1967, 606 U.N.T.S. 267 (Refugee Convention); entry into force 4 October 1967; 146 States Parties, status as at 30 November 2018. A parallel compact is being developed to address governance frameworks specifically in relation to refugees; see Report of the United Nations High Commissioner for Refugees, Part II, Global Compact on Refugees, Official Records of the 73rd session, Supp. 12, UN Doc A/73/12 (Part II) (2018).

in a country that is not the home of their birth, for whatever reason. Legal frameworks tackling the migration phenomena distinguish between the countries of origin, transit and destination. The country of origin is the state from which the individual migrant begins his or her journey – recognising that this may not necessarily be the country of birth and/or nationality. The country of transit is the state through which the individual passes en route to the intended destination state – the ultimate state to which the individual seeks to adopt as his or her residence.

The contribution of migrants to cultural, social and financial change in this age of global interconnectivity and interdependence is undoubtedly significant and it follows that migration is a 'defining feature of our globalized world'.[8] And while globalisation has pushed migration numbers higher, the impetus for economic migration has always existed to facilitate the development of global economies.[9] In 2017, the UN estimated that approximately 259 million people live in a country other than their country of birth.[10] Contemporary migration stems both from those traditional drivers that have led individuals to explore new opportunities across borders as well as new drivers of change, such as global warming and climate disasters. These drivers are reflected in a number of the SDGs, including, but not limited to: ending poverty in all its forms everywhere (SDG 1); ensuring inclusive and equitable quality education and promoting lifelong learning opportunities for all (SDG 4); achieving gender equality and empowering all women and girls (SDG 5); promoting sustained, inclusive and sustainable economic growth, full and productive employment and decent work for all (SDG 8); building resilient infrastructure, promoting inclusive and sustainable industrialisation and fostering innovation (SDG 9); reducing inequality within and among countries (SDG 10); and promoting peaceful and inclusive societies for sustainable development, providing access to justice for all and build effective, accountable and inclusive institutions at all levels (SDG 16). These particular SDGs reflect the cross-cutting nature of contemporary migration.

States at crucial borders or with strong economies have seen a large jump in migrant numbers in recent years and this has no doubt placed a heavy burden on already struggling economies and social systems. Nonetheless, problems such as

[8] Dauvergne, *Making People Illegal*, above fn. 5, ch. 3; Bailey, A. (2015) 'Global Migration: Current Trends and Issues', in Plender, *Issues in International Migration* above fn. 6, 13; Addicott, J. F., M. J. Hossain Bhuiyan and T. M. R. Chowdhury (eds) (2012) *Globalization, International Law, and Human Rights*, Oxford University Press.

[9] Migration Compact, para. 8; United Nations, Department of Economic and Social Affairs, *International Migration Report 2017: Highlights*, UN doc. ST/ESA/SER.A/404 (United Nations, 2017), para. 1, available at www.un.org/en/development/desa/population/migration/publications/migrationreport/index.shtml; Opeskin, B., R. Perruchoud and J. Redpath-Cross (2012) 'Conceptualising International Migration Law', in Opeskin, B., R. Perruchoud and J. Redpath-Cross (eds), *Foundations of International Migration Law*, Cambridge University Press, 1–16, at 1, 5.

[10] United Nations, Department of Economic and Social Affairs, *International Migration Report 2017: Highlights*, UN doc. ST/ESA/SER.A/404 (United Nations, 2017) (Migration Report 2017), available at www.un.org/en/development/desa/population/migration/publications/migrationreport/index.shtml

absorption capacities, access to healthcare or access to education, for example, cannot be trumped by policies that give preferment to real or imagined security issues over the rights of individuals and the needs of industry as policies of this kind tend to exacerbate rather than alleviate pressure points and disrupt regular migration. Governments of states in the throes of massive refugee influxes due to conflicts or events in neighbouring territories facilitate their citizens' disenchantment with migrants by failing to stopper the dissemination of unsupported claims about the criminality of migration. Despite prevalent negative publicity relating to a migration crisis, only an estimated 10.1 per cent of the estimated world stock of migrants in 2017 comprised refugees or asylum seekers in crisis.[11] The 'crisis' that has occupied the minds of transit and destination states over the past few years and their kneejerk policy responses has had a decidedly negative impact on regular migration – which arguably keeps most economies afloat.[12]

In an attempt to turn the tide of laws and policies that denigrate migration, the Migration Compact seeks to make sense out of current migration realities by mapping out connections between the human beings that migrate, the states that they support and the states that support them. It is possibly the largest jigsaw puzzle created to develop a picture of how the global community's collective efforts should relate in terms of form, function and practice. If successful, the Migration Compact could deliver an overarching guide as to how to coordinate the various legal frameworks that facilitate the necessary functions of migration. The following section sets out some of the most common international laws invoked in migration discourse.

International Law Frameworks

As a consistent feature of history, migration and its causes and effects have featured in international law discourse continuously.[13] A singular 'migration' treaty does not exist, yet there is no shortage of international legal agreements that relate to issues of migration. From human rights treaties and international criminal laws to environmental and labour treaties, our world is rife with 'laws' that speak to the complexities of legal issues arising from the human act of crossing a border.[14] A multitude of policy

[11] UN, Population Division, Department of Economic and Social Affairs (December 2017), Table 6, available at: www.un.org/en/development/desa/population/migration/data/estimates2/estimates17.shtml

[12] See, for example, Carswell, S. (2018) 'Tsunami of Vulnerable People Worried over Impact of Brexit', *The Irish Times*, 11 November, available at: www.irishtimes.com/news/politics/tsunami-of-vulnerable-people-worried-over-impact-of-brexit-1.3693890

[13] For a lively recap of the dawn of international relations and consular exchange see Neff, S. C. (2014) *Justice Among Nations: A History of International Law*, Harvard University Press, ch. 1.

[14] Migration Compact, para. 2. For a complete detail of the various instruments see Perruchoud, R. and K. Tömölová (eds) (2007) *Compendium of International Migration Law Instruments*, T. M. C. Asser Press. See also Chetail, V. (2012) 'Sources of International Migration Law', in Opeskin, B., R. Perruchoud and J. Redpath-Cross (eds) (2012) *Foundations of International Migration Law*, Cambridge University Press, 56–92.

frameworks and agendas also speak to migration.[15] Yet, existing laws and policies take differentiated approaches to the effects of migration, often without considering the causes or possible solutions for creating coherence from what is frequently misunderstood as chaos.

Distinguishing who is a national and who is foreign is the most rudimentary interest of most national migration laws.[16] Even with this distinction, international law has always acknowledged that 'universal hospitality' should apply to foreign individuals.[17] Therefore, international law provides rules against which states' national laws and their treatment of non-nationals, or migrants, can be assessed.[18]

As succinctly elaborated by Opeskin et al.

> The main pillars of international migration law are, first, the human rights and duties of persons involved in migration, as defined in a variety of international instruments; and second, the principles and standards deriving from State sovereignty, among which are the right to protect borders, confer nationality, safeguard national security, admit and expel non-nationals and combat smuggling and trafficking. To this, a third pillar may now be added, namely, the law promoting cooperation among States to manage the international movement of people.[19]

This section of the contribution is predominantly concerned with the first pillar and the distinct, but related, roles played by public and private international law in defining the circumstances under which pillar two functions to facilitate or thwart migration. Pillar three will be addressed in a later section.

Public International Law

Classical international law as an exclusive realm of states 'has been challenged by the emergence of individuals as international actors and the articulation of international rights attributable to individuals and opposable to States'.[20] Essentially, public international law has increasingly turned its hand to regulating obligations owed to and by individuals through the development of a range of treaties. Much of this turn has

[15] For example, the 2030 Development Agenda; UN General Assembly, Sendai Framework for Disaster Risk Reduction 2015–2030, UN Doc. UNISDR/GE/2015 (18 March 2015), paras 7, 27, 36; UN General Assembly, Resolution 69/313, Addis Ababa Action Agenda of the Third International Conference on Financing for Development, UN Doc. A/RES/69/313 (27 July 2015), paras 40, 111.

[16] Opeskin et al., 'Conceptualising International Migration Law', above fn. 9, 2.

[17] Mills, A. (2009) *The Confluence of Public and Private International Law*, Cambridge University Press, 265.

[18] Plender, R. (2015) 'Nationality Law and Immigration Law', above fn. 6, 2. See, for example, the *Nottebohm* case (*Guatemala* v. *Liechtenstein*), Second Phase, 1955 I.C.J. Reports 4.

[19] Opeskin et al., 'Conceptualising International Migration Law', above fn. 9, 6.

[20] Mills, *The Confluence of Public and Private International Law*, above fn. 17, 264. See, for example, *Jurisdiction of the Courts of Danzig*, Advisory Opinion, 1928 PCIJ, Ser B, No. 15, '[T]he very object of an international agreement, according to the intention of the contracting parties, may be the adoption by the parties of some definite rules creating individual rights and obligations . . .', 17–18.

developed as a corollary to the rise in international human rights law and international criminal law.[21] However, human rights treaties are not the sole instruments against which modern migration is considered.

Many of the international laws relevant to migration were developed to eliminate forced labour, human trafficking and slavery and these issues echo strongly in today's modern slavery discourse.[22] These instruments included the 1926 Slavery Convention,[23] conventions on statelessness[24] and early International Labour Association (ILO) Conventions that were latterly supplemented by a range of issue-specific labour agreements.[25] Today, these agreements have been joined by four instruments that expressly speak to rights and protections for migrants crossing borders under some form of duress, namely: the Convention relating to the Status of Refugees, and its 1967 Protocol (collectively 'Refugee Convention');[26] the UN Convention on the Rights of Migrant Workers and their Families;[27] the Protocol against the Smuggling of Migrants by Land, Sea and Air, Supplementing the UN Convention against Transnational Organized Crime ('Smuggling Protocol');[28] and the Protocol to Prevent, Suppress and Punish Trafficking in Persons, Especially Women and Children, Supplementing the UN Convention against Transnational Organized

[21] See, for example, International Covenant on Civil and Political Rights (ICCPR), 999 U.N.T.S. 171, 16 December 1966; International Covenant on Economic Social and Cultural Rights (ICESCR), 993 U.N.T.S. 3, 16 December 1966; Rome Statute on the International Criminal Court, 17 July 1998, 2187 U.N.T.S. 90.

[22] Opeskin et al., 'Conceptualising International Migration Law', above fn. 9, 3.

[23] Slavery Convention, 25 September 1926, 60 U.N.T.S. 254, and its 1953 Protocol.

[24] Convention relating to the Status of Stateless Persons, 28 September 1954, 360 U.N.T.S. 117; Convention on the Reduction of Statelessness, 30 August 1961, 989 U.N.T.S. 175.

[25] For example, ILO Convention No. 29 on Forced Labour, 28 June 1930; ILO Convention No. 87 concerning Freedom of Association and Protection of the Right to Organise, 9 July 1948; ILO Convention No. 97 concerning Migration for Employment, 1 July 1949; ILO Convention No. 100 on Equal Remuneration, 29 June 1951; ILO Convention No. 105 concerning the Abolition of Forced Labour, 25 June 1947; ILO Convention No. 111 concerning Discrimination in Respect of Employment and Occupation, 25 June 1958; ILO Convention No. 118 concerning Equality of Treatment of Nationals and Non-Nationals in Social Security, 28 June 1962; ILO Convention No. 143 concerning Migrations in Abusive Conditions and the Promotion of Equality of Opportunity and Treatment of Migrant Workers, 24 June 1975; ILO Convention No. 182 concerning the Prohibition and Immediate Action for the Elimination of the Worst Forms of Child Labour, 17 June 1999. All ILO Conventions available at: www.ilo.org/dyn/normlex/en/f?p=NORMLEXPUB:1:

[26] Convention relating to the Status of Refugees, 28 July 1951, 189 U.N.T.S. 150, as amended by the Protocol relating to the Status of Refugees, 31 January 1967, 606 U.N.T.S. 267 (Refugee Convention), above fn.7.

[27] International Convention on the Protection of the Rights of all Migrant Workers and Members of their Families (ICRMW), 18 December 1990, 2220 U.N.T.S. 3.

[28] Protocol against the Smuggling of Migrants by Land, Sea and Air, Supplementing the United Nations Convention against Transnational Organized Crime, 15 November 2000, 2241 U.N.T.S. 507 (Smuggling Protocol); Convention against Transnational Organized Crime, 15 November 2000, 2225 U.N.T.S. 209.

Crime ('Trafficking Protocol').[29] These are further supplemented by key human rights conventions adopted in the wake of the Universal Declaration of Human Rights in an effort to deliver universally agreed basic human rights standards.[30] Collectively, these treaties are dominated by defining the potential confrontations between individuals and the States in which they are present. Most of these clashes are then acted out, tested and adjudicated upon in national courts, parliaments and public fora.

These public international law conventions are supported by a multitude of soft law instruments and policies designed to further protect the individual upon whom each of these instruments focus.[31] The International Organization for Migration (IOM) is an intergovernmental agency that has been working to increase the understanding of the social and economic dimensions of migration since 1951. It has developed a range of policies and practice guidance to further assist states in responding to migratory ingress and egress.[32] Along with the IOM, the UN High Commissioner for Refugees is a key driver of greater institutionalisation of responses to refugee flows, but refugees represent a specific, special category of migrants that require broader substantive protections due to the drivers behind their (generally forced) migration.[33] Furthermore, the variable causes and effects of migration each tend to have their own champions, thus through specific lenses of migration, such as climate change or human trafficking and modern slavery, the dialogues will focus on the instruments most capable of effectively articulating and responding to a particular platform.[34] In many of these discussions the state is placed in a position that demands a defensive strategy thus, in due course, states have turned to offensive measures to rectify the perceived imbalance that migrants must be prioritised over the sovereign will of the state. While many recognise that public international law is increasingly 'human-

[29] Protocol to Prevent, Suppress and Punish Trafficking in Persons, Especially Women and Children, Supplementing the United Nations Convention against Transnational Organized Crime, opened for signature 15 November 2000, 2237 U.N.T.S. 319 (Trafficking Protocol).

[30] In addition to the ICCPR and the ICESCR, above fn. 21, see, for example, International Convention on the Elimination of All Forms of Racial Discrimination, 21 December 1965, 660 U.N.T.S. 195; Convention on the Elimination of Discrimination against Women, 18 December 1979, 1249 U.N.T.S. 13; Convention against Torture and Other Cruel, Inhuman or Degrading Treatment or Punishment, 10 December 1984, 1465 U.N.T.S. 85; Convention on the Rights of the Child, 20 November 1989, 1577 U.N.T.S. 3, and its Optional Protocols; International Convention for the Protection of All Persons from Enforced Disappearance, 20 December 2006, 2716 U.N.T.S. 3.

[31] For example, ILO Declaration on Social Justice for a Fair Globalization, 10 June 2008. See www.ilo.org/wcmsp5/groups/public/---dgreports/---cabinet/documents/genericdocument/wcms_371208.pdf

[32] International Organization for Migration (IOM) website at www.iom.int

[33] Loescher, G. and J. Milner (2011) 'UNHCR and the Global Governance of Refugees', in Betts, A. (ed.), *Global Migration Governance*, Oxford University Press, 189–209.

[34] See, for example, Schierup, C. U., R. Munck, B. Likić-Brborić and A. Neergaard (eds) (2015) *Migration, Precarity, and Global Governance: Challenges and Opportunities for Labour*, Oxford University Press; McAdam, J. (2011) 'Environmental Migration', in Betts, A. (ed.), *Global Migration Governance*, Oxford University Press, Ch. 6; Martin, S. and A. Callaway (2011) 'Human Trafficking and Smuggling', in Betts, A. (ed.), *Global Migration Governance*, Oxford University Press, Ch. 9.

ised', and responsive to the rights of individuals,[35] there is a question as to whether this recognition should be presented as 'opposable' as this suggests an agenda that is antagonistic to states, the results of which only exacerbate migration dilemmas.

Private International Law

Prior to the point at which international law diverged into two distinct paths, public and private international law simply covered all norms that were accepted as universal and maintained rules to negotiate those that were not. Today, private international law delivers instruments that determine, *inter alia,* which law applies to resolve situations involving private actors in a transboundary context.[36] Take, for example, the issue of labour migration, which has been a key driver of law and policy in the area of migration; the expansion of this collection of laws has increased manifold, in particular in relation to ILO agreements.[37] The discourse around labour migration is often framed as a tension between restrictive migration regulation versus migrants' rights.[38] For this reason, with the expansion of private international laws on migration there has been an increasingly reflexive reach toward public international law instruments as a reference point for laying a baseline of protection for labour migrants. The International Convention on the Protection of the Rights of All Migrant Workers and Members of Their Families (ICRMW)[39] is a clear example of this proffered connection.

It has been argued that the further instrumentalisation of private international law has increased restrictive national migration laws and policies.[40] In effect, laws that coordinate certain social aspects at a national level that are given effect in another state through private international law may engender further restrictive policies designed to defend against the facilitative private international law. These claims are raised in response to the increasing entitlements of non-nationals to social and economic benefits, particularly in the context of the European Union. For example, van den Eeckhout has noted that recognition of a foreign marriage or its dissolution is

[35] Katz Cogan, J. (2011) 'The Regulatory Turn in International Law' 52 *Harv. Int'l L.J.* 321; Mills, *The Confluence of Public and Private International Law* above fn. 17, Ch. 3; Knop, K. (2016) 'Lorimer's Private Citizens of the World', *European Journal of International Law* 27: 447–75.

[36] Van Loon, H. (2018) 'Private International Law and Global Governance Issues: the Present and Prospective Contribution of Global Private International Law Unification to Global Legal Ordering', paper delivered at NYU, Conference, 16 November 2018, 1.

[37] Likić-Brborić, B. and C. U. Schierup (2015) 'Labour Rights as Human Rights: Trajectories in the Global Governance of Migration', in Schierup, C. U., R. Munck, B. Likić-Brborić and A. Neergaard (eds), *Migration, Precarity, and Global Governance: Challenges and Opportunities for Labour*, Oxford University Press, 223–44. For an examination of labour migration in the context of integration, see the chapter by Carballo Piñeiro in this volume.

[38] Likić-Brborić and Schierup, 'Labour Rights as Human Rights', above fn. 39.

[39] Signed 18 December 1990 and entered into force on 1 July 2003; 54 Parties to date.

[40] For example, van den Eeckhout, V. (2005) *Instrumentalisation of and by Migration Law. Instrumentalisation and Private International Law*, Lecture, Leiden University, 9 December 2005, available at: https://openaccess.leidenuniv.nl/handle/1887/13855

a typical issue handled through private international law that can affect the validity of residence or other claims and, if manipulated in certain ways, can ensure a negative impact for a foreign national.[41] However, it is also argued that private international law reduces transnational conflict between substantive private laws; indeed, that is its overarching purpose.[42] Here we consider how and why private international law should and does engage with public international law norms as part of the increasing (re)integration of the public and private international law fields. This section focuses on the non-EU context of migration as the EU has its own highly developed, yet not unproblematic, regulations.[43]

Across the globe people cross borders to work, conduct business and to pursue private relationships. Certain instruments of private international law aid these endeavours. For example, the Hague Convention Abolishing the Requirement of Legalisation for Foreign Public Documents has made using foreign-issued birth certificates, marriage certificates and death certificates far less cumbersome when applying for passports, bank accounts or business permits in the states that have ratified the convention.[44] Most migrants will also have family members and, thus, issues of family law naturally arise for consideration. When family members cross borders, private international laws are generally triggered to settle questions of creation, reunification, separation, dissolution and so on. Several chapters in this volume examine issues related to cooperation between states, including enhanced cooperation in the EU, in international family law matters.[45]

National Law and Policy

Despite the broad range of international agreements that invoke issues fundamental to individuals on their migration journeys, states have always prefaced any discussion of migration with a reminder of their right to include and exclude non-nationals.[46] This is possible even where a state has ratified any number of the aforementioned treaties crafted to give priority to the human condition, as ratification does not equate to the treaty being in force at the national level.[47] Thus while treaties are in and of

[41] Ibid., 2–4.

[42] Van Loon, 'Private International Law and Global Governance Issues', above fn. 36, 1.

[43] Migration and free movement across EU Member States is currently being given plenty of coverage in the lead-up to Brexit.

[44] Hague Convention Abolishing the Requirement of Legalisation for Foreign Public Documents, 5 October 1961, entered into force on 24 January 1965; 117 States Parties, status as at 30 November 2018.

[45] See, in particular, the chapter by Espinosa Calabuig in this volume.

[46] Chetail, 'Sources of International Migration Law', above fn. 14, 56, quoting the US Supreme Court decision in *Nishimura Ekiu* v. *United States*, 142 US 651 (1892), para. 659; Migration Compact, paras 7, 15.

[47] Aust, A. (2007) *Modern Treaty Law and Practice*, 2nd edn, Cambridge University Press, 178; Staberock, G. (2011) 'Human Rights, Domestic Implementation', in Wolfrum, R. (ed.) *Max Planck Encyclopedia of Public International Law*, paras 14–18.

themselves exercises of sovereignty, how these obligations are interpreted at the national level does not necessarily enjoy universal agreement.[48]

Major Challenges

In terms of subject matter there is a great deal of overlap across public international law, private international law and national law in relation to migration.[49] The variable issues stemming from recent migration crises must be addressed using an approach that integrates public and private international law as well as more nuanced national laws. In particular, private international law has the capacity to harmonise and capitalise upon its role as resolver of inter-systemic conflicts, between national laws, non-national rules of law and international commitments.[50]

But, as recent history has demonstrated, resolving conflicts relating to migration demands a far more nuanced approach than necessary in other types of transnational conflicts as migration pits individuals' rights and market demands against the state's sovereignty claims. 'The internationalisation of rights here is in tension with the pluralism respected by the principle of subsidiarity.'[51] Mills has argued that 'the collapse in [the] distinction [between international law and national law] also collapses the traditional boundary between rules of public and private international law' thus 'international norms should be recognised and given effect in private international law . . . because of the special character of private international law as a set of national rules with an international systemic function'.[52] This makes sense when reflecting on the specific nature of migration, which sees individuals traversing borders and, depending on the situation into which they travel, in need of protections that follow them across these borders. Pushing a return to more joined-up treatment of individuals between public and private international law does not take too much of a stretch into the history of the fields, which were very much conjoined until just before the turn of the nineteenth century.[53]

This chapter now turns to an examination of the Migration Compact and how it attempts to play a re-connective role between the fields in the pursuit of stabilising legal and policy approaches to contemporary migration.

Contribution of the Global Compact on Migration to More Coherent Migration

Since the turn of the twenty-first century, migration has featured in international dialogues partly in relation to globalisation and partly as a result of multiple conflicts.[54]

[48] McNair, A. (1961) *The Law of Treaties*, 2nd edn, Oxford University Press, 35.

[49] Chetail, 'Sources of International Migration Law', above fn. 14, 67.

[50] On these capacities see further Ruiz Abou-Nigm's final chapter in this volume.

[51] Mills, *The Confluence of Public and Private International Law*, above fn. 17, 269.

[52] Ibid., 271.

[53] For a fuller discussion of this lack of distinction between the two disciplines in relation to individuals, see Knop, 'Lorimer's Private Citizens of the World', above fn. 35, 447–51.

[54] Migration Compact, para. 2.

Recalling that migration has been instrumental to the development of domestic economies throughout history, there is decided benefit in concerted action toward developing global migration strategies, rather than leaving such issues to the constantly shifting political priorities of individual states. While some question the legitimate purpose of migration in achieving the cosmopolitan objective,[55] the demonstrable benefit of coordinated approaches to migration is that legitimate workforce and economic considerations can be coupled with ensuring the basic rights of all migrants. The goal of the Migration Compact is to give effect to the New York Declaration on Refugees and Migrants (New York Declaration) and to recognise that both groups face similar vulnerabilities.[56] It is a direct response to the long-running calls for better global migration governance to address the multifaceted causes and effects of migration.[57] Regular migrants are not necessarily vulnerable but can become so quite easily. Consider the *kafala* system operating in many states, such as Bahrain and UAE, which enables guest workers on citizen-sponsored work visas to labour in many Gulf States but is repeatedly linked to ill-treatment of those workers and the facilitation of illegal workers.[58] It also acknowledges that addressing the factors that prevent individuals from 'building and maintaining sustainable livelihoods in their countries of origin, and so compel them to seek a future elsewhere' is a shared responsibility of the international community.[59] As a non-binding international instrument,[60] the Migration Compact aims to effectively translate international law and UN policy into effective practice. While international law can define some aspects of migration, only state-level implementation, cooperation and capacity-building will deliver the Migration Compact aims.

The Migration Compact presents a path toward achieving greater predictability and certainty for all stakeholders, including states, migrants, business and society. While 'States may distinguish between regular and irregular migration status, including as they determine their legislative and policy measures for the implementation of the Global Compact',[61] suggestions that democracies are able to navigate the com-

[55] Rodríguez, C. M. (2017) 'Regulatory Pluralism and the Interests of Migrants', in Knight, J. (ed.), *Immigration, Emigration and Migration: NOMOS LVII*, New York University Press, 277–307.

[56] Migration Compact, paras 3, 13; Johns, F. E. (2004) 'The Madness of Migration: Disquiet in the International Law Relating to Refugees', *International Journal of Law and Psychiatry* 27: 587, 590.

[57] Opeskin et al., 'Conceptualising International Migration Law', above fn. 9, 9–10; Addis Ababa Action Agenda, para. 111: 'international migration is a multidimensional reality of major relevance for the development of origin, transit and destination countries that must be addressed in a coherent, comprehensive and balanced manner'.

[58] For a good overview, see Gardner, A. M. (2010) 'Engulfed: Indian Guest Workers, Bahraini Citizens, and the Structural Violence of the Kafala System', in de Genova, N. and N. Peutz (eds), *The Deportation Regime: Sovereignty, Space, and the Freedom of Movement*, Duke University Press, 196 ss.

[59] Migration Compact, para. 12.

[60] Ibid., para. 7.

[61] Ibid., para. 15. States may distinguish between regular and irregular migration status, including how they determine their legislative and policy measures for the implementation of the Global Compact.

plexities of migration without overarching coordination has proved untenable.[62] The promise of coherent migration in response to rapid globalisation has generated a great amount of migration pathways but without direction – a situation of connectivity without a compass. This, in turn, has resulted in defeating regular, necessary migrants from successfully clearing the difficult processes increasingly imposed by states and thus their positive contributions to the economy are lost. All migrants, no matter their path, are entitled to fundamental human rights protections, safety and dignity and the strong human focus of the Migration Compact underscores the centrality of this in effective migration governance. Though some have cast doubt on the potential of global governance, even soft governance, of migration,[63] the Global Compact is crafted to overcome such doubt and dismissals. As the preambular paragraphs of the Migration Compact entreat: 'It is crucial that international migration unites us rather than divides us. This Global Compact sets out our *common understanding*, *shared responsibilities* and *unity of purpose* regarding migration in a manner that makes it work for all.'[64]

The final draft sets out twenty-three objectives based on the New York Declaration.[65] Key issues include: the use of accurate and disaggregated data to develop evidence-based policies (objective 1); effective communication of migration status and processes (objective 3); availability and adequacy of documentation (objective 4); flexible pathways to migration (objective 5); addressing underlying causes and responses to vulnerable migrants that fall victim to a myriad of issues running afoul of international criminal laws and abuses of human rights (objectives 6, 7, 8, 9, 10); more coordinated borders, migration procedures, consular protections, portability of earnings (remittances) and social security entitlements (objectives 20, 22).

To achieve these objectives, existing private international law conventions offer model instruction and a potential framework for reconnecting public and private international law in a way that could aid in addressing migration challenges. The Intercountry Adoption Convention shares similar objectives in that it is designed to facilitate cooperation across states in terms of both preventing illegal activity, such as abduction or the trafficking of children, and recognising the legal decisions of courts in other states.[66] In line with the UN Convention on the Rights of the Child (UNCRC),[67] the Intercountry Adoption Convention prioritises the best interests of

62 Rodríguez, 'Regulatory Pluralism and the Interests of Migrants', above fn. 55, 279.

63 Opeskin et al., 'Conceptualising International Migration Law', above fn. 9, 10.

64 Migration Compact, para. 9.

65 UN General Assembly, Resolution 71/1. New York Declaration for Refugees and Migrants of 19 September 2016, UN Doc. A/RES/71/1 (3 October 2016) (hereinafter 'New York Declaration').

66 Hague Convention on Protection of Children and Co-operation in Respect of Intercountry Adoption, fn. 37, Arts 1, 8.

67 The UN Convention on the Rights of the Child was concluded in New York on 20 November 1989, 1577 U.N.T.S. 3, and entered into force on 2 September 1990; 196 States Parties, status as at 30 November 2018.

the child and the views of the child and includes obligations relating to tracking the progress of the process.[68] Thus the Convention integrates both transnational governance structures as well as public international law by reference to human rights treaty standards, namely the UNCRC. It mandates that each Contracting State designate a Central Authority to discharge the duties under the convention, which includes coordination between the Central Authority of the state of origin or receiving state for each case (Chapter III, Articles 6–13). It also articulates precise procedural requirements that must be followed by the Central Authority, including the preparation of a report detailing 'information about their identity, eligibility and suitability to adopt, background, family and medical history, social environment, reasons for adoption, ability to undertake an intercountry adoption, as well as the characteristics of the children for whom they would be qualified to care'.[69]

The twenty-three objectives of the Migration Compact also set a path toward comprehensive integration in both the horizontal and vertical senses. Horizontal in that it sets out the need for coordinated efforts across states' distinct sovereign jurisdictions. The vertical implications are that the Compact employs the now-familiar SDGs as well as the familiar language of other public international law treaties. Tracking the Intercountry Adoption Convention, the Migration Compact's aims of encouraging 'flexible, rights-based and gender-responsive labour mobility schemes' demand coordination of information across local and national organs in the public and private sector in terms of labour market needs.[70] This also requires keeping track of how many people are 'in the system' in terms of awaiting processing for work visas across all levels – unskilled, highly-skilled and so on – on a non-discriminatory basis which will also serve to better secure borders (objective 11) and strengthen predictability of migration procedures (objective 12). Tracking the 'Decent Work Agenda' set out in many International Labour Conventions,[71] coordination would also aid in facilitating a fair and ethical recruitment and decent work conditions (objective 6) as well as empower migrants to confidently take part in local society (objective 16), also noted in the ICRMW.[72] While it has been argued that lower-wage economic migrants might be willing to sacrifice certain rights, such as freedom from exploitation or freedom of movement, in exchange for the opportunity to work in a new country, it is extremely shortsighted to consider a 'voluntary' degradation of

[68] Intercountry Adoption Hague Convention, fn. 37, Art. 4 (best interests and wishes/opinions of the child), 16, 21.

[69] Intercountry Adoption Hague Convention, fn. 37, Art. 15.

[70] Migration Compact, objective 5(d).

[71] International Labour Organization, Decent Work Agenda, available at www.ilo.org/global/topics/decent-work/lang--en/index.htm; see discussion in Hyland, M. and R. Munck (2015) 'Labour, Migration, and Regional Integratin', in Schierup et al., *Migration, Precarity, and Global Governance: Challenges and Opportunities for Labour* above fn. 37, 281–2.

[72] The ICRMW serves to ensure that all migrant workers are able to exercise their rights in society without discrimination, reflecting those rights also set out in the ICCPR.

rights as acceptable.[73] This simply feeds discriminatory practices by distinguishing between those who are worthy of protection and those who are not. The fact that it has been reasoned that migrants who give up some of their rights in order to work in another country might change their minds and 'begin to demand fair and even equal treatment'[74] offends the fundamental cosmopolitan principle that all humans are born free and equal in rights and dignity.[75]

Encouraging ethical and fair procedures and social cohesion also tracks the aims of the Intercountry Adoption Convention in Chapter IV and Article 26, which set out the range of procedural requirements necessary to facilitate an adoption and the clarification of what recognition of that adoption means – a substantial stepping stone for a child and adoptive family in terms of integration into the new familial relationship. Establishing central authorities in states similar to the system employed in the Intercountry Adoption Convention to handle regular migration could facilitate migration flows in a similar way. As demonstrated by the Intercountry Adoption Convention, key concerns regarding legality of documentation, status in the process and transferability of work permits could be remedied through a centralised organ and aid objectives 3 and 4 of the Compact. Furthermore, close cross-border coordination will also assist in preventing migrants from sliding into vulnerable situations through substantial human rights or labour violations, or through criminal activity (objectives 7, 9 and 10), reflecting the Trafficking Protocol. Importantly, it is fundamental that governments commission and utilise accurate, disaggregated data regarding migration and work to clarify the positive role played by migrants in enriching the work force, the economy and society more generally as reflected in objective 1.

A major contribution of the Migration Compact is also its capacity to highlight that in addition to stabilising migration processes, states must also work to minimise the negative drivers that compel people to leave their homelands, as this is essential to stabilising migration flows (objective 2). Echoing the 2030 Agenda for Sustainable Development, the Migration Compact couples streamlined processes with key SDGs mentioned above. Essential to this is concerted programming to end poverty (SDG 1) and promote sustainable and inclusive economic growth through decent work (SDG 8), which should be coordinated through private actors as well as public policy. Reducing inequalities within and among different states (SDG 10) also speaks directly to reducing the drivers of migration, particularly from the Global South to the North and from South to South.

The bottom line is that the Migration Compact, much like the Intercountry Adoption Convention, opens up the possibility of global governance[76] that is predicated

[73] Rodríguez, 'Regulatory Pluralism and the Interests of Migrants', above fn. 55, 281.

[74] Ibid., 281.

[75] UN General Assembly, Universal Declaration of Human Rights, Resolution 217 of 10 December 1948, Art. 1.

[76] See further Ruiz Abou-Nigm, V. 'Private International Law and Global Governance Issues:

on integrated public and private international law aims and structures. Even if often viewed as a 'tension between the ideal and the possible',[77] private international law has demonstrated that coordination across national regulatory bodies is possible. While public international law, whether through the SDGs or a range of human rights treaties, provides fundamental principles that should be prioritised, private international law delivers examples of successful coordination frameworks that can facilitate the specific aims of the Migration Compact. Global solutions to contemporary problems, such as the migration crisis, require cross-cutting approaches and this is increasingly acknowledged at the international level.[78]

Conclusion

This chapter emphasises the need for an integrated approach to migration utilising the connective capability of private international law to foster further integration, in the understanding that integration of migrants boosts global economies and ensures that people on the move are dynamic contributors to social and economic development. While 'frictionless movement'[79] may never be achieved, existing frameworks highlight that further integrated approaches can smooth interstate processes, facilitate better responses to market labour demands, ensure individual migrant rights and enrich the dynamism of societies.

In order to respond to the legal demands of the multitude of stakeholders as well as to reflect the dynamism inherent in global migration, the Migration Compact adopts a boundary-spanning approach that reaches across different legal instruments, policies, interests of states, stakeholders and migrants to build relationships, interconnections and interdependencies. Presenting migration as 'one of the most urgent and profound tests of international cooperation in our time' suggests that it is a problem to be solved.[80] Perhaps if the opportunities presented by migration were more openly discussed and regularly facilitated, the unnecessary tether between migration and crisis could be severed. This is a key aim of the Migration Compact. 'It is with this sense of common purpose that we take this historic step, fully aware that the Global Compact for Safe, Orderly and Regular Migration is a milestone, but not the end to our efforts.'[81]

Unlocking Private International Law's Potential in Global (Migration) Governance', in Ferrari, F. and D. Fernández Arroya (eds) (2019) *Private International Law: Contemporary Challenges and Continuing Relevance*, Elgar.

77 Rodríguez, 'Regulatory Pluralism and the Interests of Migrants', above fn. 55, 289.

78 See further Ruiz Abou-Nigm, V., K. McCall-Smith and D. French (2018) 'Introduction: Systemic Dialogue: Identifying Commonalities and Exploring Linkages in Private and Public International Law', in Ruiz Abou-Nigm, V., K. McCall-Smith and D. French (eds) (2018) *Linkages and Boundaries in Private and Public International Law*, Hart Publishing.

79 Rodríguez, 'Regulatory Pluralism and the Interests of Migrants', above fn. 55, 299.

80 UN Secretary-General's Report: Making Migration Work for All, 12 December 2017, para. 1.

81 Migration Compact, para. 14.

13

Labour Migration and Private International Law

*Laura Carballo Piñeiro**

Introduction

The complexities of labour migration are manifold against the backdrop of business globalisation and the compartmentalisation of labour markets. While international agencies strive to abolish barriers to the movement of goods, services and capital across borders, the free movement of workers is separately addressed despite the close ties among all market freedoms.[1] The workforce is essential to create and produce, and thus businesses seek skilled workers worldwide; they relocate to low-wage countries, and move workers in order to provide services across borders. This, in turn, raises private international law issues, and the particular topic to be addressed in this chapter is how labour and employment conditions can be enhanced against the international/domestic divide in trade and labour matters which pulls regulatory competition downward.[2]

Conflict rules on employment matters are devised with just one type of labour migration in mind – that of workers who permanently move to a foreign country for work purposes. In principle, these rules aim to put on an equal footing domestic and foreign workers and hence they take the habitual place of work as the usual connect-

* This chapter has been co-financed by the Spanish Government under the project DER2016-80568-R and Xunta de Galicia-FEDER.

1 A clear stand against intermingling national trade policy and compliance with international labour standards was taken by the World Trade Organization (WTO) at its Singapore 1996 Session. In contrast, on the proposal to create a similar organisation for labour migrants, see Hatton, T. J. (2007) 'Should We Have a WTO for International Migration?' *Economic Policy*, vol. 22, no. 50, 339–83.

2 See Axel, M., J. Soares and W. van Acker (2015) 'The Protection of International Labour Rights: A Longitudinal Analysis of the Protection of the Rights of Freedom of Association and Collective Bargaining over 30 Years in 73 Countries', in Marx, A., J. Wouters, G. Rayp and L. Beke (eds), *Global Governance of Labour Rights. Assessing the Effectiveness of Transnational Public and Private Policy Initiatives*, Elgar, 13–41.

ing factor. While this serves for integration purposes in cases of permanent posting of workers, the same connection fuels other types of migration in search of low-cost labour markets. The most obvious one is that triggered by business relocation, which is undertaken in order to take advantage of other countries' labour and employment conditions.

Temporarily posted workers move between two or more jurisdictions, that is, although they are providing services in one country, their employment relationship is governed by the law of another country. According to Directive 96/71/EC of the European Parliament and of the Council of 16 December 1996 concerning the posting of workers in the framework of the provision of services (hereinafter 'the Posting of Workers Directive')[3] three sub-cases of this labour migration[4] can be identified: that of outsourcing chains where a subcontractor sends its employees to provide services in the country of posting; that of employees moving within a transnational group of companies; and postings undertaken by employment agencies if there is an employment relationship between the agency and the posted worker during the period of posting.[5]

The following section focuses on the conflict rules in this field, putting into question their role when it comes to enhancing working conditions and thus reducing social inequality across the world. The bigger picture shows that many countries are prone to regulatory competition on labour and employment matters as a means of achieving an economic advantage over others and in the end the much-coveted economic growth. By the same token, they are not prone to changing the status quo as to the usual conflict rules in these matters for others more proactively favouring worker protection.

As a result of these policies worker protection is undermined worldwide while economic growth is not being translated into the enhancing of labour and social conditions. In contrast, inequality in wages and salaries has dramatically increased in many countries.[6] And although the link between the scaling of social inequality and the globalisation processes is not conclusive,[7] migrants remain among the most vulnerable workers. The incorporation into a foreign labour market gives rise to many challenges that go well beyond the mere provision of services, in particular because

3 OJ [1996] L18/1.

4 See Art. 1 of the Posting of Workers Directive.

5 The WTO's General Agreement on Trade in Services (GATS) addresses the provision of services by legal and natural persons seated or domiciled in another country (Mode 4). However, the liberalisation of service suppliers is still in its infancy as the application of this Mode 4 has been made dependent on specific agreed commitments of individual states. In general, posted workers are highly skilled workers and cross-border movements are intra-corporate.

6 See OECD (2011), *Divided We Stand: Why Inequality Keeps Rising*, OECD Publishing; OECD (2015), *In It Together: Why Less Inequality Benefits All Us*, OECD Publishing.

7 For an overview of empirical studies discussing the impact of trade liberalisation on unemployment, wages, informality and labour union strength, see International Labour Office (2016) *Assessment of Labour Provisions in Trade and Investment Arrangements*, ILO, 11–16.

migrants' rights cannot be taken for granted[8] and even in those cases in which they have the same rights as local workers, labour law enforcement is a major issue on grounds of their vulnerability.[9] Private international law may help to overcome the compliance gap in cross-border settings by reinforcing the role of states and social partners in monitoring labour standards. The third and fourth sections of this chapter will address some shortcomings and advances made in that direction, while the concluding remarks will suggest how an international convention could tackle some of these issues.

Conflict Rules in Labour and Employment Matters

In accordance with the principle of 'equal pay for equal work', the first private international law response to labour migration is the submission of individual contractual relationships to the law of the habitual place of work.[10] Different considerations back up this connecting factor. First, an individual employment contract's centre of gravity is the location where the work is to be carried out, a place agreed on by employer and employee and consequently known to both parties, which means that both expect the law of this place to be applied. Second, a substantial part of labour law is made of overriding mandatory rules and thus the application of the *lex loci laboris* to employment relationships prevents operators from taking other laws into consideration when dealing with international employment.[11] Third and foremost for our purposes, this connection gives priority to the one stable factor within the employment relationship,

[8] The International Convention on the Protection of the Rights of All Migrant Workers and Members of Their Families, adopted by General Assembly Resolution 45/158 of 18 December 1990, acknowledges the problems of integration that economic migrants and their families, including irregular migrants, may encounter and strives to recognise their rights. Unfortunately, this Convention does not have a high ratification rate among developed countries. Strikingly, none of the EU Member States have ratified it, calling into question the role of the EU as a global human rights actor.

[9] Migration poses many more other issues than those related to labour matters, of course. See Corneloup, S. (2014) 'Can PIL Contribute to Global Migration Governance?', in Muir Watt, H. and D. P. Fernández Arroyo, *PIL and Global Governance*, Oxford University Press, 301–18. Focusing on migration policy in labour matters, see Castles, S., H. de Haas and M. J. Miller (2014) *The Age of Migration. International Population Movement in the Modern World*, The Guilford Press.

[10] Laid down in Art. 8 of Regulation (EC) No. 593/2008 of 17 June 2008 on the Law Applicable to Contractual Obligations (Rome I); Art. 43 of the Law of the People's Republic of China on the Application of Law for Foreign-related Civil Relationships; Art. 12 of the Japanese Act on the Application of Laws; Art. 94 of the Panamanian Private International Law Code; Art. 67 of the Tunisian Private International Law Code; Art. 27 of the Turkish Act on Private International and Procedural Law; Art. 28 of the South Korean Act on Private International Law; and Art. 121 of the Swiss Private International Law Act.

[11] With this proposal, see Art. 3 of the Resolution of the *Institut de droit international* of 3 August 1971, during the Zagreb session on 'Conflicts of Laws in the Field of Labour Law'. See further Gamillscheg, F. (1983) 'Rules of Public Order in Private International Labour Law', *Recueil des cours*, vol. 181, 285–348; Morgenstern, F. (1984) *International Conflicts of Labour Law: A Survey of the Law Applicable to the International Employment Relation*, ILO Reports, including a list of national laws that laid down this connection before its codification by the 1980 Rome Convention.

while simultaneously allowing for equal treatment of all parallel employment contracts since they are all submitted to the same law,[12] that is, the same law governs the employment relationships of all employees in the same workplace, thereby ensuring equal opportunities for them all and thus avoiding the distortion of competition and the potential social dumping which may result from this distortion.[13]

This connecting factor does not fit all workers, however, as highly skilled ones do not have the same bargaining power as low-skilled workers but generally more. Moreover, some workers lack a habitual place of work as their jobs are 'mobile' in essence, as is usually the case for pilots and other airline staff, seafarers and fishermen or other transport workers; while later developments insist that even this type of worker at least habitually discharges their duties towards their employers from a specific country,[14] the idea remains that there may be a closer law to the employment relationship than that of the habitual place of work.[15] In this vein, legal systems tend, on the one hand, to accept the role of party autonomy in these matters[16] while, on the other hand, they provide for an escape to the *lex loci laboris* in favour of a closer law.[17] The conflict rule thus gains flexibility as both mechanisms make it possible to take into account the specific circumstances of individual workers. However, there is one significant caveat to this flexible approach in that workers in the same workplace may have different working conditions as their employment contracts may be subject to different laws depending on their circumstances. As this erodes the principle of 'equal pay for equal work', it has been challenged before some domestic constitutional courts.[18] Nevertheless, the overall conclusion is that this principle is no

12 Claiming that this connection is primarily underpinned by the principle of worker protection and only secondarily by the principle of proximity, see de Boer, M. T. (1990) 'The EEC Contracts Convention and the Dutch Courts. A Methodological Perspective', *RabelsZ*, 54, 24–62, at 42.

13 In these terms, Zanobetti, A. (2011), 'Employment Contracts and the Rome Convention: the Koelzsch Ruling of the European Court of Justice', *Cuadernos de Derecho Transnacional*, 338–58, at 356.

14 See the Court of Justice's case law in CJEU, 13 June 1993, Case C-125/92, *Mulox*; 9 January 1997, Case C 383/95, *Rutten*; 15 March 2011, Case C 29/10, *Koelzsch*; and 15 December 2011, Case C-384/10, *Voogsgeerd.*

15 The same reasoning is applied to temporary migrant workers as they do not integrate into the domestic labour market given that their goal is to return to their countries of origin once the work is done. States may organise temporary foreign worker programmes and this would also require inter-country cooperation.

16 Nevertheless, as workers are at a disadvantage during the contracting process, corrections are to be introduced: for example, by not allowing the choice of law, as in Art. 43 of the Chinese Private International Law; by restricting the choice to a list of laws as provided for by Art. 121 of the Swiss Act of Private International Law; or by allowing an unrestricted choice of law provided that the choice does not deprive the employee of the protection afforded by the mandatory provisions of the law that would govern in the absence of choice of law, as required by Art. 8 Rome I Regulation, Art. 12 of the Japanese Act on the General Rules of Application of Law or Art. 28 of the Private International Act of South Korea. The latter correction achieves the protection of the weaker party without depriving him or her of the most favourable law chosen by the parties to the employment relationship.

17 This is the case of Art. 8(4) of the Rome I Regulation.

18 See, in particular, the French *Conseil Constitutionnel*, 2005-514 DC, 28 April 2005, *Droit Maritime*

longer essential, in particular as business relocation – fuelled by the free movement of goods, services and capital – puts pressure on domestic economies in order to avoid jobs migrating abroad.[19] Another troublesome outcome of this legal diversity is that workers lose collective bargaining power.

The temporary posting of workers makes the abovementioned pressure on domestic economies even more acute. This is a different phenomenon from the permanent posting of workers or business relocation as it depends on the free provision of services in integrated markets and not on the free movement of workers or the companies' freedom of establishment, namely, businesses move to another country to temporarily provide services, bringing their employees with them. These employment relationships are governed by the law of a country other than the one where workers temporarily discharge their duties towards their employer. As it is made clear by Recital (36) in relation to Article 8 of the Rome I Regulation: 'As regards individual employment contracts, work carried out in another country should be regarded as temporary if the employee is expected to resume working in the country of origin after carrying out his tasks abroad',[20] meaning that their labour standards may differ from those applicable to local workers in receiving states because posted workers remain in principle governed by the law of the habitual place of work.

The problems arising out of the distinction between the permanent and temporary posting of workers can be exemplified by the Court of Justice of the European Union (CJEU) judgment in *Rush Portuguesa*.[21] The latter was a Portuguese company subcontracted by a French company to provide services in the construction sector in France; to this end, it transferred its workers habitually working in Portugal to France. The French Immigration Office claimed, on the one hand, that this had been done without obtaining the corresponding work permits, while on the other the posted workers were being paid far below those residing in France and carrying out the same work. Noteworthy for our purposes is that the CJEU concluded that the temporary posting of workers did not entail incorporation into the labour market of the country of destination;[22] *ergo*, the free provision of services means that

> an undertaking established in Portugal providing services in the construction and public works sector in another Member State may move with its own labour force

Français, 2005, 514. See *Bundesverfassungsgerichtshof*, 10 January 1995, *NZV*, 1995, 272.

[19] Crews of convenience clearly illustrate this situation as they are set up to avoid reflagging domestic shipping and fishing fleets. See Carballo Piñeiro, L. (2015) *International Maritime Labour Law*, Springer, 20.

[20] Addressing the case of intra-corporate movements, see also Recital 36 of Rome I Regulation.

[21] CJEU 27 March 1990, Case C-113/90, *Rush Portuguesa Ltd* c. *Office nationale d'immigration*. It is interesting to note that, at the time of the preliminary question, Portugal had just entered the EU and the free movement of Portuguese workers to other Member States was still not applicable for a transition period. Accordingly, Rush Portuguesa based its defence on the free provision of services across the then European Community.

[22] CJEU 27 March 1990, Case C-113/89, *Rush Portuguesa*, para. 15.

> which it brings from Portugal for the duration of the works in question. In such a case, the authorities of the Member State in whose territory the works are to be carried out may not impose on the supplier of services conditions relating to the recruitment of manpower *in situ* or the obtaining of work permits for the Portuguese work-force.[23]

In short, temporary posted workers move across borders with their labour law, that is, that of their habitual workplace, and the country of the temporary posting is only entitled to require foreign employers to comply with its overriding mandatory rules.[24] This distinction is a significant one to the extent that it provides businesses with room for legal shopping.

In view of the 'opportunities' for social dumping, the Posting of Workers Directive was issued to level the playing field within the EU internal market.[25] To this end, the Directive lays down an intra-EU conflict rule by which the law of the receiving country will govern the employment relationship during the posting if some minimum labour standards therein laid down are more favourable to posted workers than those established in the *lex laboris*.[26] However, the application of this special conflict rule and the distinction between the permanent and temporary posting of workers give rise to significant problems, in particular in terms of enhancing labour conditions.

The first issue posed by such a conflict rule is one of information to the extent that it involves legal comparison,[27] that is, posted workers have to be informed about the

[23] CJEU 27 March 1990, Case C-113/89, *Rush Portuguesa*, para. 19. On similar terms, see Case C-43/93, *Raymond Vander Elst* v. *Office des migrations internationales*.

[24] See C-113/89, *Rush Portuguesa*, para. 18.

[25] See Recitals 10 and 11 of the Posting of Workers Directive. Art. 20 of the Rome Convention and Art. 23 of the Rome I Regulation give preference to conflict rules laid down in other EU instruments such as this Directive.

[26] See Art. 3 of the Posting of Workers Directive. From a comparative perspective, see Voss, E., M. Faioli and J. P. Lhernoul (2016) *Posting of Workers Directive: Current Situation and Challenges. Study for the EMLC Committee*, General Directorate for Internal Policies, 23, available at: www.europarl.europa.eu/thinktank/en/document.html?reference=IPOL_STU(2016)579001

[27] This is a very complex issue which has given rise to several judgments of the Court of Justice. See Case C-272/94, *Guiot, Climatec SA*; Case C-369/96, *Arblade*; Case 165/98, *Mazzoleni*; Joint Cases C-49/98, C-50/98, C-52/98 to C-54/98, C-68/98 to C-71/98, *Finalarte*; Case C-164/99, *Portugaia Construçoes*. See on this legal comparison issue, Houwerzijl, M. (2006) 'Towards a More Effective Posting Directive', in Blanpain, R. (ed.), *Freedom of Services in the European Union. Labour and Social Security Law: The Bolkestein Initiative*, Kluwer Law International, 179, 190. The most controversial issue has been how to establish the minimum wage. In its judgment of 7 November 2013, Case 522/12, *Isbir*, para. 37, the CJEU indicates that it is up to the receiving state to determine the elements of which the minimum wage is made up, being this case law reiterated in its judgment of 12 February 2015, Case 396/13, *Sähköalojen ammattiliitto ry y Elektrobudowa Spółka Akcyjna*, para. 70. See, in detail, Lhernoul, J. (ed.) (2016) *Study on Wage Setting Systems and Minimum Rates of Pay Applicable to Posted Workers in Accordance with Directive 96/71/CE in a Selected Number of Member States and Sectors*, General Directorate for Employment, Social Affairs & Inclusion.

applicable minimum labour standards in the receiving country in order to be aware of their rights.[28] This is not problematic for high- and medium-skilled workers who usually benefit from special arrangements such as choice-of-law clauses; but it is for low-skilled workers moving across borders, in particular if the language barrier is taken into consideration.[29]

The second issue is the non-compliance with the labour and employment rules of each of the countries involved in the posting of workers, as the application of two legislations leads to problems as to which state monitors employers' activities: two states are interested in the employment relationship, but the issue is which of them is enforcing the relevant labour law. For example, while the country-of-origin principle in the EU places responsibility on the country of the company's location, the fact is that a business and its workers are providing services in another country. While this requires inter-country coordination, it is not working satisfactorily in the EU, where many cases of letter-box companies established in the sending country, bogus employees[30] and fake posted workers have been reported.[31]

These and other issues have made the EU take action by issuing Directive 2014/67/EU of the European Parliament and of the Council of 15 May 2014 on the enforcement of Directive 96/71/EC concerning the posting of workers in the framework of the provision of services and amending Regulation (EU) No. 1024/2012 on administrative cooperation through the Internal Market Information System (hereinafter 'the

[28] The CJEU decision on Case C-369/96, *Arblade*, of 23 November 1999 focuses on Art. 4 of the Posting of Workers Directive and the obligation that suppliers of services have to inform their workers about the applicable working conditions.

[29] There are no precise statistics in the EU, but posted workers make up around 1 per cent of the total number of workers in the EU; this figure increased 44.4 per cent between 2012 and 2014. The posting of workers is particularly significant in specific economic sectors such as construction and public procurement; manufacturing industries; education, social and health services; and financial services. This and other data are available on the EU website at: http://europa.eu/rapid/press-release_MEMO-16-467_en.htm. See data analysis by Voss et al., *Posting of Workers Directive*, above fn. 26, 15–17. This study also distinguishes between highly skilled workers who represent 36 per cent of all posted workers and low-skilled workers who now make up around 50 per cent of this figure (ibid., 17–20). See also Maslauskaite, K. (2014) 'Posted Workers in the EU: State of Play and Regulatory Evolution', *Policy Paper. Notre Europe. Jacques Delors Institute*, 107, 24 March 2014, 1–20, at 4.

[30] See Thörnquist, A. (2013) 'False (Bogus) Self-Employment in East-West Labour Migration. Recent Trends in the Swedish Construction and Road Haulage Industries', *TheMES. Themes on Migration and Ethnic Studies*, 41, 1–43. Available at: www.ep.liu.se/PubList/Default.aspx?SeriesID=2551. See on this trend in the construction sector, Jorens, Y. (2008) *Self-employment and Bogus Self-employment in the European Construction Industry. A Comparative Study of 11 Member States*, Directorate General for Employment and Social Affairs of the European Commission.

[31] See Schiek, D. (ed.) (2015) *EU Social and Labour Rights and EU Internal Market Law*, European Parliament, Committee of Social Affairs, available at: www.europarl.europa.eu/supporting-analyses; Cremers, J. (2015) 'Letter-box Companies and the Abuse of Posting Rules: How the Primacy of Economic Freedoms and Weak Enforcement Give Rise to Social Dumping', *ETUI Policy Brief. European Economic, Employment and Social Policy*, 5, 1–5.

Enforcement Directive').[32] While the Directive seeks to undermine the documented abuses, it enhances inter-country communication, cooperation and coordination in order to enforce the relevant applicable laws in accordance with the Posting of Workers Directive. In particular, it puts emphasis on whether there is a real posting of workers, meaning that a company actually operates in the sending state and moves to the receiving state to temporarily provide services with its workers who habitually work in the posting state. While the main responsibility lies in the authorities of the sending state, receiving states may now supervise both the company and the posted workers, having the obligation to communicate any possible abuse to the sending state in addition to the power to sanction foreign companies in case of legal breaches.

The Enforcement Directive has not yet been applied, but it shows how significant state cooperation is in this field. Labour law enforcement is a very weak point even in such a highly integrated market as that of the EU. This framework also illustrates the shortcomings of private international law when it comes to enhancing labour and employment conditions. It is clear that the Posting of Workers Directive is not as effective as it could be due to lack of enforcement issues, but it is also that the intra-EU conflict rule therein enshrined does not put an end to social dumping; it does not put domestic and foreign workers on an equal footing but perpetuates differences by entitling posted workers merely to minimum labour standards. In order to tackle this issue, this conflict rule ought to be redrafted to submit posted workers to the law of the receiving country for the posting period.[33] It should not be forgotten, though, that there is much opposition to a rule of this type on the side of those countries that seek an economic advantage out of legal diversity in these matters.[34] If conflict rules leave scarce room for manoeuvre for political reasons, there are other private international law techniques that may be of avail, in particular when it comes to law compliance and enforcement. In this vein, the following sections focus on states and social partners as they are essential in making private parties comply with labour standards.

State Cooperation in Labour Matters

The fact that labour markets remain mostly domestic makes state cooperation essential in case of labour migration. The point has already been raised while addressing the temporary posting of workers. The same rationale applies when it comes to business relocation, which makes even more acute the need for a holistic approach

[32] OJ [2014] L 159/11.

[33] The European Commission presented on 8 March 2016 a Proposal for a Directive of the European Parliament and of the Council amending Directive 96/71/EC [COM(2016) 128 final]. The proposal seeks to ensure that posted workers get the same remuneration as local workers in light of the increasing differences in salary across the EU. See European Commission (2015) 'No Time for Business as Usual. Commission Work Programme 2016', COM(2015) 610 final, 8.

[34] This is illustrated by the contradictory reactions to the European Commission Proposal amending Directive 96/71/CE. See Voss et al., *Posting of Workers Directive*, above fn. 26, 49–54.

to market freedoms in order to stop a race to the bottom of labour and employment conditions. To this end, several steps have already been taken at an international level. Particularly remarkable is the role of the International Labour Organization (ILO) and the many conventions on labour matters it has drafted, although the low ratification figure is nevertheless problematic. Some voices have criticised the ILO for compromising too much to the extent that, in view of its relative success in harmonisation, it has made a controversial distinction between essential labour rights such as the prohibition of forced work and that of children, and other standards to which it takes a more flexible approach.[35] Nevertheless, the flexible approach undertaken by the ILO in convention implementation pays due regard to the legal and socio-economic background of each state, and it has been supplemented, on the one hand, by the supervisory role played by this agency,[36] and on the other hand by this agency's efforts in capacity-building.

As regards the ILO's efforts in enhancing state cooperation, the Maritime Labour Convention 2006 (MLC 2006) is a case in point.[37] On the one hand, it combines hard law and soft law rules with a view to paying attention to the particular situation of each ratifying state; while ratifying the convention, the contracting party can indicate its difficulties in implementing the MLC 2006's compulsory rules acquiring, nevertheless, the compromise of working towards establishing the labour standards enshrined in the MLC 2006. These obligations are supervised by the ILO, ensuring that the convention will be finally implemented and labour standards in the shipping sector enhanced.[38]

On the other hand, the MLC 2006 is also special in that it takes advantage of the international maritime regulatory regime based upon the international law of the sea and flag state and port state responsibilities. The latter consists of actually ensuring that states make private parties comply with the convention and the relevant national law implementing it. To this end, Title V establishes a system of certification and inspection of maritime labour conditions, of which flag states are primarily responsible. While the inspection system applies to all ships subject to this convention, only those of or over 500 gross tonnage engaged in international voyages or operating from a port, or between ports, in a country other than the one whose flag is flying, are obliged to get both the Maritime Labour Certificate and the

[35] See Alston, P. (2006) 'Labour Rights as Human Rights. The Not So Happy State of the Art', in Alston, P. (ed.), *Labour Rights as Human Rights. Collected Courses of the Academy of European Law*, Oxford University Press, 1–24.

[36] In addition to specific systems, there is one regular system for supervising the application of standards grounded in Article VI of the ILO Constitution. The Committee of Experts on the Application of Conventions and Recommendations, and the International Labour Conference's Tripartite Committee on the Application of Conventions and Recommendations are the bodies monitoring whether states are doing all they can to comply with the standards enshrined in the ratified convention.

[37] The Convention has been ratified by ninety-three states. This represents 91 per cent of world gross tonnage of ships. See http://ilo.org/global/standards/maritime-labour-convention/lang--en/index.htm

[38] See Arts VI and XIII of the MLC.

Declaration of Maritime Labour Compliance.[39] Both documents allow shipowners to navigate under a State Party flag, but also to avoid port controls which will be nevertheless undertaken if there is a complaint, or if it is obvious that the ship's conditions do not match with the prima facie evidence of compliance with maritime labour standards provided by those documents, or these documents show significant irregularities.[40] Should the ship not comply with the mandatory labour standards and the breach is not remedied, it could be detained by the authorities of either the flag state or the relevant port state.

The compliance mechanism set up by the MLC 2006 is rightly considered a major breakthrough in the international arena.[41] Moreover, it does not only place obligations on flag and port states, but also on labour-supplying countries, that is, those countries where intermediaries provide a labour force to shipowners located abroad. With a view to avoiding abuses such as charging seafarers undue fees, the making of an illegal deduction from wages, or blacklisting them,[42] these countries have to establish a standardised system of licensing and certification of any recruitment and placement service operating in their territory.[43]

In addition to these supervising powers, the MLC 2006 calls on states to ensure that recruitment and placement services establish worker protection by way of insurance or an equivalent appropriate measure,[44] meaning that if a shipowner fails to pay the salary of a seafarer, these services should have the obligation to pay for it on behalf of the shipowner.[45] A similar indication is found in Article 12 of the Enforcement Directive, but focusing on the construction sector: Member States are encouraged to make employers-subcontractors jointly and severally liable with contractors in the event that the former fail to fulfil their obligations to posted workers. Unfortunately, the latter is not mandatory.

State cooperation is also to be found in the labour provisions included in modern free trade and investment agreements, although still in timid terms:[46] while in some

39 See Regulation 5.1.3 and Standard A5.1.3 of the MLC.

40 The specific matters that must be inspected are listed in Appendix A5-I of the Convention, including the seafarers' employment agreement and the payment of wages.

41 See, for all, Chaumette, P., A. Charbonneau and G. Proutière-Maulion (2010) 'Les Conventions OIT sur le travail maritime de 2006 et 188 sur le travail à la pêche de 2007', *Scritti in onore di Francesco Berlingieri. Número Speciale di Il Diritto Marittimo I*, 337–60, at 349.

42 Couper, A. D. (1999) *Voyages of Abuse. Seafarers, Human Rights and International Shipping*, Virginia.

43 See Regulation 1.4 and Standard A1.4 of the MLC.

44 See Standard A1.4(5)(c)(vi) of the MLC.

45 See, advancing this measure, Final Report, Meeting of Experts on Working and Living Conditions of Seafarers on Board Ships in International Registers, Geneva, 6–8 May 2002, ILO Doc. No. MEWLCS/2002/8, available at: www.ilo.org/public/english/standards/relm/gb/docs/gb285/pdf/mewlcs-8.pdf, para. 64.

46 International Labour Office (2016) *Assessment of Labour Provisions in Trade and Investment Arrangements*, ILO. The number of trade agreements including labour provisions has significantly increased from only four in 1995 to fifty-eight in June 2016; there are roughly 120 country parties to

cases the amendment of domestic labour standards is part of the ratification process, in many more a cooperation framework between the contracting parties is set up with a view to enhancing working conditions, in particular through capacity-building or the strengthening of labour inspection in the countries concerned. Some treaties also include complaint mechanisms by which economic sanctions or benefits may be required or applied in case of lack of or compliance with labour standards. However, they have rarely been used.[47] As they tend to focus on internal labour matters, these labour provisions have been criticised for being a form of 'window dressing' and disguised protectionism.[48] However, they have the potential for improving labour standards by increasing the labour-related implementation capacity of the contracting parties.[49] Moreover, some agreements include specific references to ILO conventions, in particular to the 1998 Declaration of Fundamental Principles and Rights at Work.[50] While this helps to reinforce the harmonisation efforts on labour standards across the world, further cooperation activities have already been suggested taking advantage of the ILO's expertise.[51] From a private international law perspective, these labour provisions are interesting because they reinforce the role of social partners and states in monitoring labour compliance; they thereby set the table for cross-border cooperation purposes.

The Role of Social Partners and Corporate Social Responsibility in Transnational Labour Relations

If states are primarily responsible in labour compliance, social partners are essential not only in monitoring state responsibility, but also in negotiating further development of labour standards.[52] However, the conditions to undertake collective bargaining are laid down at a national level, meaning that the principle of territorialism establishes the collective labour relations' domain. This poses serious problems as to the role

this type of agreement (5). See WTO Regional Trade Agreements Information System at: http://rtais.wto.org/UI/PublicMaintainRTAHome.aspx

47 See ibid., 43.

48 See ibid., 6.

49 See ibid., 7.

50 See ibid., 31–5. See further Brown, R. C., 'Asian and US Perspectives on Labor Rights under International Trade Agreements Compared', in Marx et al., *Global Governance of Labour Rights* above fn. 2, 83–117.

51 International Labour Office, *Assessment of Labour Provisions in Trade and Investment Arrangements* above fn. 7, 97. The EU trade agreements do not usually include any reference to ILO conventions. While this is criticised as adding a further compliance problem because of the overlapping of the international instruments, the suggestion is made of enhancing coordination among ILO and the EU. See Hendrickx, F. and P. Peinovsky (2015) 'EU Economic Governance and Labour Rights: Diversity and Coherence in the EU, the Council of Europe and ILO Instruments', in Marx et al., *Global Governance of Labour Rights*, above fn. 2, 118–49.

52 Exploring the mechanisms under which trade unions try to influence global labour governance, see Koch-Baumgarten, S. and M. Kryst (2015) 'Trade Unions and Collective Bargaining Power in Global Labor Governance', in Marx et al., *Global Governance of Labour Rights*, above fn. 2, 150–69.

of collective bargaining in international settings, the efficiency and effectiveness of transnational collective agreements and the legality of transnational collective actions.[53]

Such issues are likely to arise when business relocate, taking the jobs to another country, or in those cases in which trade unions seek to enhance the working conditions of foreign posted workers. As a matter of fact, these cases have been already dealt with by the CJEU in very unfavourable terms to transnational collective bargaining. The widely criticised case law is to be found in the judgments *Viking*[54] and *Laval*.[55] The first case balanced the freedom of establishment against the right to strike while in the other the free provision of services was at stake, being the overall conclusion that the market freedoms prevail over the right to undertake collective action. In *Viking* the CJEU required industrial action not only to be legal in accordance with the relevant domestic rules, but also to be filtered through the screen of the principle of proportionality in relation to the freedom of establishment,[56] thereby making it almost impossible to undertake legal collective action. In *Laval*, the CJEU concluded that social partners cannot fight for putting local and posted workers on the same footing, as the latter are only entitled to the minimum labour standards granted by the Posting of Workers Directive.[57]

From a private international law perspective, this case law is relevant because if industrial action is held illegal it gives rise to non-contractual liability; taking into account the usual connecting factors in this field, the *forum/lex loci delicti* or the *forum/lex loci damni*, social partners may be sued in a jurisdiction and according to a law other than that of the jurisdiction where the industrial action was undertaken. While this was made clear in the *DFDS Torline*,[58] a specific conflict rule on the right to take collective action was included in Regulation (EC) No. 864/2007 of the European Parliament and of the Council of 11 July 2007 on the Law Applicable to Non-contractual Obligations (Rome II)[59] with the aim of ensuring that the *locus damni* coincides with that of the industrial action.[60] By this means interested parties may at least predict the outcome of their actions.

Although the purpose of transnational collective bargaining is usually to conclude collective agreements, the latter are meant to be territorially applied. States take a unilateralist approach to the conditions under which collective bargaining can be under-

[53] See Carballo Piñeiro, *International Maritime Labour Law*, above fn. 19, 229.

[54] CJEU 11 December 2007, Case C-438/05, *International Transport Workers' Federation and Finnish Seamen's Union* v. *Viking Line ABP and OÜ Viking Line Eesti*.

[55] CJEU 23 May 2007, Case C-341/05, *Laval un Partneri Ltd* v. *Svenska Byggnadsarbetareförbundet, Svenska Byggnadsarbetareförbundets avdelning 1, Byggetan and Svenska Elektrikerförbundet.*

[56] CJEU 11 December 2007, Case C-438/05, *Viking*, paras 81 and 84.

[57] CJEU 18 December 2007, Case C-341/05, *Laval.*

[58] CJEU 5 February 2004, Case C 18/02, *DFDS Torline A/S* v. *SEKO Sjöfolk Facket för Service och Kommunikation.*

[59] OJ [2007] L 199/40.

[60] See Art. 9 of Rome II.

taken. Accordingly, the scope of application of collective agreements seems to be limited to domestic employment relationships, with the exception of posted workers. Business internationalisation, however, makes transnational collective bargaining necessary.[61] Thus the main problem is whether transnational collective agreements will be deemed valid and binding.[62] As there are almost no specific conflict rules on these matters,[63] the general rules on contractual obligations apply[64] and the efficiency and effectiveness of collective agreements usually depend on whether they are taken into consideration to modify the terms of the employment relationship or not.[65] Beyond schemes such as the one developed by the International Transport Workers' Federation (ITF),[66] or the most recent development of International Framework Agreements,[67] transnational collective agreements are mostly relegated to the realm of corporate social responsibility (CSR). A specific conflict rule on this type of agreement, such as the one in Article 92 of the Panamanian Private International Law Code, would make them extant rules and national courts would be less reluctant regarding their application.

CSR may also help to enhance labour and employment conditions,[68] for example, by including social clauses in contracts. Surprisingly, this has also encountered

[61] The issue has not even been solved by the EU, although many efforts have been made to overcome this vacuum. In this vein, mention should be made of Ales, E., S. Engblom, T. Jaspers, S. Sciarra, A. Sobczak and F. Valdés Dal-Ré (2006) *Transnational Collective Bargaining: Past, Present and Future*, Directorate General Employment, Social Affairs and Equal Opportunities, February 2006, and Eichhorst, W., M. J. Kendzia and B. Vandeweghe (2011) *Cross-border Collective Bargaining and Transnational Social Dialogue*, Directorate-General for Internal Policies of the European Commission.

[62] If the existence and validity of transnational collective agreements is challenged before national courts, they pose significant problems as to the applicable law given that they do not usually match the conditions required to collectively bargain at a national level, as the case of *The Ship Mercury Bell* v. *Amosin* [1986] 3 F.C. 454, 27 D.L.R. (4th), 641, 66 N.R. 361, illustrates.

[63] Art. 92 of the 2014 Panamanian Private International Code: 'International collective agreements shall be governed by any clauses agreed between trade unions and the employer or, failing that, by the law of the place of performance' (my translation).

[64] Collective agreements would be subject to choice-of-law clauses and, failing this, to the closest law in view of the difficulties of determining who is characteristically performing in this type of agreements (see Arts 3 and 4 of the Rome I Regulation). See for further reference, Carballo Piñeiro, *International Maritime Labour Law*, above fn. 19, 259.

[65] See Term 1.2 and Term I.3 ITF Uniform TCC Collective Agreement for Crews on Flags of Convenience.

[66] The ITF is an umbrella organisation that coordinates all associated trade unions across the world, which makes it possible to require shipowners to sign standard collective agreements in order to avoid boycotts and other solidarity action in ports of call.

[67] See Telljohann, V., I. da Costa, T. Müller, U. Rehfeldt and R. Zimmer (2009) *European and International Framework Agreements: Practical Experiences and Strategic Approaches*, Eurofond.

[68] Seeking to promote best practices in companies, see ILO Tripartite Declaration of Principles Concerning Multinational Enterprises and Social Policy; the UN Global Compact; ISO 26000 Standard on corporate social responsibility; and the OECD Guidelines for Multinational Enterprises.

problems, as the *Rüffert* case illustrates.[69] It pitted the German state of Lower Saxony against Objekt und Bauregie, a German company that had won the tender put out by the former for the building of a prison. The contract concluded by the two parties included provisions requiring the application of the collective agreements in force at the place where the work was to be carried out. However, Objekt und Bauregie outsourced to a Polish company which was paying the Polish workers lower wages than were due to them according to the German collective agreements. Under the circumstances, Lower Saxony wanted to terminate the contract with Objekt und Bauregie and required payment of the penalty scheduled for breach of conditions. As this was challenged by Objekt und Bauregie, a preliminary question was put before the CJEU as to whether the contractual imposition of a collective agreement establishing a salary that exceeds the minimum to which the Posting of Workers Directive refers infringes the freedom to provide services. The answer of the Court in the affirmative was a significant blow for the fight against social dumping and attracted much criticism.[70] However, the CJEU seems to have reconsidered this answer in the *RegioPost*[71] case for which reason it is nowadays feasible to require all parties in the supply chain to comply with local working conditions.[72] The next stage is, of course, to ensure that those working conditions are applied.

Some Concluding Remarks

On the one hand, conflict rules, if ill-conceived or inappropriate, may contribute to jeopardising equality around labour migration to the extent that they allow for the search for a low-cost law in terms of labour standards. As this may result in a downward trend in labour standards, international and regional agencies have undertaken significant harmonisation efforts. The inclusion of labour provisions in modern trade agreements may also be of avail in this endeavour. On the other hand, however, labour compliance and law enforcement is a major issue in domestic settings, but even more so in cross-border ones. To this end, private international law techniques may help in making private persons comply with labour standards, in particular by strengthening the role of social partners and reinforcing inter-country communication, cooperation and coordination in monitoring working conditions when the employment relationship has an international element, including cases of circular migration.

The previous sections have provided an account of the international and regional agencies' efforts in enhancing compliance mechanisms, although mostly focused on specific sectors or regions. The inclusion of labour provisions in trade agreements is still in its infancy and does not seem to address other settings than the domestic

[69] Case C-346/06, *Dirk Rüffert, acting as liquidator in Objekt und Bauregie GmbH & Co. KG* v. *Land Niedersachsen*, 3 April 2008.

[70] Case C-346/06, *Rüffert* v. *Niedersachsen*, 3 April 2008.

[71] Case C-114/15, *RegioPost GmbH & Co. KG* v. *Stadt Landau in der Pfalz*, 17 November 2015.

[72] Ibid., para 66. The European Commission's Proposal amending Directive 96/71/EC also includes a provision on social clauses.

ones. Against this backdrop, it would be worth establishing a multilateral framework amongst sending and receiving states. The case has already been made by Hans van Loon,[73] the former Secretary-General of the Hague Conference, who suggested a convention including the definition of responsibilities to be placed on the contracting states; the establishing of mutual information, cooperation and coordination duties as to the implementation of the assumed responsibilities; and other monitoring tools such as follow-up meetings.[74] The main idea is not to replace other instruments, but to address some underdeveloped aspects of labour migration. More specifically, Hans van Loon[75] mentions the temporary and circular labour migration, the return and resettlement of irregular migrants, the accreditation and regulation of intermediaries and the transfer of remittances. The perspective of van Loon's proposal is broader than the issues herein addressed, but the latter neatly fit in the former. More specifically, the proposed convention ought to establish a cooperation framework in order to monitor migrants' working conditions and employment relationships in both sending and receiving countries. The added value of this convention would be the placing of specific monitoring responsibilities on each state covering aspects such as the existence and validity of an employment agreement; the effective compliance with minimum labour standards in the country where workers actually discharge their duties towards their employer; the fact that there is a real temporary posting of workers meaning that this is undertaken by a company actually operating in the sending country which brings its employees to the receiving country; or the transfer of remittances to workers' families in their country of origin. The establishing of mutual information and cooperation duties would shed light on many abuses that go unnoticed, taking advantage of the cross-border dimension of employment. In this vein, such a convention should institutionalise the role of social partners meaning that they should be granted standing at least to report abuses, and in particular to engage in social dialogue.

The role of intermediaries in labour migration is a case in point. Recruitment and placement services are increasingly important against a backdrop of growing mobility facilitated by modern means of communication and transportation. On the one hand, the establishing of a system of licensing and accreditation may greatly facilitate the control of the many documented abuses undertaken by such services as migrant workers are particularly vulnerable. On the other hand, they are the best placed to monitor employers, for which reason they ought to take responsibility in

[73] Van Loon, H. (2008) 'Vers un nouveau modèle de gouvernance multilatérale de la migration internationale. Réflexions à partir de certaines techniques de coopération développées au sein de la Conférence de La Haye', in *Vers de nouveaux équilibres entre ordres juridiques. Liber amicorum Hélène Gaudemet-Tallon*, Dalloz, 419–31; Van Loon, H. (2016) 'The Global Horizon of Private International Law', *Recueil des cours*, vol. 380, 9–108, at 77.

[74] See van Loon, 'Vers un nouveau modèle de gouvernance multilatérale de la migration internationale', above fn. 73, 424–7.

[75] See also van Loon's chapters in this volume.

those cases in which the latter disappear or dissolve without paying the employees or otherwise. To this end, it would be a very important step forward to follow the path opened by the MLC 2006 and require these services to ensure worker protection by way of insurance or an equivalent appropriate measure.

All in all, inter-country communication, cooperation and coordination have already proved their efficiency and effectiveness in enhancing labour standards. The MLC 2006 is again a case in point, but the pressure put on the EU to improve its cooperation framework in the event of the temporary posting of workers makes the significance of such a framework even more obvious. Further benefits of drafting an ad hoc international convention for this purpose come from the fact that it will create the need for further harmonisation at domestic level.[76] Accordingly, this would be a step forward in the path towards levelling the playing field in labour matters, and in winning the fight against social dumping in favour of fair competition worldwide.

[76] Remarkably, the establishing of a cooperation framework by the UNCITRAL Model Law on Cross-Border Insolvency Matters and Council regulation (EC) No. 1346/2000 of 29 May 2000 on insolvency proceedings have led to increasing aspects of substantive insolvency law being harmonised.

14

E-commerce and Consumer Protection in Integrated Markets

Beatriz Añoveros Terradas

Introduction

In European private international law rules consumer protection has acquired a new dimension that has in turn led to a new paradigm. This change arises from amendments to legislation and new case law of the Court of Justice of the European Union (CJEU) in the field of e-commerce. First, the Brussels I Regulation recast (hereinafter 'Brussels I *bis* Regulation') establishes universal rules of jurisdiction in consumer contracts.[1] The reform has eliminated the existence of two different jurisdictional regimes in matters relating to consumer contracts (the national jurisdictional regime applicable when the supplier defendant is domiciled outside the European Union (Article 2.2 Brussels I Regulation) and the Brussels I Regulation regimen applicable when the supplier defendant is domiciled in the European Union (Articles 15–17 Brussels I Regulation)) in order to create a unified European system. Second, CJEU case law concerning e-commerce transactions has shifted its focus to the conduct of suppliers instead of the traditional distinction between active and passive consumers. This new focus covers a wider range of cases in which the consumer is protected. Both changes have greatly increased the protection of the consumer when entering into an international contract. From a European perspective, this should be seen as a step further in the evolution of European consumer policy and its goals. However, difficulties arise when explaining such an expansion from an international perspective. The application of both extensions to situations connected to Third States may result in an unrealistic and inefficient overprotection of the consumer which may jeopardise any attempt to globally unify the rules on consumer protection.

[1] European Parliament and Council Regulation (EU) 1215/2012 on jurisdiction and the recognition and enforcement of judgments in civil and commercial matters (recast) [2012] OJ L351/1.

This chapter examines consumer protection rules when entering into e-commerce transactions in an integrated market (the EU) from an *ad intra* (that is, covering relationships connected to Member States) and an *ad extra* (also connected to Third States) perspective. E-commerce consumer transactions connected to non-EU states (Third States) are those that are most problematic and on which the debate will be focused. Consequently, the distinction between intracommunity situations and relationships involving Third States should be reopened.[2]

Extensions to the *Forum Actoris*

Universal Rules on Jurisdiction: Spatial Extension

One of the cornerstones of the Brussels I Regulation recast was to extend the rules on jurisdiction set up in the former Brussels I Regulation to defendants domiciled in Third States.[3] As the Commission had pointed out, access to justice within the EU was unsatisfactory in cases in which the defendant was domiciled in a Third State.[4] Except in certain cases (Articles 22 and 23 Brussels I Regulation), the Regulation was only applicable when the defendant was domiciled within the EU. When that was not the case, the international jurisdiction was determined according to national rules (residual jurisdiction).[5]

Although the proposal was to extend the European rules on jurisdiction to any cross-border situation, the Regulation recast only extended the rules in two areas: consumer and employment contracts. In those situations where a weaker party is involved, such as in consumer contracts, the lack of uniform rules on jurisdiction when contracting with parties domiciled in Third States may place the weaker party in a vulnerable position, which clearly goes against European consumer policy[6] and the proper function of the internal market. Analysis of the national jurisdiction rules showed that there was unequal access to justice for consumers which could hamper the smooth running of the internal market. In the Study on Residual Jurisdiction by

2 On this distinction see Añoveros, B. (2003) *Los contratos de consumo intracomunitarios*, Marcial Pons.

3 Borrás Rodríguez, A. (2010) 'Application of the Brussels I Regulation to External Situations: From Studies Carried out by the European Group for Private International Law to the Proposal for the Revision of the Regulation', *Yearbook of Private International Law* 333; Cordero Álvarez, C. I. (2015) 'La contratación entre consumidores de la UE y empresas de terceros Estados: evolución del DIPr de la UE', in Bergé, J. S., S. Francq and M. Gardeñes Santiago (eds), *Boundaries of European Private International Law/Les frontières du droit international privé européen/Las fronteras del derecho internacional privado europeo*, Bruylant/Larcier, 352.

4 Proposal for a Regulation of the European Parliament and of the Council on jurisdiction and the recognition and enforcement of judgments in civil and commercial matters (Recast) [SEC(2010) 1547 final][SEC(2010) 1548 final]COM (2010) 748.

5 On the Proposal see Añoveros, B. (2009) 'Extensión de los foros de protección del consumidor a demandados domiciliados en terceros Estados', IX AEDIPr 285.

6 Art. 169 TFEU (ex Art. 153 TEC).

Nuyts[7] based on national reports, some conclusions were reached which confirmed the Commission's fears.[8] Most of the Member States had special rules on jurisdiction protecting the consumer. Nevertheless, some Member States had no rules to protect consumers and therefore in those countries the consumer acting as a claimant was subject to the general rules on jurisdiction.[9] In cases where such protection was provided by the Member State the mechanisms used varied from one state to another. According to the Commission

> the good functioning of an internal market and the Community's commercial policy both on the internal and on the international level require that equal access to justice on the basis of clear and precise rules on international jurisdiction is ensured not only for defendants but also for claimants domiciled in the Community.[10]

For all these reasons the extension of the jurisdiction protective rules must be welcomed.

According to Article 6(1) of the Brussels I *bis* Regulation '[I]f the defendant is not domiciled in a Member State, the jurisdiction of the courts of each Member State shall, subject to Article 18(1), Article 21(2) and Articles 24 and 25, be determined by the law of that Member State'. Reference to national legislation continues subject to Article 18(1) of the Regulation which establishes that

> [a] consumer may bring proceedings against the other party to a contract either in the courts of the Member State in which that party is domiciled or, regardless of the domicile of the other party, in the courts for the place where the consumer is domiciled.

The application of this provision to defendants domiciled in Third States leads to an analysis with the following hypotheses.

Consumer acting as claimant domiciled within the EU v. professional acting as defendant domiciled in a Third State (*forum actoris*)

Article 18(1) Brussels I *bis* Regulation covers this hypothesis, in other words, those situations when the consumer is domiciled in a Member State and, acting as claimant, starts proceedings before the courts of his or her domicile against the professional domiciled in a Third State. In these cases the *forum actoris* is granted to the consumer.

[7] Nuyts, A. (2007) 'Study on residual jurisdiction' (Review of the Member States' rules concerning the 'residual jurisdiction' of their courts in civil and commercial matters pursuant to the Brussels I and II Regulations), JLS/C4/2005/07-30-CE)0040309/00-37 (hereinafter Nuyts Report), available at: http://ec.europa.eu/civiljustice/news/docs/study_residual_jurisdiction_en.pdf

[8] See further ibid., conclusions.

[9] States with no protective jurisdiction rules are Germany, Cyprus, Greece, Lithuania, Malta, Poland, United Kingdom, Czech Republic and Romania.

[10] European Commission, 'Review of Council Regulation (EC) No. 44/2001 on Jurisdiction and the Recognition and Enforcement of Judgments in Civil and Commercial Matters' (Green Paper) COM (2009) 175 final, 21 April 2009.

In fact, taking into account what has been said before, this was the most worrying situation before the recast and the one mostly in need of amendment.

In order to understand the true scope of this extension and its implications, it is necessary to analyse Article 18(1) in the context of Section IV of the Regulation and, in particular, taking into account its scope of application and its protective mechanisms: *forum actoris* and limitations to party autonomy. As the former Brussels I Regulation, Section IV Brussels I *bis* Regulation does not protect all consumers but only those under the conditions set forth in Article 17 of the Regulation (reproduces *mutatis mutandis* Article 15 of the former Regulation). Nevertheless, as will be shown, the new interpretation of the CJEU in the field of e-commerce has shifted the protection from the 'passive' to the 'active' consumer (that is, from the consumer who has been approached by the supplier in the consumer's market to the consumer who has moved to the supplier's market).[11] Such a shift in cases in which the defendant is domiciled outside the EU raises some doubts. In this sense it is necessary to conduct a joint analysis of both extensions (the universal application of the rules on jurisdiction and the protection of the active consumer). This change of paradigm carries significant consequences for those professionals and suppliers domiciled in Third States which 'direct' their activities to one or more Member States including the Member State of the consumers' domicile.

Another relevant issue is the link between the extension within Article 18(1) mentioned above and the limitations to party autonomy set forth in Article 19 of the same Regulation. The need for common universal jurisdiction rules in consumer contracts corresponds to the need to limit choice of court agreements in order to prevent the parties from jeopardising the efficiency of the protective rules. Article 19 is therefore essential to guarantee the inefficiency of a jurisdiction clause in certain circumstances. Article 19 also applies in cases covered by Article 18(1), that is, cases where the consumer acts as a claimant against a professional domiciled in a Third State.

The main problem in all these cases could be the eventual refusal of recognition and enforcement of the European judgment in the Third State. Even if the European judgment will freely move from one Member State to another, the risk of not being recognised in a Third State is very high.[12] In this sense, a global approach would be desirable,[13] such as a double multilateral convention on jurisdiction and recognition

[11] The CJEU case law analysed refers to Art. 15 of the Brussels I Regulation but it can be extended to Art. 17 of the Brussels I *bis* Regulation. In order to facilitate its understanding and its impact on the latest Regulation, the analysis refers to Art. 17 of the Brussels I *bis* Regulation.

[12] Espiniella Menéndez, A. (2015) 'Contratos de consumo en el tráfico comercial UE-Terceros Estados' (2014–15) *AEDIPr* 294, 295.

[13] Magnus and Mankoswski use the following words to reject the extension of the EU jurisdiction rules to defendants domiciled in Third States: 'The Community might better extend not its rules but its hand'. Magnus, U. and P. Mankowski, 'Joint Response to the Green Paper on the Review of the Brussels I Regulation', available at: http://ec.europa.eu/justice/news/consulting_public/0002/contributions/civil_society_ngo_academics_others/prof_magnus_and_prof_mankowski_university_of_hamburg_en.pdf, 1, 3.

and enforcement.[14] A universal unification of the protective fora would guarantee its efficiency. Nevertheless, the Judgments Project in its broad context has shown the difficulties in reaching an agreement with regard to consumer contracts.[15] From the beginning (1992) the impossibility of developing a consensus-based rule on consumer contracts became clear and was excluded from the project and from the 2005 Choice of Court Convention (Article 21(a)).[16] In 2011, the Judgments Project was resumed through the creation of an Experts' Group with the aim of assessing its feasibility. In 2012, the Council established a Working Group in order to prepare proposals on the recognition and enforcement of judgments, including jurisdictional filters, and requested the Experts' Group to further study and discuss the desirability and feasibility of making provisions in relation to jurisdiction.[17] In 2018, the Special Commission met from 24 to 29 May and produced the 2018 Draft Convention. Article 5 of the 2018 Draft Convention includes jurisdictional filters. Only paragraph 2 of Article 5 refers to consumer contracts, stating

> 2. If recognition or enforcement is sought against a natural person acting primarily for personal, family or household purposes (a consumer) in matters relating to a consumer contract, or against an employee in matters relating to the employee's contract of employment – (a) paragraph 1(e) applies only if the consent was addressed to the court, orally or in writing; (b) paragraph 1(f), (g) and (m) do not apply.

As can be observed, it refers to a judgment rendered against a consumer and not to a judgment against a supplier rendered in the consumer's domicile based on a *forum actoris* granted to the consumer. Taking this provision into account it is unlikely that a judgment rendered within the EU against a supplier domiciled in a Third State would be eligible for recognition and enforcement. In any case, the interpretation given in this chapter with regard to Article 17 of the Brussels I *bis* Regulation when applied to suppliers domiciled outside the EU will increase the possibility of recognition and enforcement.

An unresolved situation under the Brussels I *bis* Regulation merits further

[14] See Art. 7 of the Hague Draft Convention 1999. On this provision see Gilles, L. (2008) *Electronic Commerce and International Private Law*, Ashgate, 214.

[15] The Judgments Project refers to the work undertaken by the Hague Conference on Private International Law since 1992 on two key aspects of private international law in cross-border litigation in civil and commercial matters: the international jurisdiction of courts and the recognition and enforcement of judgments abroad. See Permanent Bureau (Prel. Doc. No. 2, April 2016), 'Explanatory Note Providing Background on the Proposed Draft Text and Identifying Outstanding Issues'. Available at: https://assets.hcch.net/docs/e402cc72-19ed-4095-b004-ac47742dbc41.pdf. See van Loon, H. (2016) 'The Global Horizon of Private International Law', *Recueil des cours*, vol. 380, 46–52.

[16] De Miguel Asensio, P. (2008) 'La tutela de los consumidores en el mercado global: evolución del marco normativo', *Estudios sobre consumo*, 27. The 2005 Choice of Court Convention is currently in force between the EU (except Denmark) and Mexico, and was also signed by the United States in 2009, Singapore in 2015 and Ukraine in 2016.

[17] www.hcch.net/en/projects/legislative-projects/judgments

analysis. It refers to the consumer, resident in a Member State, who moves to another Member State where a contract is concluded, within the terms of Article 17, with a supplier domiciled in a Third State. The question that arises is whether the *forum actoris* granted to the consumer domiciled in that state can be extended to any consumer (European or not) moving to it. From a choice of law perspective that protection has been claimed by several scholars, since Article 4 of the Rome I Regulation leads to the application of the law of the place of the establishment of the supplier. Free movement of persons, goods and services imply not only the right to move to receive a service but also the freedom of the consumer to choose between the goods and services offered in the different Member States. The CJEU has ruled that Article 34 TFEU (ex Article 28 TEC) guarantees the right of a consumer domiciled in a Member State to travel freely to another Member State in order to 'shop under the same conditions as the local population'.[18] This interpretation shall be extended to Article 56 TFEU (ex Article 49 TCEC).[19] Therefore, it would be contrary to European law to hamper the active European consumer by the fact that he or she has travelled around the internal market in order to buy goods and services. The intracommunity active consumer has to be protected by the law of the Member State where the contract is concluded.[20] The logic of integration leads to this result. The same idea can be extended to the jurisdictional benefits in the sense that the consumer should be able to use the *forum actoris* as if he or she were domiciled in that state.

Consumer acting as a claimant domiciled in a Third State v. professional acting as a defendant domiciled in a Member State

In this hypothesis, Article 18(1) in conjunction with Article 4 of the Brussels I *bis* Regulation gives the consumer domiciled in a Third State the right to start proceedings against the professional domiciled in a Member State in the courts of that Member State. This result is in principle not surprising since the rule *actor sequitur forum rei* is broadly accepted.[21] The Regulation cannot grant the consumer domiciled in a Third State the *forum actoris* since it would mean assigning jurisdiction to the courts of a non-Member State. In the case of passive consumers domiciled in Third States who

[18] Case C 362/88 *GB-INNO-BM* c. *Confédération du commerce luxembourgeois* [1990] ECR I-667, para. 8.

[19] Henning Roth, W. (1993) 'Article 59 EEC-Treaty and its Implications for Conflicts of Law in the Field of Insurance Contracts', in Reichert-Facilides, F. and H. U. Jessurun D'Oliveira (eds), *International Insurance Contract Law in the EC. Proceedings of a Comparative Law Conference held at the European University Institute, Florence, May 23–24, 1991*, Kluwer Law and Taxation Publishers, 64.

[20] De la Rosa, F. E. (2003) *La protección de los consumidores en el mercado interior europeo*, Comares, 271; Requejo Isidro, M. (2005) 'Régimen de las garantías en la venta transfronteriza de los bienes de consumo: armonización en el mercado interior y derecho nacional' 1 REDI 257, 263.

[21] Gaudement-Tallon, H. (1996) 'Les frontières extérieures de l'espace judiciaire européen: quelques repères', in Borrás, A. (ed.), *E Pluribus Unum – Liber Amicorum Georges A.L.Droz, On the Progressive Unification of Private International Law*, Martinus Nijhoff, 88.

have been attracted by European suppliers, the *forum actoris* cannot be used as a protective measure. By contrast, in terms of choice of law, given the universal scope of application of Article 6 of the Rome I Regulation, the conflict of laws rule extends the protective mechanism to all consumers regardless of their domicile (within or outside the EU).

Limitations to party autonomy provided for in Article 19 do not apply in this scenario since they do not prevent the European supplier from imposing a choice of court agreement in favour of a European court. This result is not in line with the protective aim pursued by the jurisdictional benefits when the consumer is the claimant since the need for protection still remains when the consumer is domiciled in a Third State. I agree with Espiniella when he proposes to extend the CJEU ruling in the Océano Case,[22] a purely internal case, to international situations. According to the ruling, a choice of court agreement in favour of the courts of the supplier's domicile shall be deemed an unfair term due to the existence of an imbalance of the rights and obligations for the consumer.[23] This outcome does not go against the 93/13 Directive since it does not exclude its application when the consumer is domiciled in a Third State.[24]

From the Passive to the Active Consumer: The New CJEU Case Law

The definition of 'passive' consumer and its extensive interpretation by the CJEU

In order to understand the relevant elements of the term 'passive consumer' it is important to bear their origin in mind. Both the 1968 Brussels Convention[25] and the 1980 Rome Convention[26] used a more casuistic method to identify the situations in which the consumer was attracted by the supplier within the consumer's market and therefore needed to be protected. The 1968 Brussels Convention, only protecting those entering into contracts for sale of goods or provisions of services, set forth two conditions based on the circumstances that led them to conclude the contract: (1) the conclusion of the contract was preceded by a specific invitation addressed to him or her or by advertising; and (2) the consumer took the steps necessary for the conclusion of the contract in that state. The 1980 Rome Convention added two far more specific situations in answer to certain sales techniques that were being used at that time.[27]

22 Case C-240/98 and joined cases, *Océano* v. *Murciano Quintero*, [2000] ECR I-04941.

23 Espiniella Menéndez, 'Contratos de consumo en el tráfico comercial UE-Terceros Estados', above fn. 12, 283.

24 Ibid., 283.

25 1968 Brussels Convention on jurisdiction and the enforcement of judgments in civil and commercial matters (consolidated version), OJ L299, 31.12.1972.

26 1980 Rome Convention on the Law Applicable to Contractual Obligations (consolidated version), OJ C 27, 26.01.1998.

27 Art. 5(2): 'if the other party or his agent received the consumer's order in that country, or if the contract is for the sale of goods and the consumer travelled from that country to another country and there gave his order, provided that the consumer's journey was arranged by the seller for the purpose of inducing the consumer to buy'.

The established conditions were conceived to protect consumers who entered into distance contracts with foreign companies through catalogues or door-to-door sales.[28] The seller would have had to have performed specific activities such as publicity in the media (press, radio, TV, etc.) or through catalogues aimed at the consumer's Member State or have used door-to-door sales representatives.[29] Furthermore, the consumer would have had to have taken the necessary steps to have concluded the contract. The term 'necessary steps' included any written communication arising from a special offer or advertisement. A broad term was preferred in order to avoid the problems arising from determining the place where the contract was concluded.[30] The territorial nature of these conditions caused problems when it came to contracts made on the internet which was among the main motives for reforming these provisions at the time of adoption of the Brussels I Regulation. The wording of Article 13(3) of the 1968 Brussels Convention was uncertain on this point. Therefore, one of the main objectives of the revised version of Article 15 of the Brussels I Regulation was to clarify in which situations the consumer was granted the *forum actoris* when contracting through the internet. The idea was that consumers entering into contracts through the internet deserved the same level of protection as those who responded to a special offer or advertisement in the media. The key question was to determine whether they were active or passive consumers. The result arose from a compromise between those who championed a high level of protection for internet consumers and those who wanted a restrictive application of Section IV in order to protect suppliers, especially small and medium-sized companies, from having to litigate abroad simply because they had a presence on the internet.[31]

In turn, Article 17 of the Brussels I *bis* Regulation sets out the conditions with regard to the conclusion of the contract in a more flexible way, that is to say, it is less casuistic and therefore easier to apply to new situations which are likely to deserve protection. The first condition is that the contract has been concluded with a supplier who pursues commercial or professional activities in the state of the consumer's domicile or, by any means, directs such activities within that state or several states including that state. Second, the contract must fall within the scope of such activities. In these scenarios the consumer can sue the supplier in the courts of his or her own country of domicile (Article 18 Brussels I *bis* Regulation).

The conditions formerly laid down in Article 13 of the 1968 Brussels Convention have been omitted, those being the conditions relating to the consumer having taken the necessary steps for the conclusion of the contract in his or her country of domicile,

[28] Art. 5(2): 'if in that country the conclusion of the contract was preceded by a specific invitation addressed to him or by advertising, and he had taken in that country all the steps necessary on his part for the conclusion of the contract'.

[29] Giuliano/Lagarde Report, 22.

[30] Ibid., 22.

[31] Bonomi, A. (2015) 'Jurisdiction over Consumer Contracts', in Dickinson, A. and E. Lein (eds), *The Brussels Regulation Recast*, Oxford University Press, 224.

especially significant in relation to business-to-consumer (BtoC) contracts. In such contracts, the place where the consumer concludes the contract could be very difficult to determine. As has been pointed out, with the new wording of Article 17

> we can assume that as long as the consumer has his domicile within the territory of a Member State, the e-commerce contract can be concluded not only from the State of his domicile but also while the person in question is on travel, whenever the web site where the goods or materials are being advertised is available in the Member State where the consumer has his domicile.[32]

The rule in Article 17(c) includes two components which give jurisdiction to the courts of the consumer's domicile. The first one requires the 'target activity test'. The starting point is that the supplier is the one creating the link between the contract and the consumer's domicile through targeting its activities to the market of the consumer and therefore the one with the burden of litigating abroad. As can be observed, the Regulation broadened the concept of 'passive consumer' although it is a term not always easy to determine: it requires the localisation of professional activities in the consumer's domicile. The second component requires that the contract must fall within the scope of such activities. Therefore, the contract must have been concluded as a result of such activities.

Target activity test. This is the first and fundamental element within the definition of 'passive consumer'. It includes two situations: the supplier (1) engages in commercial or professional activities in the state of the consumer's domicile or (2) directs commercial or professional activities to the state of the consumer's domicile. In the first situation, the supplier pursues commercial or professional activities in the state of the consumer's domicile, that is, it has a physical presence (permanent or temporary) in the consumer's Member State, such as through an establishment, agent and so on.[33] In this case it will be easy to prove the existence of the activities pursued by the supplier.[34]

More difficulties arise with regard to the exact meaning of 'directing activities' that is, when should a professional be considered as directing its activities to the state of the consumer's domicile or to several states including that state? As has been already mentioned, the main concern was related to the use of new technologies and, in particular, whether e-commerce consumer transactions were covered (or ought

[32] Rosner, N. (2012) 'International Jurisdiction in European Union E-commerce', *LLRX*, 1 May 2012, available at: www.llrx.com/2002/05/features-international-jurisdiction-in-european-union-e-commerce-contracts

[33] Garcimartín Alférez, F. (2013) 'Consumer Protection from a Conflict-of-Laws Perspective: The Rome I Regulation Approach', in Forner Delaygua, J., C. González Beilfuss and R. Viñas Ferrer (eds), *Entre Bruselas y La Haya. Estudios sobre la unificación internacional y regional del Derecho internacional privado.Liber Amicorum Alegría Borrás*, Marcial Pons, 449, 450.

[34] Bonomi, 'Jurisdiction over Consumer Contracts', above fn. 31, 224.

to be covered) by Section IV of the Brussels I *bis* Regulation.[35] The idea behind the jurisdictional protection granted to the consumer is that the supplier by engaging or directing its activities in the consumer's domicile is the one assuming the risk of being sued in that state, that is, the supplier has the burden of having to litigate abroad. The idea of a consumer who needs protection because he or she has been captured in his or her market is still present. Therefore, the idea of the 'passive consumer' remains.[36] The Brussels I *bis* Regulation does not clarify nor does it define the concept of 'directing activities'.[37] It is a vague concept which raises several questions of interpretation especially in the framework of e-commerce. In its leading joined cases *Pammer* and *Hotel Alpenhof*[38] the CJEU clarifies some of the interpretative questions which arise from Article 17(1)(c) of the Regulation, in particular the meaning of 'directing activities'. The question was whether online presence was sufficient to satisfy that requirement, that is, the target activity test. The CJEU confirmed the need for an autonomous interpretation of the notions 'directing activities' by reference principally to the system and objectives of the Regulation, in order to ensure that it is fully effective.[39] Furthermore, Article 17(1)(c) constitutes a derogation both from the general rule of jurisdiction laid down in Article 4(1) of the Regulation and from the rule of special jurisdiction for contracts, set out in Article 7(1) in the same instrument.[40] As with any exception, it has to be interpreted restrictively.[41] The wording must be considered to encompass and replace the previous concepts of a 'specific invitation addressed' to the consumer and 'advertising', covering, as the words 'by any means' indicate, a wider range of activities.[42] It is not clear, however, whether the words 'directs such activities to' refer to the supplier's intention to turn towards one or more other Member States or whether they relate simply to an activity turned de facto towards them, irrespective of such an intention.[43] The question that arises is whether the intention on the part of the supplier to target one or more other Member States is required and, if so, in what form such an intention must manifest itself.[44] The CJEU held that, in order for Article 17(1)(c) of the Brussels I *bis* Regulation to be

35 Case C-180/06 *Renate Ilsinger* v. *Martin* [2009] ECR – I 03961 (*Ilsinger*), para. 59 and Recital 24 RIR.

36 Garcimartín Alférez, F. 'Consumer Protection from a Conflict-of-Laws Perspective', above fn. 33, 445.

37 Joined cases, C-585/08 and C-144/09, *Peter Pammer* v. *Reederei Kart Schulüter GmbH & Co KG and Hotel Alpenhhof GesmbH* v. *Oliver Heller* [2010] ECR I-12527, para. 55 (*Pammer*).

38 Ibid.

39 Ibid.

40 Ibid., para. 53.

41 Case C-89/91, *Shearson Lehman Hutton Inc.* v. *and TVB Treuhandgesellschaft für Vermögensverwaltung und Beteiligungen mbH*, ECR [1993] I-00139 (*Shearson Lehman Hutton*), para. 16.

42 *Pammer*, para. 61.

43 Ibid., para. 63.

44 Ibid., para. 64

applicable, the supplier must have manifested its intention to establish commercial relations with consumers from one or more other Member States, including that of the consumer's domicile.[45] That intention exists in all those cases where the supplier has a physical presence in the Member State in which the consumer is domiciled and when advertising has been carried out in that Member State whether disseminated generally by the press, radio, television, cinema or any other medium, or addressed directly, for example by means of catalogues sent specifically to that state, as well as commercial offers made to the consumer in person, in particular by an agent or door-to-door sales representative.[46]

Further difficulties arise in the case of advertising by means of the internet. As the CJEU held

> since this method of communication inherently has a worldwide reach, advertising on a website by a trader is in principle accessible in all States, and, therefore, throughout the European Union, without any need to incur additional expenditure and irrespective of the intention or otherwise of the trader to target consumers outside the territory of the State in which it is established.[47]

In this regard, Recital (24) of the Rome I Regulation also embeds the terms of the joint Declaration by the Council and the Commission in relation to Article 17 of the Brussels I *bis* Regulation which stated that for this provision to be applicable the mere fact that an internet site is accessible is not sufficient. The CJEU confirmed, in *Pammer*, such interpretation. In order to determine the existence of such intention on the part of the supplier to target the consumer's market it must be established, in the case of a consumer contract, whether, before any contract with that consumer was concluded, there was evidence demonstrating that the supplier was envisaging doing business with consumers domiciled in other Member States, including the Member State of that consumer's domicile, in the sense that it was minded to conclude a contract with those consumers.[48] It follows that the distinction between 'passive' and 'interactive' websites is not decisive.[49] Even if it is clear that mere accessibility is not sufficient, it is nevertheless possible that a supplier would direct its activities to the consumer's market through a passive site. A website enabling the supplier to be contacted electronically, indeed even the contract to be concluded online by means of an 'interactive' site, does not indicate that the supplier is directing its activity to one or more other Member States, since that type of information is, in any event, necessary to enable a consumer domiciled in the Member State in which the trader is established to make contact.[50] The existence of an intention on the part

[45] Ibid., para. 75.
[46] Ibid., para. 66.
[47] Ibid.
[48] Ibid., para. 76.
[49] Ibid., para. 79.
[50] Ibid., para. 77.

of the supplier to target its activities to the Member State of the consumer's domicile is therefore the relevant element. In its ruling the CJEU gives a non-exhaustive list of elements which may constitute evidence of the mentioned intention and others which may not. The interpretative doubts raised by the abovementioned Joint Declaration by the Council and the Commission on the irrelevance of the language or currency used in a website have been clarified by the CJEU according to which when

> the website permits consumers to use a different language or a different currency, the language and/or currency can be taken into consideration and constitute evidence from which it may be concluded that the trader's activity is directed to other Member States.[51]

Among the evidence establishing whether an activity is 'directed to' the Member State of the consumer's domicile 'are all clear expressions of the intention to solicit the custom of that State's consumers',[52] for instance, 'offering its services or its goods in one or more Member States designated by name' or 'the disbursement of expenditure on an internet referencing service to the operator of a search engine in order to facilitate access to the trader's site by consumers domiciled in various Member States, which likewise demonstrates the existence of such an intention'.[53] Furthermore, the CJEU refers to other items of evidence, possibly in combination with one another, which are capable of demonstrating the existence of an activity 'directed to' the Member State of the consumer's domicile: international nature of the activity at issue, such as certain tourist activities; mention of telephone numbers with the international code; use of a top-level domain name other than that of the Member State in which the trader is established, for example '.de', or use of neutral top-level domain names such as '.com' or '.eu'; the description of itineraries from one or more other Member States to the place where the service is provided; and mention of an international clientele composed of customers domiciled in various Member States, in particular by presentation of accounts written by such customers.[54] Finally, the ruling mentions some factors which might not be considered in themselves as evidence factors, such as an email address and other contact details, or use of a language or a currency which are the language and/or currency generally used in the Member State in which the trader is established.[55]

Link between the consumer contract and the target activity. The second and fundamental element within the definition of 'passive consumer' relates to the conclusion of the consumer contract and its connection with the activity directed by the

[51] De Miguel Asensio, P. (2010) 'El asunto Pammer y el artículo 15 RBI' (7 December 2010), available at: http://pedrodemiguelasensio.blogspot.com.es/2010/12/el-asunto-pammer-y-el-articulo-15-rbi.html

[52] *Pammer*, para. 80.

[53] Ibid.

[54] Ibid., para. 83.

[55] Ibid., para. 94.

supplier to the Member State of the consumer's domicile. Both the 1968 Brussels Convention and the 1980 Rome Convention required the consumer to 'have taken in that State [the consumer's domicile] the steps necessary for the conclusion of the contract'.[56] This condition has been omitted in the following amendments (Brussels I Regulation and Brussels I bis Regulation) in favour of the more flexible 'and the contract falls within the scope of such activities'.[57] The new wording raises several interpretative questions which show the complexity of the issue. As Garcimartín has pointed out, a clear link between the activities directed by the supplier to the consumer's domicile and the contract concluded by the consumer must exist.[58] It will be shown that this second requirement laid down in the abovementioned Article 17 is somehow jeopardised by the CJEU in its case law and as a consequence the notion of 'passive consumer' has been blurred.

The need to conclude a consumer contract

The question of whether Article 17 of the Brussels I *bis* Regulation requires the conclusion of a consumer contract as a condition of applicability arose, with regard to the former Article 13 of the 1968 Brussels Convention, in the *Engler* case.[59] At that time the CJEU ruled that 'as is apparent from its wording, Article 13 clearly covers a "contract concluded" by a consumer "for the supply of goods or a contract for the supply of services"',[60] something which was not required according to Article 5 of the Brussels Convention. Some years later, in a very similar case (*Ilsinger*),[61] the same question arose, this time with regard to Article 17 of the latest Regulation. The CJEU ruled again in favour of the existence of such a requirement, arguing that according to the wording of both the introductory paragraph of Article 17(1) and Article 17(1)(c), that provision requires a 'contract' to have been 'concluded'. This finding is also supported by the heading of Section IV, which refers to '[j]urisdiction over consumer contracts'.[62]

[56] Art. 13(3)(b) 1968 Brussels Convention and Art. 5 1980 Rome Convention.

[57] Art. 17(1)(c) Brussels I *bis* Regulation.

[58] Garcimartín Alférez, 'Consumer Protection from a Conflict-of-Laws Perspective', above fn. 33, 452. According to this author, some problems arose during the negotiations of the RRI with regard to the application of this requirement in cases where the professional engaged in his or her activities in several Member States and the consumer had his or her residence in one of them but the contract did not fall within the scope of the activities carried out in the consumer's domicile. The author gives the example of a French company with several shops in France, Portugal and Spain and a consumer domiciled in Spain who travels to Paris for the weekend and concludes a contract in the French shops. In this case the supplier operates in the consumer's domicile (Spain), yet the contract does not fall within the scope of those activities carried out in Spain. For this reason. it is important to comply with the second condition provided for in Art. 15 of the Brussels I *bis* Regulation.

[59] Case C-27/02 *Petra Engler* c. *Janus Versand GmbH* [2005] ECR-I 439.

[60] Ibid., para. 40.

[61] *Ilsinger*, para. 53.

[62] Case C-375/13, *Harald Kolassa* v. *Barclays Bank plc*, para. 38.

Formal requirements as to the conclusion of the contract: not limited to contracts concluded at a distance

The second question that arose, which the CJEU ruled on in the *Mühlleitner* case,[63] was whether Article 17 requires the consumer contract to have been concluded at a distance or whether the same protection could apply to contracts concluded in person. In fact, this question came from the arguments used by the Court itself in the *Pammer* case which appeared to lead to the existence of that requirement.[64] Following a literal and teleological interpretation, the CJEU considered that Article 17 does not imply the need for the contract to be concluded at a distance.[65] There is no doubt that the provision does not expressly state the need for this circumstance with regard to conclusion of the contract. According to Advocate General Cruz Villalón, had the EU legislature wished to limit its protection to contracts concluded at a distance it would have expressly stated so.[66] Therefore, the place where the contract is concluded is irrelevant. From this we can extrapolate that the traditional distinction between passive and active consumers is now unclear. The relevant question is not whether the consumer moves or not but whether the supplier targets its activities towards the Member State of the consumer's domicile and there is a contract which falls within the scope of such activities, that is, a consumer contract linked to those activities. As long as there is such a link between the contract and the activities directed by the supplier, the place of conclusion of the contract is irrelevant. With regard to the teleological interpretation, the CJEU considers that it would be contrary to the protective aim of that provision to include further conditions.[67] Although, according to the Court, concluding the consumer contract at a distance is not a requirement for the application of Article 17, it can nevertheless be considered as an indication that the contract is connected with such an activity.

Causal link between the directed activity and the consumer contract

Assuming that the active consumer can be protected to the extent that the supplier has directed its activities to the consumer's domicile, the next question that arose was whether it was necessary for a causal link to exist between the means by which the activities were directed to the consumer's domicile (through a website) and the conclusion of the contract with the consumer. In the *Emrek*[68] case it was proven that the consumer in question had heard through friends about the supplier with which he signed the contract. Consequently, there was a question about whether the protective jurisdiction rules also

[63] Case C-190/11, *Daniela Mühlleitner* v. *Ahmad Yusufi y Wadat Yusufi*, ECLI:EU:C:2012:542 (*Mühlleitner*).

[64] *Pammer*, para. 86.

[65] *Mühlleitner*, para. 35.

[66] Conclusions AG Cruz Villalón, in *Mühlleitner*, para. 21.

[67] *Mühlleitner*, para. 42.

[68] Case C-218/12, *Lokman Emrek* v. *Vlado Sabranovic*, ECLI:EU:C:2013:666 (*Emrek*).

applied when the consumer had not been attracted by the website through which the supplier directed its activities in the consumer's market. In this regard, the *Shearson Lehman Hutton* v. *TVB*[69] case had already posed the question of whether a link should exist between the advertising done by the supplier to attract the consumer and the conclusion of the contract.[70] Although the CJEU did not give an answer to that question as it considered that Section IV was not applicable to the case, Advocate-General Darmon did so, confirming that Article 13(3) of the 1968 Brussels Convention only required that the conclusion of the contract had been preceded by publicity in the consumer's domicile. The Convention did not demand that the consumer proved the existence of a causal link between the publicity and the conclusion of the contract.[71] Apart from the fact that it would be generally impossible to satisfy such a requirement, it would also be contrary to the protective aim pursued by the referred Article 13.[72] According to Advocate-General Darmon the only conceivable limitation is one of common sense: the advertising cannot have been remote in time from the conclusion of the contract.[73]

It is reasonable to consider that proving the existence of a causal link may place the consumer in a disadvantageous situation. For this reason, the CJEU again rejected, through a literal and teleological interpretation, the need for such a causal link in order to apply the protective rule. Adding a further and implicit condition, which is, moreover, based on the conduct of the consumer, would be, according to Advocate-General Cruz Villalón, significantly upsetting for the already delicate balance put in place by the EU legislature, as well as departing from the interpretation that the CJEU has up to now put on the provision in question.[74] However, the fact that the causal link cannot be considered as a condition of applicability does not mean that it cannot be used as evidence relevant to the assessment of the second condition for the application of the protective rules: the contract falls within the scope of the activities targeted by the supplier. It seems, as highlighted by scholars,[75] that the CJEU confuses both elements and strangely enough it refers to the causal link as strong evidence which may be taken into consideration by the national court when determining whether the activity is in fact directed by the supplier, an activity that in the case at issue was already proven.[76] It would have been much more useful had the CJEU taken the opportunity to clarify the meaning and scope of that second condition, in other words, to clarify what the link between the contract and the activities needs to be in order to consider that it falls within its scope. In this sense, even if we

[69] *Shearson Lehman Hutton* c. *TVB* case.

[70] Ibid.

[71] Opinion AG Darmon, paras 83–4, in *Shearson Lehman Hutton* c. *TVB* case.

[72] Ibid.

[73] Ibid.

[74] Opinion AG Cruz Villalón in *Emrek*, para 24.

[75] De la Rosa, F. E. (2014) 'El Papel del Nexo de Causalidad en el Sistema Europeo de Competencia Internacional de los Contratos de Consumo: una Condición para el Olvido?' 14 *La Ley Unión Europea* 5.

[76] *Emrek*, para. 26.

agree on the fact that requiring such a causal link could harm the consumer, it could be used by the supplier to demonstrate that there is no link between the contract in question and the activities directed to the consumer's domicile. In other words, it could be used as qualified evidence of the lack of connection between the contract and the activities targeted through the web. On this basis, it is necessary to identify those situations where there is no such causal link and which, as a consequence, are not covered by the protective rule. In order to do so the circumstances of the contract have to be analysed in the case at issue to see where it falls under the scope of the activities targeted by the supplier to the consumer's domicile.

As de la Rosa pointed out, there will be no link when the contract concluded by the consumer has no relationship with the activity directed by the supplier to the state of the consumer.[77] In fact, Recital (25) of the Rome I Regulation refers to this idea when it requires, in relation to the application of Article 6, 'that the consumer contract has been concluded as a result of the professional pursuing his commercial or professional activities in that particular country'. The expression 'in that particular country' was introduced in the Recital to guarantee such a link.[78] The requirement of such a link between the activities directed by the supplier to the consumer's domicile and the consumer contract does not necessarily entail the need for a causal link, that is, it does not necessarily imply that the consumer has been attracted through the website.[79] In this point I agree with the result of the CJEU ruling in the *Emrek* case (regardless of the arguments used in the decision). The traditional distinction between passive and active consumers has been overturned. While the Brussels I Regulation meant the move towards the protection of the 'semi-passive' consumer (that is, a consumer who has been captured in his or her market but who does not necessarily conclude the contract in the state of his or her domicile), the lack of requirement of a causal link leads to the protection of the active consumer to the extent that the supplier has directed its activities to the consumer's domicile and the contract falls within the scope of such activities.[80] This is logical if we consider the evolution of European consumer policy and its protective aim. As will be shown in the last section of this chapter, European consumer law aims not only to protect the consumer but also to encourage him or her to participate within the internal market.

Connected contracts

In the *Hobohm*[81] case the question arose as to whether that requirement is fulfilled when the case concerns a contract concluded between a consumer and a professional

[77] De la Rosa, 'El Papel del Nexo de Causalidad', above fn. 75.

[78] Garcimartín Alférez, 'Consumer Protection from a Conflict-of-Laws Perspective', above fn. 33, 453.

[79] De la Rosa, 'El Papel del Nexo de Causalidad', above fn. 75.

[80] Thiede, T. and J. Schacherreiter (2015) 'The Recent Shift from the Passive to the Active Consumer', *Austrian Law Journal* 23, 28.

[81] Case C-297/14, *Rüdiger Hobohm* v. *Benedikt Kampik Ltd & Co. KG y otros* ECLI:EU:C:2015:844 (*Hobohm*).

which on its own does not come within the scope of the commercial or professional activity 'directed' by that professional 'to' the Member State of the consumer's domicile, but which is linked to a contract concluded beforehand by those same parties in the context of that activity. In the case at issue there were two different contracts, separated in time but with a link between them. The first was a brokerage contract in order to purchase an apartment and the second, a 'transaction-management contract'. The latter was signed in order to safeguard the consumer's interests in relation to the sale contract, when the developer of the tourist complex where the aforementioned apartment was to be located encountered financial difficulties that jeopardised the completion of the construction of the tourist complex. It was proved that the brokerage contract fulfilled the requirements for the application of Article 17 of the Brussels I *bis* Regulation since the contract was concluded due to the activities directed to the consumer's domicile by the defendant. The question arising was with regard to the transaction-management contract on which Mr Hobohm based his claim. Seen independently from the brokerage contract, the transaction-management contract did not fulfil the requirements. However, the court stated that there is a compelling material link between the property-intermediary activity 'directed' to the consumer's domicile and the conclusion of the transaction-management contract. That activity led the consumer to enter into the brokerage contract and the sale contract. Had it not been for those contracts, the transaction-management contract, which formed the basis of Mr Hobohm's claims and was intended to resolve the problems in performing the sale contract, would not have been concluded.[82] Even if the parties' obligations under the brokerage contract were fulfilled as a result of the conclusion of the sale contract, the economic objective of the brokerage contract – which was to ensure that Mr and Mrs Hobohm could also have effective enjoyment of the apartment which they acquired as a result of the intermediary activity – had not, however, been achieved.[83] This posed the question as to whether the link between both contracts justified that the transaction-management contract fell within Article 17 as well as the brokerage contract. The CJEU accepts the extension of the protective fora to cases where the contract in question does not fall within the framework of the activities directed by the supplier to the consumer's domicile, as long as there is a strong link with another contract concluded beforehand by the same parties that falls within the scope of the activities directed by the supplier to the state where the consumer is domiciled. Consequently, it was necessary to determine in which cases there is such a link and the constituent elements of that link. According to the Court the aim of the transaction-management contract was to achieve the economic objective of the brokerage contract, that is to say, the effective enjoyment of the apartment.[84] In this case, even though the transaction-management contract on its own did not come within the scope of the activity 'directed' by the supplier 'to' the Member State of

[82] *Hobohm*, para. 20.
[83] Ibid., para. 20.
[84] Ibid., para. 34.

the consumer's domicile, it was nevertheless concluded as a direct extension of that activity, and as such complementary to the brokerage contract, in that it sought to make it possible for the economic objective of that contract to be achieved.[85]

Therefore, when the linked contract has the satisfaction of the economic objective of the other contract as its aim, the CJEU considers its conclusion as an extension of the directed activities by the supplier to the consumer's domicile.[86] Consequently, even though it is accurate to establish that there is no legal interdependence between the brokerage contract and the transaction-management contract, it must be held that there is an economic link between those two contracts.[87] In order to determine whether this link exists the judge needs to take into account the constituent elements of the link which are listed, not exhaustively, by the CJEU case law: whether the parties to both of those contracts are identical in law and in fact; whether the economic objective of those contracts concerning the same specific subject-matter is identical; and whether the transaction-management contract complements the brokerage contract, in that it seeks to make it possible for the economic objective of the contract to be achieved.[88] In its ruling the CJEU uses the objectives pursued by the Brussels I *bis* Regulation itself: to enhance the predictability of the rules of jurisdiction, the principle of consumer protection and maximum avoidance of parallel proceedings. A balance between those objectives led the CJEU to confirm the possibility that contracts with no legal link but with an economic connection may benefit from the protective jurisdiction rules.

Protecting the active consumer

The extension of the protective jurisdiction rules to the active consumer conforms to the European consumer protection policy and its objectives. European consumer law does not only pursue a high level of consumer protection but also promotes and contributes to the opportunities given by the creation of an internal market which benefits both consumers and suppliers. Consumer protection and the creation of a single market have to be seen not as contradictory but as complementary policies. In order for consumers to enjoy the full benefit of the internal market it is crucial to allow the consumer to take advantage of the markets of other Member States without facing the risk of possibly having to litigate overseas.[89] This is aligned with other mechanisms also aiming to bridge and balance legal diversity and integration as discussed throughout this volume. However, neither suppliers nor consumers have total confidence in the internal market which is a factor affecting the growth of cross-border transactions. Consequently, one of the basic aims is to encourage

85 Ibid., para. 35.
86 Ibid., para. 35.
87 Ibid., para. 36.
88 Ibid., para. 37.
89 Thiede and Schacherreiter, 'The Recent Shift from the Passive to the Active Consumer', above fn. 80, 29.

more confidence.[90] For this reason, for the internal market to fully benefit European consumers, not only should the acquisition of goods and services be beneficial but also recourse to the proper remedies and compensation in case of an eventual dispute should be accessible. It is therefore essential to guarantee European consumers effective access to justice granting them the possibility to litigate at home (*forum actoris*). As the Advocate-General pointed out in the *Emrek* case, the protective fora act as incentives for trade in other Member States.[91] The protection of the active consumer is a lure (the bait)[92] to encourage the consumer to trust the single market. However, suppliers also need to trust the internal market in order to face the risk of the 'internationality' of the transaction. In this sense it is also fundamental to guarantee the predictability of the jurisdiction rules. That predictability will be guaranteed as risk of international litigation is faced by the supplier when directing its activities to the consumer's domicile. Consequently, as mentioned before, the existence of a causal link loses relevance when the supplier directs its activities to the consumer's domicile and the contract falls within the scope of such activities. The suppliers will be able to adapt their behaviour according to the interpretation of Article 17 of the Brussels I *bis* Regulation given by the CJEU.

Nevertheless, in the framework of the Digital Single Market strategy, Regulation 2018/302 on addressing unjustified geoblocking and other forms of discrimination based on customers' nationality, place of residence or place of establishment within the internal market, has recently been approved.[93] Some trade practices and techniques such as the blocking of access to websites and other online interfaces and the rerouting of customers from one country version to another or refusing delivery or payment based on the place of residence of the customer, are discriminatory and contrary to the single market since they artificially segment the market based on the customers' residence.[94] The aim of Regulation 2018/302 is to give customers better access to goods and services by prohibiting such practices. However, the relationship between the prohibition of these geoblocking techniques and the 'directed activity' criteria developed by the CJEU, and discussed above, needs to be addressed.[95] If the key element within the directing activity test is to determine the subjective intention of the trader to target its activities to the consumer's domicile, is it then reasonable to

[90] Along these lines, see Proposal for a Directive of the European Parliament and of the Council on certain aspects concerning contracts for the online and other distance sales of goods COM (2015) 635 final.

[91] AG *Emrek*, para. 37.

[92] Thiede and Schacherreiter, 'The Recent Shift from the Passive to the Active Consumer', above fn. 80, 29.

[93] OJ L 60I/1, 02.03.2018. This contribution was submitted before the adoption of this Regulation.

[94] Ibid.

[95] Von Hein, J. (2016) 'Geoblocking and the Conflict of Laws: Ships that Pass in the Night?', Conflicts of Law.net, 31 May 2016, available at: http://conflictoflaws.net/2016/geo-blocking-and-the-conflict-of-laws-ships-that-pass-in-the-night; and de Miguel Asensio, 'El asunto Pammer y el artículo 15 RBI', above fn. 51.

ban any way of preventing the trader from doing so, that is, from offering its goods and services to some customers? Aware of the issue, the Regulation states in Article 1.6 that

> [t]his Regulation shall be without prejudice to Union law concerning judicial cooperation in civil matters. Compliance with this Regulation shall not be construed as implying that a trader directs activities to the Member State of the consumer's habitual residence or domicile within the meaning of point (b) of Article 6(1) of Regulation (EC) No 593/2008 and point (c) of Article 17(1) of Regulation (EU) No 1215/2012. In particular, where a trader, acting in accordance with Articles 3, 4 and 5 of this Regulation, does not block or limit consumers' access to an online interface, does not redirect consumers to a version of an online interface based on their nationality or place of residence that is different from the online interface to which the consumers first sought access, does not apply different general conditions of access when selling goods or providing services in situations laid down in this Regulation, or accepts payment instruments issued in another Member State on a non-discriminatory basis, that trader shall not be, on those grounds alone, considered to be directing activities to the Member State where the consumer has the habitual residence or domicile. Nor shall that trader, on those grounds alone, be considered to be directing activities to the Member State of the consumer's habitual residence or domicile, where the trader provides information and assistance to the consumer after the conclusion of a contract that has resulted from the trader's compliance with this Regulation.

In spite of this and other references to private international law instruments, there is no doubt that problems of interplay between both regulations may still arise. It is therefore important to better coordinate different European policies.

When the consumer relationship has connections with Third States, the logic of integration cannot be used. Even if the affected market is the European internal market, the aim to encourage consumers to participate in the European common market cannot be pursued since one of the parties is domiciled outside of the EU. The disappearance of this European objective brings back all the relevance to the requirement of a causal link between the directed activity and the contract concluded because otherwise the protection of a consumer who has travelled is not justified. In this scenario the supplier must have targeted the consumer in his or her own domicile. Any other interpretation would prevent the final achievement of a universal convention which would unify jurisdiction and recognition and enforcement rules, which is the only way to guarantee the efficiency of the desired protection.

15

Protection of the Individual in Recent Private International Law Codification in Latin America

Sebastián Paredes

Introduction

After decades of passivity, in recent years several Latin American countries, including Argentina,[1] Brazil,[2] Panama,[3] the Dominican Republic[4] and Paraguay[5], have adapted their civil codes, or adopted – or drafted with a vicw to adoption – private international law acts in relation to specific private international law matters. Does this new normativity bring real answers to Latin American private international law dilemmas? Do these new enactments incorporate institutes and principles that facilitate real access to justice for individuals and provide them with simple and accessible methods to guarantee their rights and protect their assets?

In this postmodern, integrated world, it appears necessary to analyse these issues through the lens of human rights. The focus on the individual is a definitive factor in relation to access to jurisdiction and due process and is also influencing international judicial cooperation.[6] From a private international law perspective, but infused also with the international comparatist law approach, this chapter explores the ways in which recent Latin American codifications are embracing modern

[1] Argentina: *Código Civil y Comercial de la Nación.* This Code was adopted by Act 26.994 of 1 October 2014 and entered into force on 1 August 2015 according to Act 27.077 of 16 December 2014.

[2] Brazil: *Código de Processo Civil.* Act 13.105 of 16 March 2015.

[3] Panama: *Código de Derecho internacional privado de la República de Panamá,* 7 October 2015.

[4] Dominican Republic: *Ley N° 544-14 de Derecho internacional privado de la República Dominicana,* 15 October 2014.

[5] Paraguay: *Ley 5393 sobre el derecho aplicable a los contratos internacionales,* 20 January 2015.

[6] Jayme, E. (1995) 'Identité culturelle et intégration. Le droit international privé postmoderne. Cours général de droit international privé', *Recueil des cours*, vol. 251, 49.

conceptions of private international law centred on the individual and to what extent they are still influenced by classical solutions and methodologies regarding conflict of laws.

The analysis that follows is provided in relation to three main topics addressed in the new codifications: (1) international jurisdiction; (2) international cooperation; and (3) international commercial contracts.

International Jurisdiction

Argentina

The 2015 Civil and Commercial Code of Argentina[7] adopts several private international law principles addressing international jurisdiction that were already used by courts and judges in practice through the construction of previously existent provisions[8] or the interpretation of relevant case law.[9]

The new code contains a specific chapter (Chapter 2) on general rules in relation to international jurisdiction in addition to its content on detailed and concrete rules of jurisdiction in specific categories such as natural persons, marriage, maintenance, adoption, inheritance, contracts, consumer contracts and securities, among many others.

The general basis of jurisdiction of Argentina's private international law is set in Article 2608 as the domicile of the defendant.[10] This rule must be understood as

[7] An English-language version of the code is available: 'Argentina' (2017) in Basedow, J. et al. (eds), *Encyclopedia of Private International Law*, Elgar, 2930–41.

[8] For example, before 2015, as we will see later in the chapter, there were no provisions on the choice of court agreements. In addition, specific regulations for international securities, bills of exchange and cheques lacked rules on jurisdiction for cross-border cases. To solve these problems judges used to apply international treaties in which Argentina was a Contracting State but the other connected country was not. See also Paredes, S. and E. H. Vetulli, Case note, in Cartas Blogatorias, available online at: https://cartasblogatorias.com/2015/05/28/argentina-laguna-normativa-para-letras-de-cambio-libradas-en-brasil

[9] Another example is the incorporation of the solutions of the Supreme Court of Justice in *Exportadora Buenos Aires S. A.* c. *Holiday Inns Worldwide Inc.* of 20 October 1998 into the wording of the new Art. 2650 for international contracts. In that decision the Court 'expanded' the meaning of 'place of performance' that was set in Arts 1215 and 1216 of the former civil code to grant jurisdiction to the Argentine court in a case connected with the United States. In the case of a sponsorship contract to be performed by the Argentine national football team coach during the 1994 FIFA World Cup in the US, the Court established that 'any place of performance' was enough to grant jurisdiction to the courts of Argentina. Even given that the sponsorship activities took place in the US but a payment was made in Argentina, the Supreme Court decided that that was enough to consider Argentina the 'place of performance'. After this decision, the meaning of 'place of performance' was changed to encompass the broader 'the place of performance of any of the contractual obligations' and incorporated into the new code in 2015. The decision is available (in Spanish) in Fallos DIPr Argentina, available at: http://fallos.diprargentina.com/2007/03/exportadora-buenos-aires-c-holiday-inns.html

[10] Art. 2608, 'Absent specific provisions, actions *in personam* must be brought before the judge of the domicile or habitual residence of the defendant'.

an alternative basis to the specific bases provided for in other categories for personal claims, that is, providing for concurrent fora. The underpinning of the widely accepted domicile of the defendant basis is to facilitate the defendant's constitutional right of defence.[11]

Along with the domicile of the defendant as a general connecting factor, specific criteria are used for categories such as marriage in Article 2621 (last known effective marital domicile), maintenance in Article 2629 (claimant's domicile or where the defendant has assets), contracts in Article 2650 (place of performance of any of the contractual obligations). In turn, these special bases of jurisdiction,[12] particularly the last-mentioned, can mean different jurisdictions are competent internationally to hear the case.

The main constitutional principle on international jurisdiction, following a well-established tradition in Argentinian private international law, is set out in Articles 2594 and 2601, and provides that jurisdiction rules contained in international or regional treaties in force in Argentina prevail over those provided for in the civil code.

Forum necessitatis

Forum necessitatis is codified for the first time in the private international law of Argentina in Article 2602 of the code. This institute, whose ultimate goal is to provide effective access to justice, gives exceptional competence to Argentine judges to

> intervene with the purpose of preventing a denial of justice, provided that it is not reasonable to require initiating the action abroad and as long as the private situation presents a sufficient connection with the country, the right to defense is guaranteed, and it serves the convenience of achieving an effective decision.[13]

That is, this exceptional jurisdictional ground can only be used as a basis of jurisdiction when it is impossible for the parties to access the jurisdiction of the courts in other countries because no other country has international competence to hear the case.[14]

[11] Uzal, M. E. (2016) *Derecho internacional privado*, Thomson Reuters, 250–1.

[12] On the distinction between general and special jurisdictional bases see McClean, D. and V. Ruiz Abou-Nigm (2016) *Morris on the Conflict of Laws*, 9th edn, Sweet & Maxwell, ch. 4.

[13] Article 2602, 'In cases in which the present Code does not grant international jurisdiction to Argentine judges, they may intervene exceptionally with a view to preventing denial of justice, provided that it is not reasonable to require the initiation of the claim abroad and as long as the private situation manifests sufficient connection to the state, the right to legal counsel in proceedings is guaranteed and the expedience of achieving an effective judgment is regarded'.

[14] Fernández Arroyo explains that if there is a mere 'inconvenience' to proceed in another state then there is no *forum necessitatis*. See Fernández Arroyo, D. P. (2016) 'Main Characteristics of the New Private International Law of the Argentinian Republic', 80 *RabelsZ*, 130–50, at 140–2.

In Argentina this institute is not new. Long before there was a specific private international law rule to that effect, *forum necessitatis* was in fact brought to life in marriage cases for the first time by the courts in the leading case of *Vlasov*[15] and it has subsequently been operating as recognised by contemporary Argentinian jurisprudence.[16]

The requirements for *forum necessitatis* to operate in Argentinian courts according to the new private international law provision are as follows: it is essential to first establish the lack of international competence of the Argentine courts and then the impossibility of starting the proceedings in another country.[17] Only then, and with the aim of ensuring effective access to justice, can a judge in Argentina exceptionally exercise jurisdiction in situations in which such exercise is indispensable, despite not being internationally competent according to the provisions in force.[18] In addition, it is required that the case has enough of a connection with Argentina. This can be established by means of personal connections such as the domicile of one or both of the parties, and also by other kind of connections such as assets of the defendant located within the jurisdiction. This is in order to avoid the exercise of jurisdiction in what it could become an exorbitant forum.[19] The relevant provision orders the judges

[15] Argentina's seminal case in relation to *forum necessitatis* was decided by the Supreme Court on 25 March 1960, *Cavura de Vlasov, Emilia* c. *Vlasov, Alejandro*. In this case Mrs Cavura de Vlasov attempted to divorce Mr Vlasov but according to the jurisdiction rule on marriage in force in 1960 the internationally competent courts were those of the couple's last domicile. At the time the couple's domicile was fixed by the husband's domicile and in this case Mr Vlasov had moved some years earlier to Italy, never to return, while Mrs Cavura de Vlasov remained in Argentina. At that time, according to the rules on international jurisdiction, Argentine courts lacked competence. When she tried to serve Mr Vlasov in Italy this turned out to be impossible as he was a sailor with no fixed abode at which he could be served. The Supreme Court granted exceptional jurisdiction even though it lacked international jurisdiction based on the 'natural rights of judges' provided for in the Argentine Constitution. The case is available online in Fallos DIPr Argentina at: http://fallos.diprargentina.com/2007/02/vlasof.html

[16] It should be mentioned that in 1940 there was another case, *Vazquez*, relating to nationality issues, in which the Supreme Court acted in a similar fashion. Some cases that required *forum necesitatis* after *Vlasov* are cited in Fernández Arroyo, D. P. (2014) 'Disposiciones de Derecho internacional privado. Capítulo 2. Jurisdicción internacional', in Rivera, J. C. and G. Medina (eds), *Código Civil y Comercial de la Nación comentado*, vol. VI, Thomson Reuters-La Ley, 799–829, especially 805.

[17] As explained in above fn. 14.

[18] See an excellent analysis in Fernández Arroyo, 'Main Characteristics of the New Private International Law of the Argentinian Republic', above fn. 14, 140–2.

[19] Exorbitant fora as opposed to reasonable fora, meaning that there will be exorbitance when there is little or no connection between the case and the forum. The question of reasonability of the forum is analysed in Fernández Arroyo, D. P. (2006) 'Compétence exclusive et compétence exorbitante dans les relations privées internationales', *Recueil des cours*, vol. 223, 9–259. For Argentine international jurisdiction rules, even if before the new Code, see All, P. M. (2005) 'Las normas de jurisdicción internacional en el sistema argentino de fuente interna', in *Litigio judicial internacional*, 4 *DeCITA. Derecho del Comercio Internacional. Temas y actualidades*, Zavalía, 422–44. Also

to bear in mind the effectiveness of any eventual decision: that decision should have a real chance of being recognised and enforced abroad.[20]

Choice of court agreements

Another important modernisation included in the recent private international law codification in Argentina is the express recognition of party autonomy in choice of court agreements.[21] This provides the exclusive effect of choice of court agreements and allows the parties in certain scenarios to provide for the derogation of jurisdiction in relation to the courts in Argentina. By means of a choice of court agreement it is possible for the parties to choose national courts as well as arbitrators abroad.

Choice of court agreements with these effects were already recognised before the entry into force of the new civil code; however, this was done by means of a broad interpretation of civil procedure rules applicable in domestic cases[22] rather than a specific private international law provision to that effect.

However, the specific new provision is limited to the remit of international commercial contracts. Choice of court agreements are not recognised in relation to family law, succession, cases involving the custody or maintenance of children, and certain other excluded categories.[23] The new provision does not require the foreign court to have any connection with the case, the parties or even Argentina, since there is no express normative requirement in relation to any such connection. The code lacks provisions with regard to the validity requirements and prorogation effects of choice of court agreements selecting the courts of Argentina.

There seems to be no controversy when one of the parties has a connection with Argentina, but it is uncertain if foreign parties with no connection with Argentina

available at: https://sociedip.files.wordpress.com/2013/12/all-las-normas-de-jurisdiccic3b3n-internacional-en-el-sistema-argentino.pdf

20 See the rule in above fn. 13.

21 Art. 2605: Choice of forum agreement. In patrimonial or international matters, the parties are entitled to designate judges or arbitrators abroad, unless the Argentine judges have exclusive jurisdiction, or the choice of forum is prohibited by law.

22 The most used was Art. 1 of the Federal Code of Civil and Commercial Procedure. This Code applies to federal cases, such as those relating to ships, aircraft, copyright law, citizenship and so on, in the whole country no matter where the court is located and also for civil and commercial matters in local courts of the Buenos Aires Autonomous City and states: 'The competence granted to Argentine Courts cannot be declined. Without prejudice of international treaties provisions it could be extended when Parties agree to do so in patrimonial cases exclusively. If the case has international connections it could be extended to judges and arbitrators abroad except on those cases when Argentine courts have exclusive competence or it is forbidden by Law'. For more on this issue, see Noodt Taquela, M. B. (2003) 'Reglamentación general de los contratos internacionales en los Estados mercosureños', in Fernández Arroyo, D. P. (ed.), *Derecho internacional privado de los Estados del Mercosur*, Zavalía, 1008–10 and All, 'Las normas de jurisdicción internacional en el sistema argentino de fuente interna', above fn. 19, 430–1.

23 Such as international contracts involving consumers. The criteria to establish jurisdiction is wider for consumers than for 'regular international contracts'.

could choose Argentinian courts. It is submitted, in agreement with Fernández Arroyo, that a teleological construction of the wording of the article allows an inference to that effect, that is, if it is not forbidden, Argentine courts cannot refuse to declare themselves competent because there is no specific requirement.[24]

It would also be possible to argue in favour of a reflexive effect of the provision referred to in the previous paragraph in relation to the choice of court agreements in favour of foreign courts or arbitration (Article 2605), to the same effect.

Ultimately, it is submitted that the only requirement that an Argentine judge could require in cases where foreign parties choose Argentine courts is *ratione materia*, that is, for the case to be on patrimonial matters with international elements. This argument is inferred from Article 2605, allowing parties to choose foreign courts in international cases regarding patrimonial issues.[25] This is the construction considering what is omitted in Article 2605 in relation to the selection of Argentine courts.

These are positive changes in Argentine private international law with regard to international jurisdiction. First, *forum necessitatis* allows individuals to be protected, providing them with the opportunity of access to justice when it is really needed. Second, although there are no substantial changes to former practice, with the incorporation of rules on choice of forum agreements the code has become more in tune with the needs of postmodern society and individuals, and their needs as global citizens to further interact in cross-border scenarios.

Uruguay

Despite the intense work of Uruguayan scholars and the doubtless need to modernise certain rules of private international law in Uruguay in relation to international jurisdiction, the Draft Private International Law General Act of Uruguay is yet to get the green light from Parliament.[26] One of the most important changes it presents is to allow the choice of forum in certain specific matters. Currently, Article 2403 of the Appendix to the Uruguayan Civil Code prohibits the recognition of choice of court agreements. This reflects the Uruguayan position in the Additional Protocol to the Montevideo Treaties of 1940. The general jurisdiction rule is based on the place of performance of the obligation in question following the structure of the Montevideo Treaties on International Civil Law signed in Montevideo in 1889 and 1940.[27]

The Private International Law Draft Act reverses the traditional Uruguayan reluctance to party autonomy and allows the parties to choose the jurisdiction by

[24] Fernández Arroyo, 'Main Characteristics of the New Private International Law of the Argentinian Republic', above fn. 14, 146.

[25] See the rule in above fn. 21.

[26] Proyecto de Ley General de Derecho internacional privado. Available online at: https://legislativo.parlamento.gub.uy/temporales/4070629.PDF

[27] Still in force for some aspects, the 1889 Treaty has Argentina, Bolivia, Colombia, Peru, Paraguay and Uruguay as Contracting States. The Treaty of 1940 is in force between Argentina, Paraguay and Uruguay.

means of choice of court agreements. The Draft regulates all international jurisdiction bases in the same Chapter XII (Articles 57 to 61) at the end of the Act, and up to a certain extent the approval of the Act as presented to Parliament would put an end to the Uruguayan approach to the issue, which has been contradictory in recent years. This contradiction is reflected, for instance, in Uruguay as a Contracting State of Mercosur's 1994 Buenos Aires Protocol on Jurisdiction in Contractual Matters in force in Argentina, Brazil, Paraguay and Uruguay, which expressly allows party autonomy in jurisdictional matters.[28]

Article 60 of the Draft Act provides for the recognition of choice of court agreements in contractual matters establishing the written form as a formal validity requirement. The provision also provides for certain matters to be excluded from the scope of application of the provision, with the aim, *inter alia*, of protecting weak parties.[29] Thus, the choice of forum is forbidden for contracts relating to immovable property where the property is in Uruguay, and also in consumer, employment, insurance and transport contracts. Securities and those contracts and obligations relating to family law and succession are also excluded from the scope of application of choice of court agreements.

Overall, Uruguay's long-standing struggle to modernise its private international law on jurisdiction would come to an end with the introduction of party autonomy through the choice of forum in international contracts. This would further entrust individuals and private actors to provide for their obligations according to their own needs rather than to maintain a set of rigid rules that may differ from those of the legal systems of their main partners in private international law cases. Despite the omnipresent fears that the choice of forum can favour the stronger parties in a private international law case, the Draft Act manages to strike a balance protecting weaker parties in relation to specific issues, as well as reinforcing substantial rules in specific issues, including the provision for *forum necessitatis*.[30]

Soft Law Provisions: ASADIP and the TRANSJUS Principles

In 2014 in Porto Alegre, Brazil, the American Association of Private International Law (ASADIP) presented the TRANSJUS Principles, a soft law instrument focused on transnational access to justice as an instrument of reference for judges, lawmakers and parties to a dispute to grant and provide substantial solutions in cross-border litigation.[31] Chapter 3 of the TRANSJUS restates several principles of international

[28] Basedow, J. (2013) 'The Law of Open Societies: Private Ordering and Public Regulation of International Relations. General Course on Private International Law', *Recueil des cours*, vol. 360, 9–515, especially 168.

[29] Art. 60, with remission to Art. 50.

[30] For example, *forum necessitatis* of Art. 57.8 of the Draft Act.

[31] ASADIP. *Principios ASADIP sobre el acceso transnacional a la justicia (TRANSJUS)* presented at the VIII ASADIP Congress in Porto Alegre, Brazil on 30 and 31 October 2014. Its final 2016 version, in English, is available at: www.asadip.org/v2/wp-content/uploads/2018/08/ASADIP-TRANSJUS-EN-FINAL18.pdf

jurisdiction;[32] among the most significant is that jurisdiction must be established according to substantial connections with the forum such as the place of performance of the obligation in question, the domicile or habitual residence of the parties and the place where the property or assets of the defendant are located.

An essential role is given to party autonomy: the TRANSJUS Principles recognise the role of choice of court agreements, with the limitations necessary for safeguarding weaker parties in cases when one party is presumed to be in an unequal negotiating position, such as in consumer contract cases.[33]

Another well-established principle recognised in this regard is the severability of choice of court agreements,[34] with a validity assessment to be carried out independently of the rest of the contractual clauses. Article 3.4 establishes that the agreement may be made expressly, by any means of communication that can made be available for consultation at a later date and that evidences the free decision of the interested parties.

The TRANSJUS Principles also tackle the complex issue of exorbitant jurisdiction. Article 3.6 establishes the criteria for determining what is a reasonable forum for litigation in cross-border cases. The nationality or domicile of the litigant are considered exorbitant bases in this regard, as well as the place where the defendant is served with process, a unilateral choice of forum, and the place of casual commercial activities of the defendant.[35]

International Cooperation

Nowadays the literature of modern private international law includes international judicial cooperation as an essential disciplinary pillar.[36] The third pillar, in a classical conception of private international law, was reserved for the recognition and enforcement of foreign decisions but has been replaced in the last few decades by the broader concept of international cooperation, which includes the recognition and enforcement of foreign decisions but also service abroad of judicial and extrajudicial documents, taking evidence abroad, recognition of foreign public documents, enforcement of preventive measures abroad and access to the contents of foreign law.[37]

[32] See also French, D. and V. Ruiz Abou-Nigm (2018) 'Jurisdiction: Betwixt Unilateralism and Global Coordination', in Ruiz Abou-Nigm, V., K McCall-Smith and D. French, *Linkages and Boundaries in Private and Public International Law*, Hart Publishing, 75–104, at 97.

[33] See Ochoa Muñoz, J. and C. Madrid Martínez (2015) 'Problemas de acceso trasnacional a la justicia en el Derecho internacional privado. Perspectiva latinoamericana', in OEA (ed.), *XLI Curso de Derecho Internacional 2014*, OEA-OAS, 281–346.

[34] ASADIP's TRANSJUS, Art. 3.5.

[35] For further information on exorbitance see Fernández Arroyo, 'Compétence exclusive et compétence exorbitante', above fn. 19, 9–259.

[36] Noodt Taquela, M. B. (2016) 'Applying the Most Favourable Treaty or Domestic Rules to Facilitate Private International Law Co-operation', *Recueil des cours*, vol. 377, 121–317, especially 166.

[37] Fernández Arroyo, D. P. (2003) 'Conceptos y problemas básicos del Derecho internacional privado', in Fernández Arroyo (ed.), *Derecho internacional privado de los Estados del Mercosur*, Zavalía,

The real impact and importance given to international cooperation by states, international organisations and private international law codification fora is reflected in the increased number of international treaties on cooperation issues: bilateral, regional and universal in scale, and also in the upsurge of non-state codifications.[38]

It is submitted that international judicial cooperation has left its old, 'classical' role of being merely a set of international civil procedure rules to become central to the operationalisation of private international law objectives and in some cases this shift is evidenced in substantive provisions that allow real access to justice not only in jurisdiction disputes but also in other specific areas such as cross-border child abduction cases and cross-border maintenance.[39]

Changes to Argentina's Codification

Codification attempts relating to international cooperation in Argentina were in the past unduly complex due to the federal composition of the Argentine state. Many lawmakers argued that it was impossible for federal legislature to enact international cooperation provisions because procedural law is a provincial prerogative, that is, a devolved matter, according to the Argentine national constitution.[40] This misconception of the constitutional rule has deprived Argentina's private international law (or the internal dimension thereof)[41] of specific provisions on international judicial

39–82; also Noodt Taquela (2016) 'Applying the Most Favourable Treaty or Domestic Rules', above fn. 36, 137.

[38] For example *ALI/UNIDROIT Principles of Transnational Civil Procedure* of 2004, available at: www.unidroit.org/english/principles/civilprocedure/ali-unidroitprinciples-spanish.pdf. In June 2018, UNIDROIT was still working jointly with the European Law Institute on the *ELI-UNIDROIT Transnational Principles of Civil Procedure*, a set of rules focused on the growth of European civil procedural law and which could, according to UNCITRAL's website, lead to other regional projects adapting the ALI/UNIDROIT Principles to the specificities of regional legal cultures and paving the way to the drafting of another regional rule. For further information see www.unidroit.org/work-in-progress-eli-unidroit-european-rules

[39] See Najurieta, M. S. (2015) 'Una mirada sobre el acceso a la justicia en el nuevo Código Civil y Comercial de la Nación Argentina', in ASADIP (ed.), *El acceso a la justicia en el derecho internacional privado. Jornadas de la ASADIP 2015*, CEDEP-ASADIP-Mizrachi & Pujol, 191–212, especially 210.

[40] According to the Constitution the Federal Parliament can enact substantive codes, while the procedural codes are the prerogative of the provinces. See Fernández Arroyo's fierce criticism of this concept in Fernández Arroyo, 'Main Characteristics of the New Private International Law of the Argentinian Republic', above fn. 14, 147.

[41] The concept of 'internal dimension' refers to a set of rules on private international law (jurisdiction, applicable law and international cooperation) contained in national sources, that is, private international law codes, Civil Codes or Acts for private cases or relations with cross-border or foreign elements. The 'internal dimension' is complementary to the normativity provided by international treaties and is used when a treaty is not applicable. In most Latin American countries private international law provisions in treaties prevail over the internal dimension. The concept of internal dimension is autonomous and totally separate from domestic rules applicable to private law domestic cases.

cooperation even though it was included in the first draft of the new Civil and Commercial Code.[42]

Nevertheless, and despite this constitutional limitation, the legislators managed to include some substantive provisions that guarantee basic rules for international judicial cooperation in the code's chapter on international jurisdiction. Article 2611 provides one of the most decisive and positive rules of Argentina's new code establishing that judges should provide broad jurisdictional cooperation in civil and commercial matters and those relating to labour law.[43]

The extent of 'broad' in this context means, it is suggested, that unconditional cooperation could only be restricted or rejected by *ordre public*, that is, when the requested foreign cooperation leads to solutions incompatible with the fundamental principles of public policy underlying the Argentine legal system. In addition, it is important to underline that the reception of this substantive principle is considered as a mandatory rule for judges and obliges them to guarantee access to justice when cooperation is requested.

Furthermore, Article 2612 establishes the letter rogatory as the main communication channel with foreign authorities. This kind of request needs to be expedited *ex officio* and without delay as long as the request does not infringe Argentine public policy. However, the latter rule is reserved to foreign requests for service and taking of evidence in Argentina; in our view the wording 'any cooperation request' would have been preferable.[44]

The same Article, even if it establishes the letter rogatory as the main communication channel, leaves a window open in that it permits Argentinian judges to use direct communication – not provided for in the code – with foreign judges when the situation so requires. This window must be seen as complementary to Article 2611, giving the judges a certain degree of leeway to justify their decisions, taking in consideration the respect of due process in both legal systems.[45]

Finally, another controversial issue in Argentina's procedural system is dealt with by a substantive provision in Article 2610 establishing the right of access to justice

[42] Argentina's Parliament approves international treaties in those matters binding the Argentine Republic, and every provincial judge applies them in cross-border cases. This policy also excluded provisions for recognition and enforcement of foreign decisions approved in the first drafts and now remain regulated in twenty-four local Civil Procedural Codes (twenty-three Provinces and the Autonomous City of Buenos Aires).

[43] Article 2611. 'Jurisdictional cooperation. Without prejudice to the obligations assumed in international conventions, the Argentine judges must provide broad jurisdictional cooperation in civil, commercial and labour matters'.

[44] See Paredes, S. (2016) 'La cooperación jurisdiccional internacional en el nuevo Código civil y comercial de la Nación Argentina', in Amaral Júnior, A. and L. Klein Vieira (eds), *El derecho internacional privado y sus desafíos en la actualidad*, Editorial Ibáñez, 839–62.

[45] See Iud, C. and N. Rubaja (2015) 'Algunas herramientas para favorecer el acceso a la justicia en el nuevo Código Civil y Comercial argentino', in ASADIP (ed.), *El acceso a la justicia en el derecho internacional privado. Jornadas de la ASADIP 2015*, CEDEP-ASADIP-Mizrachi & Pujol, 237–62.

as something that must be guaranteed to all without any distinctions based on nationality or residence. This provision clashes with the traditional *cautio judicatum solvi* required by most of Argentina's provincial civil procedural codes. The requirement for the foreign litigant to have a link with the country (in terms of assets or goods) was eliminated by many private international law treaties adopted by Argentina, such as the 1954 Hague Convention on Civil Procedure, the 1992 Mercosur Las Leñas Protocol on Jurisdictional Cooperation and Assistance in Civil, Commercial, Labour and Administrative Matters and a number of bilateral agreements concluded many years ago. Yet, its continued existence in domestic procedural codes led to inexplicable internal contradictions in the legal system for many years.

The new substantive provision thus goes a long way to prohibiting any kind of pecuniary requirements for a foreign litigant who does not have a local connection. To maintain requirements of any kind would lead to discrimination. Hence, despite the fact that the civil and commercial code did not expressly abrogate the *cautio judicatium solvi* in provincial codes, it is submitted that it must be considered derogated.[46]

The New Brazilian Approach

In Brazil, the Code of Civil Procedure was modified in 2015 and entered into force in March 2016. It introduced new dispositions related to cross-border civil procedure.[47] This celebrated and long-awaited reform was praised because its predecessor had only three Articles to regulate judicial cooperation whenever the internal dimension was needed.[48]

The new set of rules has a special chapter (Chapter II) dedicated to cross-border issues in Articles 26 to 41, and there is another special chapter, Articles 960 to 965, dedicated to providing for the recognition and enforcement of foreign decisions. Article 41 adopts the provisions of Las Leñas 1992 (Mercosur)[49] and establishes that no legalisation is needed for public foreign documents when they are transmitted through Central Authorities or diplomatic channels. It is important to remember that the only channel allowed in the Las Leñas Protocol[50] is Central Authorities.

Moreover, Section II of Chapter II allows judges to connect with their colleagues through direct communications to facilitate proceedings. When the requirement

[46] See Fernández Arroyo, 'Main Characteristics of the New Private International Law of the Argentinian Republic', above fn. 14, 143.

[47] Brazil. *Código de Processo Civil.* Act 13.105 of 16 March 2015.

[48] Klein Vieira, L. and R. Alvares Gaspar, 'Habemus nuevo código procesal civil. Sus principales alteraciones en el derecho procesal internacional', Cartas Blogatorias. Available at: https://cartasblogatorias.com/2015/04/21/brasil-habemus-nuevo-codigo-procesal-civil-sus-principales-alteraciones-en-el-derecho-procesal-internacional

[49] Las Leñas Protocol on Jurisdictional Cooperation and Assistance in Civil, Commercial, Labour and Administrative Matters, signed in Las Leñas on 27 June 1992; it entered into force in Argentina, Brazil, Paraguay and Uruguay, the four constituent countries of Mercosur.

[50] See further de Araujo's chapter in this volume.

is made from abroad the foreign authorities must use the main channel (the Central Authority). Article 31 allows Brazilian judges to establish direct communications with their counterparts abroad.

Lastly, to recognise a foreign decision in Brazil it is necessary to use the *exequatur* procedure with a letter rogatory before the Superior Justice Tribunal located in Brasilia.

ASADIP's TRANSJUS Principles

The 2016 ASADIP'S TRANSJUS Principles mentioned previously not only provide for rules on jurisdiction but also establish ground rules for the judiciary and administrative authorities to provide effective cross-border cooperation.[51] Chapter 4 is entirely dedicated to international jurisdictional cooperation and affirms in Article 4.1 the obligation of judges and other authorities to provide cooperation in cross-border requests. It goes as far as establishing that non-performance by the relevant authorities in this sphere should be considered as a violation of the right of access to justice, a fundamental right.[52]

The incorporation of this principle is commendable because it reinforces the obligation to cooperate and recognises the superior nature of that obligation – just below that of fundamental human rights. In this way this principle consecrates the right of access to justice. It is submitted that this principle is of real guidance to judges, enabling them to pursue and obtain what is required to facilitate cooperation, as well as to national legislatures at the time of drafting internal private international law regulations.

The Principles also encourage states to incorporate and use direct judicial communications and digital technologies in cross-border service and the taking of evidence abroad and provides that if there is no formality required, judges and authorities can use any other means if necessary.[53] In the same way the Principles also urge judges to use judicial networks established on a bilateral, regional or multilateral basis.[54]

[51] See Ochoa Muñoz and Madrid Martínez, 'Problemas de acceso trasnacional a la justicia en el Derecho internacional privado', above fn. 33.

[52] ASADIP TRANSJUS Principles are available in Spanish, Portuguese, English and French versions at: www.asadip.org/v2/?page_id=231

[53] ASADIP TRANSJUS, Arts 4.7, 4.8 and 4.9.

[54] For example, the International Hague Network of Judges of the 1980 Hague Convention on the Civil Aspects of International Child Abduction which has most Latin American countries as Contracting States, available at: www.hcch.net/en/instruments/specialised-sections/child-abduction. On a regional level, IberRed is a network of Central Authorities from Latin American states and some European countries (Andorra, Portugal and Spain) and a US territory (Puerto Rico) dedicated to establishing communications between Central Authorities and judiciary branches of the twenty-two Parties. Its website is available at: www.iberred.org

International Contracts

The Triumph of Party Autonomy

Argentina

In Argentina, the 2015 Civil and Commercial Code expressly incorporates the possibility for parties to choose the law applicable to their international contracts. The civil code prior to 2015 did not have a specific rule for party autonomy despite Argentina's long-standing tradition of allowing parties to choose the law applicable to their contracts. The former normative 'silence' came from the 1940 Montevideo Treaties Additional Protocol, in which party autonomy is not recognised.[55]

Article 2651 meticulously details the rules and limitations for the choice of applicable law. One of the most significant provisions is that there is no requirement for any connection between the chosen law and the contract,[56] that is, the new code provides individuals with flexibility in the choice of law. For example, the choice may affect only part of the contract and may be made and modified at any time, but the contract's validity and third-party rights must always be safeguarded.[57] In addition, parties can incorporate standard clauses, such as the ICC-Incoterms, or a non-state body of rules such as the UNIDROIT Principles[58] or the Hague Principles.[59] In the absence of choice, the contract shall be governed by the law of the state of the place of performance of the obligation in question according to Article 2652.

Panama

In Panama the law applicable to international contracts is that chosen by the parties. The new 2014 codification[60] also includes the possibility for parties to incorporate commercial usages and practices generally accepted according to its Article 80. If the parties have not selected the applicable law, or if their selection proves ineffective, the code provides the connecting factor of the law of the state of the place of performance to govern the contract.[61]

Article 79 of the 2014 Panamanian code is very interesting as it explicitly

[55] Despite Argentina's and Uruguay's contradictory positions on the topic. See Noodt Taquela, M. B. (2017) 'Contratos comerciales internacionales: cuestiones que plantean', *Revista de Derecho Privado y Comunitario*, 3-2017, 461–94.

[56] Fernández Arroyo, 'Main Characteristics of the New Private International Law of the Argentinian Republic', above fn. 14, 147 and its footnote 49.

[57] Ibid., 148.

[58] The 2016 UNIDROIT Principles of International Commercial Contracts version is available on the UNIDROIT official website at: www.unidroit.org/instruments/commercial-contracts/unidroit-principles-2016

[59] Uzal, M. E. (2016) 'Los contratos internacionales en la Argentina', in Fernández Arroyo, D. P. and J. A. Moreno Rodríguez (eds), *Contratos internacionales*, ASADIP-OEA, 307–34, especially 322.

[60] Panama: *Código de Derecho internacional privado de la República de Panamá*, 7 October 2015.

[61] Ibid.

mentions the UNIDROIT Principles of International Commercial Contracts. This soft law instrument can be chosen by the parties to govern the international contract as an expression of the more general principle of party autonomy, yet it can also be used as a subsidiary law to the chosen law, or to the applicable law signalled by the conflict of laws rules, and as a means for the judges or arbitrators for interpreting and supplementing the applicable law.[62]

Uruguay

Even Uruguay, one of the most reluctant countries in Latin America with regard to party autonomy, has included in its 2016 Private International Law Draft Act the possibility for parties to choose the applicable law for an international contract, allowing even *dépeçage*. In case of absence of choice by the parties the contract shall be governed by the law of the state of the place of performance of the obligation in question.[63]

The Rise of the Principle of the Closest Connection?

In 1994, in Mexico City, several Latin American countries signed the Inter-American Convention on the Law Applicable to International Contracts.[64] This treaty recognised party autonomy as playing an essential role with respect to replacing the outdated conceptions of the Montevideo Treaties and the 1928 Bustamante Code. Yet, this Inter-American Convention has apparently had very little impact in the region because it entered into force in only two states.[65]

Nevertheless, it is considered to be an important reflection of the developments in the field, including the introduction in Article 9 of the flexible connecting factor of the closest connection, in the absence of choice by the parties.

The Latin American pioneer in this sphere was the 1998 Venezuelan Private International Law Act.[66] This national enactment adopted the ideas of the 1994 Inter-American Convention and the 1980 Rome Convention[67] introducing in its Article 30

[62] See Boutin, G. (2016) 'El régimen jurídico de los contratos en el nuevo Código de Derecho internacional privado panameño', in Fernández Arroyo, D. P. and J. A. Moreno Rodríguez (eds), *Contratos internacionales*, ASADIP-OEA, 203–34, especially 218.

[63] Uruguay. Proyecto de Ley General de Derecho internacional privado. Available online: https://legislativo.parlamento.gub.uy/temporales/4070629.PDF

[64] Inter-American Convention on the Law Applicable to International Contracts, signed in Mexico City on 17 March 1994, at the Fifth Inter-American Specialized Conference on Private International Law (CIDIP-V). In force only between Mexico and Venezuela since 15 December 1996.

[65] Mexico and Venezuela. The text of the treaty is available at: www.oas.org/juridico/english/treaties/b-56.html

[66] Venezuela. *Ley de Derecho internacional privado*. Official Gazette No. 36.511 of 6 August 1998.

[67] Convention on the Law Applicable to Contractual Obligations, signed in Rome on 19 June 1980; it entered into force on 1 April 1991, later replaced by the Regulation (EC) No, 593/2008 of the European Parliament and of the Council of 17 June 2008 on the Law Applicable to Contractual Obligations (Rome I), which entered into force on 17 December 2009.

the closest connection as a connecting factor for the ascertainment of applicable law to international contracts in the absence of choice by the parties.[68]

This is also the case in the Dominican Republic where international contracts as provided for in its 2014 Private International Law Act[69] are to be governed by the law chosen by the parties and in the absence of choice Article 60 and 61 follow the solutions of the 1994 Inter-American Convention and provide for the closest connection principle. To establish the closest connection judges must consider all the objective and subjective elements of the contract to ascertain the law of the state with which the contract has the closest ties.

Argentina's approach towards the closest connection in international contracts is a highly exceptional one: Article 2653 of the Civil and Commercial Code establishes that in contractual matters courts will have the prerogative to correct the applicable law to international contracts when it is incompatible with the reality of the case but only upon the request of the party.[70]

Argentine legislators preferred the traditional solution of 'place of performance' regulated in Article 2652 when there is no party autonomy and ruled the concept of place of performance with a complex set of definitions and 'characterisations'.[71]

This means that 'closest connection' is relegated to third rank after party autonomy and the subsidiary rule of place of performance. Therefore, judges will only use the closest connection solution upon party request when the connecting factor of 'place of performance' indicates the law of a country with no or little connection with the case.

This rule clashes with the general provision of Article 2597 that allows judges to apply the law with the closest connection to the cases for all other private international law categories – *ex officio* – where party request is not necessary.[72]

[68] Venezuela. *Ley de Derecho internacional privado*, above fn. 66.

[69] *Ley No. 544-14 de Derecho internacional privado de la República Dominicana*, 15 October 2014. See above fn. 4.

[70] Art. 2653. 'Exceptionally on request by a party, and having regard to all the objective and subjective elements which can be inferred from the contract, the judge is authorized to decide on the application of the law of the state with which the legal relation has the closest connection'.

[71] Art. 2652. 'Determination of the law applicable absent choice by the parties. Absent choice by the parties on the applicable law, the contract is governed by the laws and usages of the state of the place of performance. If it is not designated or it cannot be inferred from the nature of the relation, the current domicile of the debtor of the most characteristic performance of the contract is deemed to be the place of performance. In the event that the place of performance cannot be determined, the contract is governed by the laws and usages of the state of the place where it was concluded. The conclusion of contracts between distant parties is governed by the law of the place from which the accepted offer is made'.

[72] There is a clash because there is a dual approach to the closest connection upon party request rule (international contracts) and the other rule where the request is not necessary. See Fernández Arroyo, 'Main Characteristics of the New Private International Law of the Argentinian Republic', above fn. 14, 143–4 where the author criticises this 'dual' approach. Article 2597: 'Exception clause. Exceptionally, the law designated by a conflict of laws rule must not be applied when, having regard

Paraguayan Revolution

The most revolutionary of the recent Latin American codifications of private international law regarding international contracts is the Paraguayan Law on the Applicable Law to International Contracts enacted in 2015.[73] Its revolutionary aspect lies in its main source: the Hague Principles on Choice of Law in International Commercial Contracts which, paradoxically, was approved some months later than the Paraguayan Act.[74]

Among many solutions found in the new Act following the Hague Principles is Article 4.4 which reproduces Article 2.4 of the Hague Principles and prescribes that no connection is required between the law chosen and the parties or their transaction.[75] Another milestone in Paraguay's new internal dimension is Article 5 that states – following the Hague Principles – that a reference to law includes 'rules of law' of a non-state origin that are generally accepted as a neutral and balanced set of rules. One of the questions that remains unanswered in practice is which sets of rules are 'neutral' or 'balanced' and which are not.[76]

Which Private International Law for Latin America?

At the end of this journey we must analyse in which direction the recent private international law codification in Latin American countries is evolving and if these newer solutions meet twenty-first-century needs with regard to cross-border relationships.

The decisive upsurge of human rights principles in private international law conventions and national private international law frameworks puts the protection of individuals at the top of the hierarchy and establishes the protection of individuals as its main focus. This postmodern approach seems to respond to the needs of the

to the factual circumstances of the case, it is manifest that the situation has connections of little relevance to that law, but has manifestly close connections to the law of another state, whose application is foreseeable and under whose rules the relation has been validly created. This provision is not applicable when the parties have chosen the law applicable to the case'.

73 Paraguay. *Ley 5393 sobre el derecho aplicable a los contratos internacionales.*

74 Hague Conference on Private International Law. *Principles on Choice of Law in International Commercial Contracts.* Available at: https://assets.hcch.net/docs/5da3ed47-f54d-4c43-aaef-5eafc-7c1f2a1.pdf

75 For example, the USA in its Restatement (Second) of Conflict of Laws, Art. 187(2)(a), 59. However, the current trend is seemingly moving towards the abandonment of any requirement for specific connections. For further information on the Paraguayan Law, see Moreno Rodríguez, J. A. (2016) 'The New Paraguayan Law on International Contracts: Back to the Past?', in UNIDROIT (ed.), *Eppur si muove: The Age of Uniform Law Essays in Honour of Michael Joachim Bonell to Celebrate his 70th Birthday*, vol. 2 Rome: UNIDROIT 1146–78.

76 See Michaels, R. (2016) 'Non-State Law in The Hague Principles on Choice of Law in International Commercial Contracts', in Fernández Arroyo, D. P. and J. A. Moreno Rodríguez (eds), *Contratos internacionales*, ASADIP-OEA, 153–86, where he criticises this concept. For a viewpoint in favour, see Moreno Rodríguez, ibid., 1164–6.

people engaged in cross-border relationships. The mobilisation of citizens of the world carries across the globe different identities, cultures and traditions, all in need of converging in a single multidimensional legal order.

Any solutions to this must therefore start with the first pillar of private international law, that of international jurisdiction. Access to justice must prevail over the previous paradigm of a complex set of hard rules and provide for international competence with reasonability as the main criterion in accordance with the needs of the parties engaged in international trade, belonging to an international family or seeking the protection of children. Cross-border jurisdiction, in turn, must relate to the extraterritorial effect of decisions and requests to guarantee parties concrete access to justice. The needs of individuals and global citizens must be fulfilled effectively and precisely, and this is the place for international judicial cooperation.

As shown in this chapter some changes in the national private international law regulations (the internal dimension of private international law) in Argentina and Brazil have improved their overall approach and their efforts are providing much better access to justice for individuals in cases where there are no international treaties applicable. It is argued, however, that these codifications missed the chance to go further since they did not specifically incorporate provisions to the effect of maximising the use of new technologies to accelerate foreign cooperation requests.

More positive changes we unravelled in the law are applicable to international contracts incorporating party autonomy and giving freedom of choice to the parties to regulate their own contracts. In addition, flexible connections in the absence of choice are a novelty in Latin American countries with Paraguay's striking move to incorporate the Hague Principles and the closest connection to the contract to avoid the application of a law with little connection with the case.

Overall, in the new codifications analysed in this chapter different approaches are adopted in order to answer the questions and meet the requirements of the highly complex global society that exists at the end of the second decade of the twenty-first century, and the role of individuals at the centre of this normativity. Some countries used soft law, privatising private international law and branching out to incorporate other actors of global governance. Others are trying to open up their own laws and to conquer their fears about party autonomy. Perhaps the key for Latin America is to keep the momentum going in reforming private international law as a means to continue to show the world the cosmopolitanism that has traditionally characterised the great Latin American private international law schools of thought.

16

The Challenges of the New Social and Scientific Realities in Private International Family Law – The Latin American Experience

Nieve Rubaja and María Mercedes Albornoz

Introduction

Private international family law is being challenged by the impact of the social changes that have recently taken place. Nowadays, this impact is shaped by increasing globalisation, new types of families and, especially, by technological and biomedical developments. National legislatures have been slowly updating their substantive law provisions to encompass these new scenarios. Profound differences between these developments can be observed, principally because of their diverse conceptions of family, a reflection of the particular idiosyncracies and values of each society. This legal diversity is a fact in Latin American countries. Existing private international law methodologies and techniques are insufficient to face these new challenges, both at national and international level. Some Latin American countries have developed new national private international law provisions for this purpose or are planning to do so. Although global consensus is arguably the best solution, the feasibility of new international instruments is a perennial challenge of the discipline. While widely recognised human rights standards are an important stepping-stone towards this goal, the international public policy exception tends to function as a barrier to foreign solutions in this sphere; nevertheless, its scope to accept developments in social realities is essentially variable and evolving.[1]

In this chapter, we describe some difficulties that arise from these new scenarios as well as the possibilities and challenges that the most relevant multilateral legal instruments currently in force in Latin American countries face in this field. We then explore the current work of the international community in order to achieve international protection of families and, in particular, of the rights of children.

[1] For the role of the public policy exception see the chapter by de Aguirre in this volume.

The Impact of Changing Social Realities

Over recent decades, it has become evident that there is not one unique type of family; on the contrary, the variations in the conceptions of families have widened this legal category. Today, from a legal perspective the concept of family includes, at least, matrimonial unions, cohabitation outside marriage – between heterosexual or homosexual partners – and single-parent families. Same-sex marriage has been accepted in some Latin American states although it is still prohibited in many others. Argentina was the first Latin American country to provide for same-sex marriage, doing so in 2010.[2] Since then, countries including Brazil,[3] Uruguay[4] and Colombia[5] have made the same provision. In December 2009, Mexico City was the first jurisdiction in the region to incorporate same-sex unions into its legislation.[6] Mexico's constitution does not prohibit same-sex marriage but most Mexican states do not allow it.[7] Yet, according to the jurisprudence of the Mexican Supreme Court of Justice, any law that stipulates procreation as the purpose of marriage, or that describes marriage as the union between a man and a woman, is unconstitutional.[8] Furthermore, some states recognise legal effects to civil partnerships;[9] some, however, only admit heterosexual unions.[10] As in many other fields of law this is an example of legal diversity in a sphere that requires the methodologies and techniques of private international law to guarantee the cross-border continuity of legal relations despite these differences in substantive domestic laws.

[2] Law 26.618 of 15 July 2010.

[3] The Supreme Federal Court recognised families of same-sex couples for the first time in 2011. The National Council of Justice, in Resolution No. 175 of 14 May 2013, stated that same-sex marriages were equal to heterosexual ones.

[4] Law 18.246 of 10 January 2008.

[5] In 2011, the Constitutional Court admitted these unions for the first time; in 2016 the same Court in a plenary session stated that it was in favour of same-sex marriage; since then same-sex marriages have been allowed.

[6] Civil Code for the Federal District, reform of 21 December 2009.

[7] Only thirteen out of thirty-two Mexican states recognise same-sex marriage. See Salinas Hernández, H. M. (2017) 'Matrimonio igualitario en México: la pugna por el Estado laico y la igualdad de derechos', *Cotidiano - Revista De La Realidad Mexicana*, vol. 32, no. 202.

[8] Mexico's Supreme Court of Justice, Thesis: 1a/J. 43/2015 (10a), *Gaceta del Semanario Judicial de la Federación*, 19, June 2015, vol. I, 536.

[9] For example, Art. 91 of Law 1/92 of 15 July 1992 in Paraguay. See further HCCH (2015) 'Private International Law Issues Relating to Cohabitation Outside Marriage (Including Registered Partnerships)' questionnaire (e).

[10] Peru (Law 30007/2013 of 17 April 2013, and Art. 5 of the Constitution); Honduras (Art. 112 of the Constitution); Nicaragua (Art. 72 of the Constitution); El Salvador (Art. 33 of the Constitution) and Venezuela (Art. 77 of the Constitution).

The Latin American Legal Landscape

Argentina. Civil partnerships are regulated in the 2014 Civil and Commercial Code[11] (CCC), enabling partners to conclude financial agreements and adopt children, as well as to have access to assisted reproductive techniques (ART). Registration of civil partnerships is not a requirement for their recognition. The Title on Private International Law in the CCC includes specific provisions for civil partnerships for any kind of claim (except for maintenance, for which there are special provisions in Articles 2629 and 2630). Article 2627 provides for jurisdiction of the place where the partnership has its effective common domicile, or where the defendant has his or her domicile or habitual residence, and Article 2628 provides for the applicable law to be that of the place where the partnership produces its effects.

Chile. Civil partnerships are regulated by means of Law 20830 of 2015, which provides the possibility for partners to choose a community property regime and grants them inheritance rights. Chilean law also includes a title for civil partnerships entered into abroad. It states that those partnerships must be recognised in Chile, provided they follow the requirements of Chilean law. Same-sex marriages celebrated abroad will be considered as civil partnerships.

Mexico. There is no uniformity across the country; the states of Mexico City and Coahuila both accept same-sex and heterosexual civil unions.

Uruguay. Civil partnerships have been provided for since 2007,[12] and same-sex marriage since 2013.[13]

Ecuador. Since 2015, the civil code has regulated both same-sex and heterosexual unions, stating that they are equal to marriage.

Panama. Provisions to this effect are currently included in the Constitution. Article 58 states that unions between same-sex couples with the legal capacity to get married that have lasted five years or longer, and are monogamous and stable, have all the effects of civil marriage.

Guatemala. The Constitution does not distinguish between heterosexual and homosexual unions.

Brazil. The Supreme Federal Court recognised same-sex couples' families for the first time in 2011. Several Latin American countries do not recognise civil partnerships nor do they provide for same-sex couples to have the right to marry. In many of these countries there is a constitutional provision to that effect.[14]

In this complex scenario, the scope for party autonomy has also been diverse in the family law sphere in Latin American countries. Some legal systems admit party

[11] Civil and Commercial Code, Law 26.994 of 1 October 2014.

[12] Law 18.246 of 27 December 2007.

[13] Law 19.075 of 10 April 2013.

[14] Paraguay (Art. 51 of the Constitution); Peru (Law 30007/2013 and Art. 5 of the Constitution); Honduras (Art. 112 of the Constitution); Nicaragua (Art. 72 of the Constitution); El Salvador (Art. 33 of the Constitution) and Venezuela (Art. 77 of the Constitution).

autonomy but with some limitations based on a certain degree of state intervention in order to protect certain values, such as familial solidarity (as reflected, for instance, in the protection of the family home). The possibilities of agreeing on family issues regarding children, including cross-border relocation, and choosing a matrimonial property regime or financial arrangements for non-marital unions, are increasingly within the realm of party autonomy. In this context, new challenges have appeared in addition to those perennial problems that private international law is used to facing. Those challenges include recognition of effects to same-sex marriages celebrated abroad or to same-sex or different-sex unions in other states – registered or not; adoption or recognition of adoptions established in other countries for these modern family structures; access to ART; agreement on family issues (like relocation, maintenance, visitation) and their enforcement abroad.

The Impact of Human Rights and the Doctrine of the Inter-American Court of Human Rights

For an in-depth analysis of the Latin American legal reality it is essential to examine the impact of human rights and the doctrine of the Inter-American Court of Human Rights (ICHR). In the case of *Atala Riffo* v. *Chile*[15] the ICHR considered for the first time the sexual orientation of parents as a variable in order to analyse the principle of the best interest of the child. The case concerned the custody rights of three girls who had been born within a heterosexual marriage; after divorcing the father of the children, the mother began a stable relationship with another woman. The ICHR stated that the sexual orientation of a person is part of his or her privacy and it cannot determine the person's aptitude as a parent. To do the opposite would have meant making unfounded assumptions and stereotypes on the capability and suitability of a parent, which is not an appropriate way to guarantee and promote the welfare and development of the child in line with his or her best interests. The Court concluded that the sexual orientation of a person is not a valid argument for rejecting a right; on the contrary, pursuant to Article 1.1 of the American Convention on Human Rights, discrimination in general is forbidden, including in categories such as sexual orientation.[16] Furthermore, in *Fornerón* v. *Argentina*[17] the ICHR decided that single-parent families must be considered as any other family in which children are cared for and in which they are able to grow up and be nurtured. The Court stated that the day-to-day reality of life confirms that there is not necessarily a maternal or a paternal figure in

[15] Case of *Atala Riffo and daughters* v. *Chile*. Judgment of 24 February 2012. Series C No. 239.

[16] See also *Ángel Alberto Duque* v. *Colombia* (ICHR, 2/4/2014), in which Colombia's denial to the right of pension of Ángel Duque, who had been in a homosexual partnership, was evaluated. The Court held (by four votes to two) that Colombia had violated the petitioner's right to equality and non-discrimination as provided for in the American Convention on Human Rights. See judgment of 26 February 2016, para. 62.

[17] Case of *Fornerón and daughter* v. *Argentina*. Judgment of 27 April 2012. Series C No. 242.

every family, and that does not imply any obstacle in the way of the family being able to offer the necessary well-being for the development of their child.

Undoubtedly, states must give the same protection to all types of families, and domestic regulations are gradually including provisions to that effect. The diversity of legal systems in this field at national level lead to special difficulties when cases have links with more than one state. Private international law should serve the purpose of protecting human rights while managing these differences. The following sections in this chapter examine the lawscape in Latin America in order to reach this goal in the current scenario and explore the new solutions that are being developed in global fora.

The Impact of New Technologies

Two aspects of new technologies have an impact on private international family law: (1) information and communication technologies (ICT), which in turn enhance international cooperation, and (2) biomedical developments both bring about new challenges in this field.

International Cooperation

When it comes to international cooperation, ICT is a valuable tool to improve and facilitate direct contact between the authorities of different countries and it also allows instant information sharing. Information regarding, for example, who is the authority that should take part in a certain procedure, the content of the applicable law and how that law has been applied by courts can all be made available in cyberspace. General or specific government networks are established by international agreements. Depending on the needs of each network, ICT allows the creation of secure channels to guarantee the secrecy of communications. The existence of secure ways to transfer sensitive data is necessary when the connected authorities are dealing with confidential and sensitive matters. There are different international and domestic sources of law that provide for the recourse to ICT to facilitate international cooperation in family law cases. Additionally, ICT tools are more often used in judicial proceedings, facilitating cooperation and helping to guarantee the rights of children.

Judicial Networks

In Latin America valuable efforts have been made in order to create networks of judges[18] and other authorities specialised in international family law proceedings, incorporating the use of ICT. Moreover, several countries in the region actively participate in universal networks. Three networks in which different Latin American countries interact are worth mentioning:

[18] An already consolidated and successful experience in the field of international cooperation is the European Judicial Network in Civil and Commercial Matters. This network, which encompasses family law, has operated since 2002. For more on the work of these networks, see van Loon and Goicoechea's and Wisdahl's chapters in this volume.

The network of hemispheric legal cooperation in the area of family and child law

The Organization of American States (OAS) was instructed[19] to create an Inter-American project on legal cooperation and mutual assistance in this field. The network was created as a concrete measure to strengthen legal and judicial cooperation in the region, with an emphasis on the rights of children. The OAS supported the initial activities of the network by uploading information to the website. It was also looking forward to activating a secure electronic communication system, which was crucial for the operability of the network. Unfortunately, the essential financial support for setting it up was, in the end, not provided by the OAS.

Ibero-American network for international legal cooperation (Red Iberoamericana de Cooperación Jurídica Internacional: IberRed)

This network was created in 2004 with the aim not only of optimising legal cooperation in civil as well as criminal matters, but also of establishing and maintaining a database on the different legal systems of the countries of the Ibero-American community.[20] Article 9 of the IberRed Regulation provides that the contact points of the network will use the most appropriate technical means to respond promptly and effectively to all requests submitted to them. Moreover, the network has shown interest in offering online courses and in developing other virtual products that might improve the management skills of the judicial sector.

The International Hague Network of Judges

This network[21] was created in 1998 as part of the umbrella of the Hague Conference on Private International Law (HCCH)[22] and seeks to improve international cooperation through communications of a general nature as well as direct judicial communications with regard to specific cases.[23] Judges must use the most appropriate technological

[19] Eighth Meeting of Ministers of Justice or Other Ministers or Attorneys General of the Americas (REMJA-VIII, Brasilia, 2010).

[20] Argentina, Bolivia, Brazil, Chile, Colombia, Costa Rica, Cuba, Dominican Republic, Ecuador, El Salvador, Guatemala, Honduras, Mexico, Nicaragua, Panama, Paraguay, Peru, Uruguay and Venezuela are members of this network.

[21] Judges from Argentina, Barbados, Belize, Brazil, Chile, Colombia, Costa Rica, Dominican Republic, Ecuador, El Salvador, Guatemala, Guyana, Honduras, Mexico, Nicaragua, Panama, Paraguay, Peru, Saint Kitts and Nevis, Uruguay and Venezuela (as well as other Caribbean countries) are members of this network.

[22] Electronic resources available via the HCCH website (at www.hcch.net) include INCADAT, the Judges' Newsletter on International Child Protection, guides to best practice, information on the application of Hague instruments, ongoing projects, iSupport, etc.

[23] HCCH (2013) 'Direct Judicial Communications Emerging Guidance Regarding the Development of the International Hague Network of Judges and General Principles for Judicial Communications, Including Commonly Accepted Safeguards for Direct Judicial Communications in Specific Cases, Within the Context of the International Hague Network of Judges', available at: www.hcch.net

facilities and, in the case of oral communication, telephone or videoconferencing may be used in order to communicate as efficiently as possible.

Regional and domestic provisions of ICT: hard and soft law

ICT offers a valuable set of tools to facilitate international direct judicial communications. Some steps have been taken nationally and internationally to promote and improve these practices, and to give them a basis in legislation. The Ibero-American Convention on the use of videoconferencing in international cooperation among justice systems, signed in Mar del Plata in December 2010, and in force since 2014, provides specific rules aimed at encouraging and regulating the adequate use of videoconferencing in civil, commercial and criminal proceedings where international cooperation is needed. An Additional Protocol on costs, language and procedures for sending requests complements those rules.[24] Argentina, Costa Rica, Dominican Republic, Ecuador, Mexico and Spain are States Parties to both instruments, while Panama is only a Party to the Convention. Moreover, the Ibero-American Judicial Summit adopted an Ibero-American Protocol on International Judicial Cooperation[25] with an Annex on International Child Abduction.[26] Both contain recommendations on the use of new technologies to improve international cooperation. Furthermore, in November 2016, the American Association of Private International Law (ASADIP) approved the ASADIP Principles on Transnational Access to Justice (TRANSJUS).[27] This soft law instrument favours the use of new ICT.

In the domestic realm the use of ICT is also promoted and encouraged. For example, when the situation requires it, Argentine judges are empowered to establish direct communications with foreign judges if due process and security guarantees are respected.[28] Another example is the Mexican Network of Judicial Cooperation for the Protection of Children.[29] It was created in 2010, intending to articulate common objectives between the country's different Superior Tribunals of Justice in order to improve the delivery of justice and the effective protection of children's rights. Its bylaw[30] provides that members shall support the judges of the International Hague Network of Judges and contact points of IberRed; they shall act as active intermedi-

[24] Mar del Plata, 3 December 2010.

[25] Santiago de Chile, 2014.

[26] Protocolo Iberoamericano de Cooperación Judicial Internacional, adopted on 4 April 2014 by the Presidents of the Supreme Courts and the Councils of the Judiciary of the twenty-three states that constitute the Ibero-American Judicial Summit (Andorra, Argentina, Bolivia, Brazil, Chile, Colombia, Costa Rica, Cuba, Dominican Republic, Ecuador, El Salvador, Guatemala, Honduras, Mexico, Nicaragua, Panama, Paraguay, Peru, Portugal, Puerto Rico, Spain, Uruguay and Venezuela).

[27] Principios ASADIP sobre el Acceso Transnacional a la Justicia (TRANSJUS), of 12 November 2016.

[28] Art. 2612, CCC.

[29] Red Mexicana de Cooperación Judicial para la Protección de la Niñez, created on 15 January 2010.

[30] Bylaw of the Red Mexicana de Cooperación Judicial para la Protección de la Niñez of 15 January 2010.

aries to facilitate international judicial cooperation oriented to the protection of the children with the greatest possible flexibility and speed.

Judicial decision-making

In *PROD* v. *DDMV*,[31] a case concerning Panama and Venezuela, a mother who had abducted her child argued that she had left Venezuela with the child because they were victims of domestic violence by the father. Nevertheless, when analysing the suitability of the child's return from Panama to his country of habitual residence, such allegations were dismissed, based on the analysis of several Skype calls held during the proceedings, which were proof of the good communication between the child and his father. The fast evolution of ICT means that judges must make good use of technology while handling cases (direct communications, for example), and must take into consideration in their decision-making information obtained through ICT.

In another reported case,[32] a mother domiciled in Panama requested access to her child, who lived in the United Kingdom with his father. Among the conditions established by the UK authority were that the mother was not allowed 'to make any video or sound recordings of the child which sought to transmit his future wishes and the parents' relationship or use any of such recordings in any custody-related proceedings'.

ICT can undoubtedly be very helpful during proceedings and at the time of issuing judicial decisions; the limits to this consideration should be reduced to the exceptional cases in which public policy is violated. ICT could also be a way to facilitate or enforce rights of access when one of the parents and the child live in different countries, provided that, in the concrete case, this corresponds to the best interests of the child.

Biomedical Developments

Just as in the field of international cooperation, technology has also an important impact on biomedical developments, such as those that allow for ART. In the last few decades ART has become globally available.[33] Experts agree that Latin America is still lagging behind in biomedical developments, and that it needs to start generating its own knowledge specific to the region and to increase its contribution to the global research community.[34] Yet, Latin America is also diverse in this sphere. Many different cultural and sociological influences converge in this region. In this sense,

[31] HC/E/PA 1341, Panama, tribunal of first instance, 10 September 2014.

[32] Panama, Juzgado Segundo de Niñez y Adolescencia (tribunal of first instance), ruling No. 393-05-F, HC/E/PA 872, 5 July 2005.

[33] Inhom, M. C. and P. Patrizio (2015) 'Infertility Around the Globe: New Thinking on Gender, Reproductive Technologies and Global Movements in the 21st Century' *Human Reproduction*, vol. 21, no. 4.

[34] Benedetti, V., G. Echeverria and I. Riquelme (2016) 'Biomedical Research in Latin America: We Can Do More' *The Lancet*, vol. 387, no. 10022, e22.

the prevalence of Catholicism has had an important impact on reproductive issues.[35] In addition, ART treatments tend to be very expensive, and legislation on ART procedures differs widely from country to country.

The legal landscape

In *Artavia Murillo y otros* v. *Costa Rica*[36] the ICHR had to analyse if the declaration of unconstitutionality by the Constitutional Chamber of the Supreme Court of Costa Rica, of the Executive Decree 24029-S-1995, which regulated access to ART in that country, and that in practice had been implying a prohibition of these techniques, violated fundamental human rights. The ICHR concluded that the rights to private and family life and to personal integrity in relation to personal autonomy; to choose to have biological children through ART; to sexual health; to enjoy the benefits of scientific and technological progress; and to non-discrimination provided for in the Inter-American Convention of Human Rights[37] had been violated. The ICHR also concluded that, among the obligations imposed on Costa Rica, appropriate measures had to be taken to render ineffective the prohibition of ART and to include the availability of ART within its healthcare programmes and infertility treatments, in accordance with the duty of guaranteeing the non-discrimination principle.[38] In other countries, for example in Argentina, the availability of these techniques is provided for,[39] guaranteeing comprehensive access to ART for heterosexual and homosexual couples and for single women; in addition, the CCC included ART as a new source of filiation, both in domestic and private international law provisions.[40]

The Latin American Registry of Assisted Reproduction was established in 1990 and, a few years later, was incorporated into the larger framework of the Latin American Network of Assisted Reproduction.[41] This network has been taking advantage of ICT by facilitating access to data from every participating centre. Moreover, new software was developed and implemented, which allows the gathering of individualised case-by-case data and information from every treatment cycle.[42]

[35] Luna, F. (2001) 'Assisted Reproductive Technology in Latin America: some Ethical and Sociocultural Issues', in Vayena, E. et al. (eds), *Current Practices and Controversies in Assisted Reproduction*, World Health Organization, 31.

[36] ICHR, 28 November 2012.

[37] Arts 5.1, 7, 11.2 and 17.2, in relation to Art. 1.1 of the ICHR.

[38] The ICHR supervised the enforcement of the decision but found that Costa Rica did not comply with it (Acc. Resolution of the ICHR, 26February 2016).

[39] Law 26.862 of 5 June 2013.

[40] Arts 558, 2631 and 2634 of the Civil and Commercial Code 2014.

[41] The Red Latinoamericana de Reproducción Asistida was created in 1995. At present, it is made up of 195 centres that offer ART in different Latin American countries.

[42] Zegers-Hochschild, F., J. E. Schwarze, J. A. Crosby, C. Musri, M. do Carmo and B. de Souza (2014) 'Assisted Reproductive Technologies (ART) in Latin America: The Latin American Registry, 2012' *JBRA Assisted Reproduction*, vol. 18, no. 4.

Surrogacy

An interesting development that has become possible thanks to the evolution of ART is surrogate gestation. International surrogate arrangements (ISAs) are contracts concluded between intending parents domiciled in one country and a woman domiciled in another, who will carry a baby with whom she may or may not have a genetic link; after the birth, the child is to be considered the son or daughter of the intending parents. Surrogacy is legal only in a few Latin American countries; it is permitted in the Mexican states of Tabasco and Sinaloa, but foreigners no longer have access to it. The state of Tabasco witnessed complicated outgoing cases, which led to a modification of the legislation to require that all parties to the surrogacy arrangement must be Mexican.[43] Latin America also witnesses incoming cases concerning children born through ISAs abroad. Outgoing and incoming ISA cases pose specific challenges to private international law.

Relevant Multilateral Legal Instruments in Force in Latin American Countries

The aim of this section is to provide an overview of international instruments in force in Latin America by reviewing their status and some of their provisions, partly in order to consider the challenges posed by these new scenarios. Each instrument should be analysed in terms of its scope and adaptability to the new social realities, in particular the modern family structures (such as civil partnerships and same-sex marriages) discussed in the first section of this chapter. The analysis also focuses on observing the protection of human rights, especially the best interest of the child, when relevant. Undoubtedly, the scope of the public policy exception has a crucial role in this regard, as do conflict solutions if they lead to an applicable law with a restrictive position on modern family structures. Besides, in all the instruments based on cooperation schemes, or those that provide cooperation mechanisms (such as the designation of Central Authorities), the use of ICT implies an improvement in the expeditiousness and the quality of cooperation.

United Nations Maintenance Convention – New York 1956[44]

This is the convention mainly relied upon for cross-border maintenance issues in Latin America because it is the instrument that provides answers to most of the

[43] Art. 380 Bis 5, incorporated into the Civil Code of Tabasco on 13 January 2016. It is nevertheless considered that the best way to avoid the country being perceived as a 'surrogacy paradise' would be to choose domicile or residence instead of nationality as a factor to restrict access to this practice in Tabasco. Albornoz, M. M. and F. López (2017) 'Marco normativo de la gestación por sustitución en México: desafíos internos y externos', *Ius*, vol. 11, no. 39, 179.

[44] Convention on the Recovery Abroad of Maintenance, New York, 20 June 1956; entry into force 25 May 1957. The Convention is currently in force in sixty-four countries, ten of which are in Latin America: Argentina, Brazil, Chile, Colombia, Ecuador, Guatemala, Haiti, Mexico, Suriname and Uruguay, status as at 15 November 2018.

maintenance cases in the region. It has been highly efficient in its application, especially in providing legal assistance to creditors. However, some difficulties that mar its effectiveness have been identified, the most significant of these being unavoidable expenses, such as the translation and legalisation of documents, and international transfer fees.[45] Mechanisms provided for in this instrument are mainly of an administrative nature; lack of jurisdictional and applicable law rules has been criticised.[46]

Montevideo Treaties

Two instruments regarding family law issues are worth mentioning: the 1889 Montevideo Treaty of Civil International Law, in force between Argentina, Bolivia, Colombia, Paraguay, Peru and Uruguay; and the 1940 Montevideo Treaty of Civil International Law, in force between Argentina, Paraguay and Uruguay.[47] Their scope of application covers marriage (validity, recognition, personal and property effects and divorce), maintenance,[48] parental responsibility and parentage, and the 1940 Treaty also includes adoption.[49] They include jurisdictional provisions and applicable law rules; the former based on *forum causae* and forum of the defendant, with the possibility of choice of courts agreements only for property issues and *post litem natam* (Article 56); the latter generally by means of conflict of law rules. Furthermore, recognition and enforcement of judicial decisions are regulated in the Montevideo Treaties on Civil Procedure of 1889 and 1940. These instruments had an impact in all the national private international law provisions of the States Parties. It is remarkable that consensus was reached in such a sensitive field of law at that time. However, the scenarios unfolded by modern family structures and the recent biomedical developments mentioned above, as well as the new framework imposed by human rights standards, are beyond the scope of application of the mechanisms provided for in the Montevideo Treaties.

Bustamante Code[50]

This was drafted during the 6th Pan-American Congress that took place in Havana, Cuba, in 1928. It regulates marriage and divorce, parentage, maintenance, parental responsibility and adoption, among other categories of private international law.

45 Rubaja, N. (2014) 'Argentina's Regulation of Maintenance Obligations: Implementation of the 2007 Hague Convention', in Beaumont, P., B. Hess, L. Walker and S. Spancken (eds), *Recovery of Maintenance in the EU and Worldwide*, Hart Publishing.

46 Ibid.

47 All the Member States to the Montevideo Treaties are parties to the Inter-American Conventions; thus, in those areas in which the latter include special provisions they shall prevail.

48 The Treaties only offer tangential solutions on maintenance.

49 Arts 23 and 24 regulate conditions and effects in international adoptions. The Treaty requires that the laws of both the adopter's and the adoptee's domicile apply in each case; thus, even though this would imply a higher protection, these provisions have not been applied.

50 This Code is in force between Bolivia, Brazil, Costa Rica, Cuba, Chile, Ecuador, El Salvador, Guatemala, Haiti, Honduras, Nicaragua, Panama, Peru, Dominican Republic and Venezuela.

In general terms, the code provides rules on applicable law, with a preference for personal law, especially regarding the impossibility, at that time, of defining this law by domicile or nationality (Article 7 leaves this decision to domestic laws). In the recognition of situations originating abroad the code aims to coordinate cross-border legal diversity in sensitive subject matters (for example, a marriage that is valid in accordance with the law of the place where it was celebrated will be valid in the other States Parties). In some areas, the code introduced innovations appropriate for the time in which it was developed. However, this instrument contains some provisions that are nowadays unacceptable with regard to fundamental gender equality rights (for example, if the laws of both spouses differ, the husband's law will prevail for determining the right to protection and the duty to obey, and the wife's obligation to follow the husband if he changes residence, as well as for determining the patrimonial aspects of marriage (Article 43)). Recourse to the public policy exception is widespread throughout the instrument, probably as a result of the compromise needed to reach consensus on the final text.[51]

CIDIPs[52]

Inter-American Convention on Conflict of Laws Concerning the Adoption of Minors[53]

Adopted in CIDIP III, held in La Paz, Bolivia, in 1984, this binding instrument contains not only applicable law rules, but also rules to ascertain jurisdiction. The Convention provides that the authorities of a State Party may refuse to apply the law declared applicable under this convention when that law is 'manifestly contrary' to their public policy (Article 18). Such an exception could be invoked if the adopters are single, a same-sex couple or in a civil partnership and the law of domicile considers them capable to adopt but the law of the country of habitual residence of the minor denies them the right to do so. Nevertheless, in practice, this Inter-American convention is rarely used.

Inter-American Convention on the International Return of Children[54]

Adopted in CIDIP-IV, held in Montevideo, Uruguay, in 1989, in overall terms the objectives, main provisions and the cooperation system through Central Authorities of

[51] Samtleben, J. (1983) *Derecho Internacional Privado en América Latina. Teoría y práctica del Código Bustamante*, Depalma.

[52] Texts of the Inter-American Conventions are available at: www.oas.org

[53] In force between Belize, Brazil, Chile, Colombia, Dominican Republic, Honduras, Mexico, Panama and Uruguay. It is worth noting that Honduras is the only State Party to this convention that is not a State Party to the 1993 Hague Convention on Protection of Children and Cooperation in Respect of Intercountry Adoption.

[54] In force between Antigua and Barbuda, Argentina, Belize, Bolivia, Brazil, Colombia, Costa Rica, Ecuador, Mexico, Nicaragua, Paraguay, Peru, Uruguay and Venezuela. Antigua and Barbuda is not a State Party to the 1980 Hague Convention on the Civil Aspects of International Child Abduction and

this instrument provided for therein are very similar to those of the Hague Convention. Despite this, the Inter-American instrument has some differences, such as the length of some of the time limits and the possibility of requesting the child's return with the competent authorities of both the requested and requesting states. Moreover, the exception to the duty to order the immediate return of the child to the country of his or her habitual residence contained in Article 25 of the Inter-American Convention is very similar to the one sought under Article 20 of the Hague Convention, but in the former, the specifications regarding human rights instruments may imply a narrower margin of interpretation. Article 20 of the Hague Convention allows the possibility to refuse the return of the child if 'this would not be permitted by the fundamental principles of the requested State relating to the protection of human rights and fundamental freedoms'; while in the Inter-American Convention, the condition is that the return would be 'manifestly in violation of the fundamental principles of the requested State recognised by universal and regional instruments on human rights or on the rights of children'. Thus, the violation must be manifestly against principles recognised in human rights instruments.[55]

Inter-American Convention on Maintenance Obligations[56]

Adopted in CIDIP-IV, held in Montevideo, Uruguay in 1989, this instrument (Article 1) seeks

> to establish the law applicable to support obligations and to jurisdiction and international procedural cooperation when the support creditor is domiciled or habitually resides in one State Party and the debtor is domiciled or habitually resides or has property or income in another State Party.

The support obligations falling within the material scope of this convention are 'child support obligations owed because of the child's minority' and 'spousal support obligations arising from the matrimonial relationship between spouses or former spouses' (Article 1). A state may declare that the Convention will also be applied to support obligations in favour of other creditors (Article 3). For instance, Colombia extended the Convention's scope to descendants, ancestors, adopted children, adoptive parents,

is not a member of the HCCH. Even though Bolivia is not a member of the HCCH, it acceded to the Hague Convention on 13 July 2016. In accordance with the Inter-American Convention, amongst the States Parties to both international instruments, the Inter-American Convention should prevail (Art. 34).

[55] The interpretation of both instruments would probably be very similar in practice. There are no reported cases in which the refusal for the return was based only on this exception. Rubaja, N. (2012) *Derecho internacional privado de la familia. Perspectiva desde el ordenamiento jurídico argentino*, La Ley, 511.

[56] In force in Argentina, Belize, Bolivia, Brazil, Colombia, Costa Rica, Ecuador, Guatemala, Mexico, Panama, Paraguay, Peru and Uruguay.

siblings, an individual who made a substantial donation and a constant partner in a common-law marital union.[57]

Pursuant to Articles 6 and 7, support obligations, the definition of support creditor and debtor, the amount of support due and the timing and conditions for payment, who may bring a support claim on behalf of the creditor, and any other condition necessary for enjoyment of the right to support, shall be governed by the law of the state of domicile or habitual residence of the creditor, or by that of the state of domicile or habitual residence of the debtor, whichever the competent authority finds the most favourable to the creditor. This result-oriented conflict of laws rule receives the *favor creditoris* principle through alternative connecting factors, from among which the authority shall choose the one that favours the creditor the most. Thus, possibilities of including modern family structures depend on each state's criterion.

Regarding jurisdiction, a series of alternative fora with several options for the creditor is provided in Article 8. Furthermore, the Convention sets a basic framework for international cooperation, focused on the recognition and enforcement of foreign support orders, which might be refused recognition only if they are manifestly incompatible with fundamental principles of public policy of the forum (Article 22). Considerations regarding civil partnerships or same-sex marriages could bring about recourse to the public policy exception; nevertheless, the best interest of the child must always be a paramount consideration in this analysis in cases where children are involved. Unfortunately, several problems have been identified regarding this Convention: the cooperation system is not so expeditious;[58] the transfer of funds entails a cost;[59] the Convention is not widely circulated, therefore it is not well-known and not frequently used by the relevant legal operators; and several States Parties have failed to designate their respective Central Authorities.[60]

Inter-American Convention on International Traffic in Minors[61]

Adopted in CIDIP-V, held in Mexico City in 1994, the goal of this instrument, 'with a view to protection of the fundamental rights of minors and their best interests, is the prevention and punishment of the international traffic in minors as well as the regulation of its civil and penal aspects'.[62] Therefore, states assume three main commitments: (1) to ensure the protection of minors in consideration of their best interests; (2) to institute a system of mutual legal assistance among them; and (3)

57 Ibid.

58 Arts 11 to 18.

59 Nevertheless, Article 20 provides that '[t]he States Parties undertake to facilitate the transfer of funds required for compliance with this Convention'. See Rubaja, 'Argentina's Regulation of Maintenance Obligations', above fn. 45, 229.

60 See Rubaja, 'Argentina's Regulation of Maintenance Obligations', above fn. 45, 229.

61 In force between Argentina, Belize, Bolivia, Brazil, Colombia, Costa Rica, Dominican Republic, Ecuador, El Salvador, Honduras, Nicaragua, Panama, Paraguay, Peru and Uruguay.

62 Art. 1.

to ensure the prompt return of minors that are victims of international traffic to the state of their habitual residence.[63] International cooperation is the cornerstone of this Inter-American Convention, which seeks criminal and civil cooperation. States Parties shall cooperate even with non-States Parties,[64] reflecting the pivotal place of international cooperation in this Convention. The use of new ICT developments is important to facilitate cooperation in this field.

The HCCH Conventions[65]

Convention on the Civil Aspects of International Child Abduction[66]

This instrument seeks to secure the prompt return of children wrongfully removed or retained, and aims to guarantee that rights of custody and of access granted under the law of a State Party are respected in other States Parties.[67] The law of the state of the habitual residence of the child before the wrongful removal or retention will govern the rights of modern family structures in relation to custody and access, and other states, in application of the Convention, should recognise the decision adopted based on the relevant applicable law. Exceptions to the prompt return of the child are restricted to those expressly provided for in Articles 13 and 20. The international cooperation sought by the Convention, as well as the system established by the Inter-American Convention in this sphere, is the key to achieving the objectives proposed by these frameworks. Indeed, the main means to implement cooperation through the conventions are Central Authorities, competent authorities and judges belonging to the International Hague Network of Judges. ICT is a valuable tool in this regard and can be used to expedite proceedings and to establish direct judicial communications.

Convention on Protection of Children and Co-operation in Respect of Intercountry Adoption[68]

This Hague Convention has three objectives: (1) to create safeguards to ensure that intercountry adoptions are done in the best interest of the child; (2) to establish a

[63] Ibid.

[64] Art. 4.

[65] Under this section, reference will only be made to the more recent international conventions in the area of international family law, to which Latin American countries are States Parties, and in which ICT can help to facilitate cooperation. Texts of the conventions are available on the HCCH website at www.hcch.net

[66] Latin American States Parties to this convention are: Argentina, Bahamas, Belize, Bolivia, Brazil, Chile, Colombia, Costa Rica, Dominican Republic, Ecuador, El Salvador, Guatemala, Honduras, Jamaica, Mexico, Nicaragua, Panama, Paraguay, Peru, Saint Kitts and Nevis, Trinidad and Tobago, Uruguay and Venezuela.

[67] Art. 1.

[68] Latin American States Parties to this convention are: Belize, Bolivia, Brazil, Chile, Colombia, Costa Rica, Cuba, Dominican Republic, Ecuador, El Salvador, Guatemala, Haiti, Mexico, Panama, Paraguay, Peru, Uruguay and Venezuela.

cooperation system among States Parties to ensure these safeguards; (3) and to secure the recognition of adoptions made in accordance with this convention in all States Parties.[69] Doubts arise in relation to the application of this convention to ISAs.[70] Nonetheless, it should be kept in mind that international adoptions and ISAs respond to different realities.[71] The possibilities of adoption by civil partners or people in same-sex marriages will depend on the agreement of both the state of origin of the child and the receiving state, according to their respective domestic laws. With regard to the effects of intercountry adoption, any adoption duly certified by the competent authority of the state of the adoption and in accordance with the stipulations of the Convention shall be recognised by operation of law (*ipso iure*) in the other States Parties.[72] This parameter should also be applied to encompass modern family structures.

Convention on Jurisdiction, Applicable Law, Recognition, Enforcement and Co-operation in Respect of Parental Responsibility and Measures for the Protection of Children[73]

In accordance with the four pillars of private international law,[74] this Convention provides rules on jurisdiction, applicable law, recognition and enforcement of foreign judgments and international judicial cooperation.[75] As in the other Hague Conventions on international cooperation in the field of family law, a network of Central Authorities has been set up. Regarding the applicable law, the authorities of the States Parties shall apply their own law. Nonetheless, for protecting the person or the property of a child, authorities may, extraordinarily, apply the law of another state with which the case has a substantial connection (Article 15). In addition, the 'attribution or extinction of parental responsibility by operation of law . . . is governed by the law of the State of the habitual residence of the child' (Article 16), as well as the exercise of parental responsibility (Article 17). Besides, parental responsibility acquired abroad (even if the parents are unmarried or a same-sex couple) shall be upheld in the new country of residence (see Article 16.3).

69 Art. 1.

70 See HCCH (2012) 'A Preliminary Report on the Issues Arising from International Surrogacy Arrangements'.

71 Ibid., especially note 171.

72 Art. 23.

73 Latin American States Parties to this Convention are Cuba, Dominican Republic, Ecuador and Uruguay; Argentina signed it but has not yet ratified it.

74 See the chapter by Noodt Taquela in this volume.

75 Art. 1.

Convention on the International Recovery of Child Support and Other Forms of Family Maintenance[76]

The object of this Convention is 'to ensure the effective international recovery of child support and other forms of family maintenance'. It applies to maintenance obligations arising from a parent-child relationship (Article 2(1)(a)), regardless of the marital status of the parents (Article 4), thus all family forms are included. Spousal support obligations are also sought under certain provisions, and others deal with maintenance arrangements (Article 30). One of the cornerstones of this Convention is the provision for ICT as facilitative of intercountry cooperation; the iSupport system[77] is an excellent example.

It is desirable that more Latin American countries become parties to this Convention, especially because of the advantages that it could bring for fulfilling human rights. However, several challenges could arise in some jurisdictions: need for training, lack of resources (legal, technological and human) and further dissemination.

Current Work of the International Community on International Protection of Families and, in Particular, of the Rights of Children

Cohabitation outside Marriage

It is a fact that nowadays an increasing number of people prefer to live and form a family without getting married. This reality has resulted in many states developing their regulations by including provision to guarantee minimum standards of familial solidarity; some other states treat them as though they were married, while in others still these kinds of unions and families have no rights recognised at all.

These realities also impact and bring important challenges to private international law and the management of legal diversity when a union is registered or formed in a particular state and needs to be recognised or to produce effects in another state that has a different legal system; the lack of recognition of these unions or of the obligations between partners or in relation to third parties may affect the right to family life of all the family members. In these cases, special attention must be paid to the protection of the rights of children born through ART or adopted.

The HCCH has included this topic in its agenda and has been monitoring the private international law aspects of 'unmarried couples' or 'cohabitation outside marriage including registered partnerships', as the matter has been referred to since

[76] Latin American States Parties to this Convention are Brazil and Honduras. Regarding this subject matter see also the 2007 Protocol on the Law Applicable to Maintenance Obligations; no Latin American country is part of this instrument at the time of writing.

[77] The iSupport system is an electronic case management and secure communication system for the cross-border recovery of maintenance obligations, developed by the Hague Conference of Private International Law.

1987.[78] Initially, the research was focused on applicable law, but since 1995 it has included jurisdiction, applicable law, and the recognition and enforcement of judgments in respect to unmarried couples.

In April 2013, the Council on General Affairs and Policy (Council) invited the Permanent Bureau (PB) to continue working in this area and to update a 2008 study,[79] especially in the light of the increasing number of individuals in this situation, changes to legislation, as well as the jurisprudence at national and international levels. The studies conducted by the HCCH[80] have shown the increase of this kind of family and the different positions that legislations have adopted in this regard: some states do not have a registered partnership scheme, while others do. Among the latter, some reserve their registered partnership schemes exclusively for opposite-sex partners, others for same-sex partners, and still others include them both.[81] In addition, some countries have introduced provisions on international jurisdiction and applicable law. However, this legal diversity, as well as the absence of regulation in a large number of states, has led to legal uncertainties (such as negative conflicts of jurisdiction or the existence of conflicting private international law rules that may lead to forum shopping and to a 'rush to court').[82] To face and explore these problems in depth, the latest study has focused on examining issues of jurisdiction and applicable law and issues related to the recognition of foreign registered partnerships, and has also explored the possibility of applying international instruments already in force to registered partnerships, in particular to the 2007 Child Support Convention, the 2007 Protocol on the Law Applicable to Maintenance Obligations, the 1980 Child Abduction Convention, the 1996 Child Protection Convention and the 1993 Intercountry Adoption Convention.[83] The study concludes that the variety of approaches of the different states to this topic, both at domestic and international levels, leads to legal uncertainty for the partners as well as for their children. Even though some aspects of the family life of registered partners fall within the scope of selected Hague Conventions, there is no international instrument at the global level dealing with the private international law aspects of cohabitation outside marriage in a comprehensive way.[84] Hence, to assess the need and feasibility of a global

[78] HCCH (2015) 'Update on the Developments in Internal Law and Private International Law Concerning Cohabitation Outside Marriage, Including Registered Partnerships'.

[79] HCCH (2008) 'Note on Developments in Internal Law and Private International Law Concerning Cohabitation Outside Marriage, Including Registered Partnerships'.

[80] Especially HCCH, 'Update on the Developments in Internal law and Private International Law', above fn. 78.

[81] Ibid., 30.

[82] Ibid., 36.

[83] See van Loon, H. (2014) 'Hague Conventions on Private International Law, Same-Sex Marriage and Non-Marital Institutions', in Piers, M., H. Storme and J. Verhellen (eds), *Liber Amicorum Johan Erauw*, Intersentia, 290–1 and 293–4.

[84] See HCCH, 'Update on the Developments in Internal Law and Private International Law', above fn. 78.

instrument in this field, a questionnaire was circulated and several answers received during 2016.

The answers to the questionnaire were analysed and divided into two parts: Part A, registered partnerships, and Part B, unmarried cohabitation.[85] With the former, it was noted that a large number of jurisdictions would not recognise a partnership registered abroad, and that those jurisdictions that would recognise it would probably require additional conditions for it to be recognised domestically.[86] Also, the answers showed that diverse approaches are possible in order to determine the jurisdiction and the law applicable to the effects of these partnerships. It was concluded that, from the limited number of responses received (forty), it did not seem that there is enough support at the moment among the Members to initiate any work on the development of new private international law rules.[87]

In relation to Part B, in order to determine which legal effects would be recognised and which would not, it seems that most jurisdictions would apply their own laws, including general conflict of laws rules.[88] It is worth mentioning that, according to the answers, many jurisdictions seek to protect children of unmarried cohabitees and to avoid undue discrimination between children from married and unmarried parents.[89] It was concluded that the answers did not reflect the desirability of further work on this topic;[90] and regarding the feasibility of developing such an instrument, the conclusion was that this would need to be discussed further.[91]

Finally, in March 2017, the Council decided to remove the item from the agenda; it authorised the PB to continue monitoring this area, and, if necessary, to bring any significant developments to its attention.[92]

Family Agreements involving Children

Conflicts that arise in family life have special characteristics when the parents of the child do not reside in the same state. The possibility of reaching solutions by consensual agreement between the parents has innumerable advantages over the solutions imposed by a judge. However, this possibility needs sufficient legal certainty to be efficient and guarantee the rights of children. It is likely to be necessary for these agreements to have effects in more than one state, and their efficiency may be affected by the diversity of criteria and treatment proposed by the different legal systems in this field. Agreements may involve relocation, parental responsibility

[85] HCCH (2017) 'Private International Law Issues Relating to Cohabitation Outside Marriage (Including Registered Partnerships) – Summary and Brief Analysis of the Responses to the Questionnaire'.
[86] Ibid., 16.
[87] Ibid., 21.
[88] Ibid., 27.
[89] Ibid., 31.
[90] Ibid., 39.
[91] Ibid., 41.
[92] HCCH (2017) 'Conclusions and Recommendations Adopted by the Council on General Affairs and Policy of the Conference (14–16 March 2017)', Section 8.

and issues surrounding protection measures, access and maintenance obligations, among others; in fact, they usually involve several issues ('package agreements'). It is remarkable that all the existing conventions encourage agreements between parents as the most adequate mechanism to solve conflicts. However, their recognition and enforcement may become complex and the international existing frameworks may not offer an integral solution for all these packages. In addition, the coordination of existing conventions may offer particular difficulties, such as when different Central Authorities – designated for the operation of each convention – must intervene in the same case. Challenges may also arise when not all the countries involved in a case are parties to all the existing conventions and, consequently, the criteria and requirements for recognising and enforcing these agreements may differ among countries. Hence the question regarding the need for and feasibility of a new international instrument to guarantee the effectiveness of the circulation of these kinds of agreements and the children's rights involved was brought into the HCCH's agenda. In 2012, the Council mandated the establishment of an Experts' Group to carry out further exploratory research on the topic. The Group met three times (2013, 2015 and 2017). During the first meeting, the work comprised the identification of the nature and extent of the legal and practical problems, including jurisdictional issues, and an evaluation of the benefits of a new instrument, whether binding or non-binding, in this area. In 2014, a questionnaire developed by the PB circulated among different countries with a view to the second Experts' Group meeting in order to further consider the role that existing Hague Family Law conventions play in cross-border recognition and enforcement of agreements in international child disputes, as well as the impact that an additional instrument might have on the practical use and 'portability' of these agreements across borders. As a result of the second meeting, the Group proposed to the Council that the mandate had to continue to further explore the development of two eventual instruments: (1) a non-binding navigation tool to provide best practices on how an agreement made in the area of family law involving children can be recognised and enforced in a foreign state under the 1980, 1996 and 2007 Hague Conventions; and (2) a binding legal instrument that would establish a 'one-stop shop' for agreements in a cross-border context pertaining to custody, access, child support and other financial arrangements (including property issues) and provide more party autonomy by giving parents the possibility of selecting an appropriate authority. The instrument would allow for the conferral of jurisdiction exclusively on one court or authority for the approval of such agreements and would provide for simple mechanisms for recognition and enforcement of the decision of that court or authority. It would build on and supplement the 1980, 1996 and 2007 Hague Conventions. At the 2016 Council, it was decided to mandate the PB to develop a non-binding navigation tool to provide best practices on how an agreement made in the area of family law involving children can be recognised and enforced in a foreign state under the 1980, 1996 and 2007 Hague Conventions. It was also decided that the need for and feasibility of developing a binding instrument in this field would be revisited by the Council, based on further information which would result from the work on the navigation tool.

In 2017, the Group met for that purpose and presented the Draft Practical Guide to Family Agreements under the Hague Conventions to the Council in March 2018. The Group held a fourth meeting in June 2018, and finalised the practical guide in light of the discussions that took place at the Seventh Meeting of the Special Commission on the practical operation of the 1980/1996 Hague Conventions, on the shift of habitual residence following a non-return agreement. The Group will provide the Practical Guide to the Council at its 2019 Meeting.[93] It is likely that the Council will, at that meeting, take the opportunity to also consider the continuity of the Project with regard to the binding tool.

Parentage/Surrogacy

Over the last decades the advances of ART together with the advent of new family patterns have been challenging the laws on parentage. In the context of this novel reality, it is becoming more and more difficult to be certain about who is/are the legal parent/parents of a child. As states have different approaches to both parentage and surrogacy, and there is no international legal instrument on these topics, children and their families involved in this kind of private international law case often find themselves down a blind alley where their human rights are violated. The increasing number of ISAs concluded under no regulation, incomplete or unclear rules, or even under banning provisions, has triggered the emergence of a business[94] and a whole industry of 'reproductive tourism'.[95] To tackle this problem, in 2013 the HCCH sent questionnaires on private international law issues surrounding the status of children, including those arising from ISAs, to states, legal practitioners, health professionals and surrogacy agencies. The answers received were a rich source of information for the study on the topic prepared in 2014 for the attention of the Council,[96] which deals with the establishment and contestation of legal parentage in national law, with private international law and cooperation rules, and with the specific phenomenon of ISAs. Following that study, in 2015 the Council determined that an Experts' Group be convened to explore the feasibility of advancing work. The Group should first consider the private international law rules regarding 'the legal status of children in cross-border situations, including those born of international surrogacy arrangements'.[97] It is worth underlining that this mandate embraces all cross-border situations of parentage and it is not exclusively focused on ISAs. Thus, in 2016, the first meeting of the Experts'

[93] HCCH (2018) 'Conclusions and Recommendations Adopted by the Council on General Affairs and Policy of the Conference (13–15 March 2018)', Section 12-13.

[94] González Martín, N. and M. M. Albornoz (2016) 'Aspectos transfronterizos de la gestación por sustitución', XVI *Anuario Mexicano de Derecho Internacional*.

[95] Lamm, E. (2013) *Gestación por sustitución: Ni maternidad subrogada ni alquiler de vientres*, Universidad de Barcelona, 193 ss.

[96] HCCH (2014) 'A Study of Legal Parentage and the Issues Arising from International Surrogacy Arrangements', Preliminary Document No. 3 C.

[97] HCCH (2015) 'Conclusions and Recommendations Adopted by the Council on General Affairs and Policy of the Conference (24–26 March 2015)', Section 5.

Group was held. There, it was decided that, due to the complexity of the subject and the legal diversity of states' approaches to it, definitive conclusions could not be reached, and that work should continue, focusing the feasibility analysis primarily on recognition.[98] A further meeting was held in January–February 2017 where it was agreed,[99] in principle, the feasibility of developing a binding multilateral instrument dealing with the recognition of foreign judicial decisions on legal parentage,[100] to tackle the existence of a diversity of approaches with respect to the determination and to the recognition of the legal parentage when recorded in a public document.[101] Owing to the complexity of the subject and the diversity of approaches by States in cases of ISAs, definitive conclusions could not be reached as to the feasibility of the possible application of future agreed general private international law rules on legal parentage to ISAs, and the possible need for additional rules and safeguards in these cases and in cases of ART.[102] In 2018, the Group held its third meeting; following its recommendations, the Council decided that the Group should hold: (1) a fourth meeting in September 2018 to deepen the discussion regarding uniform applicable law rules on parentage, including how such rules might operate together with public documents which record legal parentage, and further analysing the possibility of recognising or accepting foreign public documents which record legal parentage, as well as refining possible provisions regarding the recognition of foreign judicial decisions; (2) a fifth meeting in February 2019 focusing specifically on ISAs, to consider the feasibility of the possible application of future agreed general private international law rules on legal parentage to ISAs, and the possible need for additional rules and safeguards in these cases, including the possibility of a Protocol for ISAs.[103]

98 HCCH (2016) 'Report of the February 2016 Meeting of the Experts' Group on Parentage/Surrogacy', Preliminary Document No. 3.

99 HCCH (2017) 'Report of the Experts' Group on the Parentage/Surrogacy Project (Meeting of 31 January – 3 February 2017)', February 2017, Section 38.

100 The fact that states already have regulations on the recognition and enforcement of foreign judicial decisions would facilitate reaching consensus in this field, even though special safeguards might be needed.

101 While birth certificates issued in some states record legal parentage, those issued in some others do not. Such a difference makes it difficult to agree on a common solution; different approaches will probably be needed for each context. A possible way of overcoming this problem, especially in those cases in which the legal parentage is established by operation of law, could be (as suggested by some members of the Group) having a uniform new stamp or document ('international certificate of parentage').

102 An urgent need for practical solutions was noted, with one of the key aims being to secure continuity in the parent-child legal status. In addition, the Group agreed that all children, irrespective of the circumstances of their birth, should be treated equally. Concerns at the international level and the consequent public policy considerations relating to surrogacy arrangements including, for example, the potential for exploitation were also recognised. Several members of the Group noted the importance of children knowing their origins, which some characterised as a right, and the preservation of records. Ibid., Sections 24 and 25.

103 HCCH, 'Conclusions and Recommendations', above fn. 97, Section 6.

The fourth meeting of the Experts' Group took place in The Hague from 25 to 28 September 2018. On the need for common solutions, during the fourth meeting the Group agreed that any new instrument should seek to provide for certainty and cross-border continuity of legal parentage, taking into account the best interests of children.[104] It also agreed that combining different private international law methods might be the most effective path to follow.[105]

The Group analysed the possible methods to use, in both the absence and the presence of a judicial decision. For the first scenario, it discussed the topic in the absence of applicable law rules in a possible future instrument (acceptance of a public document as a rebuttable evidence of the legal parentage recorded therein, and cross-border recognition of legal parentage established by operation of law or following the act of an individual), and with uniform applicable law rules in a possible future instrument. In the case of an applicable law approach being followed, the Group identified several connecting factors that would require further consideration: the state of the child's birth, the state of the child's habitual residence at the time of birth and the state with which the child has a real and substantial connection.[106]

For the second scenario, when legal parentage was established by judicial decision, the Group agreed on the feasibility of developing a hard law instrument on the recognition of foreign judicial decisions on legal parentage and it noted that refined provisions would be necessary.[107]

In the end, the Experts' Group decided to reserve its final conclusions and recommendations on future work pending the fifth meeting.[108]

Private international law solutions for practical problems relating to legal parentage and ISAs demand urgent solutions. It is hoped that the Group will succeed in reaching consensus on an international instrument, and that it could be accepted by states and finally applied in real-life cases with the ultimate goal of protecting the best interests of children and the rights of all persons involved in these situations.

Conclusions

Private international family law is affected by new social and scientific realities. Two axes may be identified: first, social and biomedical developments are challenging traditional methodologies and techniques relating to private international law, which must provide solutions to these new issues; second, international cooperation ('the architecture of engagement')[109] highly benefits from ICT. Regarding the latter, several examples taken from the Latin American experience were examined in this

[104] HCCH (2018) 'Report of the Experts' Group on the Parentage / Surrogacy Project (Meeting of 25–28 September 2018)', October 2018, Section 6.

[105] Ibid., Section 8.

[106] Ibid., Section 26.

[107] Ibid., Section 34.

[108] Ibid., Section 48.

[109] See further Part II of this volume.

chapter, and many more were the focus of analysis in the previous part of this volume. As to the former axis, national private international law sources in Latin American countries are making efforts to gradually include provisions to capture these new scenarios. Moreover, the framework of international legal instruments currently in force in Latin American countries might provide solutions to some of the new problems. It is crucial to coordinate these instruments and results via guiding principles such as those in favour of the most vulnerable parties. Principles of this kind could become of pivotal importance at the time of interpretation and application of these multiple and, at times, overlapping sources. Yet, as some international treaties were created many years ago, some of them reflect cultural, religious and social conceptions which have become outdated by new social and technological realities and by fundamental human rights that today prevail in the states of the region.

PART IV

PRIVATE INTERNATIONAL LAW IN PRACTICE

17

The Key Role of Judges in the Development of Private International Law: Lessons Learned from the Work of the Hague Conference on Private International Law

*Ignacio Goicoechea and Hans van Loon**

Introduction

In practical terms, the purpose of private international law is to provide the means to solve international legal issues of private parties; to provide legal security to individuals, families and companies as well as other entities, despite the differences between legal systems. This is also the (unstated) objective of the 'progressive unification of the rules of private international law', which is the mandate of the Hague Conference on Private International Law (hereinafter 'the Hague Conference' or 'HCCH').[1]

The working cycle of the Hague Conference is based on the idea that there is a need to: (1) identify those legal cross-border issues that require tackling with private international law tools, foremost multilateral treaties or conventions; (2) develop a private international law tool to address the identified legal issue; (3) implement the new tool in the respective jurisdictions; (4) apply the new tool to the given case, in order to provide an effective solution to the issue; and (5) assess the operation of the given tool to make sure that the problems are now solved, or, if there is a need to improve the operation of the tool, develop the required support side-tools or devices, or develop a new instrument.

The Hague Conference has been, in particular, a pioneer in identifying the importance of the implementation (3), operation (4) and assessment (5) phases in the development of its Conventions as an integral part of the process of establishing them as effective, practical instruments. Indeed, the Hague Conference has pioneered the development of a range of devices to support national authorities in their implementation and operation of the Hague Conventions.

When we reflect in more general terms on the development of private international

* The views expressed in this article are those of the authors and should not be attributed to the Hague Conference.

[1] Statute, Article 1, available at: www.hcch.net/en/instruments/conventions/full-text

law, and those playing a prominent role therein, we may think, at the international level, of: senior government officials and other experts who participate in private international law-making fora such as the Hague Conference, and who, in the framework and supported by the staff of such organisations, negotiate and assess new international tools. Then there are, at the national level, legislators in each country that enact domestic private international law rules and approve international conventions. In addition, the following actors also have a role in the development of private international law: judges who apply international and domestic private international law rules and adjudicate 'international cases'[2] (their role in the development of private international law is very prominent in jurisdictions which do not have comprehensive private international law legislation, common law jurisdictions in particular); academics who study the reality, identify gaps and suggest solutions; practitioners who represent and advise clients in international cases; and non-governmental organisations (NGOs), whose work in one way or another may touch on private international law matters.

The aim of this chapter is to discuss the role of judges in the development of private international law. First, we will highlight the changing role of judges in the context of contemporary globalisation. Second, we will argue that as a result of the expansion of their international duties, judges, in a way that is analogous to the working cycle of the Hague Conference, also have a role in identifying legal issues that must be addressed by private international law, developing tools to tackle those issues, ensuring the implementation and operation of these tools, and assessing their effectiveness. In this regard we will also highlight their contribution to the development of Hague Conventions. Finally, we will describe the very important role of Latin American judges in the development of special devices to promote the implementation, operation and assessment of the 1980 Hague Child Abduction Convention in Latin America.

Private International Law in the Twenty-first Century and Implementation of Private International Law Instruments

Contemporary globalisation is giving increasing visibility to private international law, since there are more and more cases with relevant international elements that have great impact on the lives of people and the conduct of business. Globalisation has encouraged the proliferation of private international law-making at national, regional and global levels. It has given a huge boost to private international law activities of legislators as well as judges around the world. At the regional level, in the Americas, the Organization of American States (OAS) and Mercosur have adopted a wide range of private international law instruments, while in Europe, the European Union has acquired powers to legislate in the field of private international law, and has made

[2] Cf. the section below on Operationalising Private International Law Instruments.

ample use of these powers. In addition, the Hague Conference has seen impressive growth of both its membership and the range of States Parties to its Conventions.

Globalisation also has an impact on the general outlook and methods of private international law. Where the nation state is no longer its sole anchoring entity, private international law must transcend its traditional boundaries, and, adapting its methodologies while preserving its integrity, must orient itself towards the idea of an emerging global community. This adaptation process has both a vertical and a horizontal dimension.

The vertical dimension appears in the growing link that manifests itself in modern private international law – and in particular in global and regional private international law instruments – between the international legal order and the national, or domestic, legal order. We see, for example, an increasing influence of global and regional human rights norms on the development of private international law. This vertical dimension is further reinforced by the activities of international organisations, such as the Hague Conference, aimed at fostering the legal regime established by their Conventions, and in particular their correct implementation and proper operation by their main protagonists, including judges.

A comprehensive view of the role of judges in international cases, therefore, requires a double focus: it must be understood both from a perspective anchored in the state – the judge remains an organ of his or her state – and from a perspective anchored in the international legal ordering – the international convention which supports or mandates the role of the judge. In other words: judges increasingly fulfil a double role: not only do they function as national organs; they also act, at the same time, as informal agents of a 'decentralised' international – regional or global – legal system.[3]

The horizontal dimension appears in the increasing need for coordination of the powers of different national administrative authorities and judges (and of the laws they are called to apply), and for mechanisms for communication and cooperation between them in cross-border civil cases. The mere volume and complexity of transnational civil legal issues in the context of contemporary globalisation make such coordination, communication and cooperation a growing necessity.

The Role of Judges in the Development of Private International Law

In light of the scenario that has been described above, we will now try to elaborate on the contribution of judges to the development of private international law.

Due to their particular role, judges are in a unique position to contribute to this

[3] As the French internationalist Georges Scelle would say, their role undergoes a *dédoublement fonctionnel*. For a discussion of the effects of globalisation on the nation state, on the proliferation of private international law sources, and new approaches in private international law, including the enlarged role of the courts, with a focus on the Hague Conference and its work, see van Loon, H. (2016) 'The Global Horizon of Private International Law', *Recueil des cours*, vol. 380, 1–107 (Chapter I, D and Chapter II).

development. Clearly, their most relevant function and contribution comes from their natural task of adjudicating cases. They are the ones who normally have the last word in interpreting and applying private international law tools, whether of national, regional or global origin, to international cases (the 'operational phase', to put it in terms of the working cycle of the Hague Conference referred to above). In doing so, they develop private international law jurisprudence, which may then guide judges in later cases. However, as we will argue below, in addition to the operational phase, judges can also contribute in other phases of the development of private international law.

Indeed, we may consider the role of judges in the development of private international law in terms of the various stages of the working cycle developed by the Hague Conference, and, most eloquently, in their very role in the development of private international law by the Hague Conference.

Identification of International Legal Issues (People's Needs)

During their daily work of adjudicating cases, judges are often exposed to legal gaps that they need to fill by applying their creativity and sense of justice. Those gaps are sometimes due to the lack of private international law regulations on a topic that has not been addressed before (such as international surrogacy arrangements, international tourist protection, and so on), or to incomplete regulation of issues by existing private international law instruments, which might require the development of complementary tools (such as Protocols, Principles and Guides to Good Practice).

Judges have their own fora where they meet with colleagues to discuss matters of their concern. These meetings occur within their jurisdiction at the national and international levels. The latter are set up by different public and private organisations, such as the Commonwealth Magistrates and Judges Association, the Ibero-American Judicial Summit, the International Association of Women's Judges, the Association of Family and Children Judges; there are also different meetings organised by their respective national and international judicial networks (such as the International Hague Network of Judges). In many of those meetings judges address matters relating to private international law, so as to identify possible gaps, and may even make suggestions for dealing with them. All these gatherings of judges may help not only to identify a possible legal gap, but also to measure its magnitude and geographical impact. If we consider that one of the problems worldwide is the lack of statistical information, and that the field of private international law is one that is particularly difficult to develop, we may agree that judges, and their respective meetings, are an extremely valuable source of information for identifying and assessing the existing and prospective needs of private international law. By way of example we can mention, at the national level, a recent meeting of Panamanian judges, held on 27–8 March 2017, during which the judges concluded that their current procedural norms were not suitable to deal with child abduction cases and that there was a need to develop a specific procedure tailored to meet the 1980 Hague Child Abduction Convention's requirements. At the regional level, in the recent Inter-American meeting of Central

Authorities and Hague Network Judges of the Americas, held in Panama on 29–31 March 2017, participants invited states to consider joining the 1996 Hague Child Protection Convention.[4]

Development of Private International Law Instruments

Considering that private international law tools (both hard law and soft law) are supposed to be interpreted and applied by judges, it seems advisable to include judges, or at least to solicit their views and take these into account, when drafting such norms. This is all the more necessary when drafting instruments that include a judicial cooperation component. Naturally, their involvement should be fully respectful of the division of responsibilities between legislators and courts of the given state.

The Hague Conference has a long tradition of involvement of judges as experts or representatives of their governments. As an early example, no fewer than ten judges took part in its first post-Second World War diplomatic session in 1951. Since then, there has been continuous participation of judges in national delegations during the negotiations of its Conventions.

There are also judicial fora that develop soft law tools to facilitate the operation of existing instruments. For example, in the field of insolvency, EU judges have worked together as part of the 'European Cross-border Insolvency: Promoting Judicial Cooperation' project to develop non-binding Principles and Guidelines for cross-border communication and cooperation in support of the EU Insolvency Regulation[5] (EIR);[6] while the Ibero-American Judicial Summit developed the 'Ibero-American Protocol on Judicial Cooperation', applicable to civil, commercial and criminal cases (approved at the 17th Ibero-American Judicial Summit that took place in Santiago, Chile on 4 April 2014).[7]

Likewise, some Supreme Courts, such as those of Panama and Uruguay, have the power to propose draft laws to Congress, while some others, like the Supreme Courts of Chile and Dominican Republic, are entitled to enact procedural regulations. We will provide some concrete examples of judicial regulations below, when presenting the implementation of the 1980 Hague Convention in Latin America.

[4] Conclusion and Recommendation No. 29, available at: https://assets.hcch.net/docs/4388950c-c5c2-4a1c-bb7d-7a92384ddfa7.pdf

[5] See EU Cross-border Insolvency Court-to-Court Cooperation Principles, available at: www.tri-leiden.eu/uploads/files/EU_Cross-Border_Insolvency_Court-to-Court_Cooperation_Principles.pdf

[6] Recital 45 and Articles 41–4 and 56–9 EIR Recast, available at: http://eur-lex.europa.eu/legal-content/EN/TXT/PDF/?uri=CELEX:32015R0848&from=EN

[7] Among other things, the Protocol recommends that states incorporate different international conventions, and incorporated as an annex is the full text of the 'Emerging Guidance regarding the development of the International Hague Network of Judges and General Principles for Judicial Communications, including commonly accepted safeguards for Direct Judicial Communications in specific cases, within the context of the International Hague Network of Judges', available at: www.cumbrejudicial.org/c/document_library/get_file?uuid=0db452e9-4509-43cb-bf2e-629fa183db53&groupId=10124

Implementing Private International Law Instruments

The successful development of a private international law convention only goes halfway to helping people resolve their legal problems. Often, the challenge of implementation is no easier than its development – 'implementation' is here understood in a broad sense, encompassing incorporation into the national legal system, adjustment of internal regulations or procedures, training of operators and publicity about the availability of the convention.

Some authors prematurely conclude that a convention is failing to fulfil its purposes, either because it only has a small number of States Parties, or because its application in some cases shows undesirable results. A brief comment on both points may be useful.

Practice indeed shows that it takes several years for a convention to enter into force, and many more years, sometimes decades, for a convention to receive a considerable number of ratifications. There may be different reasons to explain such delays, but certainly one of the most relevant is the lack of political support from decision-makers in the relevant states. Political agendas at state level are very much driven by urgent, short-term concerns, and the analysis and implementation of a new private international law instrument is rarely seen as an urgency, and is therefore left for 'less busy times' which hardly ever come. As a result, very useful and straightforward instruments may take many decades to achieve a considerable number of States Parties (for example, the Hague Legal Cooperation and Litigation Conventions, and many other instruments produced by other fora both at global and regional levels). Often, the efforts of stakeholders advocating the incorporation of a new convention are required for many of these instruments to receive the necessary political attention to undergo analysis by different agencies in the executive, and later on to navigate the difficult waters of congresses, until they are finally approved and incorporated into the relevant legal systems.

On the other hand, even if a convention has been incorporated into a legal system, this does not guarantee that it works smoothly in serving its purposes. First, this is because there may still be a need to adjust internal regulations, or coordinate the work of relevant authorities (in particular when establishing a Central Authority to operate the convention). Second, there is often a need to train users in the operation of the instrument (including judges). Last but not least, there is often a need to raise awareness among the public so they know that they can benefit from the new tool.

Judges can essentially only apply a convention once it has been implemented in their country. Otherwise, when faced with a situation addressed in the convention that has not (yet) entered into force for their jurisdiction, they are forced to apply less efficient solutions or mechanisms to their cases. Often this implies either considerable delays – such as the taking of evidence abroad via ordinary letters rogatory, instead of using an efficient mechanism such as that provided by the Hague 1970 Convention on Taking of Evidence Abroad; or accepting less satisfactory results – for example, in the case of a child support order that needs to be enforced abroad, where the judge's country is not a Party to the Hague 2007 Child Support Convention.

Faced with the limitations of their legal systems in the absence of a convention, judges can also be considered stakeholders regarding the call for the ratification of (or accession to) and implementation of the relevant private international law tool. In fact, some supreme courts have assumed this role, and have addressed executives and parliaments, requesting them to join certain conventions. For example, the Supreme Court of Uruguay has addressed its Ministry of Foreign Affairs, requesting the incorporation of the Hague Legal Cooperation and Litigation Conventions, while the Supreme Court of Argentina has urged Congress to consider regulating an adequate procedure to apply the Hague Child Abduction Convention.[8]

Finally, another key aspect of the implementation phase is the raising of awareness of the existence of the new tool and training users in operating it. Naturally, if legal actors (including judges) do not know about the existence of the tool, it will not be applied (and people will not benefit from it). If it is not duly applied, it might generate undesirable outcomes in cases. Judges may need to be trained to make better use of judicial cooperation mechanisms to mitigate this risk.

Judicial authorities have been instrumental in many jurisdictions to implement the necessary adjustments to the internal legal system and to train judges in the operation of international conventions.

Operationalising Private International Law Instruments

Judges' adjudicatory role makes them the primary interpreters of private international law techniques and the actors in charge of an appropriate application of these tools to do justice in an international case. This prominent role of judges in the development of private international law is increasing as a result of the developments described above, as the following examples may illustrate.

In the first place, the mere notion of 'international case' is undergoing a paradigm shift. Traditionally, private international law instruments require a foreign element for their application, such as only applying between parties having their habitual residence in different states. This reflects a perspective from within the nation state that views the international as the exceptional, and the domestic as the common situation. By contrast, recent instruments, such as the 2005 Hague Choice of Court Convention, which entered into force in 2015, and the 2015 Hague Principles on Choice of Law, take the opposite view. Both apply 'in international cases' only. According to both, however, cases are 'international', unless the parties are resident in the same Contracting State and the relationship of the parties and all other relevant elements regardless of the location of the chosen court or the chosen law, are connected only with that state. Thus the paradigm shifts: the international (transnational) dimension,

[8] Supreme Court of Argentina, case G., L. si por su hijo G.P., T. por restitución s/ familia p/ rec. ext. de inconstit. – casación, of 27 December 2016, consideration No. 22.

rather than being viewed as the exception, becomes the normal scenario for the application of the instrument, with the purely internal case as an exception.

In this way, both the 2005 Convention and the 2015 Principles encourage judges to transcend the boundaries of their own legal system. Moreover, the 2005 Convention requires a court other than the chosen court to determine the validity of the choice of court agreement in terms not of its own law, but of the law of the chosen court.[9] A similar rule applies to the court requested to enforce the judgment of the chosen court. Thus the judge must put him or herself in the shoes of the chosen court. Moreover, the Principles make a bold step by opening the door for courts to apply non-state law, such as the UNIDROIT Principles on International Commercial Contracts – something arbitrators have been doing for a long time.

The enlarged international role of the judge emerging from both these recent Hague instruments follows from the enlarged recognition of the role of party autonomy. Once broadly applied, these instruments will significantly improve the coordination of adjudicatory jurisdiction and applicable laws, and increase the involvement of judges in commercial dispute resolution through civil courts.

A second example is the expanding role of judges in the field of cross-border judicial and administrative cooperation. Initially, the lead in this area was taken by the development of cross-border cooperation through Central Authorities (1965 Convention on Service of Documents Abroad, 1970 Convention on the Taking of Evidence Abroad, 1980 Access to Justice Convention). The 1980 Child Abduction Convention then enlarged the role of the Central Authority, and at the same time made necessary more intense cooperation between Central Authorities and judges. The next step was the development of direct cross-border communication between judges themselves. Both the latter developments initially raised concerns about possible tensions with the principle of judicial independence, but their increased use, and benefits to secure effective operation of justice are gradually consolidating their application.

For the purpose of this chapter, it is worth highlighting the invaluable benefits of developing a smooth and efficient working relationship between judges and Central Authorities. The operation of the Child Abduction Convention has provided ample examples where improving their working relation has resulted in improving the overall operation of the Convention in the given country.

Direct judicial communications (DJCs) refer to communications that take place between sitting judges concerning a specific case.[10] Their use has been expanding

[9] Readers familiar with the 1980 Hague Child Abduction Convention will be reminded of the rule of Art. 3(1)(a) of the 1980 Hague Child Abduction Convention, which requires the court of the state of refuge to apply not its own law but the law of the state of the previous habitual residence to determine whether or not there is a breach of rights of custody.

[10] As defined in 'Emerging Guidance Regarding the Development of the International Hague Network of Judges and General Principles for Judicial Communications, Including Commonly Accepted Safeguards for Direct Judicial Communications in Specific Cases, Within the Context of the

considerably during the last years in the commercial area in the field of international insolvency, and notably in the application of instruments dealing with the mobility of children and families, foremost the Hague Child Abduction and Child Protection Conventions, which provide for coordination of judicial powers.[11] It is precisely because two judges, two different jurisdictions, two different legal systems, are involved, that practice has shown that it is also crucial for these judges to be able in certain cases to exchange information. The information may relate to laws on custody and access, but also to measures of protection that may be ordered, for example to protect the child's safety when the return is ordered despite allegations of domestic violence or abuse by the left-behind parent. In short, such information, shared directly or through Network Judges, may well be essential as a means of building the trust that is necessary to make the return mechanism work. It is conceivable that the scope of application of these cross-border communications between judges could be extended to other matters than insolvency and child protection, such as access and proof of foreign law; recognition and enforcement of precautionary measures and civil protection orders; and recognition and enforcement of foreign judgments in civil and commercial matters.

Obviously, the fact that judges may now be in contact with their counterparts in other countries also widens their horizons, empowers them and supports them in cultivating the international outlook which they need to develop, alongside their firm grounding in their own domestic legal system, to apply the international instruments in an international spirit.

Assessing and Improving the Operation of Private International Law Instruments

Private international law instruments that are focused on or include a component of international legal cooperation may greatly benefit from periodic reviews that assess their operation. The reason for this is that their efficacy basically depends on the evolving practice of their application.

The Hague Conference has been a pioneer in monitoring and assessing the operation of this type of convention, starting with its first Special Commission on the operation of the Hague Service Convention in 1977. Such a Special Commission brings together the primary actors in the operation of the legal cooperation Conventions, that is, Central Authorities and judges, to discuss and exchange experiences about

International Hague Network of Judges', 12, available at: www.hcch.net/en/publications-and-studies/details4/?pid=6024&dtid=3. For further explanation on the Hague Network and DJCs, see Lortie, P. and I. Goicoechea (2013) 'The Future of Judicial Co-operation: Building on Recent Innovations', *International Family Law*, special issue in Honour of The Rt Hon. Lord Justice Thorpe, Head of International Family Justice for England & Wales, 107–218, at 129–33.

11 The coordination of the dynamic balance between the jurisdiction of the court of the state to which a child has been removed or where the child is retained (the state of refuge) and the state of the former habitual residence (the state of origin) is even crucial for their proper operation, cf. Arts 12–20 Child Abduction Convention, and Arts 7 and 11 1996 Convention.

the following sort of questions: is the Convention working properly? Are there any problems which have been identified in its operation? Is there a need to achieve greater consistency in certain aspects of interpretation? Are there still gaps not covered by the Convention, and, if so, might they be filled by developing a side tool to the Convention? This has laid the basis for a rich variety of gatherings and tools to promote, monitor and support the operation of Hague Conventions. Since the 1993 Intercountry Adoption Convention,[12] a standard article in Hague Conventions provides that 'at regular intervals . . . a Special Commission [shall be convened] in order to review the practical operation of the Convention'.

At the regional level there are also fora that assess the operation of conventions. In Ibero-America, IberRed organises meetings of experts/contact persons to assess the international cooperation developed in civil and criminal law, including specific topics such as child abduction, adoption and child support. The assessment operation is also developed in national jurisdictions, in many cases in the framework of judicial meetings or seminars, notably during the meeting of national judicial networks (for example in Spain, Mexico and Argentina). As mentioned above, in March 2017 the Supreme Court of Panama, in partnership with the Hague Conference Regional Office for Latin America and the Caribbean (ROLAC), organised a Judicial Seminar. One of its main purposes was to assess the operation of the Hague Child Abduction Convention in Panama, identify challenges and suggest concrete actions to be implemented in order to improve the Convention's operation. The exercise proved to be extremely helpful and produced a concrete road map of implementing measures, which was submitted to the Supreme Court for its consideration.

In all these meetings at the global, regional and national levels, judges play a key role, contributing their unique experiences in operating relevant instruments, and making suggestions for recommendations that should lead to a more efficient operation of the conventions.

The Implementation of the 1980 Child Abduction Convention in Latin America

We have described above the outstanding importance of the implementation phase in order to secure the correct operation of Hague Conventions, in particular those that include judicial and administrative cooperation mechanisms.

In the case of the Hague Child Abduction Convention, after more than thirty years of application and numerous meetings to assess its operation (seven times at the global level),[13] there are some practices that have consolidated as key recommendations when thinking of the implementation of the Convention. Among the most relevant recommendations are the following: (1) review and where necessary adjust procedural regulations so as to have cases decided expeditiously, as required by the Convention; (2) develop international cooperation through the work of Central

[12] Art. 42.

[13] See www.hcch.net/en/instruments/conventions/publications1/?dtid=57&cid=24

Authorities and Judicial Networks, by promoting the use of DJCs and encouraging a smooth and efficient working relationship between Hague Network Judges and Central Authorities; (3) consider concentration of jurisdiction as a possible means to facilitate the development of judicial expertise, and more efficient handling of cases; and (4) train judges in the interpretation and operation of the Convention.

The described practices are gradually being considered and many of them implemented in Latin American jurisdictions, to a considerable extent thanks to the work of judges. This judicial action has been promoted and developed by Latin American members of the Hague International Network of Judges (IHNJ), Supreme Courts and other judicial authorities in the region.

Reviewing Procedures

If we take the recommendation to review procedures, the first milestone in the region has been the development of the Inter-American Model Law of Procedure (hereinafter 'Model Law'), which was mostly developed by Latin American Hague Network Judges (adopted in Buenos Aires during the 2nd Expert Meeting on Child Abduction that took place on 19–21 September 2007).[14] The Model Law has been a primary source for many states that have regulated, or are in the process of regulating, their procedural norms applicable to the Child Abduction Conventions (both the 1980 Hague Convention and the 1989 Inter-American Convention on the International Return of Children). Since the adoption of the Model Law, the Dominican Republic, Uruguay, Chile and Venezuela have regulated the child abduction procedure, while several others, namely Panama, Peru, Paraguay, Mexico and Argentina, are working on draft laws. In some of the cases it was the Supreme Court that regulated the procedure, in others it was, or it is going to be, the legislator; but in all cases draft laws have been developed by or with the participation of the respective Hague Network Judge.

Judicial Networks and DJCs

The second recommendation, on judicial networks and DJCs, was initiated with the official designation of Hague Networks Judges in the region. The IHNJ started its development in Latin America in 2005, when Mag. Ricardo Perez Manrique from Uruguay was officially designated by the Supreme Court of his country as a member of the Network. The IHNJ then developed at swift and constant pace,

[14] The initiative was decided in a judicial meeting held in The Hague in margins of the 2006 SC. Central Authorities and Hague Network Judges that participated in the meeting realised that one of the greater challenges in the application of the Convention was to decide cases within the limited timeframes envisaged by the instrument. There was agreement that many procedural codes or regulations in the region did not provide for such a swift procedure, and that law reform should be considered. Therefore, the development of a model law was recommended, in order to encourage and facilitate the work of those states that would be willing to review their procedures. In early 2007, under the coordination of the HCCH, a group of Uruguayan judges prepared the first draft Model Law of Procedure, which was then reviewed and enriched by most of the Latin American IHNJs.

and a few years later each of the seventeen Latin American states, then parties to the Hague Convention, were represented in the IHNJ (Bolivia, who joined the Convention in 2016, is currently the only Latin American country that has not yet designated a Judge to the Hague Network). Judicial authorities have supported the IHNJ by being receptive to the underlying idea of the Network, making designations and supporting the work of the Network Judges. From their side, Network Judges have been supporting the operation and implementation of the Convention, and the progressive use of DJCs. Furthermore, some of them have promoted the creation of National Networks in their own jurisdictions (Argentina and Mexico). Others have promoted the regulation of DJCs in their own system. DJCs are now specifically regulated in procedural laws (Uruguay[15] and Chile)[16] and in Civil Codes (Argentina)[17], and they have also been incorporated into the Ibero-American Protocol on Judicial Cooperation[18] (another purely judicial initiative).

Concentration of Jurisdiction

The third recommendation, on concentration of jurisdiction, has been promoted by Hague Network Judges and implemented by respective judicial authorities in Uruguay, Peru, Mexico City, Guatemala, Brazil and the province of Cordoba in Argentina.

Training

Finally, in terms of *training*, Hague Network Judges have been promoting and developing judicial training in their respective jurisdictions, and have become key partners to ROLAC in these endeavours. ROLAC, in partnership with the judicial and administrative authorities of states in the region, has organised more than fifty judicial training sessions in the region in the last decade.

Although we have mentioned above that the described recommendations/good practices are gradually being implemented in the region (as part of the long and progressive process of implementation of conventions), practice is confirming their value with measurable results. In the Latin American region we can refer to the following examples, all linked to the work of judges:

Uruguay

The Uruguayan example can be seen as the model example of implementation, because it is the jurisdiction where the four abovementioned recommendations have been fully implemented. The judicial procedure was regulated by Law No. 18.895,

[15] Art. 28, Law 18.895.

[16] Art. 13, Supreme Court Acta No. 205-2015

[17] Art. 2612, Argentine Civil and Commercial Code.

[18] Available at: www.cumbrejudicial.org/c/document_library/get_file?uuid=0db452e9-4509-43cb-bf2e-629fa183db53&groupId=10124

adopted on 11 April 2012. This law developed a new specific procedure for the application of the Hague Convention, which has been tailored to meet the requirement of speed of the Convention. It also establishes the role of the Hague Network Judge and provides for the development of DJCs. Likewise, the Supreme Court enacted a complementary regulation, Acordada No. 7758, on 24 December 2012, which concentrated jurisdiction and organised the role of the Hague Network Judge (which includes being informed about every incoming case, and the task of producing statistics on the length and outcome of cases). Uruguayan statistics on incoming cases decided after the implementation of these procedural regulations show that the average time needed to obtain a decision decreased from one year for a first instance judgment (to which the second instance and an appeal in cassation to the Supreme Court of Justice must be added) to sixty days for a final second instance judgment, without the possibility to appeal.

Dominican Republic

The Dominican Republic experience should also be noted. Its statistics show that for cases tried after the new regime implemented by the Supreme Court Regulation No. 480-2008, enacted on 6 March 2008 (fully inspired by the Inter-American model law, and proposed by the Hague Network Judge), the length of procedures diminished considerably: from four to twelve months under the old regime, to two to four months under the new procedure (provided no appeal is lodged with the Supreme Court).

Chile

The Hague Network Judge prepared a draft law which was adopted by the Supreme Court through Acta 205-2015 of 3 December 2015. It established a swift procedure which diminished the length of the judicial procedure, saving about 120 days in comparison to the former procedural regime.

There are many other examples of implementing efforts that have been developed in coordination with Hague Network Judges. Among others, in Mexico, one of the Hague Network Judges promoted and assisted with the implementation of concentration of jurisdiction in Mexico city. In Nicaragua, the Hague Network Judge drafted the Administrative and Judicial Procedure that is currently applied to Hague cases, and together with the Judicial School has developed the first specialised diploma programme on child abduction. In Guatemala, the Supreme Court passed a Regulation which concentrated jurisdiction and determines that the swiftest available internal procedure should be applicable to return procedures. In Venezuela, the Hague Network Judge drafted the procedural regulation applicable to Hague cases, which was adopted by resolution of the Supreme Court of the country.[19] In Argentina, the National Network of Judges adopted a Protocol to be applied to the Hague and

[19] Resolution 2017-0019, 4 October 2017, Tribunal Supremo de Justicia de Venezuela.

Inter-American Child Abduction Conventions,[20] while the Hague Network Judge promoted and assisted with the implementation of both concentration of jurisdiction and a procedural law for the Province of Cordoba.[21]

Despite the above described actions, it is to be acknowledged that the Child Abduction Convention does not always work smoothly in Latin America. Statistics show that the challenge of delays in deciding cases is still there, and probably can be singled out as the most severe obstacle to overcome in the next few years. We can choose to see the glass half full or half empty, but there is certainly a lot of work to be done if we would like to see the Convention fulfilling its objectives in most of the cases. In this regard, the regional assessment of the Convention's operation that took place in Panama on 29–31 March 2017 with the participation of Central Authorities and Hague Network Judges of the Americas left us with some helpful recommendations that are strongly worth supporting.[22] One of the most important messages that arose at the meeting was probably the Network Judges' conclusion that 'there was a need to review their internal procedures to assess whether they allow for decisions to be taken within the timeframe of the 1980 Child Abduction Convention (cf. Article 11), and if not, to adjust the relevant procedures accordingly'.

Conclusions

This chapter has shown the prominent role that judges have in the different phases of the development of private international law. While they naturally have a primary role in adjudicating cases (and operating international instruments), they may also have a role in identifying international legal issues, developing private international law instruments, implementing them, and assessing and improving their operation.

The levelling of the global economic playing field and the increasing interconnectivity of societies and people worldwide in practically all areas of life – that is, globalisation – which is overwhelmingly a matter of private initiative, increases the role of private international law and thereby that of judges in the development of private international law. This role is bound to expand further in the future.

We have also highlighted the importance of the implementation phase, in particular in the case of private international law instruments that include a legal cooperation component, and have provided several examples of the active role that judges have played, and are playing, in this phase in the Latin American region, especially regarding the 1980 Hague Child Abduction Convention.

Against this background, we would hope that international organisations and

[20] The Protocol, which has been officially recommended by the Supreme Court of Argentina, can be accessed at: www.cij.gov.ar/adj/pdfs/ADJ-0.305074001493756538.pdf. For further references on the Protocol, see All, P. and N. Rubaja (2017) 'El Protocolo de Actuación para la Sustracción Internacional de Niños', *Revista La Ley*, 14 June 2017 (AR/DOC/1426/2017).

[21] Law No. 10.419 adopted by the Provincial Legislature on 21 December 2016.

[22] The report of the meeting and its conclusions and recommendations can be accessed at: www.hcch.net/en/news-archive/details/?varevent=551

state authorities that are tasked with the development of private international law consider judges as relevant stakeholders and invaluable partners in their endeavours to develop private international law, all the more so when dealing with matters involving cross-border judicial cooperation.

Finally, in relation to the Hague Conference, it should be noted that currently judicial meetings of the International Hague Network of Judges are lacking a solid formal (and financial) foundation. Such a firm footing would be helpful to secure regular meetings, efficient participation in the Hague Conference's relevant work and sustainability of essential tools to support the Network – such as the Judges' Newsletter or the regular collection and analysis of statistics – all of which are also crucial in linking judges and Central Authorities. Likewise, the useful 'Emerging Guidelines regarding the development of the International Hague Network of Judges'[23] have no formal status. This informality has advantages: it provides flexibility and makes further organic growth possible. However, it comes at a price, because for want of a formal basis the system is fragile, and its continuity is not guaranteed.[24] We would hope, therefore, that efforts to obtain a firm legal and financial basis for these tools will be continued and intensified. Input from the judges themselves in these efforts is of course, in our view, vital.

[23] See above fn. 10.

[24] In this respect the European Judicial Network in civil and commercial matters, based as it is on a decision of the European Council (2001, and since 2009 also of the European Parliament) has a more solid foundation. The Red Iberoamericana de Coopéracion Juridica Internacional (IberRed) would also seem to benefit from a more solid supportive framework.

18

Private International Law and International Commercial Arbitration – A Dialogue about the Usefulness and Awareness of the Former for the Latter

Giuditta Cordero-Moss and Diego P. Fernández Arroyo

Introductory Note

This contribution is different in many ways. It is not in the format of a traditional book chapter but it replicates, without some conversational ingredients, the keynote debate between Giuditta Cordero-Moss (GCM) and Diego Fernández Arroyo (DFA) that took place at one of the conferences in Edinburgh in the context of the PILIM project. This chapter explores the role played by private international law in international commercial arbitration. It highlights the relevance of private international law's thinking for the practice of international commercial arbitration and discusses the advantages and disadvantages of conflict rules in arbitration proceedings where the parties have made a choice of law, examining also the limitations of choice of law clauses. The debate was chaired by Verónica Ruiz Abou-Nigm (VRA), principal investigator of the PILIM project.

The Debate

GCM: We have seen the role of private international law highlighted from different perspectives. I expected coming to a seminar on private international law to see and hear a consistent support for the idea that private international law is important for arbitration, but I have heard a little bit of both points of view. This is good because I will speak about how important private international law is, and if everyone agreed it would be quite boring. Diego has generously agreed to play the role of devil's advocate in this debate, that is, to challenge the usefulness of private international law in the context of international commercial arbitration. We thought that we might start with some general brief comments and then approach some specific issues including jurisdiction, procedure, law applicable to the substance, and challenge and enforcement of the arbitral award.

DFA: I must confess my sceptical views on the usefulness of private international law in arbitration, at least if we take 'private international law' in its classical conception. I have several observations underlying my scepticism to share with you. In my own experience as an arbitrator I have never seen my colleagues very worried about private international law in general. Actually, some months ago, a colleague mentioned to me that he brought up the question in a case in which he is involved as the presiding arbitrator. Considering his character of private international law scholar, he tried to expose an issue relating to the applicable law to the merits from the traditional perspective of private international law, underlying how important this perspective was. His co-arbitrators were astonished: 'What? What are you talking about?' After a short discussion, they decided to submit the question to the parties, who answered immediately that the law of country A was applicable and that they could not see any problem there. I suspect that the same reaction would arise in any single opportunity a similar question is raised.

That said, let's go to my observations, from a very general point of view. The first one is particularly addressed to people here who are not familiar with private international law or who are not private international law specialists. Private international law scholars (also known as conflict scholars in England and North America) are convinced that private international law is the centre of the universe, at least of the legal universe. According to a private international law scholar, colleagues from other fields deal with legal science and technique; conflict scholars deal with an art. Actually, they feel like artists. They are much more sophisticated than ordinary lawyers. They solve disputes that lack a common legal framework. That is to say, disputes involving several legal orders. Solving disputes whose elements are all related to a single legal order can be relatively straightforward in terms of technique. Even a student in the first semester of law school can attempt to provide an answer to a legal problem if all the elements involved therein are related by a single legal order. Conversely, solving a dispute involving many legal orders is an art only reserved to a few specialists. That is what conflict scholars tend to think about themselves. Needless to say, generally speaking, the other legal scholars and practitioners do not share this impression.

The second observation concerns methodology. As you know, the most renowned conflict scholar ever, Friedrich Carl von Savigny, coined a methodology which has proven to be successful. I said successful, which does not always mean useful. In other words, many legislators and courts followed and still follow that methodology even if its flaws seem more numerous than the solutions it offers, particularly in some fields. The idea of private international law that has been shared by many conflict scholars until now is based on a notion of a world divided into national states and national legal orders. Given that there are many legal relationships that are linked to more than one legal order, it would be necessary to rely on a mechanism to select one single law to govern each legal relationship. The key notions of this classical assumption of private international law are domestic law, national law and the use of an indirect mechanism, a mechanism of localisation, to deal with international legal relationships. That is to say, we would need a sort of particular methodology to adjudicate a particular legal outcome to legal relationships related to several legal orders. This kind of mechanical tool to select one legal order to be applied to relationships that are related to several legal orders is enforced in many systems and still attracts lawmakers all over the world, even in the most recently enacted acts on private international law.

Thirdly, when arbitration started its evolution toward a modern disputes settlement mechanism – I am talking about the idea of the immediate post-World War II period, in the 50s and 60s – classical private international law was still influential. So modern international arbitration was born under a conflicts pattern, that is, under the classical private international law pattern described above. You can see that in the 1958 New York Convention, in the 1961 Geneva Convention and even in more recent private international law domestic Acts. The main example is the Swiss Private International Law Act adopted in 1987, which includes a chapter on arbitration, from a very classical private international law approach. The reason is perhaps that this law was made when international arbitration was not so important in Switzerland. In Latin America, this approach from a private international law perspective in arbitration no longer exists, but we have the example of the 1975 Panama Convention and the Mercosur Agreements in international arbitration made in 1988. The latter is in force but it remains practically (and fortunately) unapplied, maybe because of the approach used in the drafting of those agreements.

Lastly, international arbitration today is not what it used to be in 1958 when the New York Convention was made. Today, it is rather transnational in nature. There are common terms, common practices, the same leading arbitrators, and the most significant institutions compete to develop the most attractive legal offer for transnational business. In this framework, that panorama of classical private international law is not necessarily adapted to the field of arbitration. If we took private international law in another sense, from a more modern perspective (I mean including soft law rules and substantial considerations), perhaps it could be interesting to deal with certain situations. Yet, private international law based on the selection of a national law according to the location of some connecting factors is practically irrelevant for arbitration, or at least it should be. Rules on arbitration are mainly substantive rules. Within the context of arbitral proceedings, that is to say, proceedings conducted by arbitral tribunals, the use of classical private international law is exceptional. Private international law may have a role only at the limits of the arbitral proceedings, or outside of them. I mean when parties go to the courts before, during or after arbitral proceedings requesting judicial support for arbitration proceedings, but not for the proceedings as conducted by arbitral tribunals themselves. Courts, in their assistance of arbitration, may have recourse to private international law tools, but even in court proceedings related to arbitration, private international law is becoming rare, for two main reasons: modern arbitration law is mostly substantive law, and its notions are transnational rather than international. Whenever the question about the applicable law arises, the best answer in arbitration is almost always a transnational substantive rule.

GCM: I noted four main points that I would like to comment upon, firstly, regarding how often private international law is relevant in practice. On this point we had nice exchanges with colleagues showing how this usually is a question of awareness. You may have a disputed contract and, if you don't know that private international law exists, you may think that the contract doesn't have any problems of private international law. But as soon as you know it exists, you become aware of all the problems. Yet, you could still 'live happily' without an awareness of those private international law problems. So, it's not that in most arbitration cases you would need to take recourse to private international law, but there is a good number of situations in which the outcome depends on whether you apply one law or another. And you have cases where one party is really gaining from the application of one law and the other party is really gaining from the non-application of that law, and that is the situation where private international law rules become really practical and relevant. This is actually an assumption I wanted to lay out underpinning the observations that I am going to make during this debate. There are situations in which this is not relevant, such as when the parties agree to apply the same law (choice of law clause), or where the possible applicable laws provide for the same substantive regulations. However, except for these kinds of situations, private international law conflict rules should provide the answer. Not in an artistic way, but in a positive way.

I had never thought of it like this, but I must say I like the idea of being an artist. Rather than as an artist, I consider the private international lawyer as a good technician. The private international law lawyer is dealing with meta law, a regulation on which regulations are going to decide the substance. I would consider it more as meta law than as an art. The point is to contribute to foreseeability in the dispute or the potential dispute. I drafted contracts for many years, and I wanted to know which law would be applicable so that I could draft the contractual clauses accommodating that. In order to do that, I need a set of rules to tell me which law is going to be applicable to that contract in the event of a dispute. Actually, a more creative and artistic approach is required, in my mind, in situations where there is no private international law. Because when there isn't private international law you don't really know the criteria according to which the applicable law will be chosen. That becomes sort of an art, not necessarily in a positive way. Here I would quote the Danish professor Ole Lando, whom everybody of course knows, wonderful academic and person, who started as a private international law lawyer and gradually turned to think that private international law was not important after all, and that transnational law gives all the solutions. In one of his many publications he said: 'Why do we have to worry about private international law in arbitration? You know arbitrators are not normal lawyers; they are more like social engineers.'[1] You just leave the matters in the hands of the arbitrators. You don't have to give the arbitrators any parameters,

[1] Lando, O. (1985) 'The Lex Mercatoria in International Commercial Arbitration', *International and Comparative Law Quarterly*, vol. 34, no. 4, 747–68, at 752.

criteria, any rules because they are social engineers; they are creating the rules and the frameworks while they are making the decision. Described like that, the idea of arbitrators as social engineers may be very appealing, but I can't help being reminded of Franz Kafka's wonderful 'The Trial'. This poor guy was accused of something and he didn't know what he was accused of nor did he know the applicable rules. Try to defend yourself and plead your case before a social engineer without knowing which rules he's going to create. That is more like art than private international law. I am not saying private international law is perfect, but it is better than the alternative, which is a sort of full discretion. The alternative assumes that you have to go to an arbitrator and plead your case before you find out under which law that case should have been pled. These are my preliminary comments on the artistic side of the question.

Thirdly, I will comment on the idea that private international law is based on relatively outdated concepts of domestic law and national states, whereas the very nature of international arbitration and international disputes is that they are based on international transactions and relationships. It is true that international disputes are based on international relationships, but as long as the awards have to be enforced by national courts, it is still necessary to relate them to the old-fashioned understanding of the law and to produce an award that can be recognised and enforced by a court that is still thinking in terms of domestic legislation. We have the New York Convention, which refers to national laws and national courts in several contexts that are quite important, that I think we are coming back to when we discuss different topics later during this debate. Invalidity of an award is regulated by national law and certainly depends on the criteria of national law, and enforceability depends on the criteria of the New York Convention, which refers to national law in some contexts. Not taking into consideration this structure of domestic legal systems may be tempting and less anachronistic than sticking to the domestic systems, but it does not fit with the regulation on invalidity and enforceability. If you abandon the traditional approach, you may have a less anachronistic award, but it might be one which is not valid or enforceable. Lastly, on these lines, being 'transnational' does not necessarily remove the need to interpret a contract or a transnational system or the need to apply rules that belong to domestic legal systems. There are several illustrations that can be made of this point, which I will leave for the later discussion on specific topics.

DFA: Let's talk about the four topics mentioned by Verónica. The first one is jurisdiction. Jurisdiction in arbitration is based on the will of the parties. I think we can share this point of view without any problem. Giuditta agrees with me. Arbitral tribunals have the competence-competence principle. So, they decide on the basis of the arbitration agreement and the generally recognised arbitration principles. National laws in this context are not relevant; therefore, classic private international law is not relevant. That is generally applicable to commercial arbitration, but if you think particularly of institutional arbitration, whenever the parties cannot solve a specific problem, it is the institution that is in charge of solving such problem on the basis of the material rules and practices of the institution. National jurisdiction is not relevant because parties have chosen arbitration as a dispute settlement mechanism in order to avoid national courts. Comparative law shows a trend towards the exceptional character of national courts' intervention in arbitral proceedings. According to this trend, national courts can only intervene in a very limited number of issues during arbitral proceedings. Some legal systems are quite tough with judges who violate this restriction. For example, the Peruvian arbitration act expressly states that judges are liable whenever they interfere with arbitration outside the few specific situations provided by Peruvian arbitration law. In my opinion private international law is not relevant for transnational issues for concrete reasons. Firstly, except for exceptional circumstances, arbitration agreements block state jurisdictions. All modern arbitration laws recognise this. Secondly, it is not clear what would be the applicable sources of private international law, since arbitral tribunals do not have a forum. If you say that a conflict rule shall apply but the arbitral tribunal can select the one it finds most appropriate (as was the common assumption in the past), we would end up in a useless, artificial intermediation. Thirdly, even if domestic rules were necessary within arbitral proceedings, arbitrators are in general free to apply them or not. Ultimately, when a domestic court intervenes in arbitration it might apply substantive rules and principles to solve jurisdictional issues. Even with regard to internationality, the answer to the question about when a specific arbitration is international is treated from a substantive perspective in some national systems. For example, Article 1504 of the French Code of Civil Procedure establishes that arbitration proceedings are international when trade interests are at stake. That is to say, the old-fashioned rule that arbitration is international if one of the parties has a different nationality from the other, or the headquarters of the company or the legal administration of the parties are in different countries . . . that does not exist any more for the French legal system. I mention France, but also other modern codifications in arbitration law assume – at least partially – a substantive point of view to deal with international arbitration. That shows the different perspectives and approaches to arbitration.

GCM: I agree with everything that you said, which can be summarised by saying that there is a widespread arbitration-friendly attitude in regulations. So, you have international conventions as well as national domestic laws providing that the agreement to arbitrate prevails and if parties have agreed to arbitrate then courts cannot in principle exercise jurisdiction. So, there is an arbitration-friendly framework. The arbitral tribunal has the competence to decide on its own competence; indeed the competence-competence principle is very well established in arbitration. This, however, does not mean that courts do not have any jurisdiction or anything to say on this matter. Because even if the tribunal has competence-competence, it is the court that ultimately decides on the validity or the enforcement of an arbitral award. And, as I was mentioning earlier, the courts do apply national law when they decide on the invalidity of an award, and in several respects they also apply national law in connection with the enforcement of the award. The most important examples are the form of the arbitration agreement, which is regulated uniformly in Article 2 of the

New York Convention, but, as we know, today there are many domestic legislations that have a more favourable regulation when it comes to the form of the arbitration agreement; for example in Norway and Sweden, the arbitration agreement may be oral, it does not have to be in writing, whereas it has to be in writing under the New York Convention.

You have the possibility to apply the more favourable law according to the New York Convention, but the question is which law is applicable to the form of arbitration agreements. This is a private international law question, and this question is solved in this case by the New York Convention itself, which has a rule in Article v that states that unless the parties have agreed otherwise, the award cannot be enforced if the arbitration agreement was invalid under the law that the parties agreed to, or if the parties have not agreed, then under the law of the place of arbitration. That is a private international law rule in the New York Convention that is very useful in the framework of international arbitration.

DFA: I have already said that the New York Convention was under the influence of classical private international law. Furthermore, the ground you mention and all grounds of Article v, paragraph 1 only apply if one of the parties invokes it. That is to say that the rule is not as mechanical as traditional conflict rules. Furthermore, coming to the enforcement of arbitral agreements, nothing prevents the use of a substantive presumption of validity, as it is the case in France.

GCM: The French approach is very special. But in the remaining 191 countries, the approach is that of the New York Convention. Another example is about legal capacity. The rule again in Article v of the New York Convention says that an arbitral award cannot be enforced if it turns out that one of the parties to the arbitration agreement was under some form of incapacity under that party's own law. That is private international law – the capacity is governed by the law of each of the parties to the arbitration agreement. And that is of course a conflict rule that is not perfect, because it does not say which law is 'each party's law', which means private international law becomes relevant to find out which law each party is subject to, when it comes to its own capacity. There are many other examples of situations where the validity and the enforceability of an award is subject to the local laws when the courts examine the arbitral award, in connection with the arbitrability, in connection with the scope of the arbitral agreement, with the substantive validity of the arbitral agreement, and then of course with public policy. I won't talk about these, but since I started talking about legal capacity, I started by saying that legal capacity has a special conflict rule in Article v of the New York Convention, which is not perfect and assumes application of another conflict rule.

I would like to go back to what Diego said and what was said earlier today as well – that arbitration has no forum, and therefore there is no private international law which an arbitrator could look at. That is something I am not very convinced of, because arbitration has a forum in many different contexts. The law of the place of arbitration is relevant, for example, when it comes to the validity of the arbitration agreement, the default mechanism for appointing the arbitrators, the default mechanism for challenging the arbitrators, the procedure of the arbitration proceeding, which powers the tribunal has, for example, when it comes to interim measures, which possibilities the court has to give assistance for the arbitral tribunal, for example in producing evidence, and then, of course, the challenge of the arbitral award and then the public policy and the arbitrability rules. All these aspects are regulated by the *lex loci arbitri*, the law of the place of arbitration. So, in my mind, arbitration does have a forum, as all these examples show. And then I wonder why should the forum not also be relevant when it comes to private international law rules? I know that recent modern legislation is trying to sever the link between arbitration and private international law of the place of arbitration – there are many different approaches. I am not sure that this is a good development, because, since the law of the place of arbitration is so important in all these aspects that I have mentioned, I don't really see why it should not also be employed when it comes to private international law. The gist of what I am saying here is that, yes, arbitration and jurisdiction of arbitrators are based on the will of the parties, and yes, the relevant laws and international conventions give plenty of room to the arbitration agreement and to the parties, but there are very important aspects where the validity and enforceability of an arbitration award depend on the arbitral tribunal having applied the right law – the right law is determined either by special conflicts rules provided for in the New York Convention or in other arbitration instruments, for example, or in some other system of private international law. I think it should be the legal system of the place of arbitration, but there are different solutions in different systems. And this is something that is useful not only for the validity and enforceability of the award, but also for the parties' ability to predict which law is going to be applied, whether they have the legal capacity or not and so on.

DFA: Before going into issues of procedure, I would like to rebut two of Giuditta's arguments. First, Giuditta said that ultimately it is a court that decides about the jurisdiction of the arbitral tribunal. That is not totally true. The court has the right to express the last word; that is the rationale of the competence-competence principle, which is based on the priority given to the arbitral tribunal in order to avoid bad practices in arbitration. Remarkably, in the overwhelming majority of cases, the court's last word is not pronounced. In other words, in the vast majority of cases the decision of the arbitral tribunal on its own jurisdiction is final and binding – there are no challenges, there is nothing for the court to decide. I do not have statistics, but my impression is that in most cases, the decision of the arbitral tribunal on its own jurisdiction is the last word. So private international law is maybe relevant, but marginally relevant. The other comment is that almost every time you mentioned for all those examples the application of the so-called *lex loci arbitri* by the courts, the law of the forum, you called it forum, or *lex loci arbitri*, or the law of the seat. That means, courts normally apply their own arbitration law. For that, no private international law is necessary.

Private international law is not necessary when the only real option is the application of the *lex fori*. I imagined that private international law was more sophisticated than that. Just to say that the law of the seat is applicable – we don't need all the complex apparatus of private international law. Courts already did that before the existence of private international law, in the Dutch statutes. We had already the application of the *lex fori* before Savigny, Mancini and everyone after that.

GCM: Just a very brief reply: in some situations, private international law will point to the law of the court; in some other situations it does not – for example, in relation to the legal capacity of the parties to enter into the arbitration agreement.

DFA: In almost all the examples you gave, the application was the law of the forum, the *lex loci arbitri.*

GCM: Not when it comes to legal capacity and not when we are talking about enforcement. Now you are assuming that you are in a challenge situation, but if you are trying to enforce the award in a different country then . . .

DFA: But that is in our last point [below].

GCM: But you are taking me there! OK, we'll leave the reply to the last point.

DFA: Let's discuss procedure. I will be brief now. Procedure is governed by the parties' agreement and parties normally choose arbitration rules of an institution or the UNCITRAL arbitration rules for ad hoc arbitration. In addition to that, arbitrators have international sources, such as the IBA rules on taking of evidence, and generally recognised principles (equality of the parties, due process, etc). Recourse to national law is not necessary and is not advantageous in general in arbitral proceedings. So private international law is not that necessary either in this point. The arbitral tribunal – by means of the so-called procedural order number one – settles what the parties have not previously agreed upon. That is the practice of arbitration. If the parties have not agreed upon some procedural aspect, the arbitral tribunal solves this by applying the rules it has established or relying on inherent powers. Whenever procedural issues are exceptionally brought before domestic courts, courts do not necessarily use private international law criteria to decide; they systematically apply their own law without considering any connecting factor and we can say that they apply the *lex fori* in general, which is an option within private international law discourse, I know, but it is rather a denial of private international law. The principle of territorialism is not even pre-modern private international law.

GCM: That is a difficult one. I do not really have so much to say about procedure because I think that, on purpose, most modern arbitration laws do not have an extremely detailed regulation on the procedure and the regulation that they have is usually a default regulation unless there are, of course, the important principles like *audi alteram partem* (you know, both parties have to present their case), and due process and several other well-recognised principles. But otherwise most of the procedural rules can be derogated from the contract of the parties and they are integrated by the arbitration rules if the parties have chosen institutional arbitration. And all this flexibility is on purpose because the parties should be able to regulate their proceeding as they see fit. So, I have not seen a lot of private international law issues arising in the context of procedure; probably the most relevant areas would be the interface between the courts' power and the arbitral tribunals' powers when it comes to preliminary or preventive measures, or the production of evidence. There was an interesting discussion in the UNCITRAL working group on arbitration in the last session when we were talking about the notes on the organisation of the arbitral proceedings: someone talked about the possibility that the parties would choose a procedural law different from the law of the place of arbitration, which is a possibility that anybody reasonable speaks badly about. But there is this possibility under French law, as far I know, and what was interesting was that the whole room was for once in complete agreement that there is no such possibility. And the French delegate was there, and I went during the break after and asked him, 'Don't you have in French law the possibility to choose a different law?' and he answered, 'Yes, indeed, but it is not so important'. So, it seems that the territoriality principle in the context of procedure is actually living a quite unchallenged and happy life.

DFA: We are talking about procedural issues arising before a domestic court. For an arbitral tribunal the problem is not a real problem because all arbitrators will be using substantive rules agreed by the parties or decided by the arbitral tribunal. Article 1509 of the French Code of Civil Procedure, it is true, allows parties to choose another procedural law, that is to say another arbitration law. That was included coupled with the intervention of the French *juge d'appui*, the judge acting in support of arbitration, just to permit another supplementary intervention of French courts in arbitrations whose seat is outside of France. And that is because in France the perception is that French arbitration law is so worthy that everyone deserves to be governed by French arbitration law.

GCM: That is very kind of them.

DFA: Yes, it would be like a gift for people of other countries.

Moving to the applicable law, I think we have heard many interesting thoughts today and several approaches to this issue, as indeed the very rich contributions to this volume, so we should not have so much to add. Nevertheless, there is, I think, an evolution in the matter of the applicable law in international arbitration, in particular regarding the merits. I am talking about the evolution from the *voie indirecte* to the *voie directe* in national acts on arbitration, in arbitration rules, and – most importantly – in lawmakers' mentality. There is also an evolution from the use of the term 'law' to the use of the term 'rules of law' and there is a common assumption that trade usages and the terms of the contract must be considered in any event. So, the space for classical private international law seems to be reduced. I cannot say it has been totally eliminated but it is significantly reduced. Talking specifically about the law applicable to the merits, concerning the arbitration agreement, back to the first issue, some legal systems have already evolved towards a substantive approach governed by the validity principle, that is autonomous of all legal systems and only subject to international public policy. And that is the French system I mentioned before. In 1993, there was a famous case in the French Supreme Court for private law matters, the *cour de cassation*, the *Dalico*[2] case; this case dealt with a contract between a Danish company and a Libyan municipality that refused to arbitrate because the mandatory provisions of Libyan law imposed formalities to the arbitration agreement that had not been fulfilled in the case. The *cour de cassation* considered that the arbitration agreement was valid, and that the fact that some formal requirements were missing did not affect its validity because an arbitration agreement must be addressed without reference to any national law. This is, I think, a manifestation of an evolution of the concept, even if I can accept that in some particular cases the law applicable to the arbitration agreement is still important and that in other legal systems, traditional conflict rules are still enforced. But this is not the idea, for example, in the new version of the UNCITRAL Model Law. As you probably recall, the Model Law was revamped in 2006 and one of the modifications was about the form of the arbitration agreement. There are now two options, and one of the options is no form at all for arbitration agreements. Maybe in the future, it will become a trend. And if no formal requirements are established for the arbitration agreement in international arbitration obviously we do not need a conflict rule to say which law governs the formal requirements.

GCM: I leave the form of the arbitration agreements because I spoke already about that; actually, I would like to add just one comment, that is, if there is uncertainty whether it is French law or Austrian law, which I think is a little bit more formal when it comes to the requirements, then private international law becomes very important because you have to decide whether the agreement was subject to one or the other. So, the fact that some national laws are becoming very liberal when it comes to the form of the arbitration agreement only enhances the need for choosing between the laws, rather than making that need less relevant. But I have some comments regarding the laws applicable to the substance of the case. You were mentioning the *voie directe* – there is a trend towards the possibility for the arbitral tribunal to directly identify the law applicable without going through the mechanism of the choice of laws, so without necessarily applying whatever connection criteria would be applicable. As I said earlier, speaking about the social engineers and Kafka, I don't think that trend is

[2] See *Municipalité de Khoms El Mergeb* v. *Société Dalico*, 20 December 1993, Case No. 91-16828.

necessarily helping because it does not really contribute to foreseeability when you don't know in advance on the basis of which criteria the law is going to be chosen.

DFA: That is in the case where parties have not chosen . . .

GCM: I know.

DFA: So, parties have the possibility . . .

GCM: They may not have chosen the law, for example, because the one informed party knew that under the applicable private international law the contract would be subject to a certain law, and that is the law that party wants, so there was no need to bring the matter up with the other party. Or the parties, without speculating on that, might have assumed on the basis of private international law that the contract would be subject to a certain law and therefore there was no need to regulate the choice of law. In any case, even if the parties have forgotten or were not aware when they drafted the contract, when a dispute arises and the parties start evaluating which possibilities they have, that is the time when they need to find out which law is applicable, because that is when they need to work out if it is worthwhile to go to arbitration, or if they should rather aim to settle the matter outside any adjudication procedure. For making that kind of assessment the parties should have the possibility to take recourse to some criteria, some objective criteria, to allow them to ascertain the law that is applicable. And if they have to wait for the social engineer to decide which law is applicable, it means that they have already started the arbitration, so they have already gone through all the costs that are connected with that. And then the arbitrator says, 'Oh sorry, it was the law according to which you are time-barred, so you don't have a claim'. So that's a little bit too late to identify the governing law. That was the point I wanted to make earlier in relation to foreseeability.

There are two further points that I would like to make on the question of the governing law and how private international law is useful in this context. One is relating to the choice of law made by the parties in the contract. According to classical private international law, the parties are allowed to choose the law that applies to the contractual aspects of their relationship. This a conflict rule known as party autonomy. If they have a complicated contract, like a shareholder's agreement that has also some company law aspects, or a transaction where there is some pledge or some mortgage or some other property law aspects, or a contract with intellectual property aspects, those are areas (legal categories) where party autonomy does not apply. Those are fields, issues, that are outside the scope of the choice made by the parties, notwithstanding that the parties have written in the contract 'this contract is to be governed by Swedish law'. The choice of law made by the parties does not necessarily have effects on every aspect of the business transaction. Limitations apply to competition law, labour law, property law, *inter alia*.

DFA: It depends on the legal system. Moreover, if you say that in a contract on intellectual property no party autonomy is admitted, that would not be true.

GCM: Well, of course. If you are licensing your property you can choose the law. Whether you have a patent that is valid or not, that is something different.

DFA: But that is not a contractual issue.

GCM: But that is exactly my point. You may have a contract that is complex. And you may have a contract that has implications of company law, of property law, of intellectual property law in the sense of patents, for example the validity of the patent. Of course, we all know that the law chosen applies only to the contractual aspects, but if the contract is complex and has also implications for several other non-contractual legal issues, what law shall govern those issues? The parties might believe that their choice of law applies also to those aspects, and that is where private international law comes in and tells you that 'sorry, your choice applies to the contract, and not also to whether you had the capacity to enter into the contract or not', for example. That is a very typical example where the parties get very surprised and say, 'What? I have chosen Swedish law, why do they say that under Ukrainian law my contract is not valid because the other (Ukrainian) party didn't have the legal capacity? I didn't choose Ukrainian law, I chose Swedish law'. And that's where an awareness of private international law is useful, because it permits the parties to determine in advance the scope of the choice of law they are making. This is something that becomes relevant again when we talk later about enforcement.

And then the other point that you made about parties choosing more and more rules of law and not necessarily only laws, meaning that there are more and more transnational sources that make the choice of domestic legal systems redundant. It is true to a large extent, of course. But there are situations where even those instruments of transnational law need to be interpreted and they need to be supplemented. They don't cover everything and what do you interpret with, and how do you supplement them? With the applicable law. So, this is another example, another situation where the modern trends do not render private international law redundant. They might reduce its scope, but they don't make it redundant.

DFA: Only marginal, not redundant. Let's go to the last point, enforcement.

GCM: Yes.

DFA: I will make only three very short points. The first one is that the vast majority of awards are enforced all over the word without any necessity for court intervention. That is a matter of fact. The second point: whenever a party applies for enforcement before a domestic court, the award is enforced in most cases. That is to say that we have a reduced number of cases where we go to court in order to enforce, to ask for the enforcement of an award. And there are an even more reduced number of cases in which there is a real problem, in which – maybe – private international law issues will arise. And the third point deals with the grounds for the refusal of enforcement or the challenge of an award, which are quite standardised due to the strong impact of the New York Convention. And I already mentioned that the New York Convention is at the beginning of the modern era of arbitration and because of this, it should change in the future. And even within the context of the application of the New York Convention as it is, if you look at Article V, paragraph 2, that is to say the problem of public policy and arbitrability, again, not real private international law is there, but a sort of control of domestic compatibility, court members do not need particular private international law skills to do that, to say 'this decision is against our public policy'. They should know their public policy principles. And finally, we have Article V, paragraph 1, and there some small space for private international law considerations appears, due in particular to paragraph 1a, which deals with the situation already mentioned of the law applicable to the arbitration agreement. And, once in a blue moon, we have a problem about capacity. In such a case you need to say, 'Ukrainian law says . . .' That is indeed very rare; it would be one case out of thousands of cases. That is the reality of the practical use, I mean of the usefulness of private international law in arbitration.

GCM: It is, luckily, true that the great majority of arbitral awards are enforced voluntarily, without having to go to court. And of those that need assistance by the courts, there are not necessarily always private international law aspects. However, this does not mean that you should not regulate those aspects. So, I do not think I should spend more time on that. And I will not spend time reading again the list of all the subjects in the first sentence of Article V, where private international law is relevant, because it is the same as I mentioned at the beginning in connection with challenge. There is one further point that I would like to make very quickly. I mentioned when we talked about the law applicable to the substance of the dispute that private international law is useful because it gives you an understanding of the scope of party autonomy. And it gives the arbitral tribunal the tools to understand how far the choice of the parties goes, and what the criteria are for choosing the law in the other aspects (company law and labour law, *inter alia*) where party autonomy does not reach. Why do I mention it again in connection with the enforcement of the arbitral award? Let's think, for example, that the parties have a contract that has competition law relevance in Europe. They do not want to be subject to European competition law. They chose Russian law instead. They go to arbitration and they instruct the arbitrator specifically to apply Russian law according to the choice made by the parties. We all know that the arbitral tribunal has to follow the will of the parties. So, if the arbitral tribunal says, 'I cannot apply Russian law to the competition law aspects, I have to apply European law, otherwise the contract is not enforceable in Europe', then the arbitral tribunal runs the risk of exceeding its power. And excess of power is reason for not enforcing the award. So, the arbitral tribunal has actually to follow the will of the parties, the instructions given by the parties, to apply Russian law. On the other hand, if the arbitral tribunal disregards the relevant provisions on European competition law, we know that the Court of Justice of the European Union said that European competition law is public policy and therefore the arbitral award runs the risk of not being enforceable in Europe. So, what should be done in this situation? Does the arbitral tribunal have to decide between non-enforceability because of excess of power on one hand, or non-enforceability because of conflict with public policy on the other hand? That is a very bad position to be in. That is where private international law comes to the rescue, because that is where an awareness of private international law allows the parties to understand that 'yes, arbitrators have to follow the will of the parties, but the parties did not have the power to choose a different competition law from European law in this scenario'. Party autonomy only gives the parties the power to choose the law for contractual matters. So the law that was chosen by the parties had effects within the contract law aspects and not beyond. The arbitrators are to apply Russian law within the contract law aspects. When it comes to competition law, party autonomy does not cover competition law. So private international law gives the tools for the arbitral tribunal to understand and to explain to the parties what is the scope of party autonomy and avoid the risk of providing reasons for the award as if they had exceeded their power.

VRA: Thanks very much to our excellent world-renowned debaters! It was a very engaging debate. There is plenty of food for thought on both sides, I have to admit. Thank you very much indeed.

19

Demystifying Private International Law for International Commercial Contracts

Guillermo Argerich and María Laura Capalbo

Introduction

Demystifying the difficulty in understanding the theoretical approach that private international law has traditionally adopted and translating this into a suitable framework for drafting relevant contractual clauses in international commercial contracts is the focus of this chapter.[1] This is examined from a legal practice's perspective. The relentless process of globalisation requires the conceptual discourse of private international law to be understood by legal operators at large, specialists and non-specialists in this field. This is an indisputable reality nowadays; private international law must be seen and operationalised as a useful resource that is capable of solving practical issues. Exploring ways to enhance the practical day-to-day role of private international law for practitioners and somehow overcoming the limitations that have been associated with private international law as a discipline of only theoretical and even philosophical importance is considered by the authors as a priority for private international law in present times. This has begun to appear as a concern for national law-makers[2] as well as international ones.[3]

[1] Juenger, F. K. (1987) Lecture of 24 March 1987, Universidad de la República, Montevideo, Uruguay. Juenger stated that the archaic discourse of private international law prevented dialogue and that the concepts and approaches frequently used did not facilitate the analysis but obscured the perception in relation to the practical needs that are the main concerns of the discipline. Much has changed in the thirty years since this lecture yet there is still much more to be done to bring private international law closer to the needs of the individuals that the discipline aims to connect, protect and engage with.

[2] For example, this concern was expressed before the Uruguayan Parliament at the time of the discussion of the Private International Law Act. National legislators expressed the need to democratise private international law. See appearance of the Bar Association of Uruguay before the Commission of Constitution, Code, General Legislation and Administration of the Uruguayan Parliament, 29 July 2015, available at: https://parlamento.gub.uy/documentosyleyes/ficha-asunto/38377/ficha_completa

[3] The Hague Conference (see, *inter alia*, the programme of the conference celebrated in Buenos Aires in August 2018 to celebrate the 125th anniversary of the HCCH).

Businesses conduct their activities across borders and all over the world. Companies that operate internationally interact in different jurisdictions and engage with a variety of rules and business partners residing in other countries. This means that executives, legal counsellors, lawyers and other practitioners need to understand the consequences of doing business in a global environment characterised by legal diversity. This requires as much knowledge of the relevant facts as it does of the potentially applicable laws, rules on international jurisdiction and procedures necessary for the recognition and enforcement of judicial and arbitral decisions in different countries.

This chapter stresses the importance of understanding private international law methodologies for non-private international law experts so often in charge of drafting international commercial contracts due to the ever-increasing developments of this discipline as a result of the globalisation process. Its understanding is pivotal for lawyers, mediators, judges and arbitrators who are in charge of interpreting contractual clauses. The reflections offered in this chapter are based on a perspective developed by the authors with a focus on Argentine and Uruguayan law.

Therefore, this chapter analyses, in turn, (1) the objectives of private international law with a special focus on integration processes; (2) the characteristics of an international contract; (3) the function of jurisdiction and applicable law rules. It is decisive that anyone entering a contract with an international dimension should know beforehand the rules of the game.

The Context: Private International Law, International Commercial Contracts and Integration Processes

Private international law has had important developments since the process of codification started in the nineteenth century. However, in the field of international commercial contracts, traditional private international law solutions had never been enough because the extant treaties bind only a certain number of countries, such as the International Civil Law Treaties of Montevideo of 1889[4] and 1940,[5] and substantive harmonisation that could cover all commercial contractual matters is not plausible. In this sense, the United Nations Convention on Contracts for the International Sale of Goods (Vienna 1980) that provides 'a modern, uniform and fair regime for contracts for the international sale of goods',[6] ratified by eighty-nine parties and considered a complete success,[7] regulates some aspects of international sale of goods as defined therein. In turn, the conflictual Inter-American Convention on the Law Applicable to International Contracts,[8] which represents real innovation in international contracts allowing party autonomy and recognising the valid choice of non-state law – *lex*

[4] Ratified by Argentina, Bolivia, Colombia, Paraguay, Peru and Uruguay.

[5] Argentina, Paraguay and Uruguay ratified the 1940 Treaties on International Private Law of Montevideo.

[6] See www.uncitral.org/uncitral/en/uncitral_texts/sale_goods/1980CISG.html

[7] See www.uncitral.org/uncitral/en/uncitral_texts/sale_goods/1980CISG_status.html

[8] Signed in Mexico on 17 March 1994.

mercatoria – was only ratified by Mexico and Venezuela. International solutions are always therefore selective and inchoate, with gaps left. For example, in the Mercosur countries international contracts for the provision of services have not been appropriately regulated by multilateral private international law rules. Hence soft law solutions give important assistance to private international law, to fill the gaps, to contribute to elucidating interpretation issues, to provide guidelines as to how to bring together different overlapping relevant sources, and also at times to provide per se substantive rules. Soft law instruments such as the UNIDROIT Principles on International Commercial Contracts[9] and The Hague Principles on the Choice of Law in International Commercial Contracts[10] have substantially contributed to the development of cross-border solutions for international commercial contracts in the past few decades.

The first edition of the UNIDROIT Principles on International Commercial Contracts was issued in 1984, the second in 2004, the third in 2010 and the fourth in 2016, showing the developmental approach to providing for appropriate solutions to regulate international commercial contracts and setting forth common rules distilled from the best experiences of existing legal frameworks.

The Hague Principles on the Choice of Law in International Commercial Contracts of March 2015 also have this supplementary and developmental nature, as set forth in the preamble, to 'affirm the principle of party autonomy with limited exceptions, may be used as a model of national, regional, supranational or international instruments, to interpret, supplement and develop rules of private international law'.[11]

The efforts of the Inter-American Juridical Committee of the Organization of American States (OAS) in the preparation of the Guide on the Law Applicable to International Commercial Contracts in the Americas[12] is also noteworthy.[13] A survey was prepared in order to unearth the empirical reasons behind the lack of support for the Mexico Convention in the American countries.[14] The results of the enquiry as explained by the rapporteur of the Guide, Jose A. Moreno Rodríguez, attributed the causes of the lack of ratification as follows: (1) the legal community in 1994 was not prepared to ratify a document of that nature; (2) certain formulas arise from diplomatic compromise, such as Articles 9 and 10, for example; (3) some of the terms did not achieve an accurate translation into English.[15] In this context, the

9 See www.unidroit.org/instruments/commercial-contracts/unidroit-principles-2016

10 See www.hcch.net/es/instruments/conventions/full-text/?cid=135

11 Hague Principles on the Choice of Law in International Commercial Contracts, 19 March 2015, Preamble.

12 See www.oas.org/es/sla/cji/docs/DDI-doc-1-18.pdf. See also http://www.oas.org/en/sla/dil/newsletter_DDI_CJI_Guide_applicable_International_Commercial_Contracts_Americas_March-2019.html

13 Inter-American Juridical Committee (84th regular session, Rio de Janeiro, March 2014). Elizabeth Villalta put forward the topic in order to promote the ratification of the Inter-American Convention on the Law Applicable to International Contracts (Mexico Convention).

14 See www.oas.org/es/sla/cji/docs/DDI-doc-1-18.pdf, 14.

15 See www.oas.org/es/sla/cji/docs/DDI-doc-1-18.pdf, 17.

rapporteurs proposed to the Committee the adoption of a guide of principles that can facilitate the interpretation and understanding of complex concepts, as well as serve as a model to facilitate national law reform and expand the scope of solutions in this matter. Moreno presented the objectives of the Guide, taking into consideration elements of the Convention of Mexico of 1994, *inter alia*, to facilitate the adoption of solutions through various mechanisms (urging the Member States of the OAS either to adopt the guiding instrument of the OAS or provide for the principles embedded therein in their internal laws); to serve as an interpretative guide and even as a lingua franca for judges, referees and contractors; and to facilitate in the region the acceptance of solutions universally extended with respect to party autonomy and acceptance of non-state law. Consequently, the guide, besides being the first in the region, will serve as an instrument bridging the work developed by different organisations. It is based on the main principles of the Mexico Convention on the Law Applicable to International Contracts, on the Hague Principles on the Choice of Applicable Law on International Contracts and the most important international instruments in this matter, such as the UNIDROIT Principles.

In this sense, the soft law solutions and especially the OAS Guide have an added value in trying to modernise the Inter-American normative system by incorporating harmonising solutions into national systems; the objective of the guide is to standardise the rules in a clear manner so that when contracts are concluded between parties located in different jurisdictions, those parties can work in a harmonious way and thus promote international business in order to find more pragmatic formulas to facilitate international trade.

In the context of integration, processes to harmonise substantive and conflictual solutions in contractual matters and to generate a common core for the judicial interpretation of international commercial contracts seems particularly important. In the European Union much has been advanced with this aim, and EU private international law instruments such as the Rome Regulation, and later the Rome I Regulation, have been pivotal to developments in this field.

In the Mercosur zone the integration process has not advanced on these lines. Through the Mercosur Free Trade Agreement,[16] concluded in 1991, Argentina, Brazil, Paraguay and Uruguay constituted the common market of the southern part of South America (Mercosur).[17] This integration process has its focus on commercial matters as set forth in the Preamble: 'Considering that the expansion of their domestic markets, through integration, is a vital prerequisite for accelerating their

[16] The Treaty Establishing a Common Market between the Argentine Republic, the Federal Republic of Brazil, the Republic of Paraguay and the Eastern Republic of Uruguay was concluded in Asuncion on 26 March 1991 and entered into force on 29 November 1991; Venezuela has also been party to the Asuncion Treaty since July 2012. See https://www.mercosur.int

[17] Venezuela has had all its rights and obligations suspended (Art. 5, para. 2 of Protocolo de Ushuaia). Bolivia is in the process of accession. Chile, Colombia, Ecuador, Guyana Peru and Surinam are associate states.

processes of economic development with social justice'.[18] Article 1 of the Treaty establishes '[t]he commitment by States Parties to harmonize their legislation in the relevant areas in order to strengthen the integration process'. On these lines several Protocols[19] have been concluded in this framework, yet mostly using traditional private international law (conflict of laws) rules and not substantive harmonisation. The preference for conflictualism rather than substantive harmonisation has been justified on the basis of the lack of a common legal identity of the block, an aspect that is considered a corollary to the adoption of substantive uniform rules. In 2015[20] Didier Opertti contended that Mercosur was going through a true 'identity crisis' and a 'decrease in institutional self-esteem', not only for the economic results, but also for the lack of social acceptance of Mercosur as a project. Later, in 2016, Mercosur experienced an institutional crisis mainly associated with the institutional, political, social and economic crisis of Venezuela. The political interests once again surpassed the economic and commercial interests. The different approaches of the states in the block in relation to how to manage the crisis in Venezuela led Mercosur to enter an unprecedented state of paralysis.[21] This socio-political context is important to understand the lack of a comparable reality to that of the EU.

Coming back to international contracts in the sub-region, there is no common ground between States Parties of Mercosur; the main principle of party autonomy as established on the Inter-American Convention on the Law Applicable to International Contracts, on the UNIDROIT Principles on International Commercial Contracts and on the Hague Principles on the Choice of Law in International Commercial Contracts is not unanimously received; it is rejected by Brazil and Uruguay.[22] In this scenario soft law solutions could be an alternative for commercial parties in the region; Uruguayan parties could incorporate uniform soft law solutions into their

[18] See www.rau.edu.uy/mercosur/tratasp.htm and www.worldtradelaw.net/document.php?id=fta/agreements/mercosurfta.pdf

[19] Las Leñas Protocol on International Judicial Cooperation (1992), Buenos Aires Protocol on Jurisdiction in Contractual Matters (1994), Ouro Preto Protocol on Provisional Measures (1994), San Luis Protocol on Traffic Accidents (1996), Santa María Protocol on Jurisdiction on Consumer Relations (1996); the latter is not in force.

[20] See Opertti Badán, D. (2015) 'Ideas para reformar al MERCOSUR en lo institucional' Estudio 09/15, Consejo uruguayo para las relaciones internacionales (CURI), '*escribo sobre la realidad de un MERCOSUR que estaría atravesando una verdadera . . . "crisis de identidad" y "disminución de autoestima institucional". Esto último tiene mucho que ver no sólo con los resultados económicos sino con la aceptación social del instrumento MERCOSUR y su progresiva ausencia del imaginario uruguayo - que no podría desconocer, como una solución a sus problemas, de los que en la versión extrema, se alega con exageración que el causante sería precisamente el propio MERCOSUR*'. Available at: http://curi.org.uy

[21] Bartesaghi, I. (2017) 'La crisis del MERCORSUR en 2016', *Informes sobre Integración Económica (ISIE)*, No. 4 (April).

[22] Basedow, J. (2016) 'Theory of Choice of Law and Party Autonomy', in Fernández Arroyo, D. P. and J. A. Moreno Rodríguez (eds), *Contratos Internacionales*, Biblioteca de Derecho de la Globalización. Asociación Americana de Derecho Internacional Privado (ASADIP), 18–19.

agreements, with well-known techniques such as incorporation by reference,[23] to overcome difficulties and promote uniformity within the region.

Legal Thinking and International Commercial Contracts

Most lawyers are used to applying the law of the legal system in which they have trained as practitioners. Yet, faced with cross-border cases lawyers need to become familiar with private international law methodologies and techniques. The first issue to be considered is the identification of the international nature of a contract. Determining if the legal relationship contains relevant elements of 'alien status' is a must; the legal framework to provide the route to the relevant answers will depend on the 'international' nature of the contract and the specific legal systems that the contract is connected to.

When a legal operator is drafting a contract, all the attention is focused on clauses relating to its performance, price, default provisions and remedies. These are the core material issues in a contract since they are the key elements of the deal being concluded between the parties, and in turn need the conclusion of the contract to enable them. This applies equally in relation to domestic contracts, that is, to contracts with no foreign elements, and to international contracts. In relation to international contracts, the role of ICT to facilitate communication at the negotiation stage and the conclusion of the contracts need not be emphasised, yet the most important characteristic of international contracts is their international nature. Obvious as it may seem, when the contract is of an international nature it may be subject to a legal system different from that of the drafters of the contract. The awareness of that is crucial for providing accurate professional legal advice. It is not uncommon for legal professionals to 'domesticate' their legal thinking when drafting a contract and forget the lateral thinking needed to analyse the effects deriving from its international character. This in turn leads to an assessment of the contractual scenario based on the legal systems of the drafter(s) rather than the potentially applicable law to the contract. This common situation entails serious legal consequences, as will be explained. Four important practical issues should be at the forefront of legal thinking in relation to international contracts. First, the international nature of the contract; second, the scope of competent courts in case of disputes; third, the scope of the governing law; and, finally, the possibilities in relation to the recognition and enforcement of an eventual foreign decision relating to any disputes arising out of the contract or related to its performance.

The International Nature of the Contract

There are different criteria for defining the international nature of a contract. Following Lorenzo,[24] three criteria might be used for these purposes. First, the legal

[23] Fresnedo de Aguirre, C. (2009) *Curso de Derecho Internacional Privado*, tome II, vol. 2, Fundación de Cultura Universitaria, 200–2.

[24] Lorenzo Idiarte, G. (2002) '¿Cuándo un contrato es internacional? Análisis desde una perspectiva

criterion, which determination arises from substantive law or from the internal law referred to by the conflict of law rules. Following this criterion only the elements expressly recognised in that law are those that determine the internationality of a contract. Therefore, private international law rules indicate the internationality of a contract. The International Civil Law Treaties of Montevideo (1889[25] and 1940),[26] as well as the Appendix of the Uruguayan Civil Code,[27] do not provide a definition of an international contract but private international law scholars, such as Fresnedo de Aguirre,[28] infer from them a specific characterisation of 'international' when the place the contract was entered into and its place of performance occur in different countries. A different stance is taken by the United Nations Convention on the International Sale of Goods (CISG). The latter focuses the 'internationality' of the contract on the fact that the buyer's and seller's commercial establishments are located in different jurisdictions.[29] The CISG does not define an international contract but in its scope of application, Article 1(1) establishes that the Convention applies to contracts of the sale of goods between parties whose places of business are in different states. In the same way, the Inter-American Convention on the Law Applicable to International Contracts (Mexico, 1994) establishes in Article 1 that 'a contract is international if the parties thereto have their habitual residence or establishments in different States Parties or if the contract has objective ties with more than one State Party . . .' Second, the theoretical criterion points to the existence of any type of foreign elements, such as the domicile of the parties, place of performance of the contract, and so on in more than one state. In this sense, Goldschmidt[30] stated that a contract is international if the place it is entered into or its place of performance occurs in different states, or if the parties are domiciled in different states at the time the contract is concluded. Finally, the objective criterion refers to the existence of objective elements, whether factual or legal. The traditional French doctrine in contractual matters limited this criterion to the existence of objective elements with economic relevance in different states.[31] Lorenzo concludes that the first two criteria are not adequate to determine the international nature of the contract. In his view the legal criterion referred to in the first place is inadequate as it is overly restrictive, since it is the rule itself which would delimit such interna-

regional', in Kleinheisterkamp, J. and G. A. Lorenzo Idiarte (eds), *Avances del Derecho Internacional Privado en América Latina. Liber Amicorum Jurgen Samtlebem*, Fundación de Cultura Universitaria, 105–32.

25 Ratified by Argentina, Bolivia, Colombia, Paraguay, Peru and Uruguay.

26 Argentina, Paraguay and Uruguay ratified the 1940 Treaties on International Private Law of Montevideo.

27 Law 10.084, enacted in 1941, which set forth the main solutions of Uruguayan national conflicts of law rules.

28 De Aguirre, *Curso de Derecho Internacional Privado*, above fn. 23, tome II, vol. 2, 143–8.

29 Ibid., 143–8.

30 Ibid., 145–6.

31 Lando, O. (1984) 'The Conflict of Law of Contrats', *Recueil des cours*, vol. 189, 233.

tionality. The international nature of a contract cannot depend on the provisions of the different treaties or the applicable national private international law rules. This kind of solution does not give legal certainty to the parties at the time of conclusion of the contract. On the other hand, the theoretical criterion is not appropriate as it is too indeterminate; it points to the existence of any type of foreign element, which is unhelpful for the ascertainment of when a contract is 'international' for the purposes of private international law. Operationalising this concept would broaden the scope of 'internationality' to cover contracts that are for the most part negotiated, concluded and performed as domestic contracts. For that reason, in cases where the nature of the contract is not properly determined, the legal operator could apply incorrect rules to regulate the contractual relationship. For instance, if a contract is entered into in state A and performed in state B, according to the said criterion this contract could be deemed international. But imagine for a moment if this contract is entered into in state A only because one of the parties is circumstantially there, and all the other contractual elements are fully located in state B, without any other points of contacts with state A or with any other state. Do we have an international contract? The answer is crucial because if we consider this agreement as an international contract, parties could be allowed to choose the applicable law and the competent jurisdiction, but if this contract is not international, the law of state B will be the only applicable law. For that reason, it is not enough to take only this type of criterion into account when considering the international nature of a contract. Therefore, the objective criterion would be the most appropriate, despite the fact that it should not necessarily be limited to those aspects with economic relevance. In that sense, the Draft Private International Law Act of Uruguay[32] provides that 'a contract is international if the parties have their habitual residence or their establishment in different States or the contract has relevant objective contacts with more than one State'.[33] In Uruguayan law the international nature of the contract cannot depend on the will of the parties; parties are not enabled in Uruguayan law to 'internationalise' the contract, that is, to agree on contractual clauses that would make a contract international in cases where the core contractual elements are essentially domestic or confined to the boundaries of one legal system.[34] The same limitation is established in the Inter-American Convention on the Law Applicable to International Contracts (Mexico Convention). Objective aspects appear, however, to be determinant of the internationality of a contract. Party autonomy to choose the applicable law is allowed only in cases where the contract is international for objective reasons.

The preamble of the Hague Principles on Choice of Law in International

[32] See https://parlamento.gub.uy/documentosyleyes/ficha-asunto/38377/ficha_completa

[33] Art. 44.

[34] The Draft Private International Law Act of Uruguay states: 'The contract cannot be internationalized by the mere will of the parties' (Art. 44 *in fine*).

Commercial Contracts[35] only mentions that it applies to 'a contract that has connections with more than one State'. No further details are provided on the definition of an international contract. It is submitted that the consequences that can arise from not pointing out the international nature of a contract are severe. To the extent that a contract is domestic, all obligations and rights that arise from it should be regulated by that national law. If the contract is international, it may be governed by the law indicated by the private international law rule that is applicable to the case, provided in conflictual or substantive solutions, or by the law chosen by the parties if enabled to so select a law by the applicable private international law framework, which could be state or non-state law. Therefore, omitting to delineate when a contract is or is not international for the sake of determining its governing law could result in the drafting of a contract according to a set of norms that would not result in the end as the governing law of that contract. As a consequence, contractual clauses could be null and/or not binding according to the law that should govern the contract or could be interpreted not in accordance with the real intention of the parties. That is, 'domesticating' an international contract with the consequential analysis from a domestic perspective could entail important modifications in the parties' rights through the life of the contract.

Internationally Competent Jurisdictions

Understanding the art and challenges of choosing 'appropriate' courts is important for raising awareness of any possible pitfalls in drafting contracts. Lawyers need to take into consideration the eventual enforcement court(s) in that selection process. A possible refusal to recognise or enforce a judgment or an award does not necessarily always imply a refusal to uphold a choice of court clause. Generally, in contractual matters private international law rules use more than one criterion attributive of international jurisdiction. As the choice remains in the hands of the claimant, if the forum is not agreed the parties will be uncertain until the dispute arises about which judge will decide. This is one of the reasons why it is usual for international contracts to provide for a choice of court or an arbitration agreement. To ascertain the international jurisdiction where disputes from a contract may eventually arise is important for various reasons: for one, it is usually easier for claimants to initiate proceedings in the courts of their own country of residence or domicile. There are, however, several other considerations to take into account, such as the existence of evidence, the language of the country or city where litigation will take place, the costs of lawyers and transfers of parties and witnesses, and the need for documents to be translated. From a strictly legal perspective, judges use their own system of private international law, so that if the dispute arises in another country, the system of private international may be different, and the applicable law may also differ.

[35] Approved on 19 March 2015.

In the absence of choice by the parties, there are several criteria to determine the internationally competent jurisdiction for international contracts, generally classified into subjective and objective criteria. The former refers to conditions related to personal aspects of the litigants, such as their domicile; the latter are linked to the dispute itself, such as the place of performance of an obligation. In Uruguayan law, both types of criteria are mixed in the different rules. The regulation of direct competence is contained in Article 2401 of the Appendix to the Civil Code, which establishes as competent the courts of the country of the law that governs the contract. This is known as the parallelism criterion. Moreover, the same provision sets forth an option for the claimant to start proceedings at the forum of the domicile of the defendant. This option is limited to certain types of actions.[36]

The *forum causae* or parallelism criterion makes possible to attribute concurrent international jurisdiction to the judges of the country whose law, according to the rules of conflicts of the forum, is applicable to the case. The parallelism technique, also known as the Asser technique, is a jurisdiction-selection technique also known as *forum-ius* alignment, by which the forum whose law results are applicable becomes internationally competent to hear the case. It is difficult to draw the lines here between theory and practice, but it is necessary to do so. In practice, *forum causae* has always been favoured by the judiciary. Judges are more comfortable applying their own law, their own framework of understanding, and, to a certain extent, that is the only thing most of them are trained to do. Courts have resorted to the *forum cause* on several occasions in the absence of rules of international jurisdiction. In the Latin American region, Boggiano argued that:

> It is reasonable to admit that if Argentine law is applicable to the case, the parties may settle the dispute before the Argentine judges. However, the jurisdiction of the Argentine judges cannot exclude, in principle, that of other foreign judges founded on procedural considerations irrespective of the applicable law.[37]

This forum-selection technique is not without flaws and indeed has received profound criticism. The main argument against this technique lies in the investment of the logical legal order by submitting the determination of the competent judge to the previous determination of the applicable law. The applicable law to the cross-border case needs to be ascertained first in order to designate the competent judge.

Moreover, in Uruguay the (im)possibility to choose the competent court for international contracts is established in Article 5 of the 1940 Additional Protocol to the Treaty of Montevideo, as well as in Article 2403 of the Appendix to the Civil Code. The parties are not allowed to choose the competent jurisdiction; unless such choice is expressly permitted in a specific positive extant norm or according to private international conflict of law rules, the governing law admits such choice. Notwithstanding the above, Uruguay has national and supranational private international law rules that

[36] Vescovi, E. (2000) *El Derecho Procesal Civil Internacional, Uruguay, el Mercosur y América*, Idea, 38.
[37] Boggiano, A. (2017) *Tratado de Derecho Internacional Privado*, 6th edn, La Ley, tome I, 265.

expressly admit party autonomy in certain specific cases, for example in the context of Mercosur, the 1994 Protocol on International Jurisdiction in Contractual Matters, Buenos Aires[38] and the Securities Market regulation[39] respectively.

The adoption of uniform rules on international jurisdiction is an imperative need in a process of integration. The Mercosur Protocol broadly accepts choice of court agreements, provided that the case is related to international patrimonial matters. No reasonable connection is required between the contract and the chosen court. Choice of court agreements cannot trump provisions on exclusive jurisdiction. The Protocol requires four conditions for the choice of court agreements to be included under its scope of application: (1) it should be an international contract between individuals; (2) one party should at least be domiciled or have its registered office in a State Party; (3) the choice of court agreement must have been made in favour of a court of a State Party; and (4) there must be a reasonable connection in accordance with the rules of jurisdiction of the Protocol.

It cannot be overlooked that some types of contract are excluded from the material scope of this Protocol.[40] The excluded matters include accession contracts or contracts in which there is a notoriously weaker party, employment contracts, consumer sales contracts, contracts of transport and insurance contracts.

International Commercial Arbitration

Frequently, the jurisdiction of the state courts is displaced in favour of arbitration tribunals because the latter are a neutral and flexible forum for resolving any dispute and have a common language all over the world.[41] Moreover, arbitration is recognised globally as the natural forum for the business world, one that is particularly suited to deal with commercial matters of a contractual nature. When parties agree on an arbitration clause at the same time they can choose the governing law applicable to the merits. International commercial arbitration has been recognised in Uruguay for more than 120 years, since the Treaty of International Procedural Law of 1889 was adopted. In the universal arena the most important treaty is the Convention on the Recognition and Enforcement of Foreign Arbitral Awards (New York 1958), considered by Goode as 'astonishingly successful'.[42] In addition, within the scope of the American region, the Inter-American Convention on International Commercial Arbitration (Panama 1975), the International Commercial Arbitration Agreement of

[38] Ratified by Argentina, Brazil, Paraguay and Uruguay. See further the chapter by Paredes in this volume.

[39] Law 18,627, enacted in 2009.

[40] Art. 2.

[41] As to the relevance of private international law for international commercial arbitration, see Cordero-Moss and Fernández Arroyo's chapter in this volume.

[42] Moreno Rodriguez, J. A. (2010) 'Los contratos y la Haya ¿ancla al pasado o puente al futuro?', in Basedow, J. D., D. P. Fernández Arroyo and J. A. Moreno Rodríguez (eds) *¿Cómo se codifica hoy el derecho comercial internacional?*, Centro de Estudios de Derecho, Economía y Política (CEDEP), 279.

Mercosur (1998) and the International Commercial Arbitration Agreement between Mercosur and Bolivia and Chile (1998) were also ratified by Uruguay. The domestic private international law regulation that governs arbitration in Uruguay is the General Code of Procedure.[43]

Moreover, in 2018, Uruguay and Argentina adopted new International Commercial Arbitration Acts[44] based on the UNCITRAL Model Law. Consequently, both countries have a positive unified legal framework that allows for the efficient recognition of arbitral clauses and the enforcement of arbitral awards. These new specific rules for international arbitration displace the previous international commercial arbitration framework in both countries.

This scenario shows that Latin American countries are finally open to international arbitration and modernising their legal frameworks.[45] After Venezuela, Paraguay, Chile and Peru, the mentioned countries have also passed new international arbitration laws. Argentina and Uruguay required their arbitration laws to be modernised. The only provisions governing arbitration were codified in their Civil Procedure Codes, and in Argentina's case in the Civil and Commercial Code. The new arbitration laws in both Argentina and Uruguay apply only to international commercial arbitration, whereas domestic arbitration will continue to be governed by the respective Civil and Commercial Codes. Uruguay and Argentina are parties to the 1958 New York Convention on Recognition and Enforcement of Foreign Arbitral Awards. Both are also parties to the International Commercial Arbitration Convention adopted by the Mercosur states in 1998.

These new arbitration enactments in the internal dimension place Argentina and Uruguay within the countries that respect international legal certainty. They are meant to stimulate foreign investment by providing a more efficient avenue for resolving international commercial disputes. In the case of Argentina this enactment completes a modernisation process and is aligned to the codification of the private international law rules in the new Civil Code.[46]

Thus, these arbitration laws emerge as tools to facilitate international commerce, bringing the law governing South America-seated international arbitrations broadly into line with international best practices to settle claims efficiently, and seeking to set Argentina and Uruguay as potential seats for international commercial arbitration proceedings. All in all, these enactments constitute a turning point in this field, achieving the recognition of the most accepted pro-arbitration principles and giving priority to the principle of party autonomy.

[43] Art. 480.

[44] Uruguay: Ley de arbitraje comercial internacional No. 19.636, adopted on 3 July 2018. Argentina: Ley de arbitraje comercial internacional No. 27.449, adopted on 4 July 2018. See: Rivera, J. C. (2018) 'La ley de arbitraje comercial internacional', *Revista La Ley*, 3 September, 1–5; All, P. M. and N. Rubaja (2018) 'Habemus ley de arbitraje comercial internacional', *Revista La Ley*, 3 September, 5–11.

[45] See further the chapter by Paredes in this volume.

[46] See further the chapter by Paredes in this volume.

Applicable Law

The determination of the applicable law is a crucial aspect when legal operators are drafting an international contract. The parties to a contract will specify which rules of law should be used to resolve any dispute between them. Particularly in international commercial transactions, the choice of law can be a significant point of negotiation among lawyers. When property passes, the governing law will determine, *inter alia*, the legal interest rate (compensatory and default interest), the possibilities of claiming for punitive damages and the impact of good faith. Parties to a contract may be in the best position to determine which set of legal principles is most suitable for their transaction. Traditionally there are several possibilities when it comes to the ascertainment of the applicable law. Three aspects appear particularly relevant: (1) first, whether the parties may or may not choose the law applicable to the merits of the contract; (2) second, and if the answer to the previous question is in the affirmative, whether this selection extends only to 'law' (generally understood to be limited exclusively to state law) or also to 'rules of law' (including non-state law) and, finally; (3) what are the criteria – the connecting factors – to ascertain the applicable law in the absence of a choice by the parties.

Party autonomy?

Basedow explains that party autonomy is universally accepted as a bedrock principle of the international law of contractual obligations. It is rooted in the pre-governmental right of individuals to subject themselves to a particular positive legal order through acts of private volition.[47] Many legal systems, if not most, enable the parties to agree on the law governing their international contracts, although this prerogative is generally not unrestricted.[48] However, there are also other jurisdictions that limit such autonomy, as in the case of Uruguay, although the most common trend is to enable the parties,[49] in scenarios of equal bargaining power, to agree on the law to govern their contractual relations.

In Uruguay, the general principle of unavailability of party autonomy in matters of applicable law and international jurisdiction is regulated in Article 5 of the 1940 Additional Protocol to the Treaty of Montevideo and in Article 2403 of the Appendix to the Civil Code.

As with international jurisdiction, discussed above, the parties are not allowed to choose the applicable law to a contract unless it is expressly admitted in a specific

[47] Basedow, 'Theory of Choice of Law and Party Autonomy', above fn. 22, 17–58, at 17 and 45.

[48] Fresnedo de Aguirre, C. (2004) 'La autonomía de la voluntad en la contratación internacional', *Curso de Derecho Internacional*, XXXI, 2004, Comité Jurídico Interamericano, Secretaria General, OEA, 323–90.

[49] On party autonomy, see Mills, A. (2018) 'Party Autonomy in Private International Law', in *Party Autonomy in Private International Law* (I–Ii), Cambridge University Press; Fresnedo de Aguirre, 'La autonomía de la voluntad en la contratación internacional', above fn. 48.

law or the relevant Uruguayan conflict of laws rule specifies the application of a national law that permits such a choice. Notwithstanding the foregoing, Uruguay contains internal regulations expressly admitting party autonomy in certain legal categories, such as the specific case of securities.[50] On the other hand, the Draft Private International Law Act of Uruguay, which is in the process of being approved by Parliament, would provide a radical change to the current paradigm, granting the parties the possibility of choosing the applicable law in the following terms:[51] (1) international contracts may be submitted by the parties to the law chosen by them; (2) the reference to the law in force in a state should be understood to the exclusion of its conflict of law rules – exclusion of *renvoi*; (3) the agreement of the parties must be express and unambiguous. The said election may refer to the entire contract or to a part thereof (*depeçage*); (4) the choice of law may be made or modified at any time. It is therefore a radical change to Uruguay's current and long-standing opposition to the stance of party autonomy.[52]

The Argentine legal framework is one of many examples of a legal system enabling the coexistence of methods to tackle applicable law issues in the sphere of international commercial contracts. The Civil and Commercial Code[53] takes advantage of the express enablement of the parties to make use of their party autonomy, by means of a choice of law agreement or the incorporation of substantive rules of law, directly or by reference. Both possibilities were already in place in the legal system before the enactment of the new Civil Code yet not as an extant positive norm but rather as a doctrinal and judicial interpretation. In relation to incorporation by reference, of particular relevance to international commercial contracts are the Uniform Commercial Terms (Incoterms) compiled by the International Chamber of Commerce.

State and non-state law?

The possibility of choosing state or non-state law has a series of consequences. Parties can choose a law or a rule of law to govern their contract. The reference to 'rules of law' enables the parties to choose non-state law and to accept the application of the international usage principles of international trade, *lex mercatoria*. Thus, the Inter-American Convention on the Law Applicable to International Contracts signed in Mexico 1994 refers to 'rules of law'[54]. It should be noted that Argentina and Uruguay did not ratify the aforementioned Convention although the Draft Private International

[50] Law 18.627 of Securities Market Law, enacted in 2009, Art. 121.

[51] Art. 48 of Draft Private International Law Act of Uruguay.

[52] See further the chapter by Paredes in this volume.

[53] Argerich, G. (2016) 'El método en el derecho internacional privado: visión en el siglo XXI', in Amaral Júnior, A. and L. Klein Vieira, *El derecho internacional privado y sus desafíos en la actualidad*, Ibáñez, 57–81.

[54] Moreno Rodríguez, J. A. (2010) 'Los contratos y la Haya ¿ancla al pasado o puente al futuro?', in Basedow, J. D., D. P. Fernández Arroyo and J. A. Moreno Rodríguez (eds), *¿Cómo se codifica hoy el derecho comercial internacional?*, Centro de Estudios de Derecho, Economía y Política (CEDEP), 321, 322.

Law Act of Uruguay also refers to the choice of 'rules of law'.[55] Clauses are usually agreed upon with the following wording: 'The contract shall be governed by the law of . . . and by the uses and general principles of law recognised by international doctrine.' This type of clause is also permitted in the field of international commercial arbitration.[56] Therefore, specifying the concepts of *lex mercatoria* and general principles of law becomes pertinent. There is no agreement on how to define *lex mercatoria* but it is generally accepted that it is a product of spontaneous generation, deriving from the international practice of traders. Following Goode, it is necessary to distinguish *lex mercatoria*, as the uses of international trade, from general principles of law, which are an autonomous source of law.[57]

On the other hand, when we refer to the general principles of law, and international commercial law principles in particular, reference must be made to those that are generally accepted and not to any principle developed by international doctrine. In that sense, the UNIDROIT Principles on International Commercial Contracts develop substantive solutions while the Hague Principles on Choice of Law in International Commercial Contracts deal with of choice of law rules, as noted.[58]

Ascertainment of the applicable law in the absence of choice by the parties

Finally, in the absence of an agreement, the applicable law to the contract will be ascertained following the relevant private international law rules. These rules may be substantive, such as the Convention on the International Sale of Goods, or they may be conflict rules, such as Article 2399 of the Appendix to the Uruguayan Civil Code, which establishes that legal transactions shall be governed by the law of the place of contractual performance, making specific reference to the solutions set forth in the Treaty of Civil Law of Montevideo of 1889 (Articles 34 to 38). Moreover, the Draft Private International Law Act of Uruguay states that in the absence of choice, or if the election by the parties proves to be invalid or ineffective, international contracts shall be governed by the law that results from applying the criteria established in Article 45 that has the same wording as Articles 34 to 38 of the 1889 Montevideo Treaty.

In Argentina, Article 2652 of the 2014 Civil and Commercial Code establishes that in the absence of choice by the parties, the contract shall be governed by the laws and customs of the country of the place of performance. This methodological pluralism in the regulation of the applicable law to international contracts is complemented by the appearance of the exclusivist method when Article 2651 establishes that the

[55] Art. 48.

[56] Goode, R. (2010) 'Reglas, prácticas y pragmatismo en el derecho comercial internacional', in Basedow et al., *¿Cómo se codifica hoy el derecho comercial internacional?*, above fn. 54, 83.

[57] Ibid., 88ff.

[58] Moreno Rodríguez, J. A. (2016) 'Más allá de la Convención de México y los Principios de La Haya: ¿Qué sigue para las América?', in Fernández Arroyo, D. P. and J. A. Moreno Rodríguez (eds), *Contratos internacionales*, Asociación Americana de Derecho Internacional Privado (ASADIP), 189–99.

principles of public policy and the internationally mandatory rules of Argentine law apply to the legal relationship, whatever the law that governs the contract; the contract may also be affected by internationally mandatory norms of those states that present economic ties relevant to the case. This method is complemented in Article 2599, which provides that international rules or 'imperatives of immediate application' (overriding mandatory provisions) will be those established not only by Argentine law but also by applicable foreign law and even by Third States with close links to the case. The construction of all these provisions together demonstrate the preponderance of methodological pluralism in private international law,[59] a combination of techniques which may in turn be considered a methodological avenue itself. This pluralism is also evident in many sources developed by different codifying bodies that apply in all or some aspects to international contracts. Each of them presents a different methodological approach to private international law, *inter alia*, international treaties, model laws, legislative guidelines, best practice guides, legal guidelines, principles, recommendations, uses of international trade, model contracts and general conditions of contract, uniform documents and unilateral codes of ethics.

Conclusion

It is particularly important to note in conclusion that international business transactions are described in the form of international contracts, containing the objective(s) and commitments of each of the parties involved and the terms that govern their transaction. When the contract has close ties with more than one legal system, private international law methodologies and techniques come into play. Since international contract law is a branch of private international law, this could, in turn, define the facilitative role of private international law for the contractual parties, giving appropriate solutions in jurisdictional issues and offering efficient alternatives for the selection of the applicable regime. Historically, merchants developed their own sort of international contract law. They wanted to trade despite differences in languages, cultures and laws, and so developed their own rules for international transactions. These rules have evolved into the private international law of today, yet it is important to bear in mind that the objective of legal frameworks is to facilitate these transactions, and this is at the root of these developments.

[59] See further the final chapter by Ruiz Abou-Nigm in this volume.

20

Public Policy in Private International Law: Guardian or Barrier?

Cecilia Fresnedo de Aguirre

Introduction

Most chapters in this book deal with international public policy in one way or another and provide multiple examples of how this exception works. Taking recourse to the international public policy exception is a traditional technique of private international law that is essential for the necessary coordination of legal diversity. It is a key instrument for enabling the necessary flexibility to articulate the integration of diversity.

This chapter will focus on the restricted character of international public policy, which has been traditionally limited – at least in Uruguay – to the fundamental principles on which each country bases its legal individuality. However, many of these fundamental principles are enshrined in human rights conventions and private international law conventions and therefore are shared by all the States Parties to that convention, which enables the integration and articulation of diversity, at either a regional or a universal level. Consequently, the identification of those shared fundamental principles should increase the predictability of results in private international law cases and soften the barrier that the public policy exception imposes regarding foreign laws and judgments. Notwithstanding this, the aforementioned statements do not mean that the role of the public policy exception will disappear.

In order to develop this argument, this chapter will explain some key concepts such as those of international and domestic public policy, *a posteriori* and *a priori* public policy, their differences and similarities. It will then examine how public policy evolves over time alongside society and how that evolution is reflected in statutory and conventional rules.

The Role of Public Policy in Private International Law

Concept

The public policy exception is a traditional mechanism of the general theory of private international law which enables the judge to reject the application of the foreign law indicated by the conflict of laws rules, or the recognition or enforcement of a foreign act or judgment, when such application or recognition contravenes a fundamental principle on which the court's legal system bases its individuality.[1] Those fundamental principles can also operate *a priori* of the conflict of laws rules through overriding mandatory rules. The latter concept will be developed later in this chapter.

For the purposes of the functioning of the public policy exception in private international law, the concept of public policy is construed, in each country, according to the fundamental principles on which that country bases its legal individuality and that cannot be set aside by any foreign law that results by virtue of the applicable private international law rules.[2] It is an exception to the normal functioning of private international law and the application of foreign law when the former indicates so.[3] Its scope is, therefore, narrower than that of domestic or national public policy,[4] which consists of each state's set of domestic substantive rules that cannot be set aside by the parties but that do not impede the application of a foreign law. The mere fact that a foreign law is different from that of the judge is not a reason for not applying it domestically. On the contrary, the court must analyse if the result or effect of applying that foreign law is or is not compatible with the fundamental values and principles that underlie its legal order.[5]

The public policy exception comes from the state towards the individual in a particular case; it operates in practice, when the state actually intervenes on the

[1] See the 1979 Uruguayan Declaration on the Scope of Public Policy, issued on the occasion of the Second Inter-American Specialized Conference on Private International Law, held in Montevideo in 1979. Its full text can be found later in this chapter and is available at: www.oas.org/juridico/english/Sigs/b-45.html

[2] Ruíz Díaz Labrano, R. (2010) *Derecho Internacional Privado*, La Ley Paraguaya, 304, includes, in what he considers is international public policy, the set of fundamental principles and those principles of universal justice vested with international value and consideration.

[3] Jayme, E. (1995) 'Identité culturelle et intégration: le droit international privé postmoderne', *Recueil des cours*, vol. 251, 228.

[4] Murphy, K. (1981) 'The Traditional View of Public Policy and *ordre public* in Private International Law', 11 *Ga. J. Int'l & Comp. L.* 591, 595, quoting Graveson et al., states that 'The characteristic feature of public policy in Anglo-American conflicts law is the restraint with which it is employed'.

[5] John, T. and L. Delahaye (2013) 'The Use of Private International Law Escape Devices to Manage the Mediate Application of (Foreign) Human Rights in Civil and Commercial Disputes in Australia', *A Commitment to Private International Law. Essays in Honour of Hans van Loon*, Intersentia, 235–52, at 245. The authors quote Judge Cardozo, in *Loucks* v. *Standard Oil Co of New York* (1918) 224 N.Y.99, 111, who remarked: 'We are not so provincial as to say that every solution of a problem is wrong because we deal with it otherwise at home'.

relationship through its courts, public registrars or notary publics.[6] The public policy exception addresses only the concrete situation[7] that would arise if the foreign law is applied as indicated by the relevant private international law rule. Therefore, the same foreign law may be rejected in a certain situation or particular case and so will be refused application in that case, but the same norm could be applied in another case scenario where, due to different circumstances, its application does not affect any fundamental principle.[8]

The public policy exception has a 'negative effect' – excluding the foreign law or judgment – and a 'positive effect': the application of another law, which in almost all cases is that of the forum.[9] This traditional private international law technique contributes to the accommodation of the diverse substantive laws applicable in a particular case.[10]

The National and International Character of Public Policy

It is international public policy that is relevant in private international law cases, no matter when and how it operates and what its effects are. The court cannot refuse the application of the foreign law indicated by its conflict of laws rule on domestic public policy grounds. However, domestic rules reflect the evolution of the fundamental principles of a certain state and thus may be relevant when determining the scope of international public policy. Let me explain this further. Public policy in private international law is construed by national courts as belonging to each country; the values it holds may vary from one country to the other. Yet, the fact is that there are some fundamental principles that do not belong merely to one legal system individually considered but are shared by many. Such fundamental principles can be found in international or regional instruments on human rights or on private international law

[6] Alfonsín, Q. (1982) *Teoría del Derecho Privado Internacional*, 2nd edn, Idea, 577; Murphy, 'The Traditional View of Public Policy', above fn. 4, 591

[7] Alfonsín, Q. (1940) *El Orden Público*, Biblioteca de Publicaciones Oficiales de la Facultad de Derecho y Ciencias Sociales de Montevideo, Section III, XIX, Peña y Cía Imp, 337–8, quoting Bar, C. L. von (1889) *Teoría y práctica del derecho internacional privado*, n.p.

[8] Blom, J. (2003) 'Public Policy in Private International Law and its Evolution in Time', *Netherlands International Law Review*, vol. 50, no. 3, 373–99, at 374–5; McClean, D. and V. Ruiz Abou-Nigm (2016) *Morris on The Conflict of Laws*, 9th edn, Sweet & Maxwell – Thomson Reuters, 4-002.

[9] Alfonsín, *El Orden Público*, above fn. 7, 339; Jayme, 'Identité culturelle et intégration', above fn. 3, 224; Blom, 'Public Policy in Private International Law', above fn. 8, 375; John and Delahaye, 'The Use of Private International Law Escape Devices', above fn. 5, 249.

[10] Lagarde, P. (1959) *Recherches sur l'ordre public en droit international privé,* Bibliothèque de droit privé, vol. XV, 238–9, said in this regard, '*La disposition étrangère n'est pas écartée parce qu'elle est contraire à un principe fondamental du droit du for, elle ne peut se combiner de façon cohérent avec les diverses dispositions de celui-ci avec lesquelles elle se trouve en relation. Si l'ordre public n'intervenait pas, la solution du litige serait insensée, puisque la disposition étrangère et les dispositions du for n'ont de sens que par leur combinaison, et que cette combinaison est par hypothèse impossible. L'ordre public intervient justement pour redonner sens et vie à l'ensemble, en procédant aux ajustements nécessaires*'.

and are therefore shared by all those legal systems of the States Parties to that convention or other kind of international instrument where those principles are enshrined.[11]

The identification of such a set of common principles shared by several legal orders in a certain region or worldwide should increase the predictability of results in private international law cases, at least regarding the operation of the public policy exception.[12] It could also contribute towards neutralising diversity and pluralism in private international law and to soften or reduce the barrier that the public policy exception imposes regarding foreign laws and judgments. These postulates are further explained in the following paragraphs.

Human Rights and Public Policy

Human rights instruments, particularly conventions, provide a set of uniform rights that should be taken as fundamental principles of the international public policy of each of the States Parties to the convention. That set of principles becomes common to all the States Parties to the convention, which shows that though international public policy principles belong to each country, they are in many cases shared by several states, which leads us to more uniform and predictable solutions regarding the resorting to the public policy exception as a traditional and specific instrument of private international law. Moreover, such uniformity and predictability regarding the public policy exception can be increased geographically when the principle at stake is enshrined in a universal convention on human rights to which the judge's country and the country whose law is applicable are States Parties. In other words, this reasoning is not only valid within a certain region but also – at least regarding certain principles – worldwide.

Therefore, the public policy exception is not only each state's legal system's guardian in so far as it protects its legal coherence within its borders, preventing the application of a foreign law or the recognition of a foreign judgment from jeopardising that set of fundamental principles and values that constitute the international public policy of the state concerned. It is also possible to argue that as the list of fundamental principles shared by several states and the list of states that share the same fundamental principles grow bigger, the need for guardians and barriers in this sense will diminish.

It is, however, very difficult to imagine that the role of the public policy exception

[11] I demonstrate this statement in Fresnedo de Aguirre, C. (2016) 'Public Policy: Common Principles in the American States', *Recueil des cours*, vol. 379, 73–396.

[12] Several decades ago, Alfonsín, *Teoría del Derecho Privado Internacional* above fn. 6, 566 identified as a practical problem regarding legal certainty and foreseeability the lack of limitation of public policy: '*en tanto el orden público carezca de límites precisos, será imprevisible el destino de las relaciones jurídicas extranacionales, pues las normas que sirven de tutela a una relación extranacional pueden tornarse inoperantes ante una ampliación inesperada de la excepción. Es preciso, pues, que el orden público fije de antemano sus límites a fin de que el* commercium *internacional obtenga seguridad*'.

will completely disappear. On the contrary, it seems feasible that the private international law system would continue working as it has done traditionally, but in a more predictable way, because the Human Rights Conventions enable the identification and prediction of the fundamental principles with which the judge of the forum will confront the application of the referred foreign law.

There could be other fundamental principles on which the country of the forum bases its legal individuality, that is, other international public policy principles that may not be shared by other countries. Only the latter is the sphere that could be reduced by the influence of human rights conventions, because there are now several fundamental principles that are common to all States Parties to each human rights convention. The same would happen with Third States, because when their laws are applicable because of the conflict of laws rules of the forum, the judge will confront them with his or her own fundamental principles of international public policy, which includes some principles that are enshrined in the human rights conventions to which his or her state is a party.[13]

The Concept and Scope of Public Policy – *a priori* and *a posteriori* – in the Codification of Private International Law

A General Approach

There are two manifestations of public policy (*ordre public*) that are habitual nowadays: the classic one, developed by Bartin, of public policy as an exception to the application of the foreign law indicated by the bilateral conflict of laws rule of the forum (*a posteriori* public policy), and the idea of *lois de police*, developed by Francescakis,[14] which imposes the preferential application of a mandatory rule of the forum, leaving aside the conflict method (*a priori* public policy). In both cases, the resorting to public policy constitutes an exception to the normal operation of private international law rules, but while the public policy exception has the negative function of refusing the application of the relevant foreign law, the *lois de police* give a positive function to public policy.[15]

Both mechanisms share some common denominators although they also have some differences. They are both based on fundamental principles embodied in the very basis of a state's legal order.[16] However, they operate at different stages of

[13] Fresnedo de Aguirre, 'Public Policy: Common Principles in the American States', above fn. 11, particularly 229–33.

[14] Though with origins that can be traced back to the Middle Ages, and lately to von Savigny, F. C. and P. E. Mancini. See Parra-Aranguren, G. (1988) 'General Course of Private International Law: Selected Problems', *Recueil des cours*, vol. 210, 121, para. 144 and 122, fn. 260.

[15] Hammje, P. (1997) 'L'ordre public et les droits fondamentaux', *Rev. crit. DIPr*, 1 ss. no 1., 153–4.

[16] Cançado Trindade, A. A. (2005) 'International Law for Humankind: Towards a New *Jus Gentium* (I)' *Recueil des cours*, vol. 316, 9–439, at 86, states: 'Every legal system has fundamental principles, which inspire, inform and conform their norms . . . It is the general principles of law (*prima principia*) which confer on the legal order (both national and international) its ineluctable axiological

the conflict of laws process: while the public policy exception appears once the conflict of laws rule has indicated the foreign law applicable, the *a priori* public policy operates before and without undergoing the process of the conflict of laws rule.

Another difference is that public policy is a narrow concept that evolves over time alongside society, but usually through a gradual process, while overriding mandatory rules or rules of immediate application tend to influence a certain conduct in certain areas, and change over time according to the evolution of public interest. Such interests may change more rapidly as a response to the needs of a certain society at a certain time, according to the particular rhythm of its development.[17] However, rules of immediate application have been considered as a species within the generic category of public policy, since while public policy is a set of principles, mandatory rules are extant norms.[18] That is a very accurate distinction, for although fundamental principles usually underlie both types of public policy, rules of immediate application are statutory rules – and may be based on a state interest or political or economic need, rather than on fundamental moral or social values – while public policy principles can be merely principles and not necessarily extant norms.[19] Rules of immediate application always aim at protecting a specific public interest that is clearly identified and designated, and that may or may not be part of public policy. These norms pursue a certain target that is particularly important for the state that issued them and that must be necessarily applied in order to reach that target.[20]

Mandatory rules have a more aggressive function: they attack rather then defend,

dimension: it is they that reveal the values which inspire the whole legal order and which, ultimately, provide its foundations themselves'.

[17] Bělohlávek, A. J. (2012) 'Public Policy and Public Interest in International Law and EU Law', *Czech Yearbook of International Law*, Juris Publishing Inc., 117–48, at 142–3. The author mentions as an example the 'developments on the capital market, which require that corrective or restrictive influence on individual investors be taken' and the related overriding mandatory rules of an administrative or financial character. He also mentions examples of 'overriding mandatory rules limiting the autonomy of contract of parties entering into contractual relationships, for instance, restrictive provisions in deposit account agreements, current account agreements, agreements on the management of security portfolios and, especially in recent times, consumer contracts (i.e. contracts made between a consumer and a commercial business entity)'.

[18] Blom, 'Public Policy in Private International Law', above fn. 8, 379–80, quoting Bucher, A. (1993) 'L'ordre public et le but social des lois en droit international privé', *Recueil des cours*, vol. 239, 34–43; Parra-Aranguren, 'General Course of Private International Law', above fn. 14, 122–3, para. 147.

[19] Nyght, P. (1995) 'The Reasonable Expectations of Parties as a Guide to the Choice of Law in Contract and Tort', *Recueil des cours*, vol. 251, 380, states that 'mandatory rules consist of specific rules, in common law countries invariably in statutory form', while public policy 'is more like an emanation from either statutory or non-statutory law invented by judges'.

[20] Bonomi, A. (1998) *Le norme imperative nel diritto internazionale privato*, Publications of the Suisse Institute of Comparative Law (33), Schulthess Polygraphischer Verlag, 218, 220.

as public policy *a posteriori* does.[21] The scope of application of mandatory rules is limited to where there are political, social or economic needs that must be met by those rules. It is usually defined by the legislator and when it is not, the courts infer their scope of application.[22] Public policy principles are not defined or listed in the norm referring to the exception mechanism.

On the whole, we could conclude with Merezhko that the public policy exception operates when the application of foreign law is absolutely unacceptable, while mandatory rules operate when their imperativity means that they are the only ones to be applied.[23]

The 1889 and 1940 Montevideo Treaties

Article 4 in both Additional Protocols to the 1889 and to the 1940 Montevideo Treaties states that: 'The laws of the other States will never be applied against the political institutions, public policy laws or good mores of the place of the proceedings'.[24] This formula was taken from Article 95 of the Draft Code on Private International Law drafted by the Uruguayan jurist Gonzalo Ramírez[25] in 1888 as a working basis to be proposed at the First South American Congress on Private International Law, which was held in Montevideo from August 1888 to March 1889.[26] The provision is categorical: those foreign laws 'will never be applied'. However, Article 4 of the Additional Protocols do not incorporate the expression in Ramírez' draft referring to the opposition to the 'fundamental principles'. It is to be noted that the latter is a basic and defining element regarding the concept and scope of international public policy, and is still in force today, as the 1979 Uruguayan Declaration demonstrates. The Montevideo Protocols make no reference to immediate application rules or *a priori* public policy.

The concept of fundamental principles as limiting the scope of international

[21] Moreno Rodríguez, J. A. (2013) *Derecho aplicable y arbitraje internacional*, CEDEP/Intercontinental Ed., 496, 520.

[22] Nyght, 'The Reasonable Expectations of Parties', above fn. 19, 382, however, states that 'most mandatory laws do not specify their ambit, leaving it to courts define same'. He adds that when that occurs, there is 'a clear analogy with modern United States doctrines based on various kinds of governmental interest analysis'. Kinsch, P. (2005) 'Droits de l'homme, droits fondamentaux et droit international privé', *Recueil des cours*, vol. 318, 9–331, at 158.

[23] Merezhko, O. (2012) 'Public Policy (Ordre Public), Mandatory Norms and Evasion of Law in Ukrainian Private International Law', *Czech Yearbook of International Law*, Juris Publishing Inc., 149–60, at 153–4, quoting Reimann, M. (1995) *Conflict of Laws in Western Europe. A Guide through the Jungle*, Transnational Publishers, Inc., 28.

[24] Free translation of the author from the Spanish text, since there is no official English text: 'Las leyes de los demás Estados jamás serán aplicadas contra las instituciones políticas, las leyes de orden público o las buenas costumbres del lugar del proceso'.

[25] See Fresnedo de Aguirre, C. (2004) *Curso de Derecho Internacional Privado*, 2nd edn, Tomo I, Parte General, FCU, 127–33.

[26] Ramírez, G. (1888) *Proyecto de Código de Derecho Internacional Privado y su Comentario*, Félix Lajouane, 59. Available at: www.bibliotecadigital.gob.ar

public policy has its first positive normative appearance in Article 15 of the 1940 Uruguayan Draft Private International Law Act, prepared by Vargas Guillemette,[27] which materialised as an Appendix to the Uruguayan Civil Code.[28] Article 2404 refers to 'essential principles' in this context. It is worth recalling what the author of this formula stated in his preliminary recitals:

> The exception does not need to be more broadly founded, since it functions as such in the doctrinal analysis of many authors and in positive formulations of international law. It constitutes the unquestionable and necessary reaffirmation of the legal order of each independent state, which cannot break the fundamental pillars on which it is based, in order to apply the law that threatens them.[29]

Other rules of the time referred to 'good morals' and similar expressions.[30]

The 1928 Bustamante Code of Private International Law

The ideas of Bustamante y Sirven regarding public policy were enacted in Article 3 of his Private International Law Code. He classified all legal rules into three categories: rules of private order or voluntary rules; rules of internal public policy or personal rules; and rules of international public policy, also called territorial or local rules. The latter are defined in Articles 4 and 5 of the Bustamante Code as the constitutional rules and all those political and administrative rules providing for individual and collective protection, unless they expressly provide something different.[31] The Bustamante Code does not clearly distinguish the concepts of *a priori* and *a posteriori* public policy.[32]

[27] See Fresnedo de Aguirre, *Curso de Derecho Internacional Privado* above fn. 25, 133–8.

[28] The Appendix to the Uruguayan Civil Code was enacted in 1941 and amended in 1994. See www.impo.com.uy/bases/codigo-civil/16603-1994

[29] Vargas Guillemette, A. (1943) *Codificación Nacional del Derecho Internacional Privado*, Barreiro y Ramos, 22. Free contextual translation by the author of the following original text: 'La excepción no necesita ser fundada con mayor amplitud, pues funciona como tal en la doctrina de todos los autores y en las articulaciones positivas del Derecho Internacional, constituyendo la reafirmación indiscutible y necesaria del ordenamiento jurídico de cada Estado independiente, que no puede quebrar los pilares fundamentales sobre los que se levanta para dar aplicación a la ley que los amenaza'.

[30] Murphy, 'The Traditional View of Public Policy', above fn. 4, 598–9, making reference to the codification of German law at the end of the nineteenth century and to the French taking into account 'the domestic French attitudes on morality and political order'.

[31] Parra-Aranguren, 'General Course of Private International Law: Selected Problems', above fn. 14, 127.

[32] Battello Calderón, S. J. (2012) *El orden público en el derecho internacional privado del Mercosur*, Advocatus, 62.

The Inter-American Specialized Conferences on Private International Law (CIDIPs)

The general rule on the public policy exception

The scope of the public policy exception as a private international law technique was first discussed within the Inter-American Specialized Conferences on Private International Law (CIDIP) codification process[33] during the first CIDIP Conference held in Panama in 1975, and specifically when analysing Article 17 in the Inter-American Convention on letters rogatory, which provides: 'The state of destination may refuse to execute a letter rogatory that is manifestly contrary to its public policy ("*ordre public*")'. Opertti Badán, acting in the name of the Uruguayan Delegation, was against the inclusion of a specific public policy exception clause in the Convention, because he considered that adopting such a defence mechanism was against the spirit of an international convention. Moreover, it would favour the use of the public policy exception, which could jeopardise the efficiency of international law. However, he recognised that the rules that are core to the identity of a state needed to be protected and enforced. The aforementioned formula on public policy was finally approved though recognising the necessarily exceptional character of its application.[34]

All the other Inter-American Conventions adopted in Panama in 1975 (CIDIP-I) maintain the aforementioned formula of Article 17 in the Inter-American Convention on letters rogatory. Such is the case of Article 7 in the Inter-American Convention on conflicts of laws concerning commercial companies,[35] Article 11 in the Inter-American Convention on conflict of laws concerning bills of exchange, promissory notes and invoices,[36] Article 12 in the Inter-American Convention on the legal regime of powers of attorney to be used abroad[37] and Article 18 in the Inter-American Convention on Conflict of Laws Concerning the Adoption of Minors.[38]

Moreover, in the Second Inter-American Conference (CIDIP-II), held in Montevideo in 1979, the aim of which this time was a general formula on public

[33] See Parra Aranguren, G. (1979) 'La Convención Interamericana sobre Normas Generales de DIPr. (Montevideo, 1979)', *Anuario Jurídico Interamericano*, OEA Consultoría Jurídica, 157–86, at 177–8, paras 22–3.

[34] Ibid., 178, para. 22.

[35] Art. 7: 'The law declared applicable under this Convention may be refused application in the territory of any State that considers it manifestly contrary to its public policy (ordre public)'. See www.oas.org/juridico/english/treaties/b-40.html

[36] Art. 11: 'The law declared applicable under this Convention may be refused application in the territory of a State Party that considers it manifestly contrary to its public policy ("ordre public")'. See www.oas.org/juridico/english/treaties/b-33.html

[37] Art. 12: 'The State of destination may refuse to execute a power of attorney if it is manifestly contrary to its public policy ("ordre public")'. See www.oas.org/juridico/english/treaties/b-38.html

[38] Art. 18: 'The authorities of a State Party may refuse to apply the law declared applicable under this Convention when the law is manifestly contrary to its public policy ("ordre public")'. See www.oas.org/juridico/english/treaties/b-48.html

policy to be included in the Inter-American Convention on general rules of private international law,[39] there was support to maintain the formula approved in Panama.[40] However, at Goldschmidt's instance, the formula was tweaked to include that the manifest contravention of the foreign law should be to the public policy 'principles' of the law of the forum. Thus, Article 5 provides that 'The law declared applicable by a convention on private international law may be refused application in the territory of a State Party that considers it manifestly contrary to the principles of its public policy ("*ordre public*")'.

It is broadly acknowledged that such express reference to the 'principles' of the law of the forum improved the formula because it made clear that the operation of the public policy exception is aimed at protecting the foundational principles upon which a positive norm of the forum has been enacted and this formula does not allow the exception to interfere with the otherwise applicable law when the foreign law only contravenes an aspect of the positive rule that develops such principles[41], and not the principles themselves. In other words, the new formula makes clear that the public policy exception protects the fundamental 'principles' of the forum, not necessarily those national substantive rules that cannot be set aside by the parties (domestic public policy). This idea can be observed in Uruguayan case law, for example in judgment 154/007 of the Supreme Court of Justice of 17 September 2007, in which the Court rejects the recognition and enforcement of a foreign judgment from the Cayman Islands because the latter did not fulfil certain Uruguayan basic procedural principles. The Court concludes that in this case the clear infringements of due process are against international public policy.[42]

The word 'manifestly'[43] indicates the absolutely exceptional character of the reservation and was included at Valladão's insistence precisely to restrict the natural tendency to extend the hypothesis where the exception can operate.[44] Nevertheless, the Uruguayan Delegation was not completely satisfied with the final drafting of Article 5 and decided to make a Declaration on the scope of public order in this context.

[39] The Inter-American Convention on general rules of private international law was adopted in Montevideo on 8 May 1979 and entered into force on 10 June 1981. It was ratified by Argentina, Brazil, Colombia, Ecuador, Guatemala, Mexico, Paraguay, Peru, Uruguay and Venezuela. See www.oas.org/juridico/english/sigs/b-45.html

[40] *Actas y Documentos Segunda Conferencia Interamericana Especializada sobre Derecho Internacional Privado (CIDIP-II)* (1980), vol. I, Secretaría General OEA (2006), 288.

[41] Parra Aranguren, 'La Convención Interamericana sobre Normas Generales', above fn. 33, 177, n. 22.

[42] http://bjn.poderjudicial.gub.uy/BJNPUBLICA/hojaInsumo2.seam?cid=473646

[43] Please note the use of this term also in the public policy exception formula of the HCCH Conventions; see van Loon's chapter in this volume.

[44] See fn. 42.

The Uruguayan Declaration on the Scope of Public Order

The Uruguayan Declaration reads:

> Uruguay wishes to state that it expressly ratifies the line of thought enunciated in Panama at CIDIP-I, reaffirming its genuine Pan American spirit and its clear and positive decision to contribute with its ideas and endorsement to the successful development of the legal community. This line of thinking and conduct has been evidenced in undoubtable form by the unreserved ratification by Uruguay of all the Conventions of Panama, approved by law number 14.534 in 1976. In line with the foregoing, Uruguay gives its affirmative vote to the formula regarding public order. Nevertheless, Uruguay wishes to state expressly and clearly that, in accordance with the position it maintained in Panama, its interpretation of the aforementioned exception refers to international public order as an individual juridical institution, not necessarily identifiable with the internal public order of each state. Therefore, the position of Uruguay is that the approved formula conveys an exceptional authorization to the various States Parties to declare in a non-discretionary and well-founded manner that the precepts of foreign law are inapplicable whenever these concretely and in a serious and open manner offend the standards and principles essential to the international public order on which each individual state bases its legal individuality.[45]

First, the Declaration aimed at making a clear delimitation of the scope of the public policy exception, highlighting that the exception refers only to international public policy, which is narrower than domestic or national public policy, and cannot be necessarily identified with the latter. Second, it provides that the judge's decision must be 'non-discretionary and well-founded'. Third, the exception can only work when the precepts of foreign law 'offend the standards and principles essential to the international public order on which each individual state bases its legal individuality', and that offence is concrete, serious and open. It has an 'interpretative' character, which consists of a unilateral act that aims at making a complete or partial interpretation of a treaty and that must not be mixed up with a reservation.[46] In Uruguay, this declaration is a mandatory legal interpretation rule (*fuerza de interpretación legal preceptiva*), since it was approved by Parliament together with the Convention.

Rules of immediate application

The 1979 Inter-American Convention on general rules of private international law does not include a special provision on rules of immediate application, or 'overriding mandatory rules' as they are best known in European private international law, in

[45] Declaration made at the time of signature. See www.oas.org/juridico/english/Sigs/b-45.html. Though signed by the President of the Uruguayan Delegation, Professor Manuel Alfonso Vieira, it was drafted by its member Professor Didier Opertti Badán.

[46] De la Guardia, E. (1977) *Derecho de los tratados internacionales*, Ábaco de Rodolfo Depalma, 187.

spite of the efforts of the Venezuelan delegation to do so.[47] Only in 1994, in CIDIP-V, did the Inter-American system expressly refer to the rules of immediate application in Article 11 of the Inter-American Convention on the Law Applicable to International Contracts, which provides:

> Notwithstanding the provisions of the preceding articles, the provisions of the law of the forum shall necessarily be applied when they are mandatory requirements. It shall be up to the forum to decide when it applies the mandatory provisions of the law of another State with which the contract has close ties.[48]

Thus, the application of mandatory rules – rules of immediate application (*lois de police*) – is compulsory for the judge when those rules belong to his or her own legal system and optional when they belong to the legal system of a Third State. The latter includes mandatory rules of the legal system of a Third State that is not the one chosen by the court's conflict of laws rule, as far as 'the contract has close ties' with it.

Mercosur

Certain private international law instruments approved within Mercosur include a public policy provision. That is the case, for example, of the Protocol on Jurisdictional Cooperation and Assistance in Civil, Commercial, Labour and Administrative Matters,[49] which refers to the 'principles of the public policy of the requested state' (Article 8), regarding the enforcement of letters rogatory. Under Article 20, judgments and arbitral awards issued in the States Parties' jurisdictions will have extraterritorial efficacy if they fulfil the conditions stated thereinafter, and paragraph (f) requires that they are not manifestly contrary to the principles of the public policy (*ordre public*) of the state where the recognition or enforcement is sought. Article 17 of the Protocol on Precautionary Measures[50] provides that the jurisdictional authority of the requested state may refuse the enforcement of a letter rogatory referred to precautionary measures, when these latter are manifestly contrary to their public policy.

However, there is no Mercosur instrument on general rules of private international law, even though all Mercosur State Members are States Parties to the aforementioned Inter-American Convention on General Rules of Private International Law. Therefore, the general rule on public policy provided for in Article 5 of that Inter-American Convention is applicable to cross-border private international law cases within Mercosur.

[47] Parra-Aranguren, 'General Course of Private International Law: Selected Problems', above fn. 14, 133.

[48] See www.oas.org/juridico/english/treaties/b-56.html

[49] Protocolo de Cooperación y Asistencia Jurisdiccional en Materia Civil, Comercial, Laboral y Administrativa, Las Leñas (Argentina), MERCOSUR/CMC/Dec No.05/92. Available at: www.mercosur.int

[50] Protocolo de Medidas Cautelares, Ouro Preto (Brazil), MERCOSUR/CMC/Dec No. 27/94. Available at: www.mercosur.int

Defining the Scope of the Public Policy Exception

It seems to be unanimously recognised that defining the exact scope of public policy is never an easy task.[51] There are helpful guidelines,[52] some of them very concrete and even mandatory, such as the 1979 Uruguayan Declaration, but a specific and complete list of fundamental principles to be taken into account for these purposes does not – and probably could not – exist.[53] However, fine-tuning criteria to enable the courts to identify and ascertain those fundamental principles for the purposes of the operation of the public policy exception as a technique of private international law would be undoubtedly helpful and would enhance predictability in private international law cases.[54] It

[51] See, for example, Merezhko, 'Public Policy', above fn. 23, 150, who adds that such determination 'depends on the concrete circumstances of the given case'. Murphy, 'The Traditional View of Public Policy', above fn. 4, 595, quoting Winfield (1929), 'Public Policy in the English Common Law', 42 *Harv. L. Rev.* 76, at 91: 'public policy occupies a unique position in the law as a vague body of moral and legal precepts, which have successfully resisted statutory formulation or judicial definition'. He adds: 'How often and by what standards courts are to reach the conclusion that foreign law is harmful remains a central question', 596. McClean and Ruiz Abou-Nigm, *Morris on The Conflict of Laws*, above fn. 8, 49; Silva, J. A. (2010) *Aplicación de normas conflictuales. La aportación del juez*, Fontamara, 280; Juenger, F. K. (1985) 'General Course on Private International Law', *Recueil des cours*, vol. 193, 200, says that the public policy exception has 'undefined dimensions', that it is a 'vague and slippery conception' and that it is like pornography – 'one knows it when one sees it', quoting *Jacobellis* v. *Ohio* (1964).

[52] Merezhko, 'Public Policy', above fn. 23, 152, mentions the following: 'Generally speaking, public policy (with regard to Ukraine) encompasses the following intertwined elements: 1) the fundamental, most important, principles of Ukrainian law, including its constitutional, private law and civil-procedural principles; 2) the generally accepted principles of morality, upon which the Ukrainian legal order is based; 3) the legitimate interests of Ukrainian citizens, legal persons and the state, the protection of which remains a major task for Ukraine's legal system; 4) the generally recognized principles and norms of international law, including international legal human rights standards'.

[53] Alfonsín, *El Orden Público*, above fn. 7, 571–2, states that 'resulta evidente que el ámbito del orden público requiere ser precisado para poder saber con certidumbre cuando se lo vulnera y cuando no'. But he concludes that 'tales formulaciones y tales enumeraciones, que por fuerza deberían ser taxativas para ser eficaces, son materialmente imposibles de realizar. Ningún Estado, por lo demás, ha de comprometer su libertad atándose las manos de este modo'.

[54] Muir Watt, H. (2012) 'Concurrence ou confluence? Droit international privé et droits fondamentaux dans la gouvernance globale', in *Mélanges à la mémoire de Patrick Courbe; le droit entre tradition et modernité*, Dalloz, 459–79, at 469, poses the following question: 'depuis leur apparition vers les années 1990 dans la discipline des conflits de lois (ou plus largement peut-être, afin d'englober l'expérience américaine, dans la régulation transnationale de la conduite des acteurs privés), la présence des droits de l'homme apparait comme éminemment perturbatrice des fondements et des méthodes établis. La vraie question est alors de savoir si cette perturbation est une tare ou une vertu, s'il faut y résister ou l'accueillir'. In my view and for the proposed aim of defining the content of international public policy, human rights are a virtue and must be welcome in private international law.

would also prevent the natural 'homing trend' of judges to reject a different foreign law and apply theirs.[55] [56]

Perhaps, then, the time has come to look into national constitutions[57] and international conventions[58] in terms of those fundamental principles – including, of course, human rights conventions[59] and other instruments – with regard to private relations.[60] The study of those rules on fundamental and human rights seems essential. Furthermore, Jayme points out that while for Foelix it was state policies that substantiated the basis of a legal system, nowadays the emphasis is put on the fundamental rights of individuals and the state as such does not play the main role regarding the scope of the public policy exception.[61] This is indeed objectionable,[62] but what is undisputable in my view is that the content of each state's public policy can also be made concrete and reinforced by transnational values incorporated in international instruments ratified by the state of the forum. However, as Jayme states, '*l'idée d'un ordre public international qui serait l'expression de l'humanité tout entière reste, pour le moment, une utopie*'.[63] [64]

[55] Merezhko, 'Public Policy', above fn. 23, 151, states: 'Sometimes public policy may be prone to abuse on the part of national courts which may, under the guise of public policy, apply their own law just because the foreign law looks alien to them.'

[56] See further what this non-recognition implies from an ethics perspective in the chapter by Michaels in this volume.

[57] See, for example, Merezhko, 'Public Policy', above fn. 23, 151; Kinsch, 'Droits de l'homme, droits fondamentaux et droit international privé', above fn. 22, 210–11; Blom, 'Public Policy in Private International Law', above fn. 8, 392 and Gamarra, J. (2012) *Neoconstitucionalismo, Código y Ley Especial*, FCU, 5.

[58] Blom, 'Public Policy in Private International Law', above fn. 8, 395 states that 'The values on which public policy decisions turn may be drawn, not only from the domestic legal system, but also from international law'.

[59] Dreyzin de Klor, A. (1997) *El Mercosur. Generador de una nueva fuente de derecho internacional privado*, Zavalía, 329–36 and De Rosas, P. E. (2003) 'Orden público internacional Tendencias contemporáneas. Orden Público en el ordenamiento del Mercosur', *Boletín de la Facultad de Derecho*, no. 22, 193–220, at 219. The authors point out that there is a tendency to strip the content of public policy from localist parameters and to redefine it according to universal values relating to human rights.

[60] Bucher, A. (2000) 'La famille en droit international privé', *Recueil des cours*, vol. 283, 22: 'les droits de l'homme et les droits fondamentaux pénètre nécessairement le droit international privé'. And more specifically Jayme, 'Identité culturelle et intégration', above fn. 3, 228. Hammje, 'L'ordre public et les droits fondamentaux', above fn. 15, 154, states: 'spécialement dans le domaine du statut personnel, le recours à l'exception d'ordre public a ainsi connu un net renforcement sous l'impulsion des droits fondamentaux . . .'

[61] Jayme, 'Identité culturelle et intégration', above fn. 3, 229. The author adds, however, that 'même les droits fondamentaux garantis par la constitution ne s'appliquent que si la situation présente un lien suffisamment étroit avec l'État du for'.

[62] Lequette, Y. (2010) 'Le droit international prive et les droits fondamentaux', *Libertés et droits fondamentaux*, 16th edn, Dalloz, 103–28, at 125: 'Nombre de règles aujourd'hui couvertes par l'étiquette des droits de l'homme sont des créations totalement artificielles, commandées non par la nature de l'homme mais par le "prêt à penser" ambiant'.

[63] Jayme, 'Identité culturelle et intégration', above fn. 3, 231.

[64] For the development of these ideas and of the concept and scope of public policy – *a priori* and *a*

The interaction between national and international law regarding not only the protection of human rights but also the scope of the public policy exception has been examined in expert writing. Blom points out that those international legal principles that recognise human rights spread their influence through public policy and demonstrate that certain domestic legal values are fundamental, which shows that public policy has different sources that coexist harmoniously and are used to solve a particular case.[65] Sometimes courts expressly mention these plural sources regarding the content of public policy while others appear implicit in their judgment. The fact is that it is increasingly frequent for courts to bear in mind the influence of national and international human rights sources regarding the content of public policy and how to solve private international law cases.[66]

It is widely accepted nowadays that although each state is free to determine the fundamental principles foundational to its legal system, such freedom is limited by the positive requirements imposed in human rights conventions.[67] Some authors also use the expression '*l'ordre public des droits de l'homme*'.[68] Foyer considers that the European Convention on Human Rights proposes a new notion of public policy[69] and that European public policy must have priority over the substantive law of a Third State referred to by the conflict of laws rule, even regarding intra-communitarian relationships. This cannot be avoided through party autonomy and a choice of law clause. The same occurs when it comes to the recognition and enforcement of judgments and awards. Undoubtedly, the European Convention on Human Rights has great impact in the determination of European public policy.[70] Other scholars are more sceptical and warn us that human rights rules must be carefully analysed to determine whether they can be considered fundamental public policy principles or not. Lequette turns on a red light on the matter that some rules are labelled as human rights while they are artificial creations[71]. It is hereby submitted that extreme approaches are dangerous

posteriori – through the codification of private international law, see Fresnedo de Aguirre, 'Public Policy: Common Principles in the American States', above fn. 11, particularly 211 ss.

65 Blom, 'Public Policy in Private International Law', above fn. 8, 396–7. See also Hammje, 'L'ordre public et les droits fondamentaux', above fn. 15, 1 ss, no. 1.

66 See Fresnedo de Aguirre, 'Public Policy: Common Principles in the American States', above fn. 11, particularly 158–61.

67 Gannagé, L. (2009) 'L'Ordre public international à l'épreuve du relativisme des valeurs', *Droit International Privé, Travaux du Comité Français de DIPr, Année 2006–2008*, Éditions A. Pedone, 205–41, at 222.

68 Bucher, A. (2000) 'La famille en droit international privé', above fn. 60, 86.

69 Foyer, J. in F. Matscher (1999) 'Le droit international privé face à la Convention Européenne des Droits de l'Homme', *Droit International Privé, Travaux du Comité Français de DIPr, Année 1996–1997*, Éditions A. Pedone, 211–34, at 232.

70 Basedow, J. (2005) 'Recherches sur la formation de l'ordre public européen dans la jurisprudence', and Courbe, P. (2005) 'L'ordre public de proximité', *Mélanges en l'honneur de Paul Lagarde. Le droit international privé: esprit et méthodes*, Dalloz, 55–74, at 72 and 227–39, at 238 respectively.

71 Lequette, 'Le droit international prive et les droits fondamentaux', above fn. 62, 125: 'Nombre de

and we should aim at achieving an appropriate balance on this issue. Human rights that have been labelled as such in human rights conventions or by the human rights courts when applying international treaty provisions to a particular case, thus adapting the former to the concrete situation, time and context, are not an artificial creation but a reality, whether one agrees with the rationale behind it or not. These human or fundamental rights are an undeniable source of substantive content for the ascertainment of the scope of the public policy exception within private international law, though that does not necessarily mean that the recognition of fundamental rights and the public policy exception[72] always operate in such an aligned way in practice. On the one hand, the scope of fundamental rights is much broader than that of private international law;[73] on the other hand, the public policy exception operates in many instances where human rights are not at stake.

Uniformity and Predictability Regarding Public Policy

The natural function of the international public policy exception is to defend the fundamental values and principles of the forum's legal system, which are those 'on which each state bases its legal individuality'.[74] As Kinsch illustrates, the public policy technique is the historic vehicle of human rights and fundamental rights, some of which are included in human rights instruments. In his analysis of French and English case law he argues that the defence of human rights in private international law against foreign law is as ancient as the development of modern private international law, that it is based on the values transmitted by human rights – which are independent from the latter's incorporation in a positive rule of law – and that such defence has been traditionally assured through the public policy exception.[75] This is also the case in some Latin American countries, such as Uruguay, where the concept of 'international public policy' refers to fundamental 'principles' that are not necessarily enshrined in positive law. However, nothing impedes some of those principles from being shared by more than one state. When a fundamental principle is embedded in a human rights convention which was ratified by several states, including the forum state, those fundamental principles 'belong' to the forum public policy, though not exclusively, since they also 'belong' to the public policy of all the other States Parties to the convention. Therefore, the international public policy exception as a private international law technique fulfils its function of avoiding the violation of

règles aujourd'hui couvertes par l'étiquette des droits de l'homme sont des créations totalement artificielles, commandées non par la nature de l'homme mais par le "prêt à penser" ambiant'.

72 Opertti Badán, D. (2013) 'Reflexiones sobre un tema esencial: derecho internacional privado y derechos humanos', *Derecho internacional privado y derecho de la integración. Libro Homenaje a Roberto Ruiz-Díaz Labrano*, CEDEP, 63–86, at 77.

73 For specific human rights issues in relation to migration, see further the chapter by McCall-Smith in this volume.

74 1979 Uruguayan Declaration on the scope of public policy, available at: www.oas.org/juridico/english/Sigs/b-45.html

75 Kinsch, 'Droits de l'homme, droits fondamentaux et droit international privé', above fn. 22, 192.

a foundational principle of a legal system and therefore protects the integrity of the legal system of the forum; for these purposes it does not matter whether the principle is one of national or international origin.

Fundamental Rights and Transboundary Continuity of Private Relationships

What are the challenges that a closer alignment between fundamental rights recognition and the public policy exception as different yet interrelated techniques of private international law entails? Might a system that admits the direct application of fundamental rights to private international relationships reduce the space traditionally left to conflict of laws and thus reduce the traditional efforts of private international law towards the assurance of transboundary continuity of private relationships?[76] In my understanding, that undesirable consequence might occur not only when human rights rules are applied directly by judges, but also if they leave aside applicable conflict of laws rules by applying mandatory rules or rules of immediate application. However, even with such an approach, it does not seem feasible that conflict of laws rules will eventually become less relevant. Human rights can help to define a minimum of common values,[77] of common principles, not only among countries with similar traditions but also among those with different ones. This set of minimum common values and principles shared by several states is compatible with the traditional view on the role of public policy in private international law.[78] Most human rights rules provide for general principles on each topic and give a mandate to the States Parties or others, but they do not provide positive rules for all aspects of each existing international private relationship. The latter will remain subject to the judge's conflict of laws system. Moreover, both human rights and conflict of laws rules coexist in the judge's legal system and can develop each other's role in a coordinated and harmonised manner.[79] If judges uses conventional human rights rules incorporated into their legal system to find some of the fundamental principles of their state's public policy, they will favour transboundary continuity, because this should lead to enhance certainty

[76] Lequette, 'Le droit international prive et les droits fondamentaux', above fn. 62, 124.

[77] Ibid., 127.

[78] This is precisely what I try to demonstrate in Fresnedo de Aguirre, 'Public Policy: Common Principles in the American States', above fn. 11, 73–396.

[79] Both sources of law are a part of a juridical pyramid. See Gannagé, L. (2001) *La hiérarchie des normes et les méthodes du droit international privé*, LGDJ, particularly 90, fn. 135, where she refers to the best interest of the child and states that: 'l'intérêt de l'enfant, apprécié de manière générale et abstraite, a permis d'élaborer un certain nombre de règles préétablies qui s'appliquent inconditionnellement aux situations de droit international privé sans varier en fonction de l'intérêt concret de l'enfant dans l'espèce considérée. Aussi, ce sont les règles de droit international privé extraites du principe, et non l'intérêt de l'enfant au regard des circonstances de l'espèce, qui permettront de régir le litige. Or, en se dispensant d'élaborer de rattachements nouveaux, pour faire une application directe du principe général lui-même, la jurisprudence aboutit à faire prévaloir de manière exclusive une approche *in concreto* de l'intérêt de l'enfant'. See further Ruiz Abou-Nigm, V., K. McCall-Smith and D. French (eds) (2018) *Linkages and Boundaries in Private and Public International Law*, Hart Publishing.

and foreseeability when it comes to ascertaining the scope of the public policy exception and therefore anticipating the limits to the application of foreign law. The parties should know in advance that fundamental rights provided for in human rights conventions to which the judge's state is a party will give force to those provisions through the operation of the public policy exception. The formerly vague and difficult to identify 'national' international public policy principles, or at least some of them, are now set forth in human rights conventions. These 'supranational' and at the same time 'national' fundamental principles will coexist with some exclusively 'national' ones, because the latter are the ultimate guarantee of each state to protect its legal individuality, and the coherence and integrity of its legal system in some exceptional cases and therefore must also prevail.

Public Policy and Integrated Markets

Is there a common public policy within each integrated market? Are there common fundamental principles shared by all national states integrated in a common market? Each integrated market has its own particularities and therefore the answer differs depending on which integrated market is analysed. In Europe, the EU private international law framework includes provisions for the operation of the public policy exception in many of the EU private international law regulations as referred to throughout this book. In EU private international law the content of public policy recognised as being within the concept of the exception as a private international law technique are those relevant content arising mostly from values and principles of the national legal order of the forum.[80] In the American region (Organization of American States, Mercosur and others), unlike in Europe, there is neither communitarian law nor delegated legislative powers.[81] Private international law instruments must be incorporated in each state's legal order through their constitutional procedures.[82] However, and bearing in mind that the starting point is different in the Americas, it is undeniable that there are some fundamental principles that have been incorporated in institutional instruments like the Mercosur treaties and covenants. What is the incidence of those principles regarding the content of public policy? Do they create a 'new' Mercosur public policy? The answer is not straightforward.

[80] Basedow, 'Recherches sur la formation de l'ordre public européen', above fn. 70, 55–6 and Courbe, 'L'ordre public de proximité', above fn. 70, 238.

[81] Dreyzin de Klor, A. (1996) 'El orden público subregional', *Revista de Derecho Privado y Comunitario*, vol. 12, 507–25, at 512.

[82] Art. 42 of the Additional Protocol to the Treaty of Asunción on the Institutional Structure of MERCOSUR, Protocol of Ouro Preto: 'The decisions adopted by the MERCOSUR organs provided for in Article 2 of this Protocol shall be binding and when necessary, must be incorporated in the domestic legal systems in accordance with the procedures provided for in each country's legislation'. See www.sice.oas.org/trade/mrcsr/ourop/ourop_e.asp

On the one hand some authors such as Dreyzin de Klor,[83] de Rosas[84] and Batello Calderón[85] argue that there is a Mercosur public policy. In Dreyzin de Klor's opinion, that sub-regional public policy is integrated by the Treaty of Asunción and its annex (the Protocol of Ouro Preto), the decisions, resolutions and directives issued by the Mercosur organs and the principles inspiring all those instruments.[86] The Permanent Revision Court of Mercosur (Tribunal Permanente de Revisión, TPR) has also made reference to a 'regional public policy' in its Advisory Opinion of 3 April 2007. After acknowledging that there is a 'national' and an 'international' public policy, the Court states: (1) that in the Mercosur integration system there is a 'regional' public policy and that it must prevail over any other concept of public policy because it is the custody and guarantee of any rule of integration law; (2) that national public policy should be interpreted according to regional public policy, which is to be interpreted by the TPR. This is due to the need to guarantee the uniform interpretation and application of Mercosur rules in connection with any eventually applicable national provisions, as well as with its common legal heritage that exists among States Parties' legal orders; (3) and that fundamental human rights can be mentioned as belonging to regional public policy.[87]

On the same lines, Ciuro Caldani refers to the universality that is respectful of particularities and to the Mercosur public policy as an exceptional institution called to defend basic principles not only of national states but of the region, as a guardian of the cultural diversity of the people that comprise it.[88]

On the other hand, some authors, such as Nascimentos Reis,[89] disagree with the TPR and assert that we cannot speak of an unconditional superposition of regional values over national values and principles if we do not first speak of delegation of sovereignty and of the will of building a deeper and supranational integration process.

Taking into account the present stage of Mercosur's integration process, it might be suggested that it is possible to identify fundamental principles in Mercosur's legal instruments but it is also important to bear in mind that those instruments must be incorporated into the legal order of each state through their own constitutional means. There is no direct efficacy because there is no delegated sovereignty. Therefore, those principles are shared by all States Parties of each particular instrument where the

83 Dreyzin de Klor, *El Mercosur. Generador de una nueva fuente*, above fn. 59, 323–44 and 'El orden público subregional', above fn. 81, 507–38, at 513, 516, 518 ss.

84 De Rosas, 'Orden público internacional', above fn. 59, 212 ss..

85 Battello Calderón, *El orden público*, above fn. 32, 82–8.

86 Dreyzin de Klor, 'El orden público subregional', above fn. 81, 507–38, at 516.

87 www.mercosur.int/innovaportal/file/PrimeraOpinionConsultiva-Versionfinal.pdf?contentid=377&version=1&filename=PrimeraOpinionConsultiva-Versionfinal.pdf

88 Ciuro Caldani, M. A. (1996) 'Introducción: ¿Optimismo o Ilusión?', in *Del Mercosur. Aduana – Jurisdicción – Informática – Relaciones Intercomunitarias*, Ed. Ciudad Argentina, 7–13, at 12.

89 Nascimentos Reis, R. (2007) 'Orden Público del Mercosur. Un introito', *Prismas: Direito Politico, Público e Mundial*, vol. 4, no. 2, 115–30, at 125.

principle is enshrined. The same happens with fundamental principles enshrined in a CIDIP Convention, a Montevideo Treaty, a Hague Convention and so on.

Therefore, there are fundamental principles that can be drawn or inferred from each international instrument – regional or universal – and that those principles are shared by all the States Parties of that particular instrument.[90] There are fundamental principles that are shared by all States Parties to a particular Mercosur legal instrument, as well as fundamental principles shared by all States Parties to the Inter-American Convention on Conflict of Laws Concerning the Adoption of Minors[91] (for example, that in Article 19) or to the 1940 Montevideo Treaty on International Civil Law (for example, that in Article 1.2). That is not exactly the same as asserting that there is a regional public policy or a Mercosur public policy. For example, after analysing the Mercosur regulations on labour relationships,[92] particularly the Mercosur Social Charter of 1998 and the Mercosur Agreement on Residence for Nationals of Mercosur States Parties of 2002, Battello concludes that Mercosur States Parties have a common concept of public policy that obliges courts not to make a restrictive application of any law, decree or other act or measure which discriminates or limits the rights of the workers of the Mercosur block.[93] I can see no relevant difference with the examples of the Inter-American Convention on Adoption and the Montevideo Treaty. In other words, all States Parties to the Inter-American Convention on Conflict of Laws Concerning the Adoption of Minors share the same public policy principle enshrined in Article 19, and all States Parties to the 1940 Montevideo Treaty on International Civil Law share the same public policy principle enshrined in Article 1.2. There is no difference between Mercosur instruments and the fact that public policy principles enshrined in them are shared by all States Parties, and what happens with the public policy principles enshrined in any other conventional instrument, either regional or universal.

Conclusions

The public policy exception as a private international law technique is a barrier to the application of foreign law or the recognition or enforcement of a foreign judgment when that contravenes a fundamental principle on which the court's state bases its legal individuality. But it is also each state's guardian in so far as it protects legal coherence within its territory, preventing the application of a foreign law, or the recognition of a foreign judgment, from jeopardising its fundamental principles.

Fundamental principles enshrined in the international treaties on human rights or private international law issues provide substantive content for the traditionally non-defined international public policy concept. Those fundamental principles do

[90] This idea seems to be shared by Battello Calderón, *El orden público*, above fn. 32, 253(b) and Dreyzin de Klor, 'El orden público subregional', above fn. 81, 520.

[91] CIDIP-III, La Paz, 1984; see www.oas.org/juridico/english/treaties/b-48.html

[92] On labour migration see the chapter by Carballo Piñeiro in this volume.

[93] Battello Calderón, *El orden público*, above fn. 32, 118–19.

not belong exclusively to each State Party to those conventions, but are shared by all of them. Therefore, it is possible to identify some fundamental common principles that constitute the core of international public policy of each and every State Party to each one of the mentioned conventions. This does not mean that there is a common public policy within an integrated region, because in some of those regions, such as the American region, not all the states are parties to the same international treaties, for instance the Inter-American Conventions (CIDIPs) or the American Convention on Human Rights.

Finally, it can be concluded that although expanding the list of fundamental principles that are shared by several states and of the list of states that share the same fundamental principles will diminish the need for guardians and barriers, legal diversity, as representative of the individuality of each nation, will (and should) survive beyond the uniformisation and harmonisation efforts. Therefore, private international law and its traditional mechanisms, as the public policy exception, will continue to be necessary to guard legal individuality thus embracing legal diversity.

21

Bridging and Balancing: Diversity and Integration in Private International Law

*Verónica Ruiz Abou-Nigm**

Introduction

When we started thinking about the PILIM[1] project several years ago, our concern was that there was something in private international law's narrative and discourse that was preventing greater contribution of the subject to integration processes, both in Europe and in the countries of Mercosur.[2] At that time the waves of isolationism threatening integration processes regionally were not at the forefront. Throughout the life of the project it became clear that part of the problem surrounding private international law's outreach was the lack of awareness of the potential that its methodologies and techniques have in contributing to the necessary accommodation of different legal cultures, and therefore for the difficult task of bridging, *inter alia*, traditions; parties' and states' interests; capitalist pressures and social and ethnographic cultural differences; and the provincial, national, regional, international and transnational normative spaces. Balancing the tensions between competing rationales is a crucial ingredient for successful inclusive integration processes. An analysis of these tensions and the potential of private international law to bridge and balance calls for a culturalist approach.

Culturalist approaches have brought invaluable insights to critical studies in

* The author would like to thank Duncan French, Kasey McCall-Smith and Ralf Michaels for their comments on previous drafts. The usual disclaimer applies.

[1] Private International Law and Integrated Markets: A Cross-Regional Collaboration (PILIM). See www.pilim.law.ed.ac.uk, British Academy funded project 2014–17.

[2] See the scoping paper for the project (in Spanish): Ruiz Abou-Nigm, V. et al. (2013) 'Reflexiones sobre el discurso conceptual, el pluralismo metodológico y el rol del Derecho Internacional Privado en la integración', in *Derecho Internacional Privado y Derecho de la Integración. Libro homenaje a Roberto Ruiz Diaz Labrano*, CEDEP, 123–46.

private international law.[3] In one of her pioneering pieces Annelise Riles[4] distinguishes between two kinds of legal scholars; on the one hand are the constitutional theorists, the legal historians, the socio-legal scholars, the legal philosophers, the literary theorists, the feminists and the anthropologists. On the other side are the economists, the political scientists, the doctrinalists and the corporate lawyers. She calls these two groups the Culturalists and the Instrumentalists, respectively. Although she distinguishes these two 'tribes', she acknowledges that few scholars would describe their scholarship in pure cultural or instrumental terms; yet, her argument is a different one: both groups have an impoverished understanding of the technicalities of legal thought. Thus her 'manifesto' is a call for all Culturalists to 'take on the technicalities' of law, and she uses the discipline of private international law ('conflict of laws') as an exemplary site for that purposes.

This chapter is a call to the Instrumentalists to take seriously the cultural insights and implications raised by private international law issues. The argument is twofold. First, the insufficient engagement of private international law with the reality of integration (what I call an 'outreach deficiency') is related not only to the complexity of its techniques, but to a failure to communicate private international law ideas effectively beyond the exclusive club of private international law scholars.[5] Bridging legal diversity is often a complex task. Yet, private international law pluralistic thinking is developed to do just that. The challenge is how to tailor the streaming of this 'intellectual style'[6] in the words of Karen Knop, Ralf Michaels and Annelise Riles, in a manner that becomes relevant to the daily life of lawyers, individuals and companies. The question is how to do that openly, effectively and in a way that engages with the relevant actors.[7] The self-perpetuating 'theoreticism' characteristic of the discipline, as referred to by Didier Opertti Badán in the foreword to this volume, is surrounded by an aura of impenetrability that disfavours the discipline and jeopardises its impact. Secondly, private international law has historically been very creative in the use of a plurality of techniques and methodologies to aim for the right balance in bridging legal diversity; bridges in need of constant maintenance as examined in many chapters of this volume. Yet, ingenuity should also focus in the paths for further

[3] This chapter has been influenced, in particular, by the inspiring work of contemporary scholars Paul Schiff Berman, Karen Knop, Ralf Michaels, Annelise Riles and Horatia Muir Watt, and to a lesser extent that of the late Werner Goldschmidt.

[4] Riles, A. (2005), 'A New Agenda for the Cultural Study of Law: Taking on the Technicalities' 53 *Buffalo L. Rev.*, 973.

[5] See further Ruiz Abou-Nigm, V. 'Private International Law and Global Governance Issues: Unlocking Private International Law's Potential in Global (Migration) Governance', in Ferrari, F. and D. Fernández Arroyo (eds) (209) *Private International Law: Contemporary Challenges and Continuing Relevance*, Elgar.

[6] See Knop, K., R. Michaels and A. Riles (2012) 'From Multiculturalism to Technique: Feminism, Multiculturalism, and the Conflict of Laws Style' 64 *Stan. L. Rev.* 589.

[7] In the words of Riles, 'the problem with Conflicts . . . is ultimately not that it is a bad set of doctrines; the problem is that the game is no longer fun to play', Riles, 'A New Agenda', above fn. 4, 982.

impact, that is, to facilitate deeper inter-disciplinary[8] and real-world dialogue.[9] To that end, an understanding of 'pluralistic thinking' as described in social psychology can contribute to a grasp of where the cognitive barriers come from, and can generate ideas in relation to the building blocks for further embracement of diversity. Hence the claim, and the one this chapter elaborates, is that private international law invites liaising between Culturalist and Instrumentalist thinking. That liaison brings to the fore the Pluralist in all of us private international lawyers.

This attempt is structured as follows. First, a glimpse at Culturalists' contributions to private international law studies is provided. Next, I introduce the concept of 'pluralistic thinking' as coined in social psychology as a valuable conceptual framework to understand legal pluralism in private international law. As this chapter is the last one of this volume I then bring together Culturalists' approaches and Instrumentalists' threads from throughout the volume reflecting on some of the techniques discussed and their fitness to embrace legal diversity in integration processes. Finally, I reflect on what this endeavour at a liaison may be telling us about the discipline's ideology more broadly.

A Glimpse at Culturalists' Approaches

Cultural concerns have always been central to private international law from Savigny[10] to modern times. Amongst Culturalist approaches of times past there is one particularly influential to one of the regions studied in this volume: the renowned German scholar Werner Goldschmidt, who lived the final decades of his life in Argentina, where he developed his theory of the three-dimensional vision of law, in its normative, sociological and axiological dimensions.[11] His vision in *Derecho Internacional Privado: Derecho de la Tolerancia* has been highly influential for many generations of private international law scholars in South America, particularly in Argentina. Another influential approach in South America, particularly focused on integration projects, is that of Erik Jayme.[12] Culturalist approaches[13] generate

[8] On the need for further interdisciplinarity see Knop, K., R. Michaels and A. Riles (eds) (2008), 'Transdisciplinary Conflict of Laws' 71 *Law and Contemporary Problems* 3, 1, 10.

[9] See, *inter alia*, Muir Watt, H. (2014) 'The Relevance of Private International Law to the Global Governance Debate', in Muir Watt, H. and D. P. Fernández Arroyo (eds), *Private International Law and Global Governance*, Oxford University Press, 8.

[10] Riles, A. (2008) 'Cultural Conflicts', 71 *Law and Contemporary Problems*, 273–308; available at: https://scholarship.law.duke.edu/lcp/vol71/iss3/13

[11] Goldschmidt, W. (1982) *Derecho Internacional Privado. Derecho de la Tolerancia*, 4th edn, Depalma.

[12] Jayme, E. (1995) 'Identité culturelle et intégration: le droit international privé postmoderne', *Recueil des cours*, vol. 251, 9–267, at 251, 120–1.

[13] Riles, 'Cultural Conflicts', above fn. 10: '[r]ethinking these cultural conflicts through the prism of recent anthropological insights about culture as a problem of empathetic description and collaborative engagement with others, moreover, both reveals the importance of conflicts as a field and draws attention to aspects of the field's methodology, such as the description of foreign law, that are given too little attention in mainstream analyses'.

further awareness of the context in which private international law is called upon to make an impact. A glimpse at some contemporary Culturalists' contributions is to follow.

Interdisciplinarity Promoters

In the words of Knop et al., interdisciplinary approaches 'demonstrate in concrete and consequential ways the remarkable ability of conflicts methodologies, whether by courts or by academics, to make what is often most pressing, most poignant, most epistemologically challenging and most politically and morally difficult about particular questions'.[14] Their contributions and those of others in *Transdisciplinary Conflicts*[15] opened new horizons to private international law thinking and discourse. One of the first interdisciplinary lenses that private international law scholars engaged with was economic analysis.[16] Other insights bearing fruit are, *inter alia*, from legal anthropology,[17] political science,[18] psychology[19] and ethics.[20] Interdisciplinarity started to flourish in North American scholarship[21] and is slowly but steadily growing in Europe; however it has yet to gain momentum in private international law studies in Latin America, particularly in Mercosur countries.[22]

The benefits of interdisciplinarity are manifold. This applies to any field of knowledge, and private international law is no exception. Interdisciplinary analysis not only allows the generation of new avenues for thinking, new models and mutual enrichment, but interdisciplinary dialogue forces us to simplify, to clarify and to 'translate', that is, to engage with other disciplines actively and efficiently, and thus throws new light on our old ways of 'doing'[23] private international law. It

[14] Knop et al., 'Transdisciplinary Conflict of Laws', above fn. 8, 10.

[15] Ibid., 1.

[16] See, *inter alia*, Muir Watt, H. (2004) 'Aspects économiques de droit international privé (réflexions sur l'impact de la globalisation économique sur les fondements des conflits de lois et de juridictions)', *Recueil des cours*, vol. 307, 25–383; O'Hara, E. A. (ed.) (2007) *The Economics of Conflict of Laws*, Elgar (2 vols); Michaels, R. (2006) 'Economics of Law as Choice of Law', 71 *L. & Contemp. Probs.* 73, 77–87; Michaels, R. (2006) 'Two Economists, Three Opinions? Economic Models for Private International Law – Cross-Border Torts as Example', in Basedow, J. and T. Kono (eds), *An Economic Analysis of Private International Law*, Mohr Siebeck, 143.

[17] Berman, P. S. (2005) 'Towards a Cosmopolitan Vision of Conflict of Laws: Redefining Governmental Interests in a Global Era', *University of Connecticut School of Law Articles and Working Papers*, 24.

[18] Whytock, C. A. (2009) 'Myth of Mess? International Choice of Law in Action', 84 *N.Y.U. L. Rev.* 719; Whytock, C. A. (2009) 'Domestic Courts and Global Governance', 84 *Tulane Law Review*.

[19] See the Pluralistic Thinking section below.

[20] See the chapter by Michaels in this volume.

[21] Knop et al., 'Transdisciplinary Conflict of Laws', above fn. 8.

[22] See the initiative led by Paula María All in Argentina, https://repensartedipr.wordpress.com/catedra-dipr-fcjs-unl

[23] Nicola Wisdahl, in her chapter in this volume, explains from an eminently practical perspective how 'doing' private international law in the context of the necessary engagement with others in international judicial cooperation practice also requires this kind of self-reflection.

also enhances the connective capabilities of the discipline, and, particularly, fosters real-world dialogue in relation to pressing contemporary issues from migration to climate change, to corporate social responsibility, amongst others. Even though interdisciplinary approaches to private international law issues do not necessarily translate into technical solutions, they enable further engagement with a much wider range of actors, issues and concerns.[24] As discussed elsewhere,[25] regional integration, as well as the intensification of global trade as rationale for the development of private international law normativity, downplays social and ethnographic cultural differences in pursuit of furthering market integration. This capitalist pressure is blatant in the European Union and Mercosur, and reality is clearly showing that the tensions generated can easily exacerbate and threaten the integration project itself.[26] Interdisciplinarity can open new dialogues to tackle these tensions.

Defenders of Technicalities

In the words of Riles, the technical character of law

> encompasses diverse and even at times contradictory subjects, ideologies, and practices. These include: (1) the ideologies – legal instrumentalism and managerialism; (2) the actors – the scholars and practitioners who treat the law as a kind of tool or machine and who see themselves as modest but expertly devoted technicians; (3) the problem-solving paradigm – the orientation toward defining concrete, practical problems and toward crafting solutions; (4) the form of technical legal doctrine and argumentation . . .[27]

Riles aimed to

> show the humanists on the one hand that the technicalities of Conflicts are far more surprising and interesting than they might imagine. And to show the instrumentalists, on the other hand, that sophisticated cultural analysis can at the very least clarify the nature of technical problems that their own methods now seem incapable of resolving.[28]

An important contribution of the technicalities defenders has indeed been to bring about the positive aspect of this characteristic feature of the discipline; rather than blaming the techniques for their complexity, this school of thought – to which this chapter adheres – shows how appreciating the value of private international law techniques, and the techniques as a way of thinking about law, is that the true worth of the discipline comes to the fore. In this sense Knop et al. explain that private international law techniques 'are not simply tools for resolving disputes, although – and this is the

[24] Knop et al., 'Transdisciplinary Conflict of Laws', above fn. 8., 10.

[25] Ruiz Abou-Nigm, 'Reflexiones sobre el discurso conceptual', above fn. 2.

[26] See further Requejo Isidro's chapter in this volume examining the potential implications of Brexit for private international law in Europe; see also the 'identity crisis' of Mercosur as referred to in Argerich and Capalbo's chapter in this volume.

[27] Riles, 'A New Agenda', above fn. 4, 976.

[28] Ibid.

trick – that is precisely how they are structured. Rather, they are first and foremost tools with which to think.'[29] Along these lines Riles argues that:

> if a judge, legislator, or scholar wished to take seriously the questions of cultural conflict raised by any conflicts issue, he or she would find that there are a number of existing conflicts doctrines that either explicitly or implicitly put these concerns at the forefront. Ironically, these doctrines tend to be among the most maligned for being excessively malleable and too complicated to apply. But if one understands the complexity and malleability of these doctrines not as technical obfuscation for its own sake, but rather as a product of these doctrines' efforts to grapple seriously with the problem of cultural conflict, then their very flaws may become their virtues.

Critical Sceptics

Critical studies of private international law epitomised in Europe by the scholarship of Horatia Muir Watt have also opened new avenues for reflection, highlighting the flaws and limitations of contemporary private international law. A very important contribution of Muir Watt is her emphasising of the value-laden nature of the discipline, demystifying the so-called 'neutrality principle': private international law is neither ascetic nor neutral in the sense that might once have been understood as a highly technical system of coordination uninterested in global values. On the contrary, it is a value-laden discipline that can only be understood in a certain socio-political context. Muir Watt puts forward values such as the 'respect for alterity, which has significant implications in terms of the perception of the relationship between the Self and the Other, the forum and the foreign',[30] and ethical connotations of hospitality[31] and tolerance. Undoubtedly Muir Watt's scholarship has been pivotal to unravelling values and policies in contemporary private international law in Europe. Her scholarship has also prompted the rethinking of the outer boundaries of the discipline and the increasing challenges to the public/private divide globally.[32] As I examine elsewhere,[33] private and public international law both have an important role to play in reconstructing the current legal landscape for the pursuit of the 'global commons'.[34] This is as essential for integration projects as it is more broadly for society at large.

29 Knop et al., 'Transdisciplinary Conflict of Laws', above fn. 8.

30 Muir Watt, H. (2014) 'Future Directions', in Muir Watt, H. and D. P. Fernández Arroyo (eds), *Private International Law and Global Governance*, above fn. 9, 374.

31 Muir Watt, H. (2017) 'Hospitality, Tolerance, and Exclusion in Legal Form: Private International Law and the Politics of Difference', *Current Legal Problems*, vol. 70, no. 1, 111–47.

32 Muir-Watt, H. (2011) 'Private International Law Beyond the Schism', 3 *Transnational Legal Theory* 2, 347.

33 Ruiz Abou-Nigm, V., K. McCall-Smith and D. French (2018) 'Introduction: Systemic Dialogue: Identifying Commonalities and Exploring Linkages in Private and Public International Law', in Ruiz Abou-Nigm, V., K. McCall-Smith and D. French (eds) (2018), *Linkages and Boundaries in Private and Public International Law*, Hart Publishing, 1.

34 Ibid., 1.

Even more relevant for this chapter and for this volume considered as a whole is Muir Watt's correlation between on the one hand 'legal pluralism and recognitive statutism as the technical avatars of hospitality' and on the other, 'multilateralism in the conflict of laws [as] correlated to liberal tolerance', explaining that:

> [a]s long as the foreign, or the other, was a marginal presence within a dominantly homogeneous society, liberalism was arguably sufficient to ensure peaceful coexistence of different lifeforms. Tolerance in the form of exceptions was adequate in terms of a collective policy towards difference, while heroic hospitality was left to individual virtue. However, dealing with difference as exception in a society composed of multiple cultures is obviously inappropriate, and liable to generate the sort of tensions which are tragically apparent in Western communities. The response has to be *more not less opening* [to the] recognition of difference.[35]

Cosmopolitan Views

Cosmopolitan perspectives have a long track record in private international law in Europe and Latin America. Yet, as a 'worldview', as a contextual framework for understanding private international law techniques and methodologies, the contemporary cosmopolitan view as portrayed by Paul Schiff Berman[36] is promising. Berman describes cosmopolitanism as a

> middle ground between universalism on the one hand and strict territorialism on the other . . . the advantage of cosmopolitanism as a choice-of-law framework is precisely that cosmopolitanism seeks to understand issues of multiple community affiliation . . . cosmopolitanism starts from the premise that community affiliations are always plural and can be detached from mere spatial location.[37]

In Berman's model '[c]osmopolitanism seeks "flexible citizenship"[38] in which people are permitted to shift identities amid a plurality of possible affiliations and allegiances'.[39] This model is indeed a manifestation of pluralistic thinking as discussed below.

Pluralistic Thinking

The *raison d'être* of private international law is the plurality of legal orders; dealing with this plurality is the quintessential function of private international law. However,

35 Muir Watt, 'Hospitality, Tolerance, and Exclusion in Legal Form', above fn. 31, 145–6.

36 Berman, P. S. (2012) *Global Legal Pluralism: A Jurisprudence of Law Beyond Borders*, Cambridge University Press; Berman, P. S. (2005) 'Conflict of Laws, Globalization, and Cosmopolitan Pluralism', 51 *Wayne L. Rev.* 1105; Berman, 'Towards a Cosmopolitan Vision of Conflict of Laws', above fn. 17; Berman, P. S. (2007) 'Global Legal Pluralism' *Southern California Review*, vol. 80, 1155.

37 Berman, P.S. (2005) 'Conflict of Laws, Globalization, and Cosmopolitan Pluralism', above fn. 36, 1113.

38 Ibid., 1115, in which Berman refers to the work of Ong, A. (1999) *Flexible Citizenship: The Cultural Logics of Transnationality*, Duke University Press.

39 Ibid., 1115.

pluralism is not only a fact in the reality of normativity; it infuses private international law in all its domains, and it is here submitted that 'pluralistic thinking' as conceptualised in social psychology by Novis-Deutsch[40] is its heart and soul, essential to 'do' private international law, in practice and in theory, in this day and age.

Her conceptualisation portrays pluralistic thinking as 'a deep form of open-mindedness, involving the recognition and endorsement of multiplicity and complexity in the world'.[41] Pluralism has been broadly described as positively valuing multiplicity.[42] 'It is used differentially to connote a multiplicity of "what is" (ontological pluralism) or to embrace a multiplicity of "ways of knowing" (epistemological pluralism)'.[43] As explained by Novis-Deutsch, '[e]pistemological pluralism refers not to reality itself but to how people perceive, interpret, and understand it . . . an epistemological pluralist believes that multiple, fundamentally different perspectives on reality, values, and lifestyles are both inevitable and desirable;'[44] it 'connotes a positive attitude towards human diversity and endorses an active dialogue between perspectives'.[45] Some building blocks are considered key motivational factors of pluralists: openness to experience, tolerance of uncertainty and empathic concern.[46]

Both domains of pluralistic thinking, ontological and epistemological, are engrained in many ways in private international law. Legal diversity, and the multiplicity of methods in private international law to bridge that diversity, both reflect ontological pluralism. Embracing diversity as a desirable outcome of that bridging and balancing speaks of epistemological pluralism.[47]

Pluralist thinking goes to the very core of the discipline's identity. For some of us,[48] pluralism is inherent not only to the methodologies and techniques of the discipline but to the very understanding of what the discipline is about. The fact that there are various understandings of the remit and objectives of private international law is not accidental; a reflection of private international law pluralistic thinking.[49]

Pluralistic thinking in private international law is also related to the awareness of the coexistence of different sources and the ability to make use of them in a

[40] Novis-Deutsch, N. (2018) 'The One and the Many: Both/and Reasoning and the Embracement of Pluralism' *Theory & Psychology* 28(4), 429–50, at 431.

[41] Ibid., 431.

[42] Ibid., 431.

[43] Ibid., 431.

[44] Ibid., 431.

[45] Ibid., 431.

[46] Ibid, 438.

[47] Novis-Deutsch, 'The One and the Many', above fn. 40.

[48] Particularly the ones who learned private international law following great scholars of the Uruguayan Institute of Private International Law; see Opertti Badán, D. et al. (1990) *Objeto y Método en el Derecho Internacional Privado*, 2nd edn, FCU.

[49] Arguably this is also reflected in the different names that the subject is known by worldwide. In English, private international law, conflict of laws, international private law. The same kind of differences appear in other languages too; in Spanish, for instance: *derecho internacional privado* and *derecho privado internacional*.

coordinated manner. Jayme's reference to a 'dialogue of the sources'[50] points to the reciprocal influences between these different sources, enabling the application of several sources at the same time, concurrently or alternately, permitting the parties to choose between instruments or even providing for an opt-out mechanism in favour of an alternative, more suitable solution.[51] For Jayme there are two main ways to resolve the possible conflicts generated by postmodern legal pluralism. The first is to give prominence to one source, discarding the other, that is, granting a certain hierarchy among them; the second involves seeking the coordination of sources. The latter methodology, that is, the 'dialogue of the sources', is an exercise of pluralistic thinking embracing legal diversity and multiplicity and making room for different normative ensembles and accommodation.[52]

The pluralistic thinking engrained in private international law may also explain the perception of difficulty of the discipline. As explained by Novis-Deutsch efforts to grasp and grapple diversity usually connote complexity.[53] It is precisely the kind of complexity at play when tackling issues of interlegality also.[54]

Pluralism in social psychology, as a specific way of engaging with diversity and multiplicity, is a modern construction entangled with the social-political and economic conditions of our modern multicultural society.[55] Novis-Deutsch argues that '[i]n promoting more complex and diversified social institutions, as well as greater social mobility and geographical migration, these changes fostered new ways of being, thinking, and behaving'.[56] As she articulates,[57] there are two types of pluralism commonly discussed by political theorists and philosophers: 'cultural pluralism' and 'value pluralism'. The former refers to how individuals and groups relate to cultural and group differences; the latter is a meta-ethical system. This means the latter takes

50 Jayme, *Identité culturelle et intégration* above fn. 12, paras 9 ff, 60 and 259.

51 See Marques, C. L. (2003), 'Procédure civile internationale et MERCOSUR: pour un dialogue des règles universelles et régionales', 1 *Uniform Law Review* 2, 465.

52 In the context of international treaties, the 'dialogue of the sources' as a methodology of normative accommodation has been considered part of a 'new general theory of law'; see Marques, C. L. (2012) 'O "Diálogo das Fontes" como método da nova teoria geral do direito: um tributo a Erik Jayme', in Marques, C. L. (ed.), *Diálogo das Fontes. Do conflito à coordenação de normas do direito brasileiro*, Editora Revista Dos Tribunais, 17, 21, 28. See further Noodt Taquela, M. B. (2016) 'Applying the Most Favourable Treaty or Domestic Rules to Facilitate Private International Law Co-operation', *Recueil des cours*, vol. 377, 121–318. Examples of coordination provisions to pre-empt and to solve these potential conflicts appear in many international treaties adopted under the auspices of the Hague Conference as well as many other international instruments. See further Noodt Taquela, M. B. and V. Ruiz Abou-Nigm (2018) 'The Draft Judgments Convention and its Relationship with Other International Instruments', *Yearbook of Private International Law*, vol. 19, 2017/2018, 449–74.

53 Ibid., 438.

54 See, *inter alia*, Wai, R. (2008) 'The Interlegality of Transnational Private Law' 71(3) *Law & Contemp. Probs.* 107.

55 Novis-Deutsch, 'The One and the Many', above fn. 40, 433.

56 Ibid., 433.

57 Ibid., 432.

as its subject not the people holding ideas, but the ideas themselves, and therefore it applies to value and moral domains. In turn, Novis-Deutsch reveals that there are different strengths of cultural pluralism, and it is possible to recognise weak and strong forms. In the terms of Walzer, the weak variant involves 'openness to the other, curiosity, respect'[58] while strong cultural pluralism is actively celebratory: an 'enthusiastic endorsement of difference: an esthetic endorsement . . . or a functional endorsement, if difference is viewed as a necessary condition of human flourishing'.[59] One of the arguments in this final chapter is that, specifically for integration projects,[60] the balance needs to tip towards the celebratory, to thrive in diversity, and private international law methodologies and techniques have the potential to be instrumental to that achievement.

Cosmopolitan Pluralistic Dialectics

What, then, are these approaches revealing about private international law roles in present times? Are private international law techniques fit to contribute to bridging and balancing legal diversity? What can we learn from a meta-paradigmatic standpoint?[61] There is no doubt that the issues involved tend to be complex and the challenges therefore far from insignificant. Culturalists argue that 'as a matter of sociology of knowledge, adhering to the constraints of form that characterize conflicts technicalities more often opens up an alternative resolution, or indeed alternative questions for theory and practice . . .'[62] What about the influences in the reverse direction? Hopefully, generating greater awareness of the cultural implications of private international law methodological choices may promote better engagement of the discipline with integration processes broadly considered, not only for the sake of promoting market integration, both in Europe and in the countries of Mercosur.

Different dimensions need to be kept in mind when reflecting on these issues; otherwise the risk is conflation, generating the miscommunication and obscurity this contribution is precisely trying to avoid. Thus, some of the insights that follow relate to (1) private international law rules (normativity); (2) private international law practice (reality); and (3) private international law as a field of knowledge (theory). These dimensions are not necessarily watertight; it is important to note the necessary cross-pollination between them, and a certain unavoidable feeling of arbitrariness when placing insights in one or another of these dimensions as some will invariably

58 Ibid., 432.

59 Ibid., 432.

60 Proponents of the highest degrees of legal harmonisation to foster integration projects may find this paradoxical, however, at least in Europe, the motto of 'unity in diversity' has been always part of the integration project's ideology.

61 See Johnson, R. B. (2011) 'Dialectical Pluralism: A Metaparadigm to Help us Hear and "Combine" our Valued Differences'. Paper presented in plenary session at the Seventh International Congress of Qualitative Inquiry, Urbana-Champaign, IL.

62 Knop et al., 'Transdisciplinary Conflict of Laws', above fn. 8, 594.

be cross-cutting.[63] With these caveats in place, what does a cosmopolitan approach reveal in relation to private international law techniques against the goals of embracing diversity and integration? In the following paragraphs a few of those insights are presented, using a dialectics model[64] to 'help us hear and "combine" our valued differences'.[65] Core to pluralistic thinking is the acceptance that there may be no clear-cut conclusions.[66]

Private International Law Rules (Normativity)

Adaptation and accommodation

As van Hoek explained,[67] the coordination of legal systems involves much more than accommodating the different domestic applicable laws or rules; it requires adaptation of those laws and rules to the reality of international cases. To manage legal diversity requires creativity in order to achieve a result that is acceptable under the different legal systems being coordinated; 'the applicable rules have to be "adapted" to fit the international case'.[68] The processes of accommodation and adaptation have always been part of private international law thinking more broadly, and as such relevant not only for judges in cross-border cases but for international arbitration proceedings as well, as shown by Giuditta Cordero-Moss and Diego Fernández Arroyo in this volume.

Culturalists' approaches connect accommodation and adaptation to pluralism.[69] On these lines Muir Watt refers to 'accommodative pluralism'[70] as not necessarily leading to the exclusive application of one or the other conflicting norms, but giving rise to adjustments and concessions. As she clearly puts it, it is precisely through such processes that the law can evolve, reflexively: 'pluralism can be seen to belong to the "balancing" paradigm, which accepts that mutual adjustment can generate a new norm'.[71]

In integration projects such as the EU, the articulation of that adaptation is

[63] The need for a better balance between theory and practice has been a constant concern of mine; see, for example, Ruiz Abou-Nigm, V. (2011) *The Arrest of Ships in Private International Law*, Oxford University Press, para. 6.3.2.

[64] See Johnson, R. B. (2012) 'Dialectical Pluralism and Mixed Research' *American Behavioral Scientist* 56(6) 751–4.

[65] Johnson, 'Dialectical Pluralism', above fn. 61.

[66] Novis-Deutsch, 'The One and the Many', above fn. 40.

[67] van Hoek, A. A. H. (2012) 'Managing Legal Diversity – New Challenges for Private International Law' NIPR 2012 FL 3, 362–70.

[68] Ibid., 362–70.

[69] On legal pluralism more generally see, *inter alia*, Berman, *Global Legal Pluralism* above fn. 36; Michaels, R. (2009) 'Global Legal Pluralism', 5 *Annual Review of Law* 243; and Michaels, R. (2005) 'The Re-State-ment of Non-State Law: The State, Choice of Law, and the Challenge from Global Legal Pluralism', 51 *Wayne L. Rev.* 1209.

[70] Muir Watt, 'Hospitality, Tolerance, and Exclusion in Legal Form', above fn. 31, 143.

[71] Ibid., 144.

shown, for instance, in the use of 'autonomous concepts'[72] in the interpretation of private international law provisions. This is primarily facilitated by the role of the Court of Justice of the European Union (CJEU) in interpreting EU legislation, and via the mechanism of preliminary rulings. Hence, for instance, when the EU private international law Regulations make reference to the 'habitual residence of a child' or to 'directing activities'[73] (the latter in the context of EU private international law rules on consumer contracts, for instance), these are autonomous concepts that cannot be interpreted according to the conceptions of any EU national legal system individually considered but have to be interpreted according to the autonomous European meaning, as discussed, for instance, by Beatriz Añoveros in her chapter in this volume. The integration project, and its demands for harmonisation, is the rationale behind the generation and interpretation of those autonomous concepts, as openly recognised in EU Regulations.[74]

This has been pivotal to the Europeanisation process, though, at times, not necessarily reflecting the 'balancing' paradigm referred to above; therefore the 'accommodation/adaptation' technique, thought to embed elasticity and inclusivity in the system, in the context of harmonisation in integration projects can acquire a tightening/exclusion effect.

Evidence shows that the tendency to interpret the EU private international law categories from the perspective of national law is quite extended and relates to the legal mindset of judges more than anything else. Trimmings and Yuksel stress in their chapter that 'even in jurisdictions where the courts have a good knowledge of EU privateEvidence showslaw Regulations, such as Scotland, the judges and the practitioners seem to struggle with interpreting the legal concepts autonomously, free from the national meanings and understanding in their jurisdiction'.[75] A Culturalist's reading of this reality may show the need to revisit the processes by which these autonomous concepts are generated, in such a way that they could resonate with the diversity of legal systems involved in the integration project and generate further inclusion rather than exclusion.[76]

Fluidity and malleability

Legal diversity features in the EU and the Mercosur countries in relation not only to their substantive laws but also to their conflict of law rules. Even though the

[72] In turn, 'autonomous interpretation' stands for a synthesis of methods; the traditional grammatical, systematic and historical method of interpretation must be supplemented by a comparative approach.

[73] Joined Cases, C 585/08 and C 144/09, *Peter Pammer* v. *Reederei Kart SchulüterSchlüter GmbH & Co KG* and *Hotel AlpenhhofAlpenhof GesmbH* v. *Oliver Heller* [2010] ECR I-12527, para. 55 (*Pammer*).

[74] See Rome I and Rome II recitals.

[75] Trimmings, K. and B. Yuksel (2017) 'National Report: Great Britain', in P. Beaumont *et al* (eds), *Cross-Border Litigation in Europe*, Hart Publishing, Ch. 5.

[76] The inclusion/exclusion dialectics is discussed below in relation to the practice domain.

EU has come a long way with its harmonisation process, it is clear that there are several spheres where diversity presents itself in these two dimensions. Carruthers' contribution to this volume is an excellent example of the challenges that this presents in the field of cross-border succession. She refers to the 'scission principle' as a conflict of laws rule of the English and Scottish legal systems, different from those adopted in the Rome IV Regulation applicable in continental European countries.

As Carruthers notes, the scission principle 'was conceived as an enlightened, outward-looking technique, a rule based in, or even fostering, comity'.[77] This idiosyncratic British scission rule, under which intestate succession to immovable property is governed by the *lex situs*, distinguishing between movable and immovable property in relation to intestate succession, was outward looking in its conception, established with a view to accommodate legal diversity 'by prioritising legal systems' interests (or perceived interests) according to the nature of property'.[78] Yet, the scission principle

> was developed at a time when wealth was equivalent to land ownership, which, in turn, was to be equated with rights of suffrage; as the economy and domestic private law have evolved, the *situs* principle in UK choice of law rules of succession has remained static.[79]

Thus, as recognised by Carruthers, the scission rule now appears anachronistic; it has lost that outward-looking perspective and it is nowadays perceived as connected to the 'tradition-bound character of the law of inheritance'.[80]

This example shows that technical rules to keep its instrumentalism need to have adaptability in the design, to allow for the reshaping of principles according to societal changes. What needs to remain central is the concrete approach to problem-solving; if the rationale at the conception of the rule was accommodating difference between legal systems and fostering comity, that underpinning should be the guidance to reshape or reformulate the rule so it can continue to provide that outcome in an evolving society. Both Culturalists and Instrumentalists recognise the need for 'maintenance' of the techniques in this sense, in the perspective of the latter. Private international law normativity in the national, regional and multilateral domains generally considers this idea. Room for revisiting and recasting is embedded in the processes of private international law development in the EU integration project,[81] as well as in the post-convention care processes at the Hague Conference (HCCH), revisiting and assessing the performance of HCCH Conventions periodically. The reform and modernisation of national systems of private international law in Latin America

[77] See Carruthers' chapter in this volume.

[78] Ibid.

[79] Ibid.

[80] Ibid.

[81] See Requejo Isidro in this volume on the evolving nature of the EU integration project as an organic project.

examined by Paredes also shows this increasing fluidity (although recognising that this has taken place after years of passivity) at the national dimension. Once private international law rules are seen as instrumental techniques, their fitness for purpose needs to be periodically tested and maintenance becomes paramount. It is to be hoped that this rationale will reach the long-awaited reform of the scission principle in the UK legal systems.

Characterisation and fragmentation

Characterisation is a technique pivotal to private international law methodologies[82] and widely recognised as a crucial part of the process of applying private international law rules. Yet, problems of characterisation are the most difficult and unsettled issues.[83] The process of characterisation seeks to allocate a certain legal issue into a private international law category.[84] This process, that is, the stepping stone of pigeonholing the case scenario into the appropriate legal category, has been abundantly discussed in private international law literature.[85]

The understanding that legal categories like 'marriage' or 'torts' have a broader and much more flexible scope in private international law mores as compared to domestic conceptualisations is something that students learn in their very first exposure to private international law methodologies. From a Culturalist perspective, as explained by Muir Watt, in the traditional private international law multilateral approach 'characterisation (a means of control of the "shape" of legal relationships) ensure[s] that more exotic forms of life [do] not intrude on the host. Through shaping the breadth and depth of these categories courts attempt to measure the degree of

[82] Alfonsín, Q. (1955) *Teoría del Derecho Privado Internacional*, Martin Bianchi Altuna.

[83] Maekelt, T. (2005) *Teoría General del Derecho Internacional Privado*, Academia de Ciencias Políticas y Sociales, 285. As revealed by Lipstein, there seems to be at least some consensus on two basic problems: what is to be characterised is a legal relation confronted with a certain system or systems of law and the aim of the process of characterisation is to reveal the function and purpose of those norms as far as that legal relation is concerned (Lipstein, K. (1999) 'Characterization' 3 *International Encyclopaedia of Comparative Law* (Ch. 5) 8).

[84] See *Raiffeisen Zentralbank Osterreich AG* v. *Five Star General Trading LLC (The Mount I)* [2001] EWCA Civ 68, (CA) (Mance LJ) [26-27].

[85] Alfonsín understood that characterisation and interpretation were the two phases of a single process. In his opinion the difference is one of perspective: from the point of view of the rule of law it is interpretation; from the point of view of the legal relation it is characterisation. Alfonsín, Q. (1982) *Teoría del Derecho Privado Internacional*, 2nd edn, Idea, 389. As to the English understanding of characterisation as a private international law technique see *Macmilland Inc* v. *Bishopsgate Investment Trust (No 3)* [1996] 1 WLR 387 (CA) 407 (Auld LJ) 'characterisation . . . is governed by the *lex fori* . . . [T]he proper approach is to look beyond the formulation of the claim and to identify according to the *lex fori*, the true issue or issues thrown up by the claim and defence. This requires a parallel classification of the rule of law'. Cf. *Raiffeisen Zentralbank Osterreich AG* v. *Five Star General Trading LLC (The Mount I)* [2001] EWCA Civ 68, [2001] 1 Lloyd's Rep 597 (CA) (Mance LJ) [26-27].

social acceptability of the foreign'.[86] This applies to national courts, but it also applies to the balancing act of the CJEU.[87]

From an Instrumentalist perspective, as examined by Espinosa Calabuig in her chapter in this volume, characterisation presents important challenges in the application of private international law rules in several countries of the EU. The 'home-trend', as referred to by the Instrumentalists, manifests itself in various fields in private international law, from the approach to problem-solving, the interpretation of rules and some rules themselves (especially jurisdiction allocating rules), and it has connotations far beyond the field of private international law rules, from the standpoint of legal education, for instance. As Michaels argues elsewhere, globalisation has not yet led to a true paradigm shift in legal thinking.[88] This is as true for Europe as it is for the rest of the world. We are used to thinking about legal issues from the starting point of our own legal system, that is the frame of reference of our legal matrix. We need to radically rethink the role and shape of law in our global changing society and this needs to start as early as someone's first exposure to legal studies.[89]

Furthermore, as shown by Carballo Piñeiro in the context of labour migration, the shaping of private international law categories is not only essential in relation to the home-foreign tension, but more broadly in relation to guaranteeing fundamental rights of equality and non-discrimination. Carballo Piñeiro shows that EU conflict rules on individual contracts of employment as devised having in mind just one type of labour migration, that of workers who move permanently to a foreign country for work purposes, strive to put on equal footing domestic and foreign workers, and for that reason they resort to the habitual place of work as the usual connecting factor. As she examines, while this serves for integration purposes in cases of the permanent posting of workers, the same connection fuels other types of migration in search of low-cost labour markets. The most obvious one is that triggered by business relocation, which is undertaken in order to take advantage of other countries' labour and employment conditions. This awareness is crucial at the stage of rule-making. Culturalist approaches can shed light on the equality implications of adopting broader or narrower categories, depending on the needs that the rule attempts to address, to strive, at the rule-making stage, to avoid systemic results contrary to the rationale of the rules themselves.

[86] Muir Watt, 'Hospitality, Tolerance, and Exclusion in Legal Form', above fn. 31, 133.

[87] As recognised by Cristian Oro Martínez in the final PILIM conference: the CJEU has exceeded what is necessary for the functioning of private international law rules, in the name of integration.

[88] Michaels, R. (2013) 'Globalization and Law: Law Beyond the State', in R. Banakar and M. Travers (eds) *Law and Social Theory*, Hart Publishing.

[89] The author is leading the ELFA European Jurist Project to build capacity along these lines for the legal profession broadly conceived in Europe.

Private International Law Practice (Reality)

Market integration and legal diversity

Private international law, explicitly or subtly, performs different roles in different contexts at different times. Historically, the various objectives from decisional harmony to the continuity of the legal relationship can be understood in terms of a particular political agenda.

In the European project of integration the adoption of uniform private international law rules has been fostered 'not only to reach harmony of solutions, but, primarily, to enhance pre-litigation predictability to the benefit of the efficiency of the internal market'.[90] As Ragno puts it, '[l]egal certainty, as a catalyst to the internal market, constitutes one of the *raison d'être* and a substantive policy of EU private international law'.[91] Enhancing the functioning of the internal market[92] was the origin of the EU intervention in private international law mores. The EU has progressively advanced its agenda, at times sacrificing legal diversity in the name of legal certainty. That is, legal certainty is directly related to fostering the development of the internal market and pursuing the objectives of the area of freedom, security and justice.[93]

Pluralistic thinking as portrayed in social psychology and explained above, however, may be pointing in a different direction in the context of integration projects. It may not only be argued that for embracing diversity in integration processes the – conflictualist – traditional private international law method is more adequate than substantive unification, and therefore takes away the 'second best' label of private international law solutions; it may also be argued, with a cosmopolitan take, that legal individuality, in its many guises, is a paramount ingredient of inclusive integration processes, and therefore needs to be safeguarded.

Harmonisation, be it at substantive level or even at secondary level – that is, harmonisation of private international law rules – is desirable for market integration as delivering legal certainty. Yet, the harmonisation endeavour needs deliverables respectful of diversity to be accepted and resonate in the integrated region as a whole. In this endeavour private international law techniques step up, from being a second-best solution, to being the only ones able to provide that bridging and balancing, that accommodation of individualities, that 'unity in diversity'. Many private international law techniques are deployed to achieve that balance, and the public policy exception is surely key to articulate and maintain legal individuality, as

90 Ragno, F. (2019) 'Certainty vs. Flexibility in the EU Choice of Law System', in Ferrari, F. and D. Fernándo Arroyo (eds) (2019), *Private International Law: Contemporary Challenges and Continuing Relevance*, Elgar.

91 Ibid.

92 Art. 81 of the Treaty on the Functioning of the EU (OJ C 115, 9.5.2008).

93 Remien, O. (2001), 'European Private International Law, the European Community and its Emerging Area of Freedom, Security and Justice' 38 *Common Market Law Review* 53, 64.

discussed by Fresnedo in this volume. Yet, what pluralistic thinking challenges is the breath and scope of the public policy exception.

Mutual trust and distrust

In the same vein and very much related to enhancing the functioning of the European area of freedom, security and justice, concepts considered the bedrocks of EU private international law harmonisation, are mutual trust, permeating the functioning of the system as a whole,[94] and mutual recognition.[95] Mutual trust is based on the assumption that the courts of all the Member States are equally competent to adjudicate jurisdiction according to the European regime. The role of mutual trust has featured particularly in the interpretation and application by the CJEU of the rules on *lis pendens.*[96] Mutual trust is used a principle to interpret and articulate techniques such as the court first seized rule in relation to the conflict of jurisdictions. This seems to work at the normative level, however, trust cannot be imposed in the reality dimension;[97] there is evidence of distrust between the legal systems of the EU in practice, and between them and the EU itself as a framework provider.

Culturalists approaches explain how distrust can also manifest itself in the tendency towards *lex forism*.[98] Culturalists want us to think about this seriously, and take foreign law seriously, yet evidence shows that difficulties in ascertaining the contents of foreign law often get in the way of the meaningful engagement required.[99] This is true for European jurisdictions, jurisdictions in Mercosur countries and globally.

Fabricio Polido in his chapter in this volume refers to distrust, in a related but arguably different vein. Let me explain. Pluralistic thinking is not without risks. It might lead to conflation. A very good example relates to the different paradigms of jurisdiction coined and examined by Michaels[100] elsewhere. Fabricio Polido refers to shades of 'mutual distrust' present at times in the room of the HCCH during the Judgments Convention Special Commission meetings. This

[94] The principles of 'comity' and 'mutual trust' are undoubtedly related but wholly distinguishable, yet are nevertheless often mentioned together. See, for example, Kenny, D. and R. Hennigan (2015) 'Choice-of-court Agreements, the Italian Torpedo, and the Recast of the Brussels I Regulation', 64 *I.C.L.Q.*, 197–209, at 199.

[95] See, *inter alia*, Mitsilegas, V. (2012) 'The Limits of Mutual Trust in Europe's Area of Freedom, Security and Justice: From Automatic Inter-State Cooperation to the Slow Emergence of the Individual', *Yearbook of European Law*, vol. 31, 319–72; Weller, M. (2015) 'Mutual Trust: in Search of the Future of European Union Private International Law', *Journal of Private International Law*, vol. 11, issue 1, 64–102.

[96] Case C-159/12 *Turner* v. *Grovit* [2005] 1 A.C. 101 (CJEU).

[97] See empirical evidence in the UNIFAM project reports.

[98] Muir Watt, 'Hospitality, Tolerance, and Exclusion in Legal Form', above fn. 31, 126ff.

[99] For a comprehensive analysis, see Nishitani, Y. (ed.) (2017), *Treatment of Foreign Law – Dynamics Towards Convergence?*, Springer.

[100] Michaels, R. (2006) 'Two Paradigms of Jurisdiction' 27 *Mich.Jo.Int.L.* 1003.

may arguably be a result of the conflation generated by the unawareness of these different paradigms of jurisdiction that Michaels examines. This fundamental non-convergence, if not acknowledged, may lead to misunderstandings. It is indeed very difficult to engage in effective communication if the actors are not aware of those different paradigms.

Culturalists' approaches can open more serious and realistic dialogue about the day-to-day difficulties in practice, in relation to collaborative harmonisation efforts, the ascertainment of foreign law[101] and the real practical challenges faced by the judiciary in the operationalisation of private international law. Goicoechea and van Loon offer a rich tribute to the supreme role of the judges in the development of the discipline. If there is to be a serious endeavour to build mutual trust from the ground up, their voices need to be in the centre of the stage. This becomes ever more important if, as explained by Muir Watt, a promising avenue is seen to be following the recognition paradigm she portrays as an 'essential ingredient for making a multicultural society work'. [102]

Inclusion and exclusion

At several points in this volume the need for further inclusion in the different dimensions and stages of action of private international law has come to the fore. The chapter by Rubaja and Albornoz in this volume refers to the lack of mechanisms to protect inclusion of individuals via private international law in some countries in Latin America, particularly in the context of recognition of same-sex marriages and surrogated filiation.

The public policy exception is the private international law technique designed to draw the line between inclusion and exclusion of 'foreignness'. Fresnedo's chapter in this volume examines the public policy exception in the context of the multilateralist methodology dominant in the legal systems of Mercosur, and particularly the operation of the public policy exception in Uruguay, and its well sustained restrictive scope, which in turn resonates with the description provided by Muir Watt in relation to the function of the public policy exception in her alternative 'recognitive statuist' methodology. This reinforces the importance of where to draw the line in the use of the public policy exception, and sheds light on what it tells us in relation to an ethical positioning; this insight is particularly timely, in view, for instance, of the current process of negotiation[103] and eventual adoption of a potential global instrument on the recognition and enforcement of foreign judgments at the HCCH, as discussed by de Araujo and Polido in their chapters in this volume.

[101] For a very comprehensive analysis see Nishitani, *Treatment of Foreign Law* above fn. 100.

[102] Muir Watt, H. (2013) 'Fundamental Rights and Recognition in Private International Law' 3 *Eur J Human Rights* 411. See further Taylor, C. (1979) *Hegel and Modern Society*, Cambridge University Press; Taylor, C. (1994) *Multiculturalism: Examining the Politics of Recognition*, Princeton University Press; Muir Watt, 'Hospitality, Tolerance, and Exclusion in Legal Form', above fn. 31, 141.

[103] In these negotiations the Uruguayan delegation put forward a motion in relation to the restrictive interpretation of the public policy exception.

However, Rubaja and Albornoz point to how the public policy exception as a private international law technique in practice in several Latina American countries at times may exacerbates the exclusion of individuals in some cases in the context of new forms of families. An Instrumentalist response to that would be to adopt a restrictive approach to the scope of the exception, but even that might not be enough to counteract the exclusion referred to by these authors. Cosmopolitan pluralistic thinking should come to reshape the boundaries of the public policy exception. Muir Watt does so in the context of the alternative private international law methodology that she proposes and calls 'recognitive statuism'. She explains the differences in the functioning of the public policy exception in Savigny's multilateralist methodology and in the alternative methodology that she proposes. In the latter, that is about 'allowing in the guest (the foreign law) in her own terms',[104]

> the threshold is placed not at the initial reception of the foreign law but at the point where the survival of the host is at stake. It must again be observed here that not only is the existence of this threshold compatible with a recognitive statutist stance, but that it has, emblematically, its proper place here. It is multilateralism, which rests on a control a priori of the conformity of foreign institutions with the forum's own categories, which has imported a tool that was not initially, or is not logically, part of its methodology. Ordre public is actually an intruder in the latter approach but is perfectly at home with recognitive statutism where it constitutes as it were the sole control mechanism, operating once the foreign-law guest has entered the home legal system, in cases where absolute incompatibility is verified in concreto.[105]

Private International Law as a Field of Knowledge (Theory)

Michaels argues that theory is 'the most important for legal thought, because paradigm shifts happen neither in reality nor in ideology but in our ways of understanding the world'.[106]

Universalism and cosmopolitanism

Universalism[107] of approach is the normative presumption upon which private international law is construed, namely, the normative equality of national legal systems in private international law, which in turns mirrors the normative equality of sovereign states in public international law.[108]As explained in the chapters of Carruthers and

[104] Muir Watt, 'Hospitality, Tolerance, and Exclusion in Legal Form', above fn. 31, 135.

[105] Ibid., 135.

[106] Michaels, 'Globalization and Law: Law Beyond the State', above fn. 89.

[107] See further Banu, R. (2018) *Nineteenth Century Perspectives on Private International Law*, Oxford University Press, Ch. 8.

[108] Mills, A. (2018) 'Connecting Private and Public International Law', in Ruiz Abou-Nigm, V., K. McCall-Smith and D. French (eds), *Linkages and Boundaries in Private and Public International Law*, Hart Publishing, above fn. 33, 13–31.

van Loon in this volume, referring to choice of law rules in European Regulations and HCCH Conventions, respectively, the principle of universality in choice of law is an important technique in the accommodation of legal diversity[109] and it speaks directly of 'equality', of treating all (national) legal systems as par. Yet, the dialectics discussed here take universalism in a different sense, as the kind of world-vision embedded in concepts such as 'citizens of the world'.[110]

As a framework of understanding, that is, in the second dimension referred to above, Berman considers universalism unhelpful, as it 'fails to capture the extreme emotional ties people still feel to distinct transnational or local communities'.[111] His cosmopolitan perspective would certainly resonate with the insights offered by Nicola Wisdahl in relation to the perspective of Scots in the United Kingdom, and also with the views of Marta Requejo Isidro in her reflections on private international law and Brexit. As Berman explains 'universalism tends to ignore the very attachments people hold most deeply',[112] and regionalism, to remain an attractive project, should strive for cosmopolitanism, for 'unity in diversity', and 'encourage recognition of multiple identifications'.[113] Evidently this vision goes far beyond the universalism v. regionalism dialectic; it can include identities based on 'belongings' within nation states themselves.[114] Hence, in Berman's model '[c]osmopolitanism seeks "flexible citizenship"[115] in which people are permitted to shift identities amid a plurality of possible affiliations and allegiances'.[116]

Cosmopolitan pluralism as portrayed by Berman seems particularly suitable for responding to the many challenges of global migration and issues such as those discussed by Kasey McCall-Smith and Laura Carballo Piñeiro in their chapters in this volume. In particular

> [t]he cosmopolitan worldview shifts back and forth from the rooted particularity of personal identity to the global possibility of multiple overlapping communities . . . '[Instead of an ideal of detachment, actually existing cosmopolitanism is a reality of (re)attachment, multiple attachment, or attachment at a distance'.[117]

Many of us migrants can certainly relate to that worldview of Berman's. In his view 'judges must see themselves as part of an interlocking network of domestic, transnational and international norms. Recognizing the "complex and interwoven forces

[109] See Carruthers' chapter in this volume.

[110] See Knop, K. (2016) 'Lorimer's Private Citizens of the World', *European Journal of International Law* 27: 447–75.

[111] Ibid., 447–75.

[112] Ibid., 447–75.

[113] Berman, 'Conflict of Laws, Globalization, and Cosmopolitan Pluralism', above fn. 36, 1113.

[114] Ibid., 1113.

[115] Ibid., 1115, in which Berman refers to the work of Ong, A. (1999) *Flexible Citizenship: The Cultural Logics of Transnationality*, Duke University Press.

[116] Ibid., 1115.

[117] Ibid., 1115.

that govern citizens' conduct in a global society," courts can develop a jurisprudence that reflects this cosmopolitan reality'.[118] This calls for private international law methodologies and *techniques*.

Technicism

Private international law's technicism is widely recognised, even though not always in the most positive sense. It is accepted that 'the discipline comes with built-in critiques' and 'it is self-conscious about its use of form'.[119] This self-awareness of the complexity of its technicalities, at times referred to as 'theoreticism',[120] may explain the timid activism of private international law scholars and the pervasiveness of the 'dismal swamp'[121] perception, which continue to jeopardise the impact of private international law techniques beyond the traditional mores of family law and commercial law where it has always operated.

Techniques such as *renvoi* and *depeçage* have been rejected in the European project, as a policy choice in the name of legal certainty.[122] The elimination of these 'escape devices', as these techniques are sometimes referred to, is not without a cost; it may foster market integration, yet these techniques are the built-in space to accommodate differences; as Riles argues

> if one understands the complexity and malleability of these doctrines not as technical obfuscation for its own sake, but rather as a product of these doctrines' efforts to grapple seriously with the problem of cultural conflict, then their very flaws may become their virtues.[123]

They speak of alternatives, of room to manoeuvre, of choice, and they necessitate 'pluralistic thinking' as an essential corollary. Culturalists appreciate that these techniques and others generally understood as part of the 'general theory' of private international law, such as 'characterization', 'adaptation', 'substitution' or 'transposition', 'provide an endorsement for the hybridization of the rules involved in a conflict'[124]

[118] Ibid., 1115.

[119] Knop et al., 'Transdisciplinary Conflict of Laws', above fn. 8, 596.

[120] See Muir Watt, H. (2011) 'Private International Law beyond the Schism', 2 *Transnational Legal Theory* 3, 347–428.

[121] After the well-known passage of Prosser, W. L. (1953) in 'Interestate Publication' 51 *Mich. L. Rev.* 959, 971. See also Cox, M. P. (2013–14) 'Choice of Law: Conflicts Doesn't Have to Be a Dismal Swamp?' 15 *T.M. Cooley J. Prac. & Clinical L.* 125.

[122] See further Ruiz Abou-Nigm, V. (2019) 'Private International Law and Global Governance Issues: Unlocking Private International Law Potential in Global (Migration) Governance', in Ferrari, F. and D. P. Fernández Arroyo, *The Continuing Relevance of Private International Law*, New York University Press.

[123] See Mills, A. (2009) 'The Application of Multiple Laws Under the Rome II Regulation', in Binchy, W. and J. Ahern (eds), *The Rome II Regulation on the Law Applicable to Non-Contractual Obligations: A New International Litigation Regime*, 133, 152.

[124] Muir Watt, 'Hospitality, Tolerance, and Exclusion in Legal Form', above fn. 31, 144.

and 'lead to hybrids – that is to a regime that does not correspond to the reality of any of the legal systems involved'.[125] Instrumentalists also value this built-in flexibility. Carruthers, for instance, refers to *renvoi* and recognises this technique's malleability[126] as 'the pinnacle of any legal system's endeavours to accommodate legal diversity'.[127] *Renvoi*,[128] as a private international law technique, can be seen as the fluidity and malleability technique *par excellence*.

As this chapter shows, culturalists' efforts to 'explore [private international law's] potential as a mode of thought or intellectual style in a context of increasing complexity'[129] are indeed very valuable. However, so far in the EU integration project, the competing rationale of simplicity in the name of predictability and legal certainty has been the preferred rationale; the latter fosters market integration, the former may be more conducive to balancing cultural approaches. *Renvoi* has also been eliminated in some of the new national codifications in Mercosur countries, as explained in Paredes' chapter. Codification of private international law worldwide has resulted in a considerable reduction in the use of this technique in modern private international law normative frameworks, particularly in integration projects.[130] Simplicity as a value has won the day. From an Instrumentalist perspective this can be understood in terms of legal certainty as a corollary for market integration. From a Culturalist standpoint it may also be understood more broadly in the light of the common resistance to 'pluralistic thinking'[131] as conceptualised in social psychology and discussed above in this chapter. In any case it may be reflecting a failure to appreciate the value of the discipline's technicalities, in the words of Muir Watt as 'geared to the coordination of legal systems, the reception of the foreign, or indeed the "management of pluralism"'.[132]

Pluralism

Legal pluralism is characterised by its breadth and depth. Different legal traditions, orders and systems continue to meet and interact at the national, regional and

[125] Ibid., 144.

[126] Riles, 'Cultural Conflicts', above fn. 10, 273, 277.

[127] See Carruthers' chapter in this volume.

[128] See, *inter alia*, Agostini, E. (2013) 'Le mecanisme du renvoi' 102 *Revue critique de droit international privé* 545; Briggs, A. (1998) 'In Praise and Defense of Renvoi', 47 *ICLQ* 877.

[129] Muir Watt, 'Hospitality, Tolerance, and Exclusion in Legal Form', above fn. 31, 114.

[130] In the EU *renvoi* has been expressly excluded as a technique in several contexts, for example, Art. 18 Rome I Reg; Art. 24 Rome II Reg; Art. 11 Rome III Reg; Art. 32 Matrimonial Property Regulation; Art. 32 Registered Partnerships Property Regulation.

[131] In the view of Novis-Deutsch, 'people opt for clear-cut solutions because complex thinking is cognitively expensive, emotionally painful, and politically embarrassing as it often involves taboo/value trade-offs'. See Novis-Deutsch, 'The One and the Many', above fn. 40, 434.

[132] Muir Watt, 'Hospitality, Tolerance, and Exclusion in Legal Form', above fn. 31, 125, referring to the 'management of pluralism' as a phrase coined by Francescakis, P. (ed.) (1975), in his preface to *L'ordre juridique*, Dalloz (the French translation of Santi Romano's *L'ordinamento giuridico*).

international levels. Legal diversity and pluralism are valuable assets in our multicultural society. In the context of regional integration pluralism also provides a rearguard against the push for normative hegemony demanded by capitalism. However, the balancing act is indeed challenging. The contributions of Paredes, Wisdahl, de Araujo, Carballo Piñeiro and others in this volume take stock of those different normative layers. There are national conflict rules, originating from national systems of private international law, and there are international conflict rules, resulting from multilateral efforts to harmonise the former so as to ensure juridical continuity of legal relations across national borders; there may be something in between, like the intra-UK rules of jurisdiction, which resemble very much the European rules of jurisdiction but with the infusion of some British flavours, such as the availability of the *forum non conveniens* plea. Or there might be devolved constitutional arrangements as to certain fields pertaining or tangential to private international law issues. This is the case in Argentina as referred to in Paredes' chapter in relation to recognition of foreign judgments as a devolved matter to provinces. In turn, in Scotland, private international law substantive issues are devolved, as explained by Wisdahl, and this presents a further layer of complexity. But there may be non-state normative orders at play, such as religious laws mentioned by van Loon in his chapter, or professional standards, or *lex mercatoria* as mentioned by Argerich and Capalbo. That is, the multi-layered nature of private international law regulation is intrinsic to the problems that private international law is there to address.

Harmonisation in integration projects, particularly in the family law and civil and commercial law fields, has been pursued, at regional levels, to facilitate commerce and to minimise the hurdles of managing diversity. This is sought to contribute to 'integrate' people, and to 'accommodate' legal systems, as examined by Requejo Isidro's chapter in this volume.

However, EU harmonisation of private international law does not capture legal pluralism in its entirety: it does not, for instance, allow for choice of non-state law as governing law. The approach is too top-down, too state-centred, with little room for manoeuvre and for further engagement with a wider range of actors.

In turn, in private international law legal pluralism is tackled with methodological pluralism. This has further implications since it may take the discipline into territories that some would consider beyond its remits.[133] In Latin American scholarship methodological pluralism[134] usually explains the use of at least two main methods: the 'uniformist' method (or unification of substantive law) and the 'conflictualist' method (or choice of law methodology). The first is used in the few departments of law where this unity is imperative and possible via multilateral instruments.[135] The traditional

[133] Reppy, W. A. (2008) 'Eclecticism in Methods for Resolving Tort and Contract Conflict of Laws: The United States and the European Union', 82 *Tulane Law Review* 2053–117.

[134] Talice, J. R. (1990), in D. Opertti Badán et al. (1990) *Objeto y Método en el Derecho Internacional Privado*, 2nd edn, FCU, 29, 53.

[135] The typical example being the United Nations Convention on Contracts for the International Sale of

view is that whenever unification of substantive law is not attainable the conflictualist method remains the only (second-best) solution. As explained by Opertti Badán elsewhere, uniform rules and conflict rules have a different objective: the first create substantive provisions for a certain cross-border legal category; by contrast, conflict rules select the applicable law among the diversity of legal systems connected to the case. Both methods are understood as pertaining to private international law by the generality of Latin American scholarship, and by many Culturalists elsewhere, including Muir Watt.[136] This methodological pluralism is seen as providing complementary problem-solving approaches to tackle legal diversity. The role of international judicial and administrative cooperation is crucial in this context, and several chapters in this volume, including McClean's and Noodt Taquela's speak to that. Moreover, there is something of the essence of private international law purview that is all-embracing and merits the cross-dimensional discussion that follows.

Bridging and Balancing: Pluralist Ideology

For many lawyers and even for many legal scholars outside the rather enclosed mores of private international law, private international law seems at best unduly technical, overly complex or inaccessible, and, at worst, marginal,[137] uninteresting and outdated. This contribution started from the premise that these perceptions are not only related to the complexity of its technicalities but to an outreach deficiency, that is, a failure to communicate its worth and potential. The perception of it as 'mere technique', that is, formulaic, deprived of any deontological concerns, is indeed harmful and prevents other disciplines from engaging in a fruitful dialogue with private international law. It generates barriers rather than bridges; exclusion rather than inclusivity. 'Pluralistic thinking', as portrayed in social psychology as indicating a 'deeper embracement of and engagement with multiplicity alongside the challenges that it entails',[138] may open a new way of thinking about what private international law strives for. In social psychology Novis-Deutsch argues that 'without an underlying recognition of irreducible multiplicity and complexity in the human world, tolerance and multiculturalism could easily crumble in situations of high social conflict'.[139] Hence, bridging and balancing legal diversity not exclusively but substantially through private international law[140] is crucial to multicultural integration projects.

Goods, which was adopted in Vienna on 11 April 1980 and entered into force 1 January 1988; 89 States Parties, status as at 30 November 2018.

[136] Other schools of thought consider international unification of substantive law for cross-border issues as beyond the scope of private international law as a discipline.

[137] See Nicola Wisdahl's chapter in this volume, where she refers to a European Commission publication in which EU private international law is reported to be 'largely unnoticed by legal practitioners' (European Commission DG Justice: 'Judicial cooperation in civil matters in the European Union. A guide for legal practitioners').

[138] Novis-Deutsch, 'The One and the Many', above fn. 40, 444.

[139] Ibid., 443.

[140] 'One does not have to venture into the higher spheres of theory on the evolution of human knowledge

This chapter has aimed to serve as a liaison between Culturalist and Instrumentalist thinking in relation to private international law techniques for the development of integration. The attempt has unearthed a need for the Pluralist in all of us, a claim that goes beyond the initial enquiry. More often than not Culturalists speak to other Culturalists: the jargon, the structure of argument, the level of abstraction, is accessible to those who are exposed to similar thinking habits and constructions, yet not so accessible to others. The same can be said about Instrumentalists and their problem-solving approach and the degree of detail of their doctrinal analysis. Not surprisingly, as explained by Riles, Culturalists and Instrumentalists find each other uninteresting, they dismiss each other's relevancy, they downplay the importance of each other's perspectives. If this is true, 'pluralistic thinking' becomes crucial for enabling further dialogue. The very outreach deficiency that we thought needed tackling at the conception of this project, and the perception of private international law as marginal (two sides of the same coin), is mirrored in the attitude of mutual indifference, of dismissal, of not taking the other seriously as between Culturalists and Instrumentalists within private international law mores.

As Riles explains:

> one cross-culturally universal truth is that in every culture, persons disagree about their cultural values . . . Cultural conflict is not just conflict between communities: it is conflict within communities as well. It is equally well established that cultures are not billiard balls; there are no 'pure' and hermetically sealed cultures.[141]

If there is something that the current political climate shows in relation to integration processes it is how patent that universal truth is. As Knop describes: 'cultures are hybrid, overlapping, and creole: forces from trade to education to migration to popular culture and transnational law ensure that all persons participate in multiple cultures at once. Cultural elements circulate globally, and they are always changing'.[142] From this point of view, '"culture" is more of a constant act of translation and re-creation or representation than it is a fixed and given thing'.[143] Riles's point is that, consequently, 'culture is neither a totalizing explanatory device for legal institutions

and scientific categories ("change of paradigms") to observe that, what at face value may be characterised as "personal" or "private"' is not only politically relevant but actually shaping collective reflection, judgment and action. In times when vanishing political, economic and cultural frontiers (euphemistically called "globalisation") are perceived as presenting both opportunities and threat, legislators and the courts will ever more frequently be called upon to identify and protect politically relevant private values and to mediate between conflicting values and expectations, not primarily but significantly through private international law": Kronke, H. (2004) 'Most Significant Relationship, Governmental Interests,Cultural Identity, Integration: "Rules" at Will and the Case for Principles of Conflict of Laws' 3 *Uniform Law Review* 467, 471.

[141] Riles, 'Cultural Conflicts', above fn. 10.

[142] Knop et al., 'Transdisciplinary Conflict of Laws', above fn. 8, 309.

[143] Riles, 'Cultural Conflicts', above fn. 10.

or legal conflicts, nor a unified singular thing agreed upon by all members of any given society'.[144]

This takes us directly to Michaels' first chapter in this volume, and the ethics of responsivity and the plea to take the Other seriously. It is the ethic of responsivity itself and its manifestation through private international law techniques and pluralistic thinking that should continue to provide those bridges, to facilitate that encounter, to make one more open to communicating, cooperating, coordinating and engaging with the Other. At the very basis of that thinking, the other, be it foreign law, a different field of knowledge, a different kind of scholarship, a perspective from another region, or another religion, or in a different language, needs to be taken seriously, and its value appreciated for its contribution; while the Self adopts a positionality of empathy.[145]

When a court adjudicating in a cross-border dispute disregards the position of other courts as a matter of indifference, when it treats foreign law as inferior, when Culturalists refer to doctrinal analysis as largely uninteresting descriptions, when Instrumentalists ignore legal theory or consider it pedantic self-indulgence, when a marriage celebrated abroad is not recognised only because that kind of marriage is not recognised in the domestic jurisdiction, when we are treated differently before judicial or administrative authorities only because we are foreigners (and the list could grow very long) – in all these instances the Other is not taken seriously and therefore there is miscommunication and lack of meaningful engagement. On the contrary, when efforts are not spared to accommodate legal diversity and all means are employed to facilitate cooperation there is serious engagement with the Other.

Conclusions

Thinking pluralistically involves a developmental trajectory.[146] Private international law exposes us constantly to the perspectives of others, and that grasp should make us more and more pluralist. Riles claims that 'one should seek to understand other people's ways of knowing the world, *on their own terms*, before passing judgment on them according to one's own moral or legal criteria'.[147]

At the time that Riles's pioneering work launched the 'technicalities' approach, private international law 'inspired more anxiety and frustration than interest or respect'.[148] This might have changed, or may be changing, and, if not, it needs to

[144] Ibid.

[145] 'A pluralistic person will take an empathic interest in different ideas, people, and cultures, enjoy diversity . . .': Novis-Deutsch, 'The One and the Many', above fn. 40, 434.

[146] Ibid., 437.

[147] Riles, 'Cultural Conflicts', above fn. 10, 275, emphasis added.

[148] Riles, 'A New Agenda', above fn. 4, 978.4. The anxiety element may be related to the understanding of the barriers to pluralistic thinking in social psychology terms. In the views of Novis-Deutsch 'people opt for clear-cut solutions because complex thinking is cognitively expensive, emotionally painful, and politically embarrassing as it often involves taboo/value trade-offs': Novis-Deutsch, 'The One and the Many', above fn. 40, 434.

change. Pluralistic thinking in the terms examined in this chapter may contribute to that trajectory fostering a drive towards embracing multiplicity and complexity. That private international law requires 'a widening of the intellectual horizon'[149] is well established, as it 'reflects a general change of views regarding the foreign'.[150]

There was a time where it was thought that legal diversity was at odds with the very idea of integration, where the trajectory was not driven by pluralistic thinking but by market integration; then, regional integration seemed to imply harmonisation at its highest possible level, not only at the secondary level of private international law rules, but even at the substantive private law level. At that time, private international law was seen as a second- or third-best, or even as a stepping stone for substantive unification. Contemporary challenges seem to be showing the need to consider alternative plans.

Bridging and balancing legal diversity and integration does not have to result in dismantling the identity of legal systems but should resonate with all peoples. We should embrace diversity with its complexities, and thrive in it.

As this volume shows, private international law methodologies and techniques, and moreover, private international lawyers' way of thinking, have an important contribution to make in this endeavour; this requires commitment and activism, and may not be for the Culturalists or the Instrumentalists alone but for the Pluralists in all of us.

[149] Husserl, G. (1940) 'The Foreign Fact Element in Conflict of Laws' 26 *Virginia Law Review* 243, at 261–2, 267, as cited by Riles, in 'Cultural Conflicts', above fn. 10, 275.

[150] Ibid.

Index